FASHION FORWARD
300 years of fashion

CREATIVE DIRECTION
MARC ASCOLI

DISCARD

FASHION FORWARD
300 years of fashion

COLLECTIONS OF THE
MUSEE DES ARTS DECORATIFS, PARIS

RIZZOLI
NEW YORK

New York · Paris · London · Milan

Translated from the French by Denise Jacobs and Liza Tripp

FASHION AT THE MUSEUM
Pierre Bergé and Olivier Gabet — p. 7

THE SYSTEM OF FASHION
Pamela Golbin — p. 9

"FROM THESE SUMPTUOUS AND INSUBSTANTIAL PHANTOMS"
Denis Bruna — p. 13

COLLECTIONS
Marie-Sophie Carron de la Carrière

Éric Pujalet-Plaà

Hélène Renaudin

Marie-Pierre Ribère

pp. 19 — 265

APPENDIXES
Captions — p. 267

Exhibitions — p. 276

Photography Credits — p. 280

FASHION AT THE MUSEUM

PIERRE BERGÉ
President of the Union Française des Arts du Costume
&
OLIVIER GABET
Director of the Musée des Arts Décoratifs

Just thirty years ago, the Musée des Arts de la Mode opened its doors in the Pavillon de Marsan, at the very heart of what was formerly known as the Union Centrale des Arts Décoratifs. And make no mistake: even though one important newspaper covered fashion's entry into the Louvre with great fanfare, the idea of an invasion into the greatest museum in the world by a subject that was then considered a minor art was hard to fathom. Let us view it instead as the installation of an evolving art form within an experimental museum open to new art movements — a laboratory that reflected French modernity, as envisioned by François Mathey, longtime director of the Musée des Arts Décoratifs and the leading proponent, during the 1960s and 1970s, of bold visions for many museums. Fashion had come not to the Louvre Museum but to the Louvre Palace, completing the circle of art history by occupying the part of the palace that had been reserved for the Musée des Arts Décoratifs since 1905. Fashion would take on a regal mantle, bringing a flash of color to history's more sober halls.

Since its founding in the nineteenth century, the exemplary industrial art museum that is the Musée des Arts Décoratifs has owned important textile collections from all over the world, including Japan, China, and the Islamic world. From the time it first opened on the rue de Rivoli, the museum presented remarkable exhibitions, such as *Tissus japonais anciens* (Vintage Japanese textiles) in 1906, *Dentelle de France* (French lace) in 1909, *Deux mille ans de mode* (Two thousand years of fashion) in 1971, and *Le costume, un patrimoine vivant* (Clothing, a living heritage) in 1980. This collection also encompasses works assembled by the prestigious Union Française des Arts du Costume (UFAC), founded in 1948 by François Boucher and directed for many years by Yvonne Deslandres, an extraordinary and endearing figure. The UFAC eventually turned over to the museum the management of its magnificent collection: a diverse grouping that included gifts from Madame de Bonneval, the collections of Elsa Schiaparelli and Madeleine Vionnet, and the wardrobe of Denise Poiret. The union of these two collections — one historic and complete, the other growing each year with both vintage and contemporary additions — forms the cornerstone of fashion at the Musée des Arts Décoratifs. It also explains the museum's continuing prestige as well as, inevitably, the accompanying controversy, paradox, and occasional tension throughout its history.

How can one forget that this adventure, born of passionate debates that continue today, was the outgrowth of a strong friendship between the benevolent François Mitterrand, the president of the Republic, who was inspired by an idea that reflected the excitement of the times, and Jack Lang, his minister of culture. It was also the product of a powerful movement by the fashion world and the titans of the textile industry in its heyday, before the more difficult times that would follow. Important to mention as well is the understated but influential role of our friend Léon Cligman, as well as the countless people who have contributed, and continue to offer, their passion and energy in the pursuit of this endeavor. Within this group are, among so many others, the successive directors of the museum, the curators in charge, the restorers who daily look after the fragile works, the generosity of the fashion houses, the donors, and the DEFI (Committee for the Development and Promotion of Apparel), which every year provides financial support that is crucial to the vitality of fashion in the museum and elsewhere.

Three decades after its brilliant inaugural year — which featured the exhibitions *Moments de mode* (Fashion moments), under the guidance of the late Edmonde Charles-Roux, who is dearly missed, and *Yves Saint Laurent: 28 années de création* (YSL: Twenty-eight years of fashion), followed by *Homage to Christian Dior* in 1987 — the Musée des Arts Décoratifs chose to celebrate this anniversary with an exhibition, held in its nave, of more than 300 pieces spanning nearly three centuries of fashion. Thanks to the remarkable and enthusiastic financial support of H&M, the show included never-before-seen pieces alongside some that have been entirely restored. Here, fashion does not speak only of fashion — though it does sometimes, out of vanity — but converses with decorative arts, scenic wallpapers, decorative paneling and interior designs by Jean-Michel Frank, life arts, and lifestyle, the very reason it is held in our museum.

What can seem at first like a startling intermingling of names, brands, and fashion houses is also a reflection of the ever-changing world of fashion. Haute couture represents one lifestyle, ready-to-wear another. Each has its own history. Is it art or applied art? No matter — in today's world, hierarchies are continuously being overthrown. Fashion is at the museum. Together, this exhibition and its catalogue create an ideal, unique, and ephemeral museum, filled with new "fashion moments." Above all, they pay homage to those who create fashion and those who wear it.

THE SYSTEM OF FASHION

PAMELA GOLBIN

There are as many ways to define fashion as there are approaches to understand it — therein lies both its strength and its fragility. Any attempt to condense it, to reduce it to a single definition, is to go against its most basic nature — one of movement, of change, an unrelenting élan that keeps pushing forward, at any cost, to reach new heights. Caught in the whirlwind, it becomes difficult to grasp the essence of fashion or measure its influence and impact. Gabrielle Chanel tried: "I would like to bring all the couturiers together and ask them, 'What is fashion? Explain it to me.' I am convinced that none of them could give me a real answer . . . and neither can I!"[1] Christian Dior offered the following interpretation: "Those who know the least about couture's secrets can instinctively sense what these extravagant collections represent in terms of effort, conscientiousness and care. They also understand — be they French or foreign — that the great adventure that is Parisian couture is not merely a Vanity Fair, but a dazzling and celebratory manifestation of a civilization that is determined to survive."[2]

Fashion has often been criticized for its provocative side, its frivolity, excess, and escalating media coverage. And yet, as its influence radiates around the globe, fashion has gained respect for its powerful impact as a creative force and a financial powerhouse. Fashion is both a marker of civilization and a passport to the world, a multicultural "open sesame" that can travel through space and time, a seductive phenomenon that attracts worldwide attention.

But before reaching this point, fashion had to find its bearings and build its own future in order to become a global force, a defining system built on a long series of spectacular events and glorious moments.

SUMPTUARY LAWS, OR HOW THE CLOTHES MAKE THE MAN

Despite their separatist and protectionist nature, French sumptuary laws, instituted in the fifteenth century, formed the foundation of the French fashion system.[3] Between 1485 and 1660, eighteen such laws were established in two phases:[4] the decrees passed between 1485 and 1583 that sought to protect the nobility from the incursions by commoners in the area of dress, thus ensuring the structure of social ranking; and the laws established between 1601 and 1660, which were mainly intended to give Louis XIV, the Sun King, exclusive access to sartorial magnificence and maintain a hierarchy within his court. Several practices were established and expanded during his reign; henceforth, the laws no longer applied only to commoners but to all the king's subjects. The sheer number and repetition of these decrees would revolutionize the dress codes. Indeed, clothes made the man: attire had to clearly identify and indicate a person's rank in order to counter the emergence of a new class of people who used their financial power to appropriate symbols of refinement. "In other words, at that time, there was an equivalence between one's manner of dress and one's title, so that an appropriation of dress was equivalent to the appropriation of a title of nobility."[5] To maintain order while transforming the rules of the game, sumptuary laws insisted on sartorial differentiation, defining it as the privilege of nobility while trying to hold off the beginnings of the long process of democratization in fashion.

> "How is it that a man's dress always speaks so eloquently if it didn't truly represent the whole man, the man and his political opinions, the man and the story of his life, indeed the hieroglyph of the man."
>
> HONORÉ DE BALZAC

These laws reinforced the obvious social divides, the clear signs of affiliation to a milieu that some, while still staunchly adhering to a caste system, tried to alter to their own benefit. It was a well-known fact that the nobility and the rising bourgeoisie would rather pay a fine than accept certain restrictions, resulting in a rivalry of ostentatious detail, a transgressive exercise that was exemplified by Brummell, the dandy of his time.

"Fashion is to France what the gold mines of Peru were for Spain," said Jean-Baptiste Colbert, minister to Louis XVI. Since silhouettes for men and women evolved slowly over the course of the eighteenth century, sartorial originality was based more on the choice of fabric, ornamentation, and embellishments than on its cut. The role of the seamstress was to provide a service: to execute the dress once the client had purchased the fabric from a mercer. Rose Bertin, Queen Marie-Antoinette's famous *marchande de mode* (purveyor of fashion), considered the embellishment process — the selection and application of decorative accessories, ribbons, colifichet embroidery, and trim — an original creative process of its own. She was the first to draw a parallel between her work and that of an artist. "Do you pay the painter Vernet only for his canvas and his paints?" mused Diderot in 1765 in his *Encyclopedia*. It would take nearly a century to address the challenge of that question.

CHARLES FREDERICK WORTH, OR THE ADVENT OF THE FIRST COUTURIER

In 1857, with one bold, simple, and straightforward gesture, the British couturier Charles Frederick Worth, official dressmaker to Empress Eugénie, revolutionized the sartorial world: he was the first to place a label bearing his name in a dress, a move that still carries the force of a manifesto. In a single stroke, the founder of Parisian haute couture and the father of modern fashion initiated the myth of the artist-couturier. Worth — who, like all established and upcoming celebrities, would be photographed by the legendary nineteenth-century photographer Nadar — invented the concept of the couturier as superstar. And just like other recognized artists, of popular or official acclaim, Worth signed each one of his dresses, or "canvases." The concept of the brand was thus born in the late nineteenth century, along with so many other innovations. Worth's signature, so personal and novel, put the finishing touch on his designs. "The women who come to me want to ask for my ideas, not to follow out their own. They deliver themselves to me in confidence, and I decide for them; that makes them happy.... My signature to their gown suffices!... My business is not only to execute but especially to invent. My invention is the secret of my success."[6]

Indeed, by imposing his vision and having the final decision, Worth redefined the creative process, with the presence of the label serving as an added value, the indelible mark of the artisan-couturier turned artist-couturier.

THE MUSEUM: A HISTORICAL PANORAMA

Once recognized as an artist, the couturier could visualize his works displayed in the ultimate temple of art: the museum, the hard drive of history, the search engine, the time machine. But not quite yet.

The "*Musée imaginaire*" (imaginary museum) as envisioned in 1947 by André Malraux, the first French minister of cultural affairs, did not include a fashion section. And the Musée des Arts Décoratifs, situated within the Louvre, opened in 1905. It has since expanded with a new wing and a permanent area dedicated to fashion. "We talked about it, wished for it for many years, we have been dreaming of it since the beginning of the century," declared Jack Lang, then minister of culture, at the inauguration of the Musée des Arts de la Mode in January 1986. "Today, the dream has become a reality. Our country finally has its own rich, prestigious fashion museum.... The excellence of French fashion descends from a long line of silhouettes, gestures, and colors otherwise known as, depending on one's perspective, *l'œil, ou le métier* [the eye, or the craftsmanship]. A fashion museum records the history of those practices and that vision."[7] The opening represented the country's validation of fashion, bestowing upon it a mantle of nobility and acknowledging its role as the showcase of French *art de vivre*.

That was thirty years ago. Fast-forward to today: the Musée des Arts Décoratifs is holding an anniversary exhibition, *Fashion Forward: Three Centuries of Fashion*, a chronological frieze of costume design and finery beginning in 1715, a celebration of the permanence of the ephemeral, and the promise of a shared spirit. This museum as sanctuary, a place of reciprocal admiration, a platform of shared savoir-faire meant to endure in our collective memory.

History, "this advocate of eternity," according to Stefan Zweig,[8] will remember that fashion made a spectacular entrance into the Metropolitan Museum of Art in New York in 1983, when Yves Saint Laurent was honored as the first couturier to be given a retrospective during his lifetime, setting a precedent for future contemporary fashion exhibitions.

"Never forget that what becomes timeless was once truly new," said Nicolas Ghesquière in a 2014 interview for French *Vanity Fair*.[9] While today's couturier superstars play musical chairs, one can ask: What is the true role of the designer in our times? Evidently, it is no longer that of a talented stylist creating collections, but rather that of an emblematic figure, a multidisciplinary genius whose role includes being the brand's ambassador, spokesperson, and master of ceremony, all at the same time; a ringmaster of the media circus, a reflection of an era, a crowned megastar who personifies fashion and defines the zeitgeist of the times. "After one fashion destroys another, it in turn will be abolished by a newer one, that will give way to the following one, that will not be the last: such is our frivolity,"[10] remarked Jean de La Bruyère in 1687. Like Proustian madeleines that evoke past times, these treasures lay hidden away in the museum's storerooms, waiting for their prince charming to bring them back to life.

In other words, "The show must go on . . . "

1 — *Coco Chanel parle: La mode, qu'est-ce que c'est?* Collection "Français de notre temps," no. 80 (Paris: Hugues Desalle, ca. 1960), sound recording [LP].

2 — Christian Dior, *Christian Dior et moi* (Paris, Bibliothèque Amiot Dumont, 1956), 236. (Translator's translation)

3 — Though sumptuary laws have existed since antiquity, periodic revisions of fashion styles began in the 14th century.

4 — Michèle Fogel, "Modèle d'État et modèle social de dépenses: Les lois somptuaires en France," *Genèse de l'État moderne. Prélèvement et distribution*, ed. Jean-Philippe Genêt and Michel le Mené (Paris: Éditions du CNRS, 1987), 227-35.

5 — Ran E. Hong, *L'impossible social selon Molière* (Paris: Nerr, 2002), 129.

6 — F. Adolphus, *Some Memories of Paris* (Edinburgh: William Blackwood and Sons, 1895), 190.

7 — Speech given by Jack Lang at the inauguration of the Musée des Arts de la Mode, January 1986.

8 — Stefan Zweig, *Fouché* (1929; reprint, Paris: Grasset, 1969).

9 — *Vanity Fair France,* May 2014, 167.

10 — Jean de La Bruyère, *Les caractères, ou les mœurs de ce siècle* (1687; reprint, Paris: Gallimard, 2013), 321.

"FROM THESE SUMPTUOUS AND INSUBSTANTIAL PHANTOMS"

—

A HISTORIOGRAPHIC PERSPECTIVE OF THE COLLECTION OF THE MUSÉE DES ARTS DÉCORATIFS

DENIS BRUNA

The exhibition *Fashion Forward: Three Centuries of Fashion*—a selection of masterpieces from the Fashion and Textile collections of the Musée des Arts Décoratifs—and its accompanying catalogue present an opportunity to review the subject. Typically, these kinds of exhibitions, characteristic of great institutions, allow museums to showcase their most treasured holdings. These might include, for instance, the remarkable collections of costumes dating from the First Empire, the July Monarchy, or the reign of Napoleon III, or the spectacular sequined dresses from the 1920s. The museum will also present, with great pride and gratitude, the generous gifts it has received, which include the prestigious wardrobes of Cléo de Mérode, the Duchess of Windsor, Princess Faucigny-Lucinge, Claude Pompidou, Denise René, and Hélène David-Weill, to name just a few. The museum's twentieth-century collections are especially rich with iconic designs by Poiret, Callot Soeurs, Vionnet, Lanvin, Schiaparelli, Chanel, Dior, Balenciaga, Saint Laurent, Miyake, Gaultier, Mugler, Alaïa, Montana, and Lacroix, among others. As the curator of pre-1800 collections, I must take this moment to express the joy I feel daily as I look after such an extraordinary collection of textiles, the oldest dating back to Coptic Egypt, as well as costumes from the sixteenth, seventeenth, and eighteenth centuries that include many rare doublets from the reign of Henri III and Louis XIII, several *robes volantes*, examples of court wear for men and women, stays (*corps à baleines*), hooped petticoats (panniers), casual robes for men, and more than 150 waistcoats from the eighteenth century.

In 1982 Jack Lang, then minister of culture, began a campaign to establish a "national museum of fashion arts" within the Union Centrale des Arts Décoratifs,[1] a movement quickly supported by the media. It was during this period of the 1980s that the historian Daniel Roche completed his monumental work *La culture des apparences: Une histoire du vêtement (xviie–xviiie siècle)*, published by Fayard in 1989.[2] The first sentence immediately caught my attention: "Whilst the last decades of the twentieth century have seen the appearance of museums of fashion, a phenomenon by definition short-lived, historians have yet to think how to write about something other than these sumptuous and insubstantial phantoms." Interviewed at the time that article was written, Roche confirmed that, indeed, it was the opening of the Musée des Arts de la Mode at the Union Centrale des Arts Décoratifs in 1986, as well as Lang's speeches on the subject, that prompted him to reconsider and examine this issue: how to record a history of clothing other than the way fashion museums have always done, through the study of their "phantoms."[3]

According to the historian, precious costumes —the topic of our study—"have taken pride of place." "Inaccessible to the majority," they are the "mark of supreme distinction." By highlighting these extraordinary pieces, Roche is also speaking of the "absentees — the less well off, the real poor. To include them, with their costume and clothes... we need a different type of history," says Roche, "one that would be written outside of fashion museums".

Using Roche's remarks as a starting point, let us consider what is missing in fashion museums. By shifting our point of view, even briefly, we can look at the styles and clothing that we do not preserve and try to extract a few facts from the following list of "negatives."

No museum can claim to possess an exhaustive collection, and the Fashion and Textiles collections of the Musée des Arts Décoratifs are no exception. For example, the museum's nineteenth-century men's clothing collection, like those of most museums, is incomplete. The dark and sober jackets and trousers from that period offered little appeal to the aesthetic eye of collectors, who were more attracted by the shimmering clothes worn by men during the Age of Enlightenment. Today, finding pieces from that period is a challenge, since so few of them have been conserved.

While we boast a fine collection of bathing costumes from the 1920s and 1930s, we regrettably have few examples of leisurewear and sportswear. A woman's hunting habit from the eighteenth century would be welcome, as would a tennis dress with its bustle from the 1880s or a woman's cycling ensemble from the 1890s. Our twentieth-century sportswear department is likewise incomplete. In addition, two other groups of clothing are missing: those that represent foreign fashion and everyday garments.

Just as in other fashion and costume museums throughout France, the collection of the Musée des Arts Décoratifs is predominantly French, though it does contain the occasional rare English or Italian piece from earlier periods. The same can be said about the great collections in Britain that favor that country's designers. However, our Parisian museum has become more internationally focused since the 1980s, as fashion has come to play an increasingly significant role on the global stage.

Furthermore, most of the museum's eighteenth-century collection illustrates the aristocracy, whereas the nineteenth-century and the first part of the twentieth-century collections represent the bourgeoisie and high society; the last decades of the twentieth century are presented in an atmosphere of "*planète mode*" (world fashion), a term coined by the fashion world and the media. As Roche pointed out, the clothes of "the less well-off" are indeed absent in our museums — an observation that applies not only to the Musée des Arts Décoratifs but to all fashion museums that, for better or worse, have made selective choices for their collections.

We should also mention that the composition of the museum's collection stems from the way in which it was originally created, through the merger of two important collections — the Union Centrale des Arts Décoratifs (UCAD), founded in 1864, and the Union Française des Arts du Costume (UFAC), founded in 1948 — as well as through other gifts, bequests, and acquisitions.

From the beginning, the UCAD had assembled a large collection of textiles that included silks, embroideries, lace, printed fabrics, and so on. Collectors and industrialists joined in this venture for the purpose of showcasing applied arts by linking industry and beaux-arts. The costumes that were already in their collection were primarily meant to illustrate textiles. The museum's rich collection of men's clothing from the eighteenth century is the result of the founders wanting to display their savoir-faire in textiles and technique, their manufacturing of velvet, shot silks, and the application of embellishments. Similarly, traditional Chinese clothing and Japanese kimonos (to mention only two examples of non-European dress) were added to the collection as further examples of the vast textile industry's technical expertise.

Founded by François Boucher, the UFAC's collections were more focused on social differentiation. Yvonne Deslandres, who began her career as the famous historian's assistant, then as an archivist and eventually the figurehead of UFAC, was responsible for substantially expanding the collection. Deslandres didn't take "everything" — as they say — that was offered to her, though everything deserved to be considered, she recalled. Seduced by the scientific research of Georges-Henri Rivière, the founder of the Musée National des Arts et Traditions Populaires, Deslandres, we have been told, wanted to feel more "connected to the people." Paraphrasing Rivière, she believed that it was as important to seek out "the typical" as it was to search for "the unique." A unique garment is

"Yes, you can build larger reception rooms,
change the shape of furniture and carriages, demolish theaters!
Go ahead! But women will no sooner
give up their crinolines than they will rice powder."

THÉOPHILE GAUTIER

the exceptional one, an haute couture creation designed by a great couturier; a typical garment is an ordinary item taken from and representative of everyday life. The museum is indebted to UFAC for its many examples of 1970s everyday clothing.

The Musée des Arts de la Mode, founded in 1986, was formed by combining the "cultural and technical" collection of textiles of the UCAD with the more "socially oriented" one of the UFAC. As its name indicated, fashion had taken precedence over fabric. But in 1997 this perceived injustice or misunderstanding — in light of the museum's vast textile collection, one of the most comprehensive in the world — was rectified when the museum was renamed Musée de la Mode et du Textile. Indeed, you should not separate clothing from fabric since one is the extension of the other.

In fact, during the 1980s and 1990s, a shift did occur, a perceptible change of direction in the way the collection was conceived.

Even the new museum's name, now specified by "des Arts de la Mode," so similar to "des Beaux-Arts de la Mode," underscores its reorientation. Is it a coincidence, then, that this name was chosen at a time when art and sculpture museums, as well as the larger cultural institutions, were examining new issues and had, at least temporarily, abandoned monographic exhibitions of "actual beaux-arts" subjects in favor of more historical and socially oriented themes?

But fashion was already very much in fashion during the 1980s. Couturiers saw themselves as creators or artists, and the media treated them like pop stars.[4] Fashion was linked to contemporary art, often addressing the same issues. Did fashion museums get caught up in this wave? Were they guilty of intellectual laziness, of abdication? Perhaps the influx of people whose training was in fashion rather than history or museum studies explains this new way of envisioning the collections.

The fashion exhibitions held at the UCAD following the opening in 1997 of new exhibition spaces in the Rohan wing — occupying 1,500 square meters (more than 16,000 square feet), one of the world's largest exhibition areas devoted to fashion — were also representative of this new dimension. The world of contemporary fashion, specifically the one derived from the dynamics of the 1980s, had taken over the lion's share of programming alongside other exhibits about the first half of the twentieth century. During the last twenty or even thirty years, shows featuring eighteenth- and nineteenth-century "historical costume" have dwindled significantly.

As we continue to enlarge our collections, looking at fashion through the elitist prism of beaux-arts will have its consequences. When selecting objects and other items meant to illustrate fashion, are we — those of us in charge of the collections — similarly influenced by fashion trends?

As mentioned earlier, everyday clothes — garments currently being manufactured and intended for the largest number of people — are underrepresented in our collections. Indeed, it has become extremely difficult to acquire modest clothing from the seventeenth and eighteenth centuries. These pieces are so hard to come by that they have achieved the status of rare antiquities when they do appear in the art markets.

And yet even pieces manufactured today, which are abundantly produced and easily available, are not reaching our storerooms.

Although we take great pride in owning denim clothing designed by Thierry Mugler, Azzedine Alaïa, Giorgio Armani, Kenzo, Martin Margiela, Alexander McQueen, and especially a wonderful collection of pieces created by Marithé and François Girbaud, we are disappointed to have so few examples of everyday jeans from before the 1970s. A pair of jeans, the most popular article of clothing in the world, probably does not have the cachet of fashion; and yet Yves Saint Laurent's greatest regret was that he did not invent them. At the Musée des Arts Décoratifs, one can retrace the history of jeans from its very beginning. One of the museum's most prized possessions is the Holker book containing, among its denim samples dating back to 1750, examples of brown and white cotton twill, described as a widely used fabric.[5] This masterpiece of our collection — the item most requested by researchers from Europe, the United States, and Asia — would be the cornerstone of a history of jeans that still needs to be undertaken by the museum.

Raise the issue of a broader, more socially relevant vision of clothing in museums — if only to point out the absence of a particular piece — and the answer is always the same: "That's not fashion; that's clothing." How strange to make a distinction between fashion and clothing. If we separate the elite from the ordinary, then there is no more elite.[6] And what should we call a garment that is not meant to be worn? In a museum it is called a "fashion piece," but in the world of fashion it is called a "museum piece."

After all, fashion is a cyclical system. How many creations intended for a privileged few were initially inspired by popular clothing? Similarly, how many haute couture and luxury ready-to-wear creations were copied to meet a wider demand? Clothing is a social system: it can separate classes who nevertheless continue to influence one another. Fashion never lives in a vacuum; everything is connected. There are countless examples of transference between one fashion world and another. For instance, what distinguishes a punk "garment" from a punk "fashion garment"? Is it because the first one is worn in the street, while the second one is a Vivienne Westwood design? Did the grunge look only become "fashionable" after Marc Jacobs showed it in his first collection for Perry Ellis? Such examples abound, but let us not lose sight of our purpose: an ordinary garment should not become the subject of attention only when it inspires a well-known designer. We should not be reluctant to speak of low-end fashion, created for mass distribution by ready-to-wear designers who are also creators in their own right. Why shouldn't an everyday garment, or a designer who creates for the masses, be recorded in history?

And what is gained by acquiring only expensive garments, those that will not be worn? It would be like studying military uniforms but focusing strictly on a French general's uniform, worn exclusively on special occasions. Would you pay attention to the robe of an archbishop only if you were studying the history of religious dress? These examples merit consideration when setting the policies of fashion museums, in France and elsewhere.

Museums face considerable challenges. Acquisitions are limited by insufficient budgets, but also by a shortage of storage space. What's more, the objectives of French museums have changed considerably during the past ten years, something that needs to be taken into account when curating a national collection. Should we continue to collect costumes from the world of the theater, as did our predecessors at the UCAD, now that the Centre National du Costume de Scène et de la Scénographie (National Center for Stage Costumes), opened in 2006 in Moulins, is predominantly focused on this genre? Should we seek to complete our collection of traditional Chinese clothing—to cite only one example—now that the Musée du Quai Branly, also opened in 2006, has such a fine collection on the subject?

And what of the couture houses, increasingly concerned with their own legacy, whose acquisitions are intended to complete their archives? We must possess the wisdom and scientific rigor to assemble examples of many sartorial styles and conventions. If the Musée des Arts Décoratifs, an institution in charge of a national collection, doesn't do it, who will?

It is easy enough to criticize the curators and directors of fashion museum collections. Historians, from universities and research centers alike, are also accountable. They have not taken the study of clothing seriously, classifying it for many years as a secondary subject matter. Negligence gave way to ignorance; several "fashion historians," many self-proclaimed, were unaware that being a historian is a profession with its own apprenticeship, tools, demeanor, savoir-faire, and code of ethics. Along with the Annales School, we had hoped for a renewed push toward a more complete history of clothing and its conventions. Except for the tireless and pioneering efforts of Françoise Piponnier,[7] and a handful of publications on the subject, it would seem that the historical movement founded in 1929 by Lucien Febvre and Marc Bloch has neglected the topic of clothing. Sixty years later, the issues raised by Daniel Roche in *La culture des apparences* are not only an exception in the field but, especially in France, have apparently failed to arouse any strong feelings about the history of fashion and clothing. What's more, although the past twenty years have witnessed an increased interest in the body, the silhouette, and one's appearance, few historians have undertaken any study of fashion or clothing. The word *fashion* has even been intentionally omitted from the titles of some research projects because it is, still today, synonymous with futility.

These observations are alarming. The absence of everyday contemporary clothing will sooner or later mean that the history of fashion will be recorded without the necessary material evidence. Some will claim that we have other sources at our disposal, an abundance of visual documentation—countless images, fashion and news magazines, brand-name catalogues, brick-and-mortar stores, online shopping as well as Internet sites, social media, and more—to study the fashion of the last few decades. Historians, by contrast, know that an image does not represent *the* reality — it is *a* reality. Are the clothes worn by peasants in seventeenth-century paintings by the Le Nain brothers a true representation, or have they been altered by an excess of realism or idealization? Without the actual clothes worn by those of modest means at that time, these questions will remain unanswered. Had these garments been preserved, we would be able to examine the textiles, the cut, the way they were assembled and finished, as well as so many other details that go into the construction of a piece of clothing. Unfortunately, we cannot, as Yvonne Deslandres explained so eloquently, "because the information we could gather does not exist in any other document."[8]

The research has already been impeded, even truncated, by this problem, for which all fashion museums are partially responsible. Indeed, where could one go to study everyday clothing from the 1920s and 1930s? Not in fashion museums, not even in ethnographic museums, or even those specializing in art and folklore. Those institutions rarely have clothes from the twentieth century; typically, they collect items that relate to certain rituals (baptism, communion, marriage, death, and other ceremonial events). Books that illustrate the "history of fashion and costume" of the 1920s and 1930s are also complicit in this elitism. Leafing through these volumes, one must maintain a sharp and critical perspective not to believe that "the" fashion of the time — as if there exists only one — was created solely by the grand couturiers. How then can we study the wardrobes of those who were not fortunate enough to wear the designs of Doucet, Poiret, Patou, Schiaparelli, Vionnet, or Balenciaga?

1 — Speech given by Jack Lang, then Minister of Culture, concerning the creation of a national museum of fashion, June 28, 1982. http:/discours.viepublique.fr/notices/823093100.html.

2 — Published as *The Culture of Clothing: Dress and Fashion in the Ancien Régime*, trans. Jean Birrell (Cambridge: Cambridge University Press, 1994).

3 — I wish to thank Daniel Roche, professor at the Collège de France, for answering my questions. This article could not have been written without the assistance of the curators who have been and still are in charge of the museum's Fashion and Textile collections; a special thanks also to Véronique Belloir, Lydia Kamitsis, and Jean-Paul Leclercq.

4 — In 2001-2 the Musée des Arts Décoratifs held an exhibit on this theme, *Couturier superstar*.

5 — John Holker (1719-1786) was a British manufacturer, established in Rouen in 1751. The *Livre d'échantillons concernant les diverses étoffes qui se fabriquent dans l'étude de la province de Lankashire en Angleterre [...]* contains 115 cotton and English linen fabric samples, with captions detailing the materials, their use, and price.

6 — Many thanks to my friend Michel Pastoureau for sharing some thoughts on the history of clothing as it is studied in museums, universities, and research centers.

7 — Françoise Piponnier's thesis, defended in 1968, is titled "Costume et vie sociale: La cour d'Anjou, xive–xve siècle."

8 — Yvonne Deslandres, *Le costume: Image de l'homme* (Paris: Albin Michel, 1976), 24.

COLLECTIONS

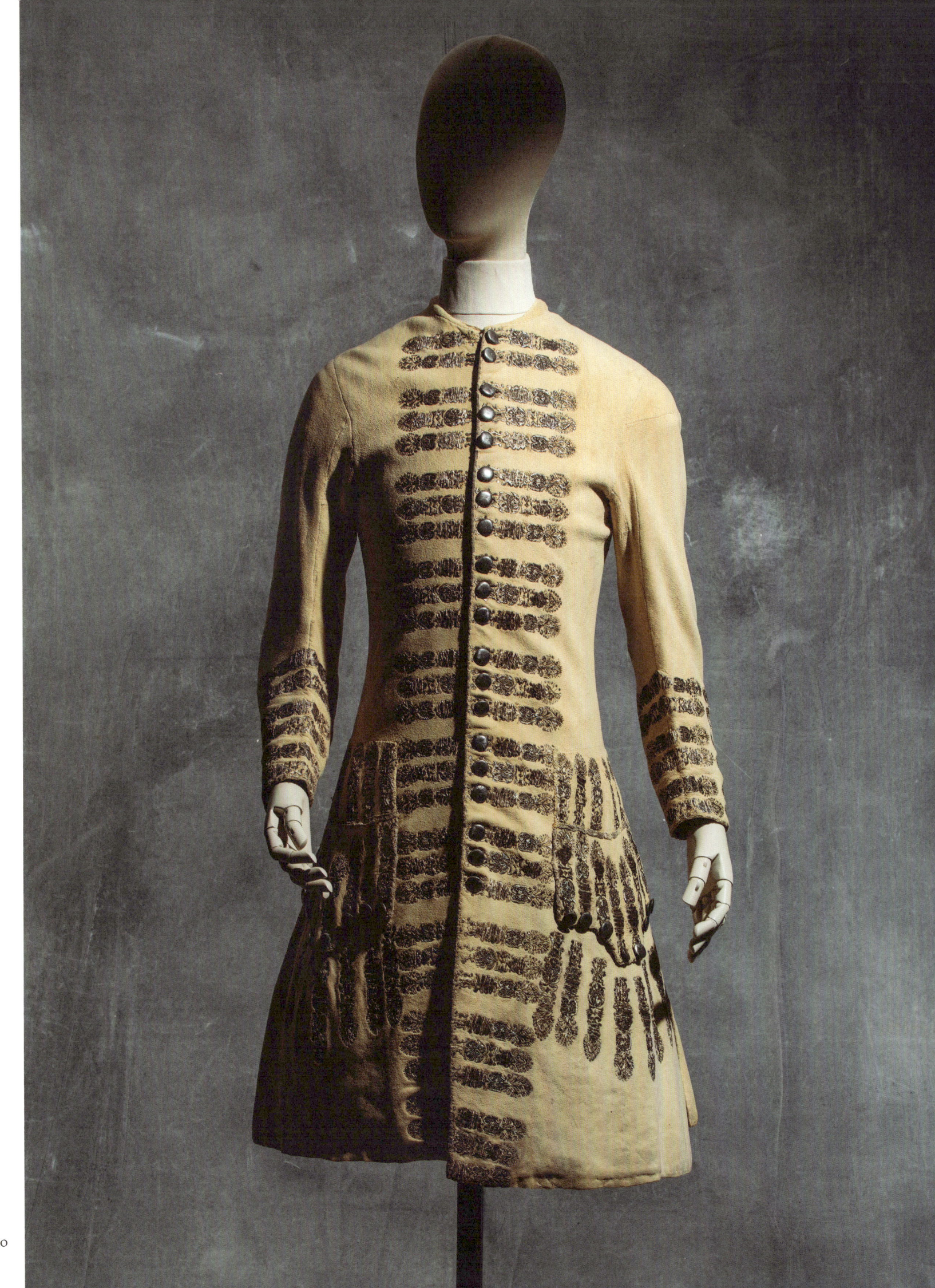

Riding Jacket
Circa 1690

Riding and hunting were favorite pastimes of the nobility during the ancien régime. At the end of the seventeenth century, participating in these activities required no specific outfits, and men wore their usual clothes: a justaucorps, a waistcoat, a shirt, and breeches. Nonetheless, some materials were favored more than others, such as animal skin, which was resistant to dirt and offered protection from the elements, as seen in this example of a waistcoat worn closed under a justaucorps. Special attention was given to the frog-closing embroideries made of metallic thread that embellish the front, sleeves, and pockets.

For women, riding was the only opportunity to wear ensembles borrowed from a man's wardrobe. Justaucorps, waistcoats, and shirts were adapted to fit their silhouette, while the breeches were replaced with a skirt.

H.R.

NICOLAS BONNART, *Gentleman Blowing a Horn*, circa 1690. Engraving. BnF, Paris; Music Department.

Children's Justaucorps
1715-1720

Until the beginning of the twentieth century, young children wore dresses, regardless of their sex. Only starting at age seven did their clothes mark the differentiation between girls and boys. Boys then wore clothes that were identical to those of adults. During the regency of Philippe d'Orléans (1715-23), young boys wore justaucorps, waistcoats, and breeches. This child-size justaucorps, with botanical and floral motifs on a solid background, is made of silk velvet embroidered with an openwork design of silk cords. Several functional and decorative passementerie buttons further enhance the front, pockets, and trim of the sleeves.

    Such decorative features show that children born into the great nobility of the eighteenth century were exquisitely dressed.

H.R.

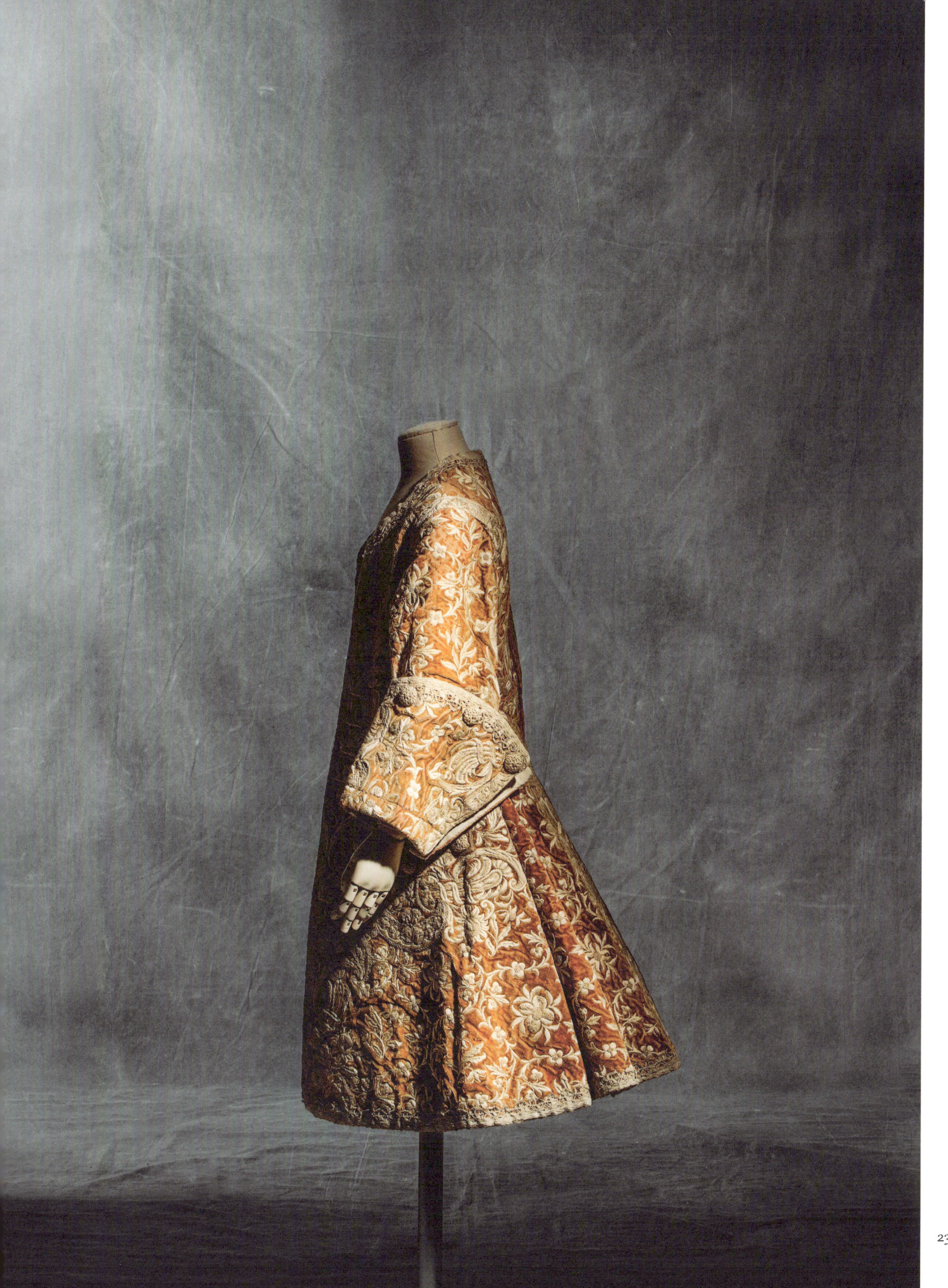

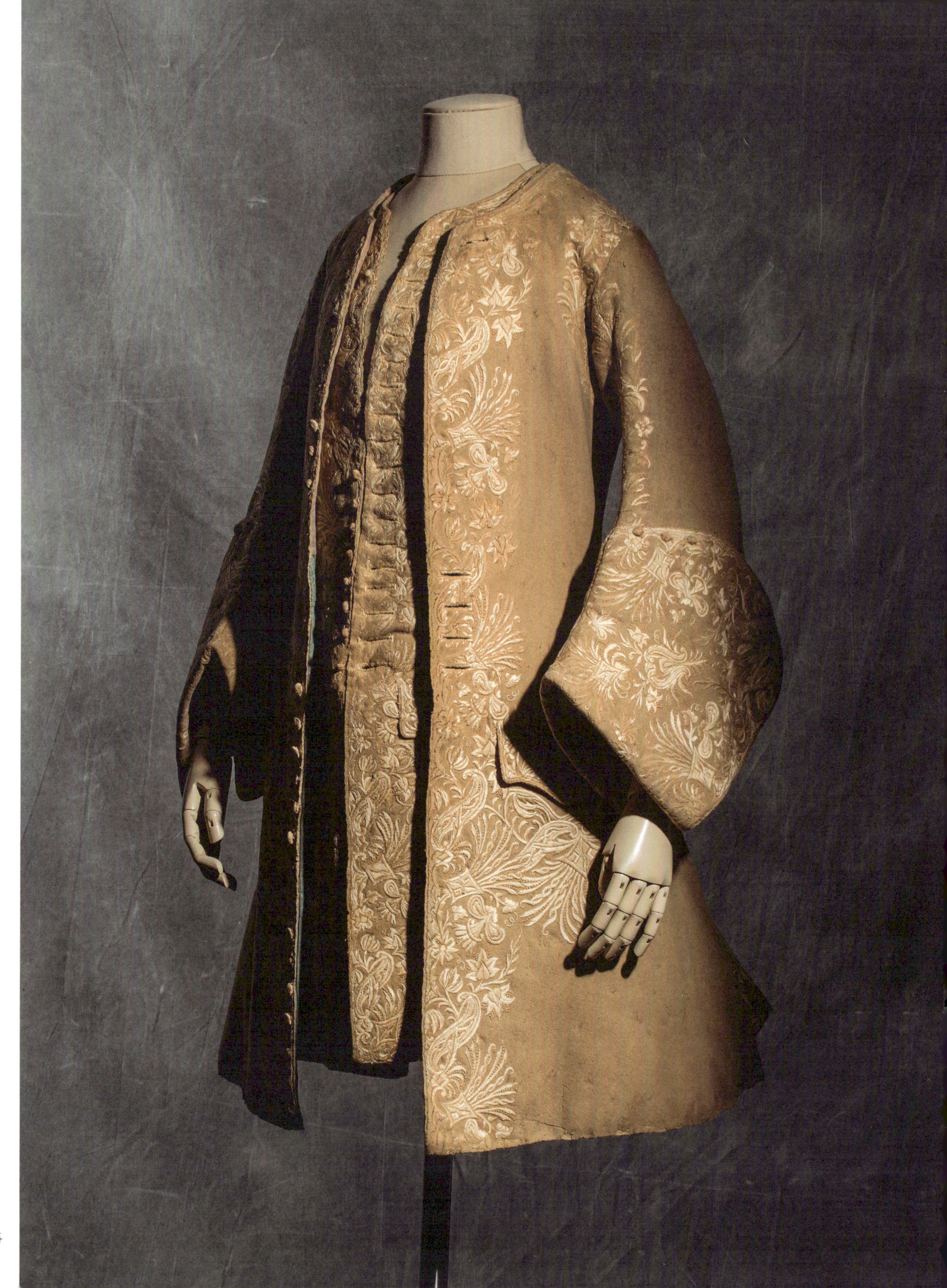

Justaucorps and Waistcoat
1720–1725

The justaucorps and waistcoat worn during the regency period were in fashion starting from the end of the reign of Louis XIV. Here, woolen cloth was used to make a warm and substantial garment. This type of fabric was favored for military uniforms and hunting clothes. While the fabric is not luxurious, the light color and lovely embroidery work lend it an elite touch. Indeed, the monochrome flat- and knot-stitch embroidery is a focal point of these two pieces, in particular down the front and across the wide trim on the sleeves of the justaucorps.

The small passementerie buttons are also decorative. Five of them serve to close the justaucorps in the accompanying buttonholes; the other twenty-two are purely ornamental.
H.R.

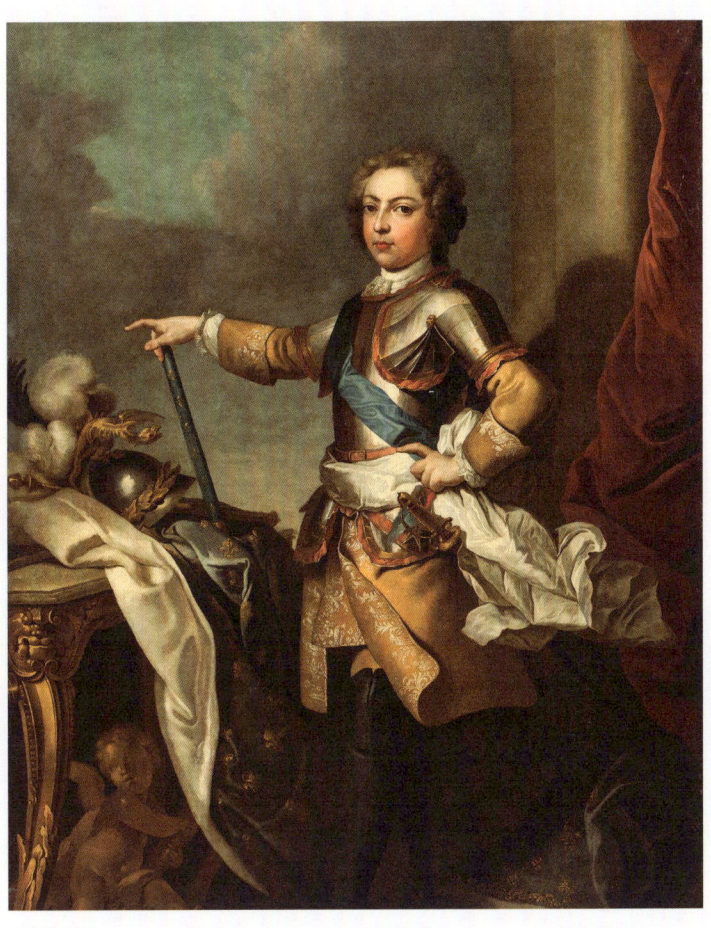

AFTER CARLE VANLOO, *Portrait of King Louis XV*, circa 1730. Oil on canvas. Musée des Arts Décoratifs, Paris; gift of Émile Peyre, 1905.

Banyan, *Waistcoat, and* Vest
1720–1730

In private life, clothes changed very little. Men eventually set aside justaucorps or suits for a banyan, an item inspired by Asian and Persian garments, which was used as a dressing gown. A waistcoat, breeches, and sometimes a vest completed the outfit, along with a negligé cap, which allowed a man to keep his head warm once he'd removed his periwig.

These at-home ensembles characteristically used a single fabric for the banyan, waistcoat, and vest, as seen in this example. This waistcoat is made entirely of silk, which was extremely rare for clothing worn outside the home. For economy's sake, the majority of these pieces contained nonvisible elements made of linen, for example on the back of the waistcoat or vest, which is not the case here. Contrary to robes of honor, the fabrics selected for banyans were close to those used for women's dressing gowns. In this piece, a decorative silk satin lampas *fond satin* "*à la dentelle*" (lace-like pattern) or "*persienne*" (Persian-style) was chosen.

H.R.

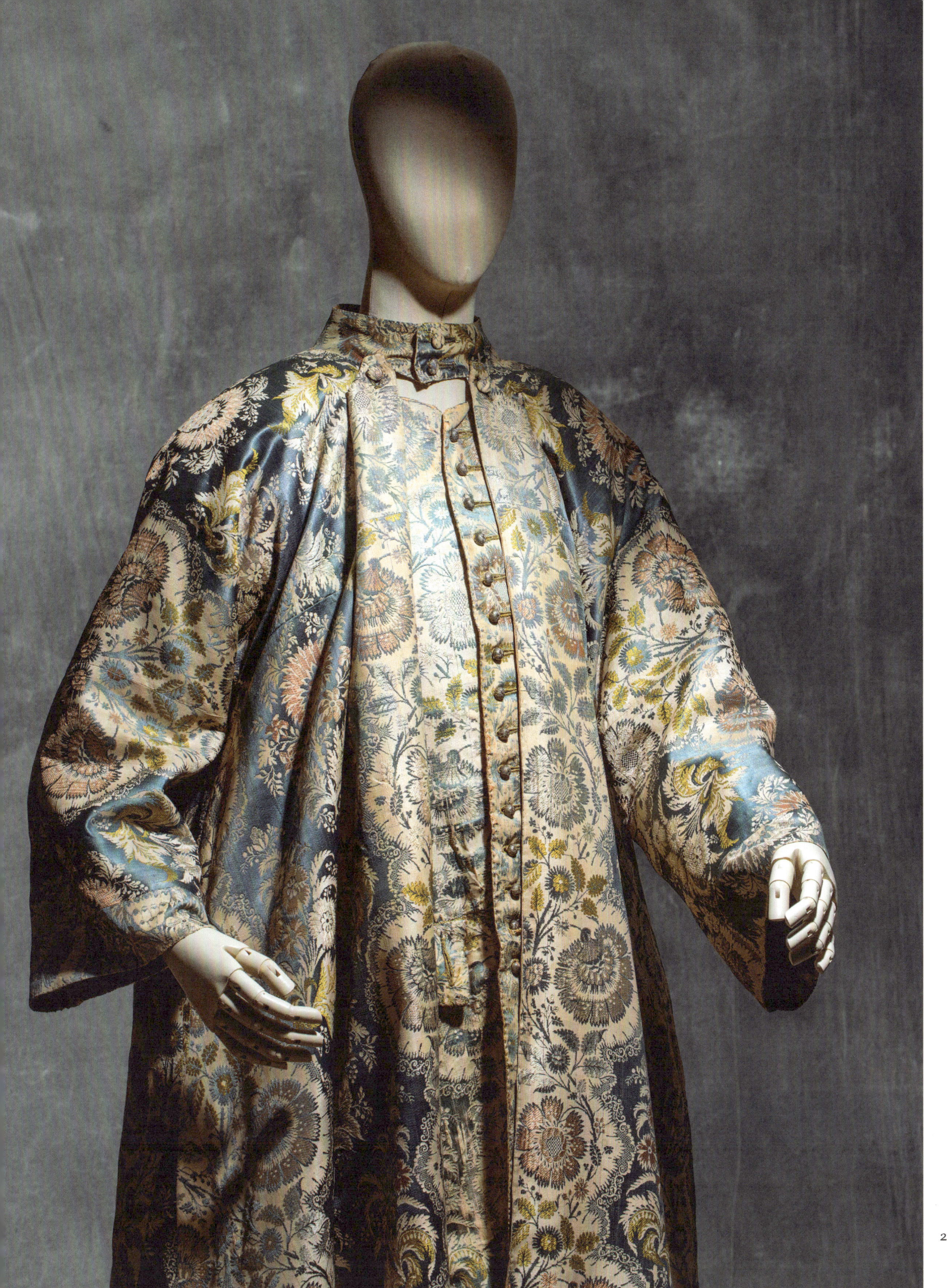

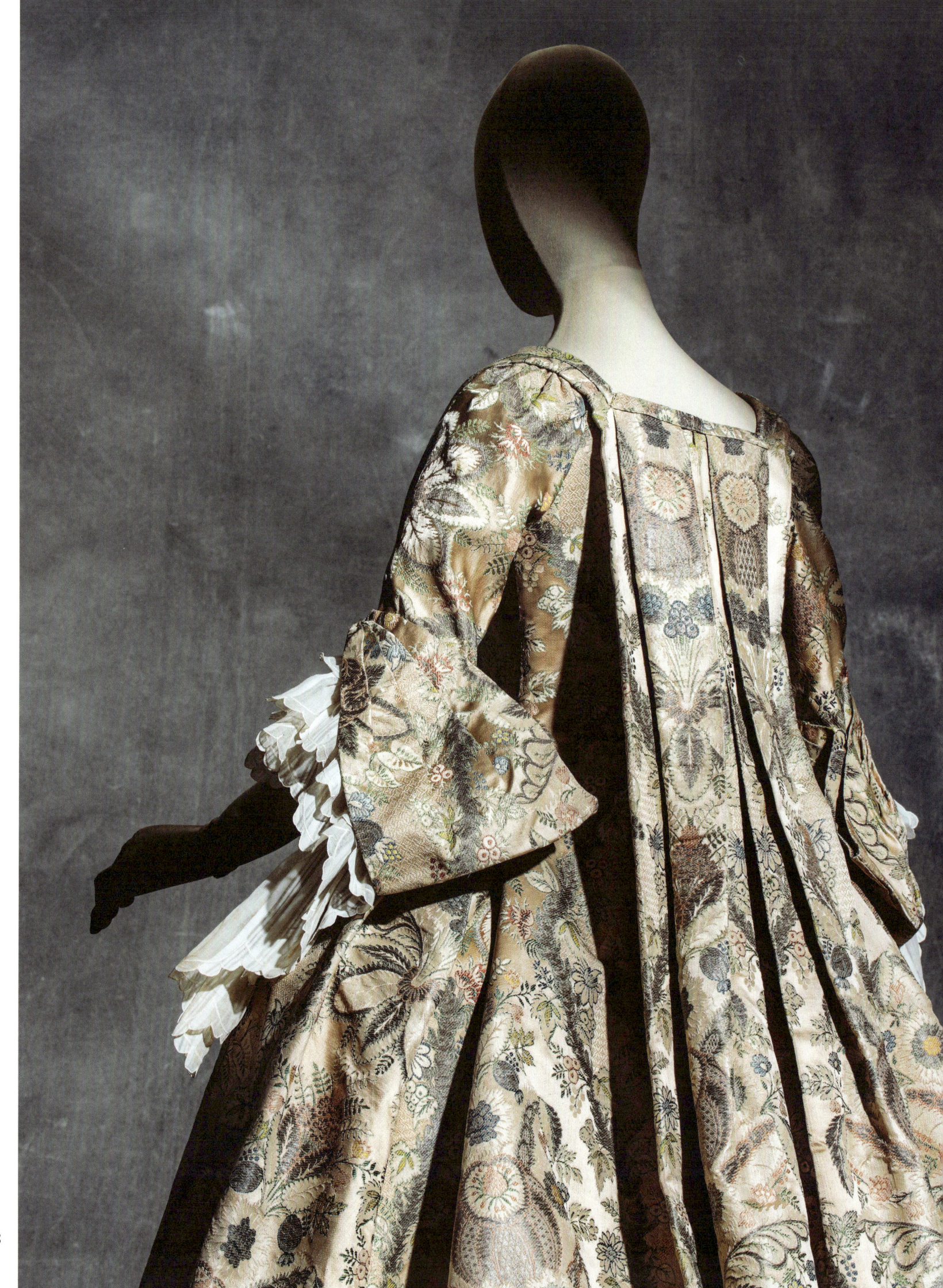

Robe Volante
Circa 1725

The *robe volante* appeared at the royal court in the early eighteenth century. With an open front revealing the stays, and embellished in the back with flat folds known as "Watteau pleats," this loose garment was somewhat reminiscent of the state of *deshabillé* (undress intended for private spaces). Madame de Montespan had already worn deshabillé in public during the reign of Louis XIV to conceal her pregnancies. The scandalous *robe volante* was disliked by women of a certain age. Princess Palatine noted in a letter dated April 12, 1721, that she found it rude to wear them, and she refused to receive women outfitted in such a dress.

This *robe volante* is made of a beautiful decorative silk lampas *"à la dentelle"* (lace-like pattern), in vogue between 1720 and 1730 and known as *"persiennes"* (Persian dresses), evoking a certain taste for exoticism in the eighteenth century.
H.R.

JEAN FRANÇOIS DE TROY, *The Declaration of Love*, 1731. Oil on canvas. Berlin Staatliche Schlösser und Gärten, Sanssouci Palace, Potsdam.

Justaucorps and Breeches
1730-1740

The male three-piece suit was created at the end of the reign of Louis XIV. It consisted of a collarless justaucorps, a coat, a waistcoat, underdrawers, and breeches. This outfit was still current during the regency and in the first years of Louis XV's reign. Unfortunately only the justaucorps and breeches remain in this beautiful example; the incredible richness of the fabric attests to the exceptional craftsmanship, and it was no doubt worn at court. The garment is made of a blue frisé velvet, edged and brocaded with silver thread.

    The false buttonholes decorating the front were done in silver thread passementerie. The buttons were also in silver thread, with embroidered and purl embellishments on a sel-patterned silver *lamella* background. The silhouette was skirted, being fitted at the waist. The justaucorps thus extended outward from the hips to the knees. The relatively short sleeves ended in so-called *"en aile"* (winged) cuffs.
H.R.

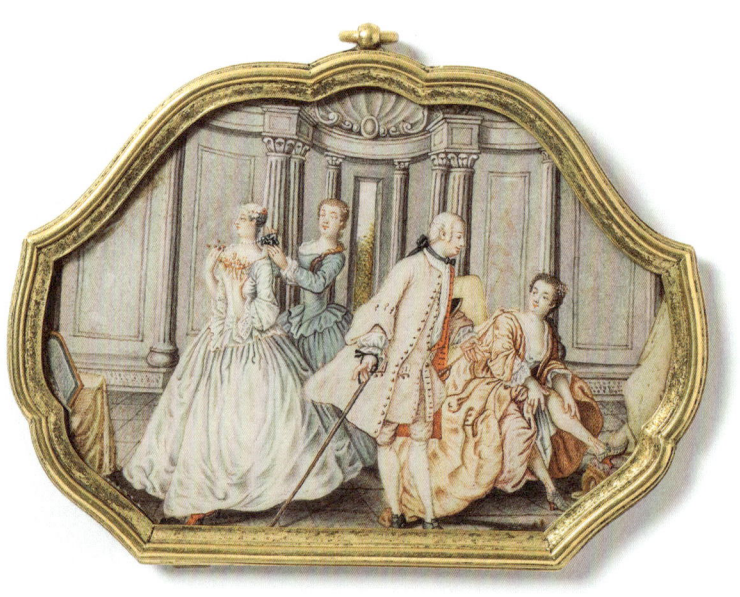

Femmes à leur toilette (Women getting ready), eighteenth century. Miniature on paper. Eighteenth century. Musée des Arts Décoratifs, Paris. Bequest of Louise Suzanne Lefebvre de Viefville, in memory of Louis Lefebvre de Viefville, 1964.

PP. 32-33 — Lampas for dress bottom or backing, 1735-1740. Silk, *fond cannetillé* (purl background) brocaded with silver thread, and polychrome silk. Musée des Arts Décoratifs, Paris; purchase, 1997.

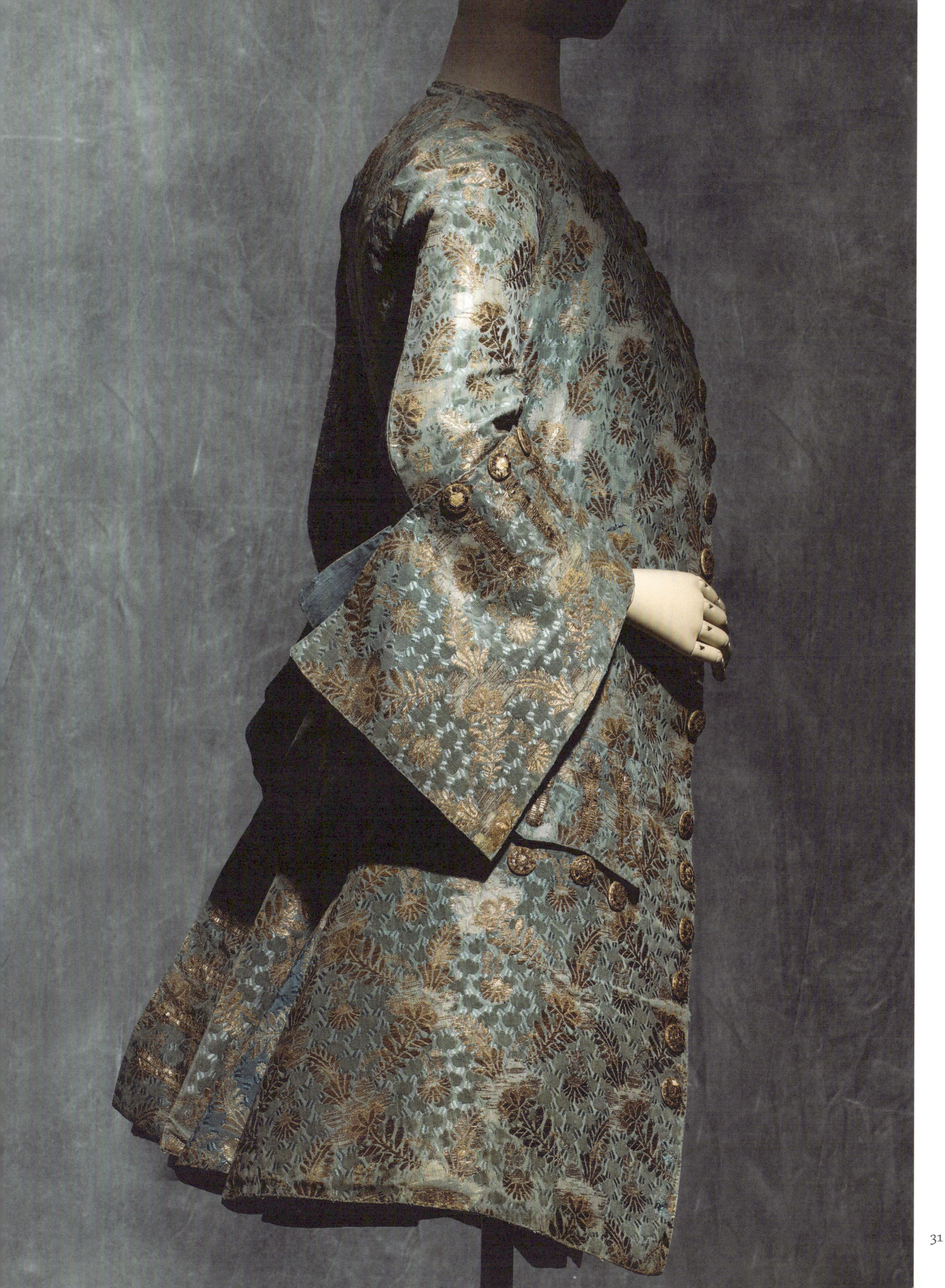

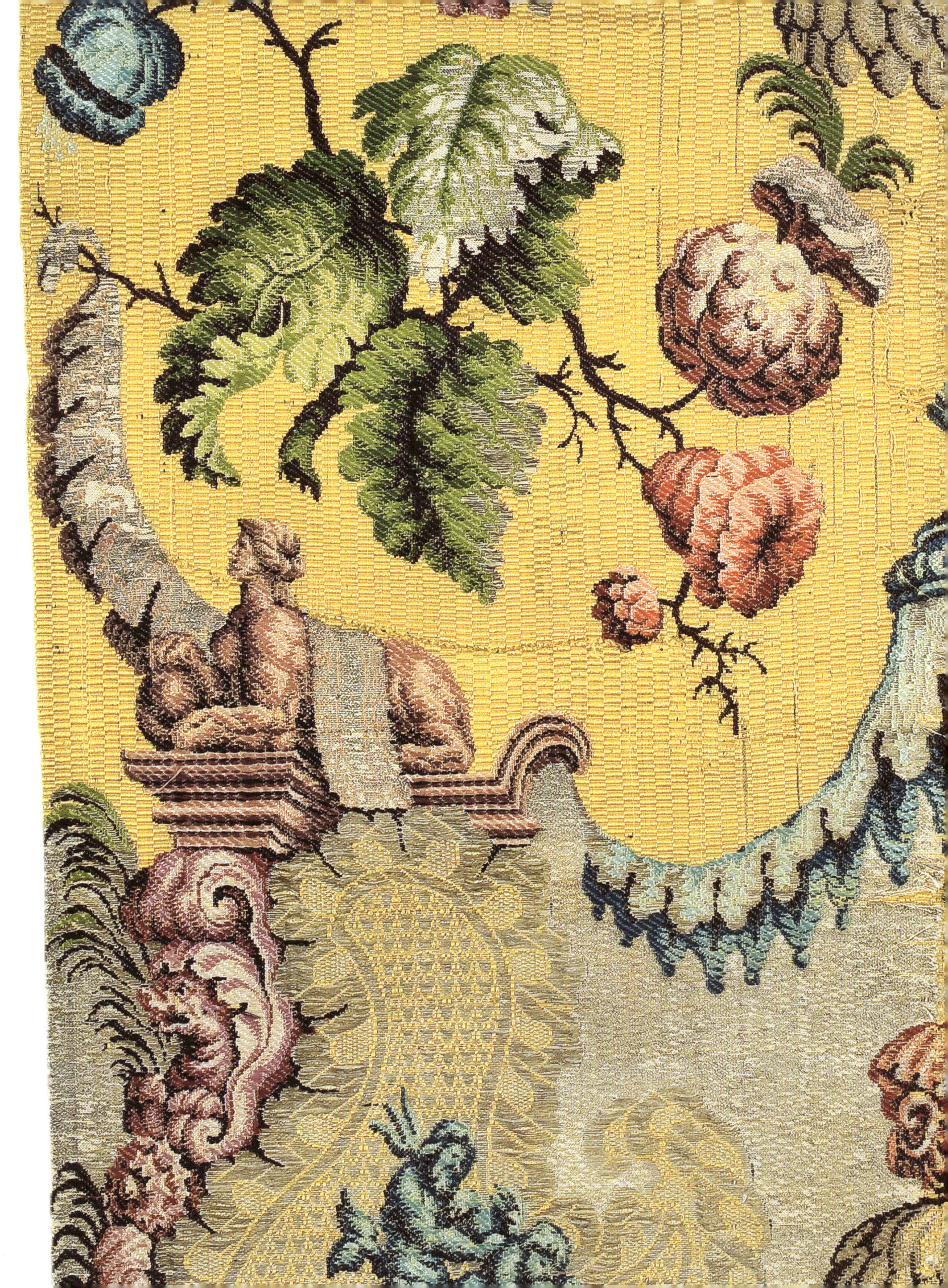

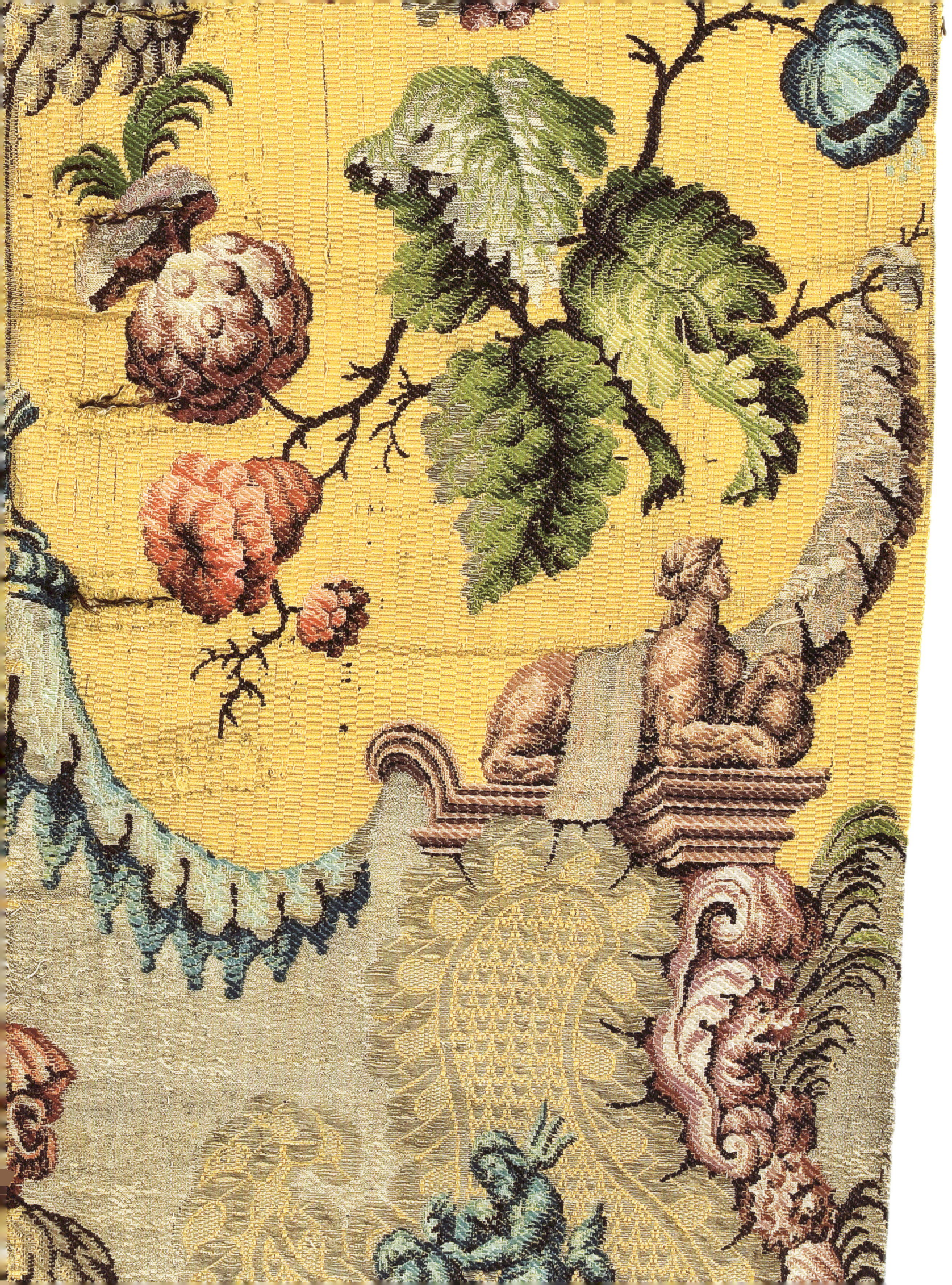

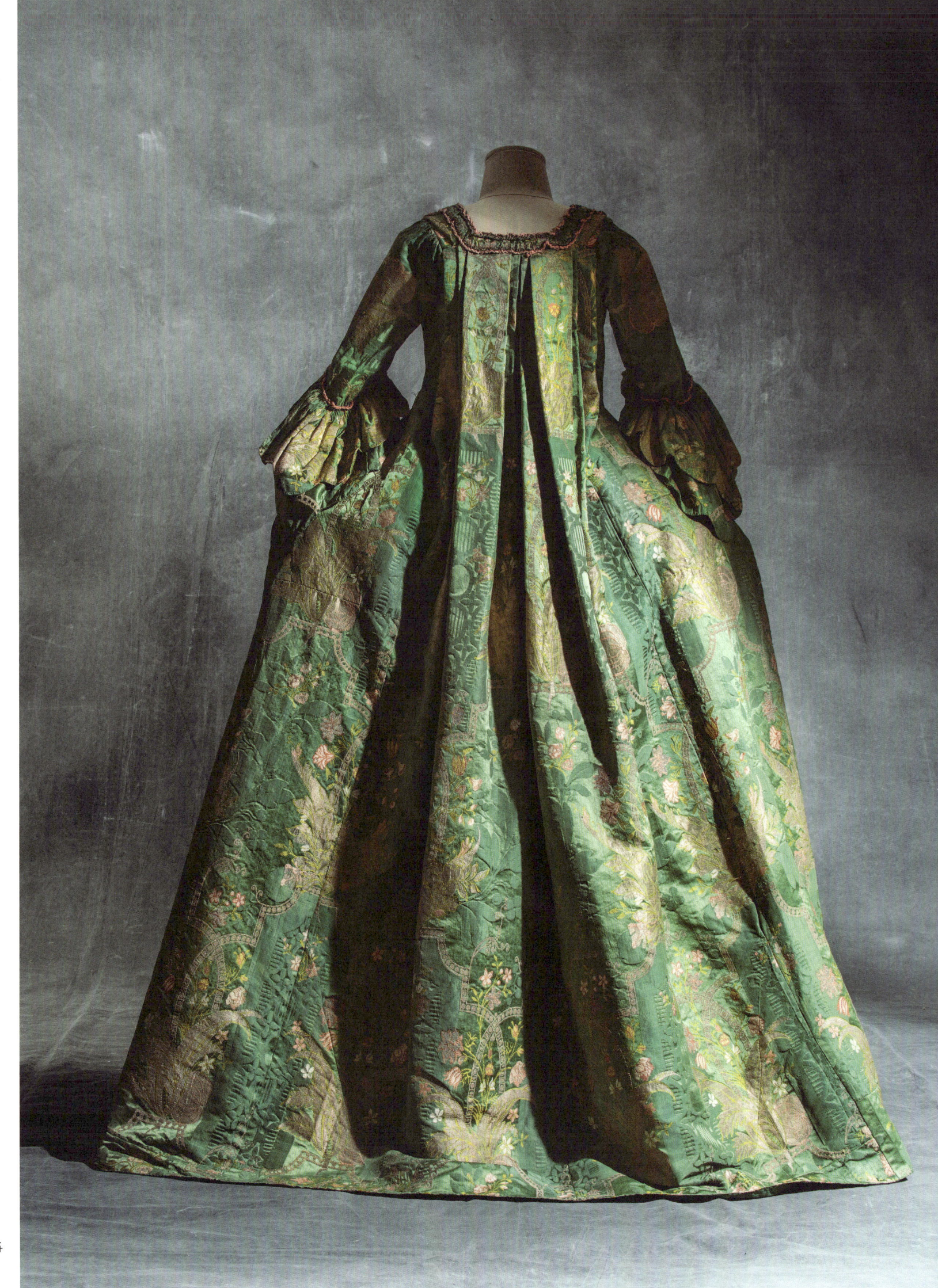

Robe à la Française
Circa 1740

Around 1740, the so-called *robe à la française* emerged from successive transformations of the *robe volante*. More fitted than its predecessor, the *robe à la française* was also completely open in front, revealing part of the stomacher that covered the stays. It consisted of an overdress and underskirt. However, the back of the overdress was similar to the back of the *robe volante*, notably due to the Watteau pleats.

The textile used on this relatively early model is extremely lavish. The green silk damask contains bouquets of flowers embroidered in polychrome silk thread. The use of gold-threaded geometric or botanical-themed embellishments provides an even more luxurious touch. The pagoda sleeves, characteristic of this period, contain two *engageantes* (false sleeves).

H.R.

Monkey's Suit
1730–1750

Monkeys often had special status vis-à-vis humans thanks to the troubling similarity of their mannerisms. People mistrusted the animals during most of the Middle Ages, and it was toward the end of that period that they were depicted in illuminations as dressed, in caricature fashion. They likewise appeared in princely menageries, and it would appear that Isabeau of Bavaria's monkey was dressed in a gray fur-lined robe. The great popularity of exoticism and chinoiserie in the eighteenth century made them well-regarded pets. Louis Sébastien Mercier noted in his *Panorama of Paris* in 1783 that women adored them.

    As with the *singeries* that adorned châteaux and private hotels, decorative scenes painted in the manner of the Age of Enlightenment (for example, Christophe Huet's *Grande Singerie* and *Petite Singerie* in Chantilly), these small animals could be dressed similarly to humans, as demonstrated by this pink taffeta suit from the mid-eighteenth century. H.R.

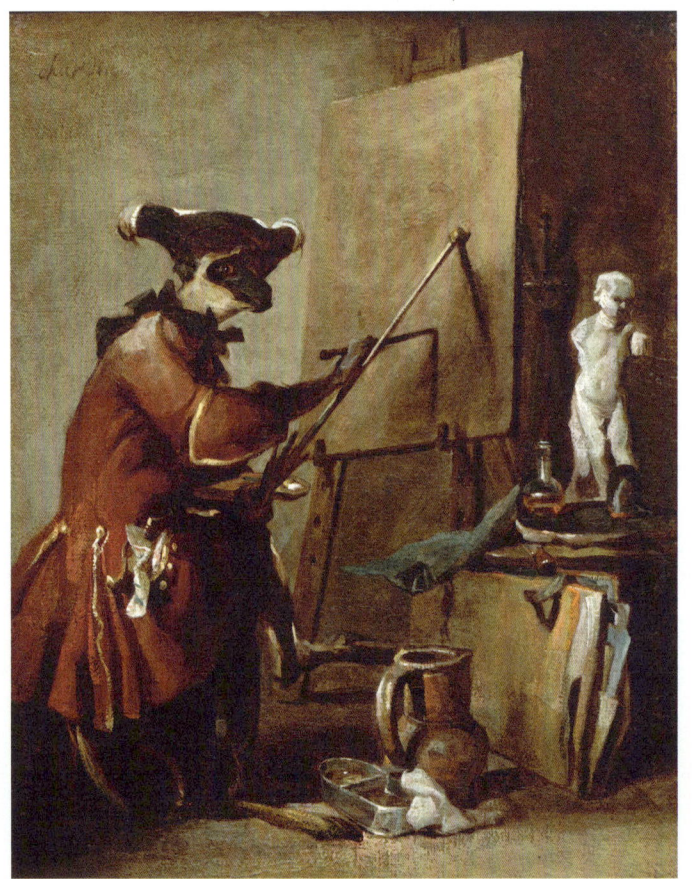

JEAN-BAPTISTE-SIMÉON CHARDIN, *The Monkey Painter*, circa 1739–1740. Oil on canvas. Musée du Louvre, Paris.

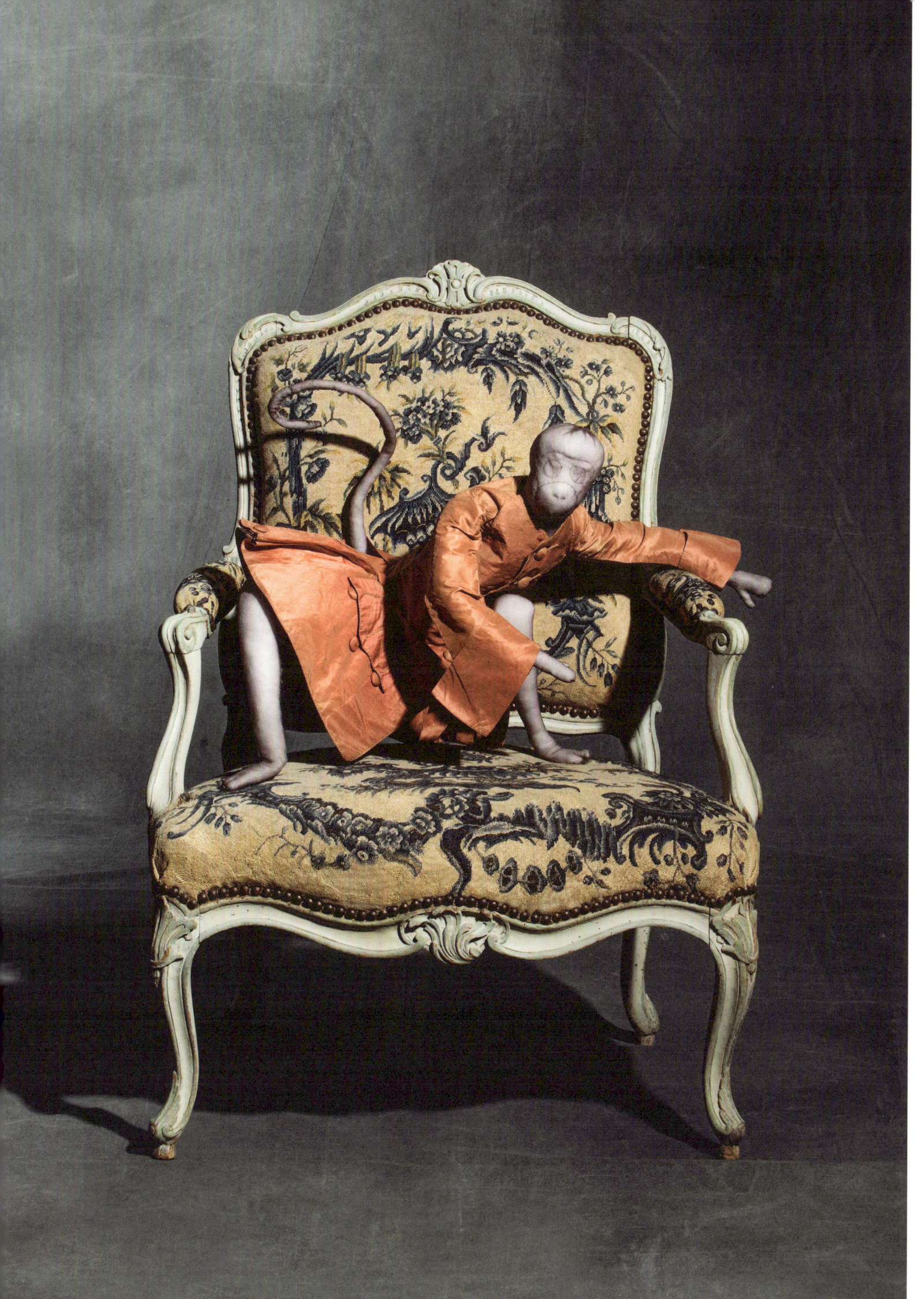

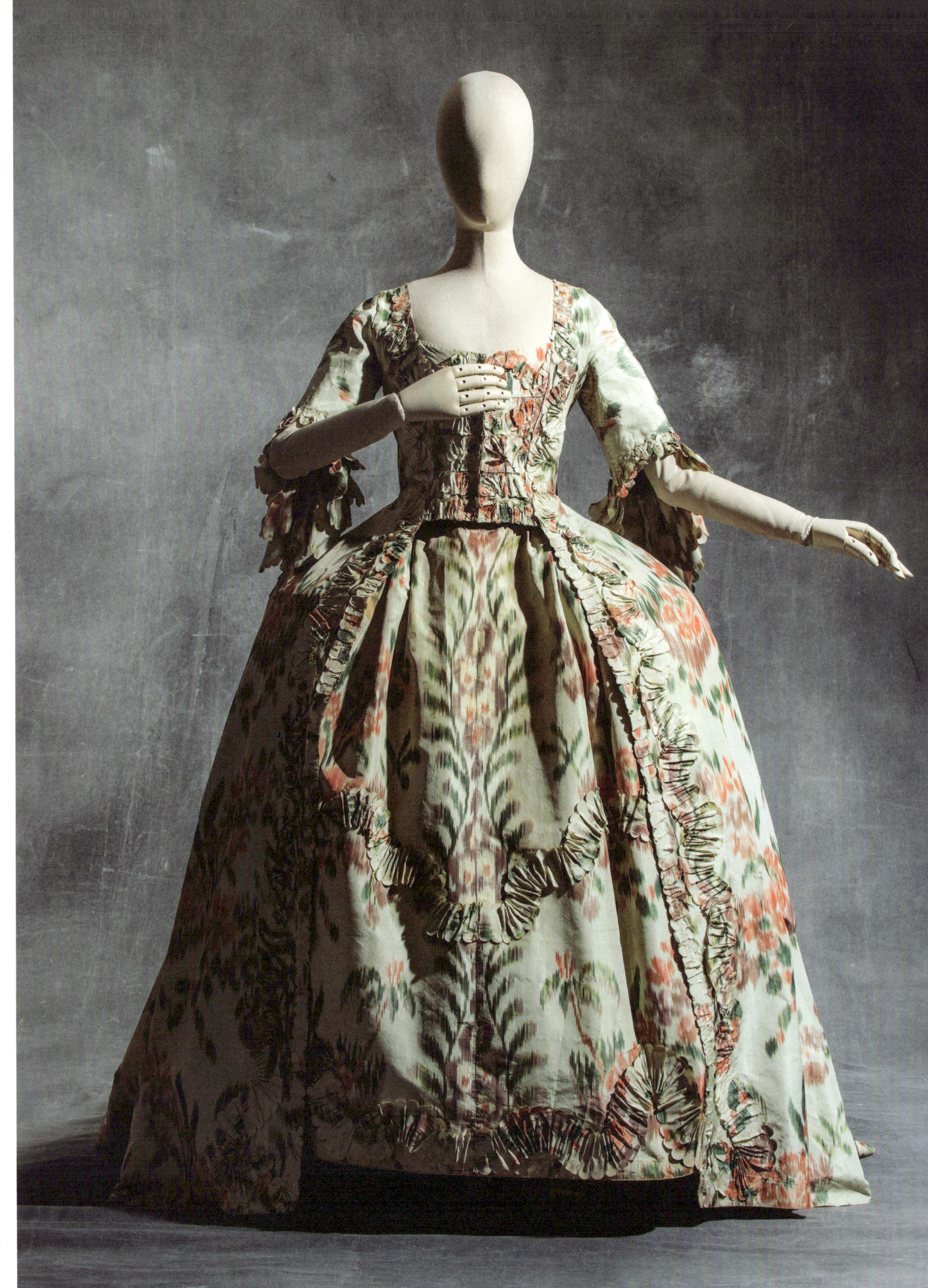

Robe à la Française
Circa 1760

This dress, consisting of a Watteau pleat overdress and underskirt, was created around 1760. Its originality is due to its then highly regarded textile, a *chiné à la branche* silk taffeta, made using the combined techniques of dyeing, printing, and weaving.

When creating this textile, only a portion of the warp threads are dyed, using a resist method. First, the entire warp is separated into packets of threads called branches and hung on a frame. The threads are partially tied in places to prevent them from being dyed during successive color baths. The packets are then positioned so that the entire warp is re-created before weaving, when the thinner solid-colored weft is left barely visible. This technique gives the final design an irregular and fluid look. In use since the sixteenth century in Lyon, this process began in Asia in the first century and once again demonstrates the popularity of exoticism during the eighteenth century.
H.R.

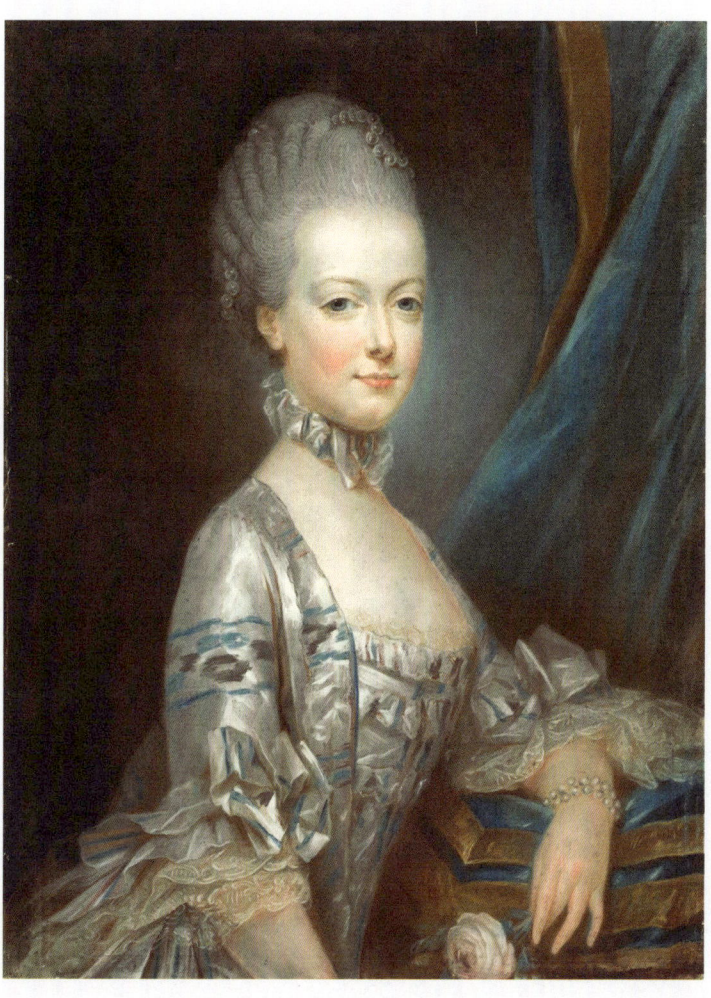

JOSEPH DUCREUX, *Portrait of Archduchess Maria Antonia of Austria*, 1769. Pastel on parchment.
Musée National des Châteaux de Versailles et de Trianon.

Men's Suit
(Habit à la Française)
1770-1780

The *habit à la française* was a three-piece suit. The suit coat was worn over a vest, which was generally sleeveless, and breeches completed the outfit. Made between 1770 and 1780, this model is entirely characteristic of court dress, as seen in the complexity of the fabric, a yellow frisé velvet with a small pattern over the smooth surfaces; it was formed by warp floats, in discontinuous broken lines. The metallic-thread-embroidered edges and buttons, with tinsel, rhinestones, sequins, and purls, lend it a luxurious look. These small ornamental elements were also found in women's clothing.

Unlike in previous years, the male silhouette became increasingly slimmer during this period, with suit coats flaring backward, flattened pleats at the lower back, and tighter breeches.
H.R.

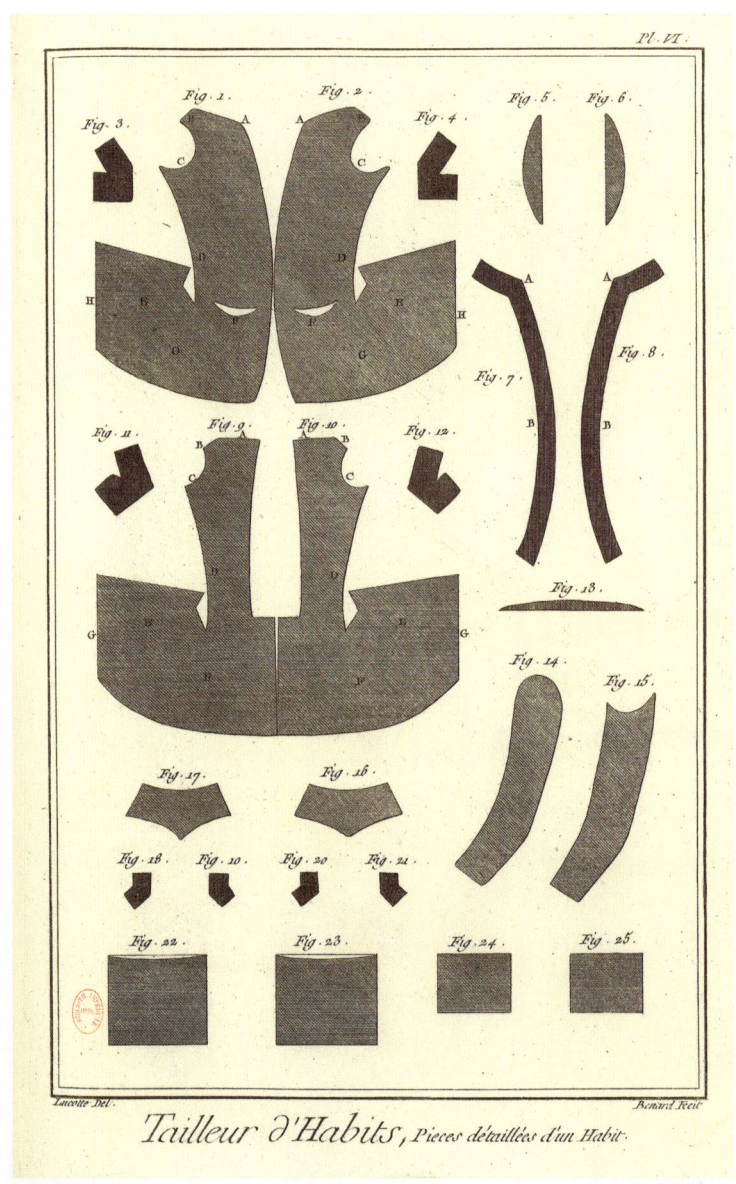

DENIS DIDEROT, JEAN LE ROND D'ALEMBERT, *Encyclopédie, ou dictionnaire raisonné des sciences, des arts et des métiers.*
Arts de l'habillement (Paris, 1743). BnF, Paris; Prints and Photographs Department.
PP. 42-43 — WIDOW OF JQ JÉROME AND ELDEST SON, Album of samples, late eighteenth century. Musée des Arts Décoratifs, Paris; Fashion and Textiles Collection, gift of Moïse de Camondo, 1919.

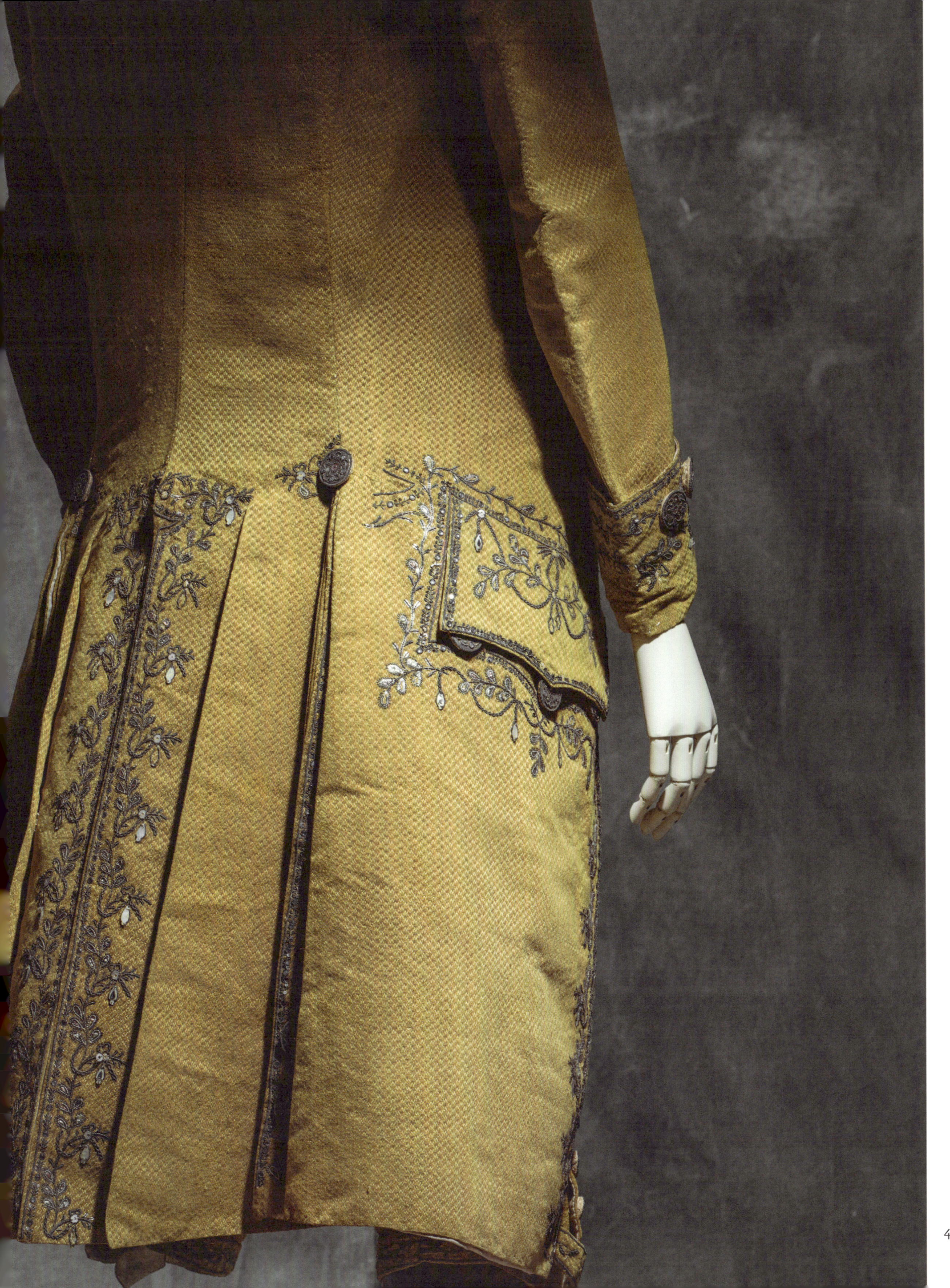

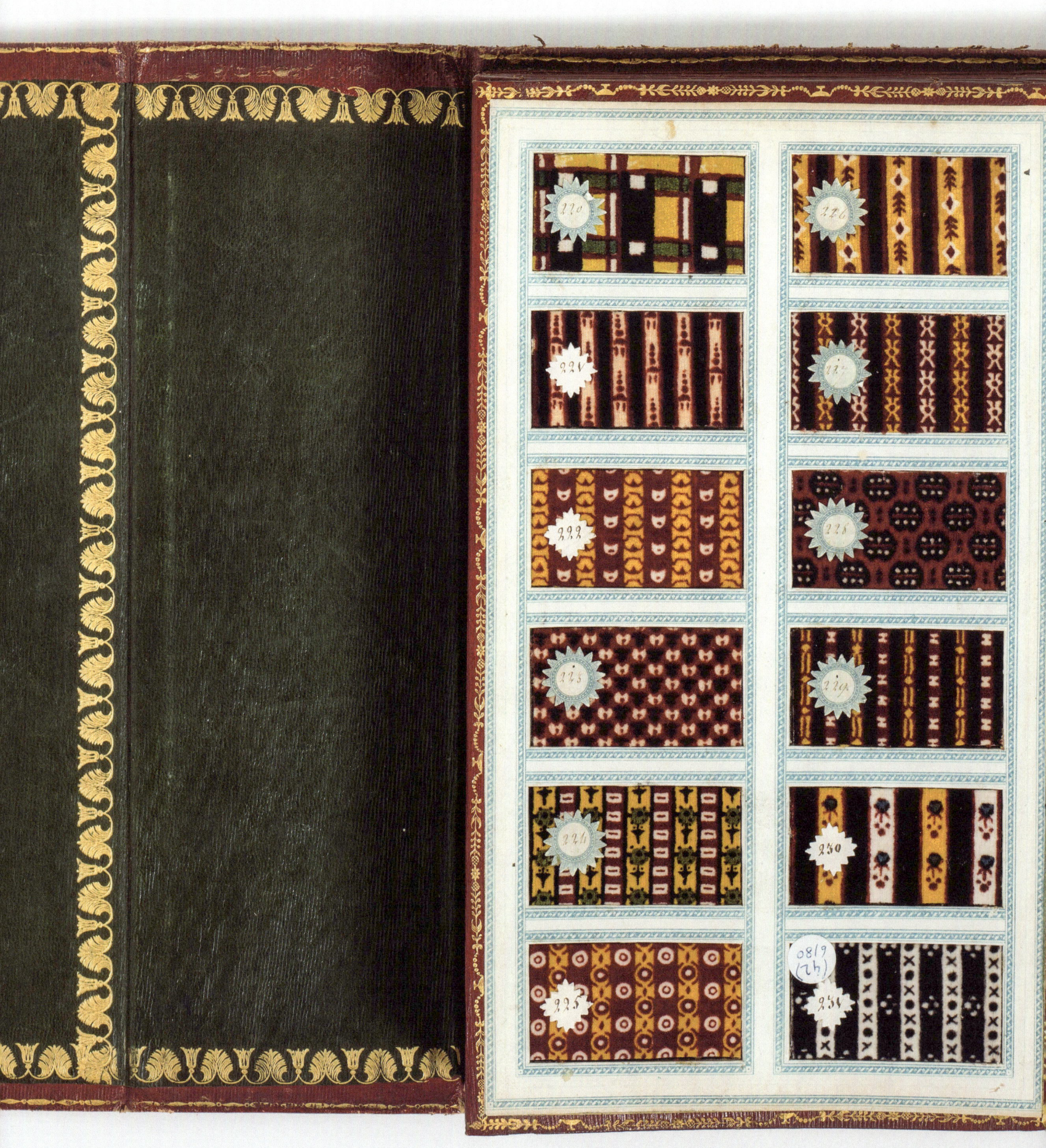

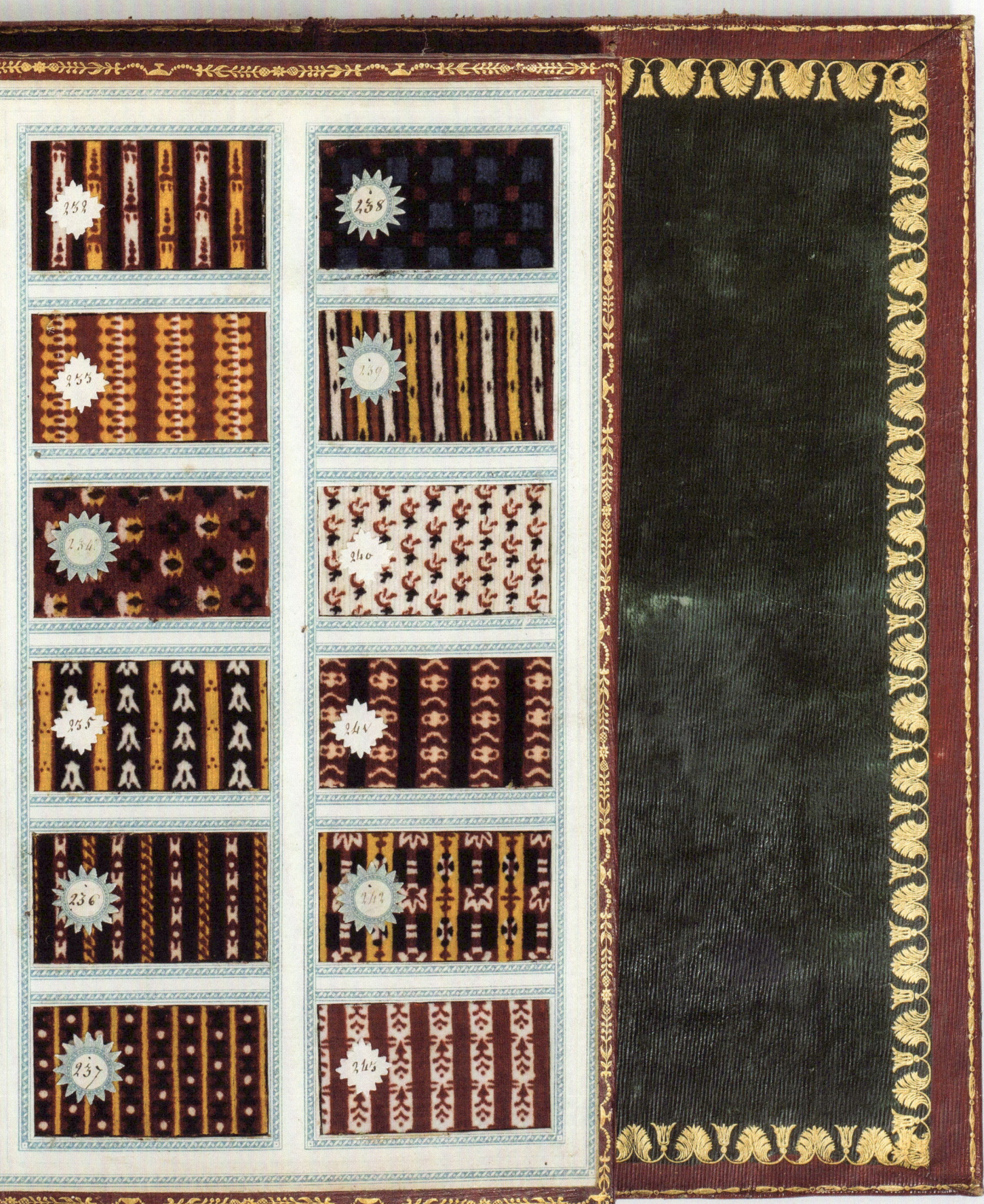

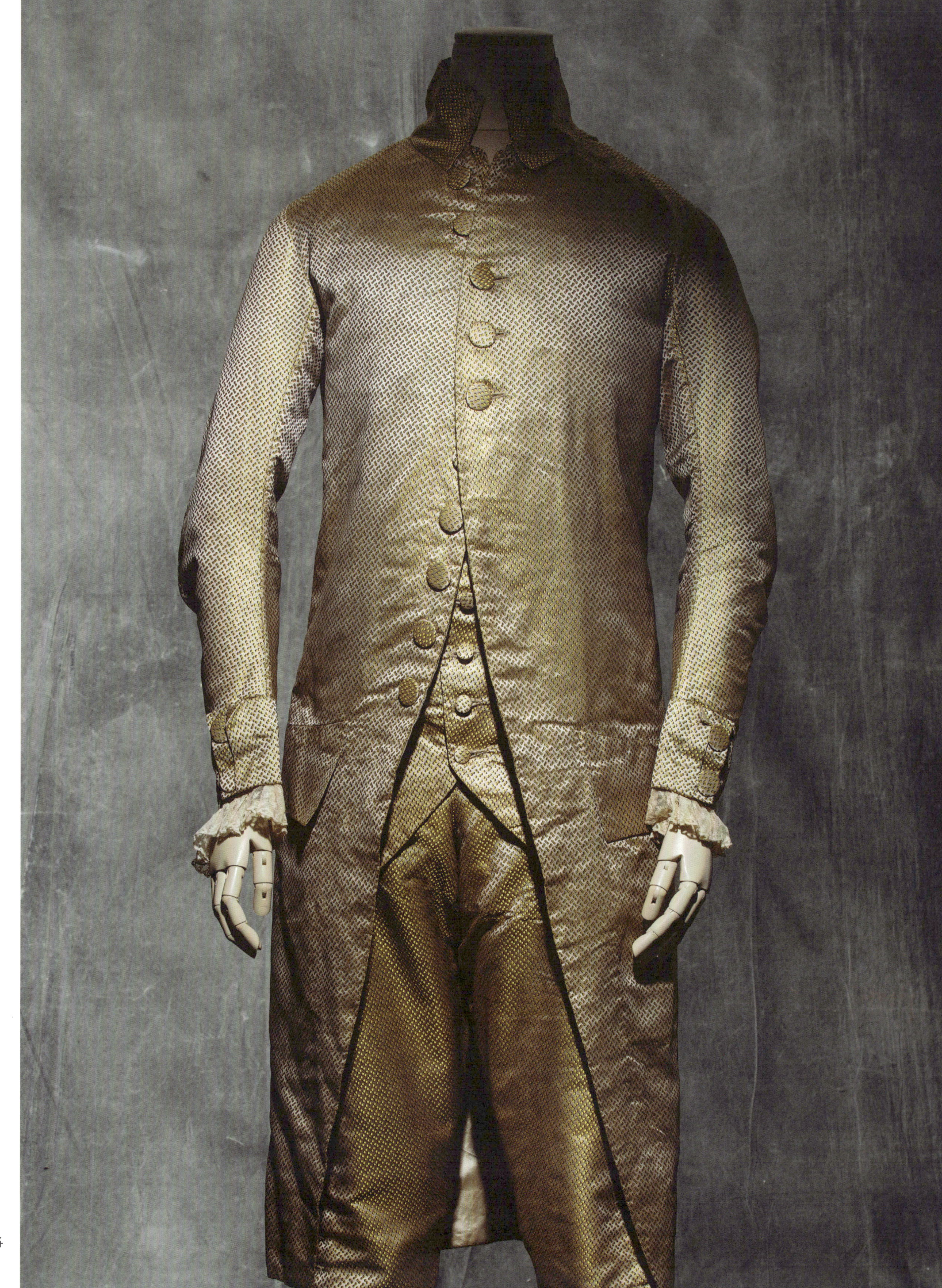

Men's Suit
(Habit à la Française)
1775-1790

This men's suit was fairly characteristic of the last years of the French monarchy. It still consists of a coat, vest, and breeches, but the sleeves are more fitted and the volume of the front of the garment flares toward the back. The neck is still high, with a turned-down collar. Although the fabric is not overly complex, the cream-colored silk satin with decorative edging and yellow and black marl lend this ensemble a look of excellent quality worthy of a respectable man. Such was the case, for it was owned by Joseph Orsel (1750-1820), lord of Châtillon, squire, secretary to the king, attorney at the high council of Lyon, and advisor in the senechalsy and *présidial* headquarters of Lyon.

This is thus a good example of clothing that belonged to a member of the Nobles of the Robe who lived in the provinces. During the Revolution, Orsel was national commander of the municipality of Saint-Jérôme and later a municipal officer in Cuires-la-Croix-Rousse.

Sentenced to death in 1793, he was imprisoned and ultimately survived the Reign of Terror.
H.R.

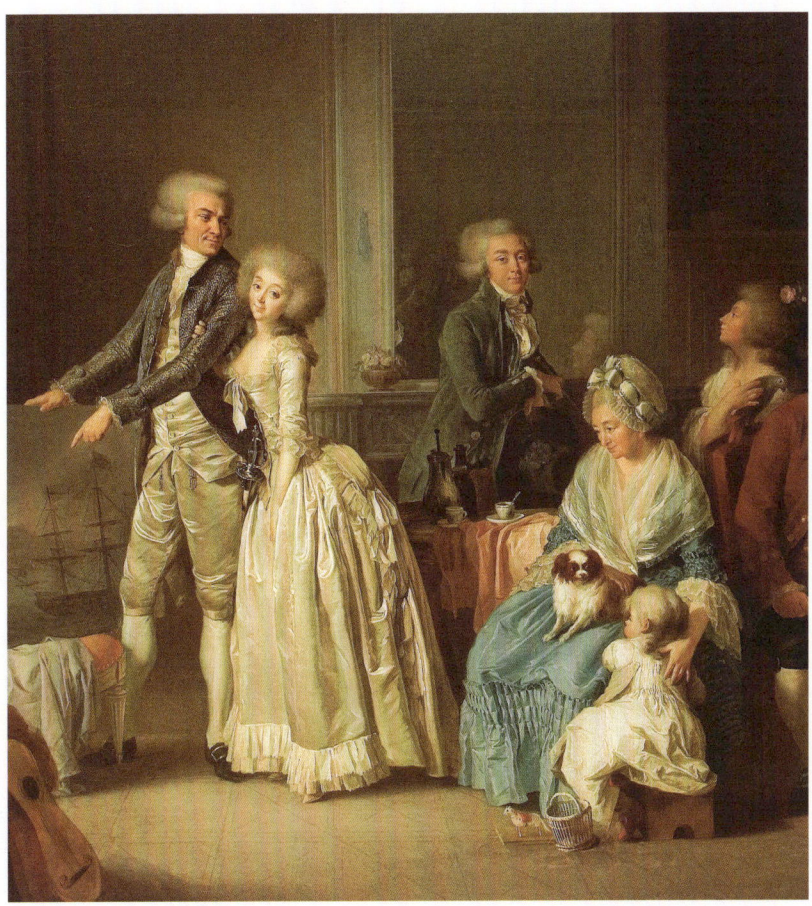

LOUIS LÉOPOLD BOILLY, *The Gohin Family* (detail), 1787. Oil on canvas. Musée des Arts Décoratifs, Paris; gift of Perrin, 1901.

Court Dress
Circa 1778

After the 1770s, the *grand habit* (with tight, rigid bodice, a wide skirt over panniers, and a train) was deemed outdated and no longer required at court. The *robe à la française* replaced it for important occasions, even though the *robe à l'anglaise* was preferred for unofficial events. This court dress made around 1778 is a bit atypical because, although its wide panniers have been maintained, the Watteau pleats that were characteristic of the *robe à la française* have been eliminated.

    This ensemble is nevertheless of high quality, for the dress is made of an ecru pekin fabric and contains taffeta, satin, *cannelé simpleté*, *cannelé fantaisie*, and decorative bands, with pile-warp floats resulting from the *cannelé*. It is decorated with satin-stitch polychrome embroidery. Tinsel encircled with purls give the overall ensemble a luxurious look. A gold lace insertion around the neckline, with small pink silk roses and foliage forming "beetle brows," provides further embellishment.

H.R.

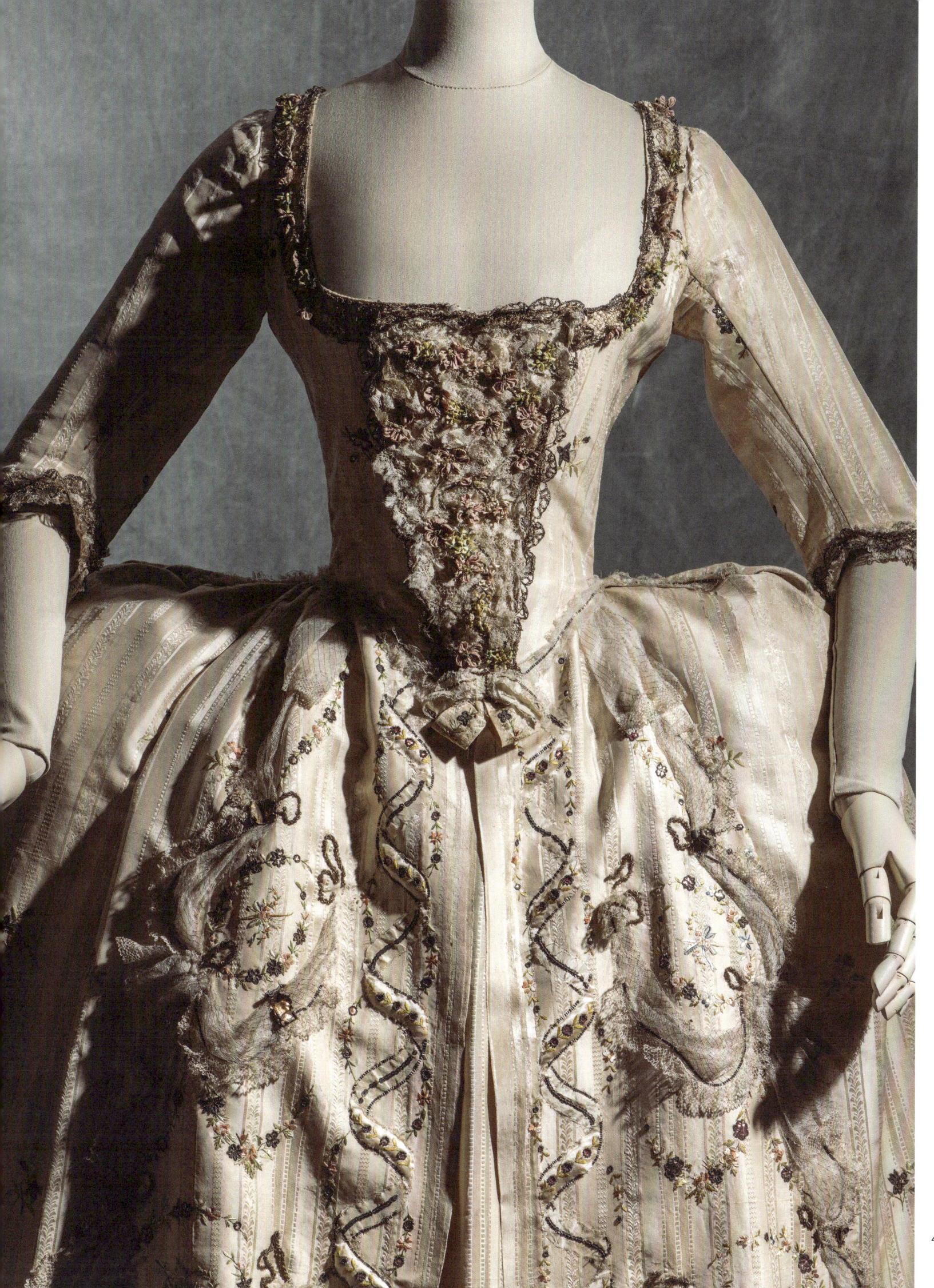

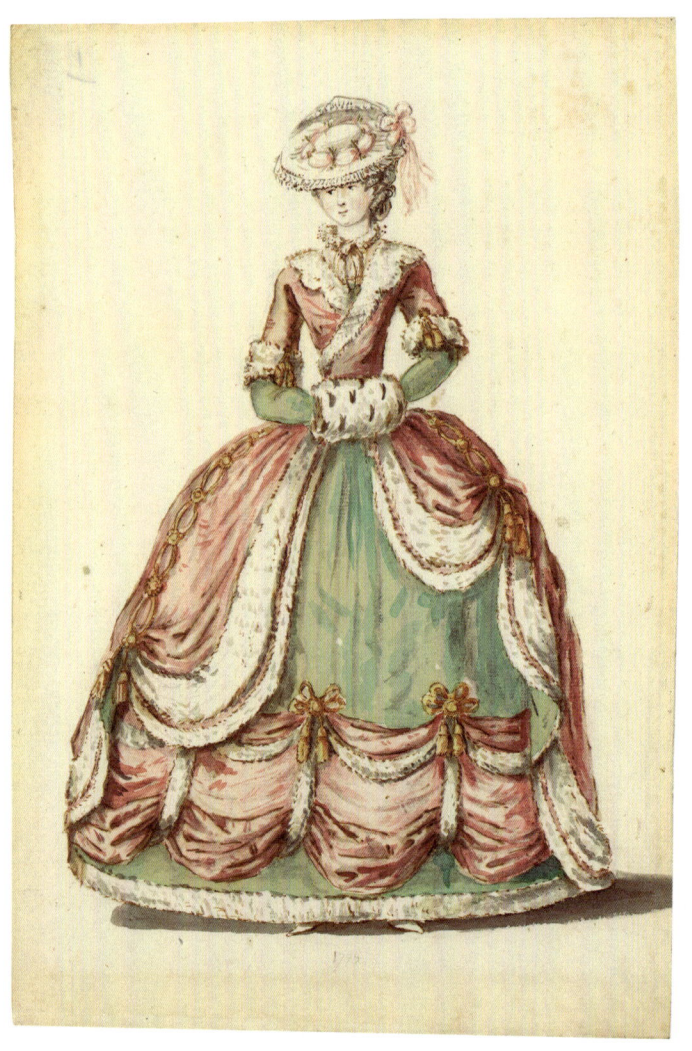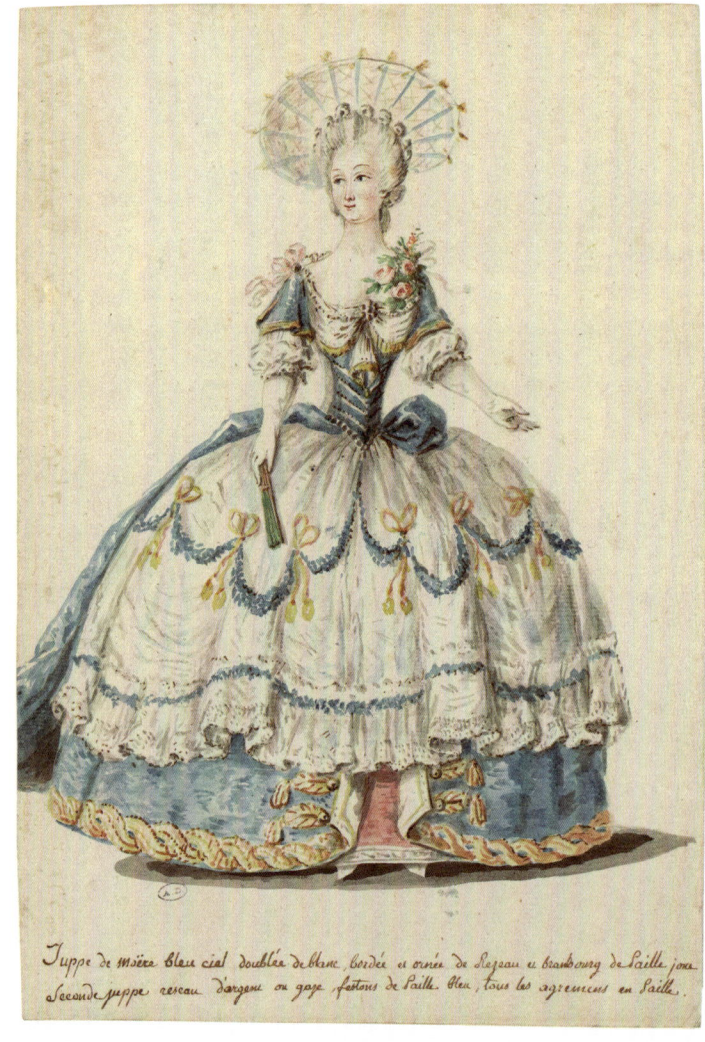

CHARLES GERMAIN DE SAINT-AUBIN, *Women in Court Dresses*, 1785-1789. Lead pencil and watercolor on gray-washed paper. Musée des Arts Décoratifs, Paris; Graphic Arts Department, purchase, 1909.

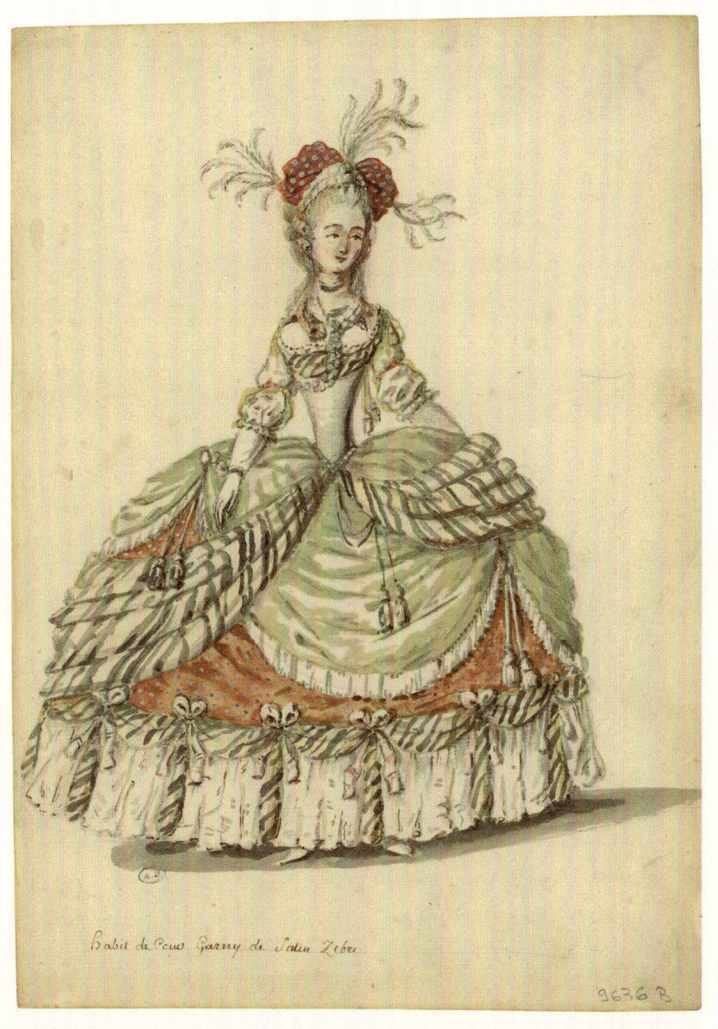

Habit de Cour garny de Satin Zebre

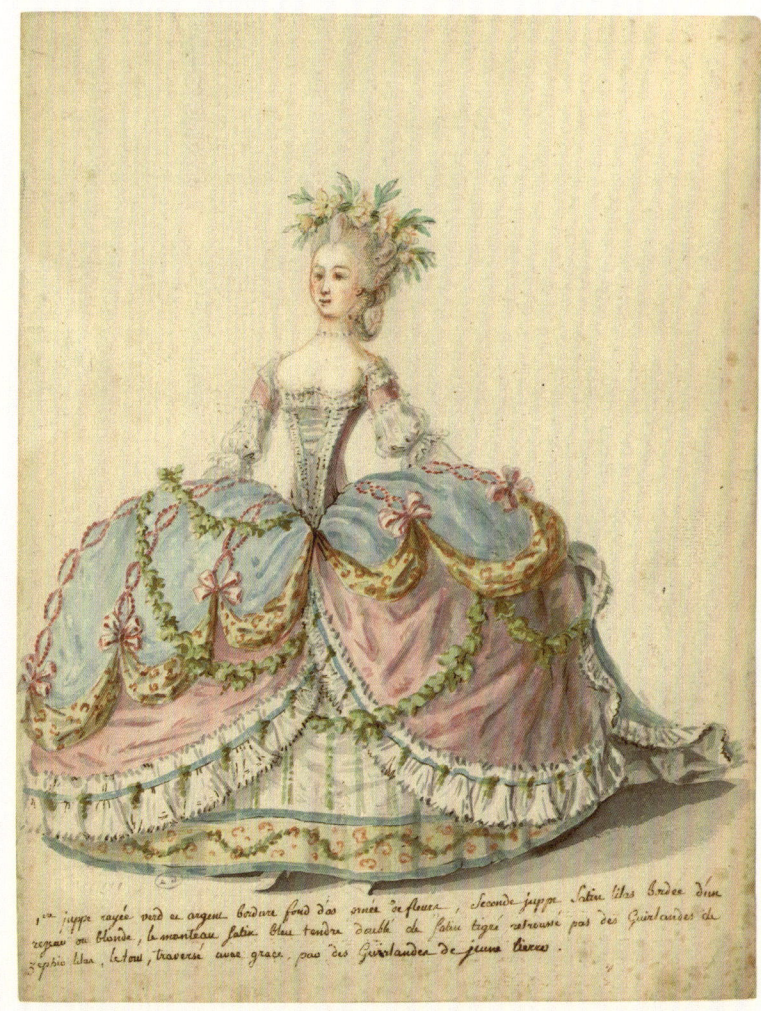

1.re juppe rayée vied et argent bordure fond d'or ornée de fleurs, Seconde juppe Satin liséré bordée d'une repeau ou blonde, le manteau Satin bleu tendre doublé de Satin tigré retroussé par des Guirlandes de Zéphir bleu, le tou, traversé avec grace, par des Guirlandes de jeunes Lierre.

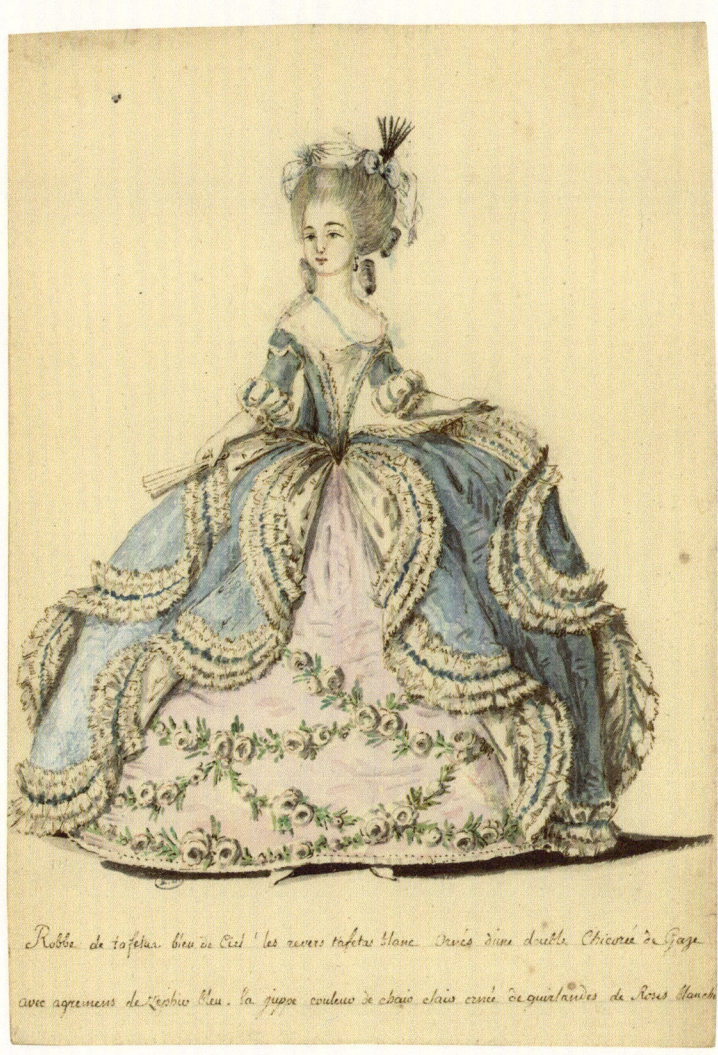

Robbe de tafetas bleu de Ciel les revers tafetas blanc. Ornée d'une double Chicorée de Gaze avec agremens de Zephir bleu. Sa juppe couleur de chair claire ornée de guirlandes de Rose blanche.

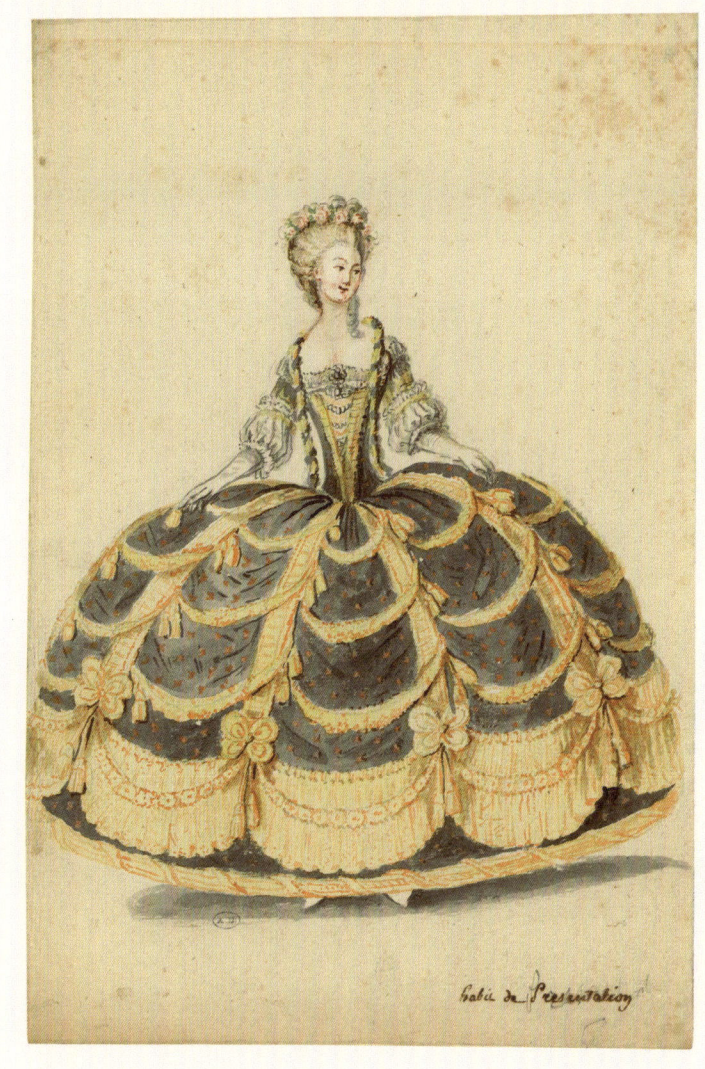

habit de Presentation

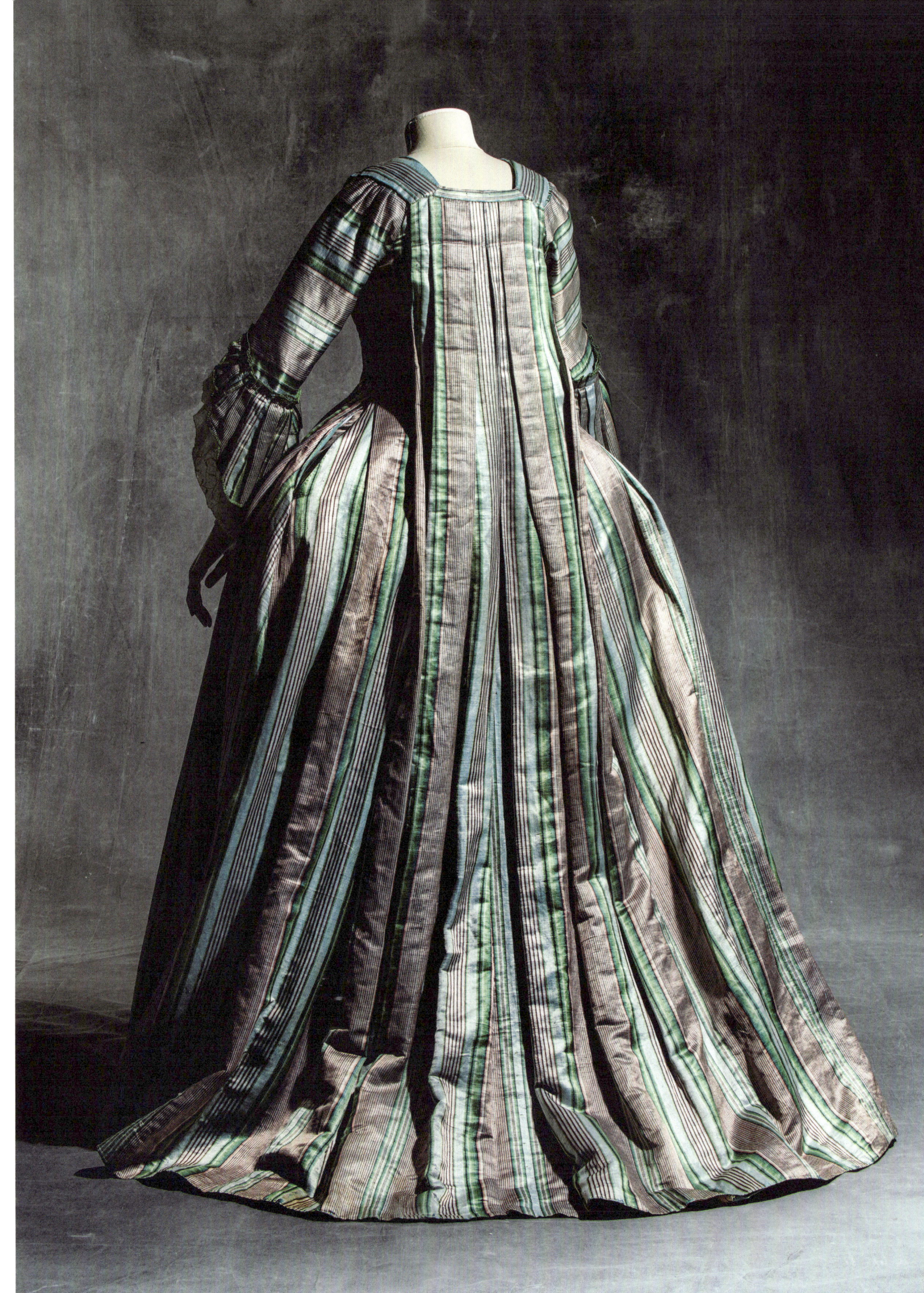

Robe à la Française
1780-1785

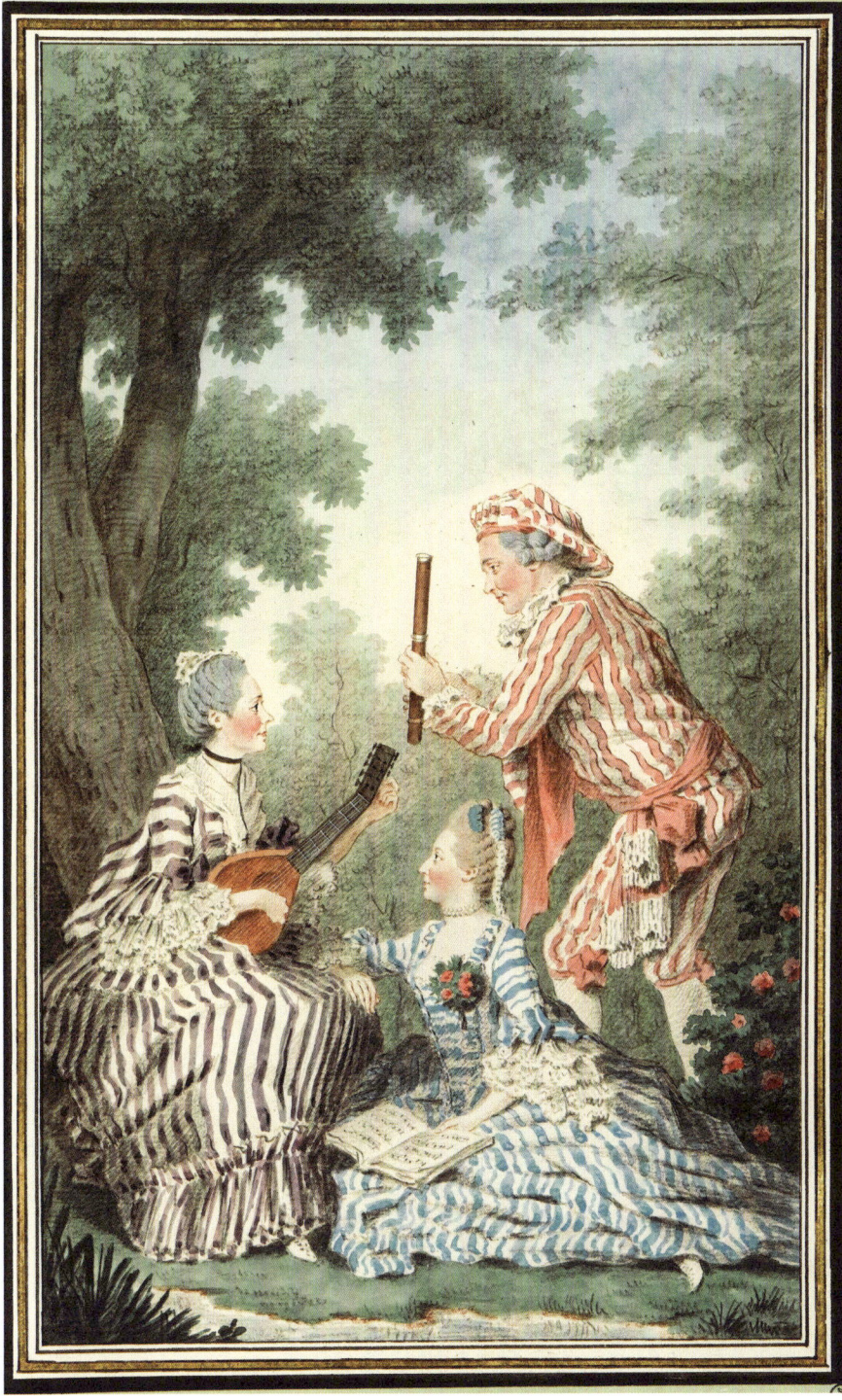

The *robe à la française* was the official outfit at court. It was also worn in other circumstances, and certain variants appeared, as shown by this example. Here, interior drawstrings allowed the underskirts to be rolled up, giving the dress a more practical dimension.

Made up of an overdress and underskirt, this ensemble was worn by an Arlesian with much more limited financial resources than courtesans enjoyed. The textile used confirms it: striped satin with a silk warp but a cotton weft, which lowered the cost of the material.

The decoration was limited to the stripes, which were produced by the single warping, using different colored threads. This decoration was highly fashionable at the end of the eighteenth century, the result of being promoted by Marie-Antoinette, who eschewed figured silks and thus roused the protests of silk producers in Lyon.
H.R.

LOUIS CARROGIS CARMONTELLE, *Madame de Meaux, Her Daughter, and Monsieur de Saint-Quentin*, late eighteenth century. Watercolor, gouache, and lead pencil on paper. Musée Condé, Chantilly.

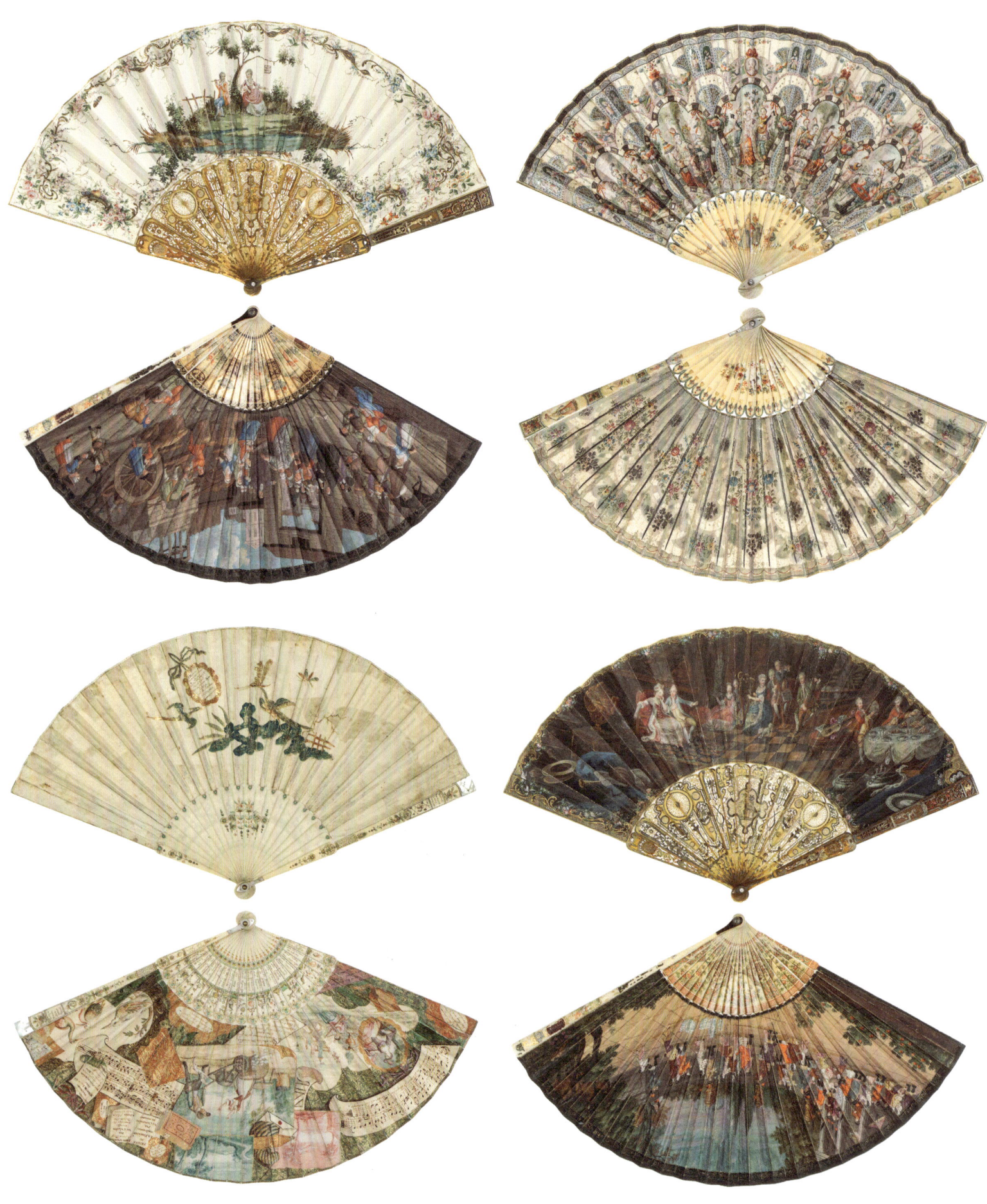

Fans, first half of the eighteenth century. Paper, silk, ivory, shell, mother-of-pearl.
Musée des Arts Décoratifs, Paris; Fashion and Textile Collection, bequest of Amélie Duquesne, 1921.

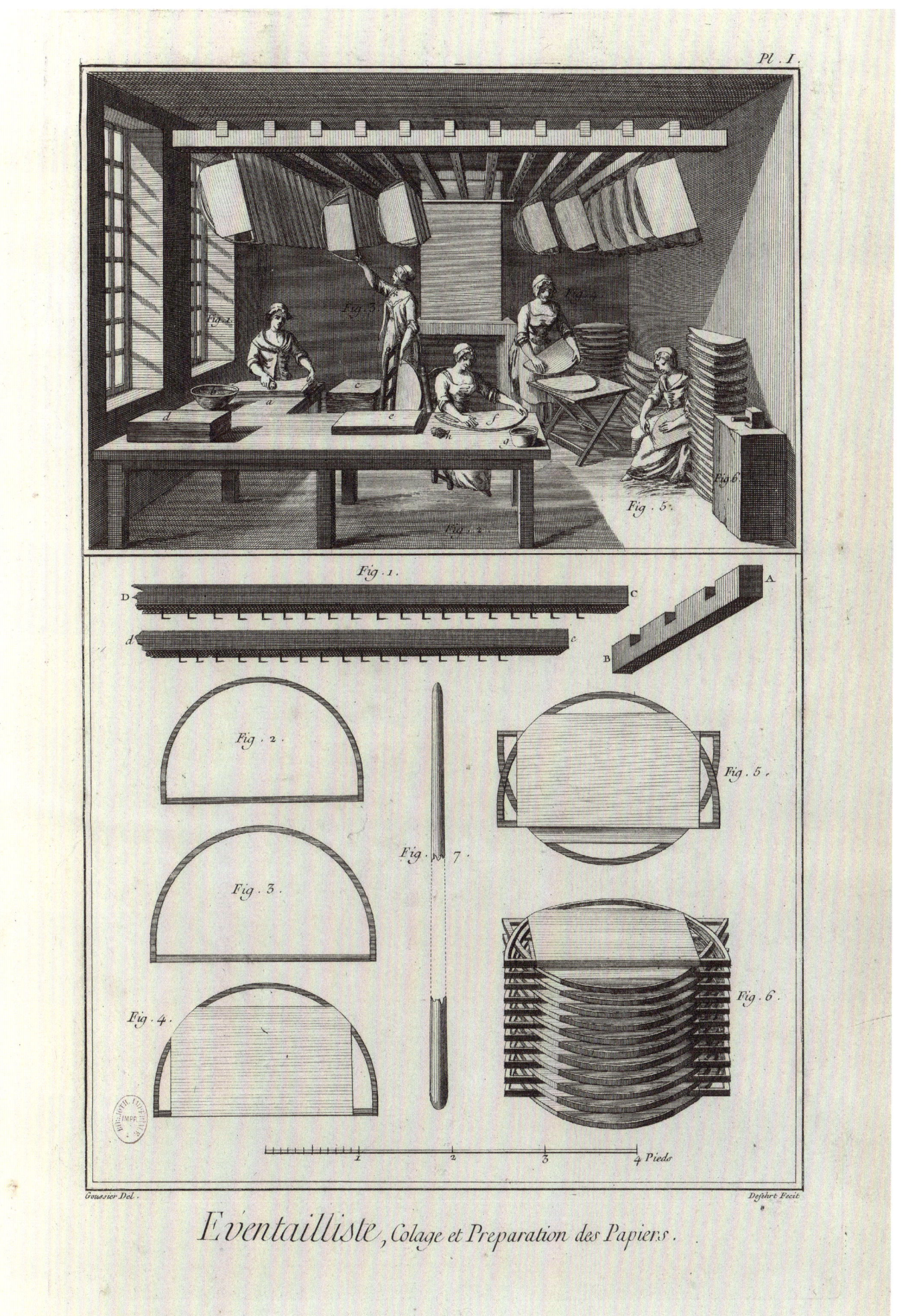

DENIS DIDEROT, JEAN LE ROND D'ALEMBERT, *Encyclopédie, ou dictionnaire raisonné des sciences, des arts et des métiers.*
Arts de l'habillement, Paris, 1743. BnF, Paris; Prints and Photographs Department.

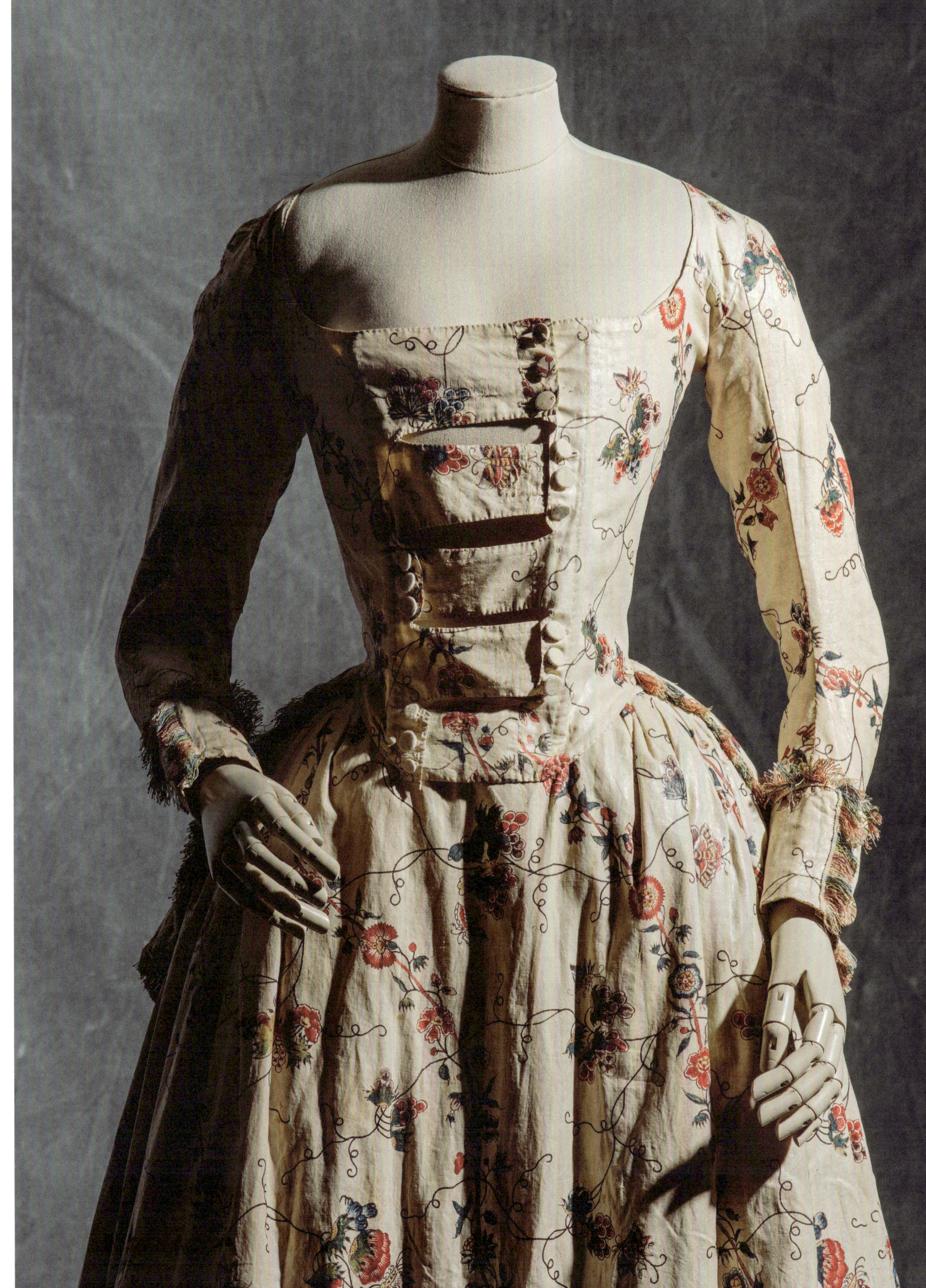

Two-Piece Dress
1775–1790

This two-piece dress consists of a boned "Pierrot" caraco, with long tails, and a skirt. The fabric is a glazed cotton percale, hand-painted with colored floral "Indian" designs, so called because they were in the style of textiles imported from India nearly a century earlier. Although Europeans were beginning their conquest of the Indian Ocean at the end of the fifteenth century, they would have to wait until 1664 for the French East India Company to be founded by royal declaration. Numerous painted canvases were then imported to France in the seventeenth century and made a great splash, notably in the form of banyans (at-home men's dressing gowns) or upholstery fabric. Above all, these fabrics were lightweight and easy to maintain.

French production was gradually organized during the second half of the seventeenth century, especially since the importation and production of true *indiennes* were prohibited starting in 1686, in an effort to protect the French industries. Despite this ban, the amount of imports remained considerable.
H.R.

Robe à l'Anglaise
1780-1785

Made between 1780 and 1785, this *robe à l'anglaise* consists of an overdress with a train and a cream taffeta underskirt with green, pink, and sky-blue stripes with black threading. The overdress formed a Basque bodice in front, with cut edges known as "chicoree," and three-quarter-length sabot sleeves. In back, the bodice comes to a point at the waist, providing volume to the overskirt. This was one of the characteristic features of the *robe à l'anglaise*, which, contrary to the *robe à la française*, did not contain panniers. Inner cords allowed the overskirt to be lifted, recalling the *robe à la polonaise*, and provided a glimpse of the underskirt while eliminating the train effect in back.

    A result of the Anglomania craze that struck France in the late eighteenth century, this model had the benefit of being less cumbersome and more comfortable than the *robe à la française*, which greatly contributed to its success.
H.R.

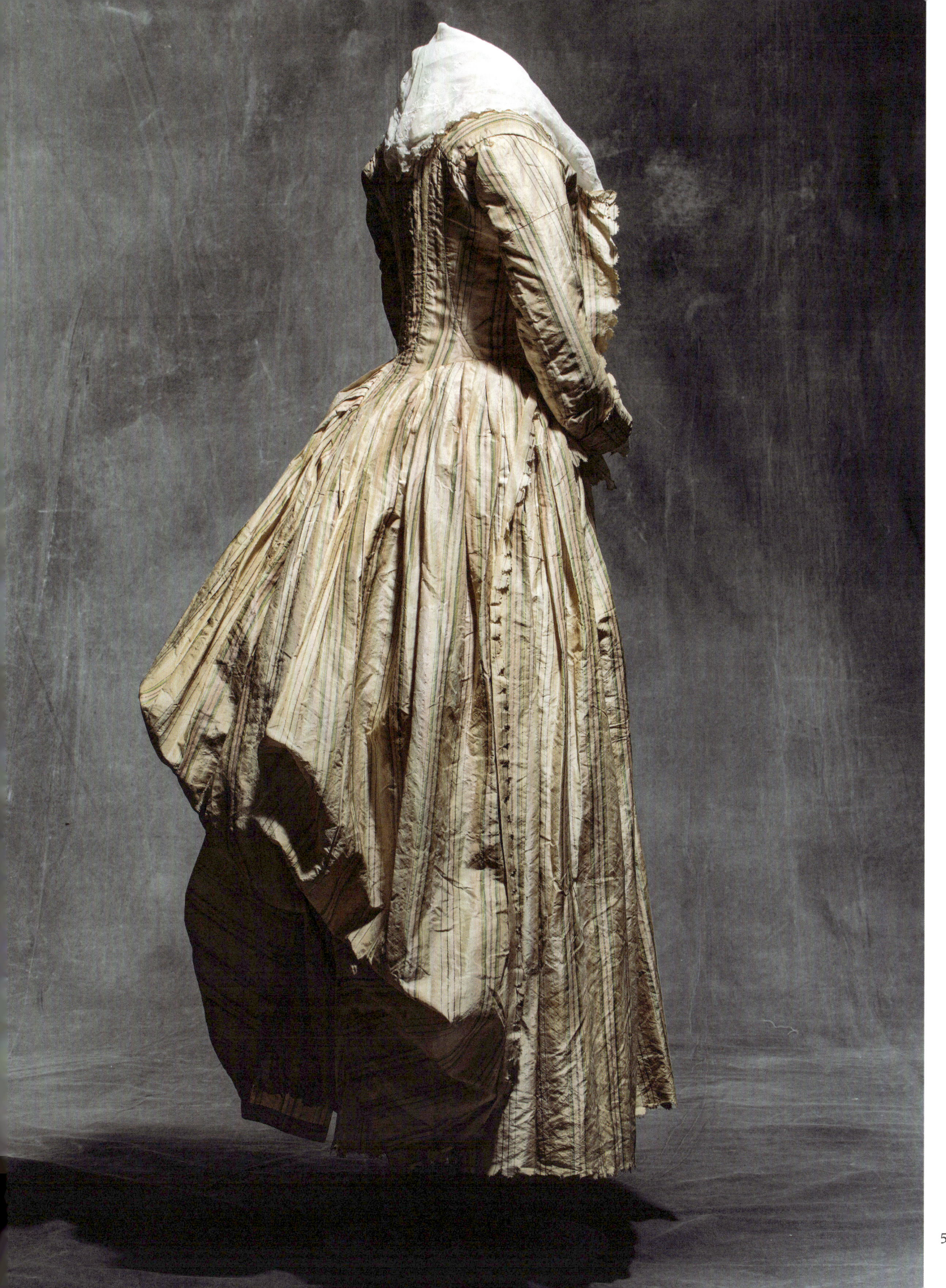

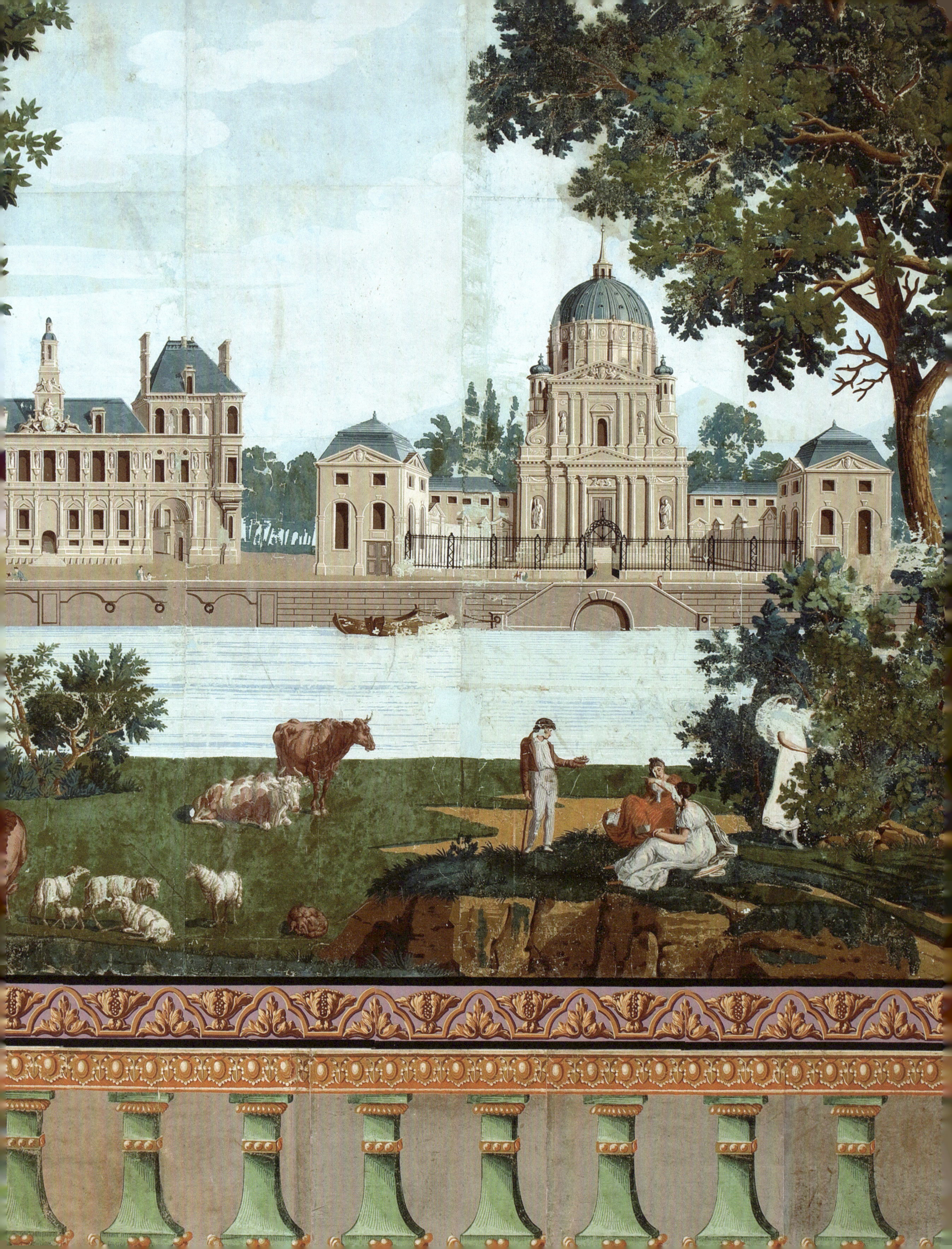

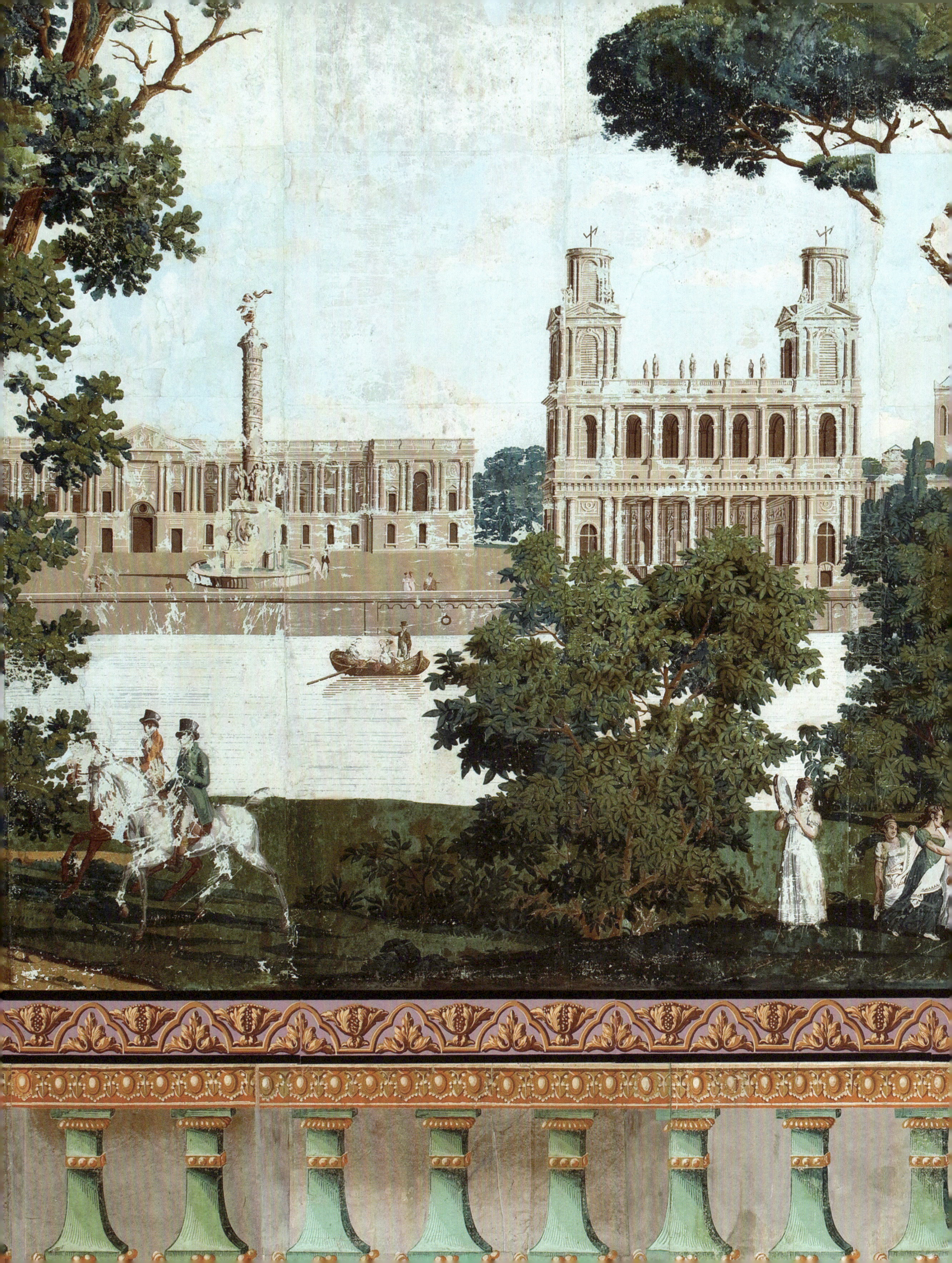

Frock Coat
1789-1791

The storming of the Bastille on July 14, 1789, marked a turning point in the history of France. The municipality distributed cockades in red and blue, the colors of Paris. On July 17, at the Hôtel de Ville, General Lafayette gave the king a cockade embellished with white, signifying the monarchy. This act was supposed to symbolize the king's union with his city. Starting on July 21, the *Magasin des modes nouvelles* proposed that its readers wear "ox-blood" colored clothes, to be paired with "blue-cornered white silk stockings." A trend emerged. The national cockades and ribbons gave way to fabrics dyed in the same colors. The November 11, 1789, issue of the *Magasin* showed a "caraco and . . . very long red, blue and white-striped satin petticoat." It also recommended the use of canvas or broadcloth fabrics instead of silk and advocated that the military uniform be used as a model for civilian clothes.

This exceptional frock coat in tricolor-striped cotton canvas, with turned-down collar and *marinière* Bavarian-style cuffs with carved copper buttons, embodied the spirit of the times.
H.R.

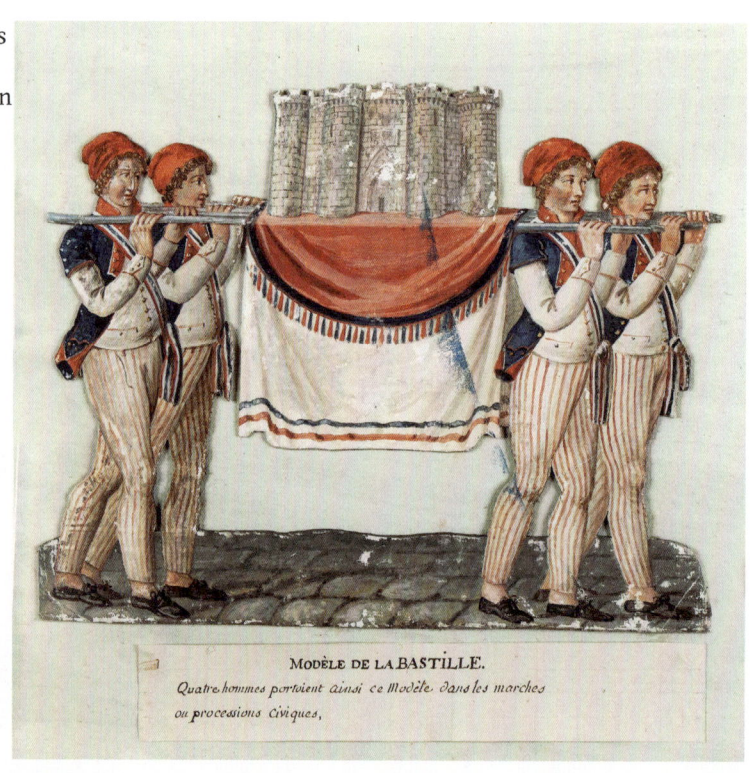

JEAN-BAPTISTE LESUEUR, *Carrying of the Model of the Bastille and Soldier Giving a Lecture to the Children*, 1790-1792. Gouache on paper. Musée Carnavalet, Paris.

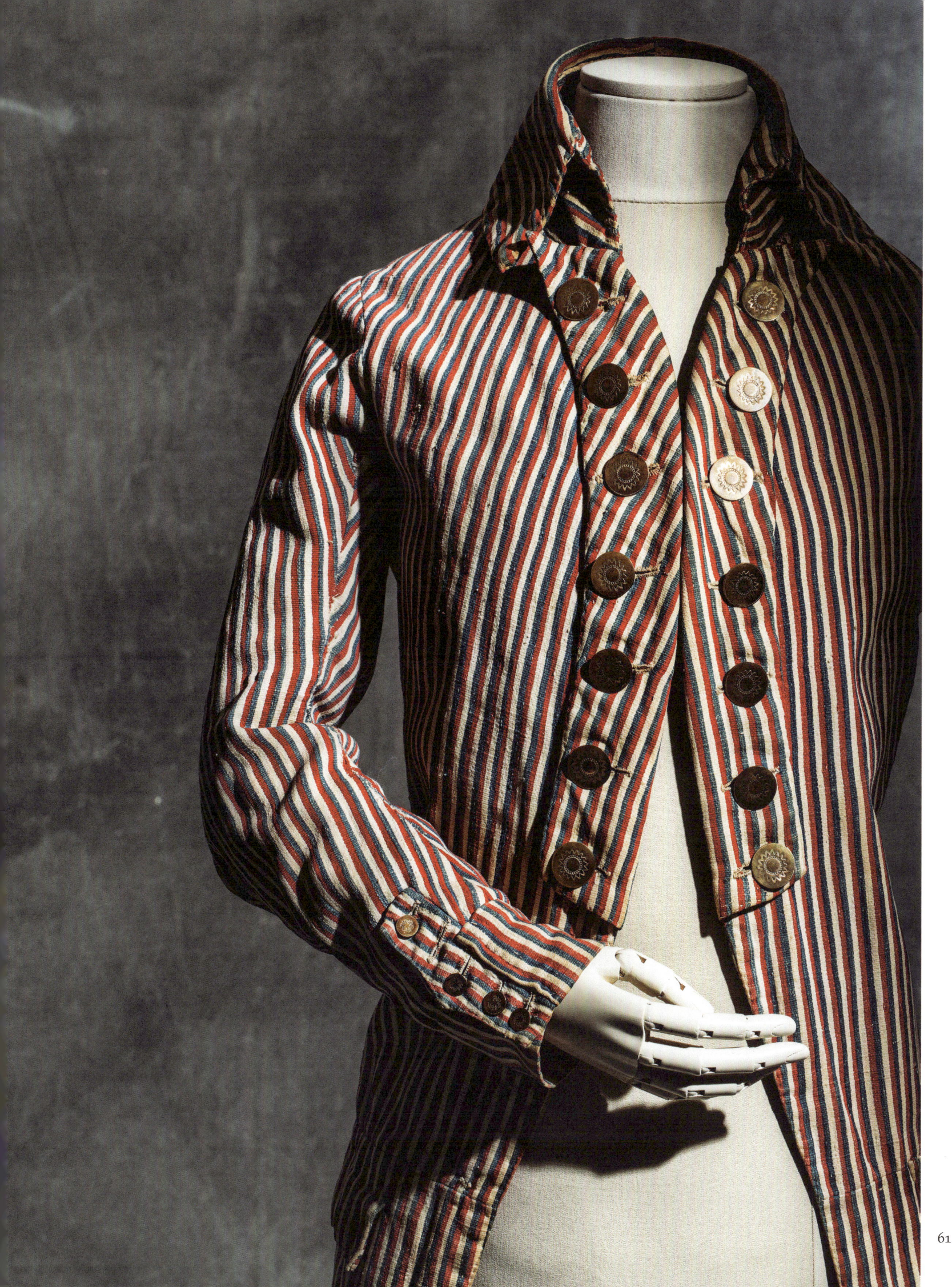

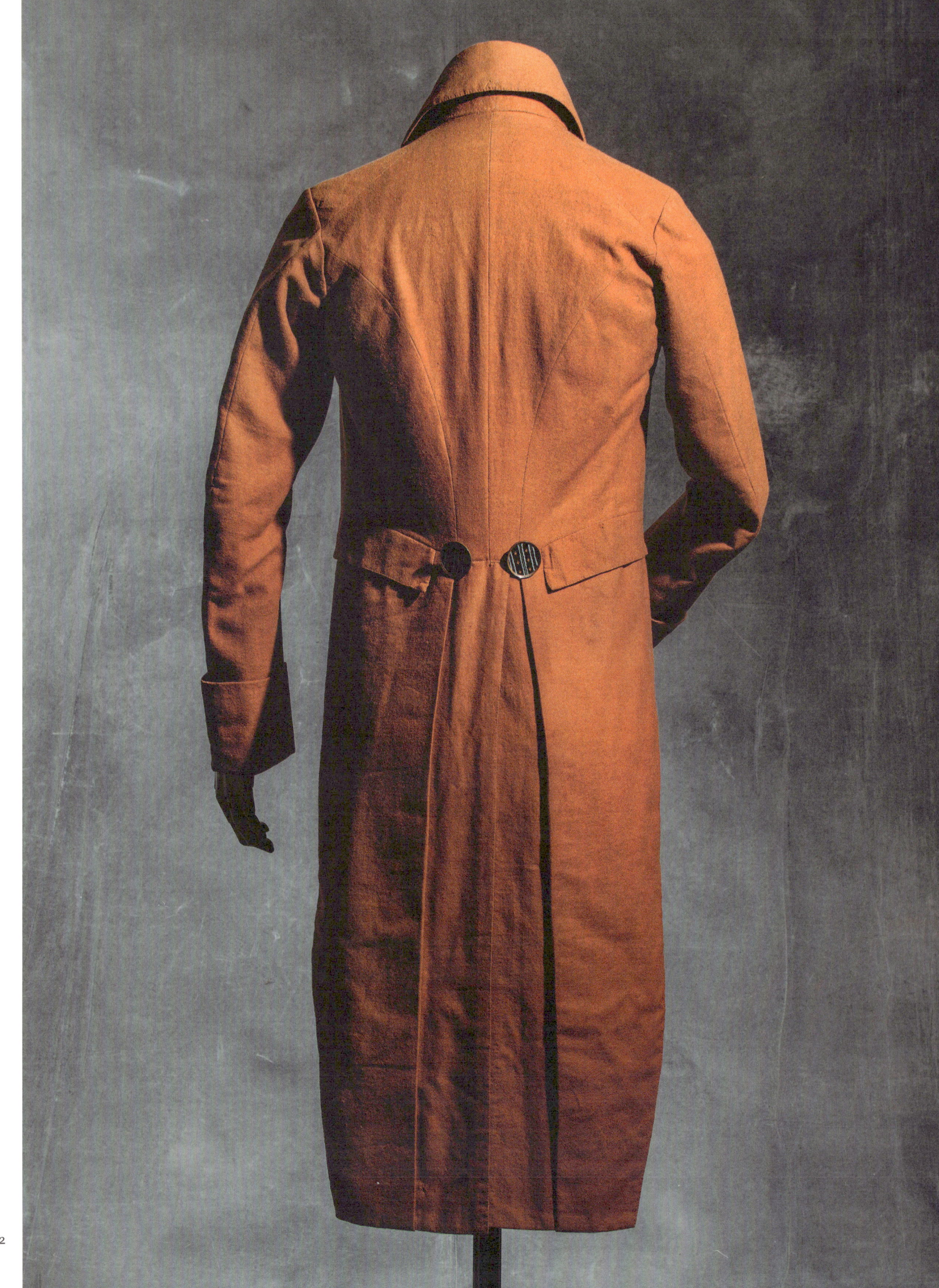

Men's Early Double-Breasted Tailcoat (Habit Dégagé)
1795–1799

While the female wardrobe underwent profound transformation, menswear changed less, though it was certainly not static. In the eighteenth century, a shift occurred from the *habit à la française* to more practical and relaxed garments, which were mainly influenced by British fashions.

This tailcoat is a perfect example. It is cut high in the front at waist level, and the back contains two tails. Its tall collar with large lapels is characteristic of clothing worn by the so-called Incroyables (men following the ostentatious fashions of the French Directoire). The sleeves are fitted. The only embellishments are the large reverse-painted glass buttons with lines and stars, set in copper. The garment was cut from stain-resistant tobacco-colored wool. Worn underneath a vest, this coat would have been topped off with either breeches or fitted pants.
H.R.

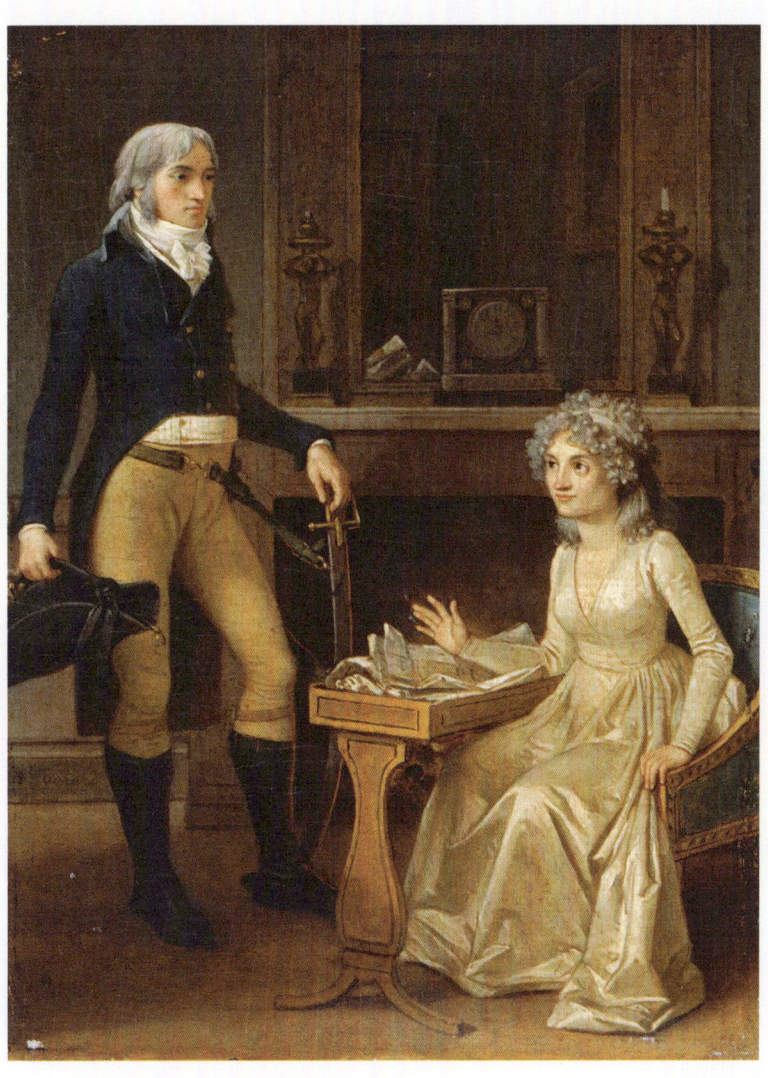

GÉRARD MARGUERITE, *Le billet de logement* (The lodging ticket), late eighteenth century. Oil on wood. Musée Magnin, Dijon.

Dress
1795–1800

A taste for antiquity began to influence fashion starting at the end of the reign of Louis XVI. It persisted throughout the French Revolution and only increased under the Directoire. Although there was indeed a transitional fashion during these troubled times, the silhouette changed radically between the 1780s and 1790s. The fairly opulent *robe à la française* transformed into fitted, high-waisted cotton dresses, most often white, which were to some extent the heirs to the *chemises à la reine*, or *gaulles*, worn by Marie Antoinette, that had shocked the public when they first appeared.

This "Merveilleuse" dress (referring to an elegant and eccentric woman of the Directoire), with a crossover bodice in front, is made of white muslin with scattered chain-stitch embroidered polychrome bouquets. It is a magnificent example of the little lightweight dresses that were favored at the end of the eighteenth century. Its long narrow sleeves end in ruffles that extend past the wrists.
H.R.

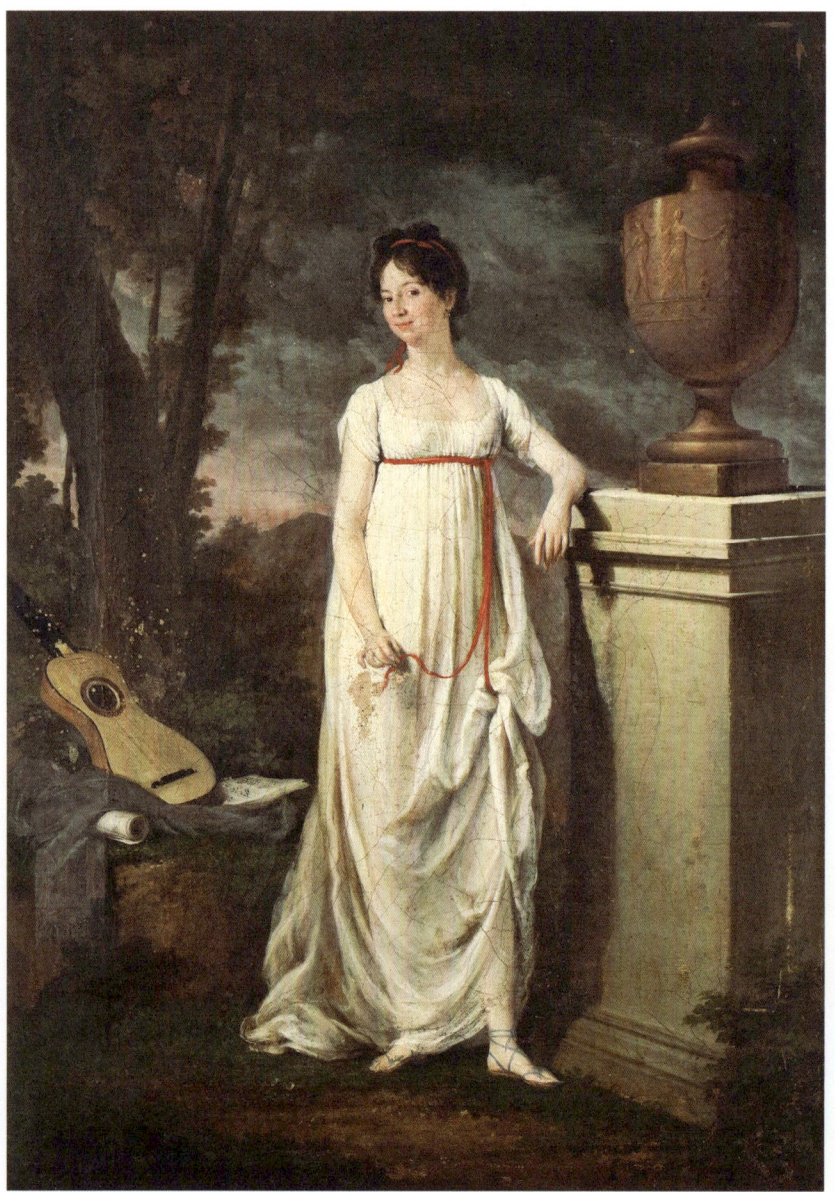

TEODORO MATTEINI, *Portrait of a Young Girl*, 1803. Oil on canvas. Musée des Arts Décoratifs, Paris; bequest of Émile Peyre, 1905.

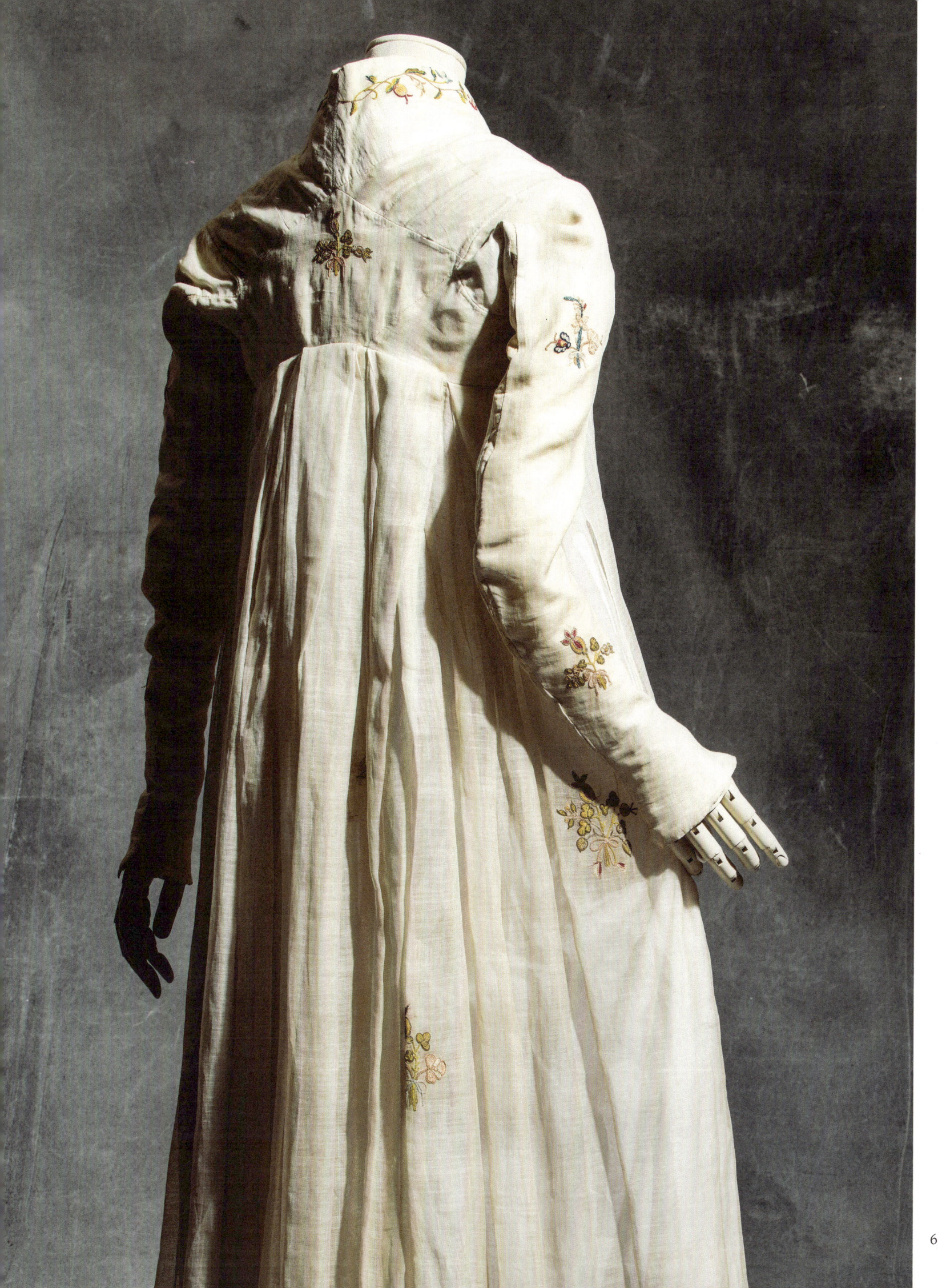

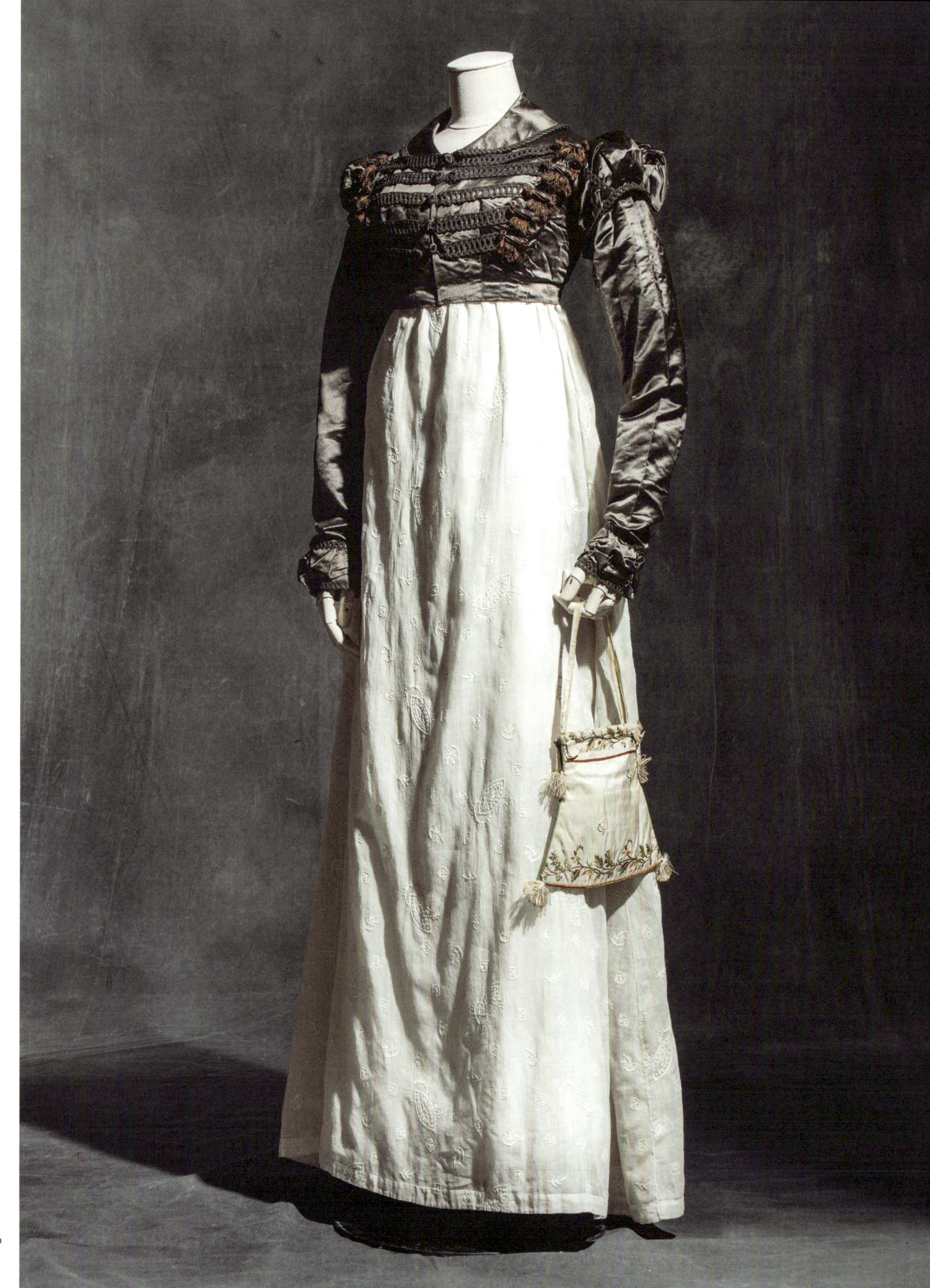

Dress and Spencer
1804-1815

This reconstructed outfit provides an example of the daily dress worn by an elegant woman under the First French Empire: an embroidered white linen dress, a spencer that preserved a wide square gathered neckline, a high drawstring waist below the bust, and a raised pleated skirt in back. A taste for antiquity favored the adoption of this streamlined silhouette, along with the choice of a light fabric on which to embroider a small, delicate design, attesting to the resurgence of needlecraft.

Named after Lord Spencer, who made the new short lapelled jacket popular, the spencer arrived from England at the end of the Directoire period. This borrowing from menswear became a cornerstone of women's clothing. Quite varied in appearance, this garment was first made from dark fabrics, which contrasted with the white of the usual neoclassical dress; gradually it became more daring, available in bolder colors and with embellishments.
This *"à la hussarde"* spencer adorned with decorative frogging demonstrates the marked influence of military dress on civilian clothes.
M.-P.R.

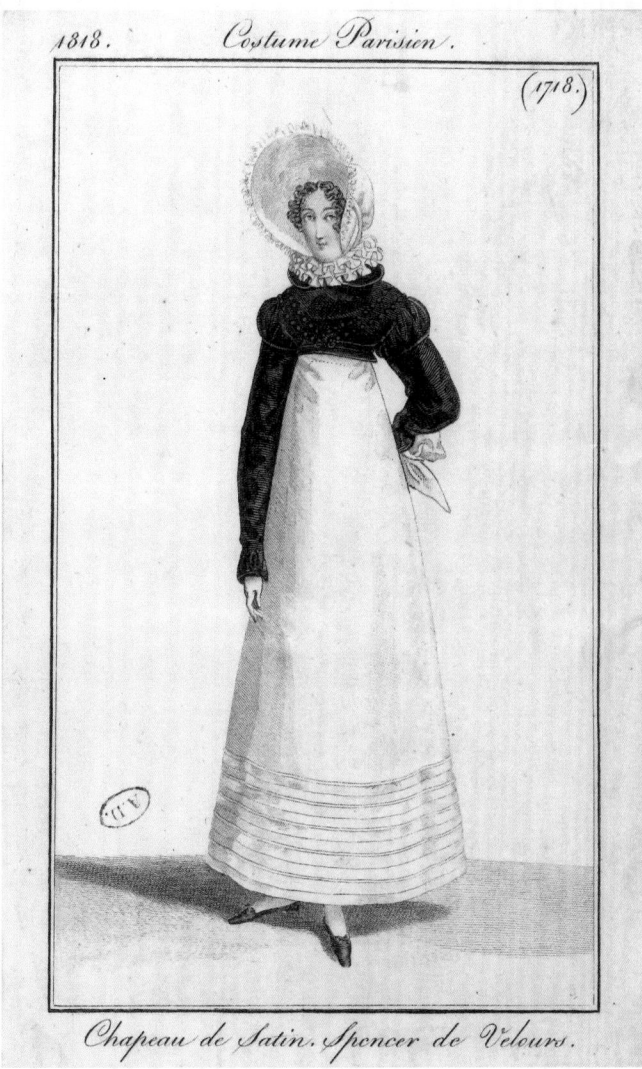

Costume parisien: Satin hat. Velvet spencer, 1818. Bibliothèque des Arts Décoratifs, Paris; Maciet Album.

Men's Suit (Habit à la Française)
1804–1815

Under the First French Empire, men without an official post who were not entitled to a uniform were required to wear an *habit à la française* in court, which, contrary to its female equivalent, was reminiscent of the dress codes of the ancien régime. Consisting of a jacket, vest, and breeches, it differed from its model in certain details: the collar of the jacket was straighter and higher, and its tails were shorter. The straight vest that had been in style for some twenty years was no longer an option. Instead, the cutaway tails that had emerged with the shortening of the jacket were reintroduced. The play in contrasting fabrics between the jacket and the vest was also a legacy from the era of Louis XVI.

In luxurious silk velvet embroidered with wide flower garlands, this example trumpeted imperial etiquette, which favored orders of fine heavy French fabrics for court dress. Topped off with a bicorne hat, sword, and buckled shoes, the outfit was likewise accessorized with a muslin collar, jabot, and white stockings.

The *habit à la française* was still the order of the day under Louis XVIII and Charles X.
M.-P.R.

CHUARD & COMPAGNIE, Wall hanging commissioned by Napoléon I for the princes' room of the royal palace of Milan, 1809. Lampas *fond satin*, silk and gold thread brocaded.
Musée des Arts Décoratifs, Paris; Fashion and Textile Collections, gift of Duplan, 1909.

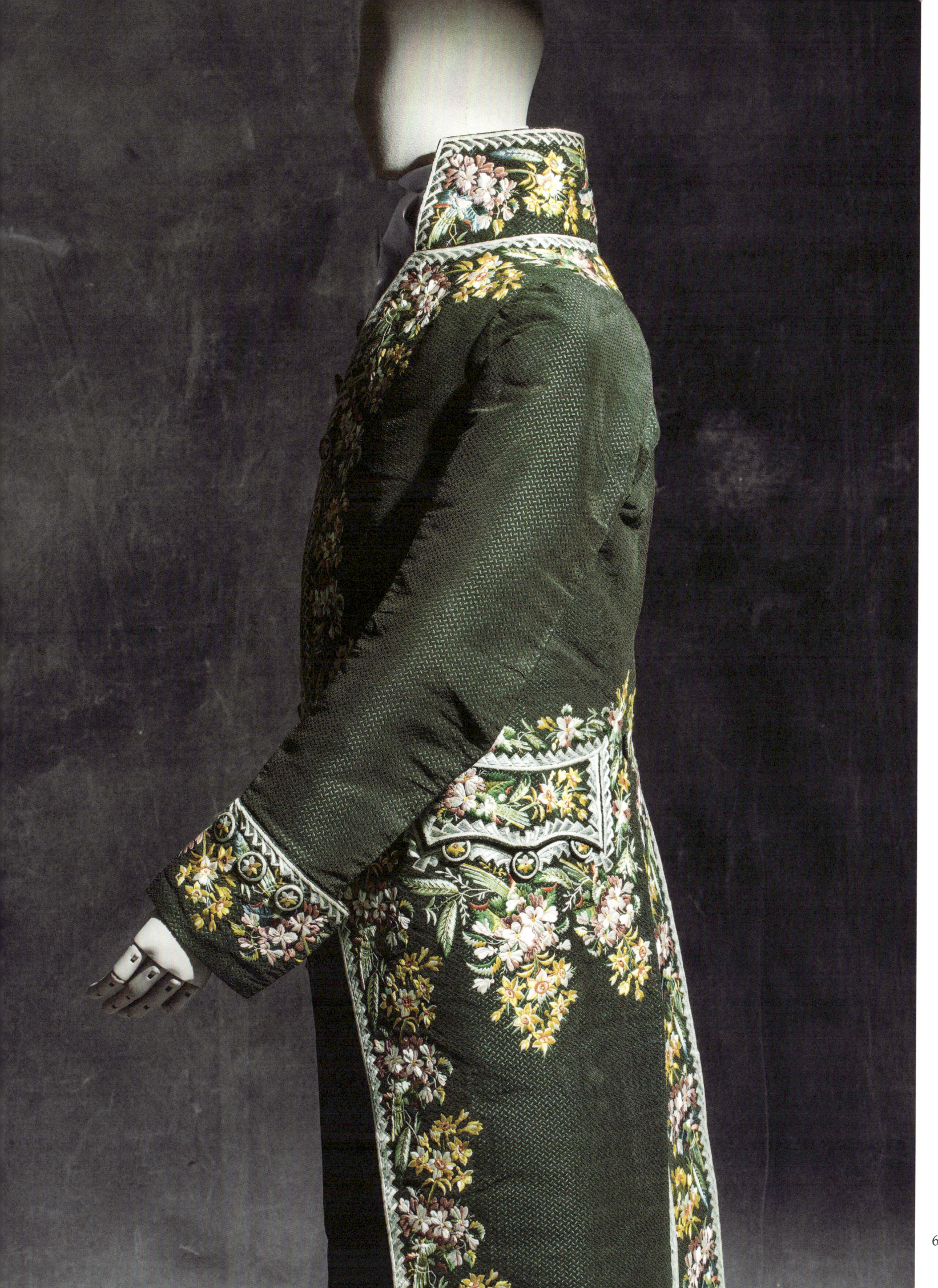

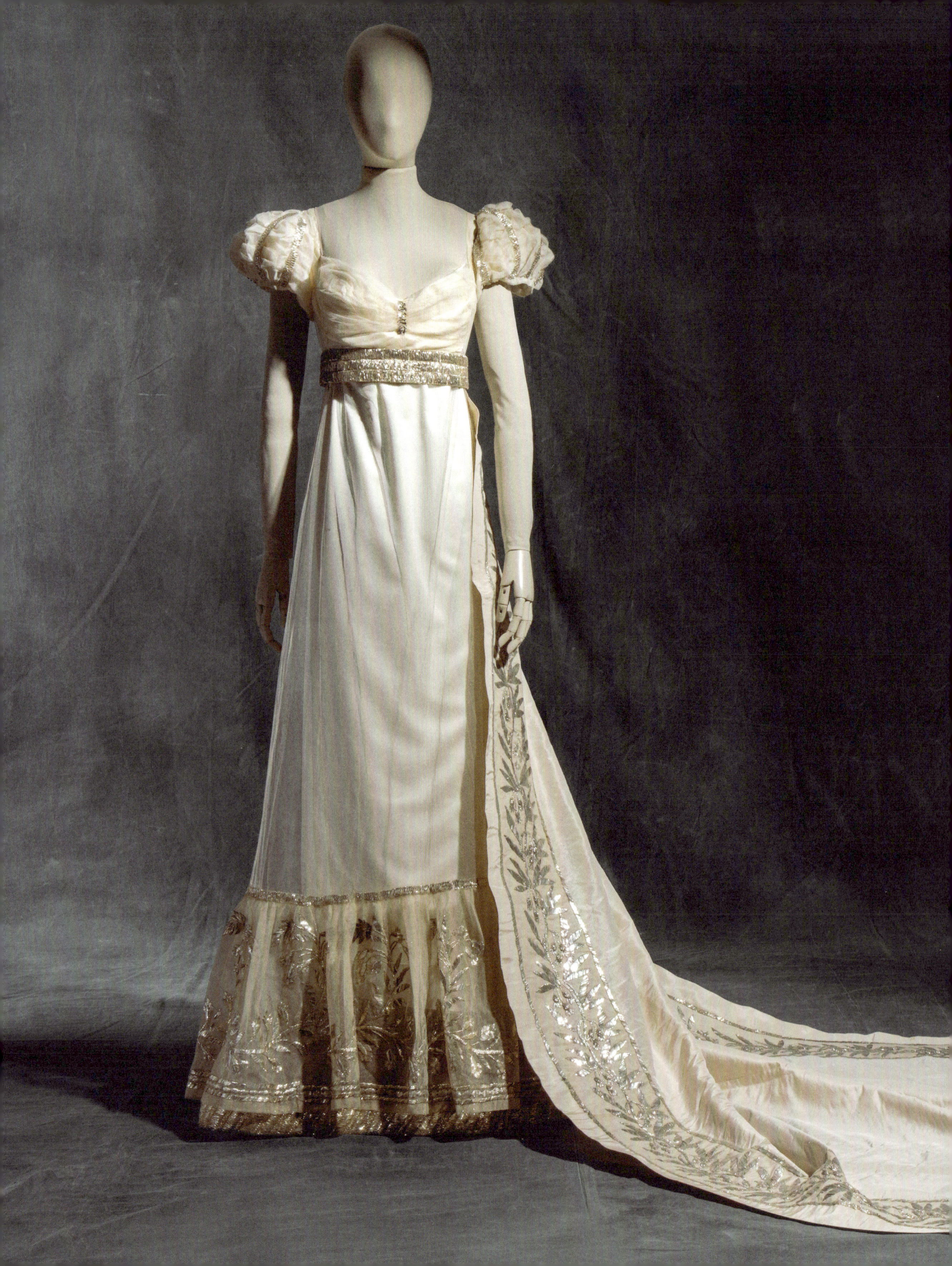

Court Dress
1815–1825

This type of court dress was one of the most original creations of the early nineteenth century. The proclamation of the Empire and the preparations for the coronation of Napoléon Bonaparte in 1804 were an opportunity, notably through the decree of the 29th Messidor of year XII, to regulate the official dress of the emperor, empress, dignitaries, and the court. Inspired by the "*petit habillement*" of Empress Joséphine designed by Jean-Baptiste Isabey for the coronation day, which served as a standard model, this dress was marked by the strict requirements of etiquette. Women admitted to court had to wear a garment made of French fabric that was of the same type as the one worn by the empress: an empire-waist classic gown, fitted with short sleeves and a removable train attached to the belt, embellished with sumptuous freehand embroidery that could not exceed a decimeter in width, according to a paragraph from the *Cérémonial de l'Empire français*, published in 1805.

This court dress later demonstrated the persistence of this type of clothing under the Restoration, when only the placement of the waist and the sleeve volume were adapted, as noted in an article from the *Journal des dames et des modes* from 1825: "Court dress for women has for a long time only varied for certain accessories in jewelry or the placements of embroideries: a long train is still attached at the waist."
M.-P.R.

Dress
Circa 1815

Dating back to around 1815, this dress is interesting for both its link to fashion and its type of fabric. The high waist and short puff sleeves were typical of the classic silhouette in vogue under the First French Empire throughout Europe, which persisted during the early years of the Restoration.

Nevertheless, certain details of this dress marked the first fruits of Romantic fashions: the inlaid belt, which considerably lengthened the bust, and the double row of chevron ruffles placed at the bottom, one of which emphasized the hem of the skirt, which is shortened to above the ankles. The adornments were carefully crafted, with cut ruffles embellished by buttons covered in the same fabric. The gauze was particularly surprising in its design, which is styled with vertical chevrons accentuated by a printed polychrome background. A harbinger of the transformations of the female silhouette that were to come, this refined dress represents a valuable milestone in the history of clothing.
M.-P.R.

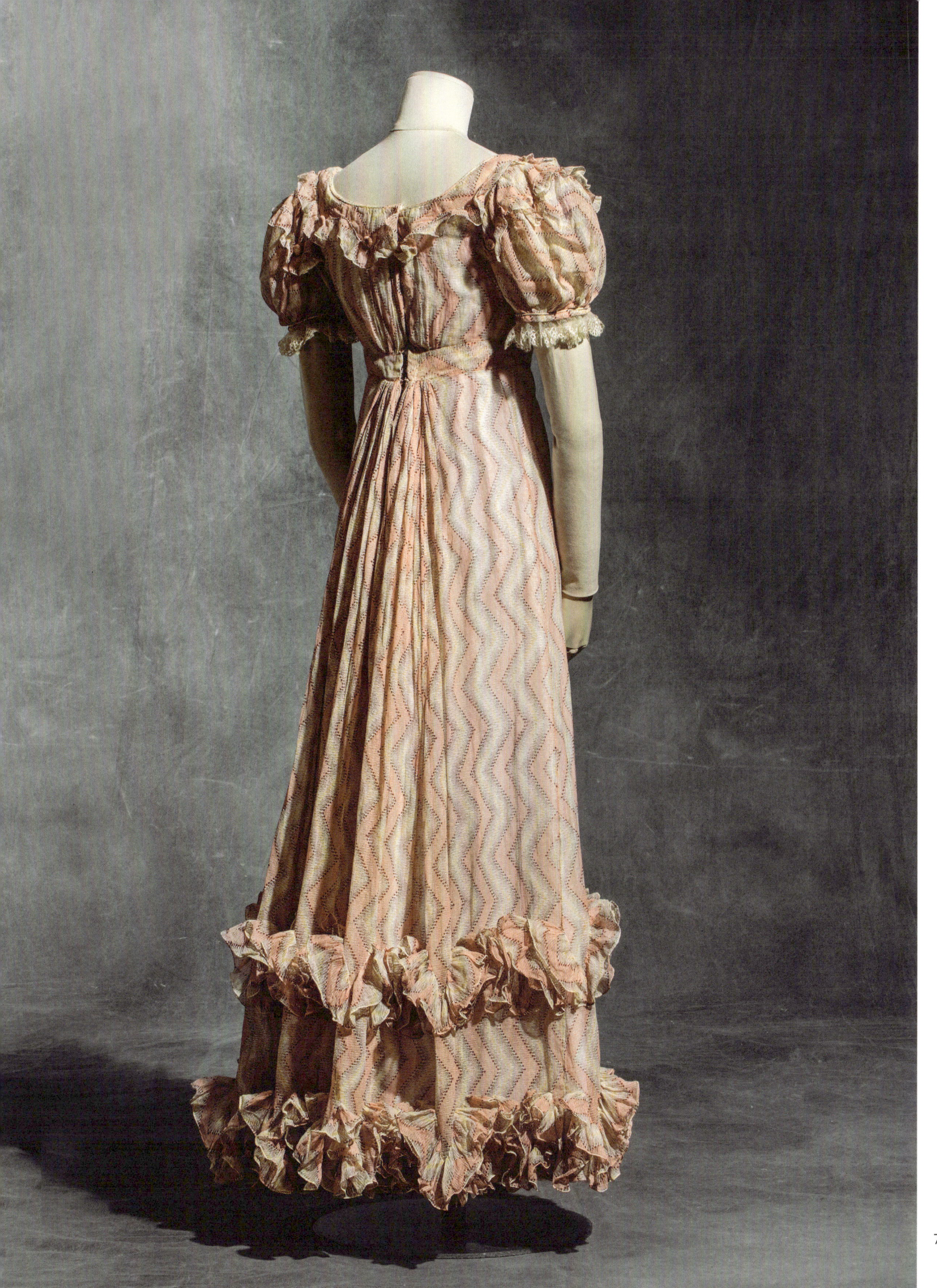

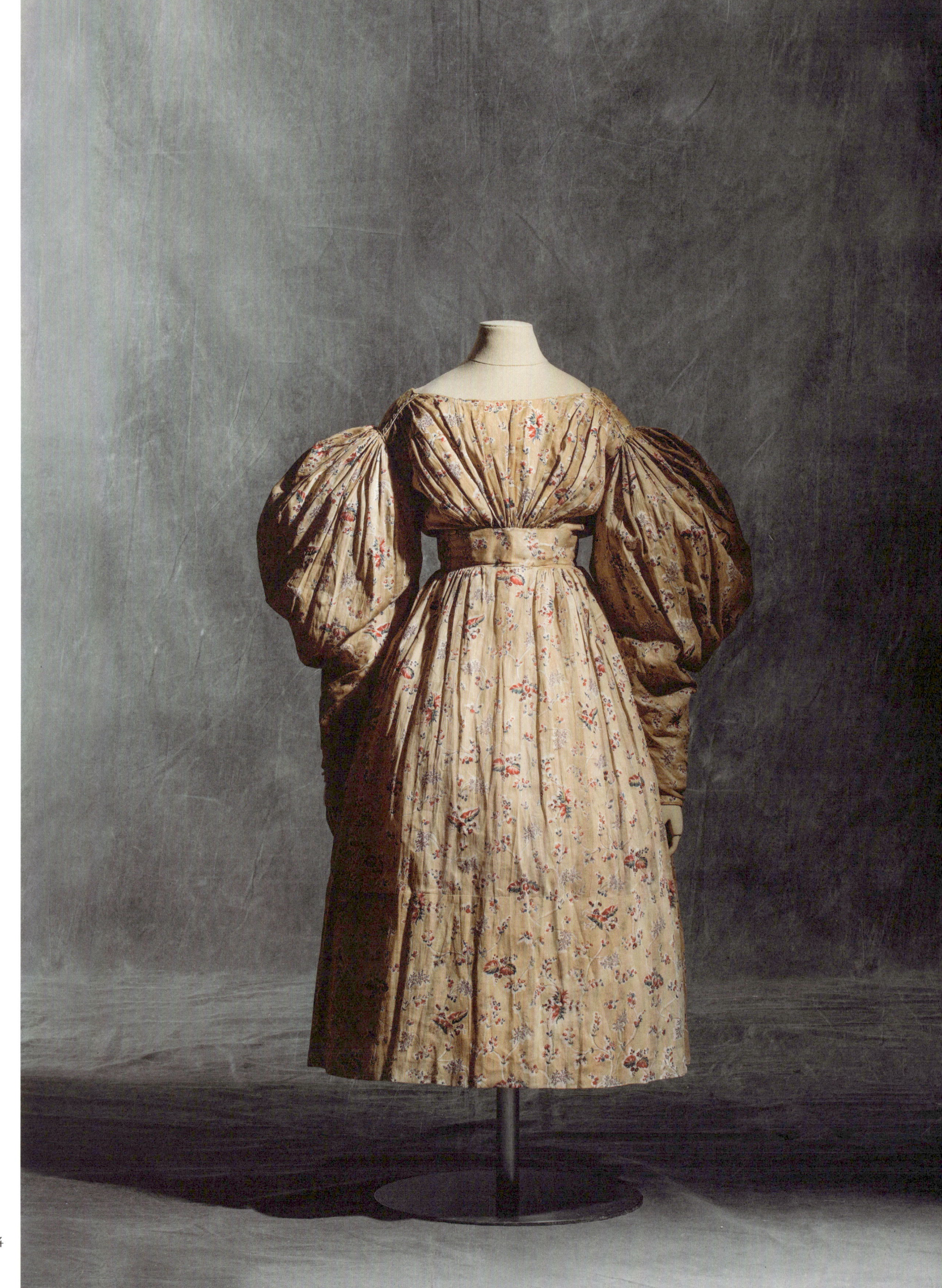

Girl's Dress
1830–1835

The subject of particular attention since the end of the eighteenth century, children's clothing benefited from the first attempts at adapting to children's specific needs. Nevertheless, under the July Monarchy, little girls still wore outfits identical to those of their mothers, reproducing their pseudohistorical nature. If we observe the fashion engravings from this period, we see a similarity of shapes. In 1831 the *Journal des dames et des modes* gave the following description of girls' clothing: "Children's fashions are more or less copied from women's fashions.... Little girls wear, like their mothers, very wide gowns cinched at the waist with a belt and billowy sleeves, covered by jockeys or a cape." It further noted in 1834: "There is a lot of coquetry in children's dress. The fabrics and styles approximate those of women's clothing."

Indeed, at this time there were still no fabrics specifically earmarked for children's clothing. In this example, the character of the floral printed designs echoes those for adults. The only formal difference lies in the skirt length, which allowed short blousy pants to be visible, a symbol of childhood that was abandoned on the date of the first communion. M.-P.R.

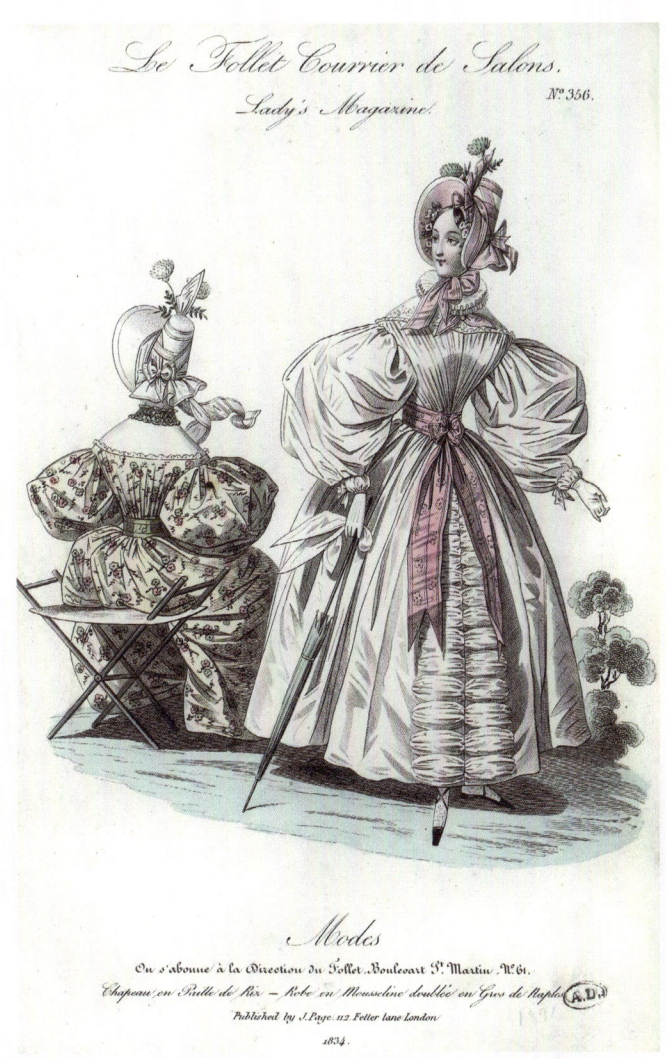

"La Follet Courrier de Salons, Lady's Magazine: Rice straw hat. Doubled muslin dress in Gros de Naples," 1834.
Bibliothèque des Arts Décoratifs, Paris; Maciet Album.

Day Dress
1830-1835

The construction and finishing on this printed cotton day dress are typical of the fashions of the 1830s. Indeed, the billowy sleeves, fitted bodice with narrow diagonal pleats, and wide gathered skirt connected to an inlaid belt lend it the hourglass shape that was so characteristic of the Romantic period. The upper part of the sleeves is tight and gathered, marking a slight stylistic change, while the fullness of the leg-of-mutton sleeves have moved to the middle of the arms. Incidentally, the female silhouette in this period was also defined by the return of the natural waistline, once again restricted by a boned corset. During the day, the neck could be covered by a guimpe, collar, or canezou, which were essential accessories at that time.

    The fabric of the dress attests to the trend of small-patterned, rolled, printed cottons, which reflected the development of the cotton printing industry, along with innovations in weaving and dyeing. Primarily located in Alsace, this industrial boom contributed to a drop in prices, making fashion more accessible.
M.-P.R.

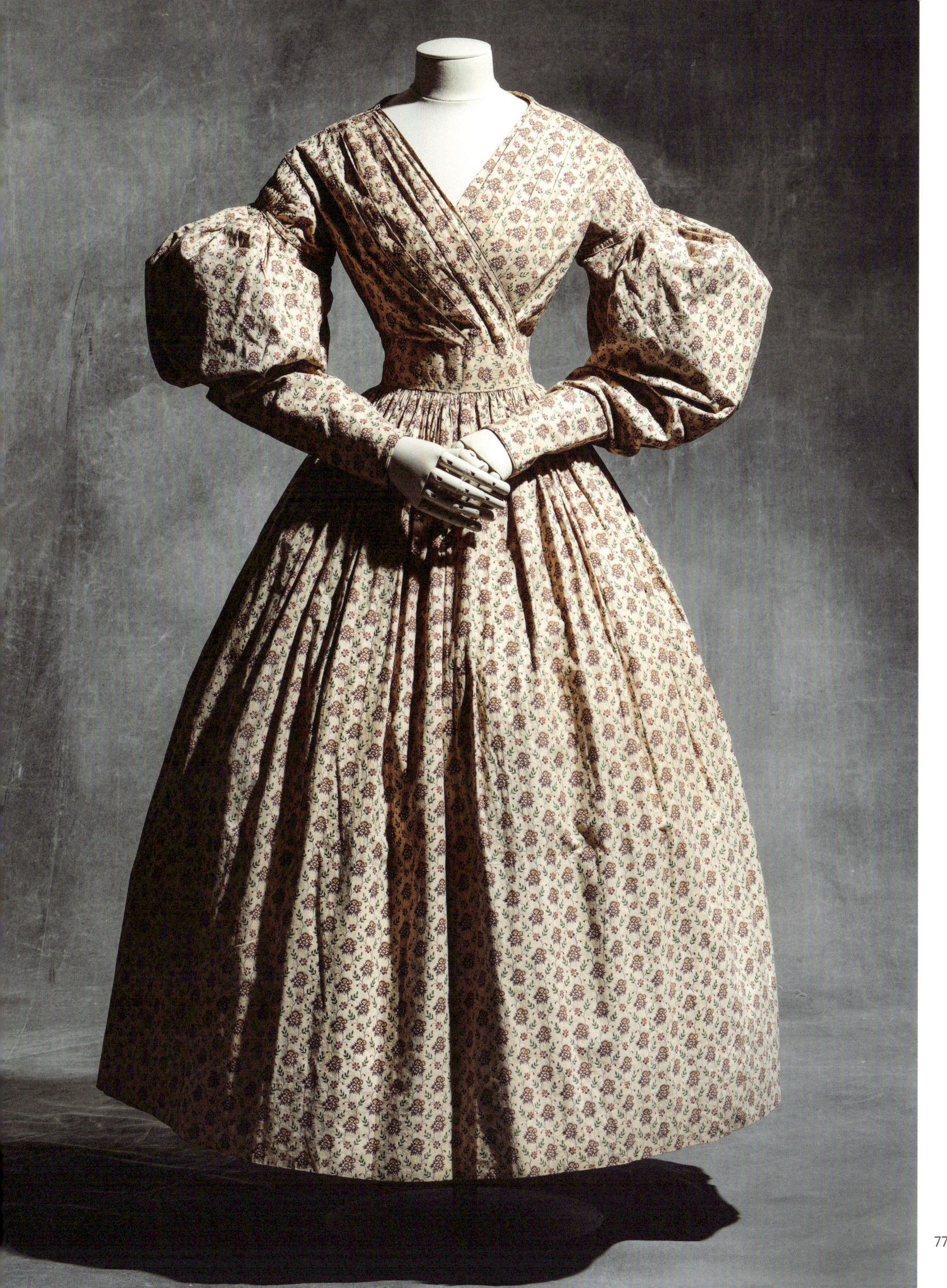

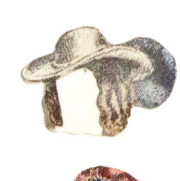
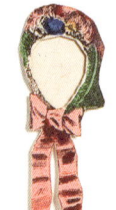
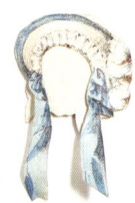
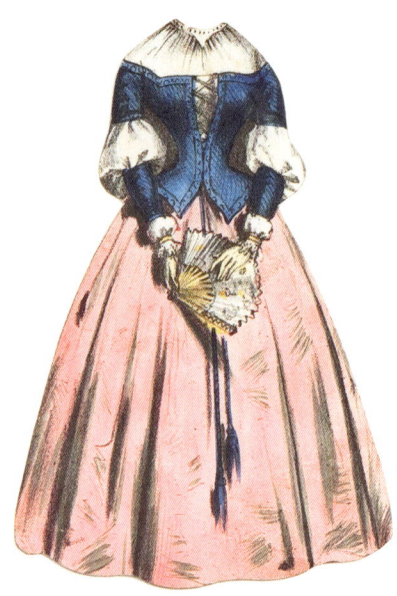
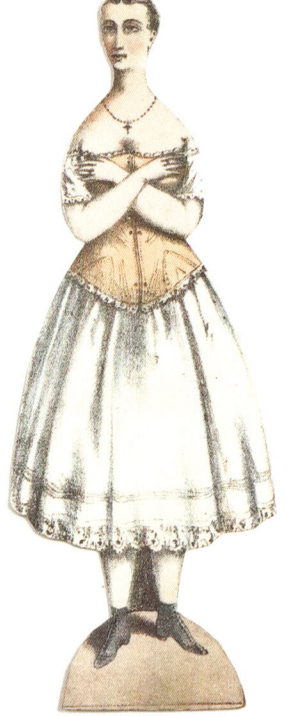
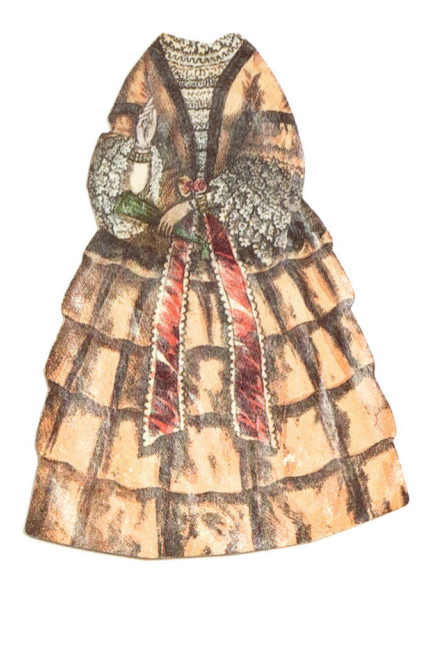
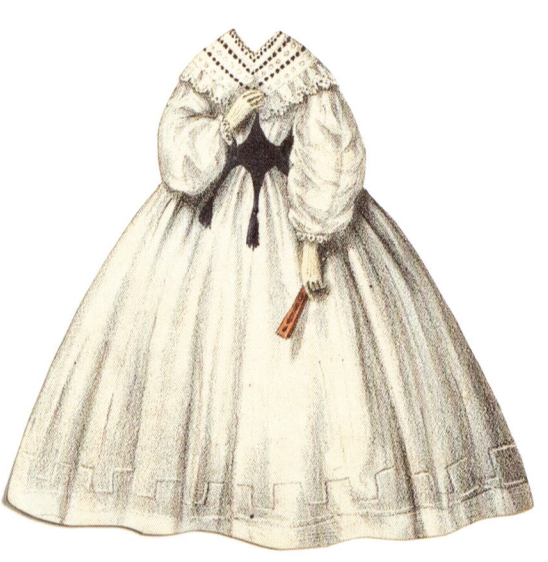
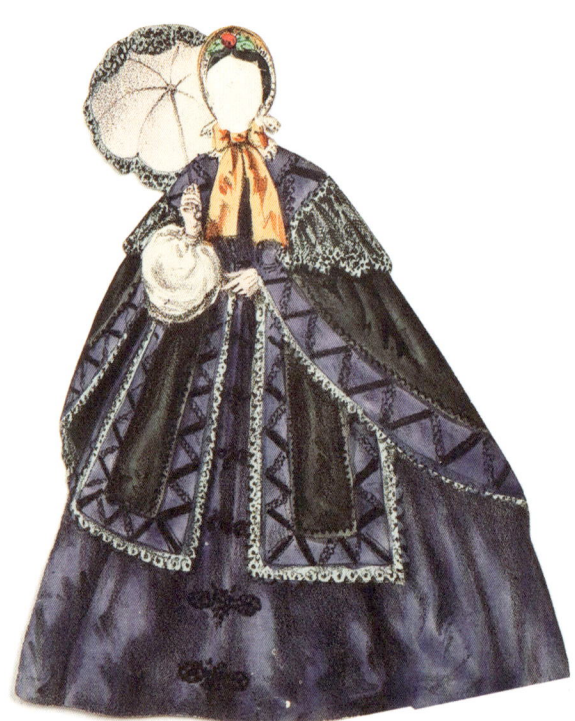
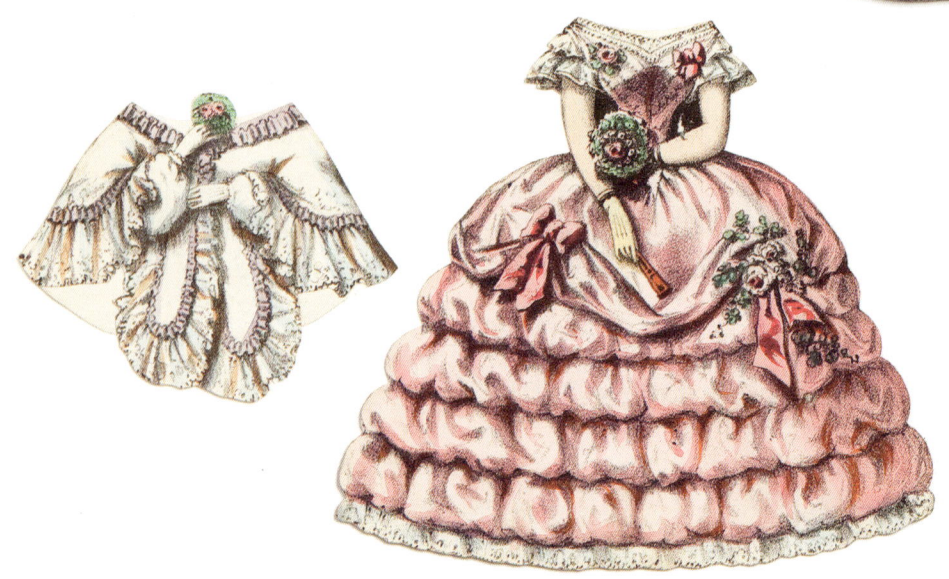
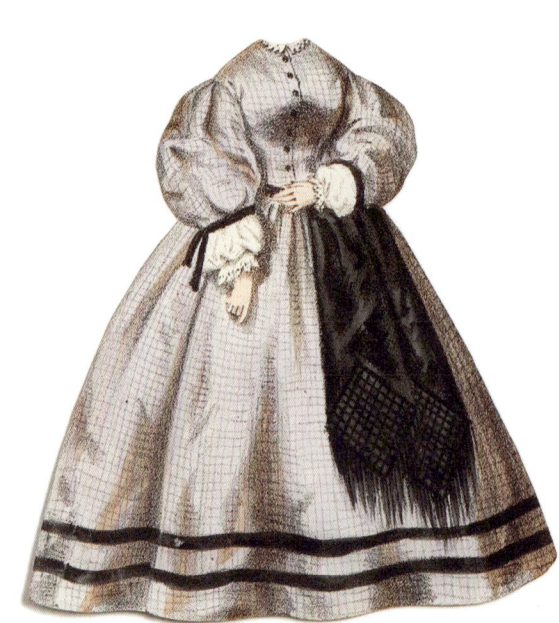

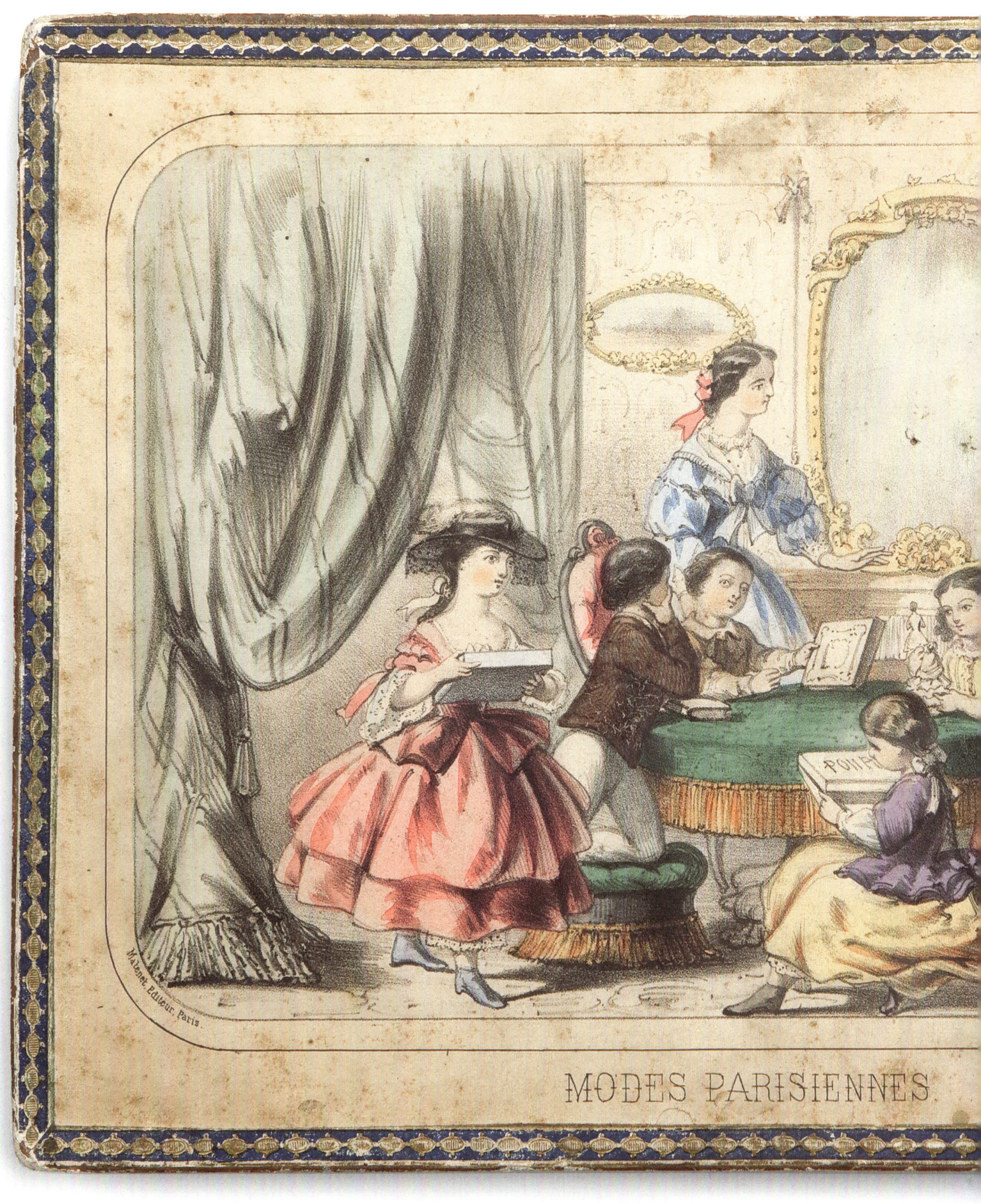

Modes parisiennes, Board game manufactured by Matenet, circa 1860. Musée des Arts Décoratifs, Paris; Games Division, gift of Contenau.
The box contains two dolls, with boxwood bases, as well as fifteen dresses and fifteen hats in cut paper.

Day Dress
1830-1835

Dating to the 1830s, this summer dress in white lawn is a remarkable example of a particular silhouette, spirit, and grace, with its "wasp" waist, overblown leg-of-mutton sleeves, and voluminous bell skirt. The romantic style had become increasingly clear in fashions of the late 1820s, and this dress was heir to the white embroidered muslin, lawn, and cambric dresses of the end of the eighteenth century and the Empire period. Indeed, hand-embroidered feather-stitched flowers, traditionally made in Paris or Nancy, adorned numerous pieces of clothing and lingerie at this time, including berthas, fichus, collars, and the like.

    Such embellishments provided an evanescent yet elegant appearance: the graceful Romantic woman embodied a feminine ideal that was personified in 1832 by the dancer Marie Taglioni, who triumphed in the ballet *La Sylphide* (The Sylph). In that role she was dressed for the first time in a white, voluminously skirted costume, a precursor of the modern tutu. The Musée des Arts Décoratifs collection contains a painting representing Taglioni in that title role, painted in 1834 by François Gabriel Guillaume Lepaulle.
M.-P.R.

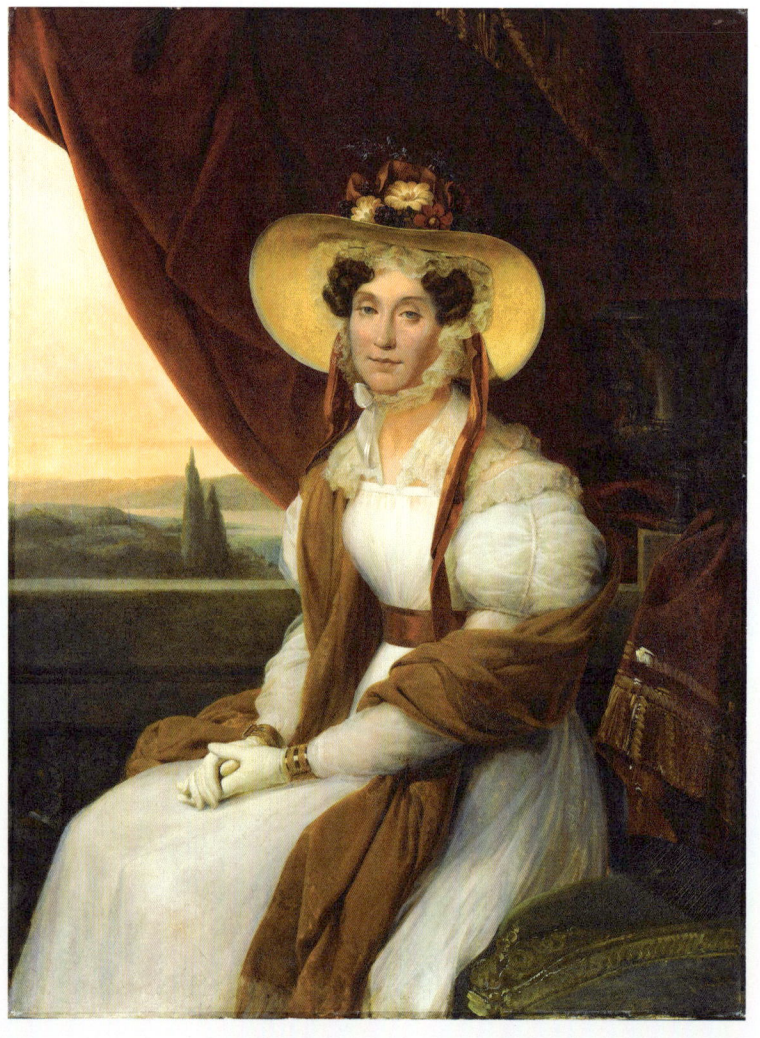

MARIE AMÉLIE COGNIET, *Portrait of Adélaide d'Orléans*, circa 1838. Oil on canvas.
Musée Condé, Chantilly.

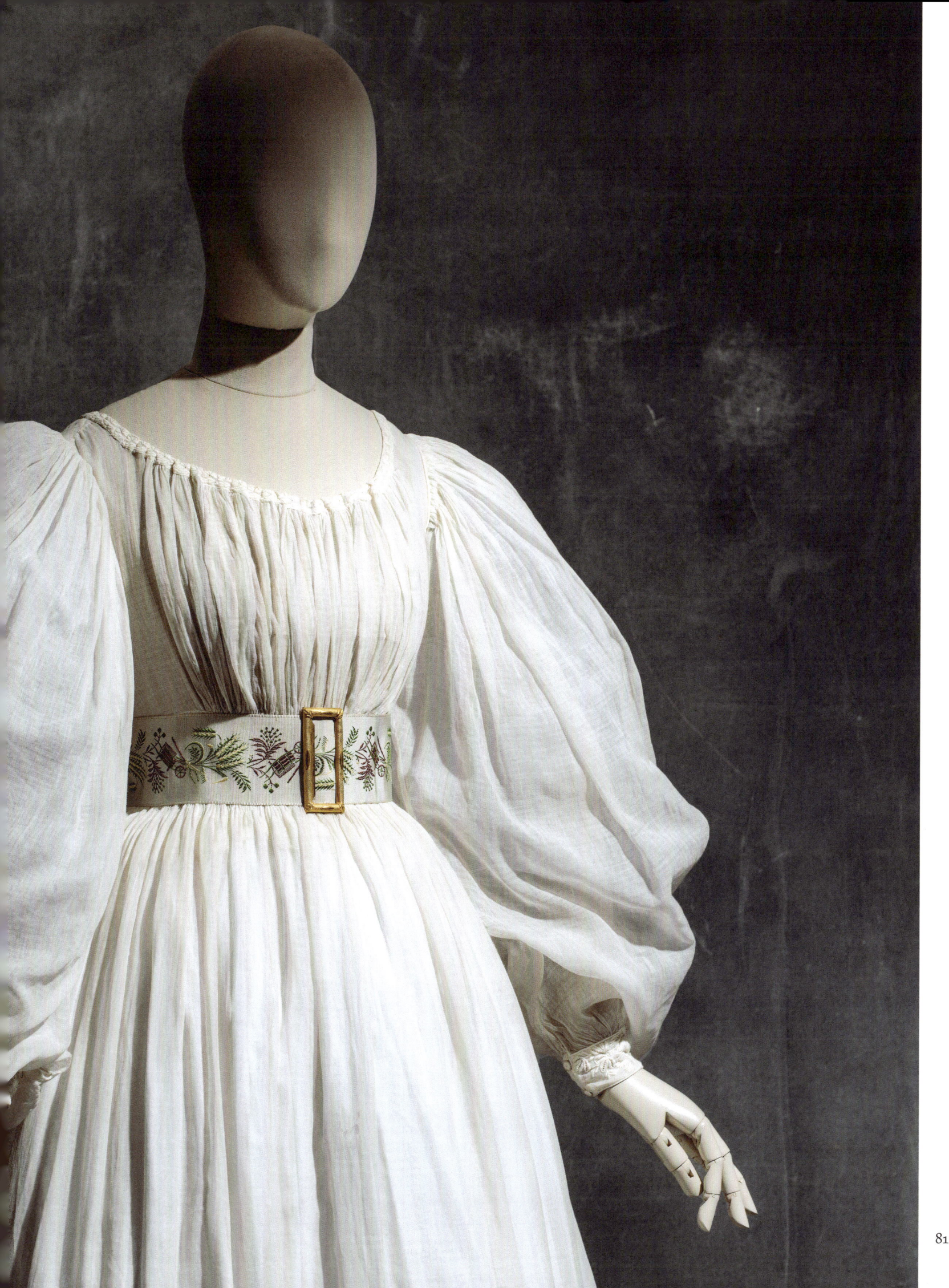

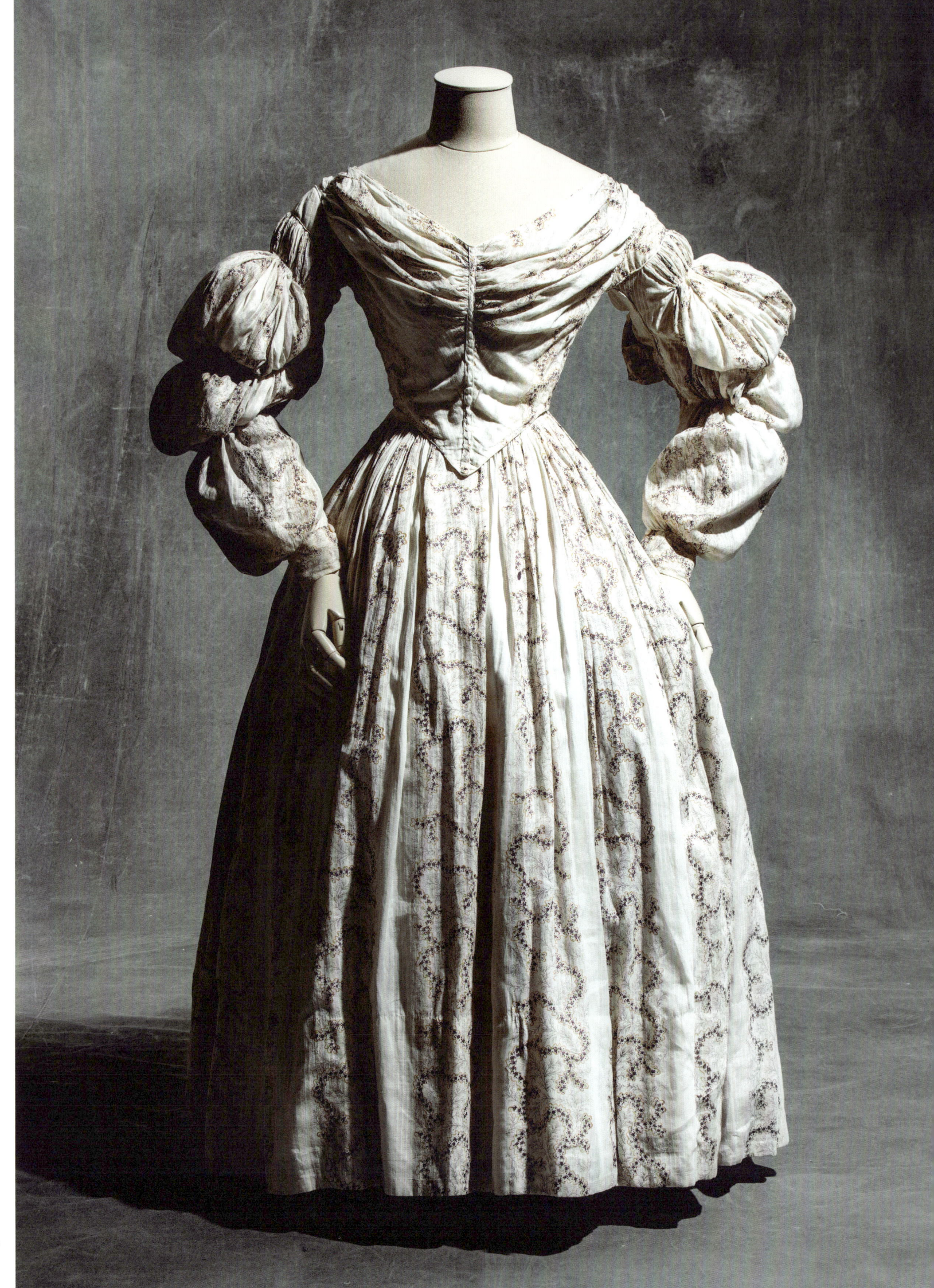

Dress
Circa 1835

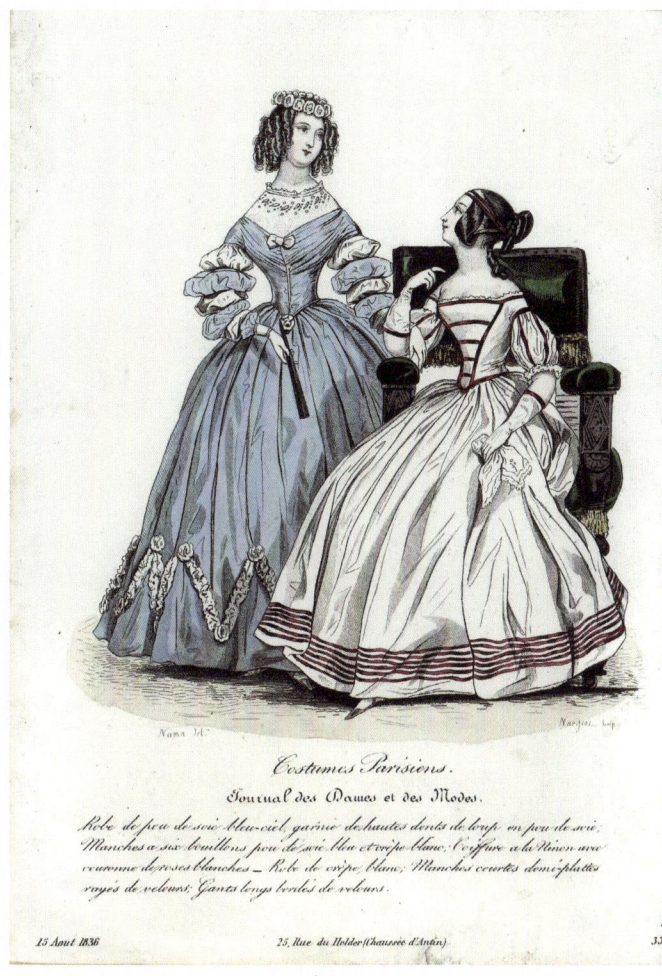

The spirit of Romantic fashion was marked by the culture of a particular historical time. Inspired by reminiscences of yesteryear, it adopted the troubadour style, which drew on the tastes of both the Middle Ages and the Renaissance. Womenswear adopted certain codes and thus reflected an entire era's fondness for an idealized past. The Duchess of Berry, Charles X's daughter-in-law, set the tone, notably by organizing a costume ball at the Tuileries on March 2, 1829. Called the Marie-Stuart Quadrille, the event embodied the spirit and elegance of her time. She also started the trend of leg-of-mutton sleeves.

This refined dress from the mid-1830s is a significant example, with its boat neck, gathered and draped V-shaped bodice, and voluminous skirt. The leg-of-mutton sleeves are bubbled with two bands, an interpretation of the sixteenth-century style. Although the embellishments are limited, the fabric is sophisticated and gives structure to the dress. The fine-striped cotton muslin is printed in wavy bands and scattered with fleurettes, with a resist of toothed, veined leaves and picot edges. This design seems to accentuate the skirt's length and shape its bias-cut bodice.

M.-P. R.

"Sky blue peau de soie dress. . . . Blue peau de soie and white crepe six-bubble sleeves. . . . White crepe dress; velvet striped semi-flat short sleeves," *Journal des dames et des modes: Costumes parisiens*, 1836. Bibliothèque des Arts Décoratifs, Paris; Maciet Album.

Dressing Gown
1830-1840

Dressing gowns are a testament to men's lifestyles. During the same period that Honoré de Balzac adopted it, this garment expressed a particular state of mind. It could be found in elegant interiors, as attested by its numerous portrayals in fashion illustrations and engravings. Although men had stopped dressing ostentatiously to go out in public starting in the early decades of the nineteenth century, the dressing gown, which could be long or short, allowed them to reconcile a bourgeois conformism with a strong desire for originality and relaxation. This piece is in the shape of a frock coat, fitted at the waist and with a crossover closure; it is marked by the particularity of its fabric and its bright-colored designs. A block-printed glazed percale contrasts with the sobriety required for city dress at that time.

  The dressing gown was also a luxurious robe of honor inherited from the splendors of the ancien régime, but one that coincided with the taste for the East so dear to Romantics. It was worn with a "Greek cap" (an embroidered velvet hat topped with a tassel) and leather slippers.
M.-P.R.

PP. 86-87 — MANUFACTURED BY ZUBER, *Les zones terrestres* (detail), 1855. Mechanical paper, hand-brushed iridescent background, polychrome woodblock print. Musée des Arts Décoratifs, Paris; purchase, 1987.

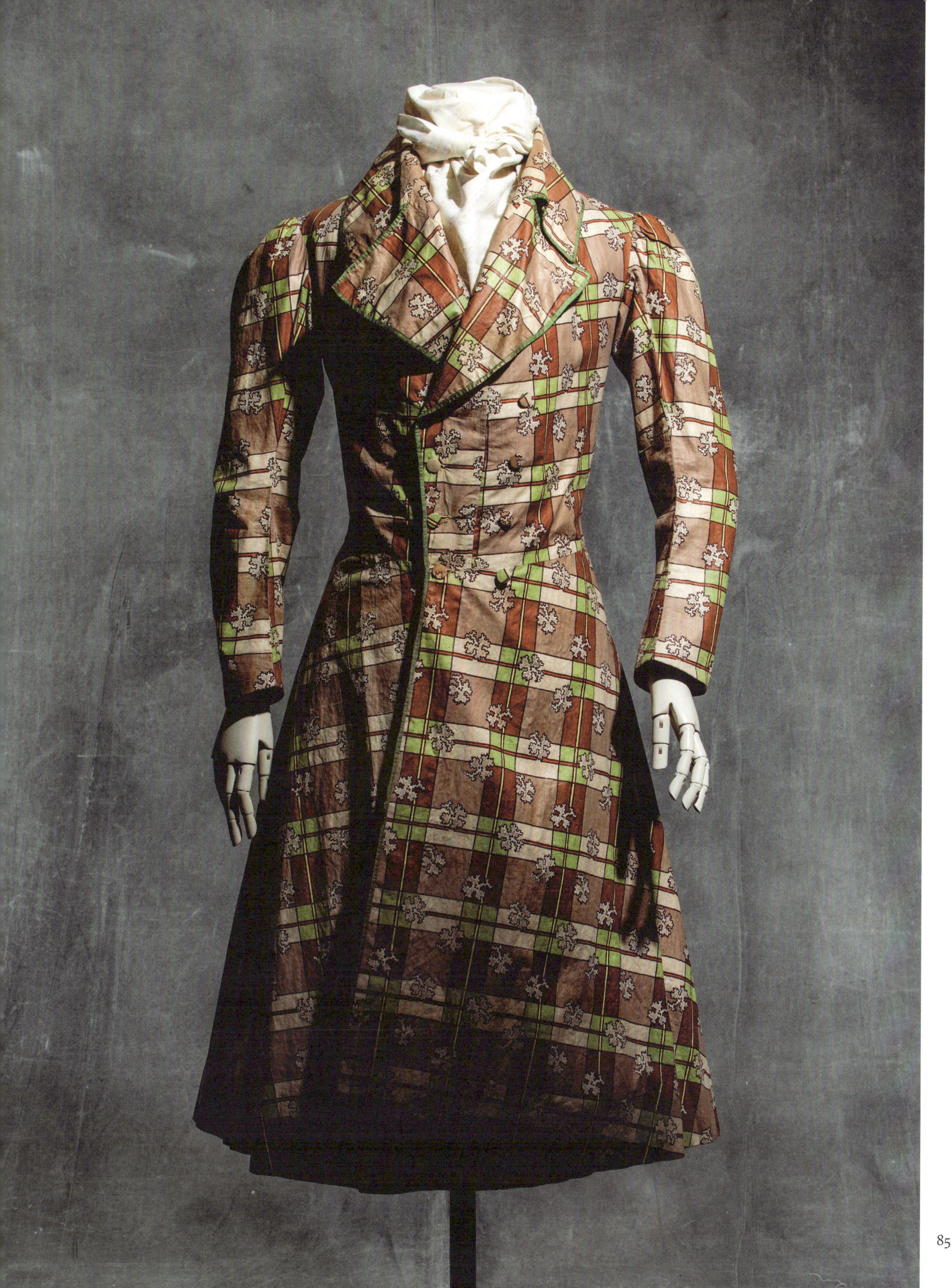

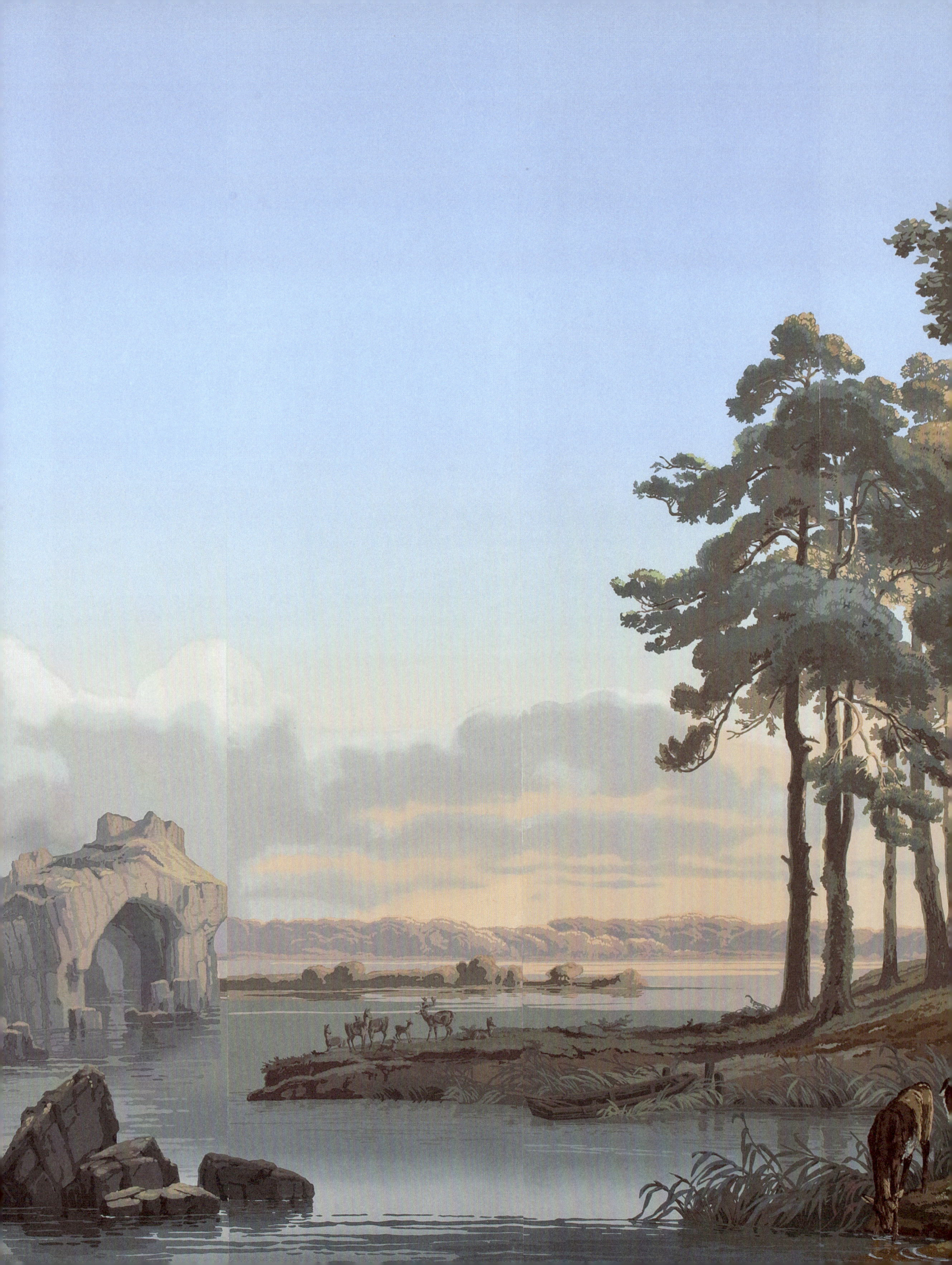

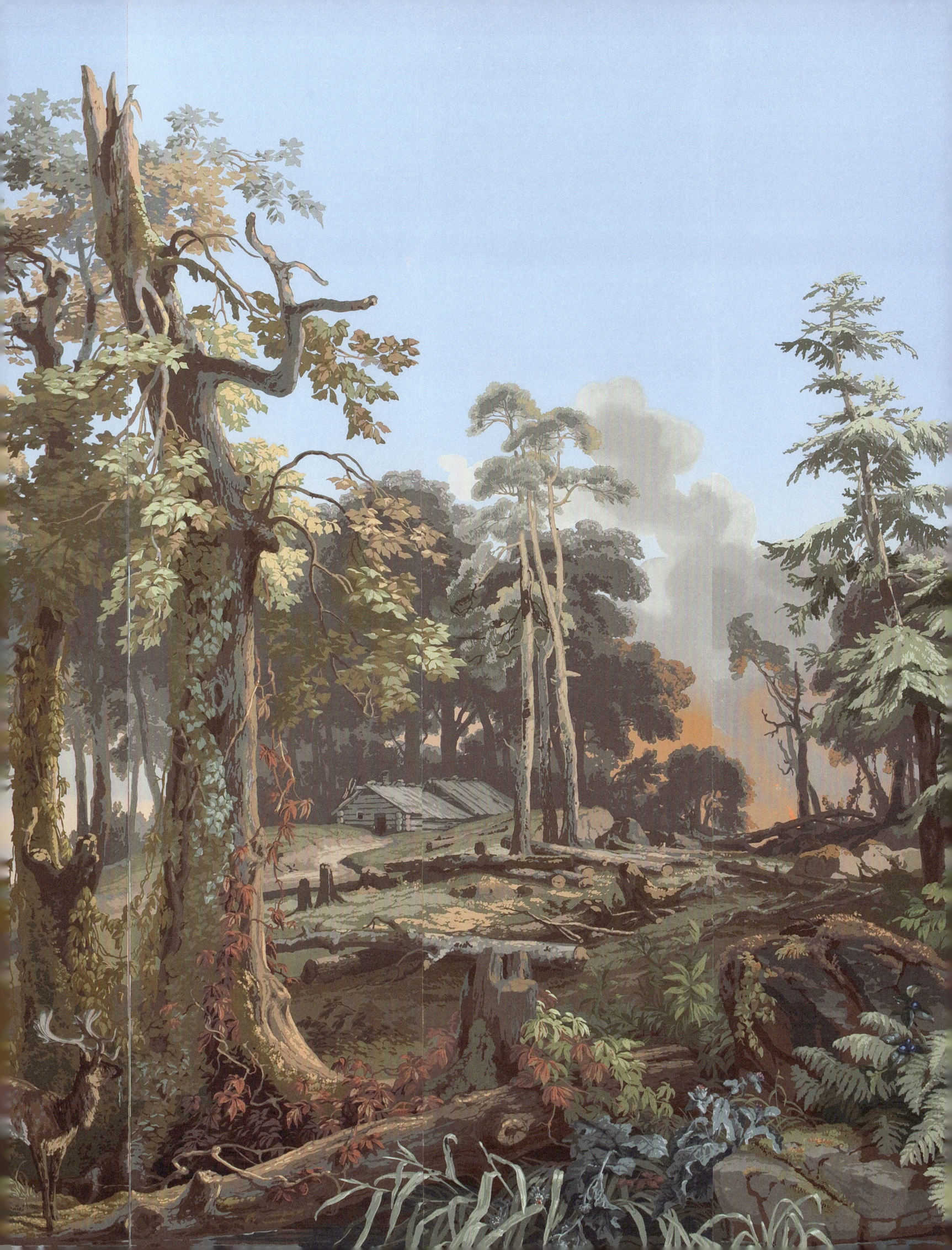

Transformation Dress (Robe à Transformation)
Circa 1862

Preciously preserved in the donor's family, this dress is emblematic of women's fashion under the Second Empire. One of its notable features lies in its name, the "transformation dress," which meant that a single skirt could easily be used to make two distinct outfits. Only the bodice was changeable, depending on the circumstances, use, and style of the dress, according to the instructions in etiquette books. For a ball, a low-cut bodice and stole were added; for day, the bodice had long fitted sleeves, placed fairly low, with the seam falling just beneath the shoulders.

Characteristic of the early 1860s, the ample skirt and train were cut to be supported with a crinoline and to project backward, accentuating the pyramid shape of the silhouette. This dress also reflects the technical advancements in synthetic dyes. The bright blue tone shows the sudden craze for intense colors, notably since the discovery of mauveine in 1856, which significantly affected the textile industry and fashion in general.

M.-P.R.

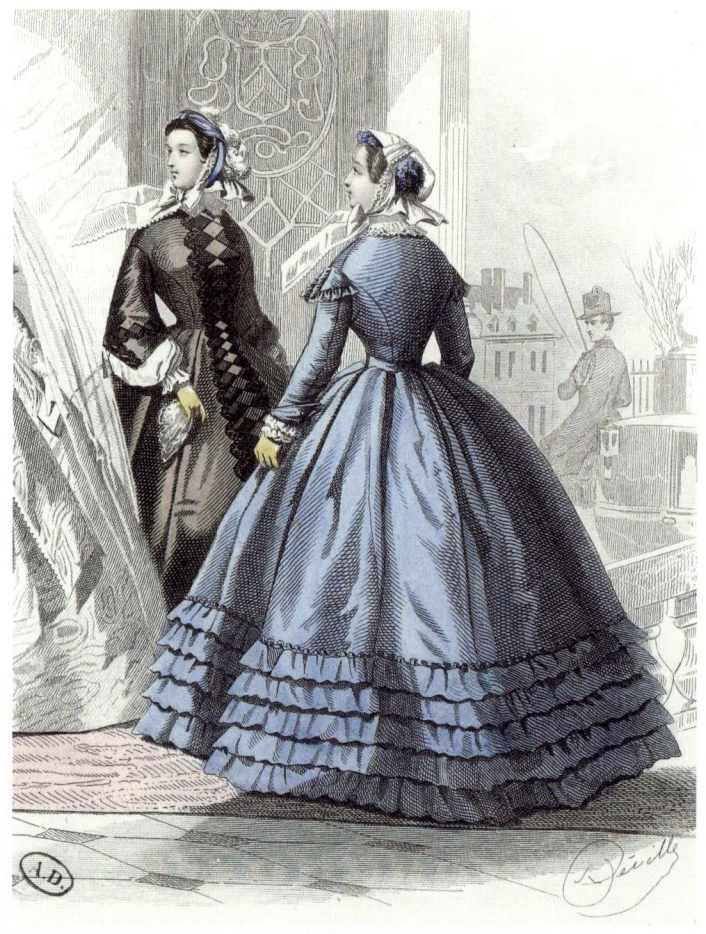

Plate from *L'écho du moniteur de la mode* (detail), 1856-1857. Bibliothèque des Arts Décoratifs, Paris; Maciet Album.

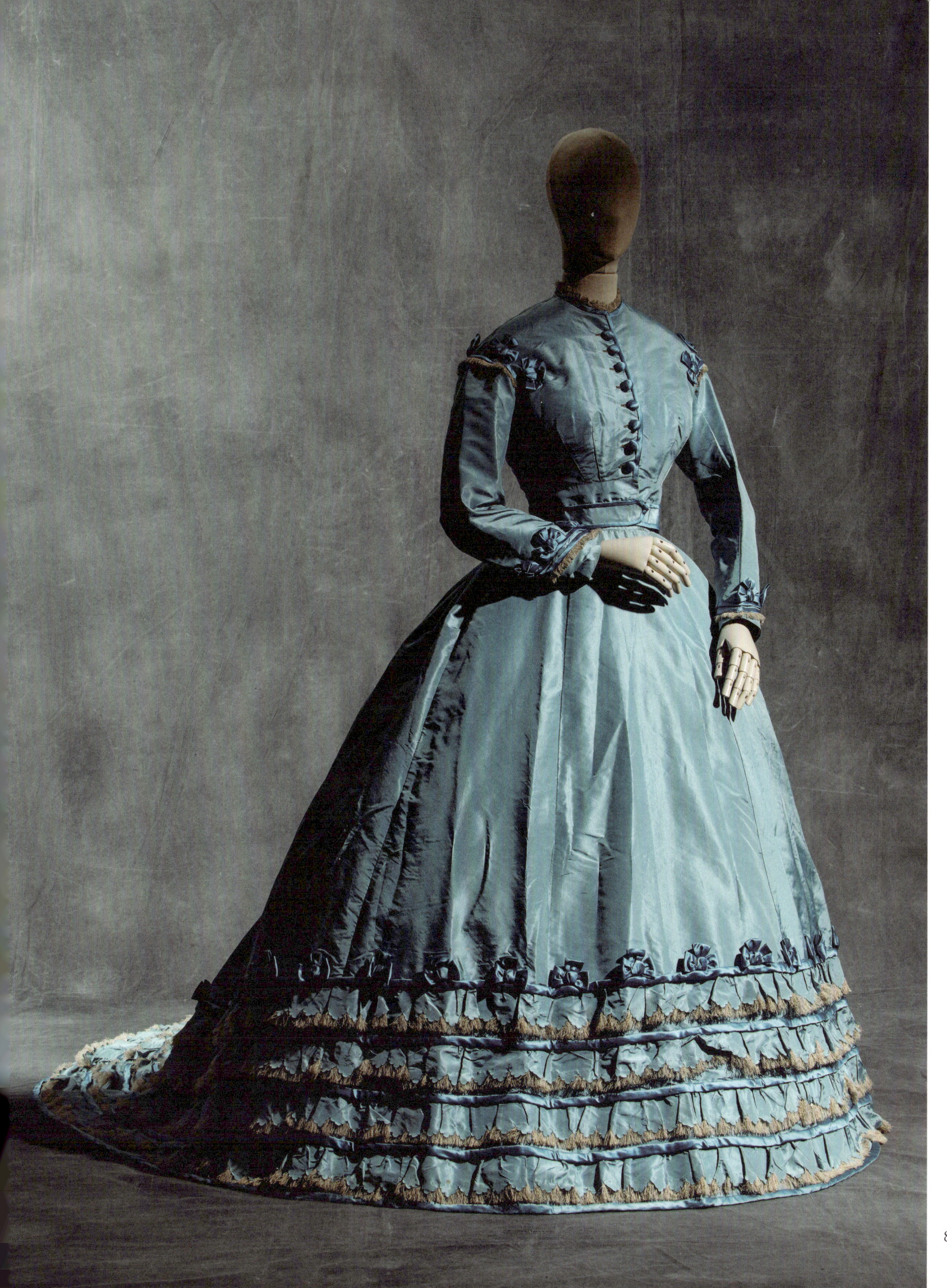

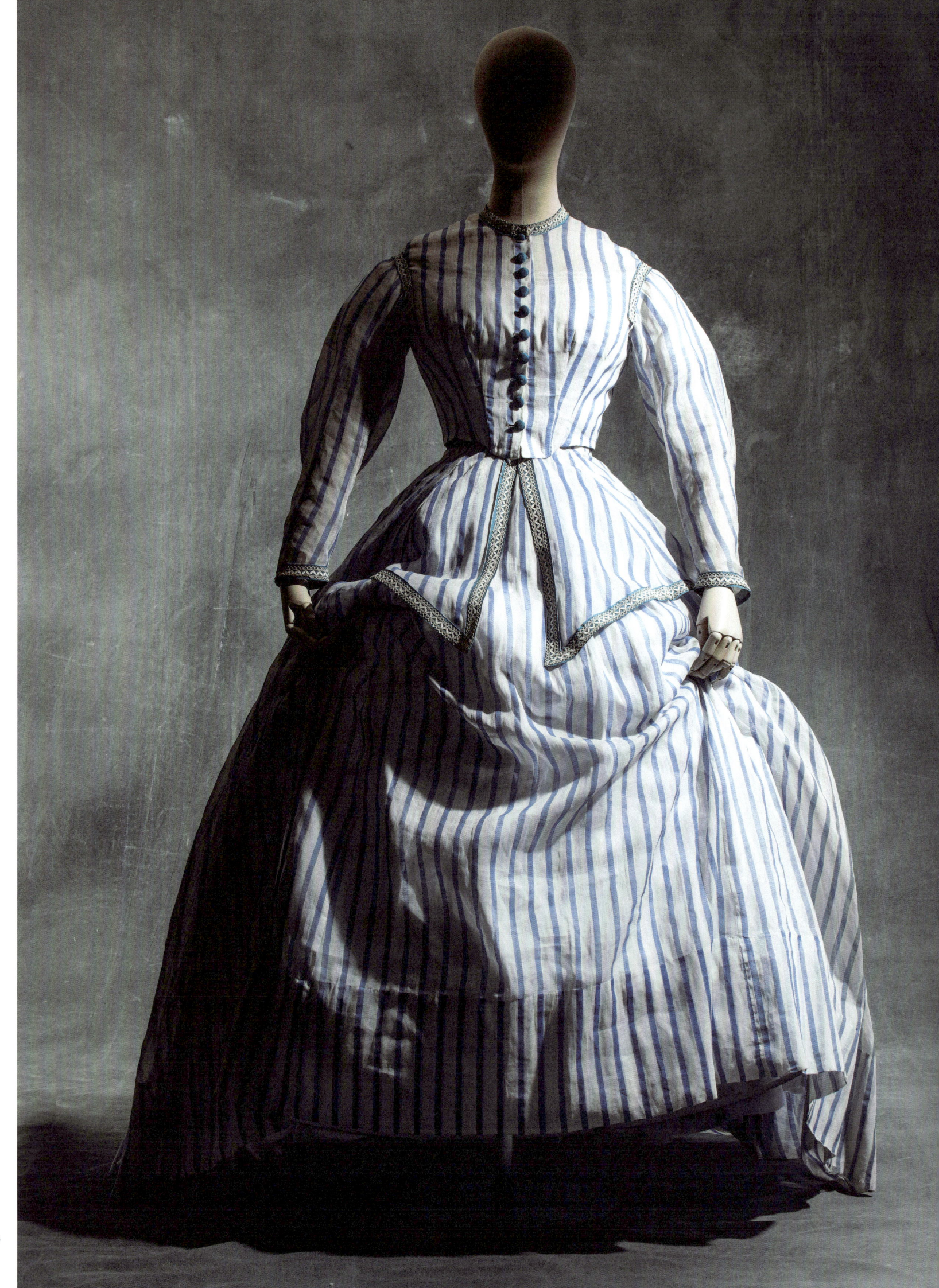

Transformation Dress (Robe à Transformation)
1868-1872

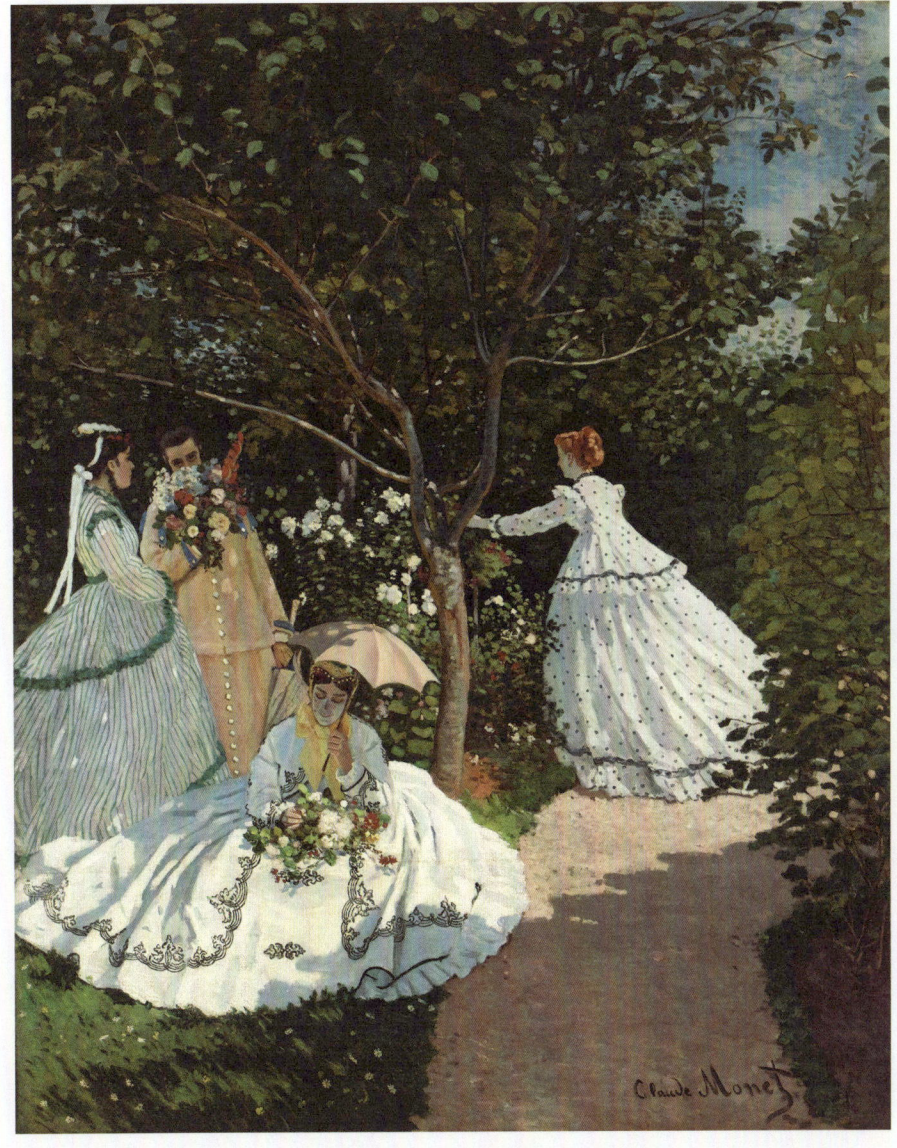

Consisting of three parts, this crinoline day dress, which concentrates most of its volume in the back, was typical of the style at the end of the Second Empire. It could be transformed into an evening gown by changing the bodice. The timelessness of this summer dress, which has been presented in recent exhibitions, highlights its aesthetic value. The couturier Christian Lacroix was fascinated by the optical effect and graphic precision of the crinoline, and he chose it for a section devoted to stripes in his *Fashion Histories* show at the Musée des Arts Décoratifs in 2007. It was then selected to appear alongside the Claude Monet painting *Women in the Garden*, in the *Impressionism and Fashion* exhibition at the Musée d'Orsay in 2012. The skirt of this dress extends into a train in the back, a nearly literal rendering of the one worn by the woman appearing in profile under the shade of the tree at the left of the painting reproduced here. The composition of Monet's canvas re-creates the moving silhouettes, which were light and lively despite the crinoline's bulk.

Some years prior, the painter Eugène Boudin, sensitive to the vibrations of natural light characteristic of the Normandy coast, had detailed elegant women vacationing for summer dressed in the crinolines that were in fashion during the 1860s. His *Vue de la plage à Trouville* is part of the collections of the Musée des Arts Décoratifs. Although it never belonged to the great dress designer, Boudin's painting now hangs on the walls of the room devoted to Jeanne Lanvin, who was a collector of Impressionist works.
M.-S.C.C.

CLAUDE MONET, *Women in the Garden at Ville-d'Avray*, 1867. Oil on canvas. Musée d'Orsay, Paris.
PP. 92-93 — EUGÈNE BOUDIN, *Vue de la plage à Trouville*, 1864. Oil on wood. Musée des Arts Décoratifs, Paris.
PP. 94-95 — Cabinet cards, second half of the nineteenth century. Musée des Arts Décoratifs, Paris; photography collections.

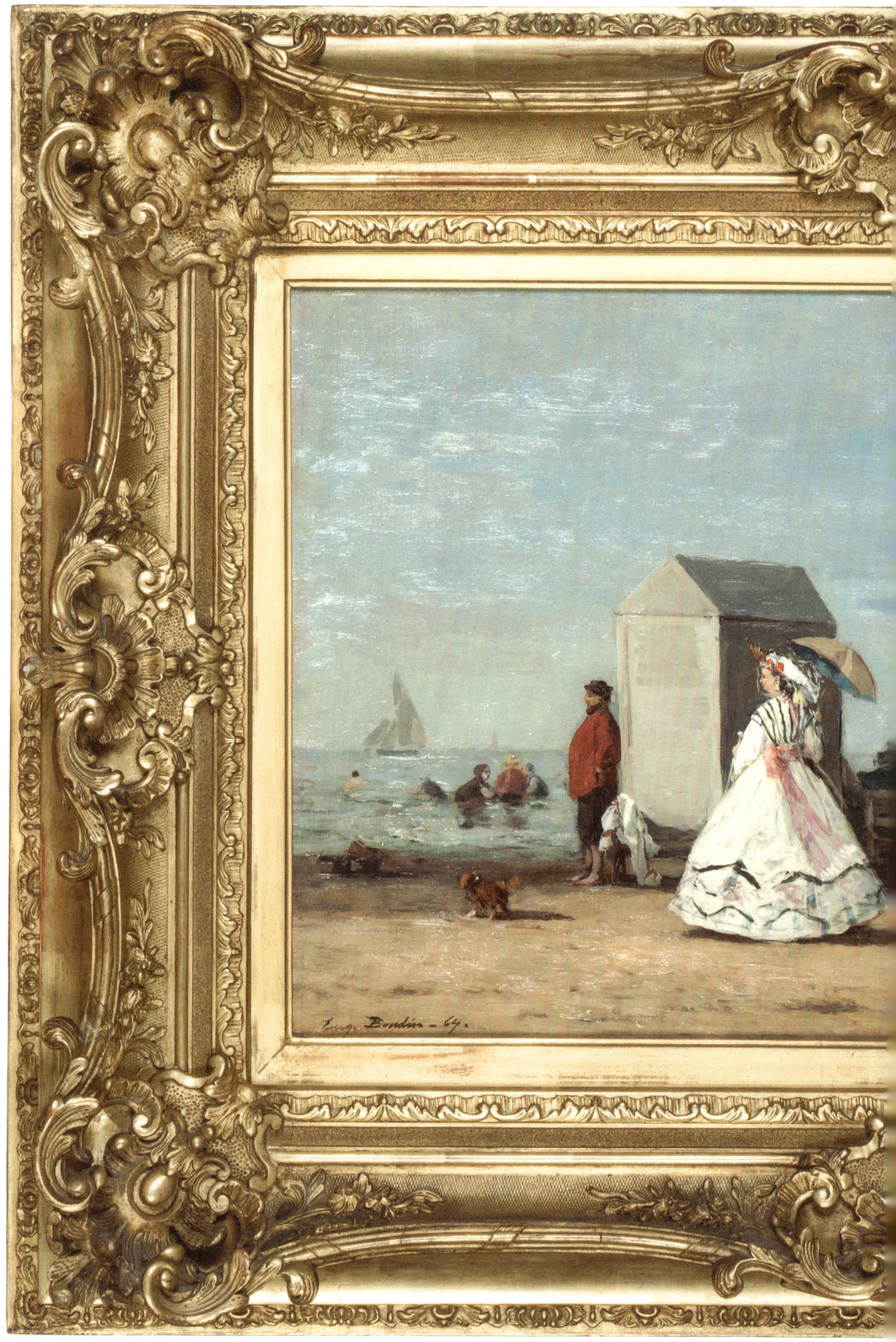

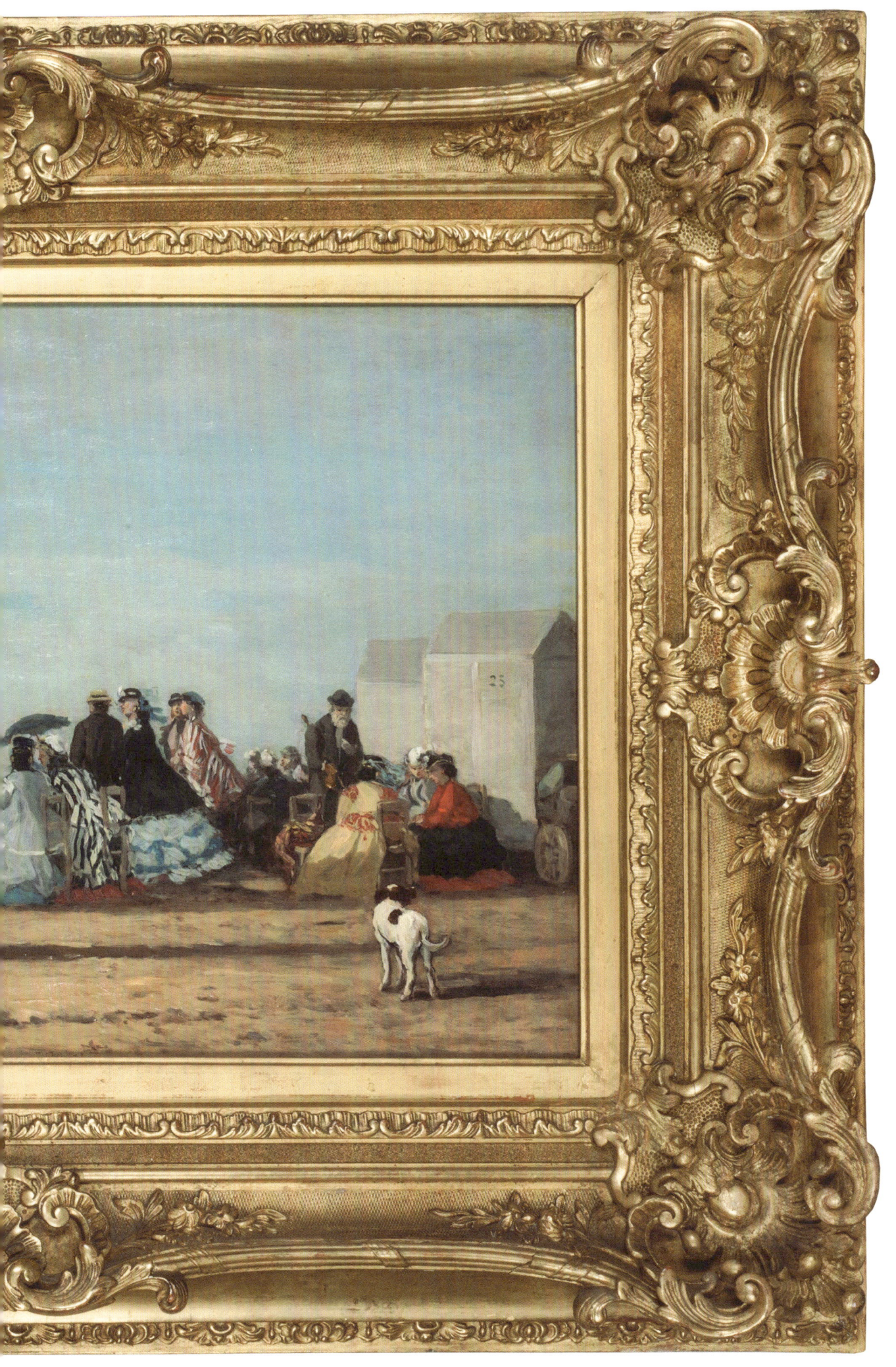

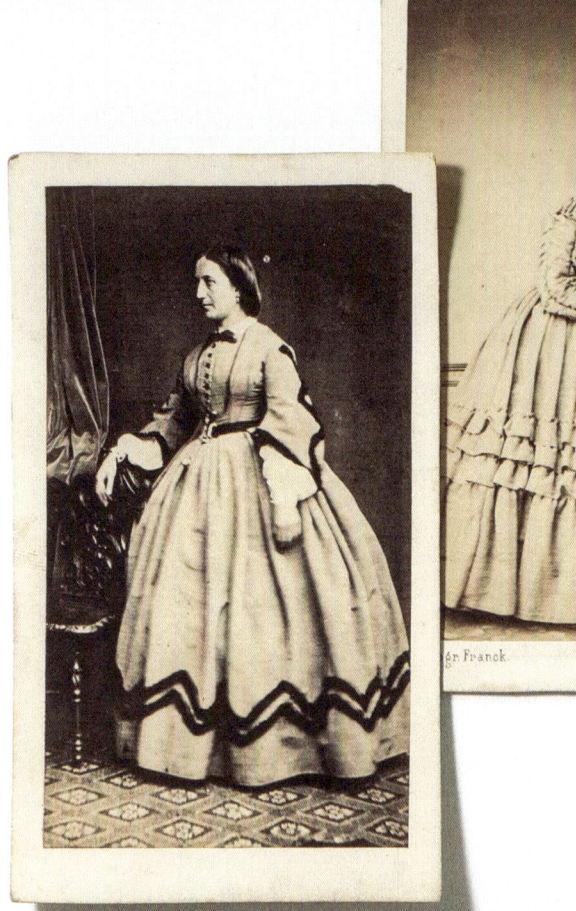
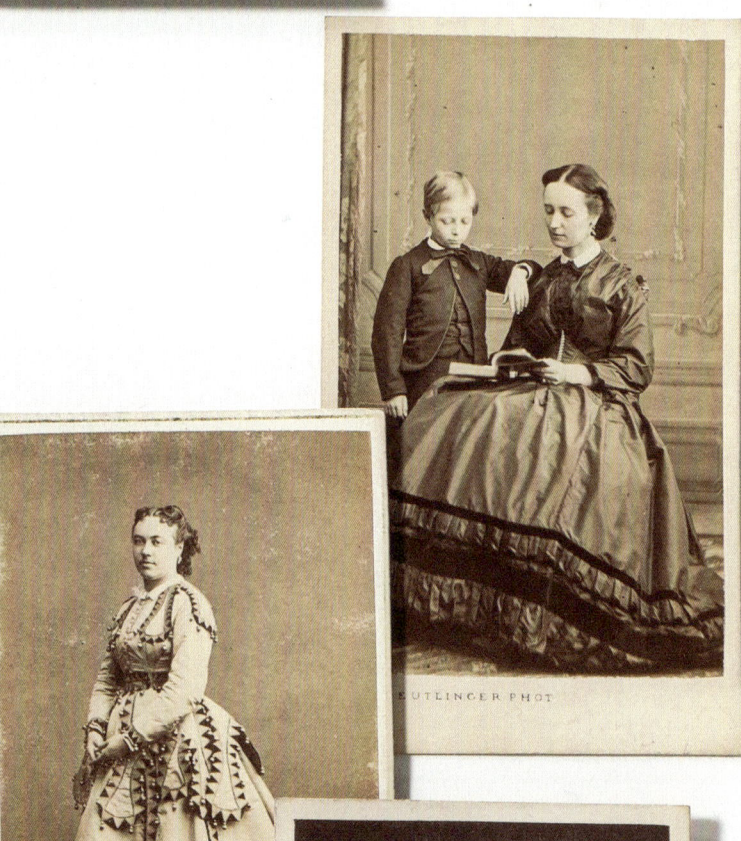
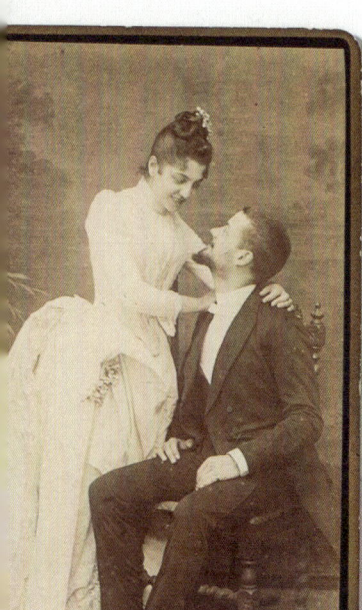
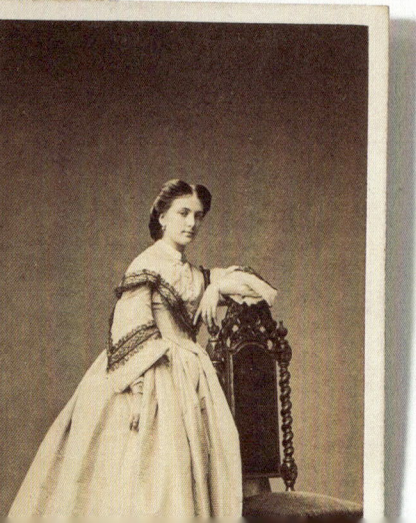
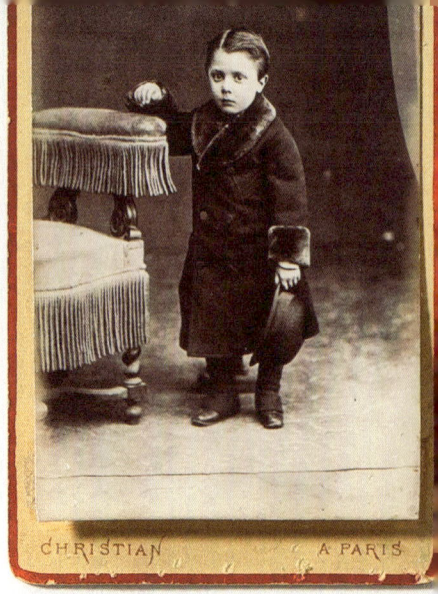
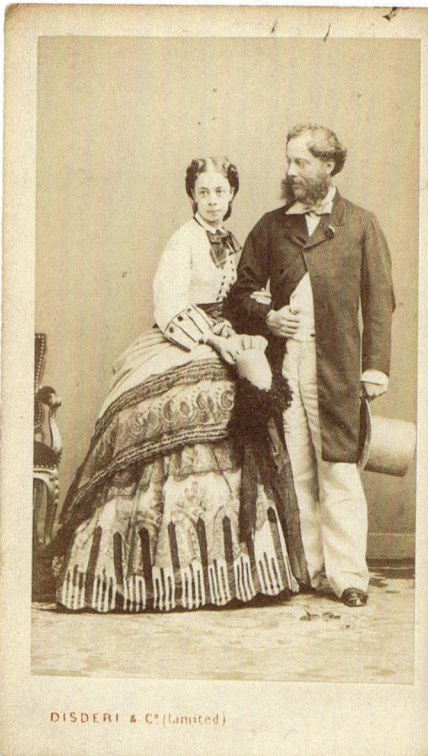
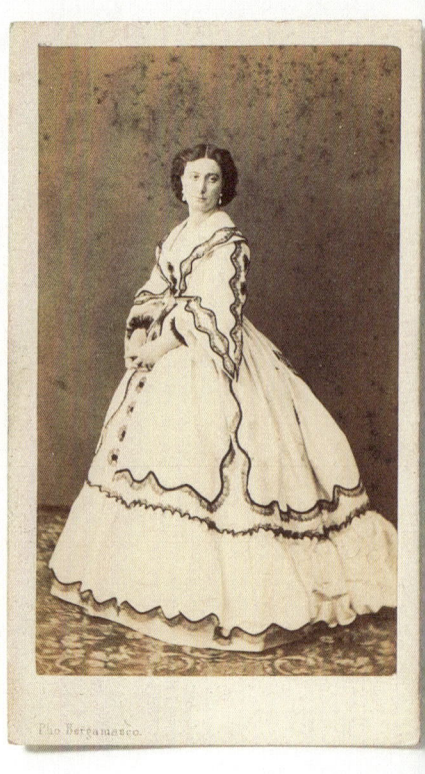

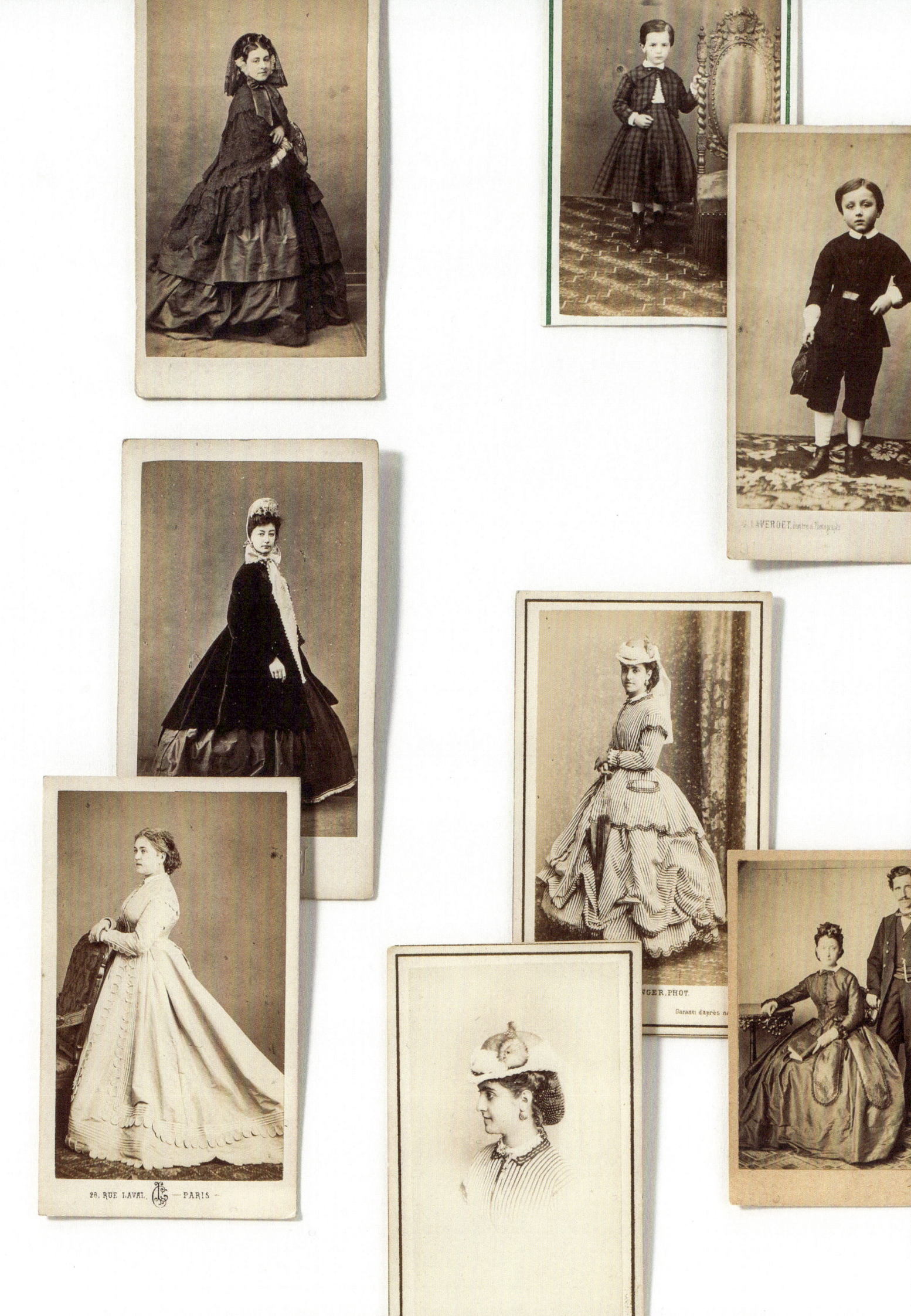

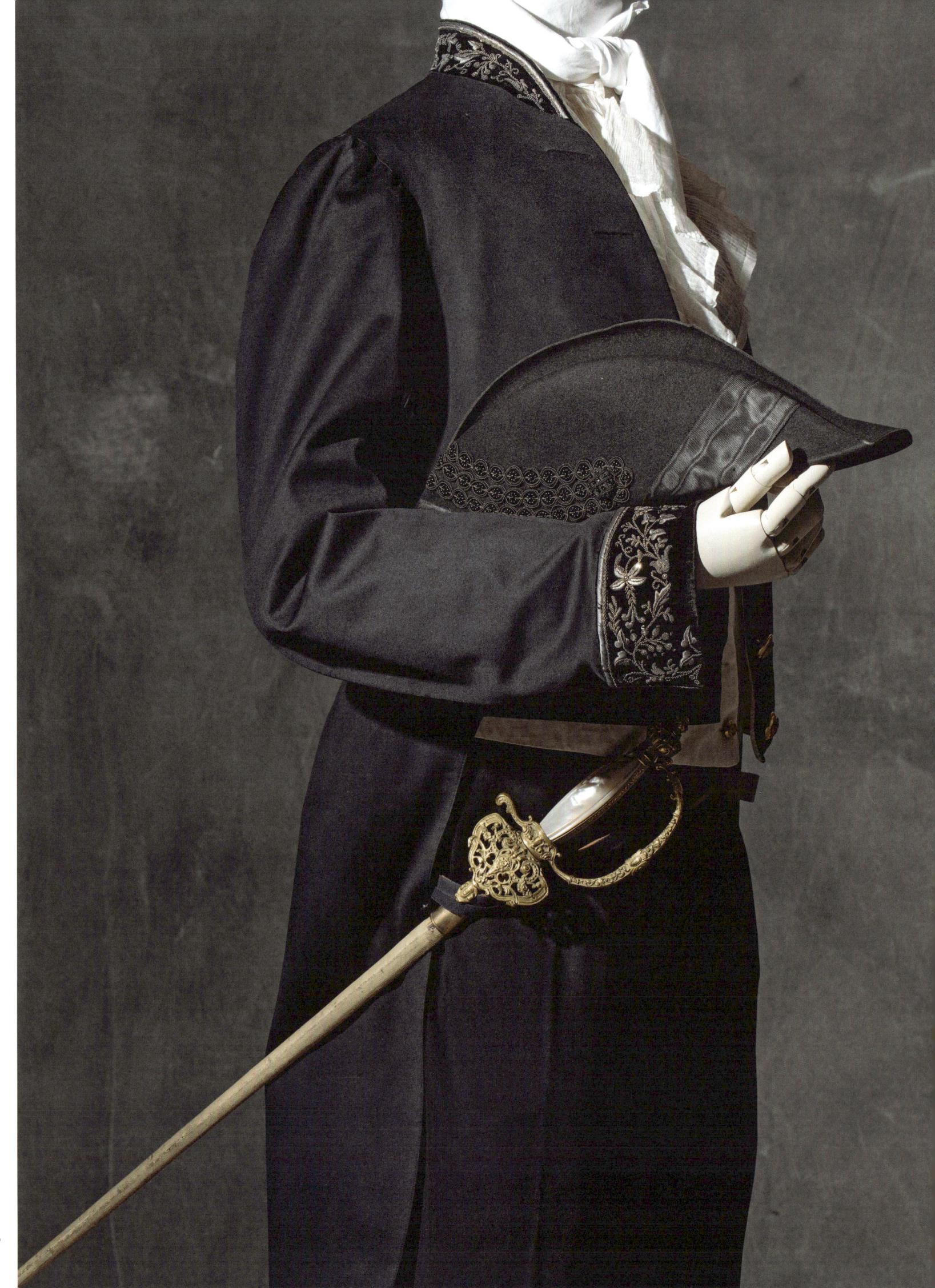

Men's Court Suit
1859

After a long absence, court dress and civil uniforms reappeared at Napoleon II's court, having been adapted to the fashions of the time. Their composition and style were marked by greater sobriety. The *habit à la française* was supplanted by a suit made of wool cloth or somber velvet, with a narrow, straight, embroidered collar; it was paired with a solid white vest, a white jabot shirt, breeches in white or matching the suit, black or white stockings, a flat bicorne hat, and a sword. Worn at court for official presentations, or during a ball at the Tuileries, this suit was intended for men who did not hold official posts.

Court dress was a symbolic language in which shapes, colors, embellishments, and accessories contributed to maintaining the proper order of the social hierarchy, rather than merely providing formal recognition of a trade. Dress-related conventions and the use of civil uniforms reached their apex under the Second Empire. Worn at major events or allotted to functionaries, they reflected the history and institutions of France.

M.-P.R.

Plate from *Tailleurs de Paris. Société philanthropique des maîtres*, 1852. Bibliothèque des Arts Décoratifs, Paris; Maciet Album.

Day Dress
Circa 1885

After having disappeared for a time, the bustle dress reappeared from 1882 to 1889 with a bigger-than-ever pouf, or "*cul de Paris.*" This two-piece midseason outfit is representative of the simultaneously skimpy and bundled-up silhouette. While mocked by cartoonists, it marked the triumph of the upholstery style (*style tapissier*) in this period.

This designer dress has a long tunic with a trompe l'oeil vest and a lateral "butterfly wing" drape, topped with a thick bow and draped apron skirt in front. Also noteworthy is the inner caging, which supported the bustle while seated. An innovation of the 1880s, this light structure with jointed half-hoops retracted to allow for more comfortable sitting and was considered a scientific breakthrough.

The matching colors of this day dress accentuate the paisley design. Here it is block printed, arranged in a band on the skirt and on the tunic's border, evoking embroidered men's suits of the ancien régime. Paisley prints were an important product for the Alsatian manufacturers of the 1880s; they were found on shawls as well as on the bibs, collars, and lapels of dresses.

M.-P.R.

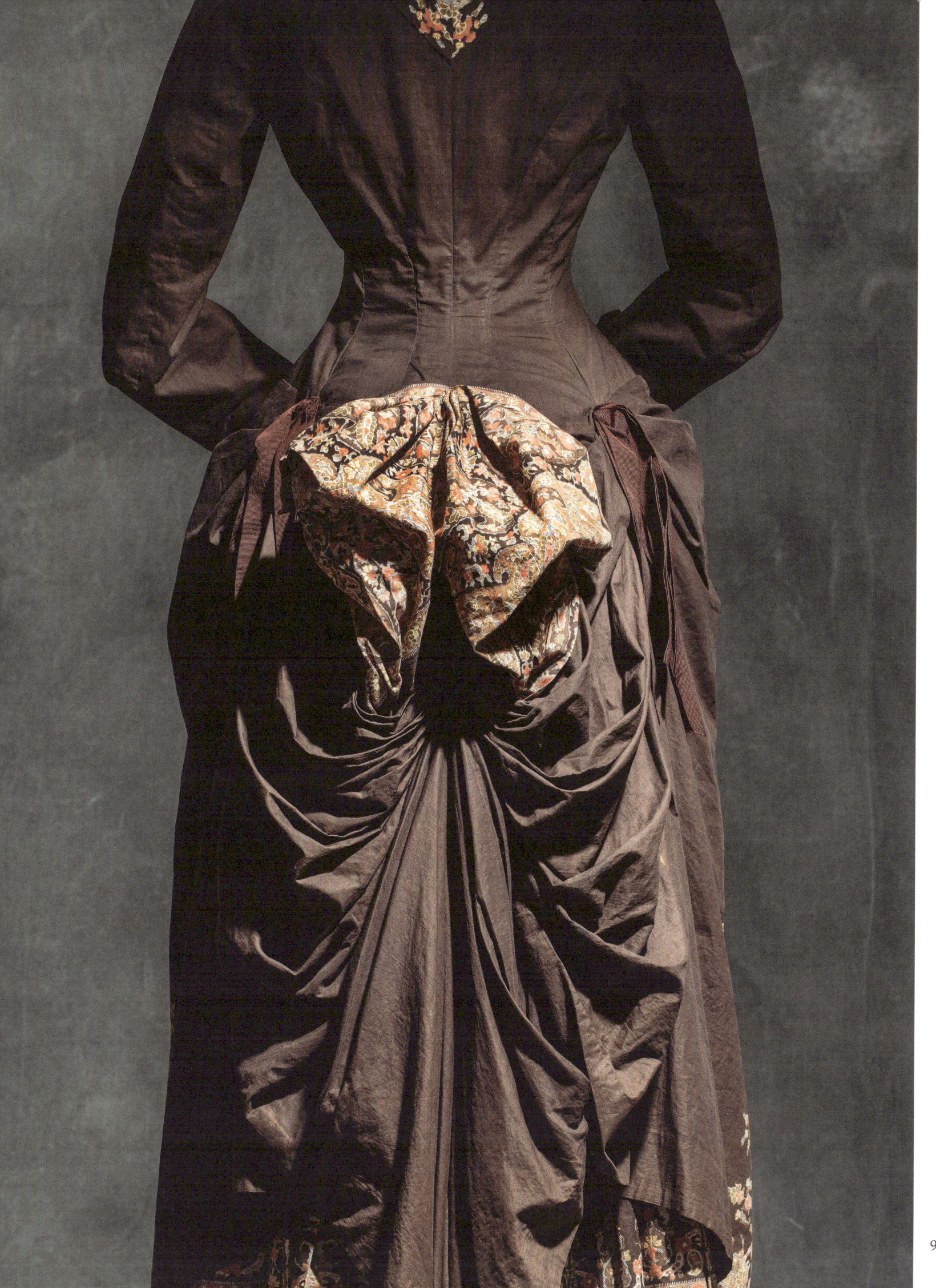

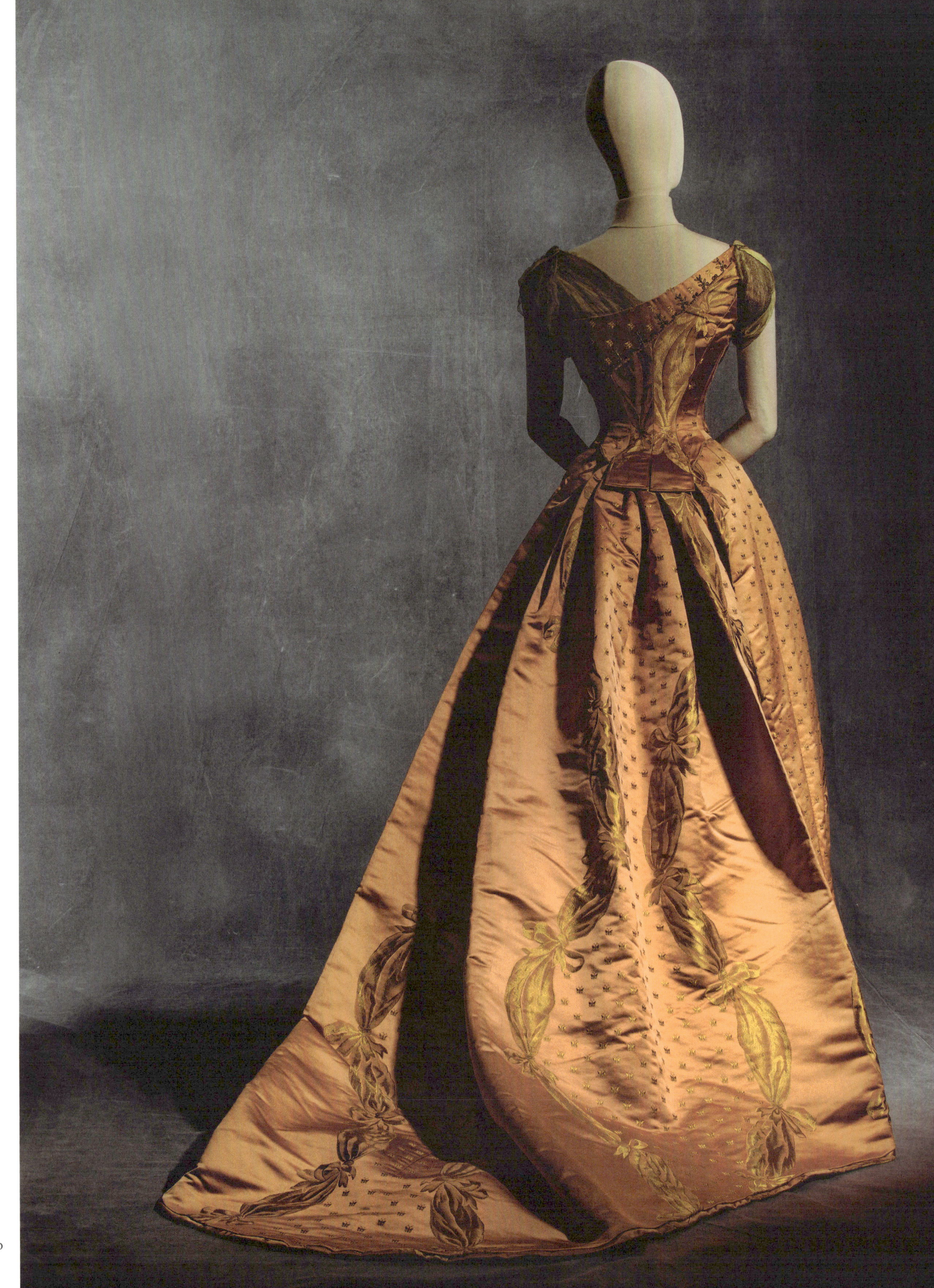

Charles Frederick Worth
Evening Gown, circa 1885

Charles Frederick Worth (1825-1895), a couturier with a penchant for European courts and a new fashionable and wealthy American clientele, designed this formal piece. This evening gown is unique in the scale of its bustle, its train, the incredible luxury of its figured satin fabric, and the magnificence of its decorative elements. It was commissioned by Mrs. Franklin Gordon Dexter (1840-1926), the wife of a rich Boston businessman, during a stay in the capital of haute couture.

In 1874 the couturier brought his sons Gaston and Jean Philippe into the family business. The latter assisted his father in the artistic management of the fashion house, developing sumptuous fabrics with Lyonnais silk manufacturers. In the frontispiece to the book *A Century of Fashion*, Jean Philippe retraces the story of the family's fashion house and pays homage to his father, the inventor of couture. The image includes a copy of a painted portrait of Queen Elizabeth I of England wearing an orange velvet dress that echoes the color of this evening gown.

Characteristic of the turn-of-the-century's taste for borrowing from history, this dress embodies the English Renaissance style of the Elizabethan era. With its sumptuous look and remarkable composition, it also reflects the couturier's desire to create an original bespoke work of art.

M.-S.C.C.

Dolman-Mantle
1870-1880

The dolman-mantle was a daily garment for outside wear that could also be adapted for evening when going out to a ball. It first became a part of women's wardrobes in 1840, later reappearing around 1870. This cinched garment with pagoda sleeves served as an overcoat, midway between a three-quarters coat and a cape. The dolman-mantle followed the curve of the waist and could be cut lower in back to account for a prominent bustle. The Musée des Arts Décoratifs houses around fifty such pieces, dating from 1870 to 1890, which attests to their extraordinary popularity.

This model is unique because it was cut from a French-manufactured paisley shawl. The fine accessory was thus recycled and, during the heyday of the upholstery style, loaded with delicate passementeries, which complemented the garment's shimmering colors. Some Parisian couturiers and fashion houses specialized in this type of transformation into dolman-mantles or even into dresses. A May 27, 1883 issue of *La mode illustrée* proposed "old Indian or French paisley" that had been repurposed by Madame Haussemberg at 46, rue du Bac, in Paris.
M.-P.R.

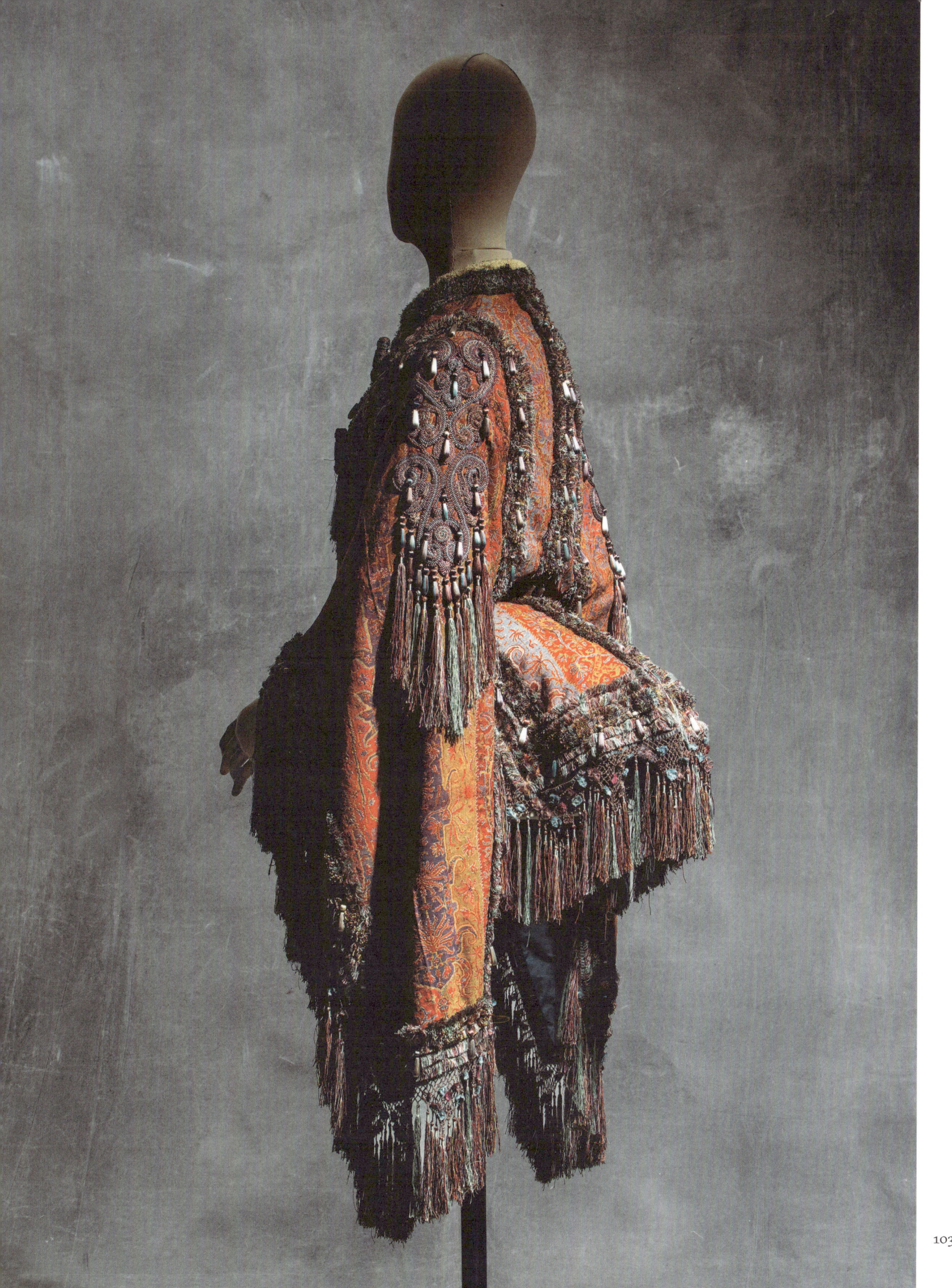

103

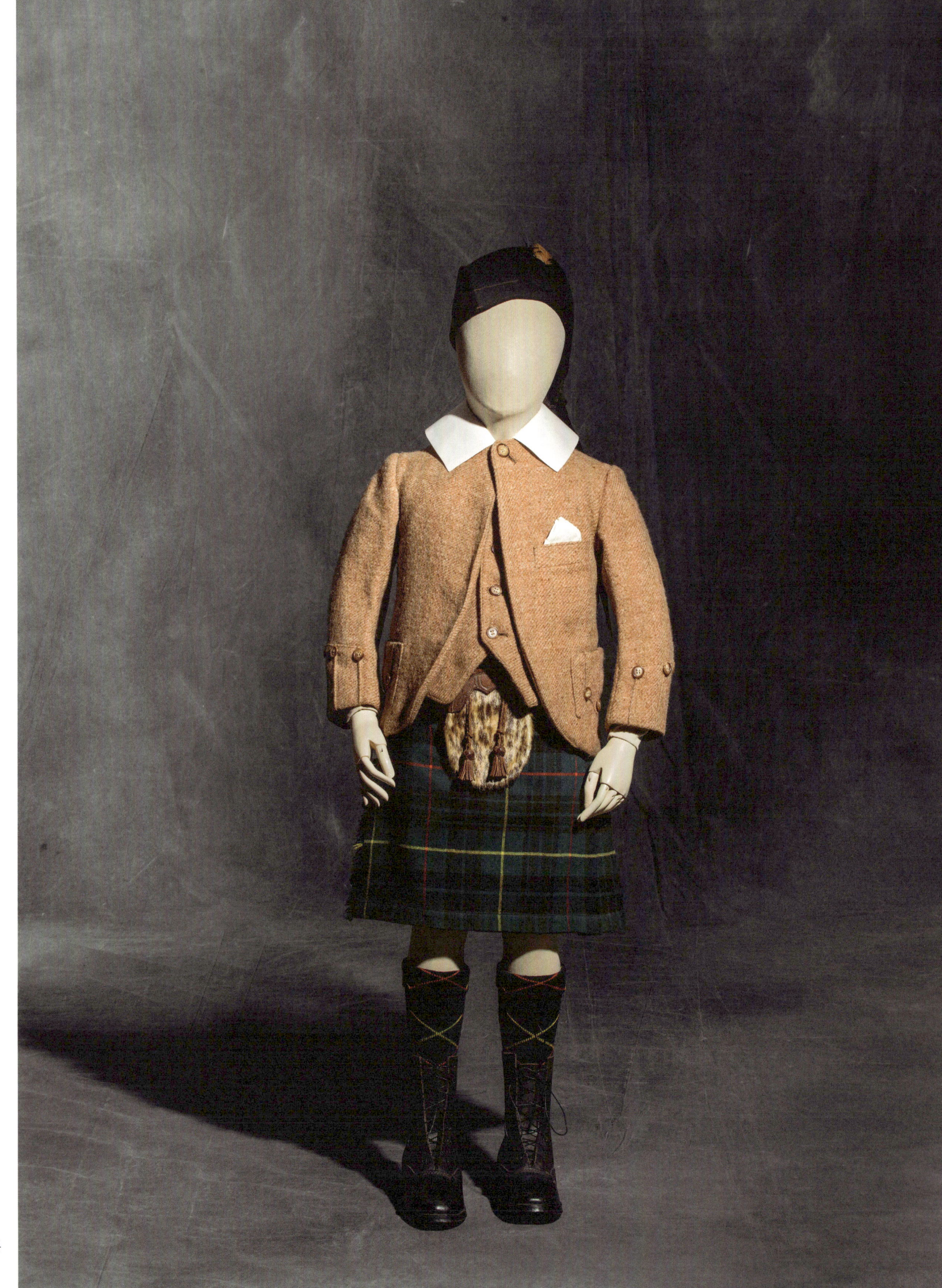

Little Boy's Outfit
Circa 1870

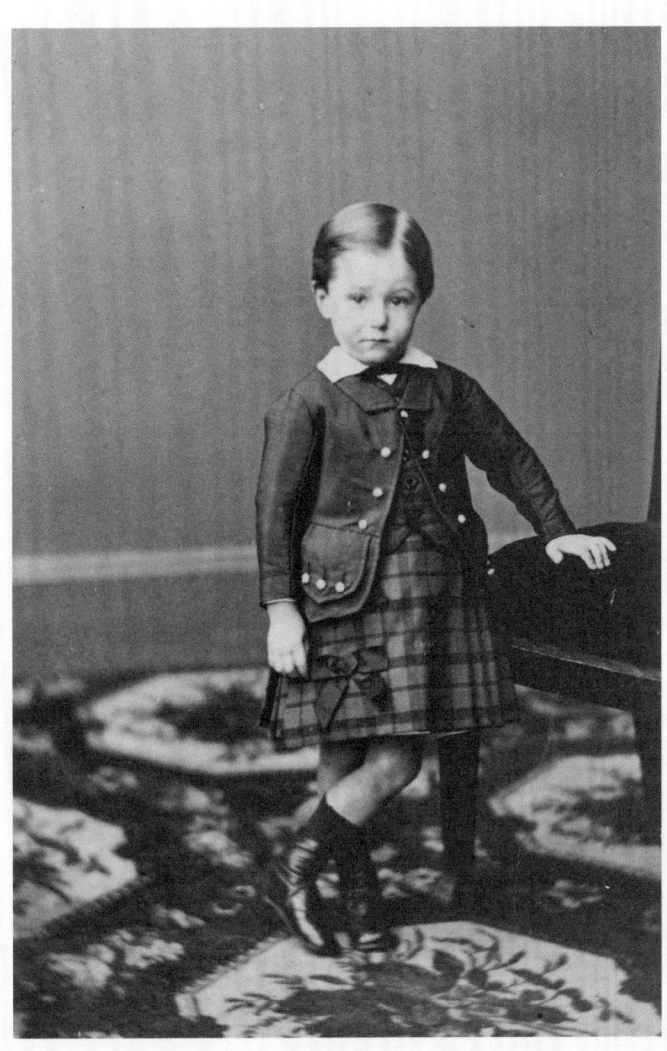

In 1855, immediately after the official visit to Paris of Queen Victoria, who was accompanied by the young Prince of Wales dressed in Scottish garb, the *Journal des demoiselles* presented its readers with detailed practical advice for creating an identical outfit, concluding: "We no longer merely see this type of dress in the little world of the Tuileries . . ." A taste for Highland clothing, and for tartan in particular, had already materialized during the Restoration, thanks to the impact of the literary work of Sir Walter Scott. Yet the adaptation of traditional dress of the Scottish clans soon became a point of reference in the wardrobes and clothing of elegant little boys, who wore dresses until the age of five or six. The Museums of the Second Empire at the Compiègne Palace house the remains of an interesting Scottish ceremonial outfit of the imperial prince, dating to 1859.

This complete ensemble consists of a tartan kilt, mounted to a black drill bodice, with long matching socks, a vest, and a tweed suit jacket with detachable starched collar. It is accompanied by a traditional sporran (small bag) and pom-pom glengarry (hat) and contains short matching tartan breeches, a more practical choice for a child.

The full outfit was later eliminated from children's wardrobes, being deemed too over-the-top.
M.-P.R.

FRANÇOIS JOSEPH DELINTRAZ, *Un enfant debout* (A child standing), circa 1870. Photograph on albumenized paper pasted on cardboard. Musée d'Orsay, Paris.

Travel Outfit
Circa 1898

In her book titled *La femme hors de chez elle: En voyage, à la campagne*, published in 1878, Marie de Saverny recommended that elegant women on the go dress comfortably, adopting sturdy and practical woolen travel attire and banishing all decorative flourishes. Although her advice preceded this outfit, it was still current at the end of the century, as emphasized by the journal *L'art et la mode* in 1895: "For a sensible woman, a travel outfit must depart a bit from our extravagances; not such a wide skirt, less enormous sleeves . . . " This outfit, created by "Mrs. Siebenmann" and consisting of a two-piece dress and jacket, was certainly modern yet conformed to the style of the time. Its silhouette displays a notable sinewy line, shaped by a corset that accentuated the curves of the waist and bosom.

    This type of Scottish-themed wool travel outfit, particularly appreciated for its practical comfort, was popular in the French press at the time. Throughout the nineteenth century, tourism related to the development of railroads favored the design of clothing that was increasingly appropriate for such activities.
M.-P.R.

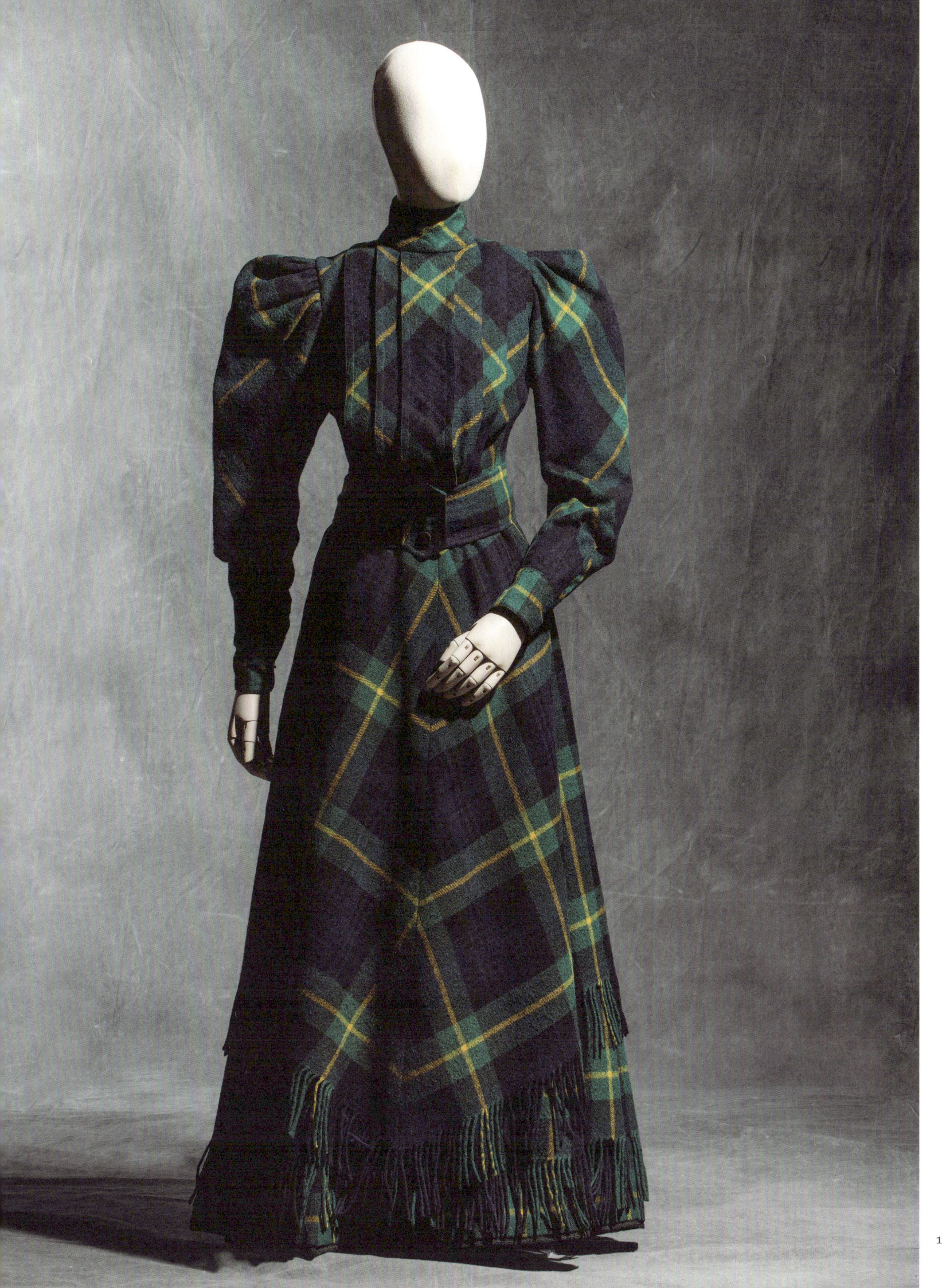

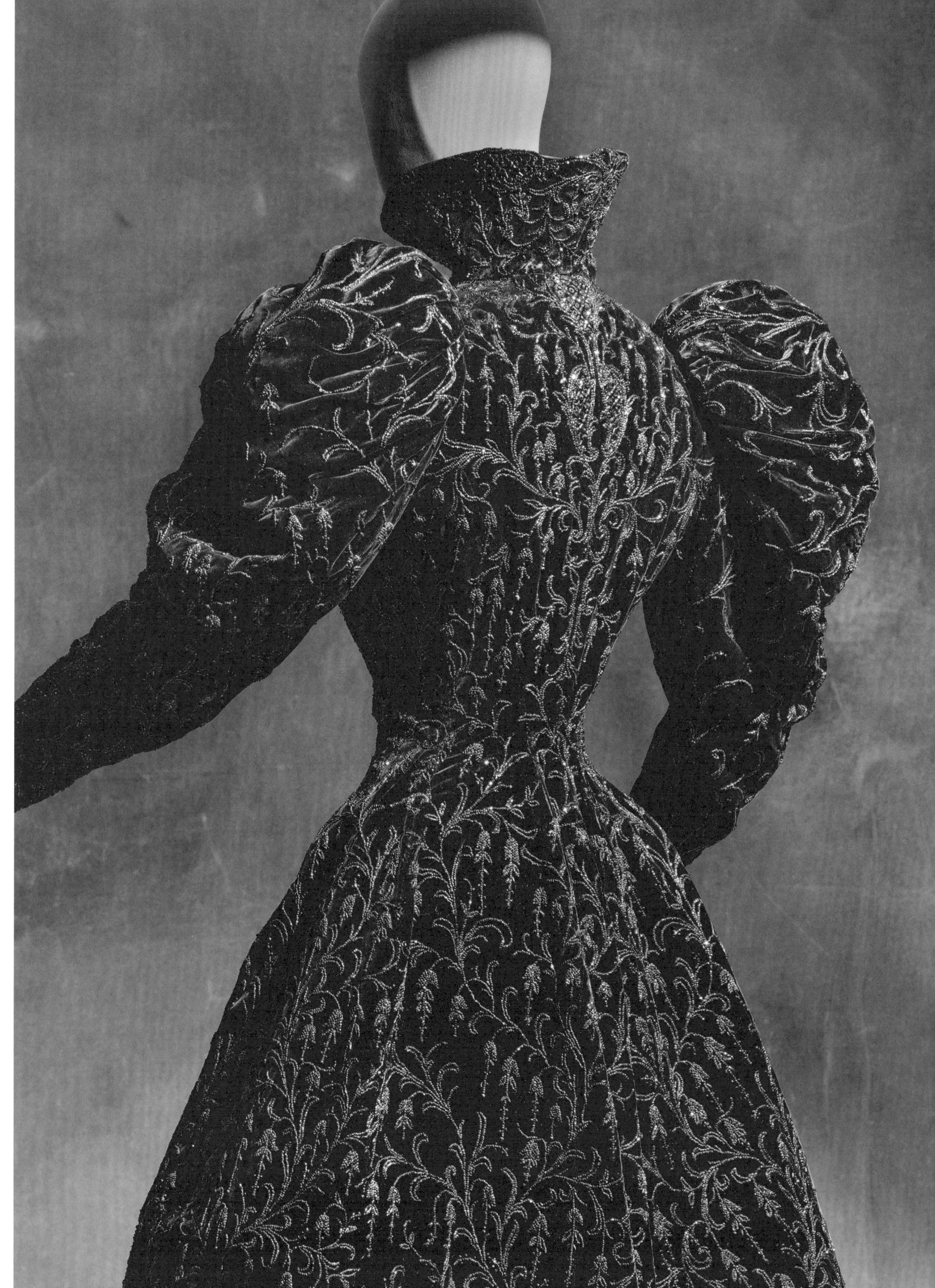

Attributed to Jacques Doucet
Jacket, 1898–1900

Numerous photographic portraits of Cléo de Mérode, reproduced on postcards in the 1900s, show her in a black velvet jacket embroidered with jet beads, similar to this one. The dark fitted jacket with a high narrow collar emphasized her face, which was framed by two flat bands of hair that covered her ears.

Elected beauty queen by the journal *L'illustration* in 1860, Cléo de Mérode (1875–1966) was a famous dancer in the corps de ballet at the Paris Opera. She was a contemporary of other Paris queens of the Belle Époque, such as Sarah Bernhardt and Réjane. In 1955 she published her journal, *Le ballet de ma vie,* highlighting her virtue and "virginal" innocence in an effort to change her reputation as a seductress and woman of the demimonde. In her memoirs, she mentions Jacques Doucet, "who was her couturier for a long time." Cléo de Mérode made several gifts during her lifetime to the Union Française des Arts du Costume. In the late 1960s her maid donated a large part of her mistress's wardrobe, including some of her stage costumes.
M.-S.C.C.

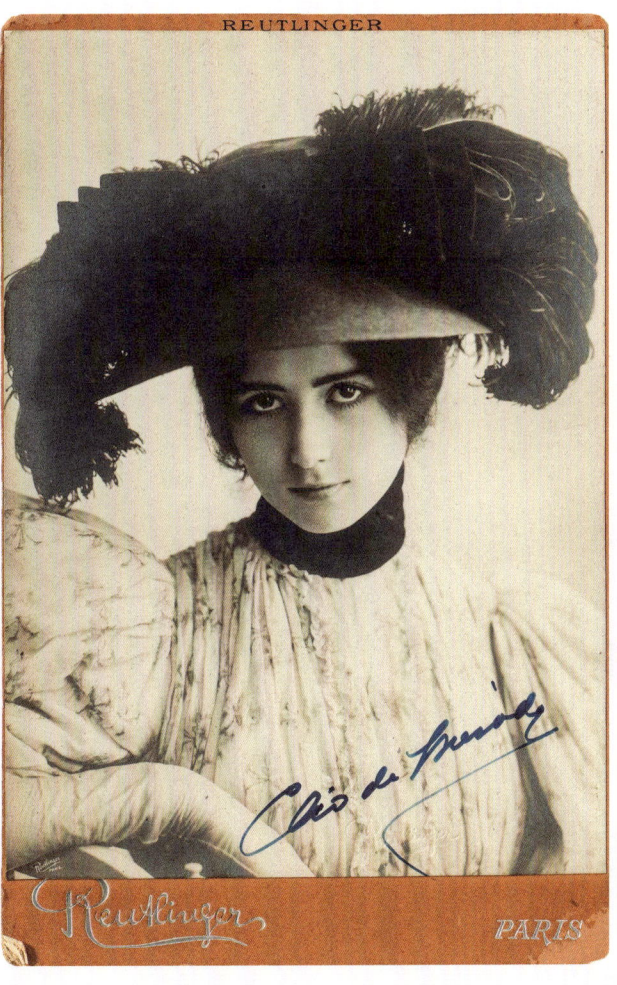

STUDIO REUTLINGER, *Portrait of Cléo de Mérode*, circa 1905. Photograph on albumenized paper.
Musée des Arts Décoratifs, Paris; Photography Collections.

Jacques Doucet
Robe à Transformation (Transformation Dress)
1900-1905

The wardrobe of Mrs. Debray, the demimondaine who owned this dress, included about ten luxurious dresses made by the Jacques Doucet couture house; these are now part of the collections of the Musée des Arts Décoratifs. Located on the rue de la Paix, it benefited from fame comparable to that of the House of Worth in Belle Époque Paris. Although referenced in *La prisonnière* by Marcel Proust's character Albertine, who desires "a particular Doucet wrapper, its sleeves lined with pink," Jacques Doucet seemed to have trouble living up to his status as couturier, being perceived at the time by the elites of "*Le Tout-Paris*" as a simple supplier. In his 1984 biography, François Chapon depicted a successful couturier, a visionary collector, and a demanding patron, highlighting Doucet's paradoxical personality and dandy-like discretion. Doucet's career was a testament to the connection between fashion and the artistic and literary trends of the 1900s.

    The Art Nouveau aesthetics of the 1900s are embodied in the undulating shapes of Doucet's dresses, which gracefully combine lace, tulle, and transparent muslin with floral motifs. This wispy style, as Guillaume Garnier defined it in his 1984 study *De la mode et des lettres*, was based on combinations of lace, pleats, and embroidery and "referred to the ideal of a disembodied, diaphanous femininity, which symbolist painting and poetry then evoked."
M.-S.C.C.

PP. 112-113 — PAUL AND HENRI VEVER, brooch and pendants, 1900. Gold, enamel, fine and precious stones, pearls.
Musée des Arts Décoratifs, Paris; gift of Vever, 1924.

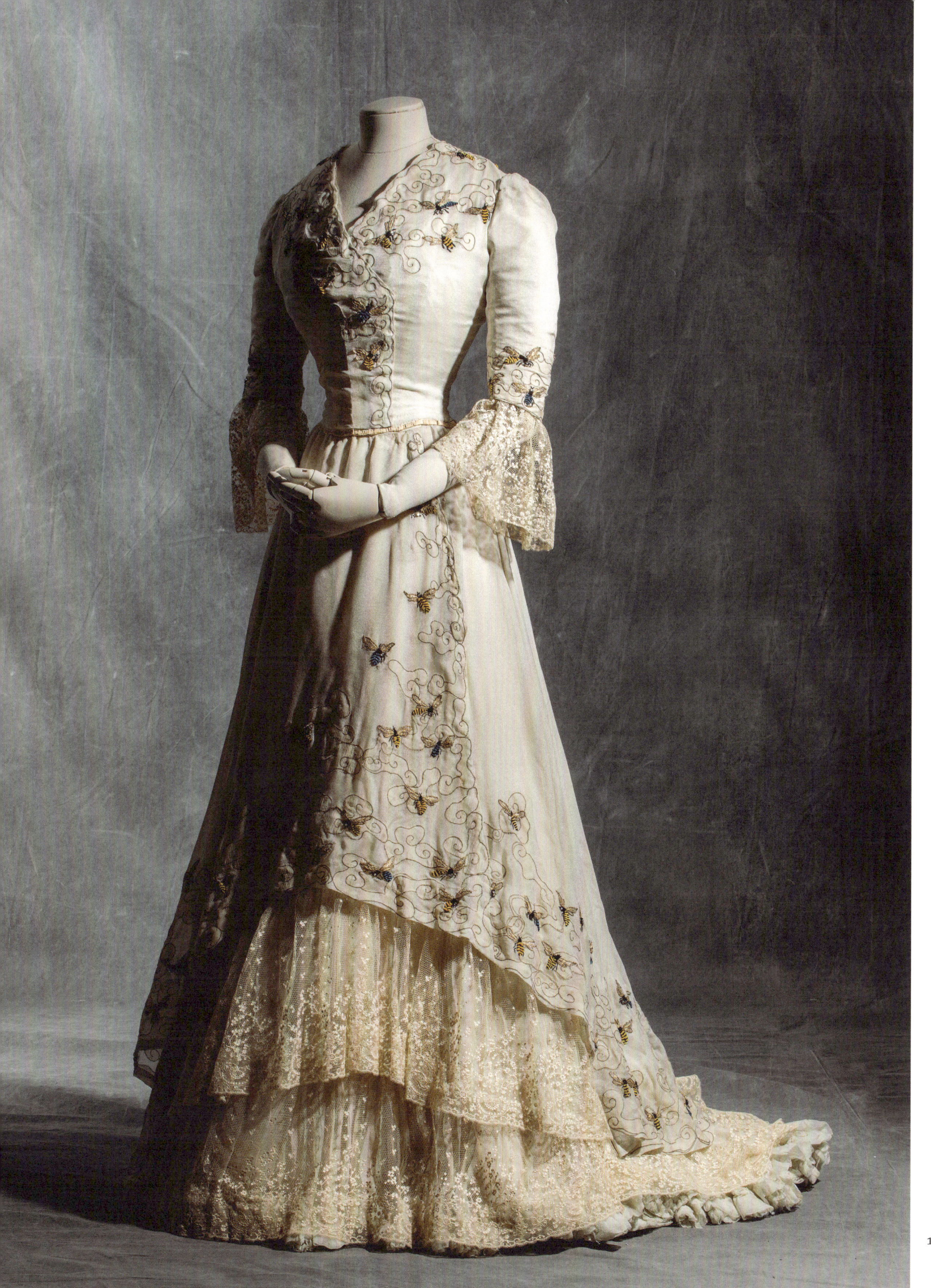

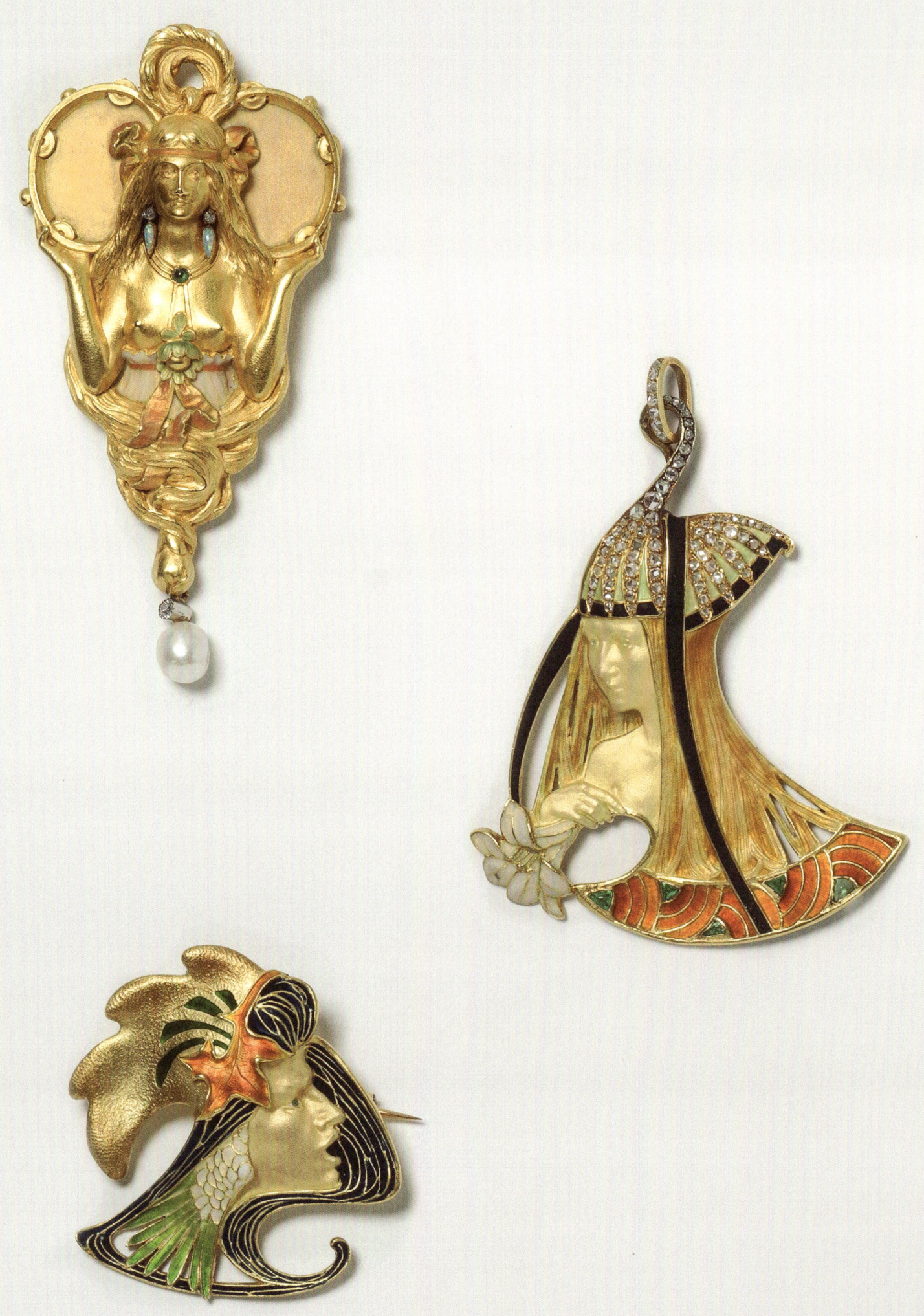

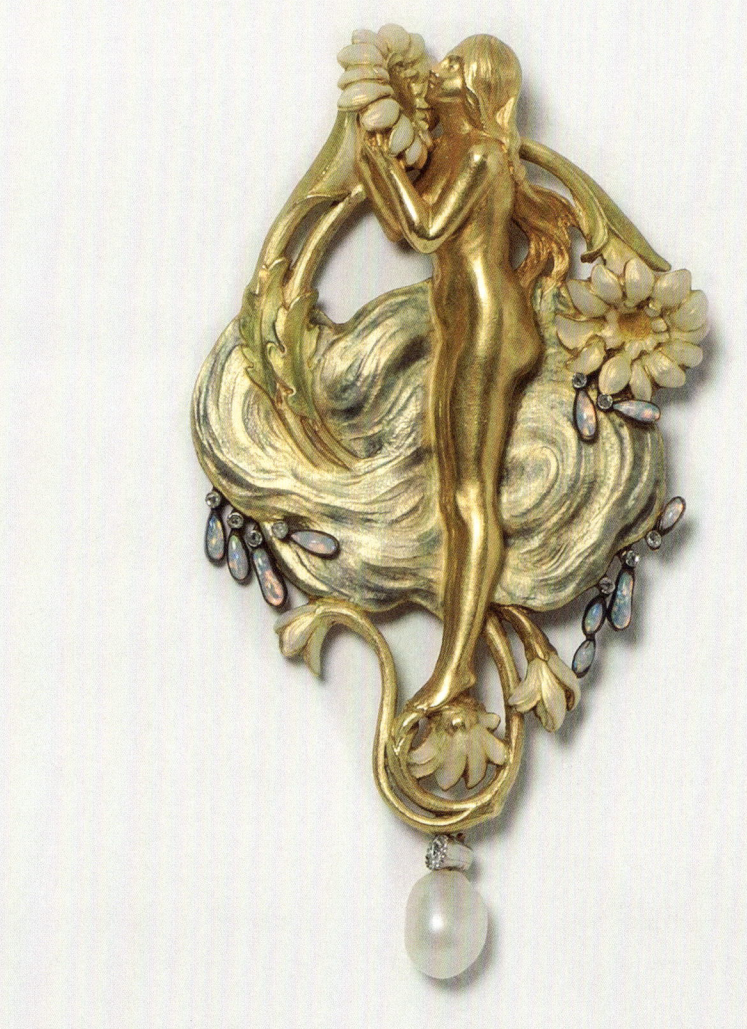
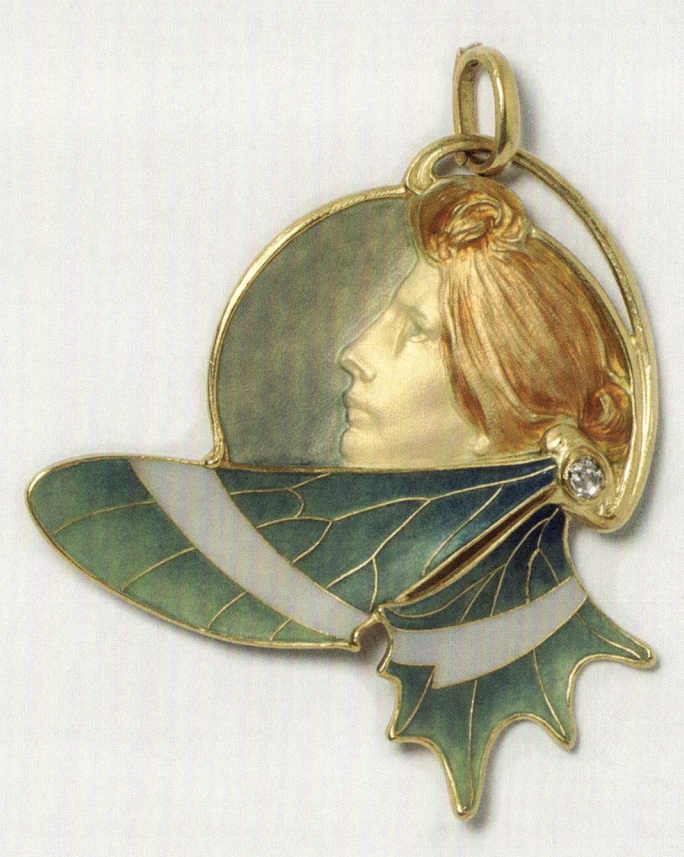

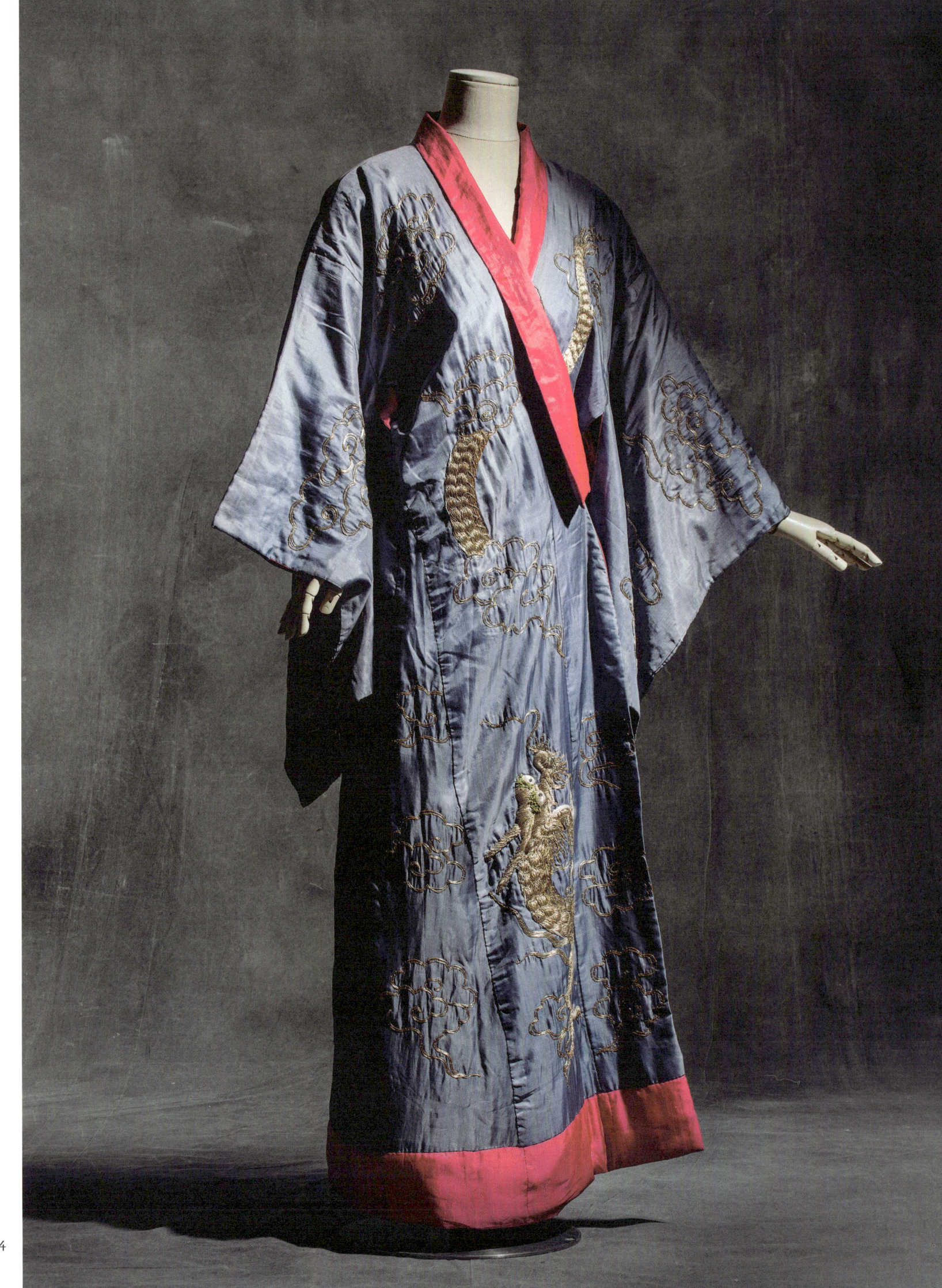

Babani
Kimono Robe, 1905–1910

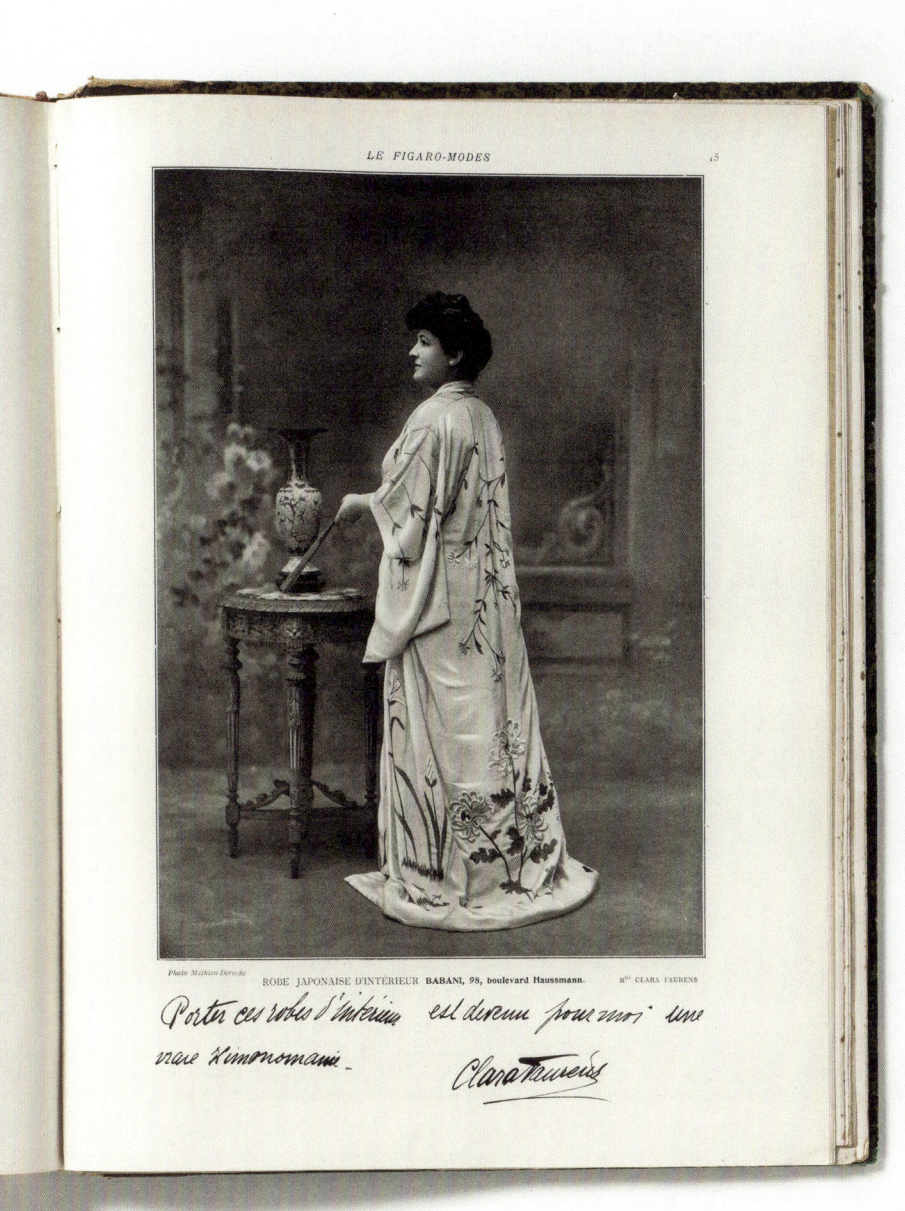

Vitali Babani opened his eponymous boutique on the Boulevard Haussmann in 1894. In addition to Mariano Fortuny's creations and fabrics from Liberty of London, the boutique specialized in the sale of art objects, silks from the Islamic world, and kimonos from Asia. The popularity of the exhibition of exquisite kimonos at the Japanese pavilion during the 1900 word's fair in Paris increased the public's interest in Japonisme and inspired Babani to create his own line of kimonos, which were manufactured in his workshops in Kyoto.

Favored by the elegant women of the Belle Époque for its wide cut and easy fit, the traditional kimono was westernized into a light pongee silk peignoir, crossed at the front and loosely tied at the side. The rolled lapel on the shawl neckline is similar to the *fuki* on a kimono. The lower part of the wide sleeves could be used as pockets.

Babani's advertisements associated the practical and comfortable kimono with glamour and sensuality. In a bimonthly publicity campaign that appeared in *Le Figaro-modes* between December 1904 and February 1906, Babani hired the Reutlinger photography studio to shoot portraits of famous actresses wearing his kimono, or "the informal Japanese robe," in various exotic settings.
M.-S.C. C.

Babani advertisement, *Le Figaro-modes,* October 15, 1905. Bibliothèque des Arts Décoratifs, Paris.
"After wearing these robes, I've become a kimonomaniac," Clara Fauren, actress

Mariano Fortuny
Delphos *Gown, 1910-1915*

Famous for having been mentioned in Marcel Proust's masterpiece, *In Search of Lost Time* ("The Fortuny dress that Albertine wore that night seemed like the tempting shadow of an invisible Venice"), the Spaniard Mariano Fortuny (1871-1949) moved in 1889 to Venice, where he set up his atelier at the Orfei palace, Campo San Benedeto. In addition to painting, engraving, photography, stage design, and developing ideas for decorative objects, Fortuny created fabrics and dresses. He conceived of art as a universal means of expression in which all aesthetic disciplines would blend together. With his French wife, Henriette, he created luxurious fabrics, overseeing the dyeing, printing, embossing, and pleating processes. He protected his research and inventions with patents; the process of permanent silk pleating, for example, was patented in Paris in 1910.

Fortuny had patented the silk satin "Delphos" gown the previous year. The straight dress slipped over the head and featured silk cord lacing that ran along the sleeves, trimmed with Murano glass beads. The gown's signature undulating pleated fabric was inspired by Ionic *chitons*, and its pearl-gray color was evocative of older fabrics that Fortuny had always favored.

Over the next forty years, the Delphos gown underwent subtle changes as Fortuny varied the colors but never the style. Appreciated for their timeless design, Delphos gowns have been worn by many artists and celebrities, including Isadora Duncan, Eleonora Duse, Sarah Bernhardt, and Marquess Casati.
M.-S.C.C.

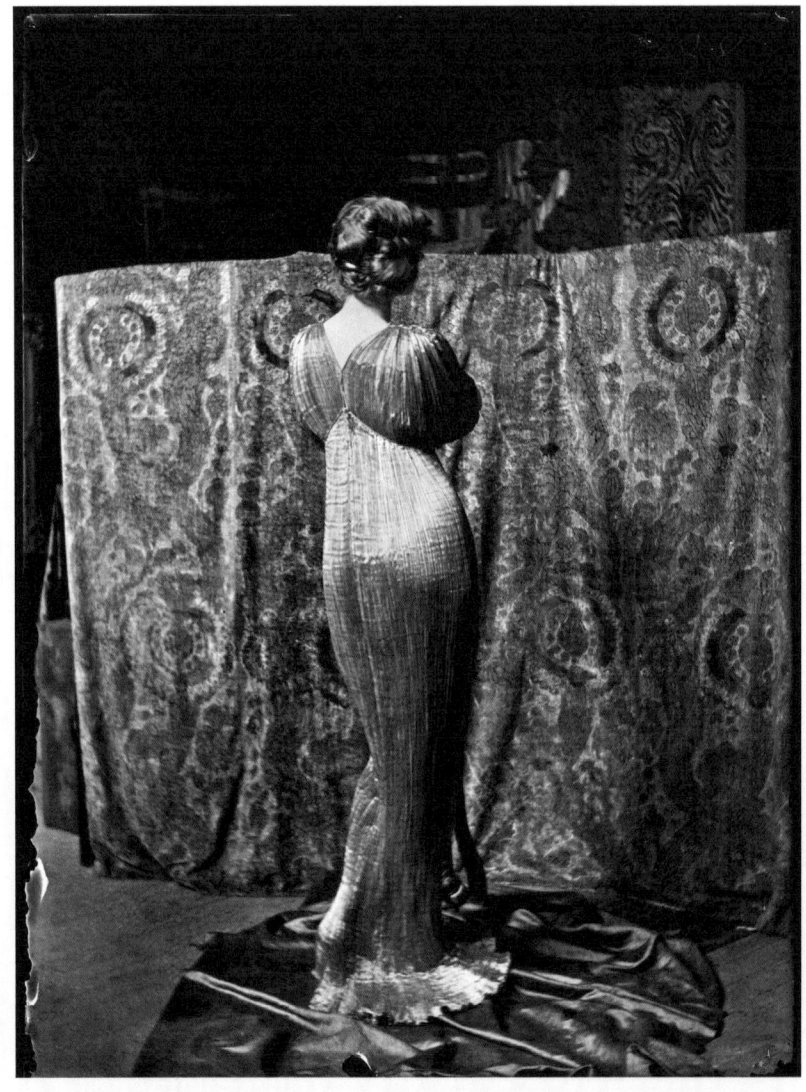

ISADORA DUNCAN wearing a "Delphos" dress, circa 1910. Photograph. Fortuny Museum, Venice.
PP. 118-119 — STUDIO TALBOT, Portrait photographs, circa 1910. Photographs printed on albumin paper.
Musée des Arts Décoratifs, Paris; The Photo Library, gift of Jas Hennessey and Co., 2007.
PP. 120-121 — GEORGES GOURSAT, KNOWN AS SEM, AND AUGUSTE ROUBILLE, *Le retour des courses ou Sem au bois*
(Returning from the races, or Sem in the Bois de Boulogne), 1907.
Color lithograph. Musée des Arts Décoratifs, Paris; Advertisement collection, gift of Goursat, 1937.

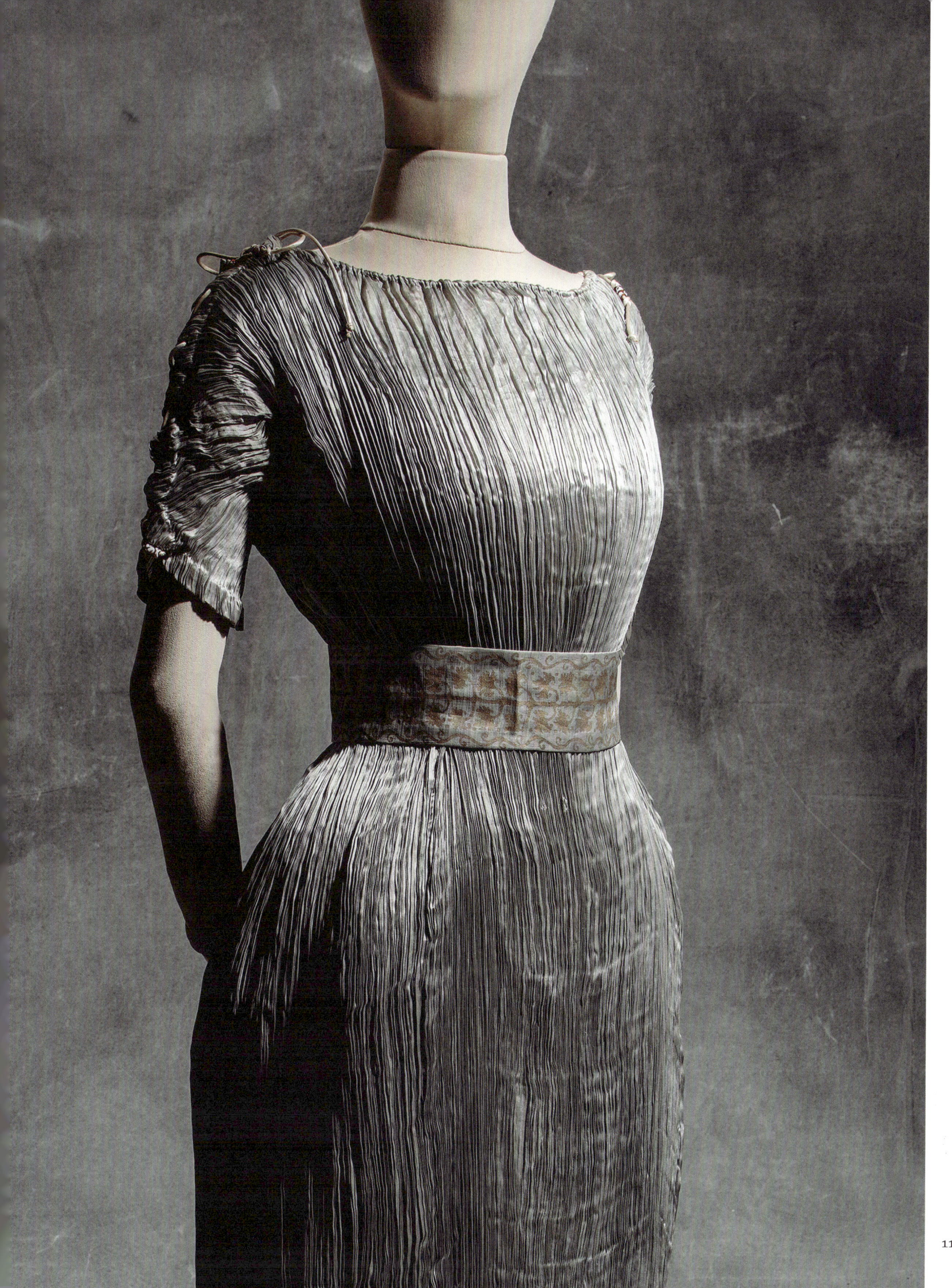

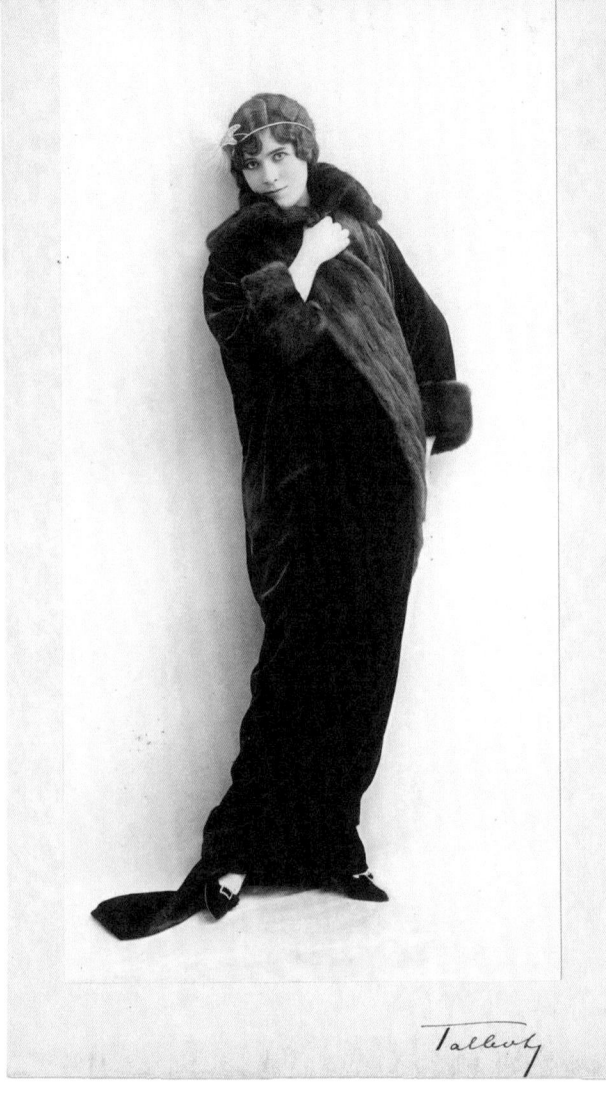
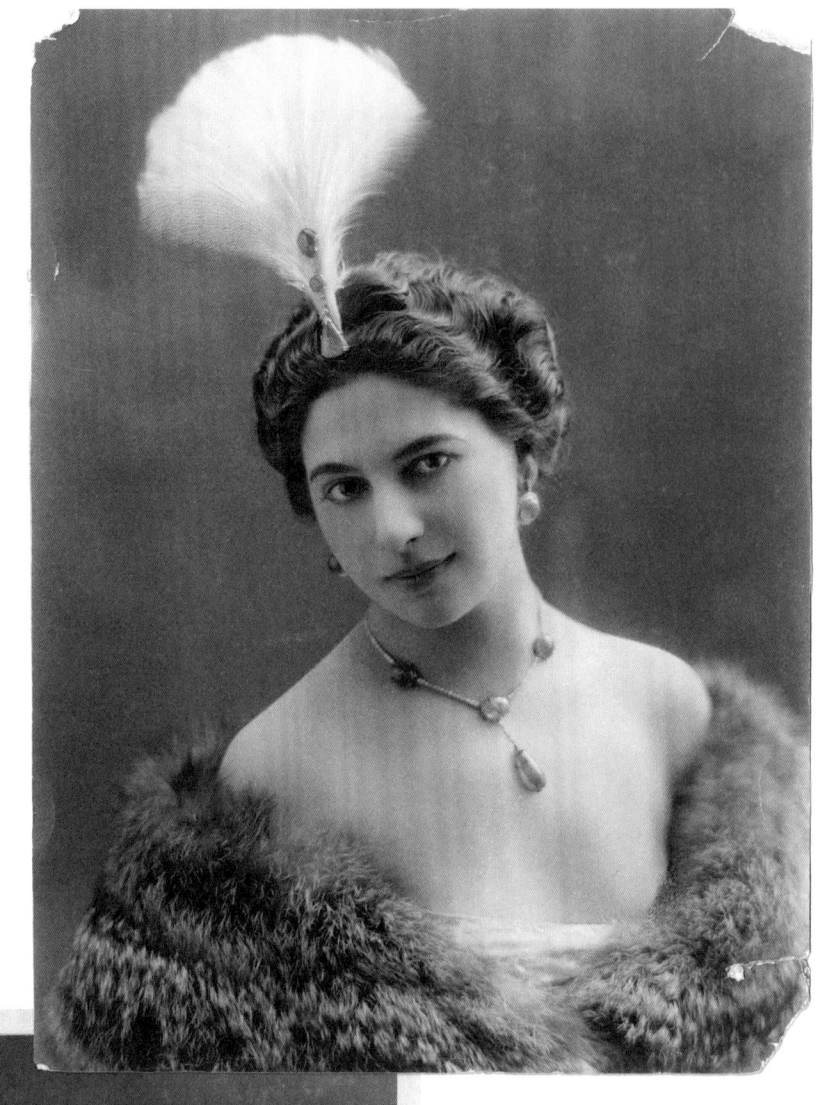
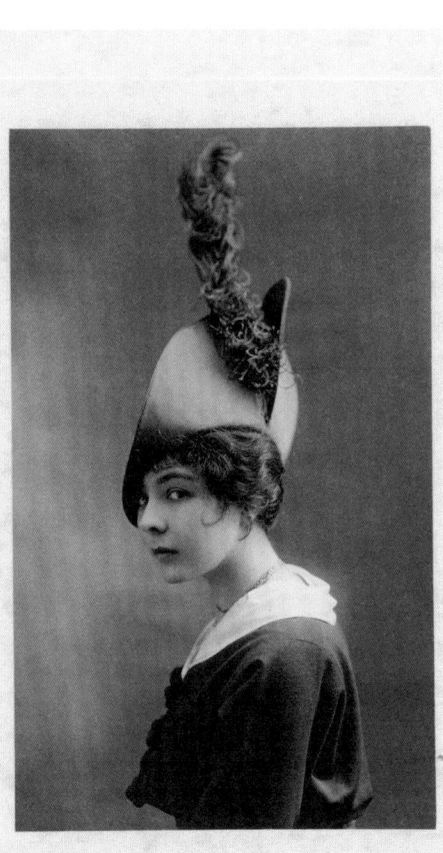
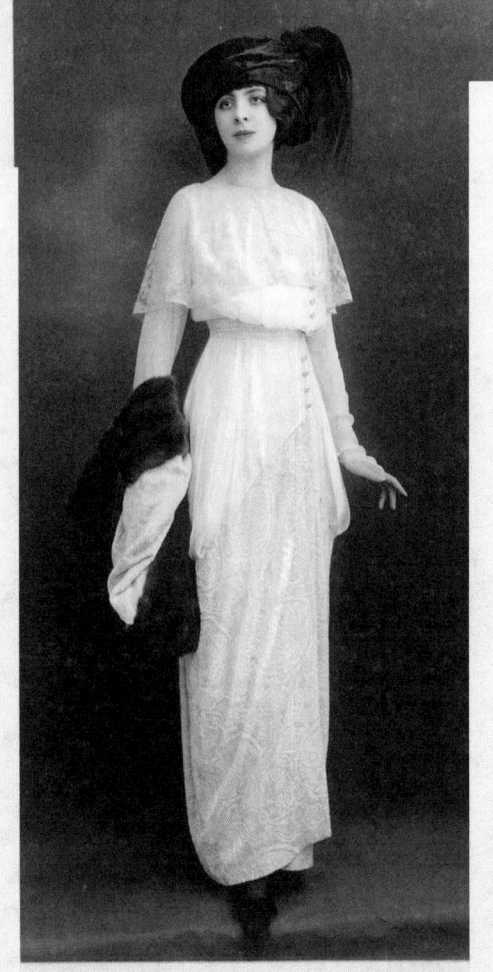
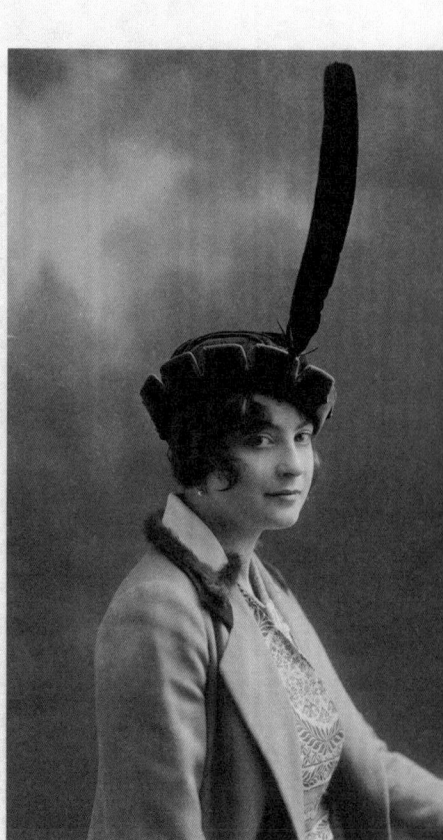

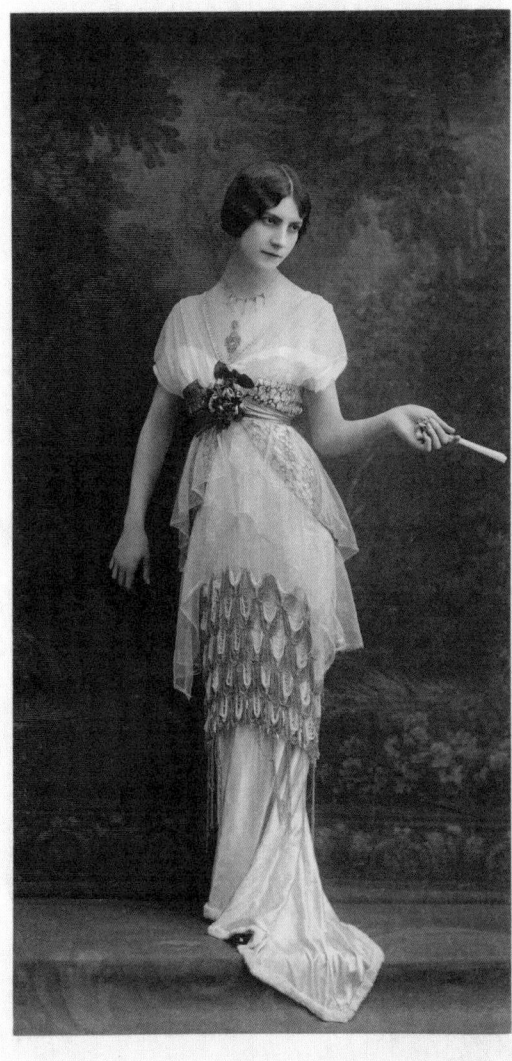
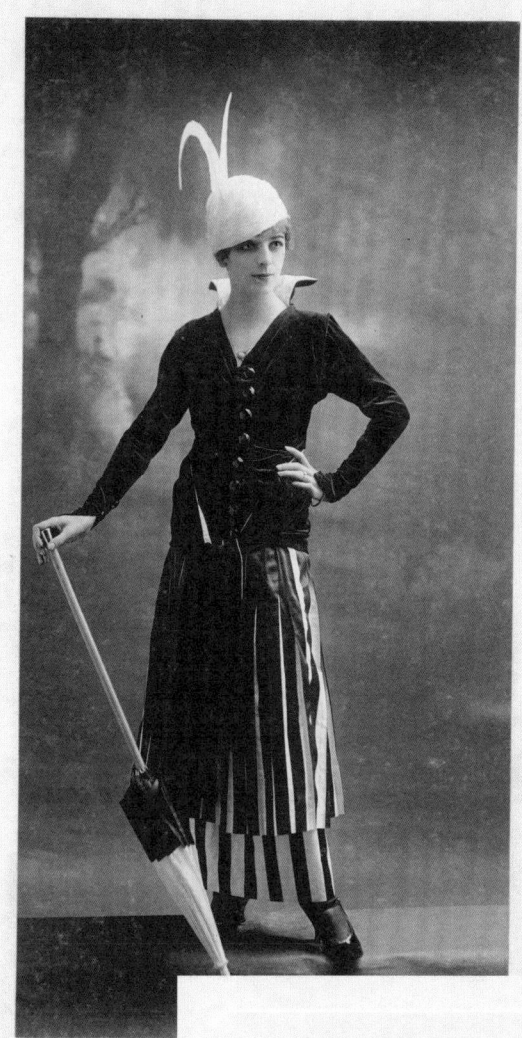
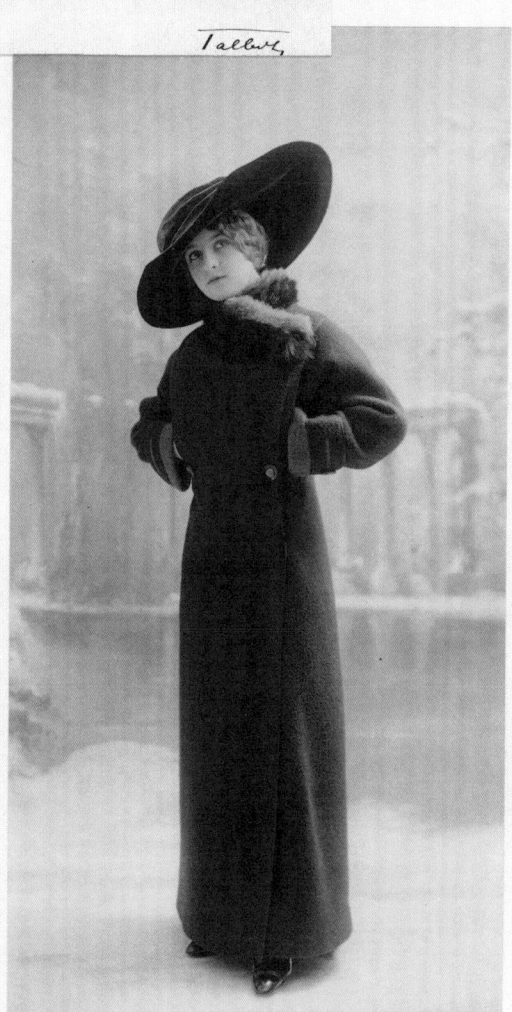
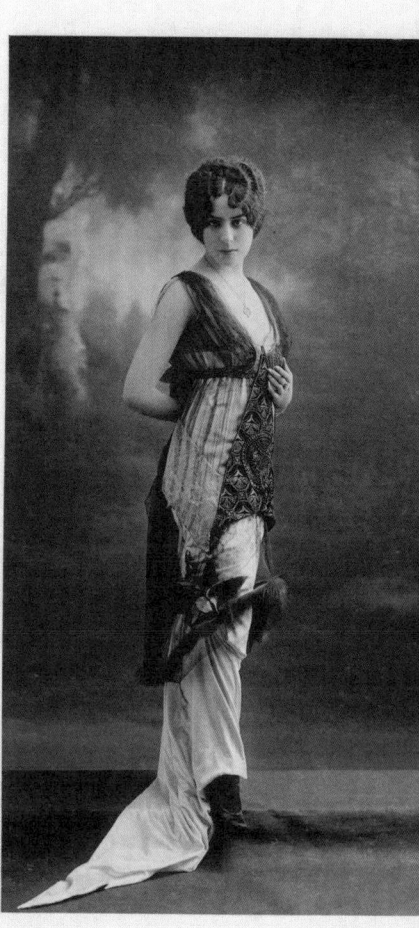

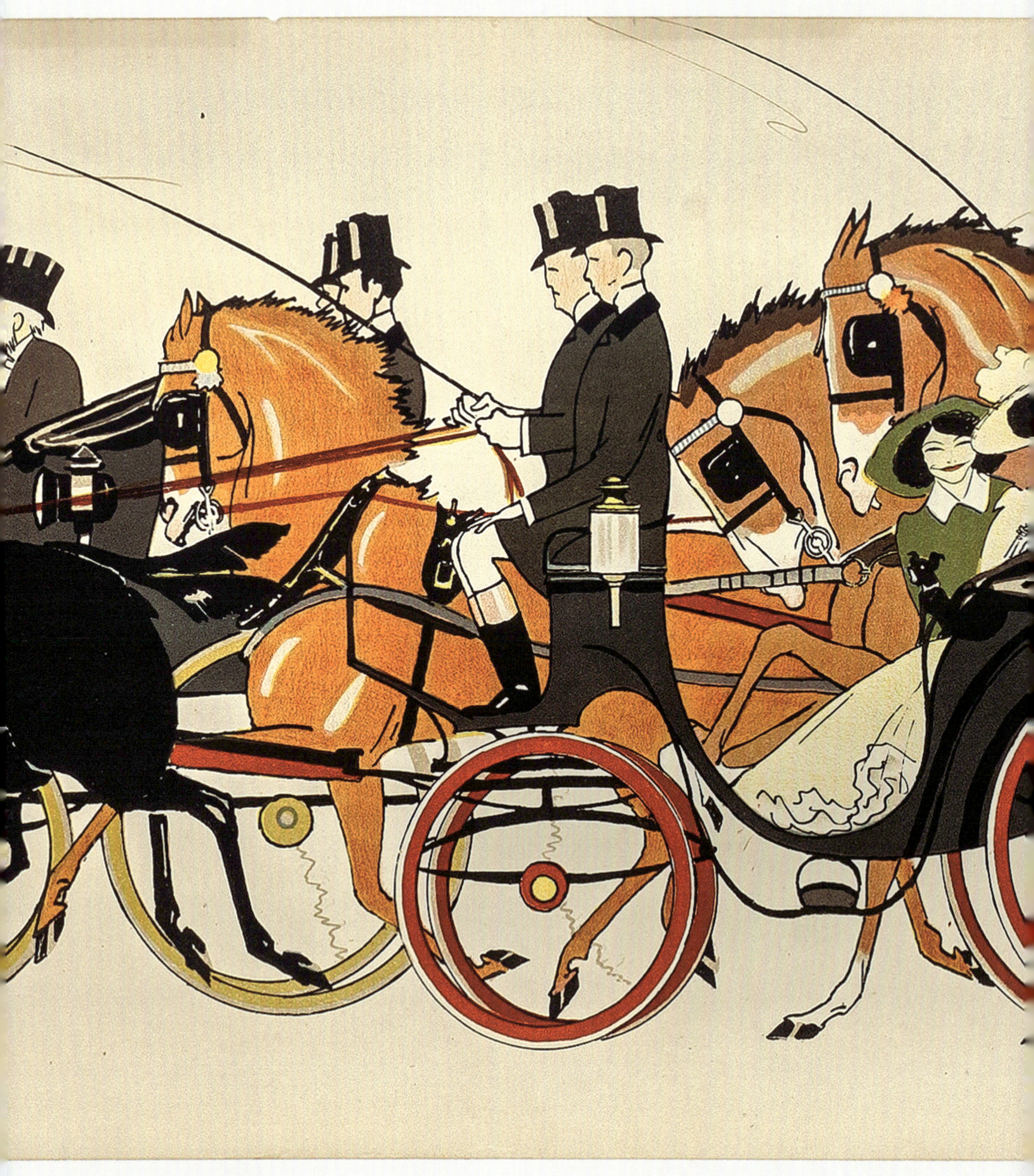

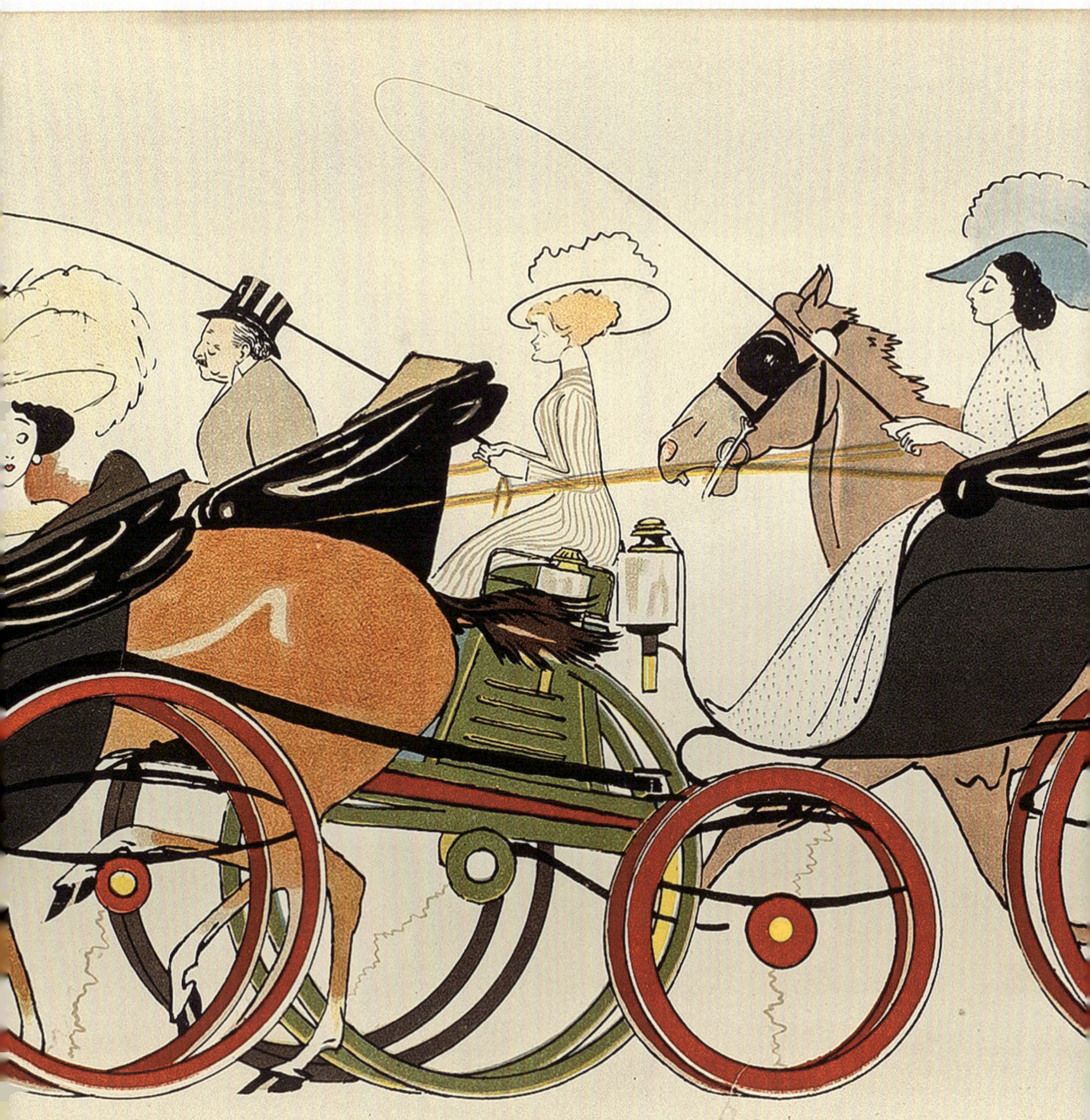

APRÈS LA COURSE — Beaucoup d'atteles mais peu d'élus.

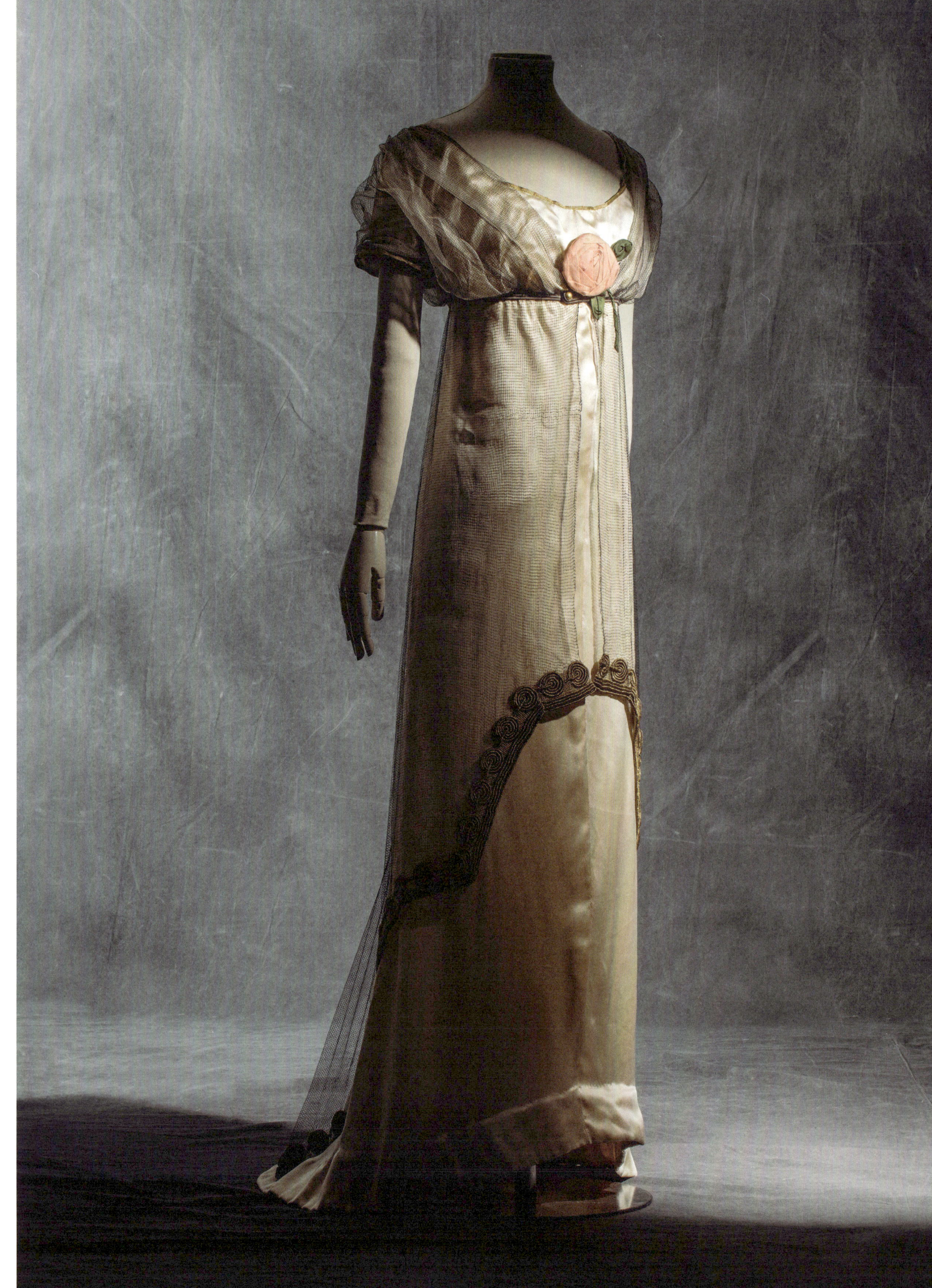

Paul Poiret
Joséphine *Evening Gown, 1907*

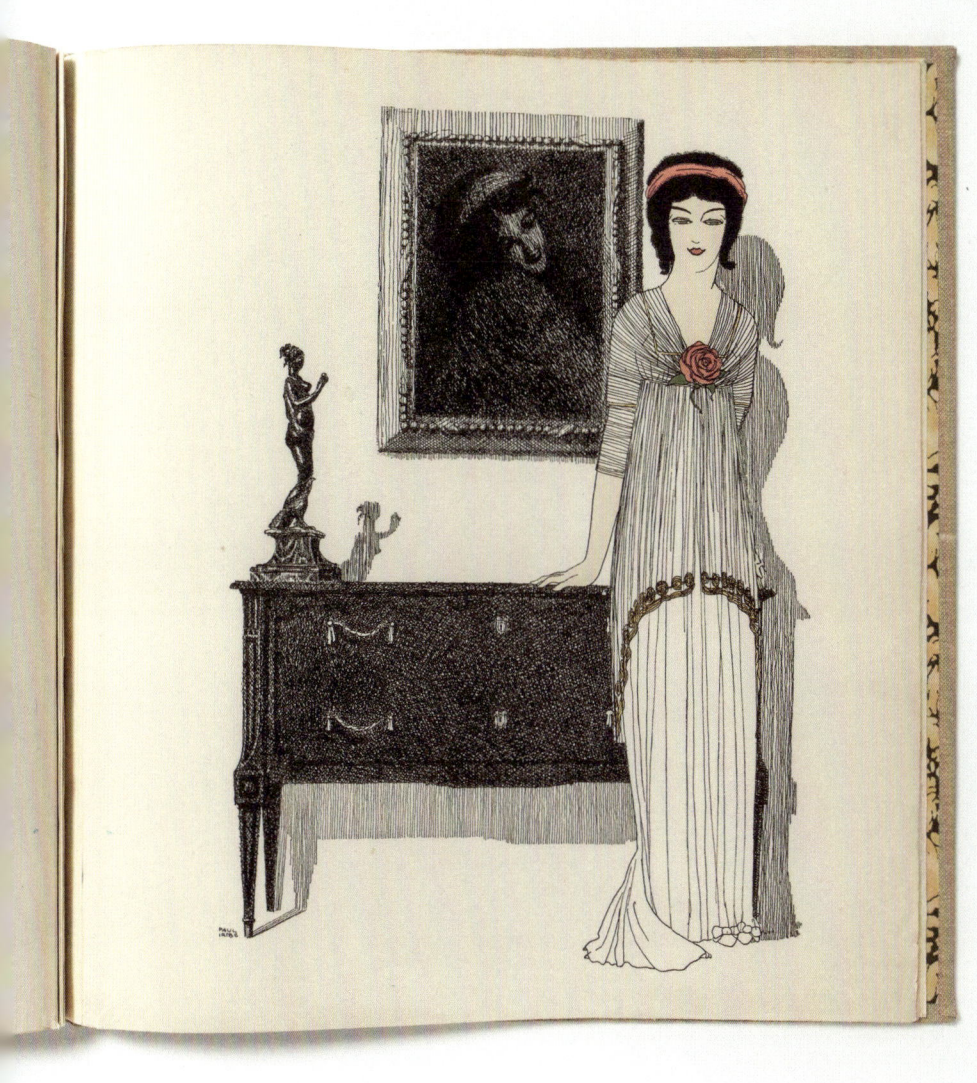

Following an apprenticeship at Doucet and, later, at Worth, Paul Poiret opened his own fashion house in 1903. He envisioned a new, simpler Parisian fashion featuring an elongated silhouette and turbans. In 1907 he designed a collection of slender, high-waisted dresses inspired by the "Merveilleuses" of the Directoire period. Though it recalled the style of the late eighteenth century, this collection was perceived as a sartorial revolution, one that would liberate women from the constraints of a corset. In its place, Poiret proposed a grosgrain band with boning supports placed under the bosom.

Poiret commissioned the artist Paul Iribe to sketch the dresses from his 1907 collection, heralding a new era of fashion illustration. The following year the drawings were published in a catalogue titled *Les robes de Paul Poiret racontées par Paul Iribe* (Poiret's dresses, as seen by Paul Iribe).

Marcel Piccioni, the grandson of Gustave Eiffel, donated the dress shown here to the Musée des Arts Décoratifs. The garment had belonged to his mother, Valentine (1870-1966), one of Gustave Eiffel's daughters and the wife of Camille Piccioni. The "Joséphine" dress was also featured in the 1999 *Gardes-robes* exhibition, along with outfits that had belonged to Solange Granet and other members of the Eiffel family.

M.-S.C.C.

Plate 10 from *Les robes de Paul Poiret, racontées par Paul Iribe* (Paris, 1908). Musée des Arts Décoratifs, Paris; The Documentation Center.

Callot Sœurs
Evening Gown, 1909-1910

After working in a shop specializing in lace and lingerie during the late 1880s, the four Callot sisters, Marie, Marthe, Régine and Joséphine, turned to couture. In 1895 three of the four women established their own fashion house, with Marie Gerber, the eldest, serving as creative director. Renowned for its use of lace and trimmings, the family-run business was one of the most important fashion houses in Paris in 1900. Madeleine Vionnet, who worked as a *première d'atelier* from 1901 to 1909, apprenticed at Callot Soeurs before founding her own fashion house.

The high waistband on this Directoire-style evening gown, made of golden yellow silk and embellished with pink and gold metallic thread tulle, is extremely fragile. Recently restored, it is being presented to the public for the first time since its acquisition in 1954 by the Union Française des Arts du Costume. The gown's bright colors, the sheerness of the draped voile, the exquisite embroidered embellishments, and the shimmer of the trimming are suggestive of orientalism. These exotic details recall the early 1910s designs of Paul Poiret, who was in turn influenced by the performances of the Ballets Russes in Paris.
M.-S.C.C.

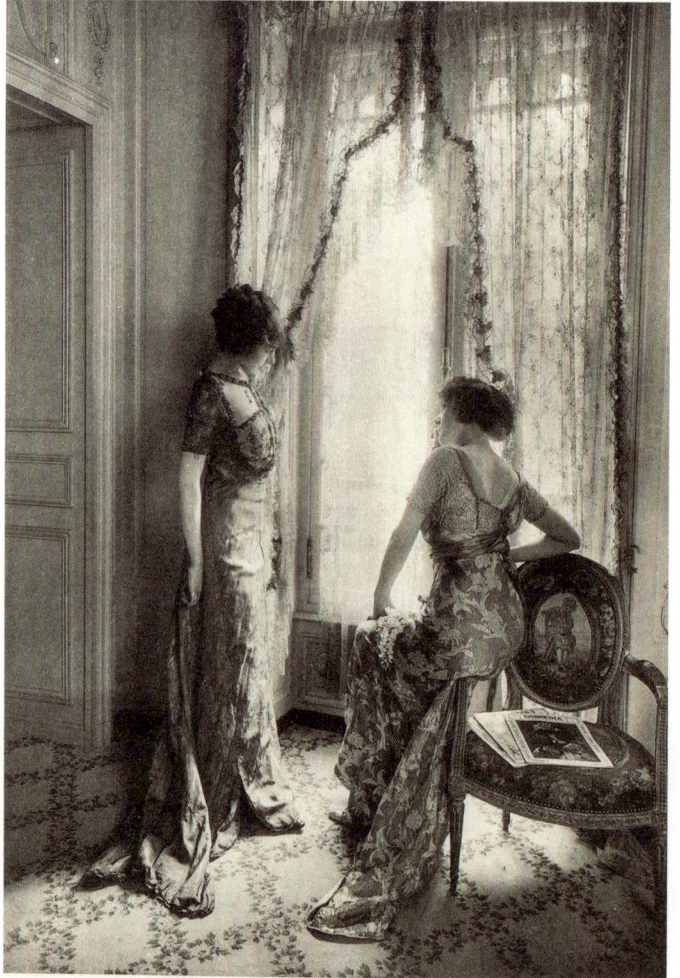

"Coin de salon. Callot Soeurs," *Les créateurs de la mode* (Paris, 1910), page 29. Bibliothèque des Arts Décoratifs, Paris.
PP. 126-127 — LÉON BAKST, Set design sketch for *Scheherazade*, 1910. Gouache, gold highlights, aquarelle, and pencil on paper. Musée des Arts Décoratifs, Paris; Graphic Arts Department, on loan from the Fonds National d'Art Contemporain.
PP. 128-129 — Figurines of women used to illustrate fashion designs from 1910 to 1917, crafted by Madame Lafitte and Madame Désirat. Musée des Arts Décoratifs, Paris; Fashion and Textile Collection, gift of Soubiran, 1939.

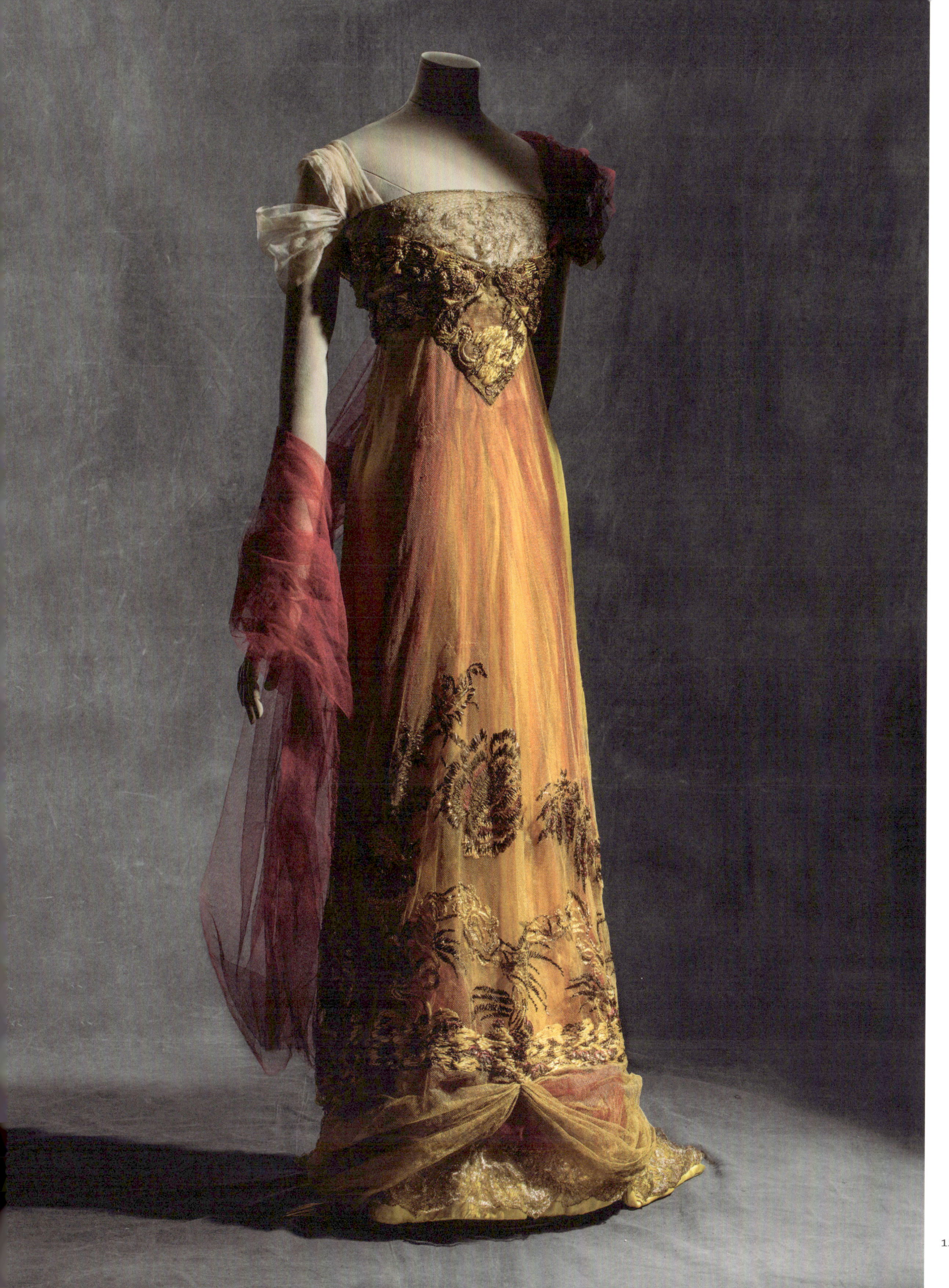

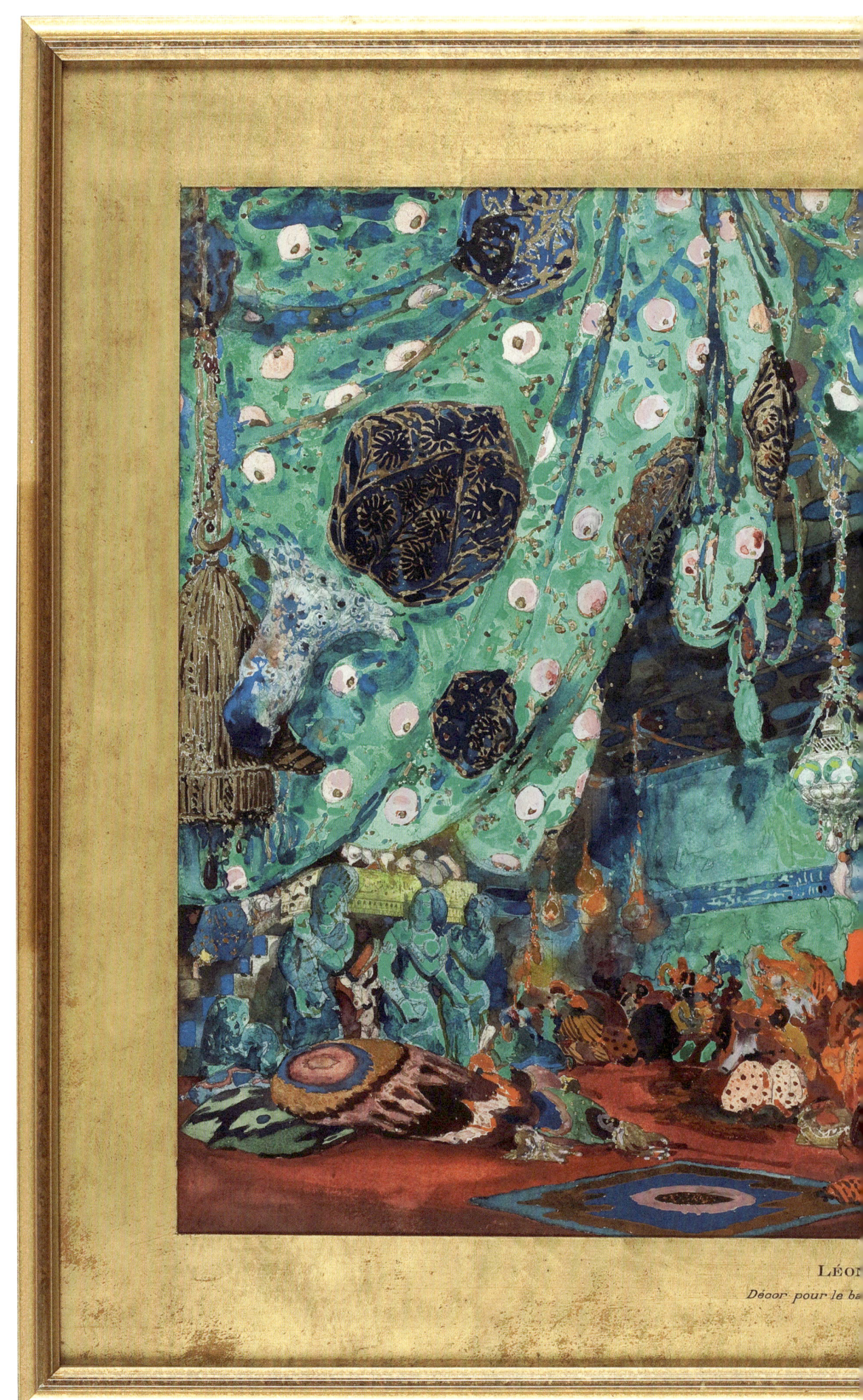

Léo...
Décor pour le ba...

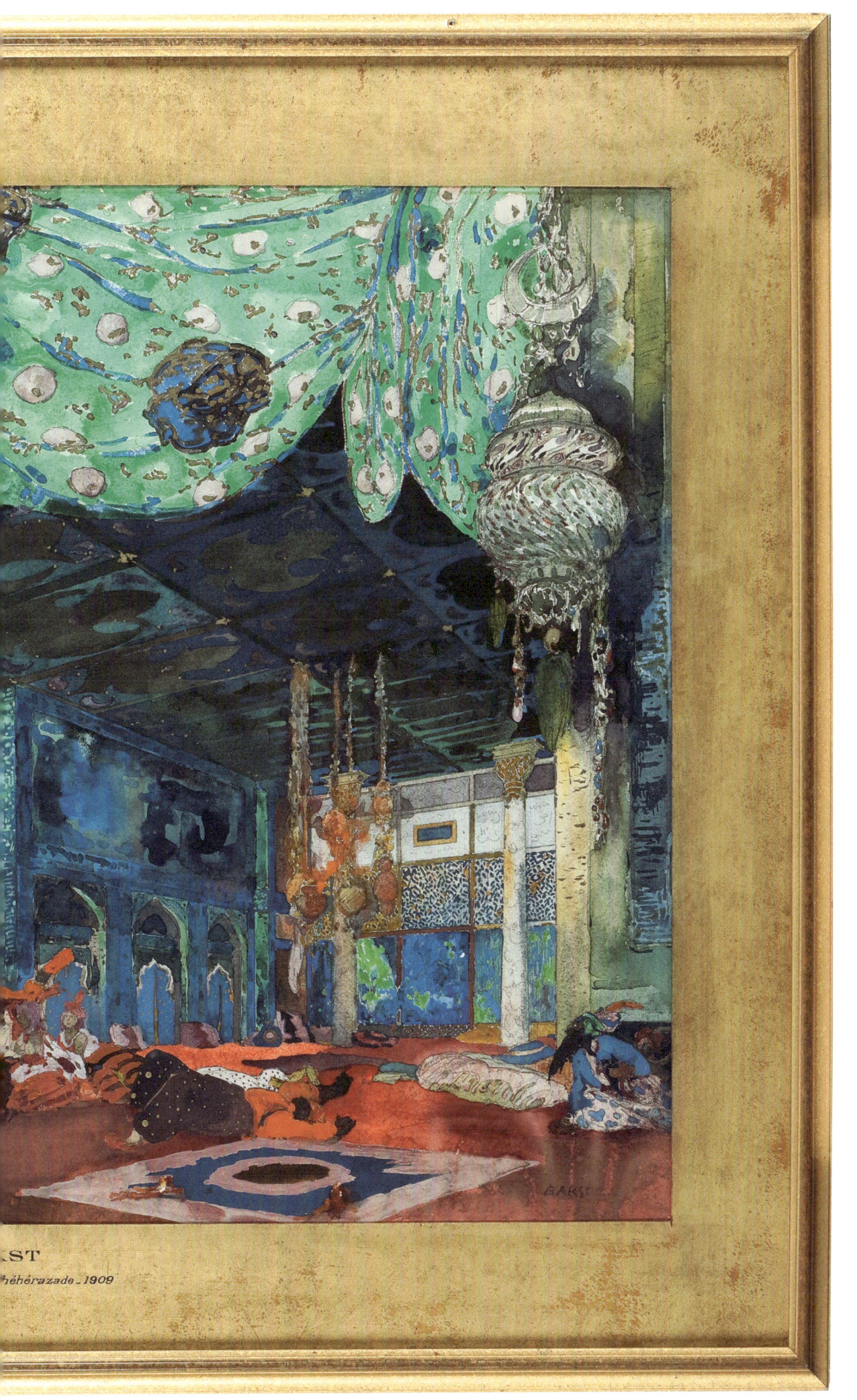

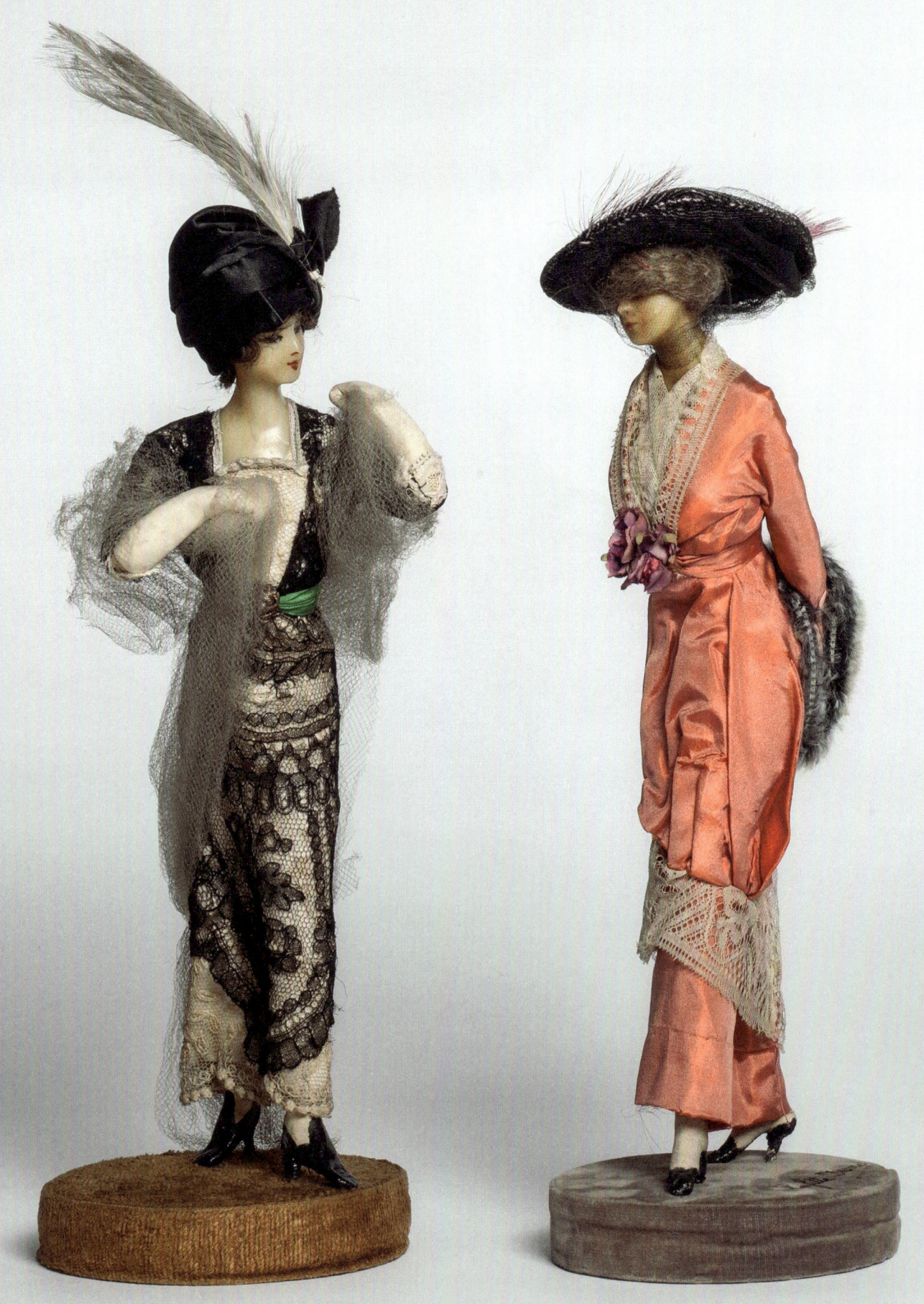

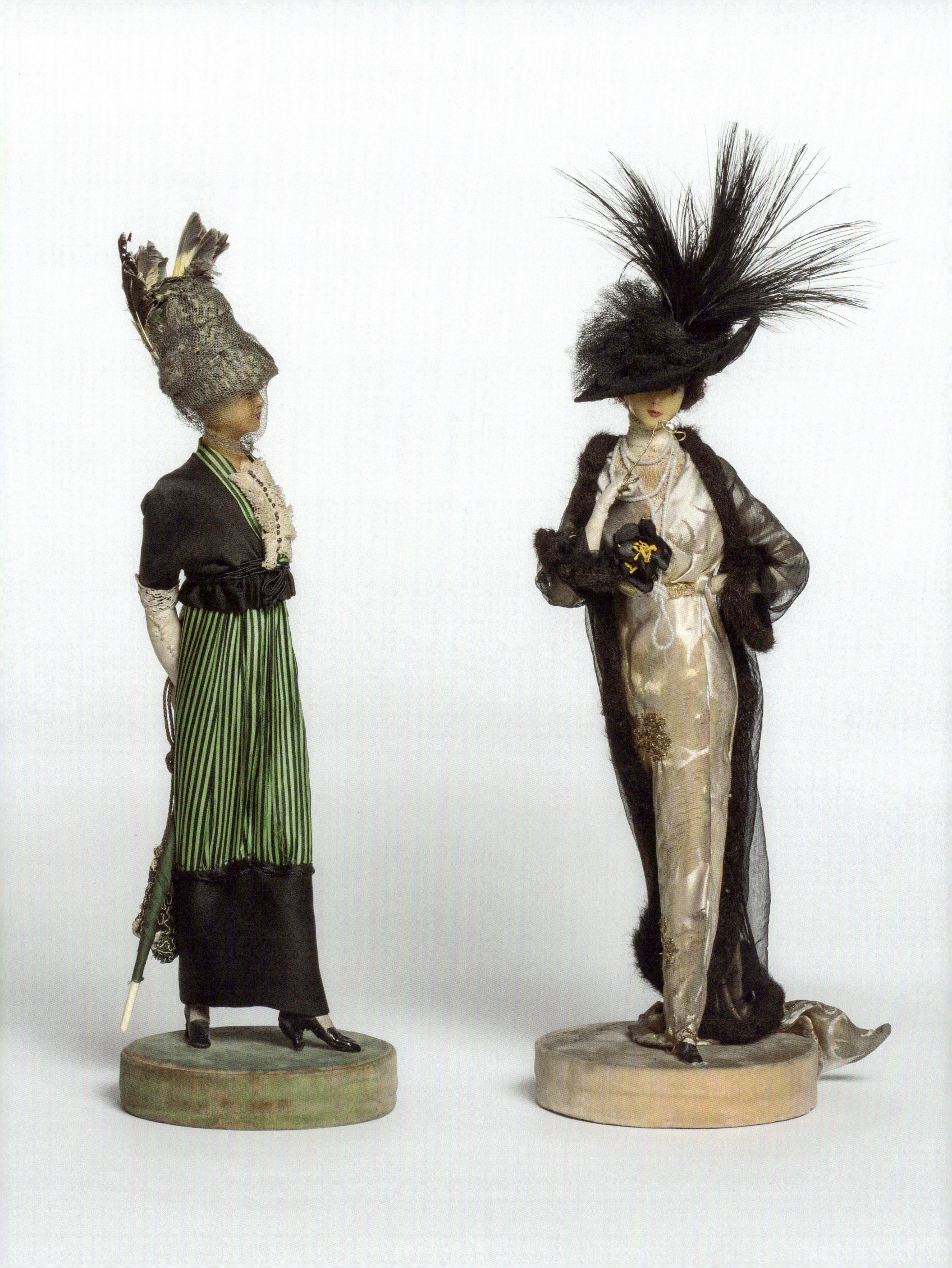

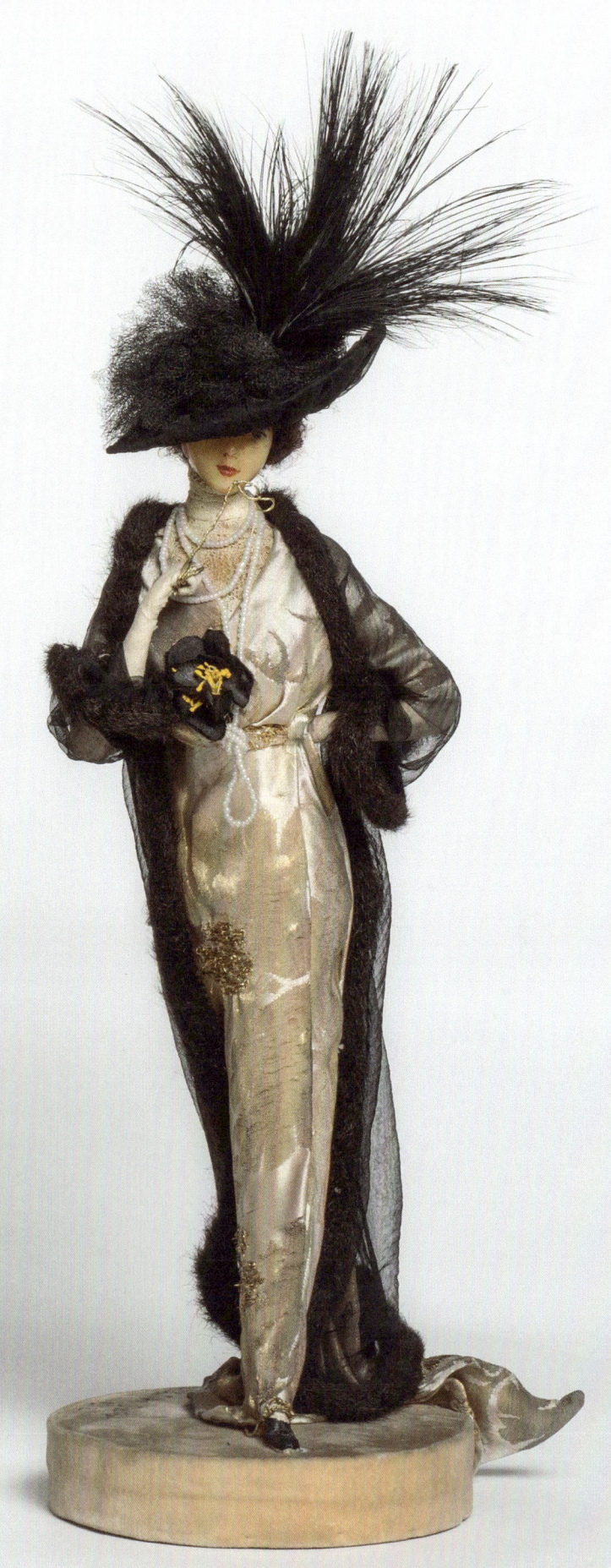

Madeleine Vionnet
Petits Chevaux (Small Horses) Evening Gown
Winter 1921-1922

Madeleine Vionnet (1876-1939) opened her fashion house in 1912, after working as *première d'atelier* first at Callot Soeurs and then at Jacques Doucet. Ten years later she would head one of the most important fashion houses in Paris. Vionnet worked out her designs on an articulated wood mannequin measuring 60 centimeters (23 ½ in), on which she would try out, drape, and pin the fabric as her ideas developed. By the end of the 1910s Vionnet had revolutionized fashion with her bias cut that hugged the body without hindering it. The straight and flat dresses from the 1920s had regained a three-dimensional look. Most couturiers of the 1930s would borrow Vionnet's bias technique.

    This dress, which was previously exhibited at the Musée des Arts Décoratifs in the 2009 retrospective of Madeleine Vionnet's work, is remarkable for its composition and aesthetic inspiration. The motif, a frieze of repeated horses and spirals, could have been borrowed from an antique Greek vase. A drawing by Florentine artist Ernesto Thayaht, published in 1924 in *La gazette du bon ton,* illustrates the stylistic similarity. This influence was further supported by a photograph of the Promonos vase found in Madeleine Vionnet's archives (owned by the Musée des Arts Décoratifs); this antique krater with a scroll design dates back to 400 BCE and resides at the Museo Nazionale in Naples. The motifs of the costumes worn by the protagonists of the unfolding play about satyrs may have served as models for the decorative embroidery of the "Petits Chevaux" evening gown. The embellishments are embroidered in a way that recalls the negative space on red-figure pottery with black background. The embroidery was produced by Maison Michonnet based on a drawing by Marie-Louise Favot (known as Yo), one of Vionnet's collaborators and the future wife of Albert Lesage, Michonnet's successor.
M.-S.C.C.

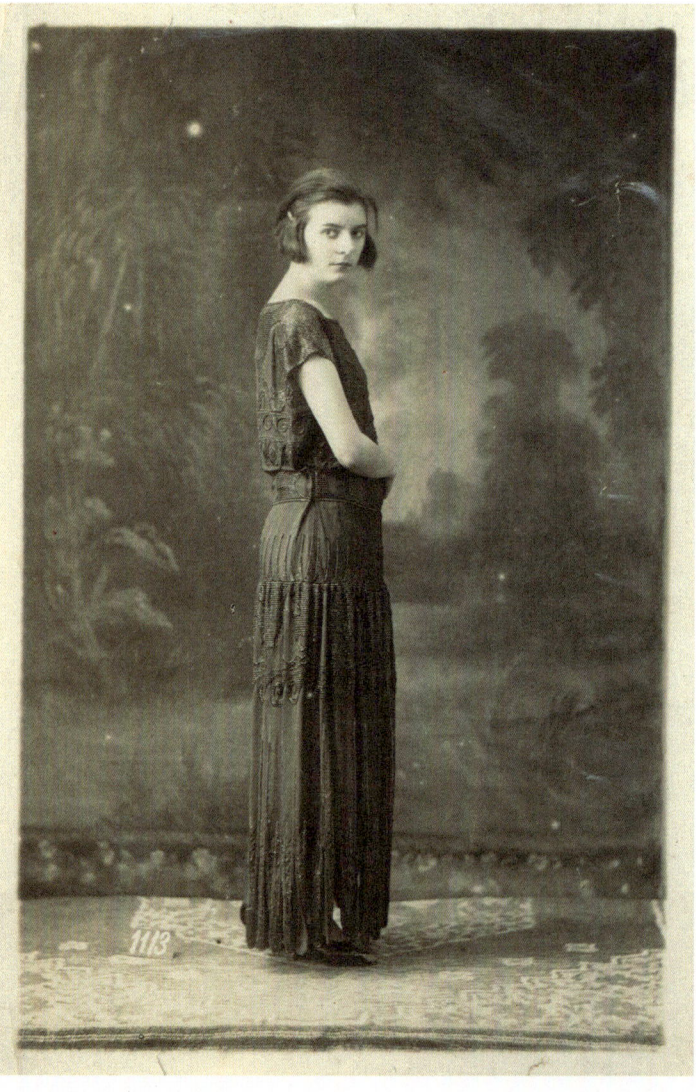

MADELEINE VIONNET, Photograph of original design no. 1113, 1921. Gelatin silver print on Baryte paper.
Musée des Arts Décoratifs, Paris; The Photography Collection.

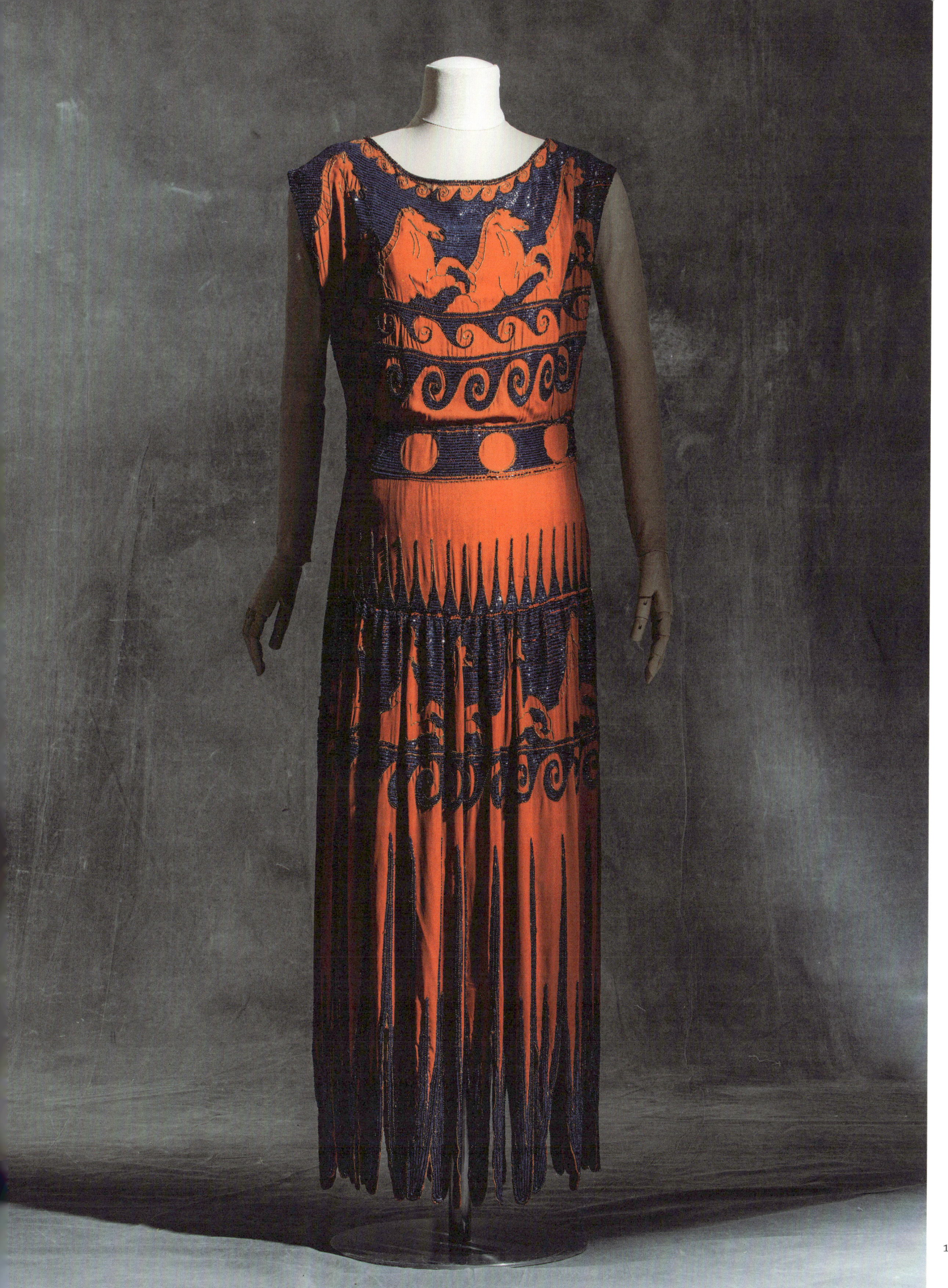

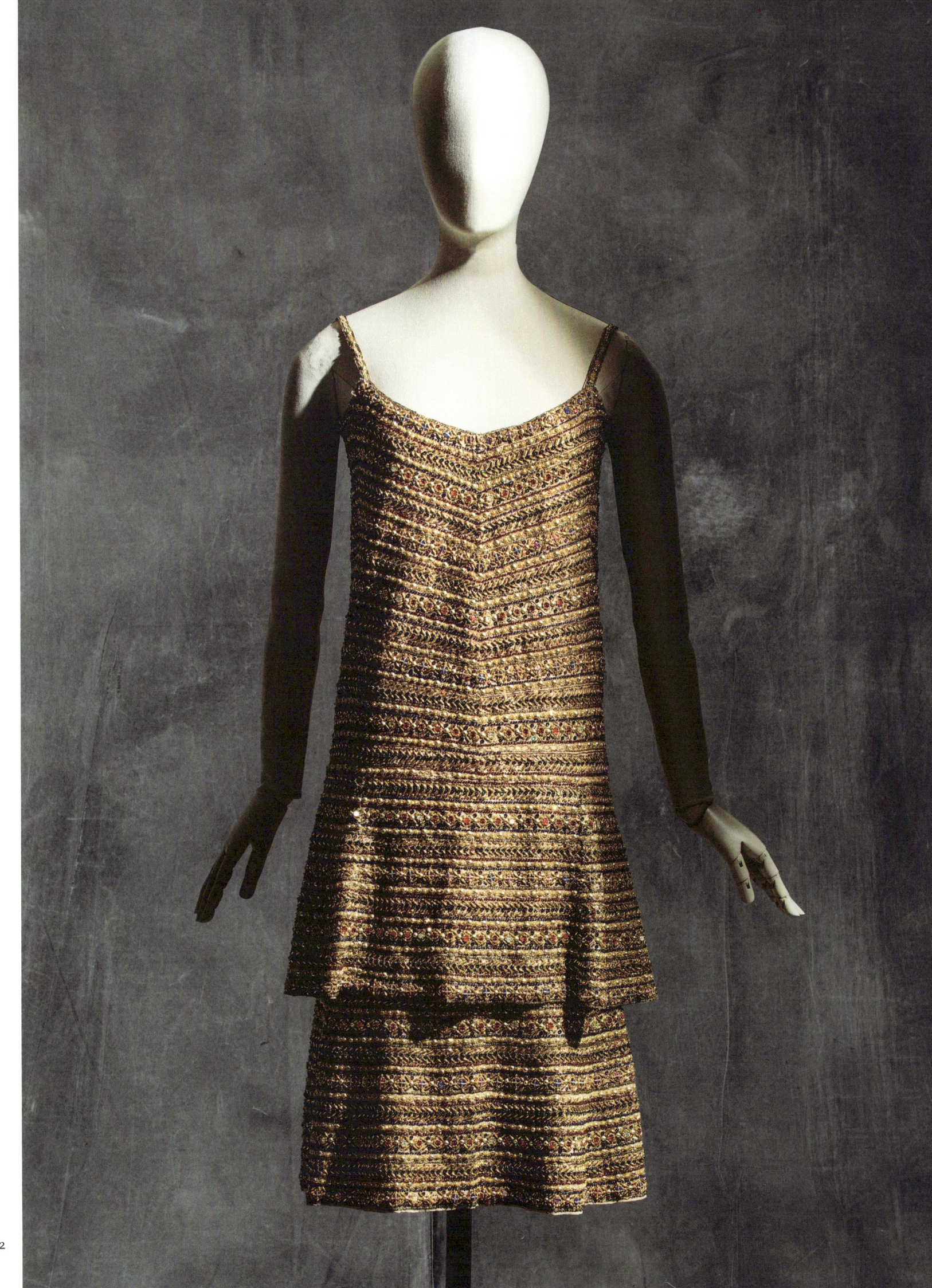

Gabrielle Chanel
Evening Dress, 1925

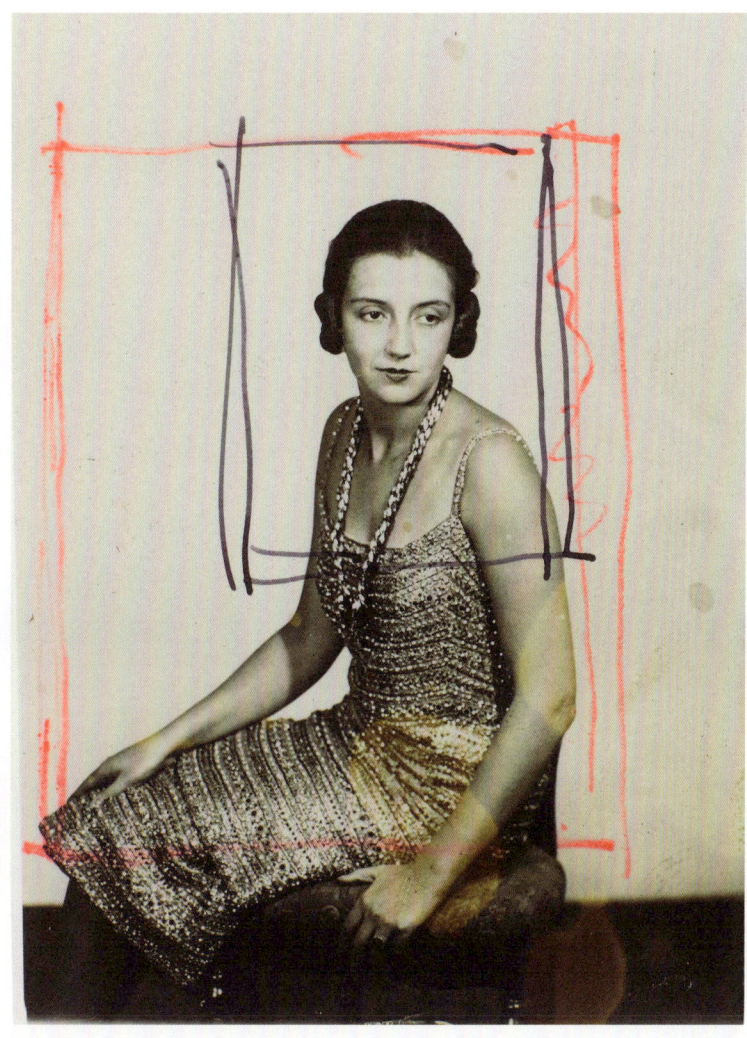

Composed of a tunic with straps, or a shorter and slightly flared dress, and a skirt attached to a full slip, this Chanel evening dress is an example of the simplified style and shorter length that became fashionable at the end of World War I.

The 1920s saw the advent of the *garçonne*, or flapper, whose bobbed hair was a style introduced early on by Gabrielle Chanel (1883-1971). Chanel was one of the main proponents of this emancipated fashion that reflected the changing role of women in society. Unlike the colorful clothes of the Roaring Twenties, Chanel's little black dress was emblematic of the radically new designs adopted by modern women.

Liberating the body and freeing the waistline, Chanel created a "new silhouette," as described by Paul Morand in his 1976 book *L'allure de Chanel*. The shorter length—above the knee—of this sleeveless, flowing dress with straps allowed for easy movement, leaving the body free to move to the beat of the Charleston or the foxtrot. The gold and multicolored embroidered embellishments caught the light as women danced the night away.
M.-S.C.C.

MAN RAY, Madame de Gaenza, 1930. Gelatin silver print. Centre Pompidou, Paris.

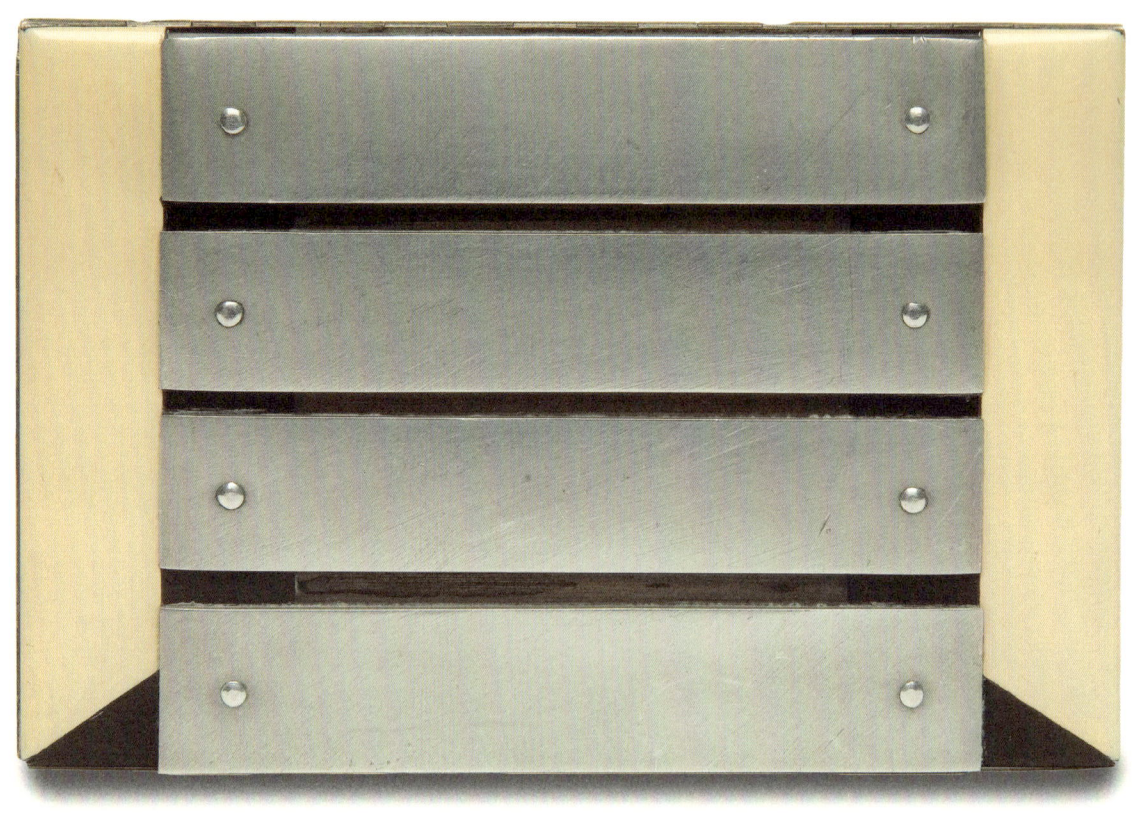

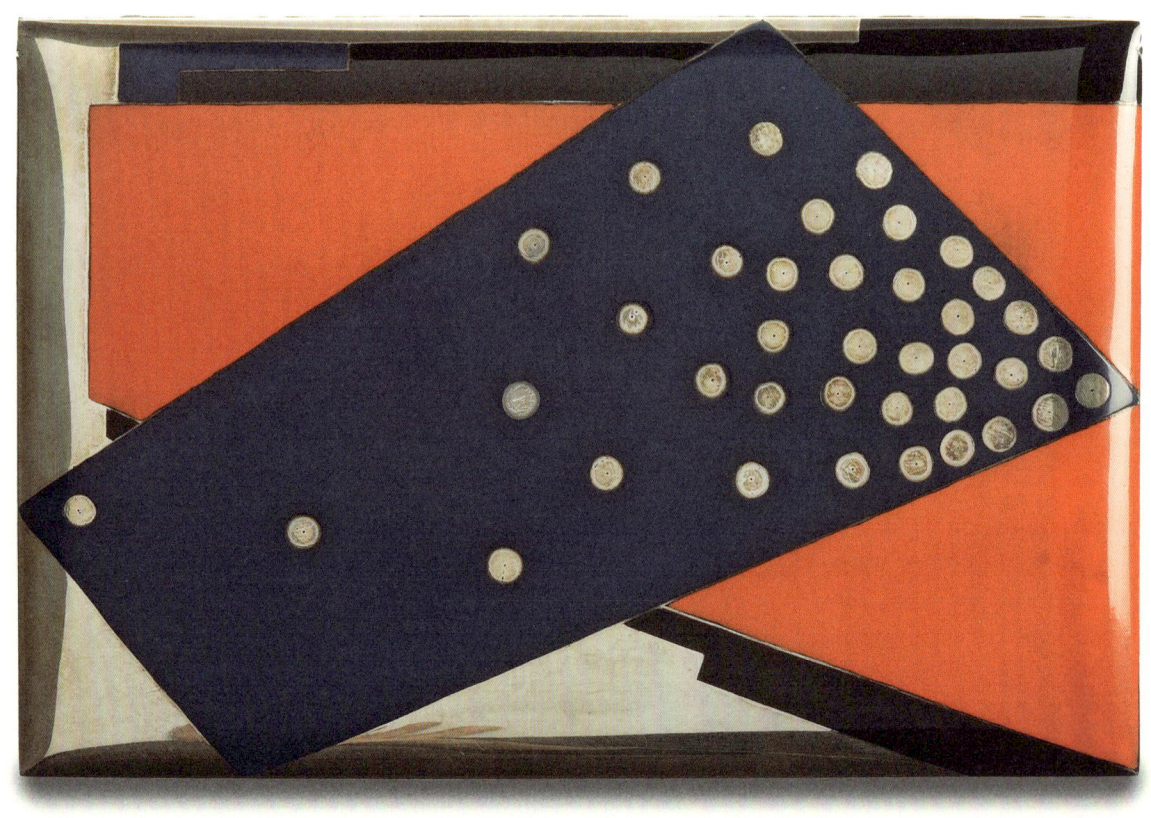

RAYMOND TEMPLIER, Cigarette cases, 1928-1930. Silver, aluminum, lacquer.
Musée des Arts Décoratifs, Paris; Gift of Raymond Templier, 1966.

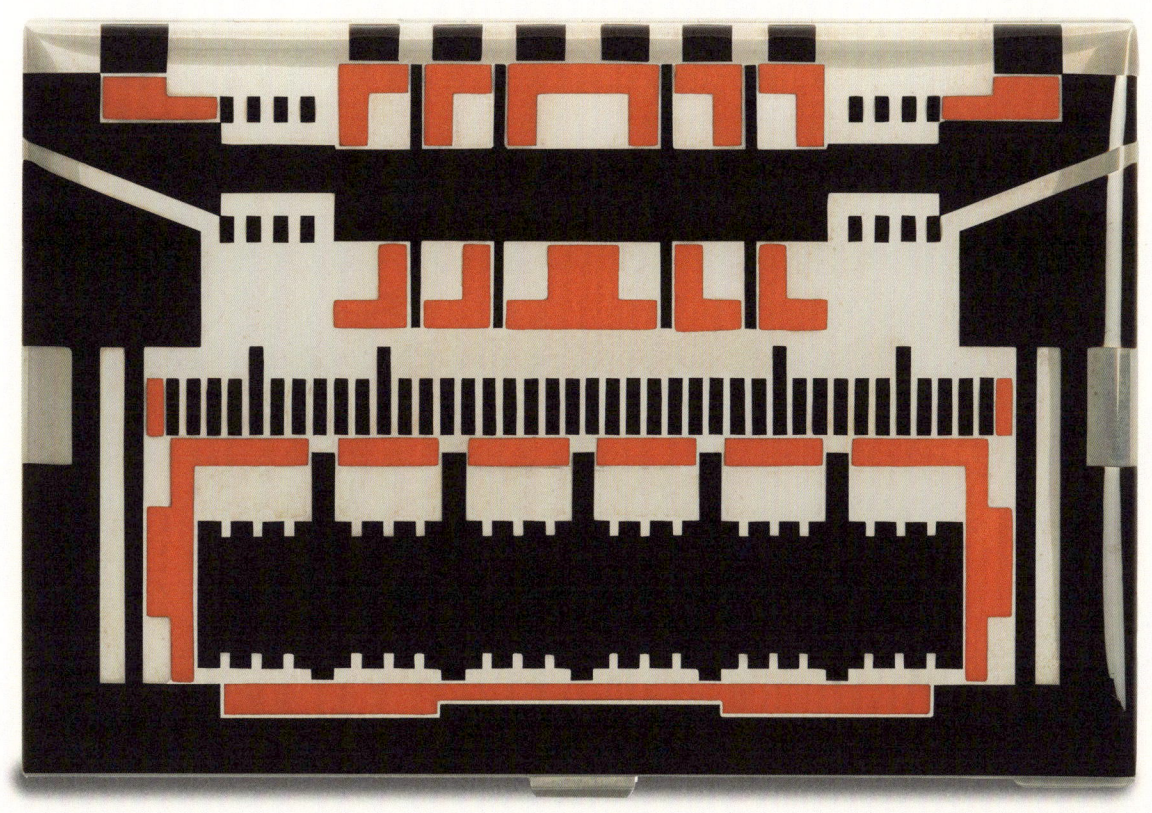
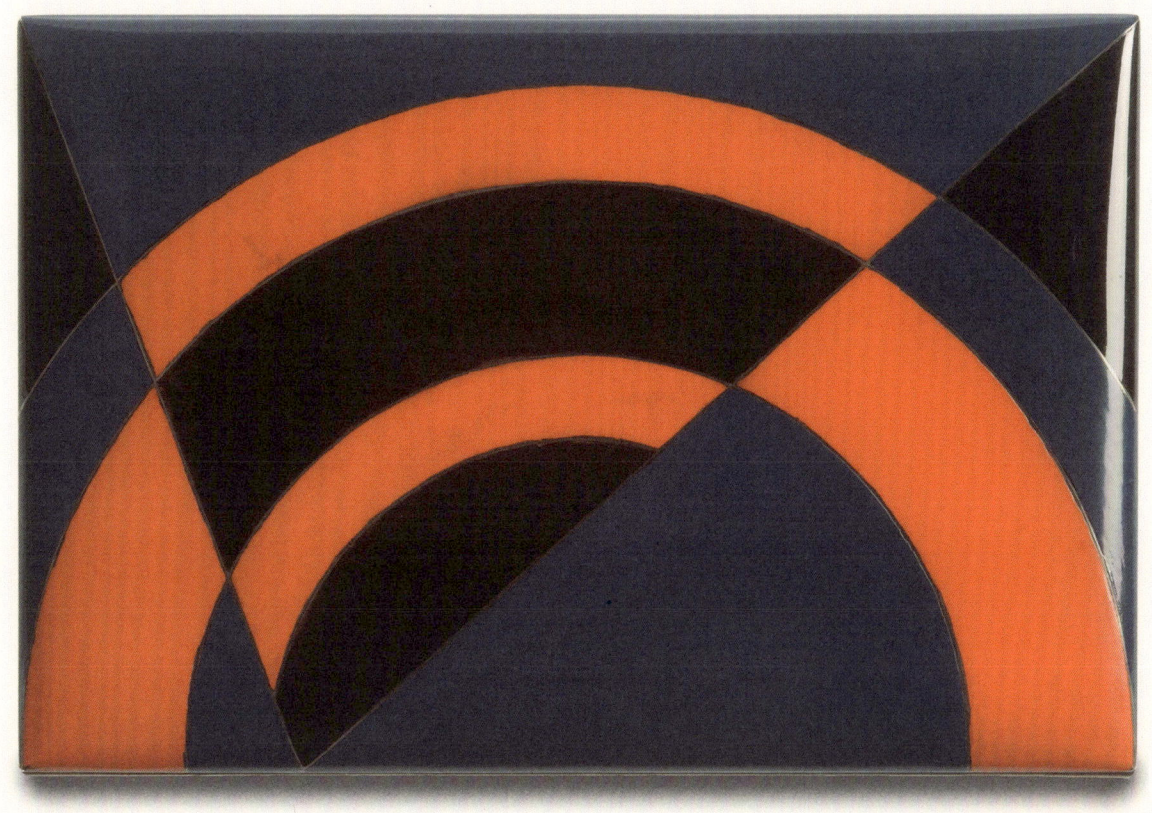

Jeanne Lanvin
Evening Cape, Summer 1923

In the era of peace that followed World War I, the lure of exotic foreign cultures that stirred the imagination made their way into the styles of the great couturiers. These seductive far-off lands also evoked the grandeur of the French colonial empire. During his travels to Morocco in 1918, Paul Poiret discovered an entirely new source of inspiration and began designing Arabian-style coats. Similarly, Jeanne Lanvin's designs were influenced by the native dress of North African countries, such as the caftan, the burnoose, or wide capes that reached the ankles and featured a tasseled hood, such as those worn by Berbers. Such orientalist fashions fueled the public's interest for travel writing, including the recounting of the 1922 Citroën rally across the Sahara Desert. Featured in the November 1, 1923, issue of French *Vogue*, an advertisement for the Compagnie Générale Transatlantique promoted the newest travel destination via elegant automobiles: "*Le voyage à la mode au pays de l'Islam et des ruines antiques Maroc-Algérie-Tunisie*" (A luxurious trip to the countries of Islam to visit the antique ruins of Morocco, Algeria, and Tunisia).

    The Berber-style evening cape pictured here features the characteristics of traditional dress. Made of silk lamé with gold and black topstitching, the cape shimmers like silver metal. Wearing such a luminous and exotic evening coat, an elegant woman could easily imagine herself as a Roaring Twenties princess.

M.-S.C.C.

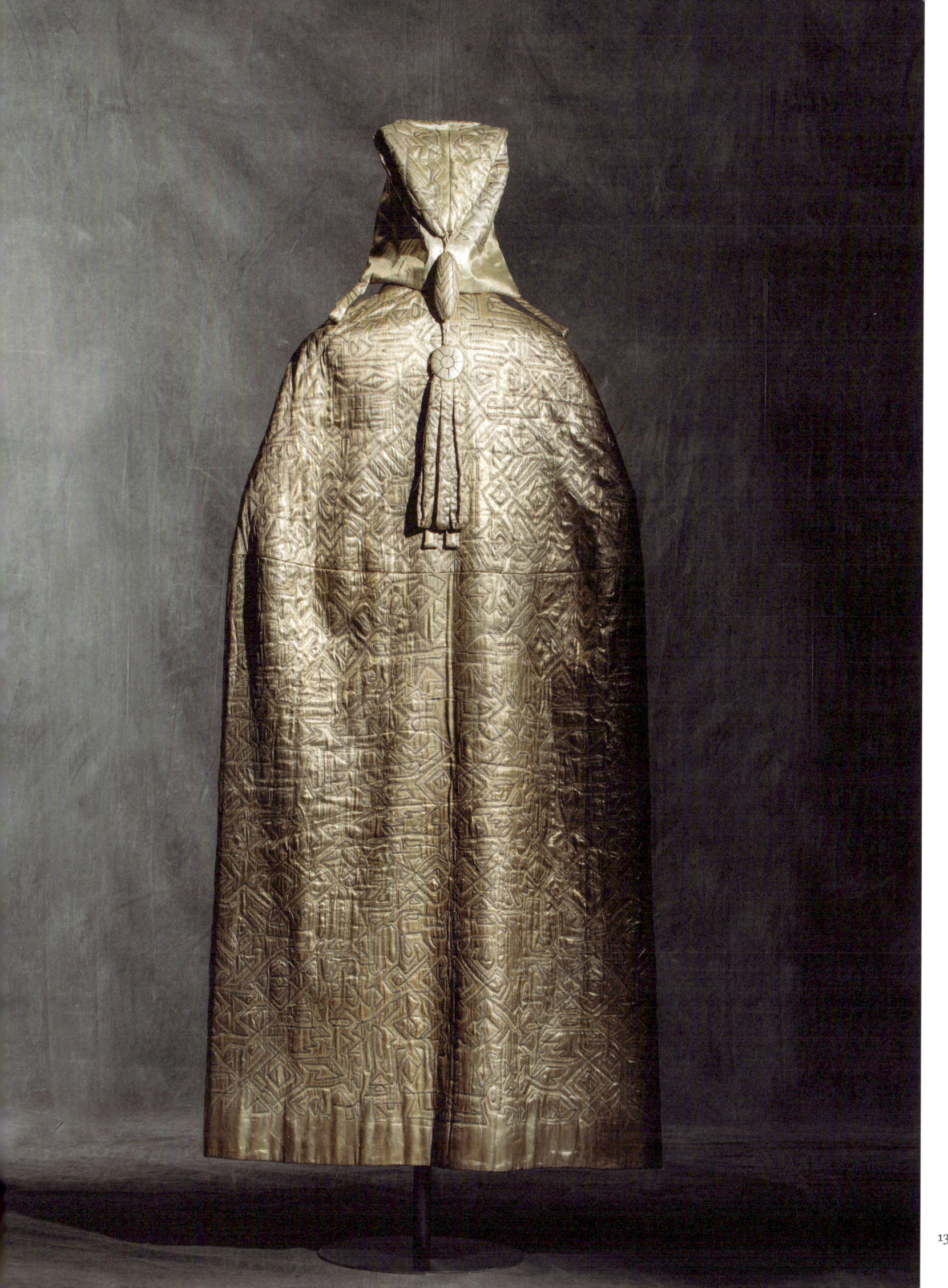

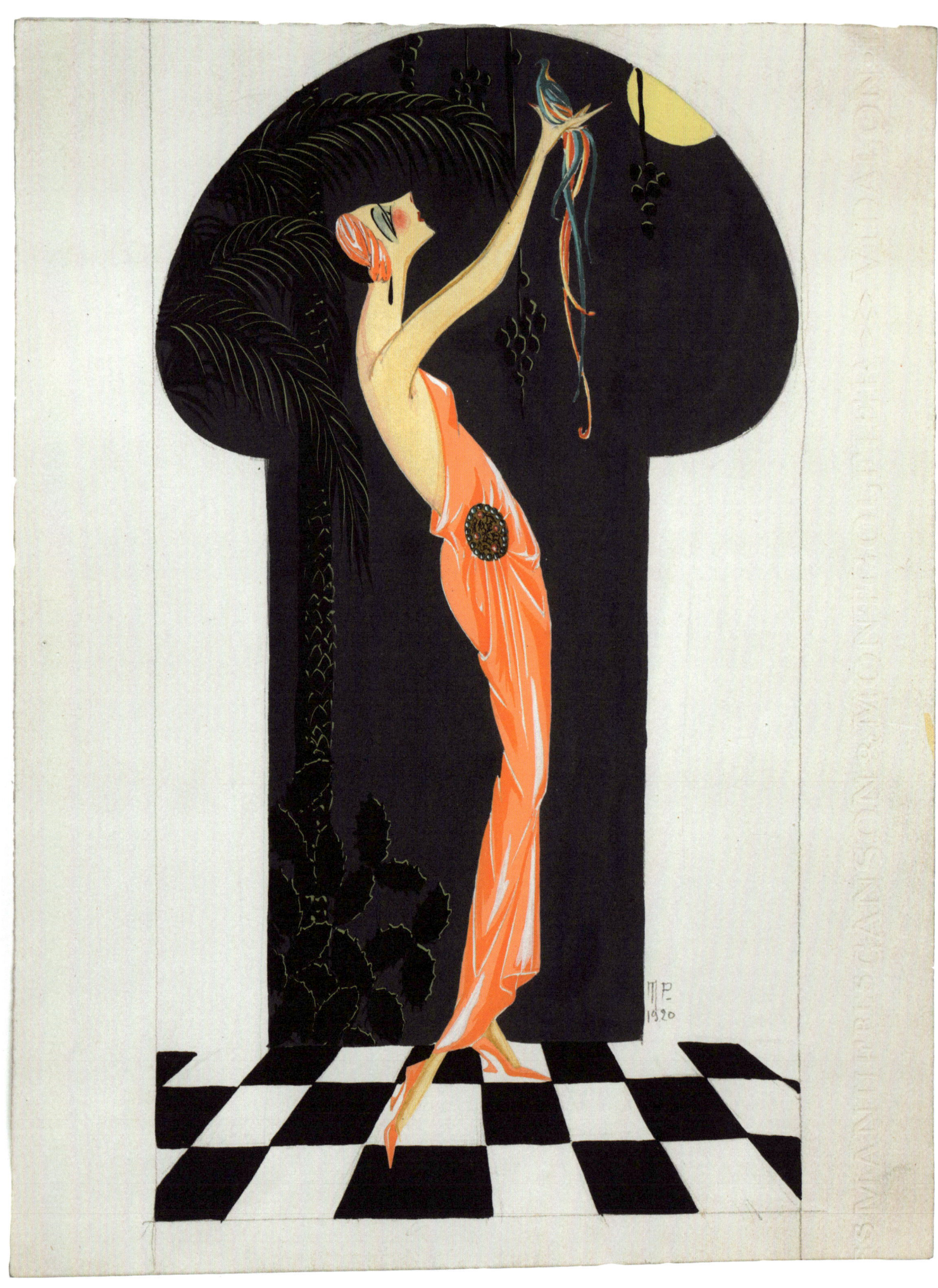

MARGUERITE PORRACCHIA, Design sketches, 1920–1930. Graphite pencil, brushwork, gouache, and black ink on paper.
Musée des Arts Décoratifs, Paris; Graphic Arts Department, gift of Bruno Gaudenzi, 2013.

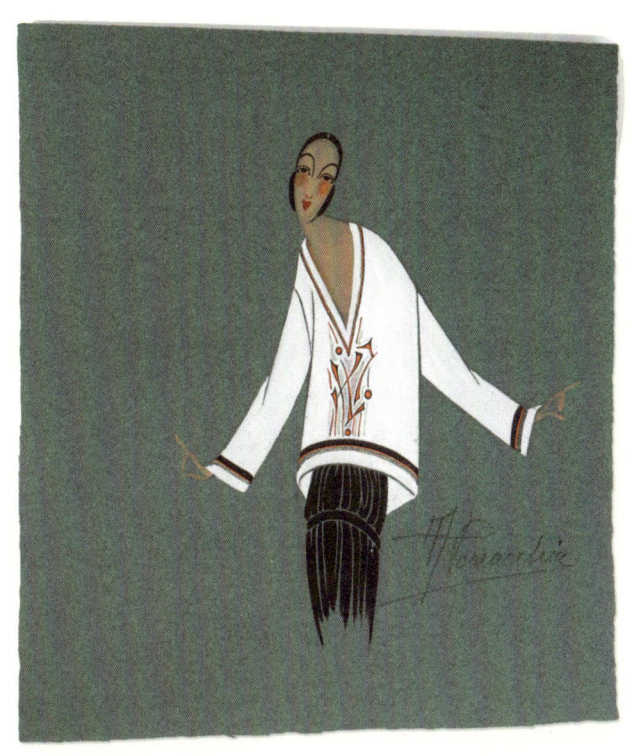
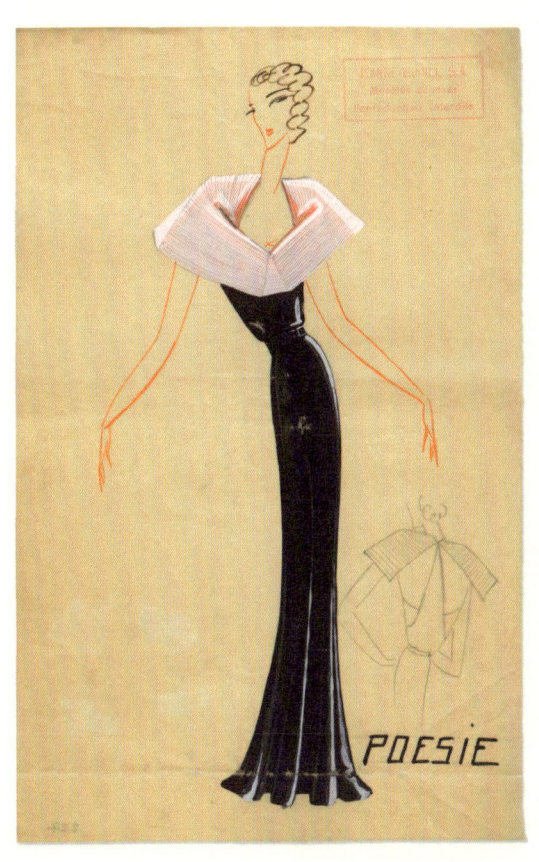
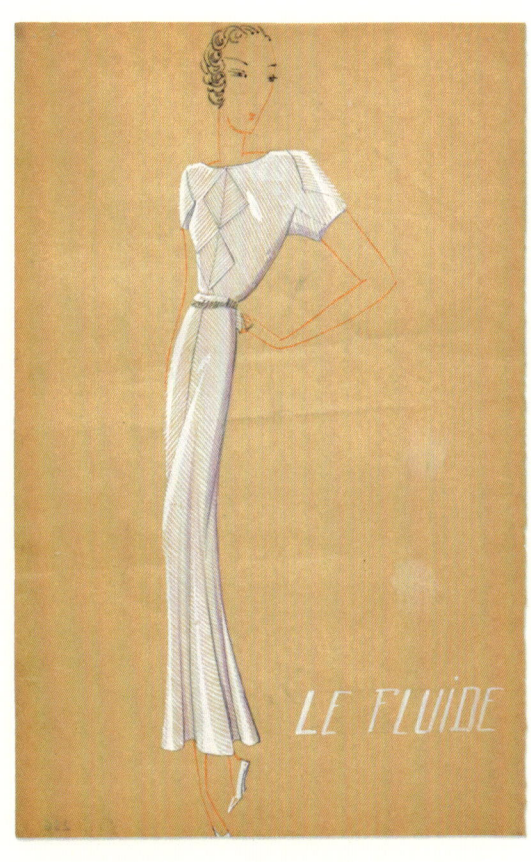
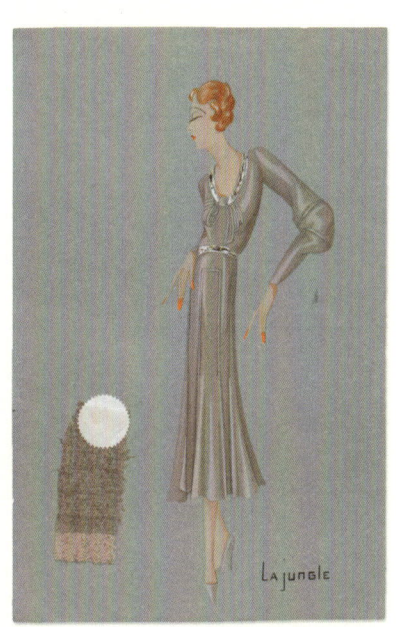
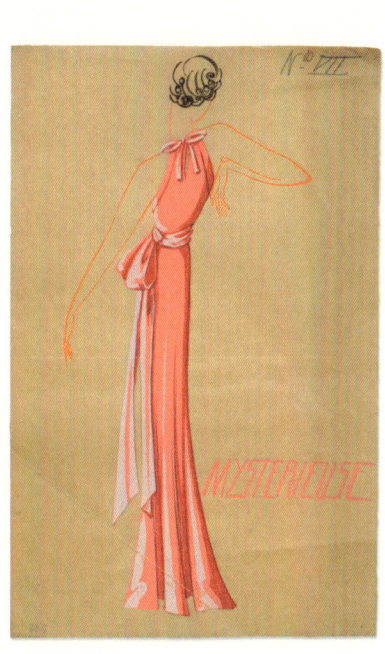

POESIE

LE FLUIDE

La jungle

MYSTERIEUSE

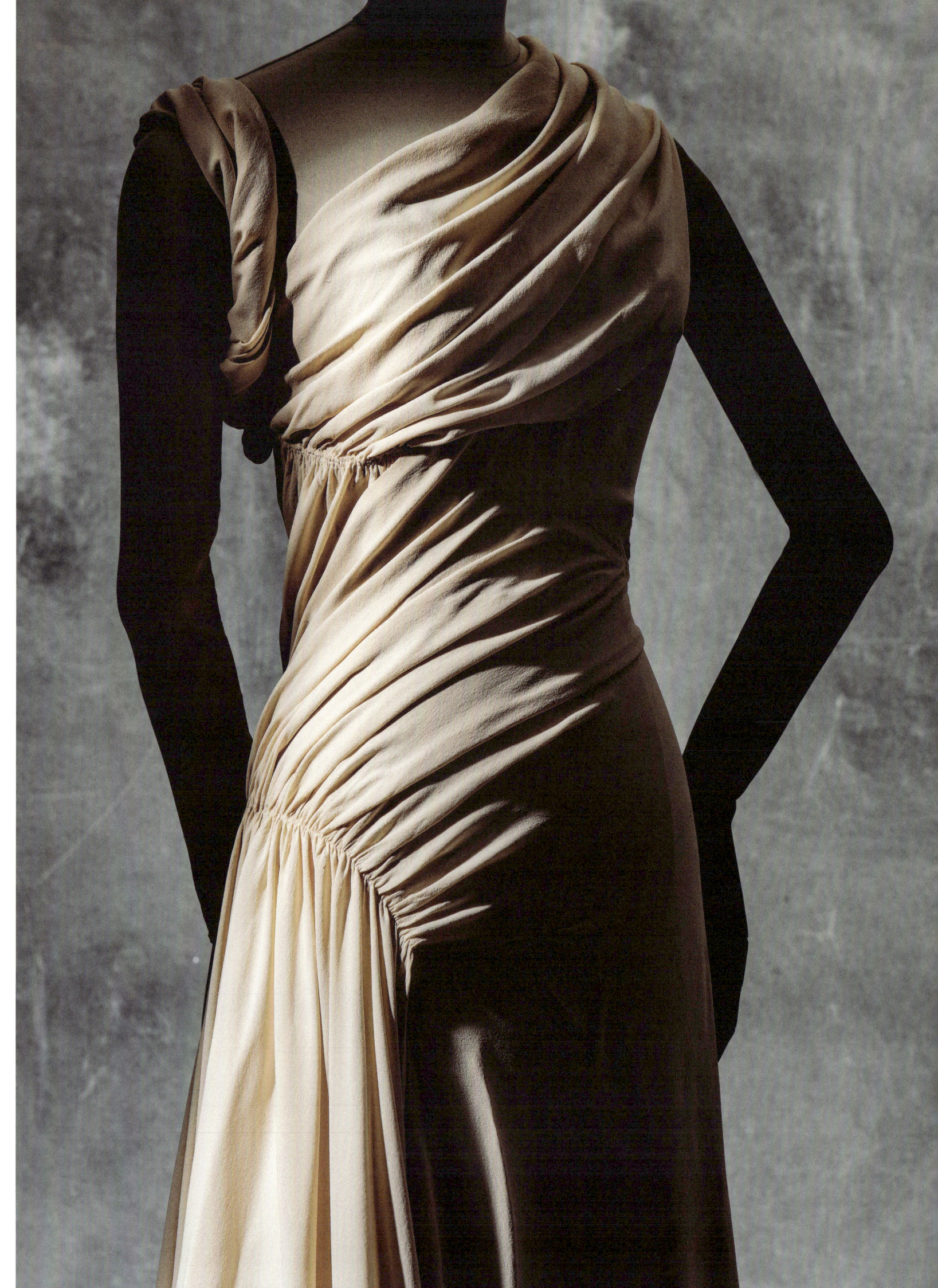

Madeleine Vionnet
Evening Gown, Winter 1935–1936

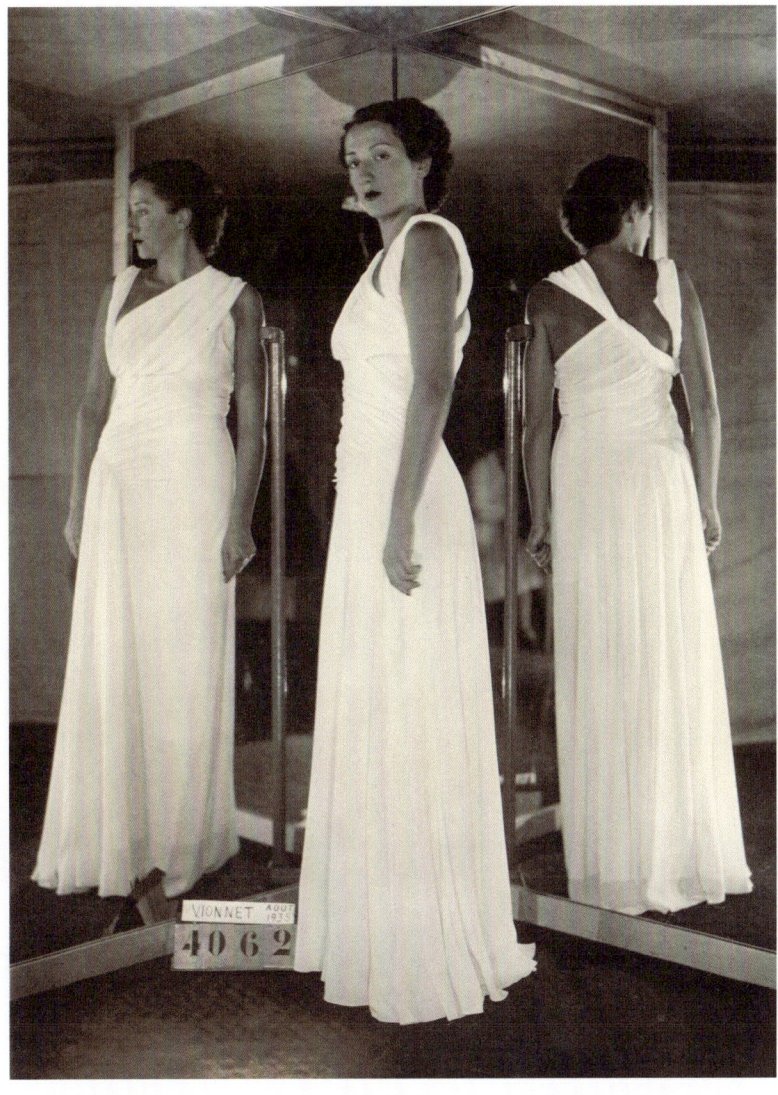

Working with volume in the manner of a master sculptor, Madeleine Vionnet reinvented Greek antiquity while meeting the needs of modern and active women. During the 1930s she streamlined her style, eliminating all literal references to antiquity, just as she had done during the preceding decade. Instead of the typical seasonal evolution of most couturiers, Vionnet created a neoclassical style that was defined not only by subtle variations of her masterful command of the drape but also by the use of fabric panels that clung to the body. In this evening gown from the 1935 winter collection, ivory crepe is draped, pleated, and coiled over one shoulder of an asymmetrical bodice. Once the dress is slipped on, the drape takes shape and finds its equilibrium. The photograph by Horst P. Horst that appeared in the October 1935 issue of French *Vogue* is a perfect illustration of Vionnet's technique.
M.-S.C.C.

MADELEINE VIONNET, Photograph of style no. 4062, 1935. Silver gelatin print on Baryte paper.
Musée des Arts Décoratifs, Paris; The Photography Collection.

Mainbocher
Evening Gown, Winter 1937-1938

The former editor in chief of French *Vogue*, Main Rousseau Bocher gave up journalism in 1929 and, the following year, became the first American to open a fashion house in Paris. The elegance of his style and the prestigious reputation of his fashion house quickly attracted Parisian high society and a wealthy international clientele to his salons on the Avenue George V. Known primarily for his evening wear, Mainbocher was also famous for his innovative use of fabric and such revolutionary creations as the strapless dress he designed in 1934. It was his style, both classical and rigorous, that attracted his most celebrated client, the Duchess of Windsor, née Wallis Simpson, for whom he designed the fabled "Wallis blue" wedding dress in 1937.

The fitted evening gown shown here is remarkable for the simplicity of its line (tubular sleeves, straight skirt, collarless) that flattered the client's silhouette. It is also noteworthy for the ingenious use of embroidery, here a sequined arabesque that serves as both fabric and embellishment.

M.-P. R.

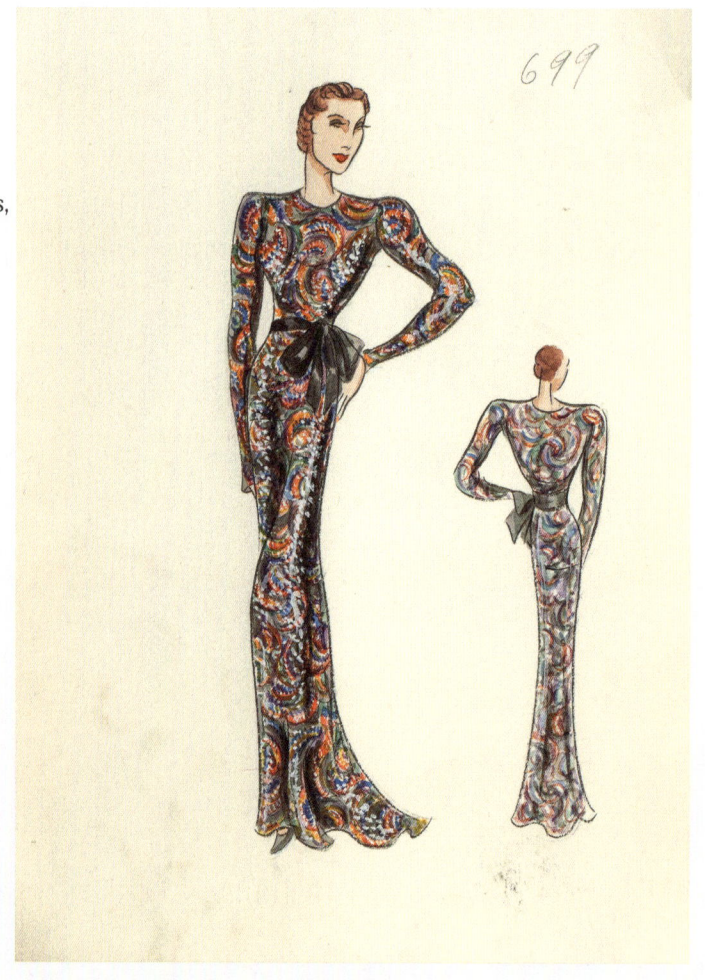

MAINBOCHER, Sketch no. 5651, August 1937. Graphite pencil and watercolor on paper.
Musée des Arts Décoratifs, Paris; Graphic Arts Department.

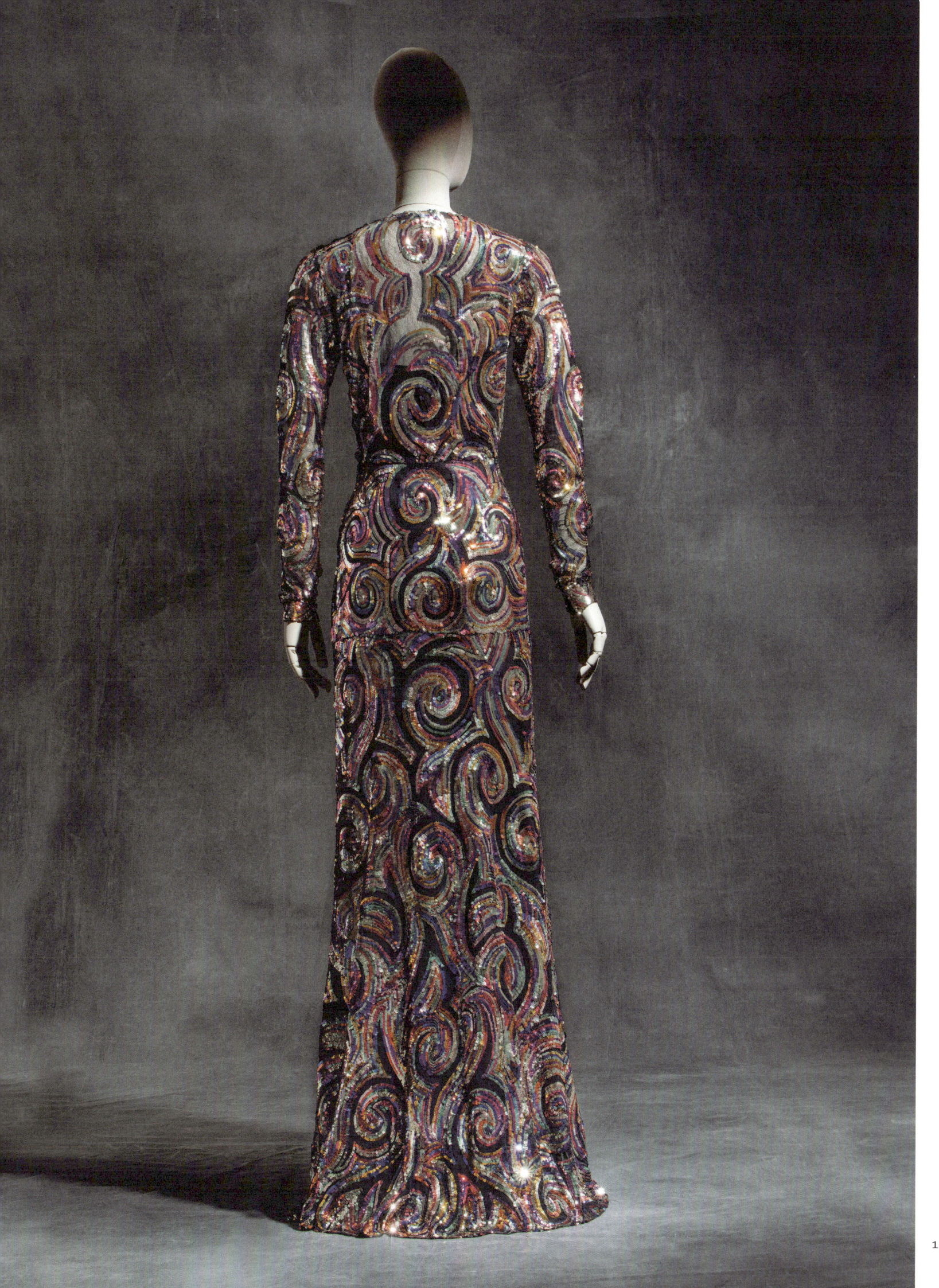

Elsa Schiaparelli
Evening Coat, Winter 1938-1939

Mrs. Arturo Lopez-Willshaw (1912-2010), the wife of a Chilean millionaire and a devoted client of the House of Schiaparelli since 1937, would always select the Italian designer's most spectacular creations. A fixture of Parisian high society who enjoyed being the focus of attention, Patricia Lopez-Willshaw developed her "own style . . . the true mark of elegance," according to the February 1939 issue of *Vogue*.

Located on the Place Vendôme, Schiaparelli's boutique was designed by Jean-Michel Frank, with furnishings by Diego Giacometti and window displays by Bettina Jones. With humor and fantasy, her collections celebrated the marriage of couture and decorative arts. Schiaparelli, who thought of herself as an inspired artist, had a marvelous circle of friends that included Salvador Dalí, Christian Bérard, Marcel Vertès, and Jean Cocteau. Their collaboration on her designs resulted in Surrealist creations that thrilled the fashionable set.

Parisian clients of the fashion houses were already familiar with the rebellious art movement, after viewing the *Exposition Internationale du Surréalisme* held in early 1938 at the Galerie des Beaux-Arts in Paris. As an American journalist for *Women's Wear Daily* noted in February of that year: "It was Schiaparelli who, eighteen months ago, introduced surrealism in couture." Gifted with a fertile sense of invention, she was the first fashion designer to give each of her collections a theme. Her Winter 1938-1939 "Cosmique" collection featured novel materials such as plastic or ceramic that were incorporated into the embroideries by Lesage or used for the buttons that embellish this black wool coat with structured padded shoulders.
M.-S.C.C.

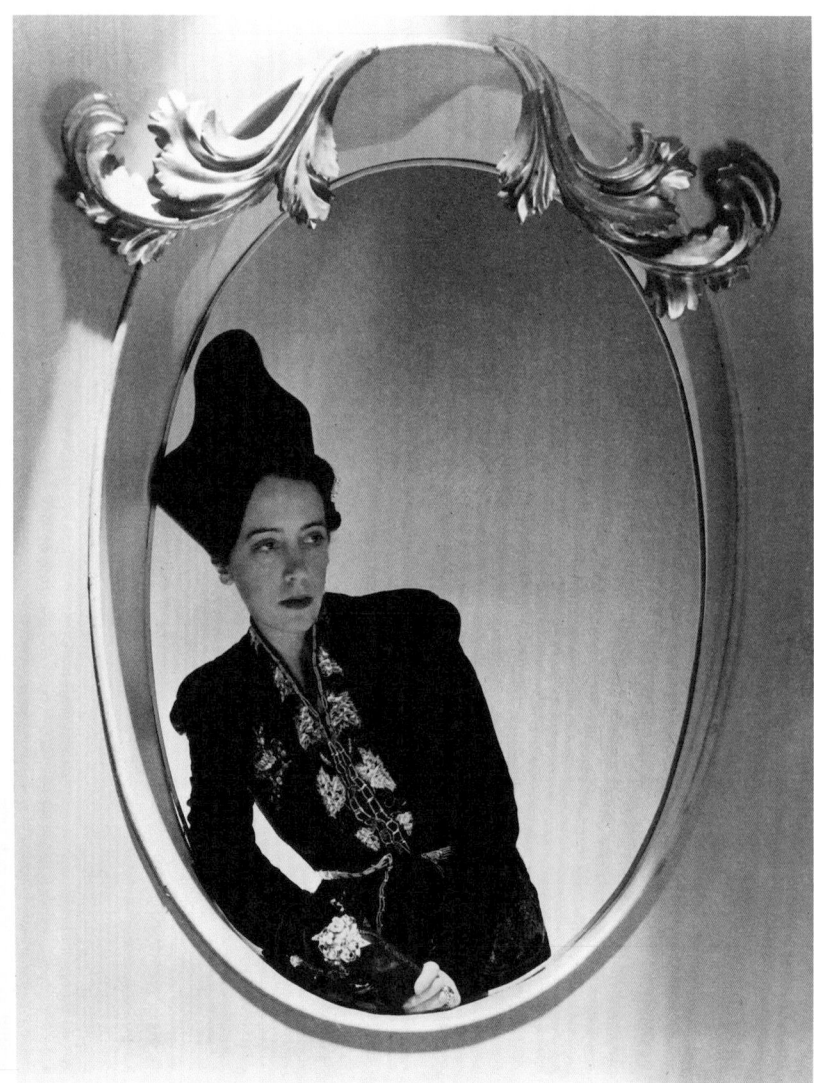

HORST P. HORST, *Elsa Schiaparelli portant un ensemble de sa collection d'hiver 1937-1938*
(Elsa Schiaparelli wearing an ensemble from her own 1937-1938 winter collection), printed and signed by Horst on silver gelatin paper.
Musée des Arts Décoratifs, Paris; The Photo Collection, gift of Horst P. Horst, 1993. Published in *Vogue*, September 1937, page 97.

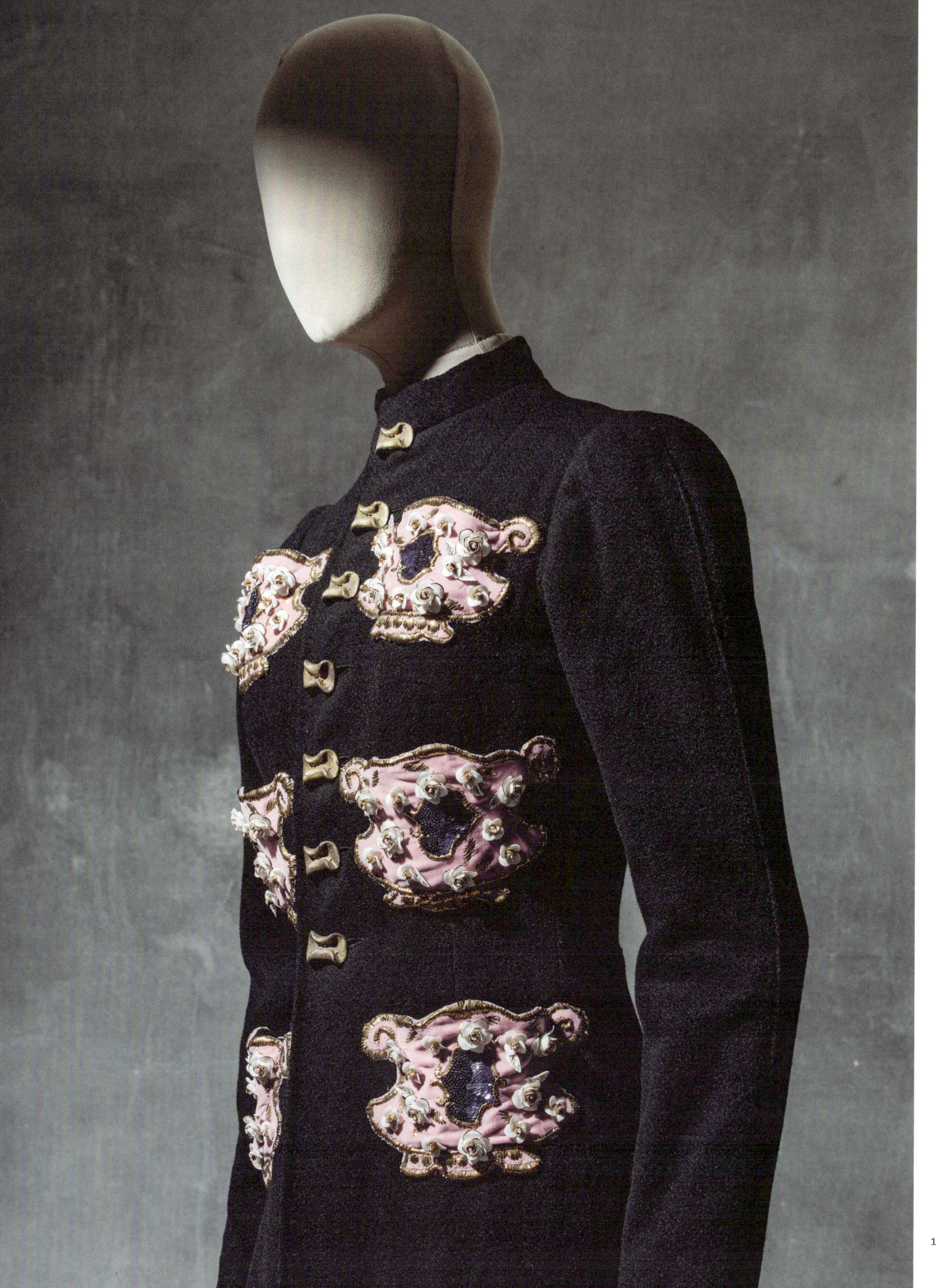

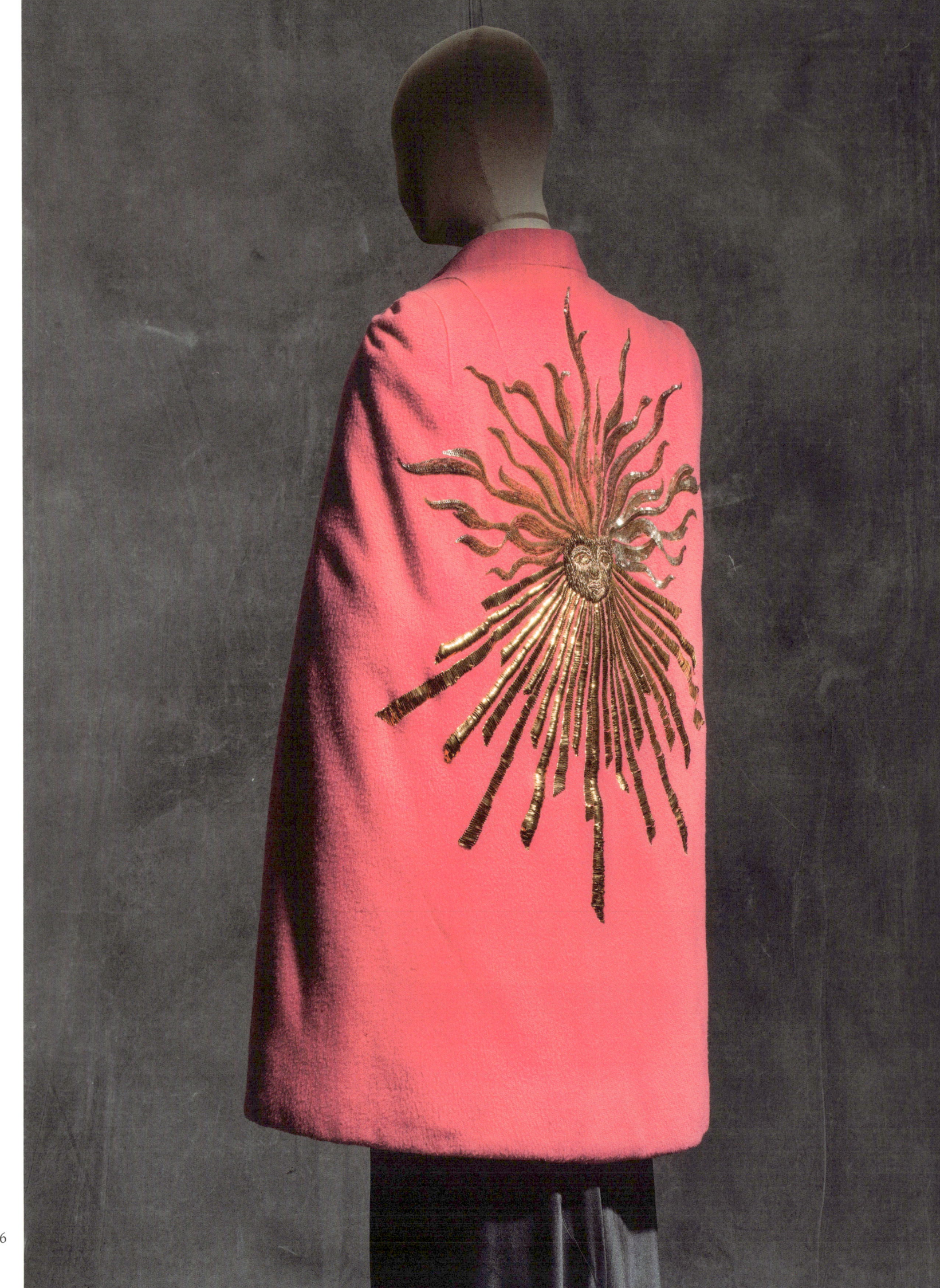

Elsa Schiaparelli
Phœbus *Evening Cape, Winter 1938-1939*

Drawn with theatrical flair by painter Christian Bérard for *Vogue* in November 1938, the "Phoebus" cape is emblematic of Schiaparelli's 1938 "Cosmique" collection, in which the eccentricity of the Lesage embroidery motifs was rivaled only by the audacity of the colors. The cape's fuchsia pink color was Schiaparelli's favorite—a shade that became her signature in 1936 when paint colorist Jean Clément created the perfect tone called "Shocking Pink." It was emblematic of her fashion house, her brand, her first perfume Shocking, launched in 1937, as well as her autobiography, *Shocking Life*, published in 1954. In a foreword to a biography of the designer in 1986, Yves Saint Laurent, who was also partial to pink in his collections, wrote that Schiaparelli demonized the color by infusing it with the spirit of red, giving it an intense and sharp dimension.

Embroidered on the back of the cape, the radiant gold mask of the sun god acts like a shield, protecting the woman wearing it. There exist only two such capes featuring the same fine embroidery: one can be found at the Palais Galliera, and the other belongs to the Musée des Arts Décoratifs, thanks to the generosity of Elsa Schiaparelli. The cape was one of 88 creations and 5,800 drawings given to the museum by the designer in 1973.
M.-S.C.C.

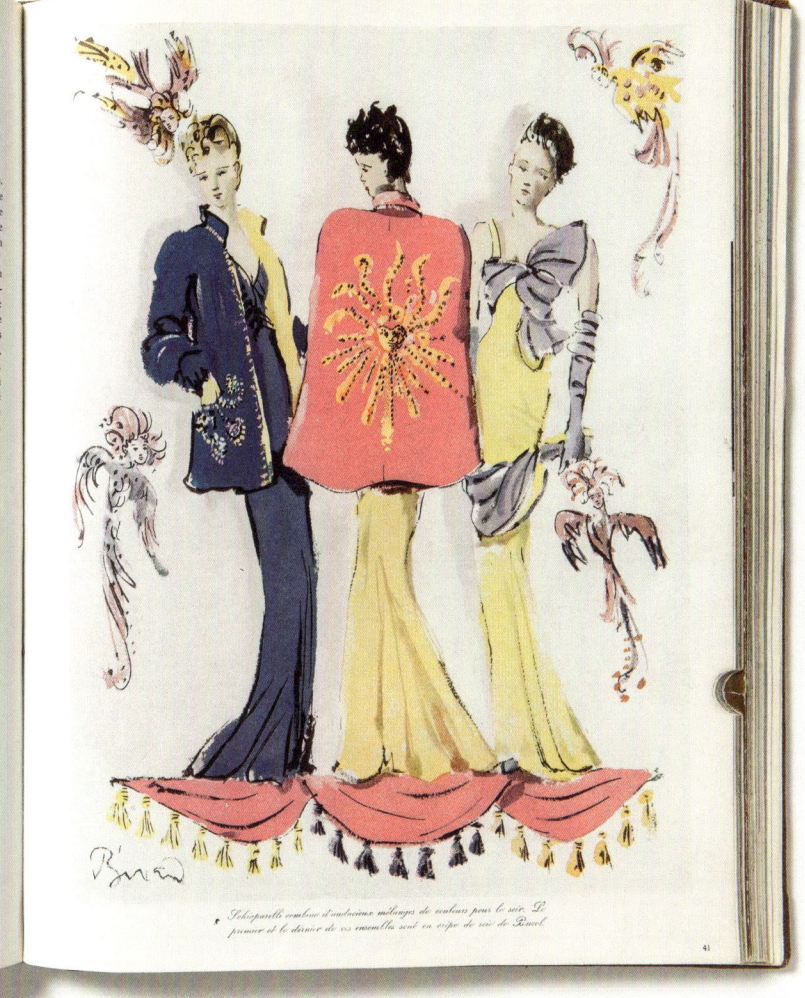

CHRISTIAN BÉRARD, Drawing published in "Poufs et pirouettes," *Vogue*, November 1938, page 41.
Musée des Arts Décoratifs, Paris; The Documentation Center.

Gabrielle Chanel
Evening Gown, Winter 1938-1939

This evening gown was featured in the *Chanel* retrospective exhibition, organized in 2005 by Harold Koda and Andrew Bolton at the Metropolitan Museum of Art in New York. A similar dress is part of the Metropolitan Museum's permanent collection. A drawing of Madeleine de Montgomery wearing that dress appeared in the February 1939 issue of *Vogue* and is also in the museum's collection. The occasion was Lady Mendl's birthday, and Madeleine de Montgomery had accessorized the dress with a pair of short gloves adorned with colored stones. The three dresses, embellished with extensive and luminous embroidery, were designed by Gabrielle Chanel and featured in her Winter 1938-1939 collection, just a few months before the outbreak of World War II. The collection coincided with the waning days of the *beau monde* of the 1930s, a time of scintillating soirées attended by an elegant and sophisticated high society. After successfully establishing both a new clothing style and lifestyle during the 1920s, Chanel decided to close her fashion house in 1939.

This piece, one of a group of evening gowns designed by Chanel and donated by Joëlle Despas, had belonged to Despas's mother, Isabelle (née Schlumberger). This ultrafeminine dress features a fitted bodice with straps, a tiny waist, and a full skirt. As the sheer and lightweight tulle comes to life and the sequins catch the light, we are reminded of Chanel's famous saying: "Be a caterpillar during the day and a butterfly at night. There is nothing more comfortable than a caterpillar and nothing more made for love than a butterfly. We need dresses that crawl and dresses that fly" (quoted by Edmonde Charles-Roux in *Le Temps Chanel*, 1980).
M.-S.C.C.

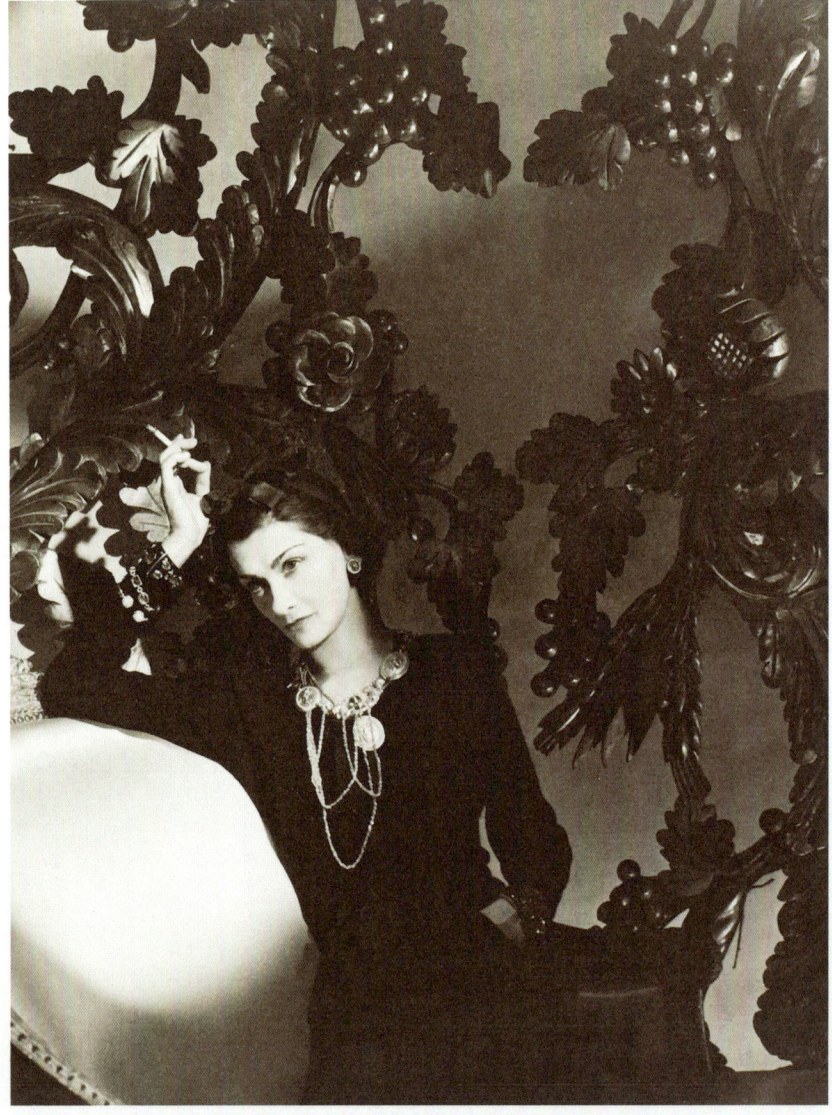

HORST P. HORST, *Coco Chanel Lying on a Chaise Longue*, 1937. Silver gelatin print (reprint). Musée des Arts Décoratifs, Paris; The Photo Collection.

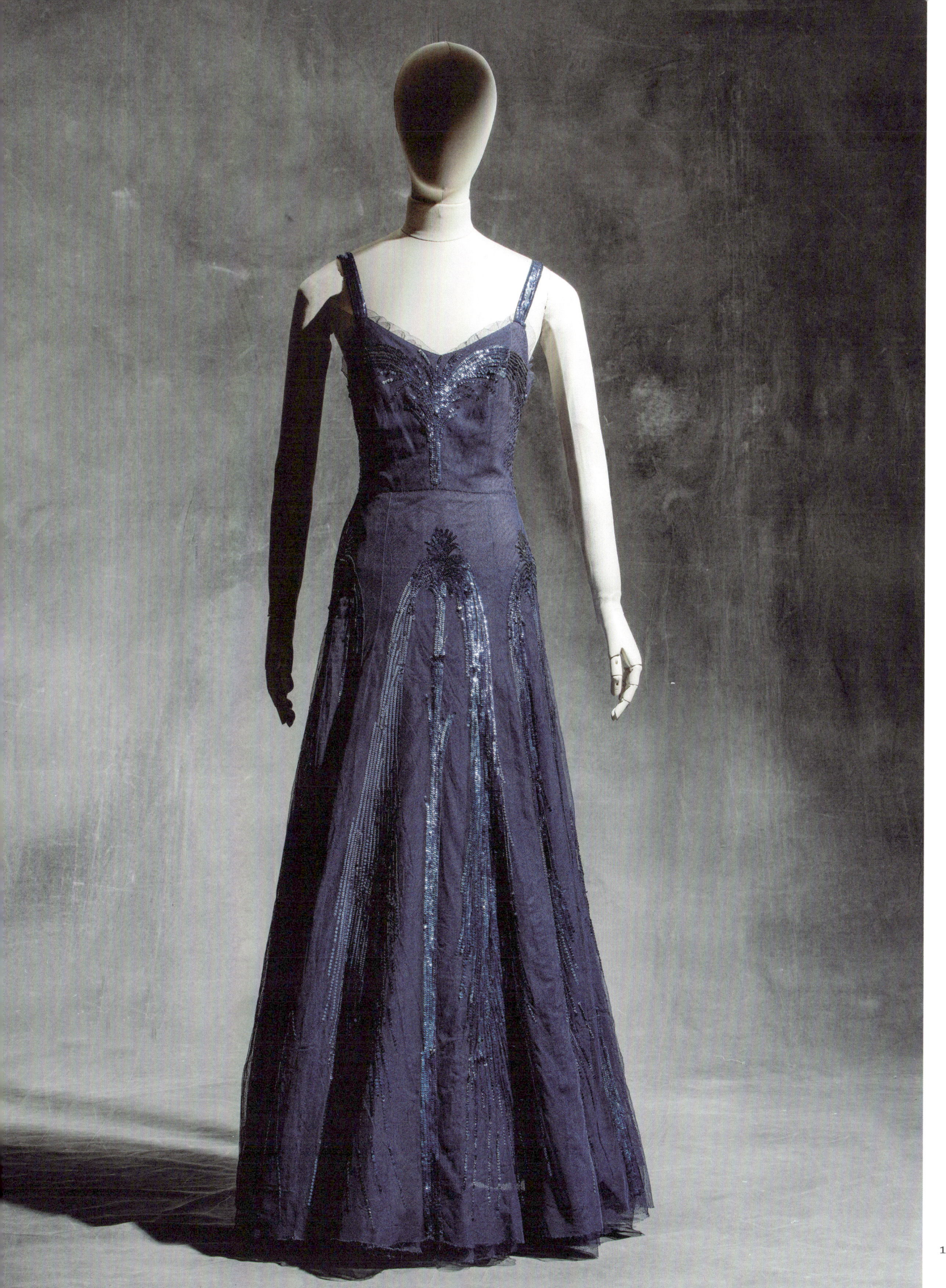

149

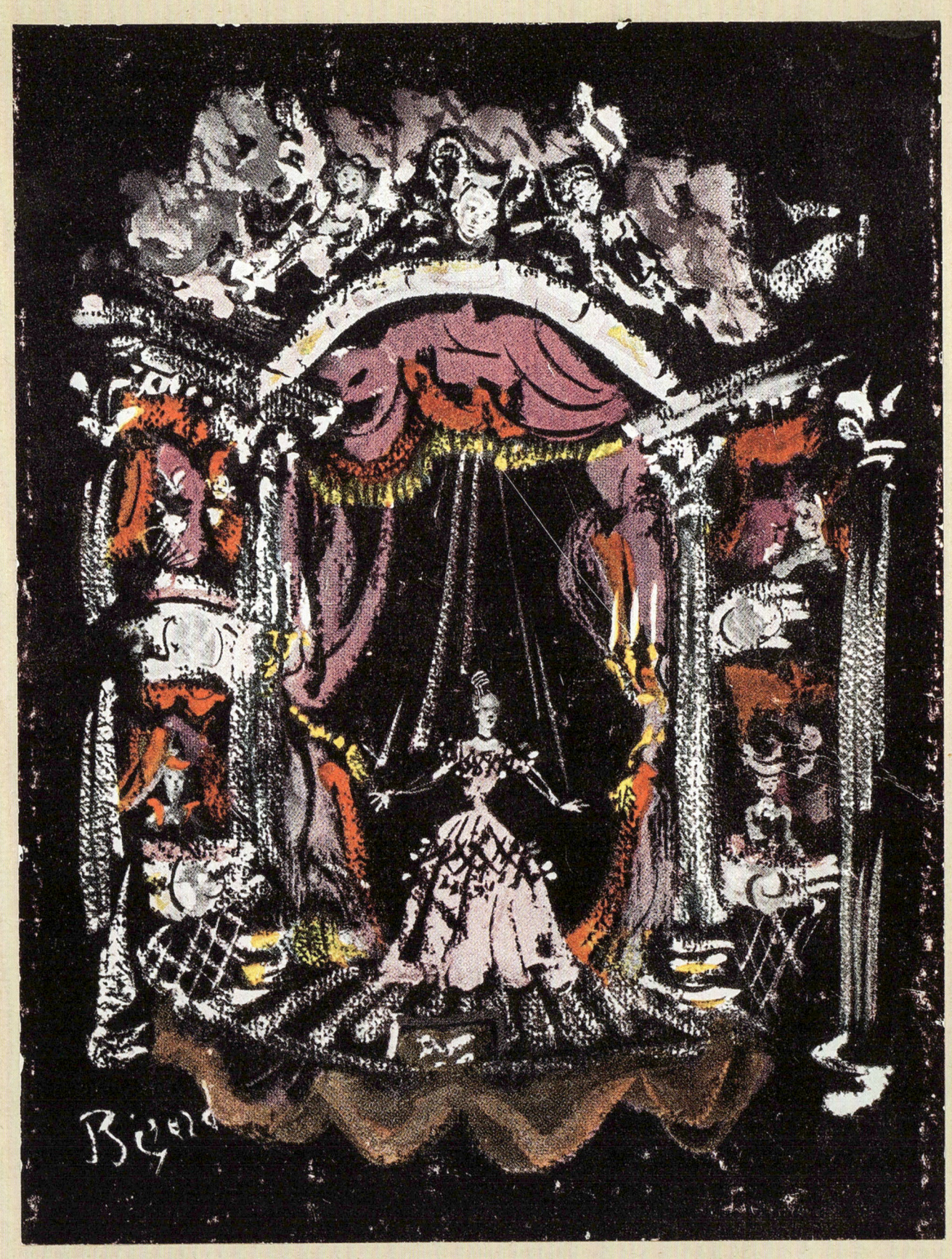

CHRISTIAN BÉRARD, Drawing that appeared on the cover of the catalogue for the *Théâtre de la Mode* exhibition, 1946.
Bibliothèque des Arts Décoratifs, Paris.

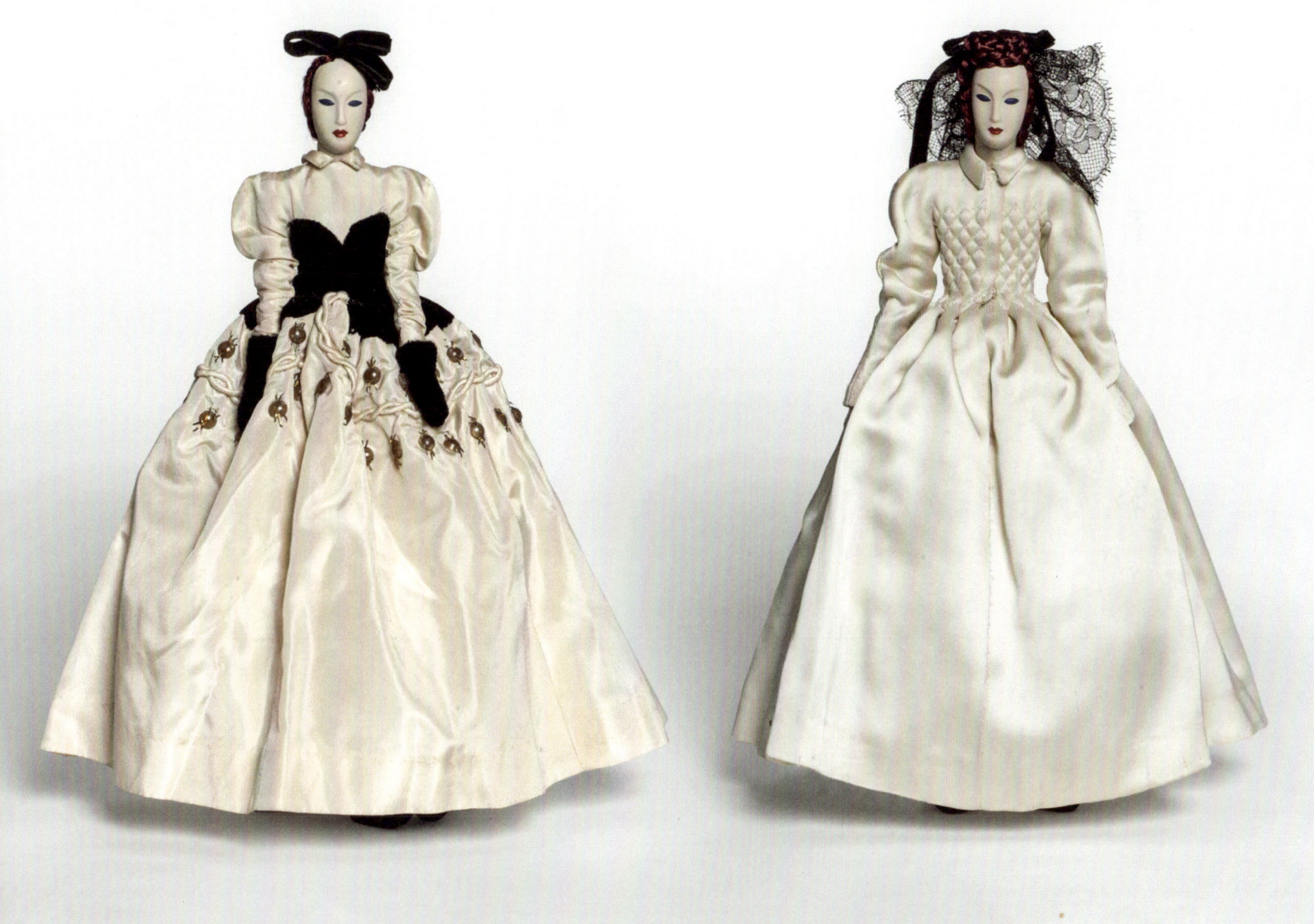

CHARLES MONTAIGNE, **Fashion dolls, 1945.** Musée des Arts Décoratifs, Paris;
Fashion and Textile Collection, gift from Charles Montaigne, 1990.
The *Théâtre de la Mode* was a traveling exhibition created in 1946 by the Chambre syndicale de la couture parisienne.
The dolls were meant to present and promote French savoir-faire in fashion.
The examples pictured here were sold in shops that welcomed the exhibition in the United States.

Jacques Fath
*Evening Gown
Autumn/Winter 1946-1947*

Jacques Fath, the imaginative couturier whose work dominated the period of the French Occupation, borrowed a page from fin-de-siècle fashion when designing this evening gown: the modest bodice that skims the hips, the draping across the midsection, and the slightly flared skirt are reminiscent of an ensemble that might have been worn by a woman traveling on the omnibus or an errand girl in a Parisian scene depicted by Gustave Caillebotte or Jean Béraud. The charm of retro fashion appealed to Fath, as it had to Elsa Schiaparelli in her Autumn/Winter 1939 collection.

This piece reflects the postwar period. The garment is cut sparingly, if cleverly, in the manner that was characteristic during times of textile shortages (the top and bottom are cut from two different fabrics, and the drape is somewhat insubstantial). Christian Dior would make a clean sweep of prewar and wartime silhouettes when he created his New Look in the 1950s.

E.P.-P.

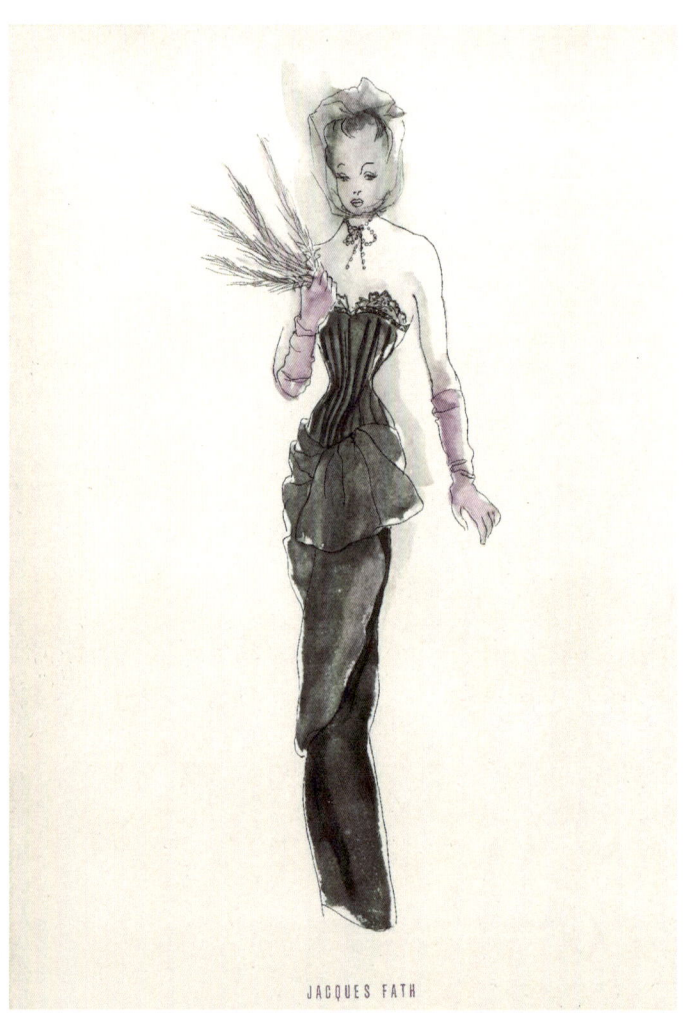

Drawing published in *L'art et la mode*, no. 2712, 1946, page 44.

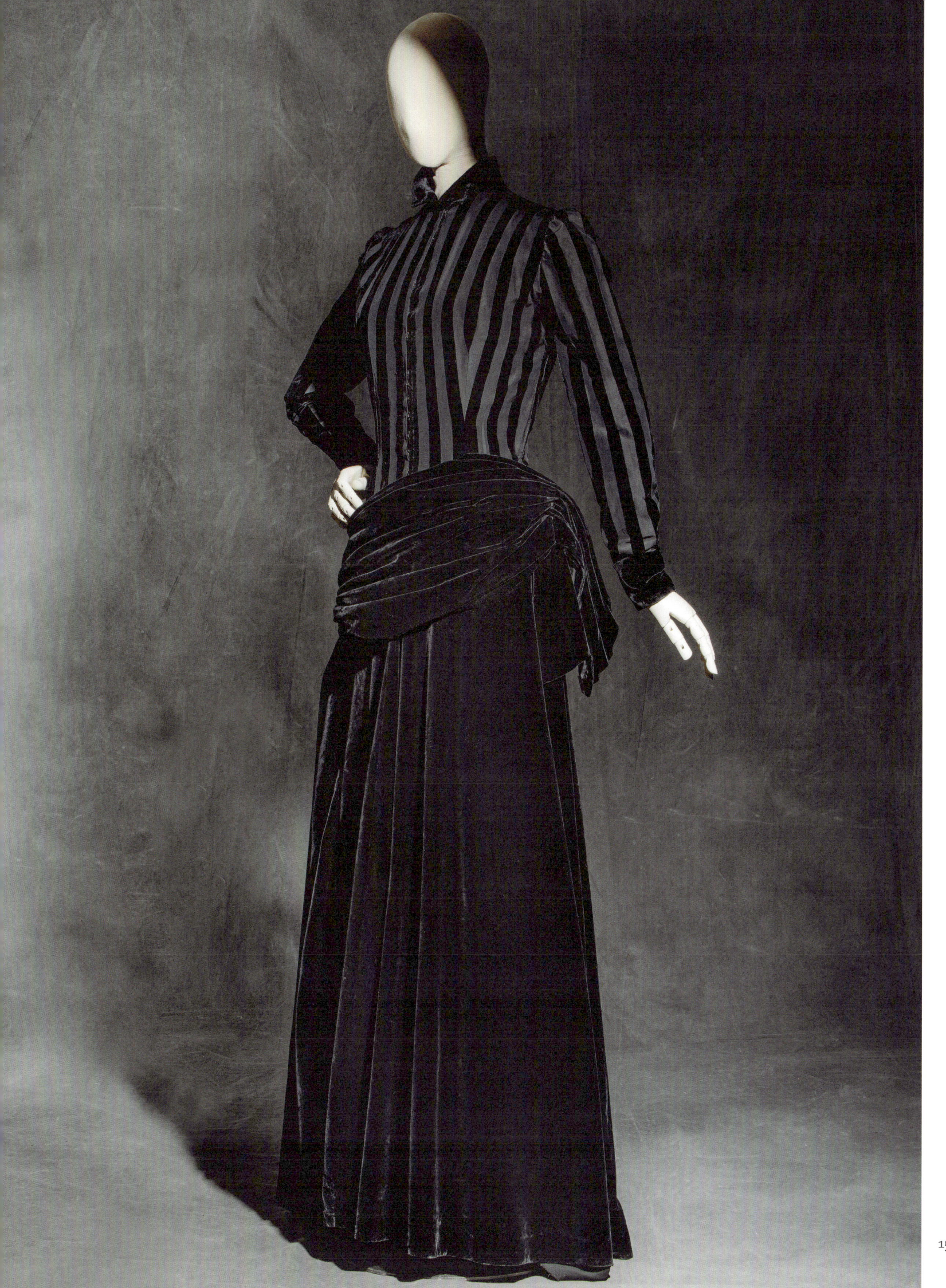

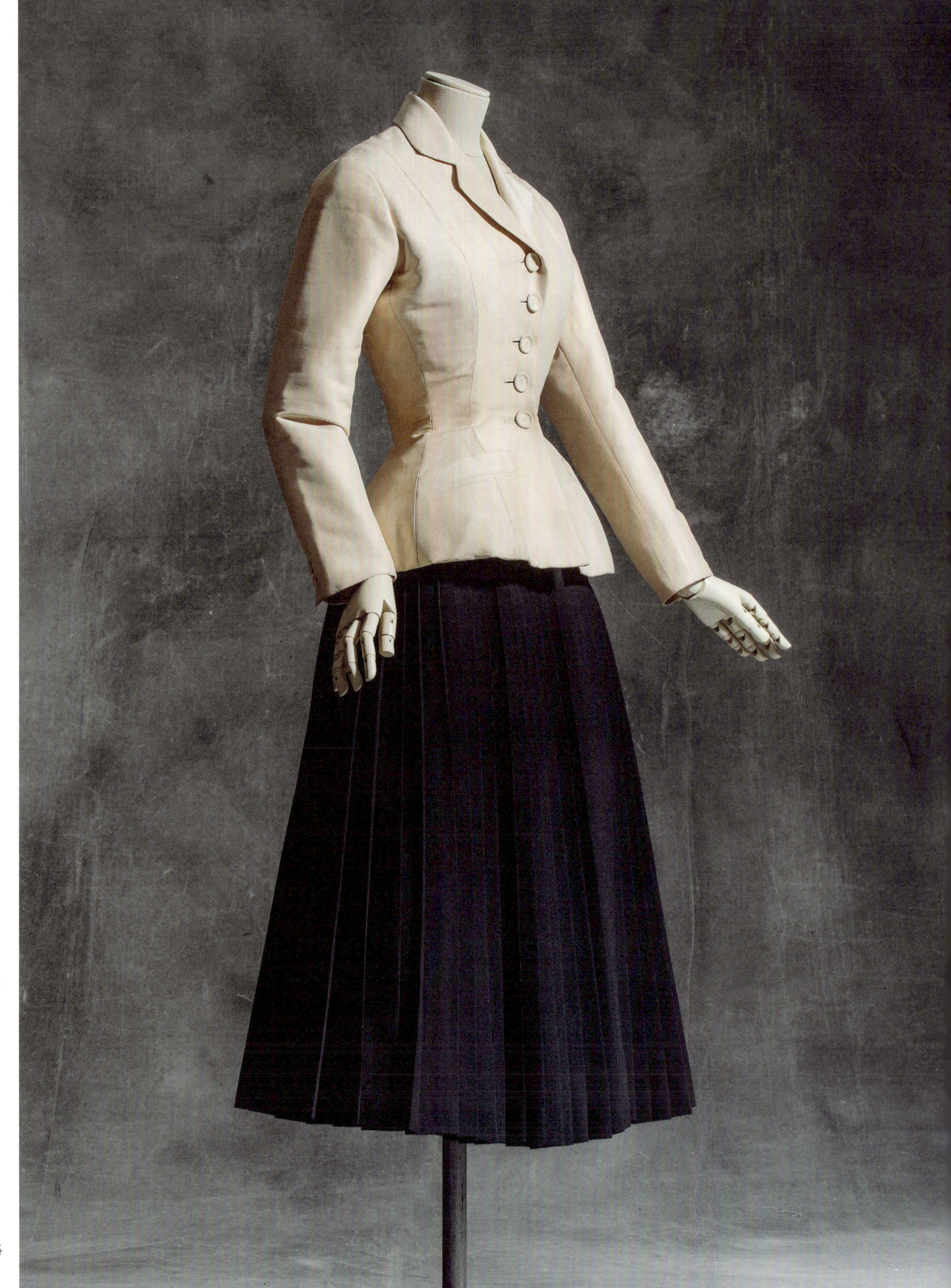

Christian Dior
Bar *Suit, Spring/Summer 1947*

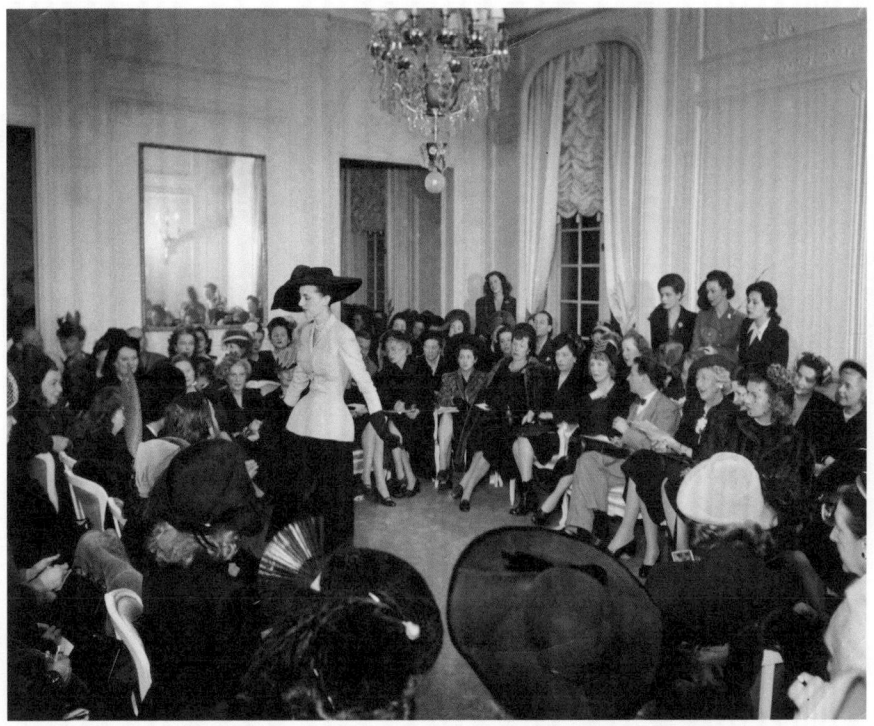

On February 12, 1947, the newly established House of Dior held its inaugural show at 30, avenue Montaigne. The collection introduced the "8" and "Corolle" styles that were immediately renamed the "New Look," an expression coined by Carmel Snow, editor of *Harper's Bazaar*: "Your dresses have such a New Look!" The "Bar" suit, emblematic of Dior's collection, was a complete departure from the styles worn during the Occupation. "We were just emerging from a period of war, of uniforms and of boxy-shaped women-soldiers. I designed flower-women with rounded shoulders, full bosoms, hand-span waists and skirts as wide as corollas," recalled the great couturier, who had previously worked in the houses of Robert Piguet and Lucien Lelong.

In the suit shown here, there are no shoulder pads, the bustline is rounded but pronounced (created with stiff interfacing), the waist is cinched, the hips are padded, and the flared pleated skirt's hemline has dropped 30 cm (9 inches) from the floor. The Bar suit required 3.75 meters (4 yards) of shantung, 3 meters (3 ¼ yards) of lining, 1.50 meters (1 ⅔ yards) of interfacing, 1.50 meters (1 ⅔ yards) of cotton canvas, 5 buttons, and most notably 5.50 meters (5 ½ yards) of wool that was 1.40 (1½ yards) meters wide — an excess of fabric that was a reaction to the frugality imposed by wartime shortages. The success of the New Look reinvigorated the entire French luxury industry and restored Paris's place as the world capital of fashion.
E.P.-P.

PAT ENGLISH, Modeling the "Bar" suit in the salon at 30, avenue Montaigne. Photograph. Christian Dior Archives.

Christian Dior
Adélaïde *Evening Ensemble*
Spring/Summer 1948

The "Adélaïde" ensemble exemplifies Christian Dior's concept of glamour — dresses that become fuller and more dramatic over the course of the day and reach their full span by the evening. The skirt of this dress flares out from the waistline into innumerable tulle folds that recall the elliptical crinolines of the Second Empire. The coat, made of shimmering duchesse satin, with three-quarter-length pagoda sleeves and a firm underlining that sustains the wide folds, is reminiscent of the overdresses worn with the *robes à la française* during the eighteenth century. The name of this ensemble refers perhaps to Marie Adélaïde, the fourth daughter of Louis XV. The historical inspiration, the astonishing amount of fabric, and the weight of this layered creation — resembling a dancer's tutu — offer a perfect synthesis of Dior's work.

"Wearing high heels, women had recovered their lively step, and their swaying stride that was accentuated by the fullness of their dresses," recalled Dior in his 1956 autobiography, *Christian Dior et moi*.

E.P.-P.

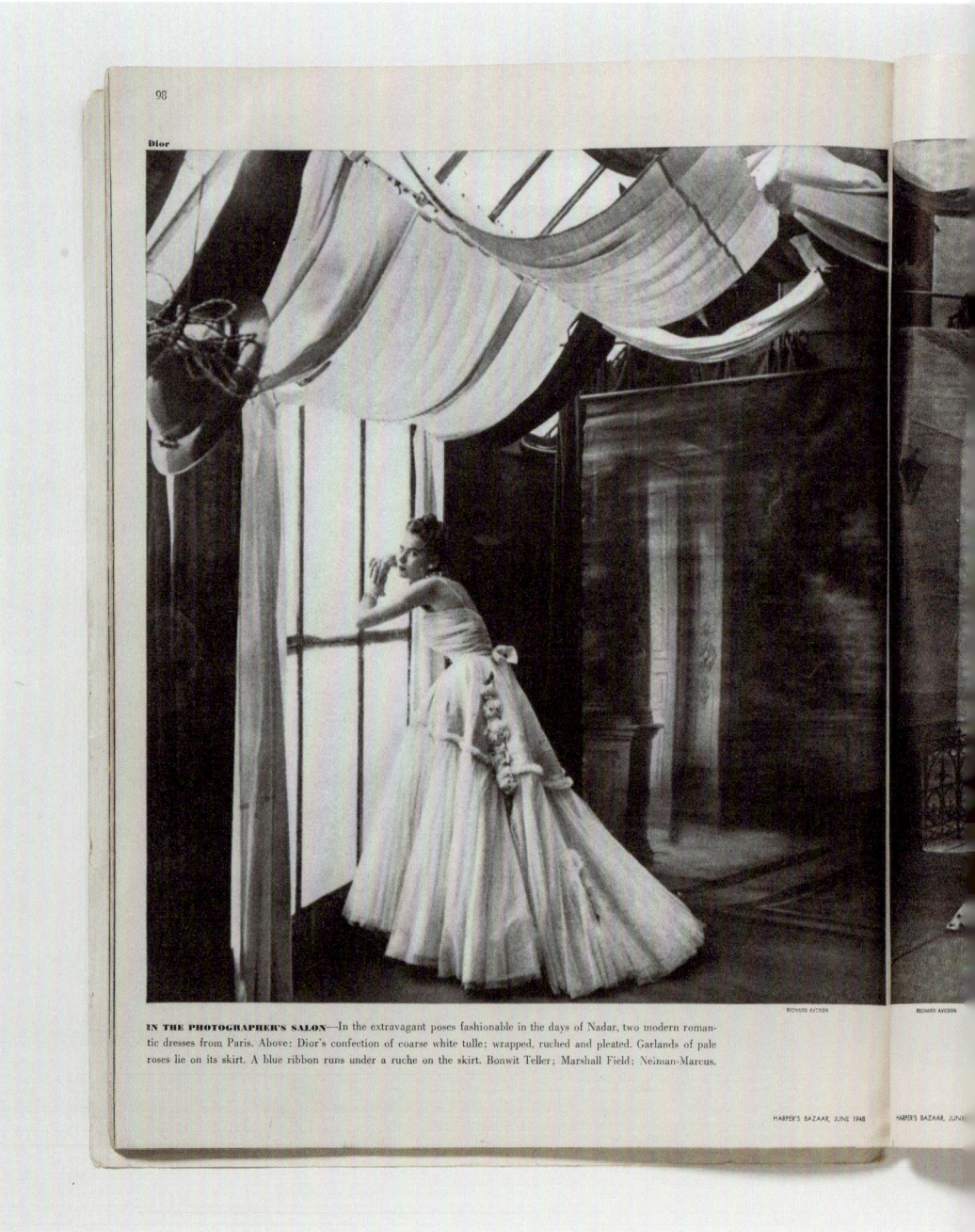

RICHARD AVEDON, Photograph published in *Harper's Bazaar*, June 1948, page 98.
Musée des Arts Décoratifs, Paris; The Documentation Center.

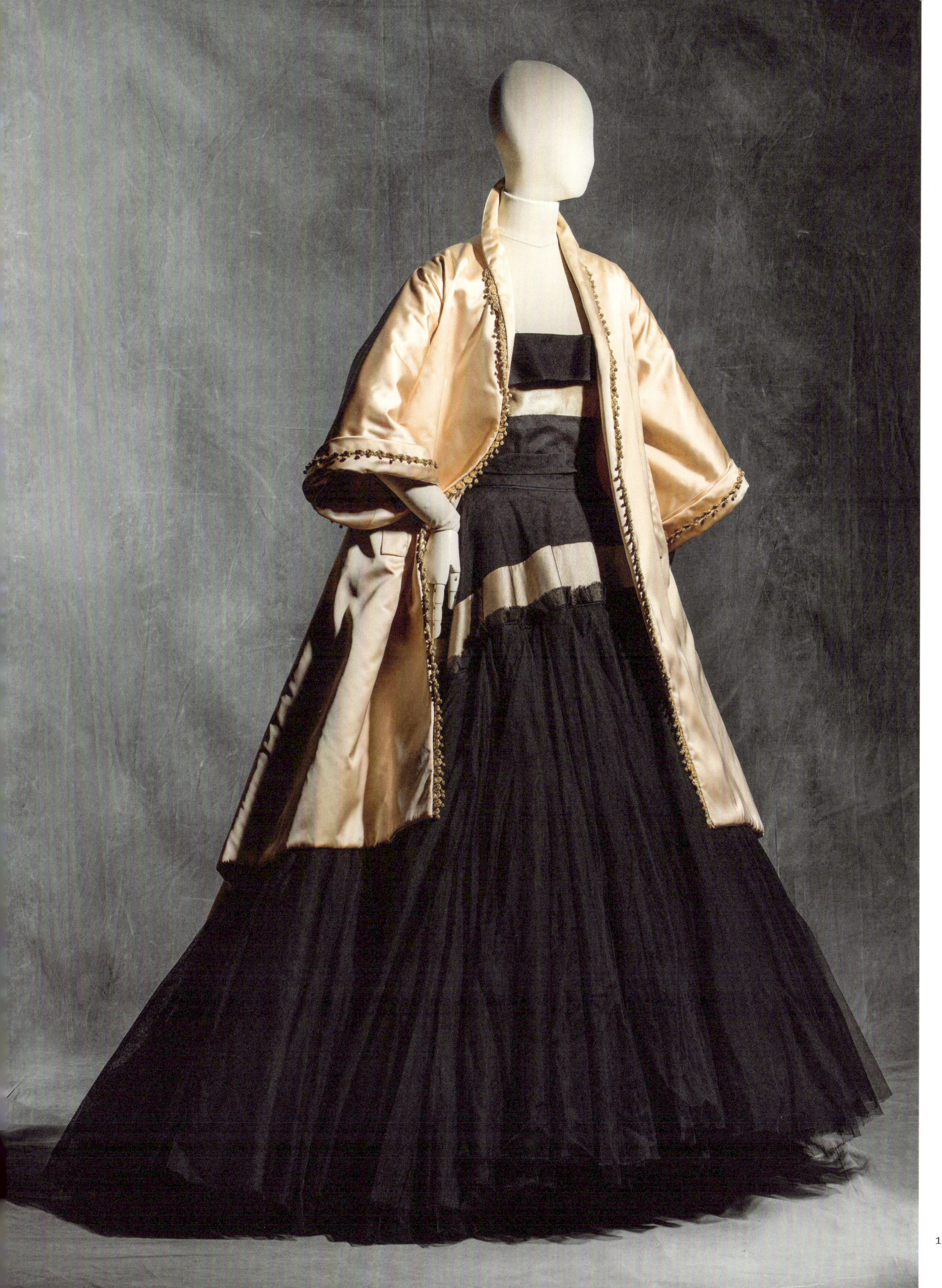

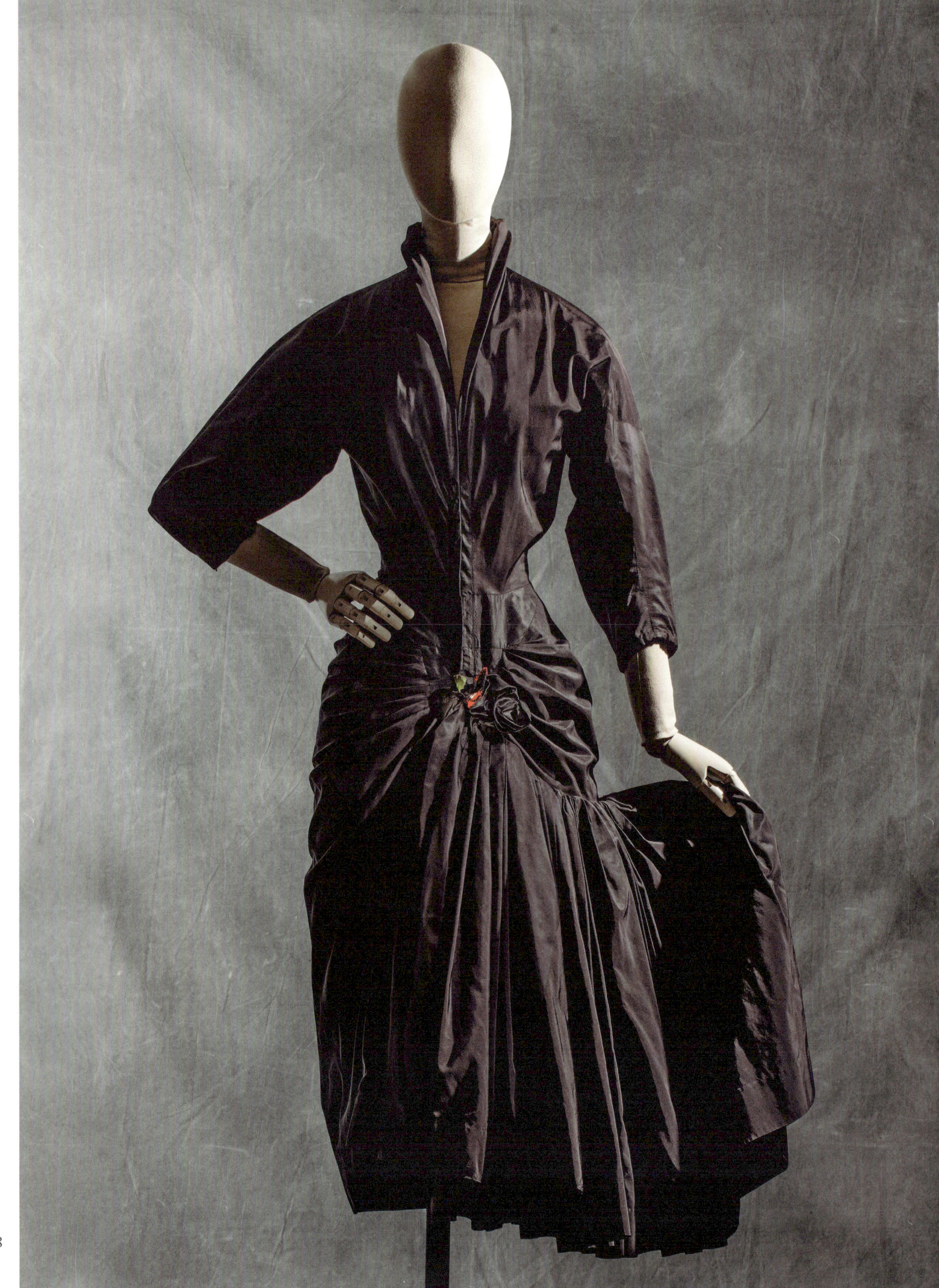

Grès
Day Dress
Autumn/Winter 1948-1949

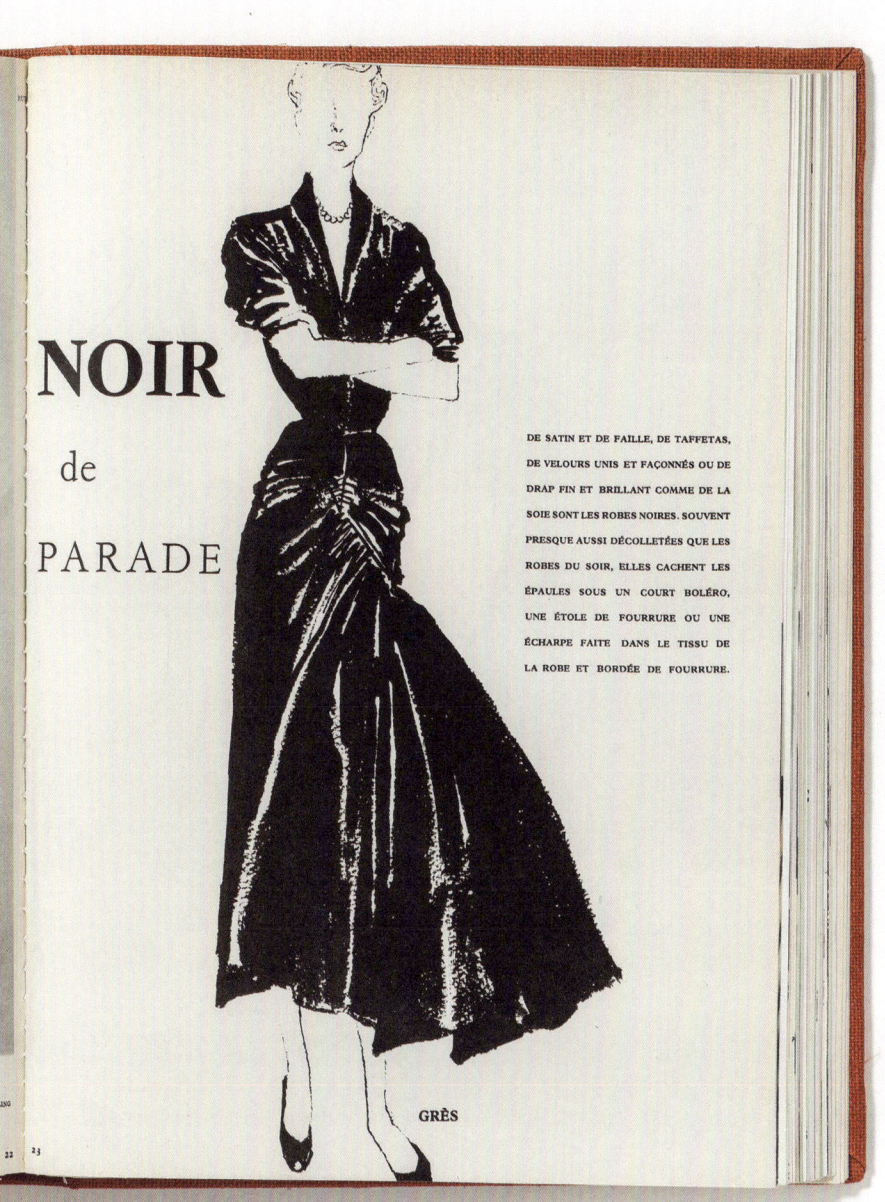

The distinctive luster and weight of gros de Tours silk inspired Madame Grès to create the fashion silhouette she had been envisioning since the 1930s. The lightweight dress does not have a fitted bodice or an underskirt, but its proportions are similar to those of the New Look: the high collar and the structure of the shoulders create a fluid line; the small waist and curve of the hips were emphasized by the draped fabric that flared dramatically below the hipline. This effect could not have been realized in jersey, yet another illustration of Dior's influence: the right fabric, in this case one similar to taffeta, determines the outcome.

This design by Madame Grès was part of a codified wardrobe that required a late-afternoon dress (between a day dress and a cocktail dress, something a woman might wear to a gallery opening): short, with a shirtwaist top, but still dressy, constructed with an asymmetric drape that flattered the body. It was the perfect dress for contemporary Parisian women. Fashionable New Yorkers could buy the garment at the Bergdorf Goodman department store.
E.P.P.

BERNARD BLOSSAC, Drawing published in *Jardin des modes*, November 1948, page 23.
Musée des Arts Décoratifs, Paris; The Documentation Center.

Christian Dior
May *Evening Gown, Spring/Summer 1953*

The "May" evening gown is composed of a bustier and a voluminous skirt created by multiple layers of tulle, a technique cherished by Christian Dior. The draped organza neckerchief is reminiscent of an eighteenth-century *fichu menteur*, or buffon. Created by Rébé, the embroidered motifs emphasize the small waist and the flare of the skirt, appearing to flow down the length of the dress and leaving behind a trail of wildflowers — dark or light red poppies, mixed with clover and blades of grass.

By its construction and use of decorative effect, the May dress — emblematic of Dior — captures the intentionally anachronistic essence of his "flower-woman." As the designer expressed in an interview at a luncheon hosted by the American Women's Group in Paris on January 10, 1955: "Our romantic evening gowns represent a necessary escape from our civilization. The civilization of our atomic age."

E.P.-P.

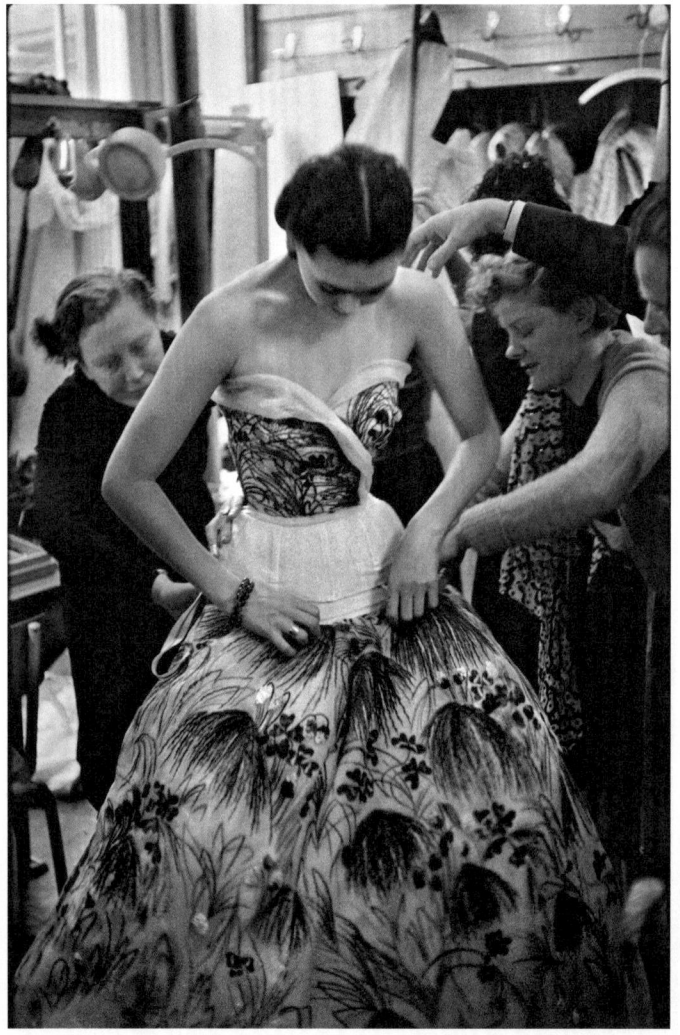

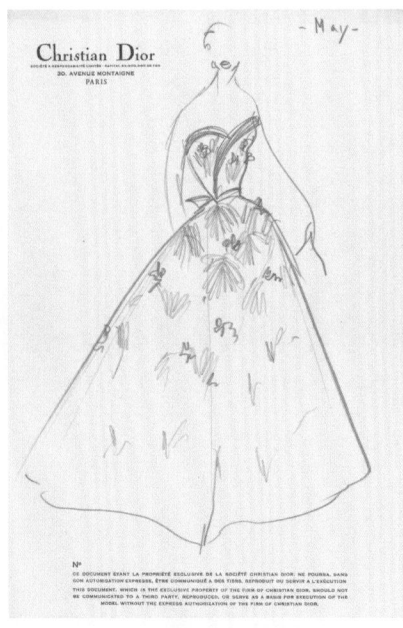

HENRI CARTIER-BRESSON, *Alla during a Fitting of the "May" Dress*, 1953. Photograph. Magnum Archives.
CHRISTIAN DIOR, Sketch for the "May" dress, 1953. Christian Dior Archives.

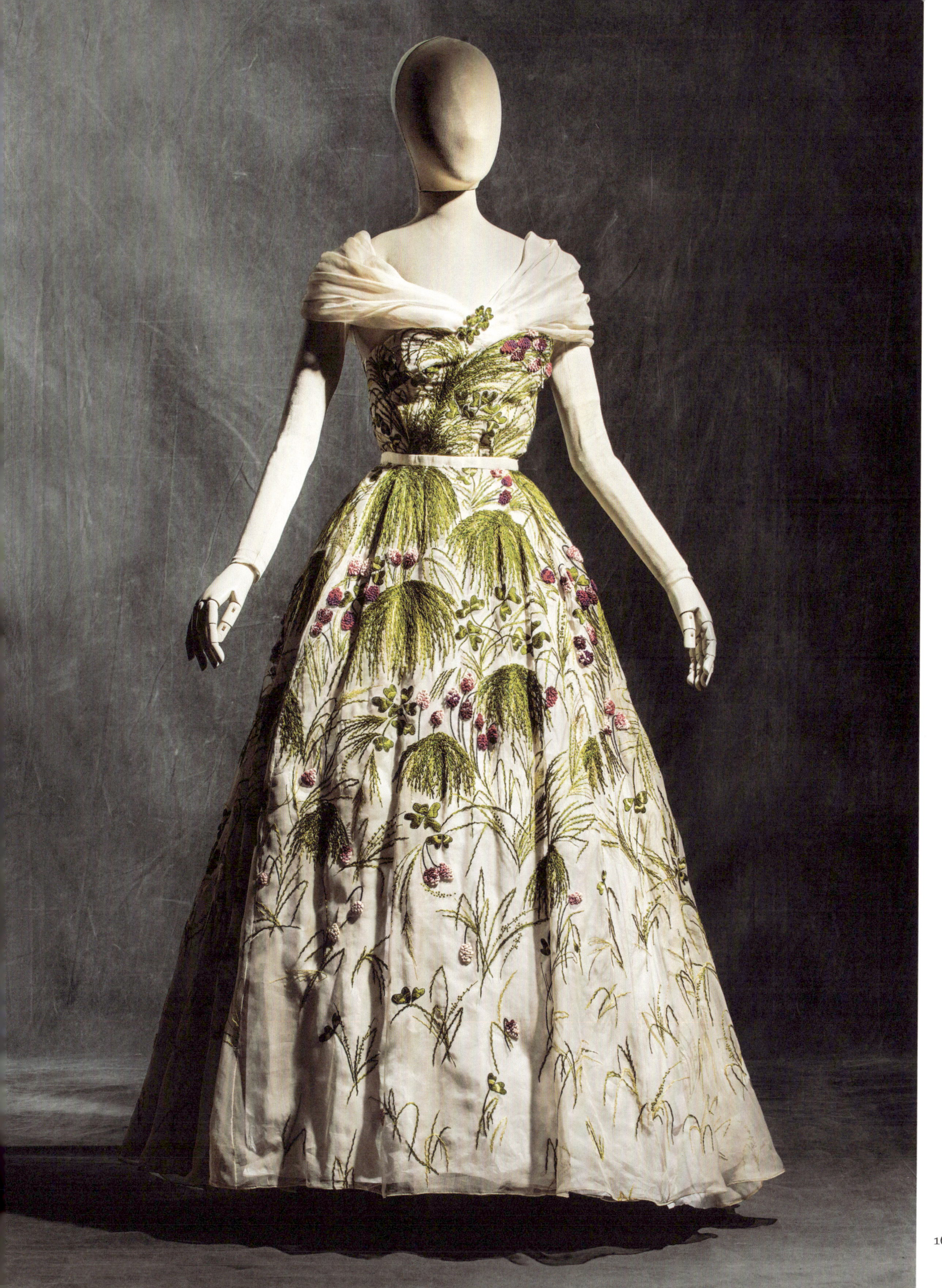

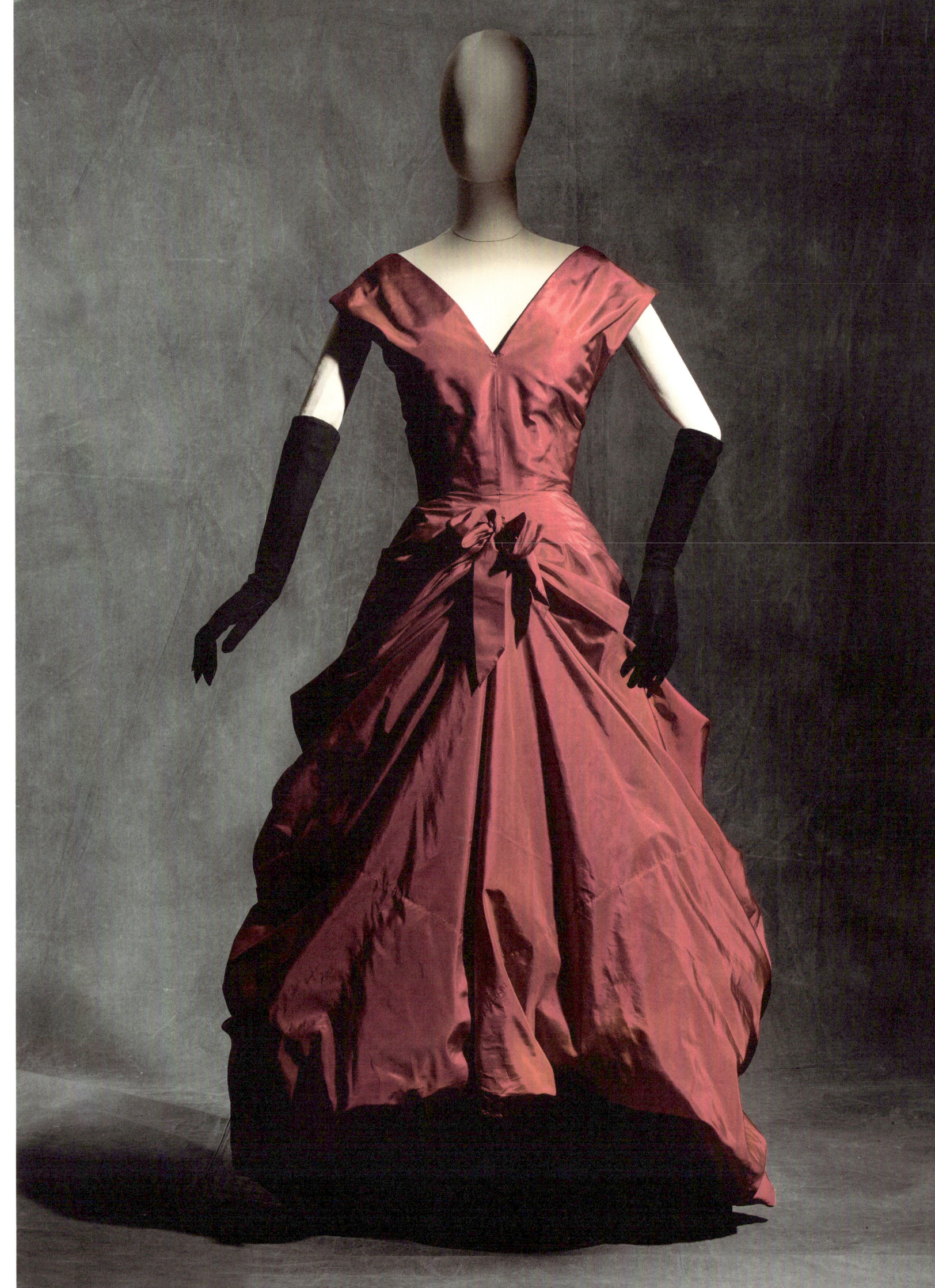

Cristóbal Balenciaga
Evening Gown
Autumn/Winter 1954-1955

The principles of the Cristóbal Balenciaga silhouette are based on fabric, construction, cut, and assembly, forgoing whenever possible the use of supports, bustiers, layering, or reinforcements. Known for his sculptural use of volume, Balenciaga created astonishing shapes by gathering and manipulating fabric and astutely fastening it in place with invisible ties. In this instance, a beautiful taffeta is molded into a billowing bubble skirt with a flounced train.

The symmetrical cut and economy of sewing of this monochromatic, majestic evening gown allow it to sway; barely skimming the body, the dress rests on the woman's shoulders. The simplicity and lightness of this design would be reprised by all of Balenciaga's disciples—Hubert de Givenchy, André Courrèges, and Emanuel Ungaro—who followed the master's credo: "A good couturier must be an architect for design, a sculptor for shape, a painter for color, a musician for harmony and a philosopher for temperance" (from *Hommage à Balenciaga,* 1985).
E.P.-P.

Charles James
Swan *Evening Gown* Autumn/Winter 1955-1956

The Anglo-American couturier Charles James lived and worked mainly in New York. His oeuvre is significant in the history of French haute couture because he was an important fashion pioneer and trendsetter. Yet he always gave the impression of being an isolated designer who struggled financially throughout his life. As quoted in Christian Dior's 1956 autobiography, he stated: "Couture, as it is still viewed in Paris, no longer really exists in America, where talented designers, such as Mainbocher, Valentine, Charles James and a few others, barely manage to survive."

The complex architecture of this design represents the apotheosis of an evening gown. The couturier achieved the effect through the use of different fabrics that were stiffened with backing, whalebone, and topstitching. He began by building a frame that extended from the bustline to the bottom of the skirt. It was then covered with layers of tulle and pleated chiffon that either spread outward in a tight drape or fell more freely in garlands or flared folds. For this particular dress, James used techniques favored by both Dior and Balenciaga, requiring significant layering and constructed volumes. The exaggerated dimensions were reminiscent of the dresses of the Belle Époque that emphasized the curves of a woman's body.
E.P.-P.

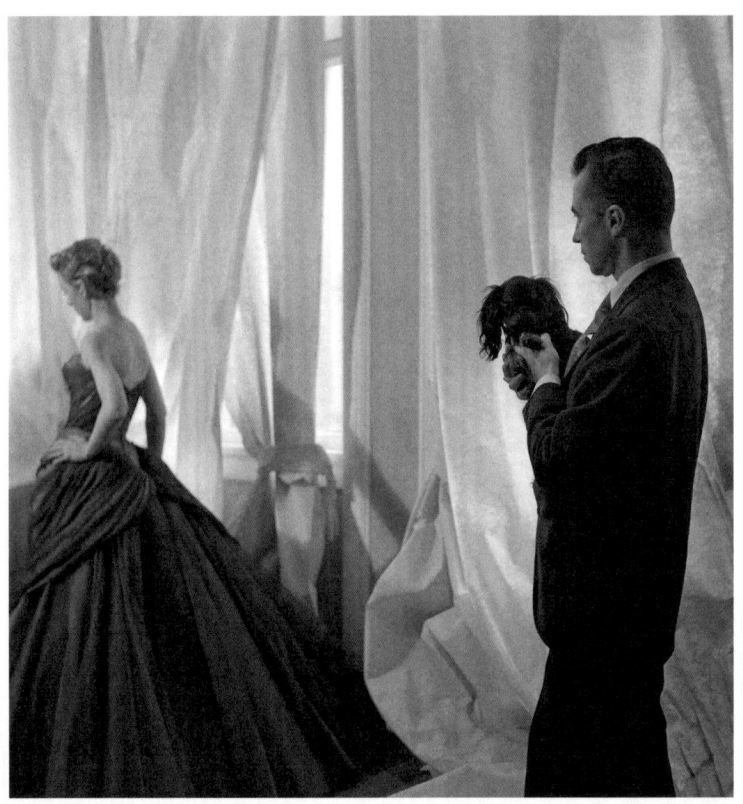

CECIL BEATON, *Charles James and One of His Models*, 1955. Photograph.
The Cecil Beaton Studio Archive at Sotheby's.

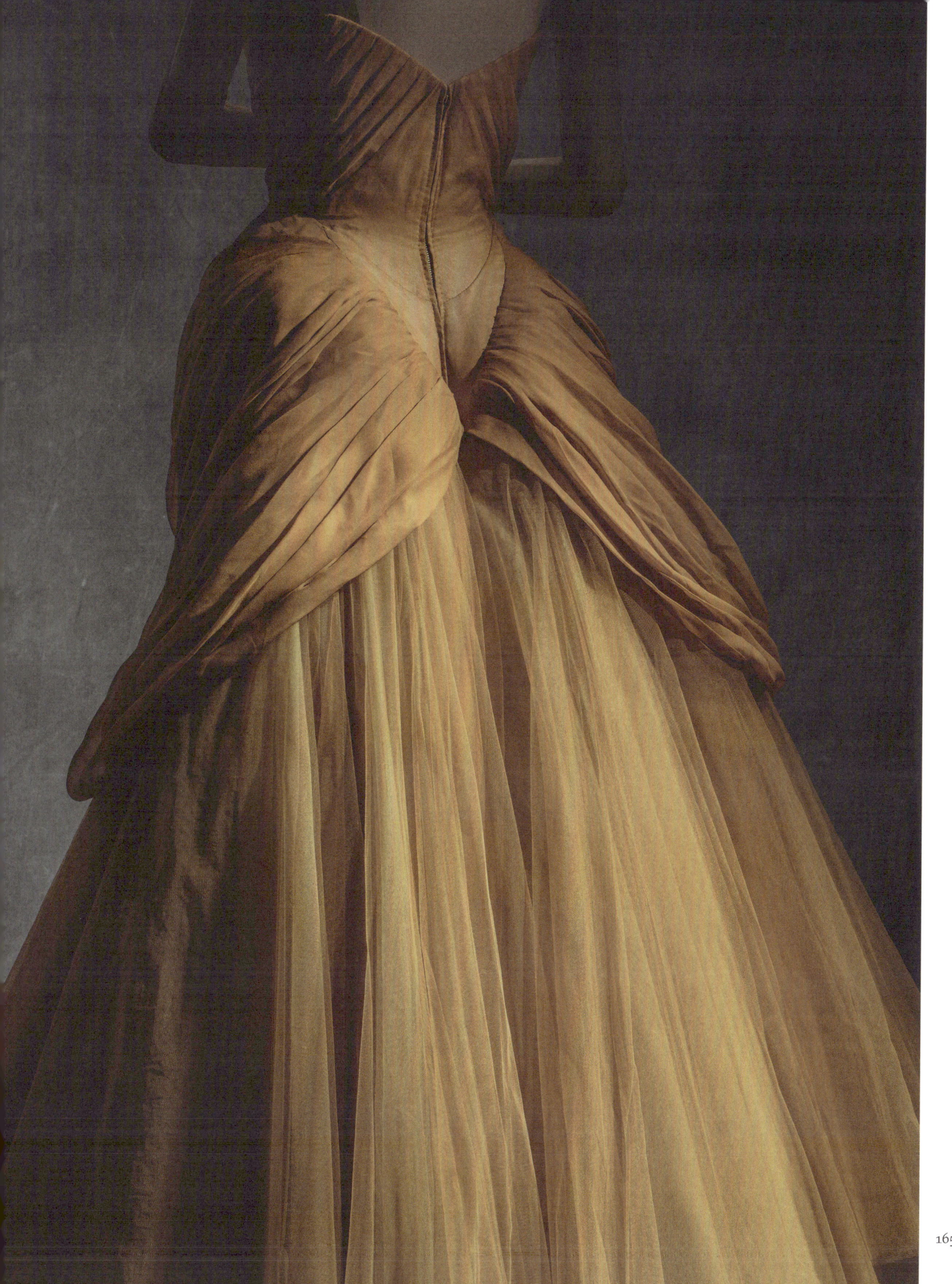

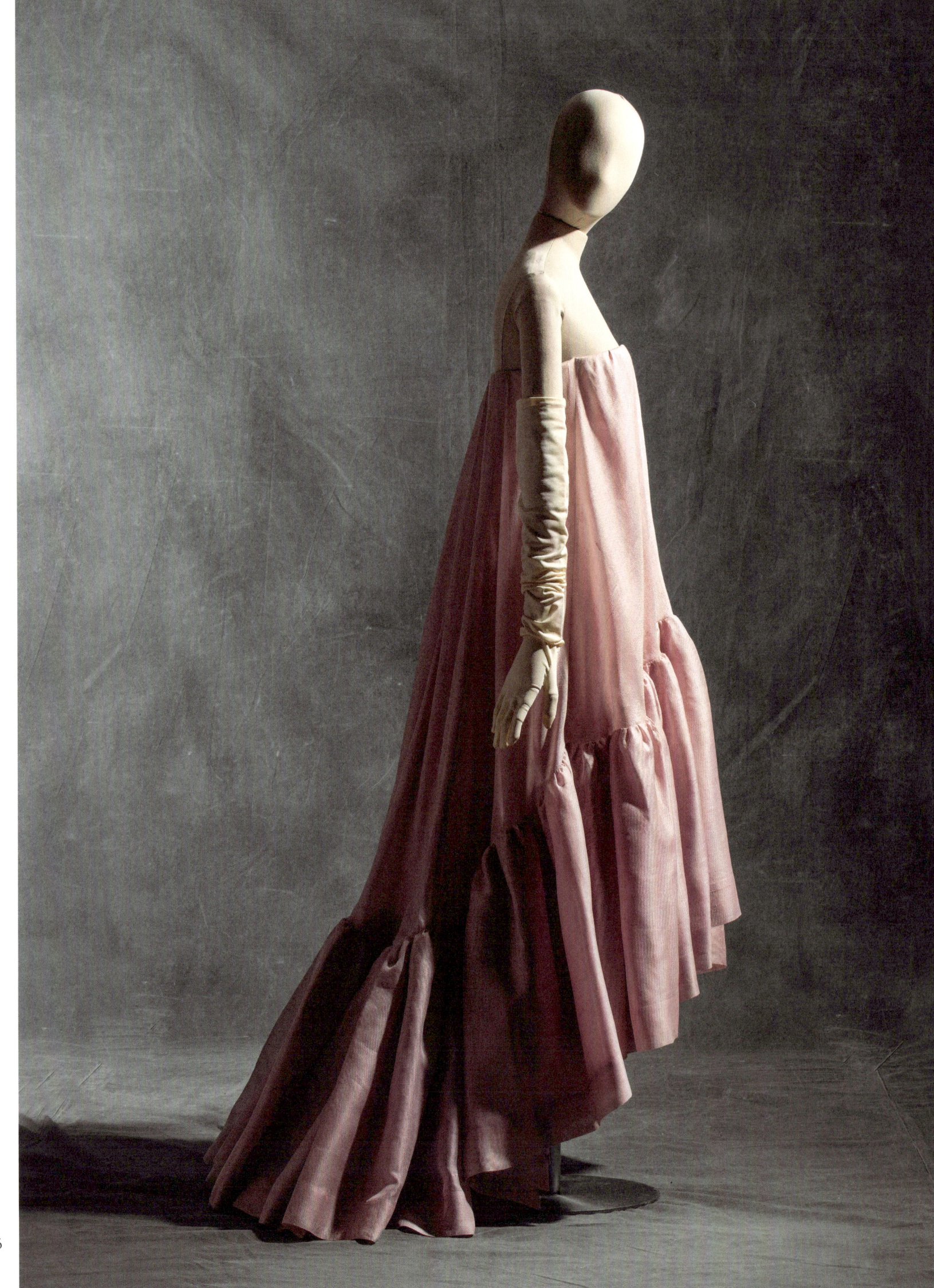

Cristóbal Balenciaga
Strapless Evening Gown, Spring/Summer 1958

Short in the front and long in the back, this dress is an example of the "peacock style *(Paon)*, one of the newest fashions in eveningwear," as described by *Vogue* in May 1958. For this design, Balenciaga reprised the baby-doll dress and added a train. The bustier is entirely covered by a flowing trapeze-shaped dress, with a wide flounce at the bottom. The *organ-laine* fabric, similar in weight to Abraham gazar — a favorite of Balenciaga — has the capacity to maintain the desired volume of this design. The simplified straight cut, similar to the dresses of little girls or dolls, reveals an interest in youth and childhood as sources of inspiration.

Indeed, Balenciaga's interest in this genre would show up during the next decade in the designs of André Courrèges and Emanuel Ungaro, whose minidresses and trapeze-shaped dresses seduced the baby boomer generation. Still, this particular dress was intended for a woman, for the sheer fabric leads us to assume the presence of a corseted undergarment.
E.P.-P.

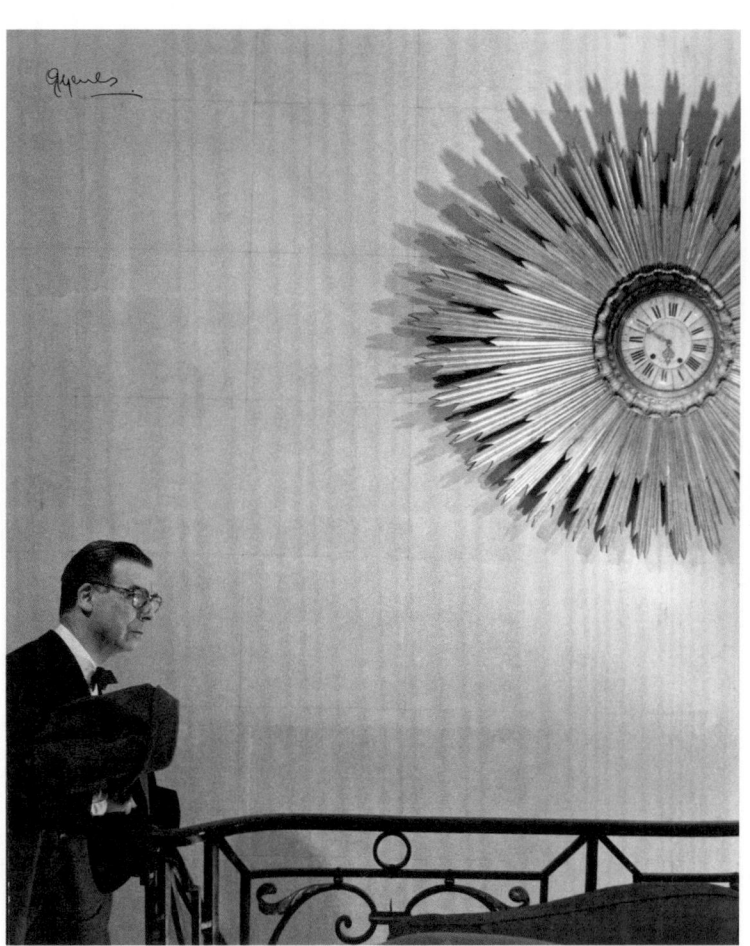

JUAN GYENES, *Cristóbal Balenciaga in His Boutique at 10, avenue George V, in Paris*, November 13, 1959.
Photograph. Biblioteca Nacional, Madrid

Cristóbal Balenciaga
*Evening Ensemble
Autumn/Winter 1961-1962*

This ensemble illustrates Balenciaga's ongoing interest in volume. The dress is shaped like a multilevel rocket ship. The accompanying bolero covers the bodice and reinforces the bubble effect of the skirt, creating an impression of stacked lanterns. This lightweight construction is feasible because of the unique texture of the lace by Marescot (a manufacturer that specializes in Calais lace). This particular *bulle* (bubble) lace is made of synthetic tulle with appliqués of matching ruched horsehair ribbon. The bubble shapes devised by Balenciaga do not correspond to the curves of a woman's body (the narrowing at the knees is the same as that of the waistline), giving the silhouette an abstract and futuristic look.

    The effect of this design relies on the quality of the fabric and is a reminder that, during the early 1960s, the materials that were essential to haute couture were still being made in France by highly specialized companies. Famous manufacturers throughout France saw their own designs and creations come to life on the works of Parisian couturiers: lace and wool fabric from the north, silks from Lyon, and printed fabrics from Alsace.
E.P.-P.

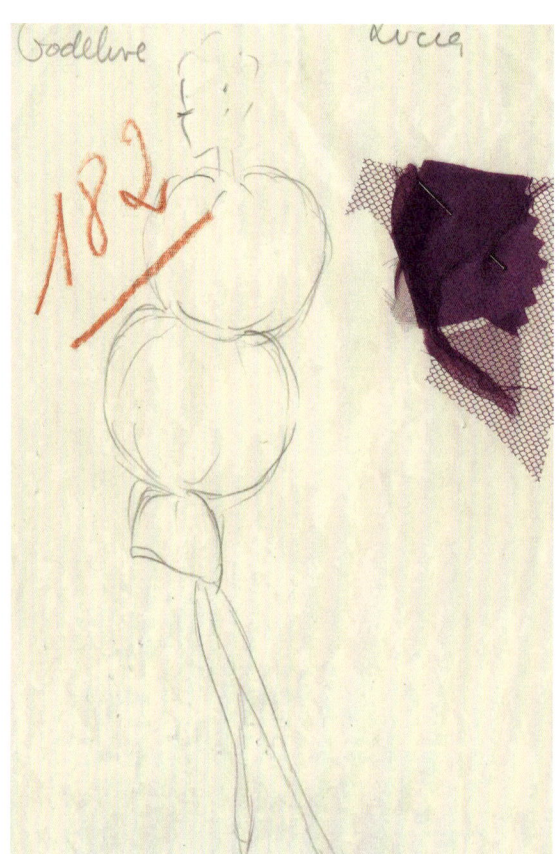

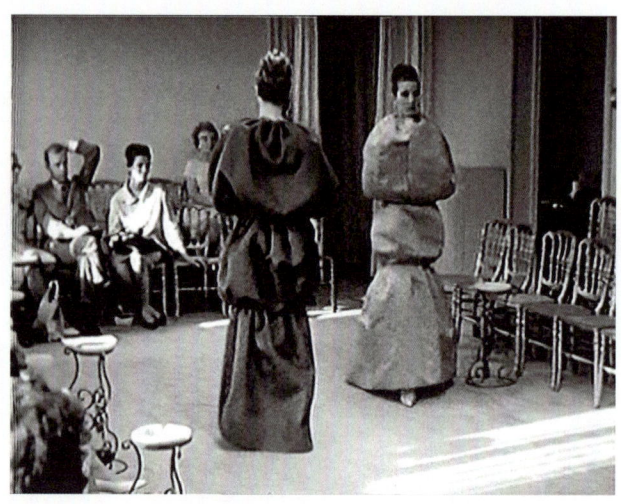

CRISTÓBAL BALENCIAGA, Sketch for the Autumn/Winter 1961-1962 collection. Balenciaga Archive, Paris.
TOM KUBLIN, Screen shot of a fashion show, 1961. Balenciaga Archive, Paris.
PP. 170-171 — Screen shot of an advertisement by Tom Kublin, Balenciaga fashion show, Spring/Summer 1966. Balenciaga Archive, Paris.

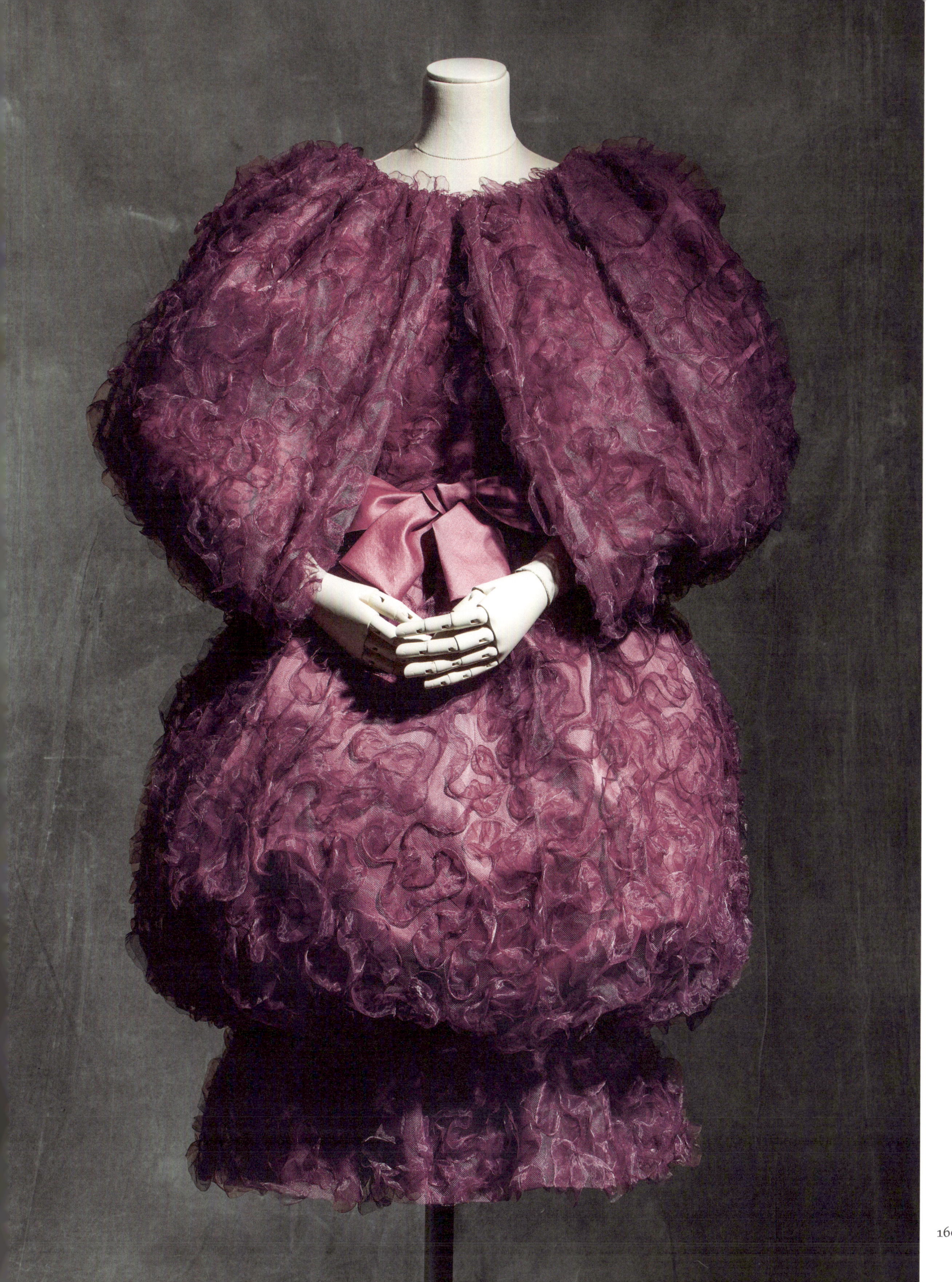

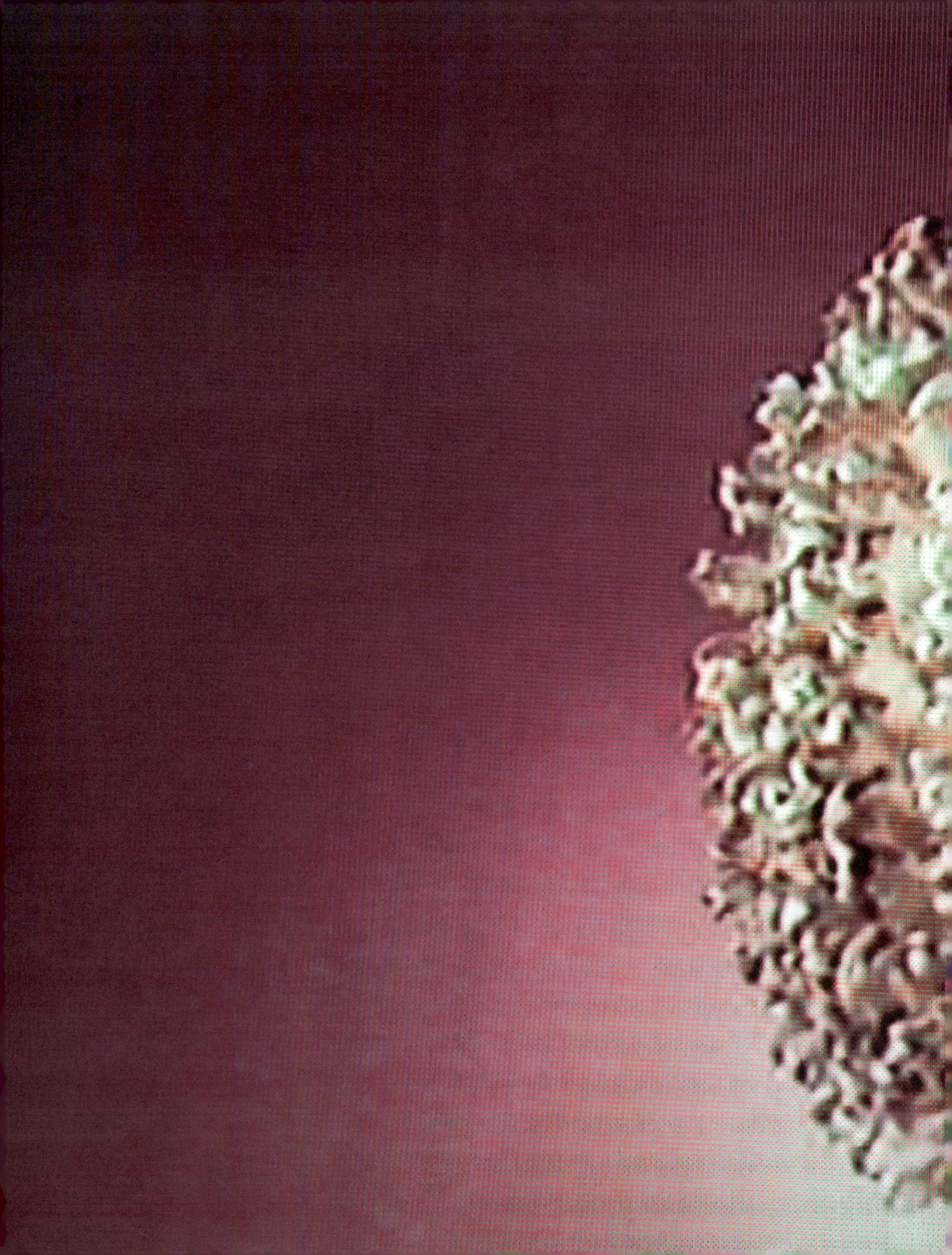

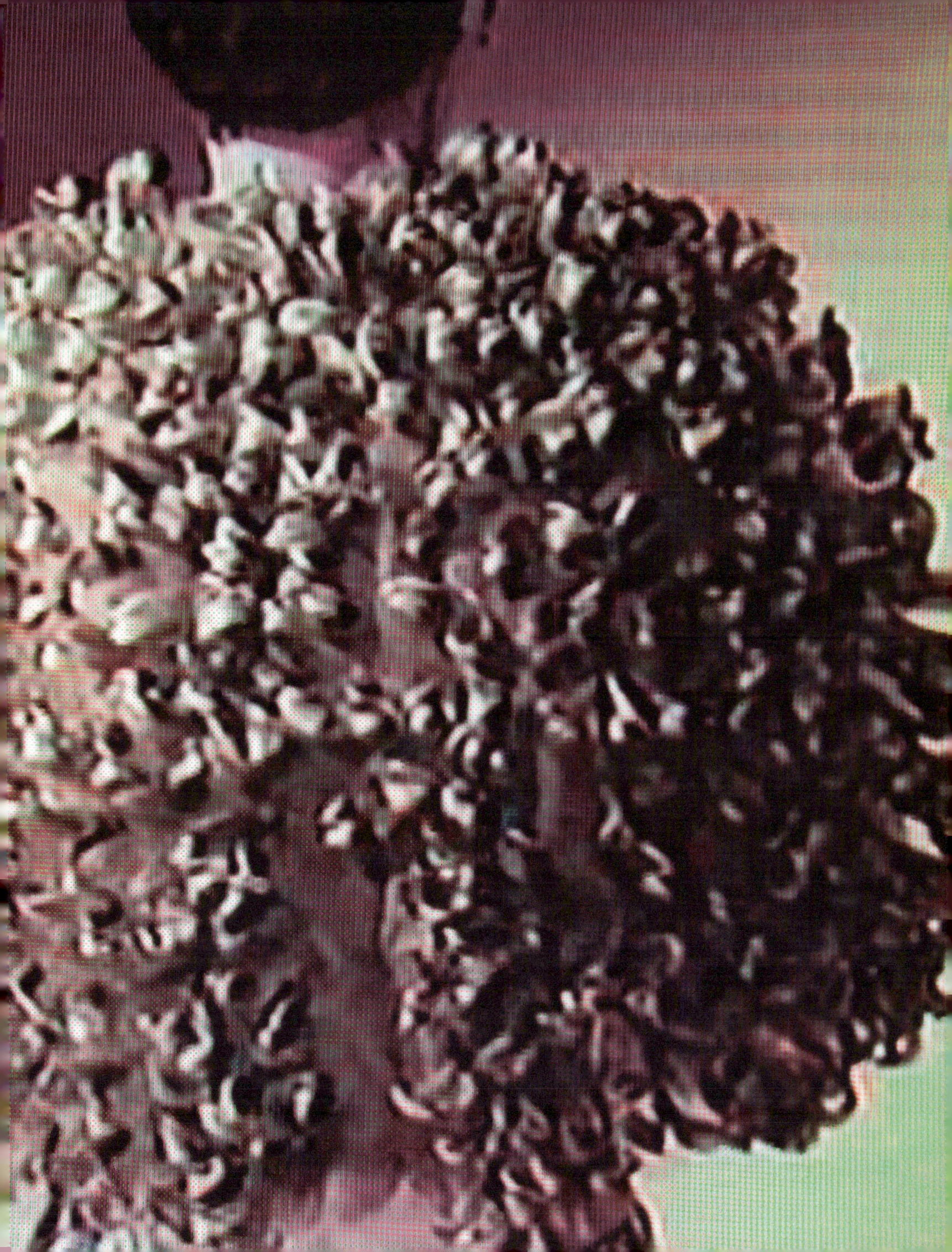

André Courrèges
Pant Suit, Spring/Summer 1965

"Courrèges, there's never been anything like it," declared *Elle* magazine on March 4, 1965. Indeed, the designer's 1965 Spring/Summer collection upended the modern woman's entire wardrobe. The "Courrèges bomb" marked the line between before and after in fashion history. Starting out with the perfect mix of existing formal elements, André Courrèges promptly began to reconsider the construction, decor, function, setting, and production of couture.

As Courrèges saw it, the only viable ornamentation was the embellished seam. The cut of his clothes allowed the body to move freely, giving movement an almost gymnastic quality. Pants and minidresses — worn for all occasions — are the main elements of this collection, along with the color white, which extends to the couturier's all-white studio at 40, rue François Ier.

Beyond the stylistic considerations, André Courrèges addressed the business of couture with the tools of industrial design and marketing. He introduced three lines at three different price points: Prototype (haute couture), Couture future (ready-to-wear), and Hyperbole (mass market). This creation from his Prototype line is a radical departure from couture collections of the past.
E.P.-P.

PP. 174-175 — PETER KNAPP, Photograph for Courrèges, 1965.
Musée des Arts Décoratifs, Paris; Advertisement Collection, gift of Peter Knapp, 2008.

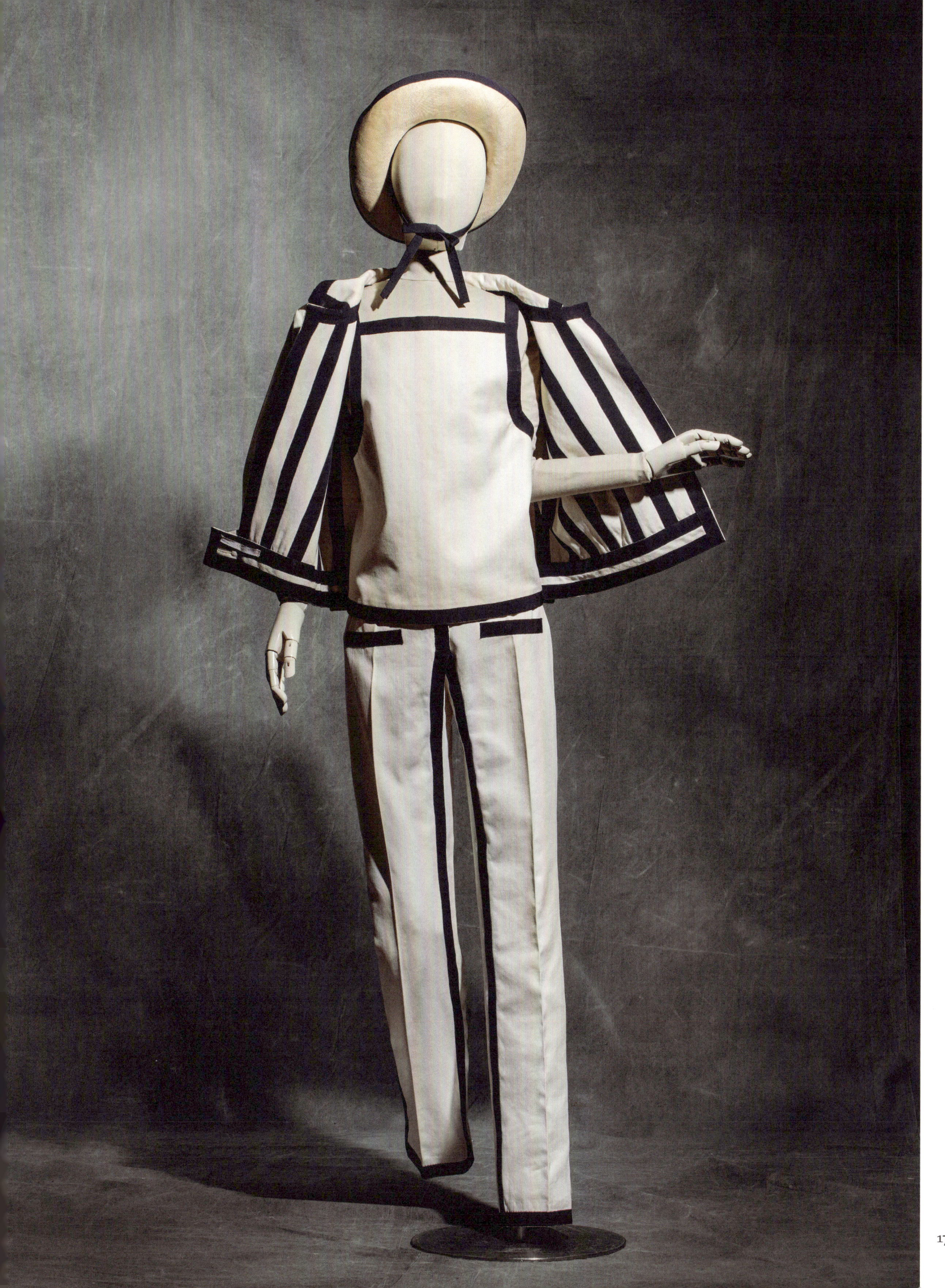

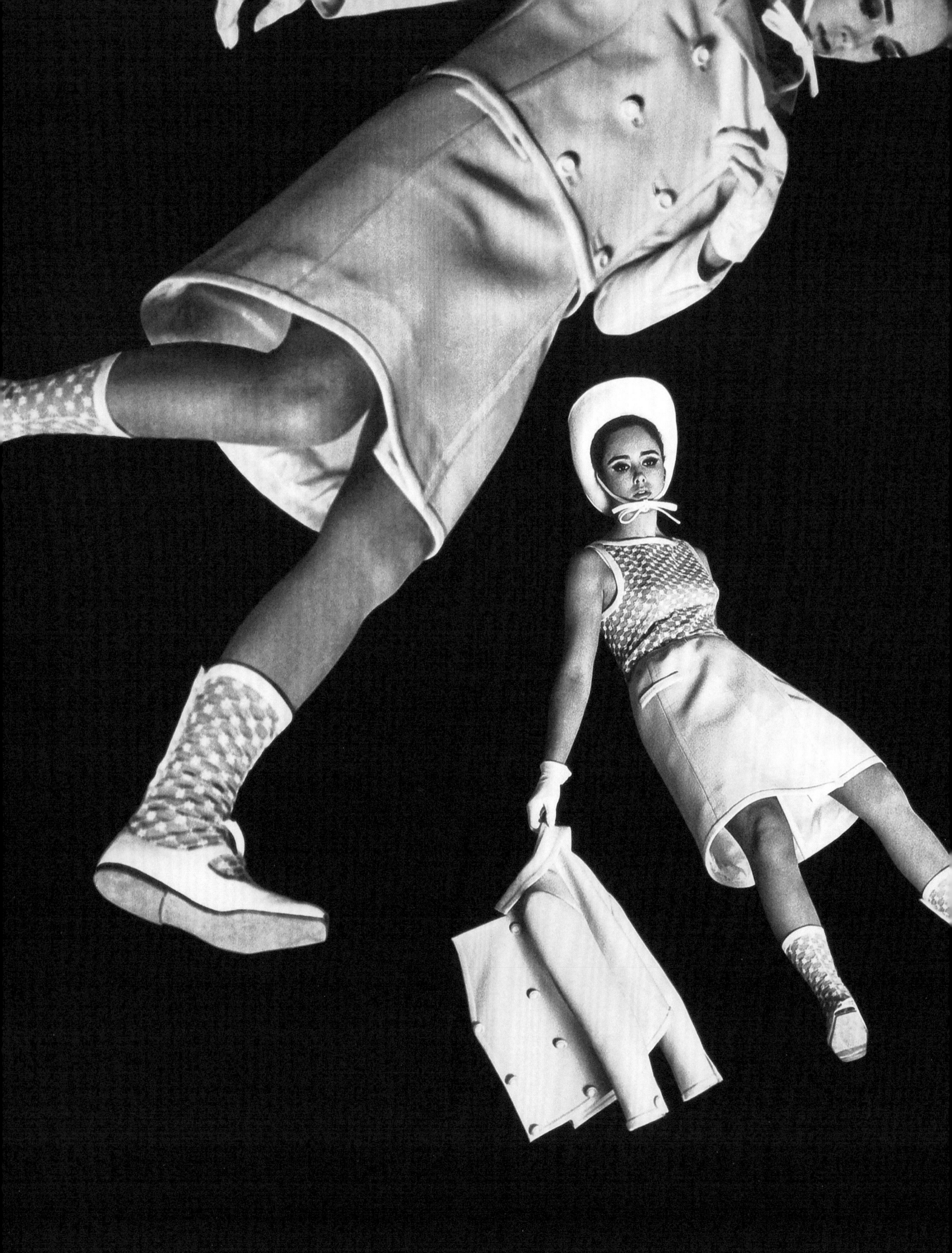

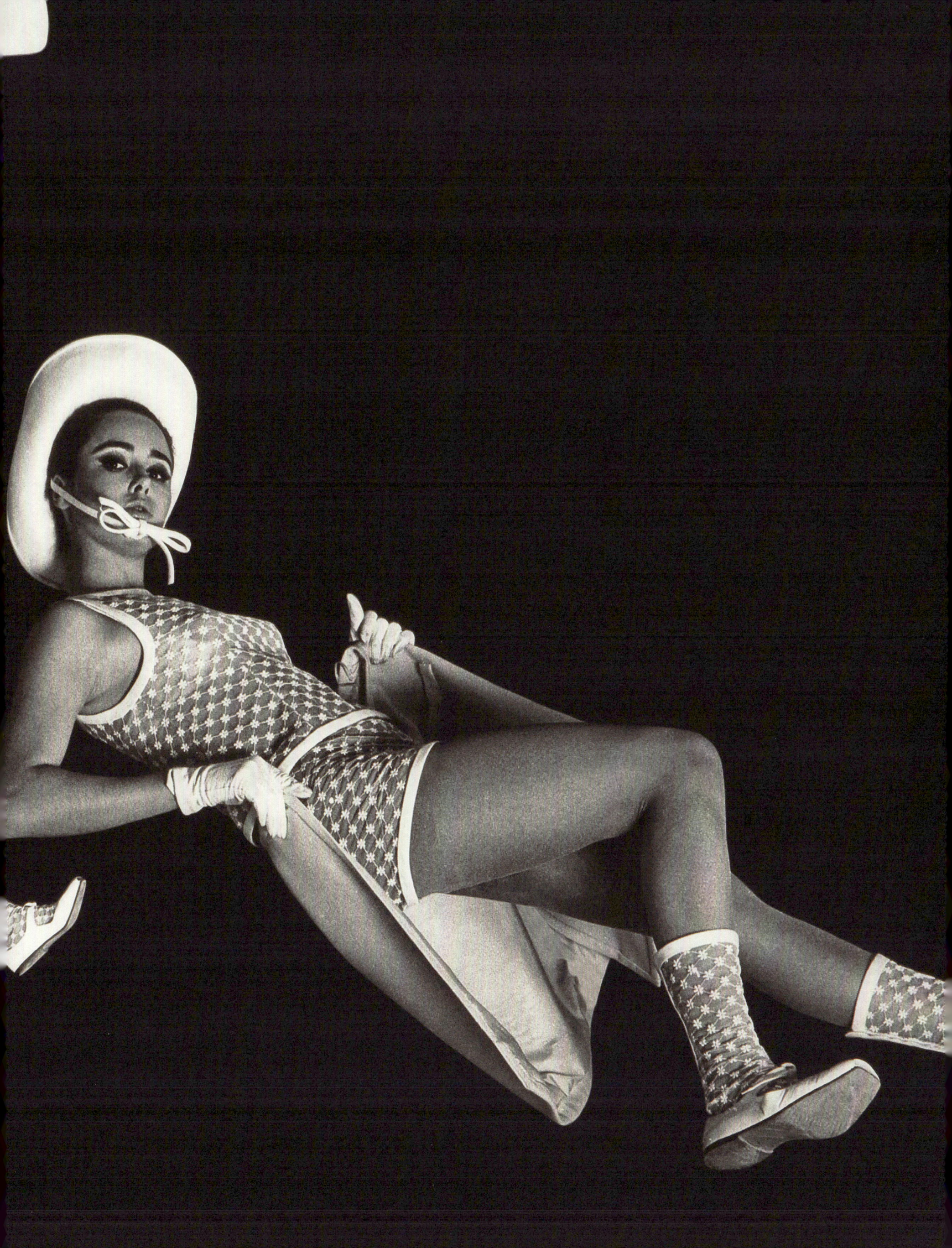

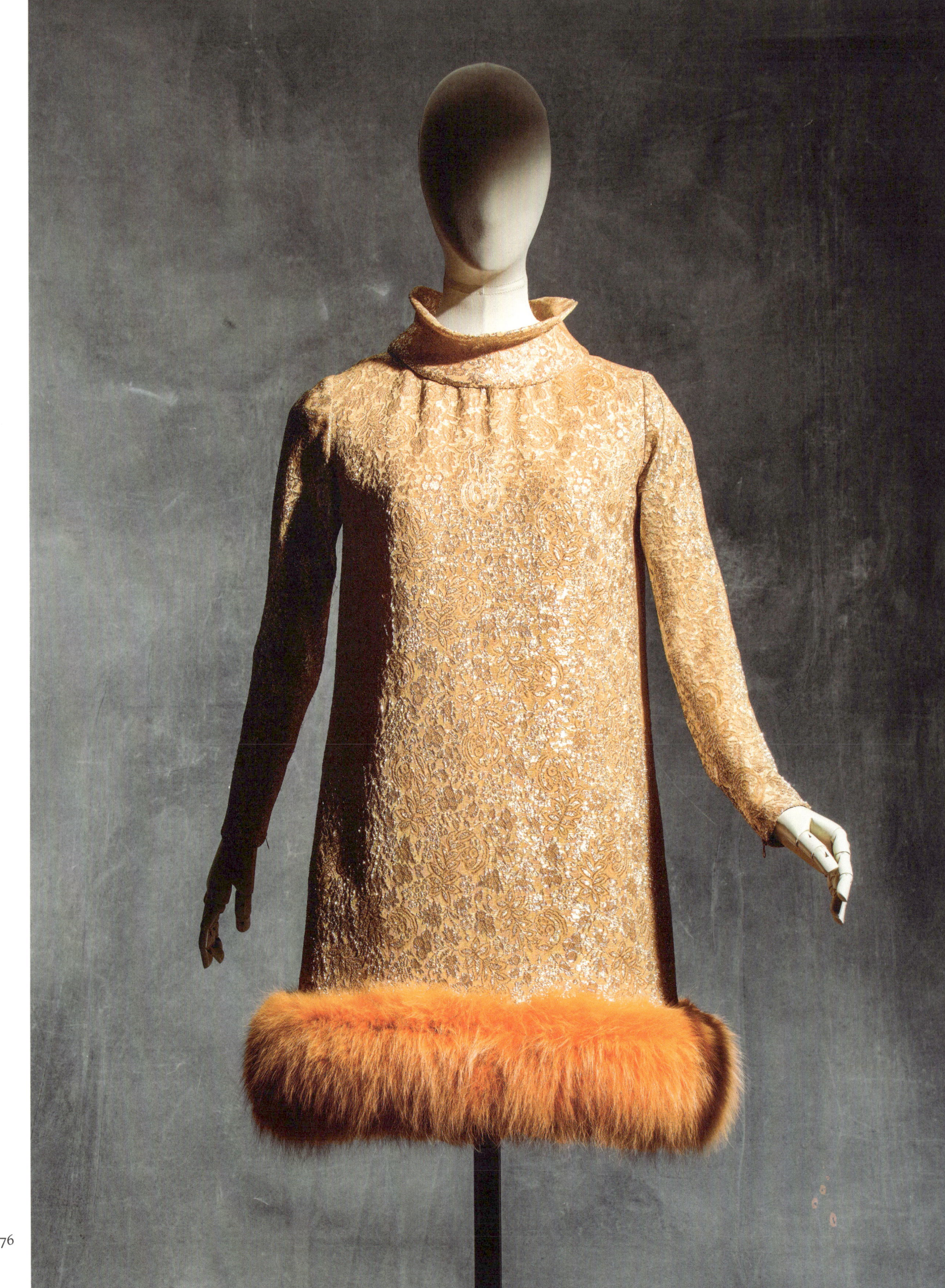

Pierre Cardin
Dress, Autumn/Winter 1966-1967

After working as head tailor at Dior, Pierre Cardin founded his own fashion house in 1957. This minidress reflects the rapid assimilation of the new style imposed by the "Courrèges bomb" in 1965 and of other influences, such as retro, exotic, and futuristic styles. This design recalls the fringe and beading of the flapper dresses from the 1920s. The paisley pattern adds a touch of orientalism. The construction is based on the circle, from the opening at the neck to the ring of fur at the bottom. These strict lines were already present in Cardin's 1964 Cosmocorps line.

Pierre Cardin, who also did costume design for the movies, was a keen observer of his time and could evoke many different women with a single outfit — a synthesis of urban sophistication and space-age aspiration.
E.P.-P.

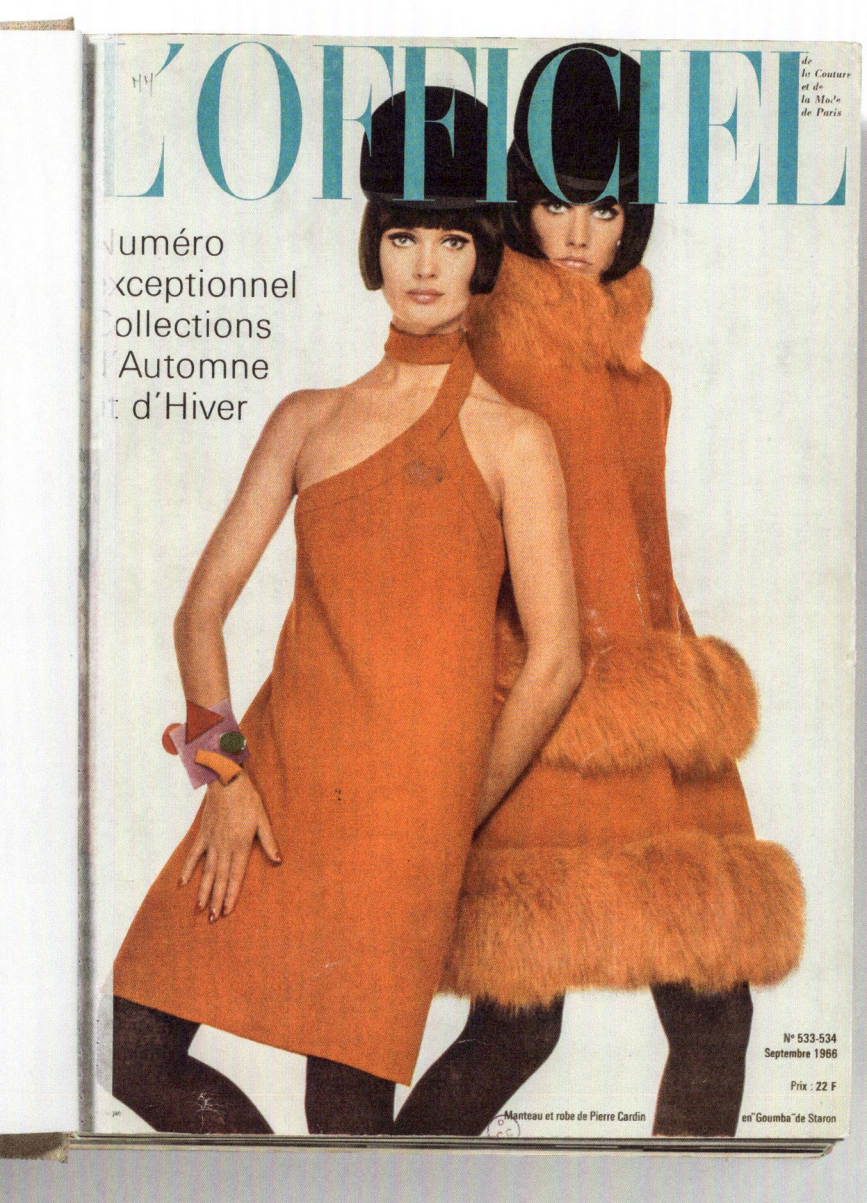

Cover of *L'Officiel*, September 1966. Archives Jalou.

Gabrielle Chanel
Evening Ensemble, Spring/Summer 1967

This evening ensemble is a variation on the Chanel suit that is usually composed of a matching jacket and skirt and can also include a blouse made from the same fabric as the lining. It is inspired by women's suits created in the early twentieth century that Gabrielle Chanel, concerned about comfort and ease, had made out of jersey.

"The Chanel suit is like a Louis XV frock coat or a Louis XVI suit," declared Yves Saint Laurent during a televised interview on the *Dim Dam Dom* show in 1986. Appropriate for any situation, it can be worn in the morning, afternoon, or evening. The suit shown here is made of metallic-plastic lamé for a lustrous, light, indestructible, and futuristic look.
E.P.-P.

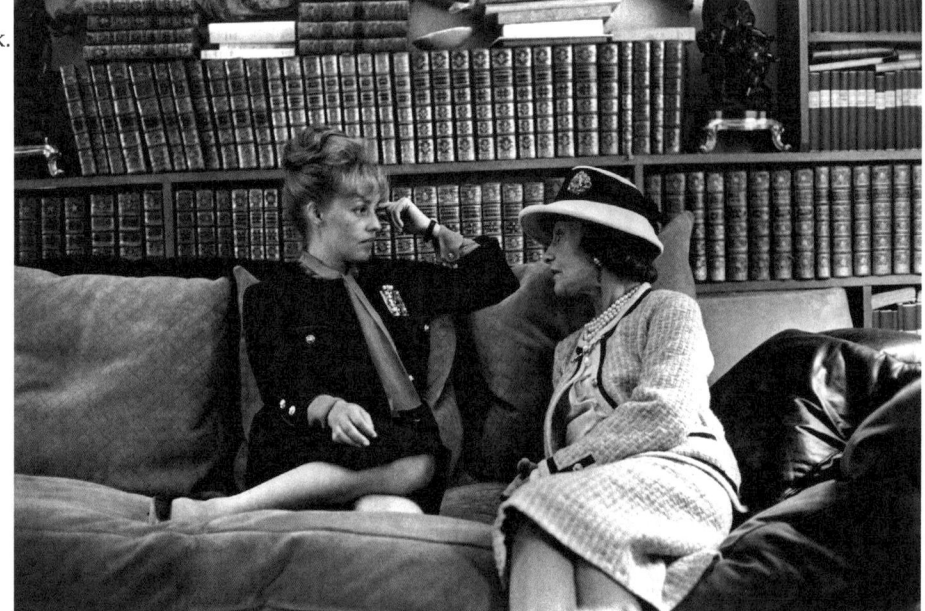

GIANCARLO BOTTI, *Coco Chanel and Jeanne Moreau in Mademoiselle's Apartment,*
31, rue Cambon in Paris, 1960. Photograph.

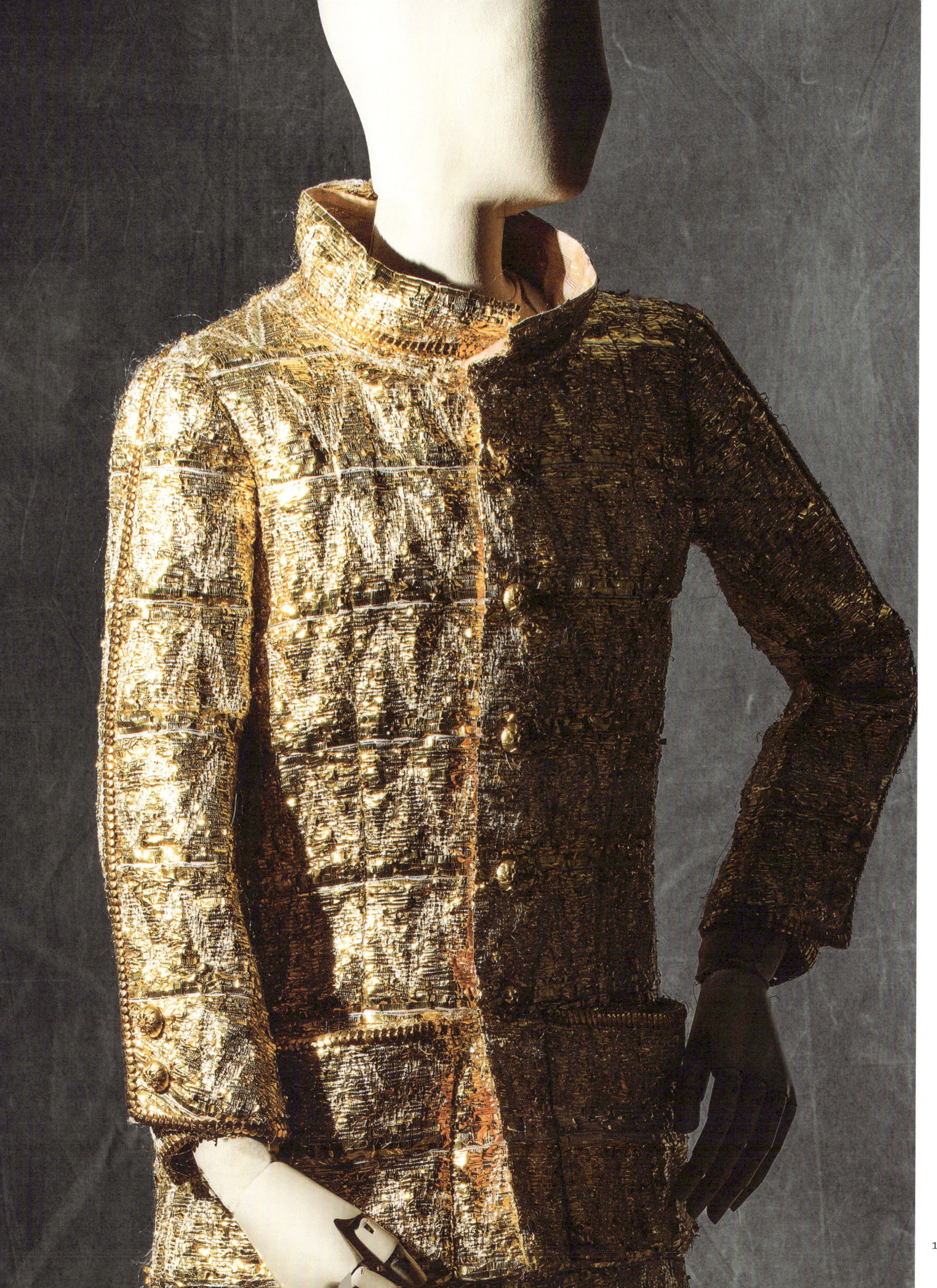

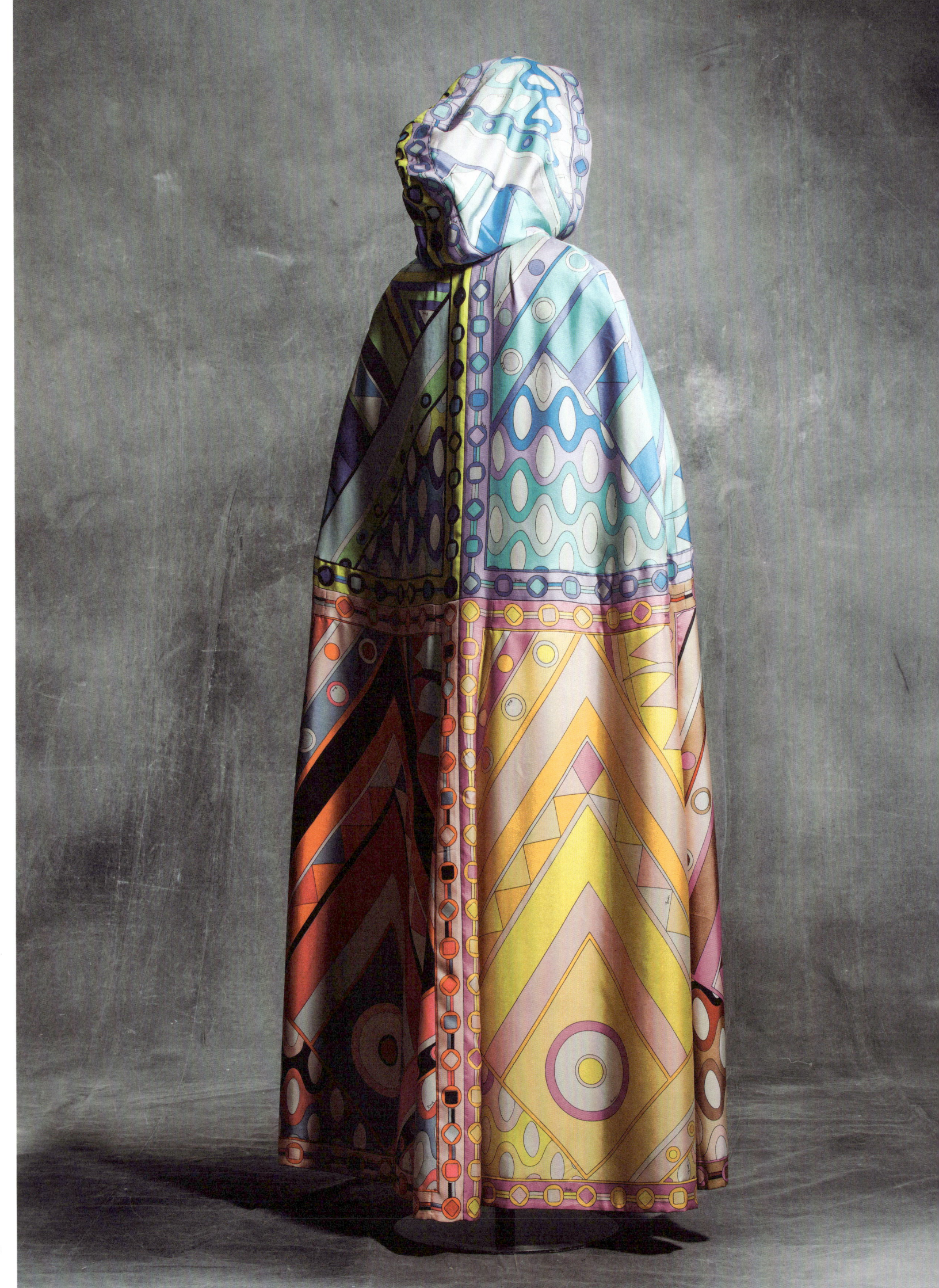

Emilio Pucci
Cape, Spring/Summer 1967

The American concept of sportswear took on significant importance during the 1960s. Designs bearing the Made in Italy label were especially vibrant. Joyous and exuberant patterns, derived from age-old decorative traditions, were adapted to the rhythms of the jet set as they descended on international resorts like Capri or Marbella, where showing off one's body was part of the fun. For the design of the cape pictured here, Emilio Pucci, a Tuscan marquis, was inspired by the costumes and standards displayed at the Palio, the traditional horse race held in Siena: the cape is made from several scarves in different colors, all featuring the same exclusive Vivara pattern.

    The seams along the back of the long hooded cape, which resembles a liturgical vestment, form a cross. While the shape is medieval in inspiration, the hypnotic motif is almost psychedelic.
E.P.-P.

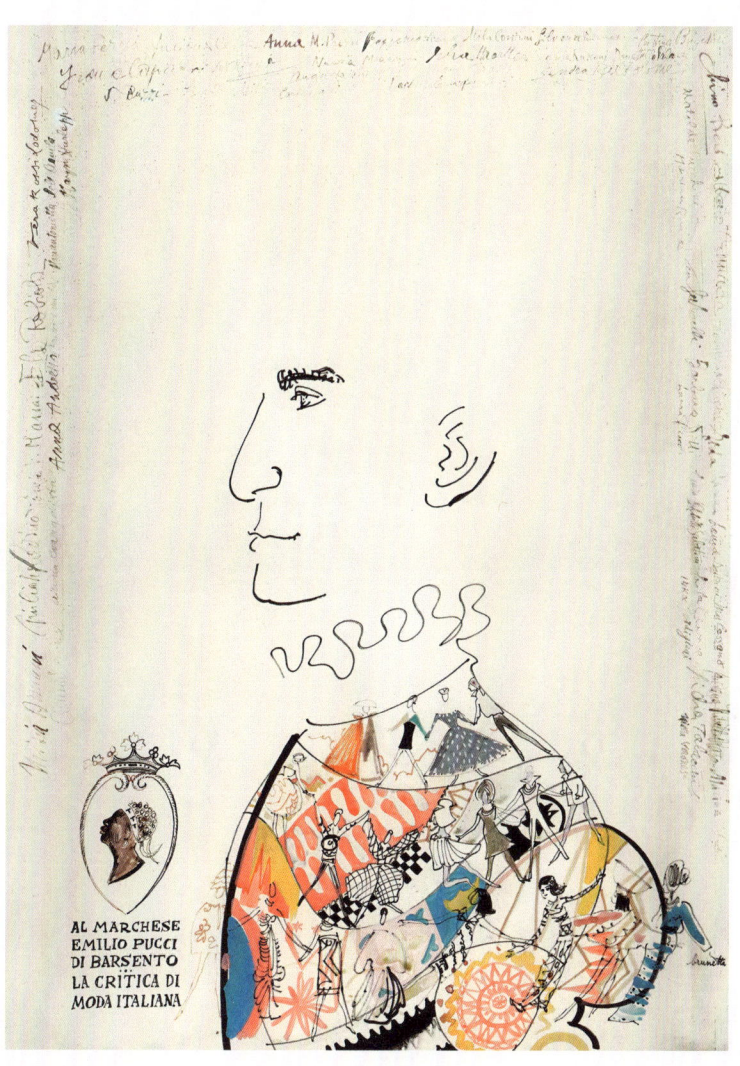

Sketch for the logo of the Emilio de Capri house, 1950. Emilio Pucci Archives.

Paco Rabanne
Evening Dress, Spring/Summer 1968

Paco Rabanne thought of himself as a technician rather than a couturier. Having started out as an accessories designer, he used techniques that were atypical of couture. Described in 1968 on the television show *Panorama* as the "metalworker of fashion," Rabanne used pliers and blowtorches to create dresses made of metal or rhodoïd that, he said, "served no purpose, offering no protection from the cold or the heat."

From the moment he presented his first fashion show in 1966, featuring "twelve unwearable dresses made of contemporary materials" and set to the music of Pierre Boulez, Paco Rabanne was an iconoclast. "A designer," he is quoted as saying in a 1995 biography by Lydia Kamitsis, "was not meant to make ready-to-wear, but to put forth an experimental fashion statement that will inspire the eternal woman in her aesthetic renewal." A darling of the French media, Rabanne dressed such popular stars as Françoise Hardy and Brigitte Bardot.
E.P.-P.

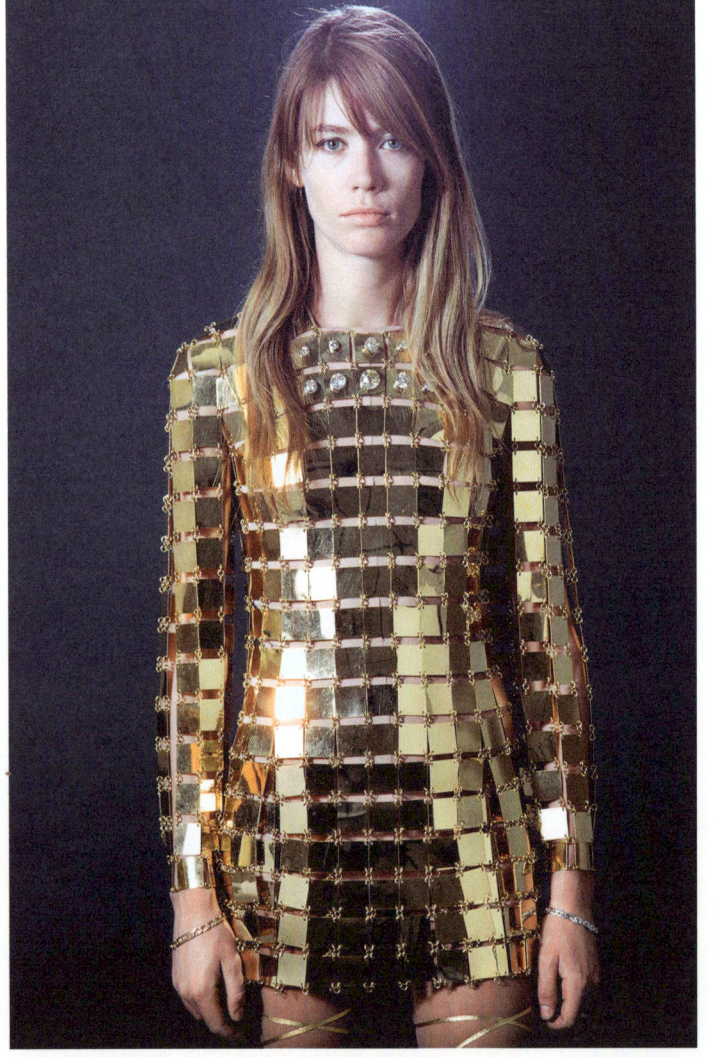

JEAN-MARIE PÉRIER, *Françoise Hardy Wearing a Dress by Paco Rabanne*, 1968. Photograph.

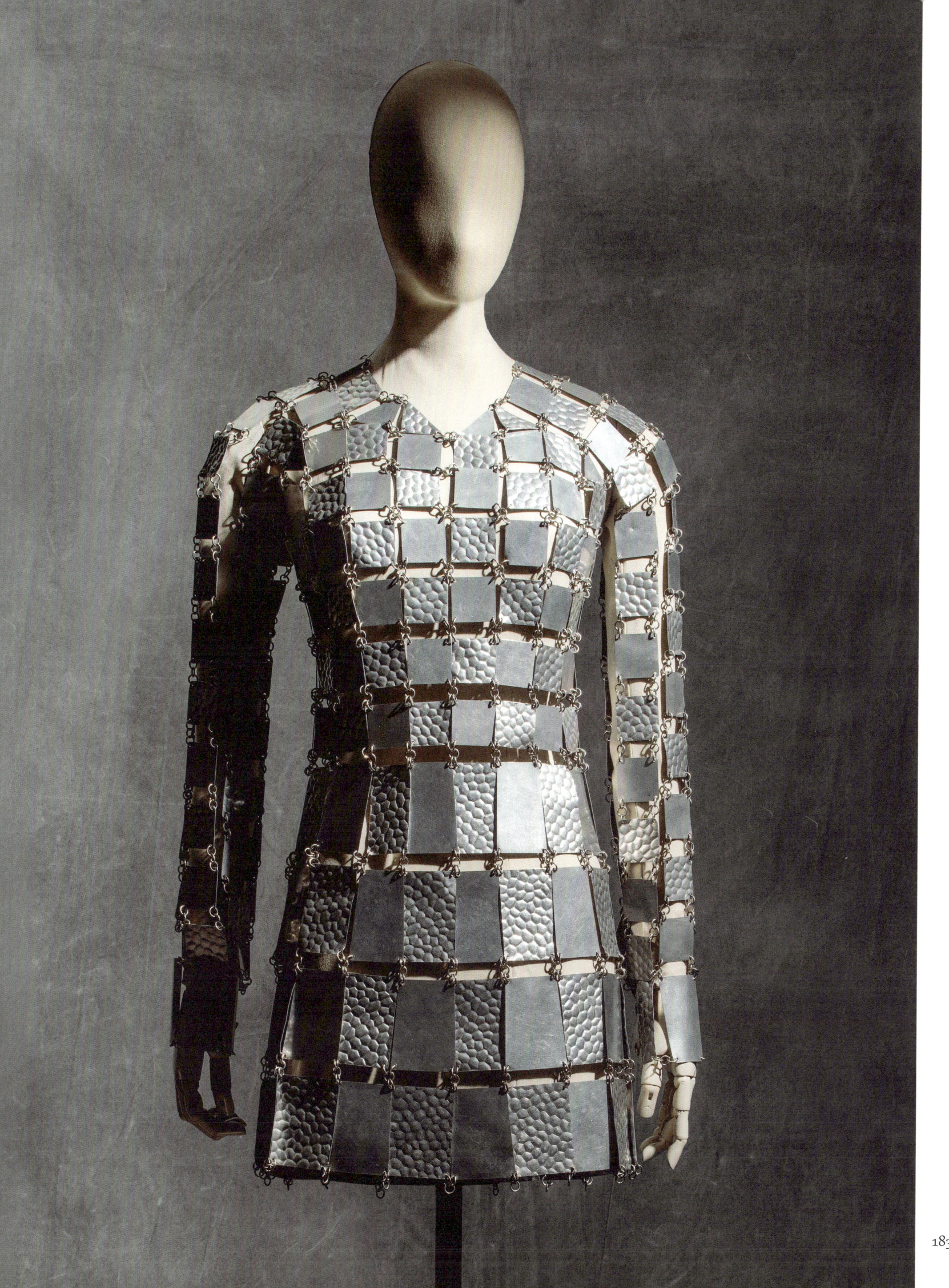

Hubert de Givenchy
Coat, Spring/Summer 1969

After working at the fashion houses of Elsa Schiaparelli and Jacques Fath, Hubert de Givenchy opened his own in 1952. From the start, he targeted a younger clientele and was one of the first couturiers to venture into the field of ready-to-wear, launching his Givenchy Université line in 1954. Around that time he met Audrey Hepburn, the American actress he would dress onscreen and off throughout their long friendship.

A friend and disciple of Cristóbal Balenciaga, Givenchy developed and maintained an ideal of couture and femininity that was founded on a specific structural formalism. Building on the success of his work from the transition years of the 1950s and early 1960s, Givenchy designed clothes that were sober, but never austere. He was mainly concerned with balance: "To create a simple dress with one single line, now that's great couture," the designer is quoted as saying in the 1998 book *Le Style Givenchy*.

This coat of carded wool reflects Givenchy's demand for perfection. The right angles of the pattern dictate the cut, but the continuity of line is addressed in many ways. In the front, the grid pattern is extended onto the sleeves to accentuate the overall shape; in the back the same effect is rendered on the slightly curved half-belt, a detail of refinement that catches the eye. The buttons also contribute to the balance of the composition, for they are specifically placed within the pattern as playfully as pieces on a checkerboard.
E.P.-P.

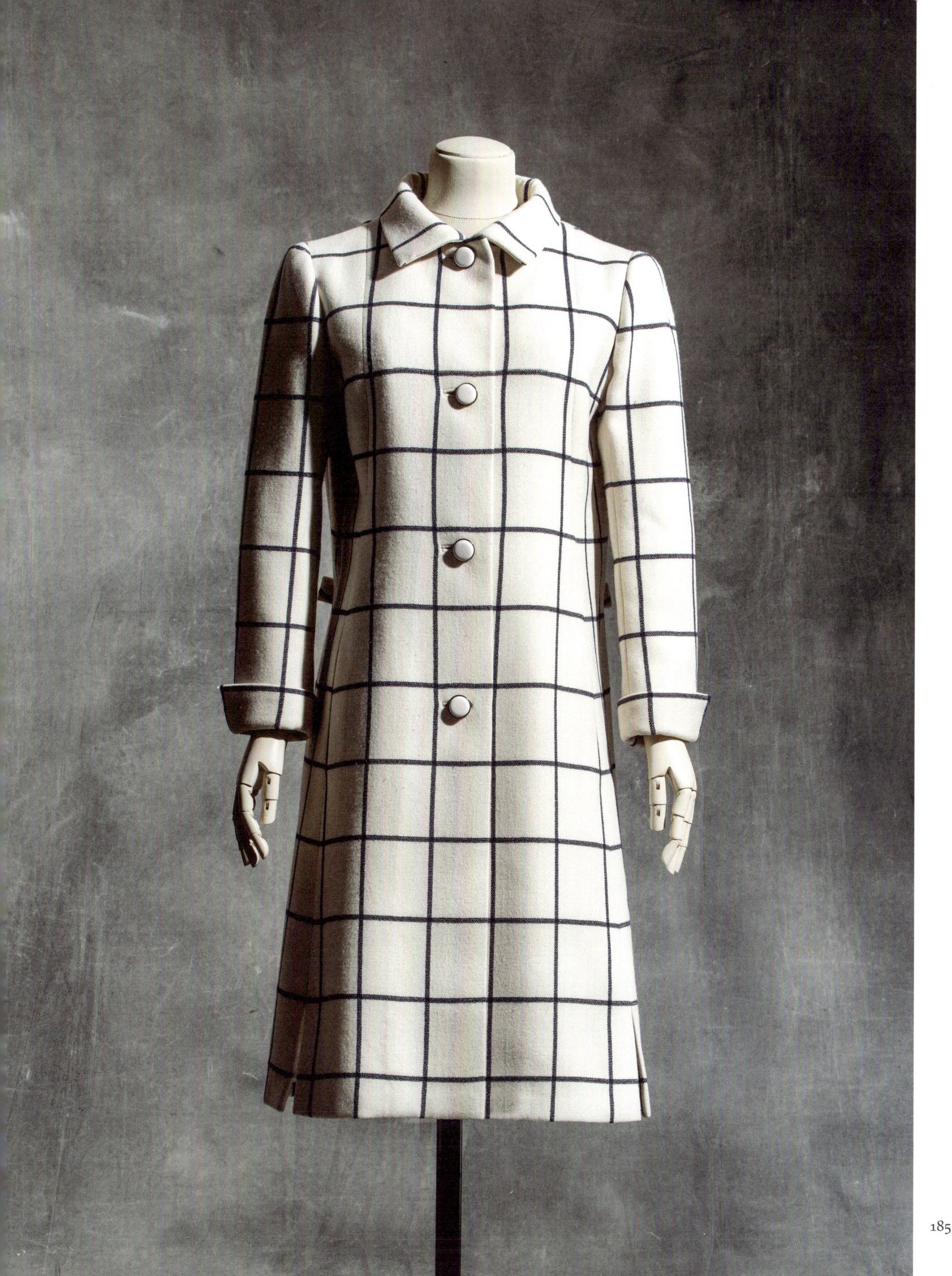

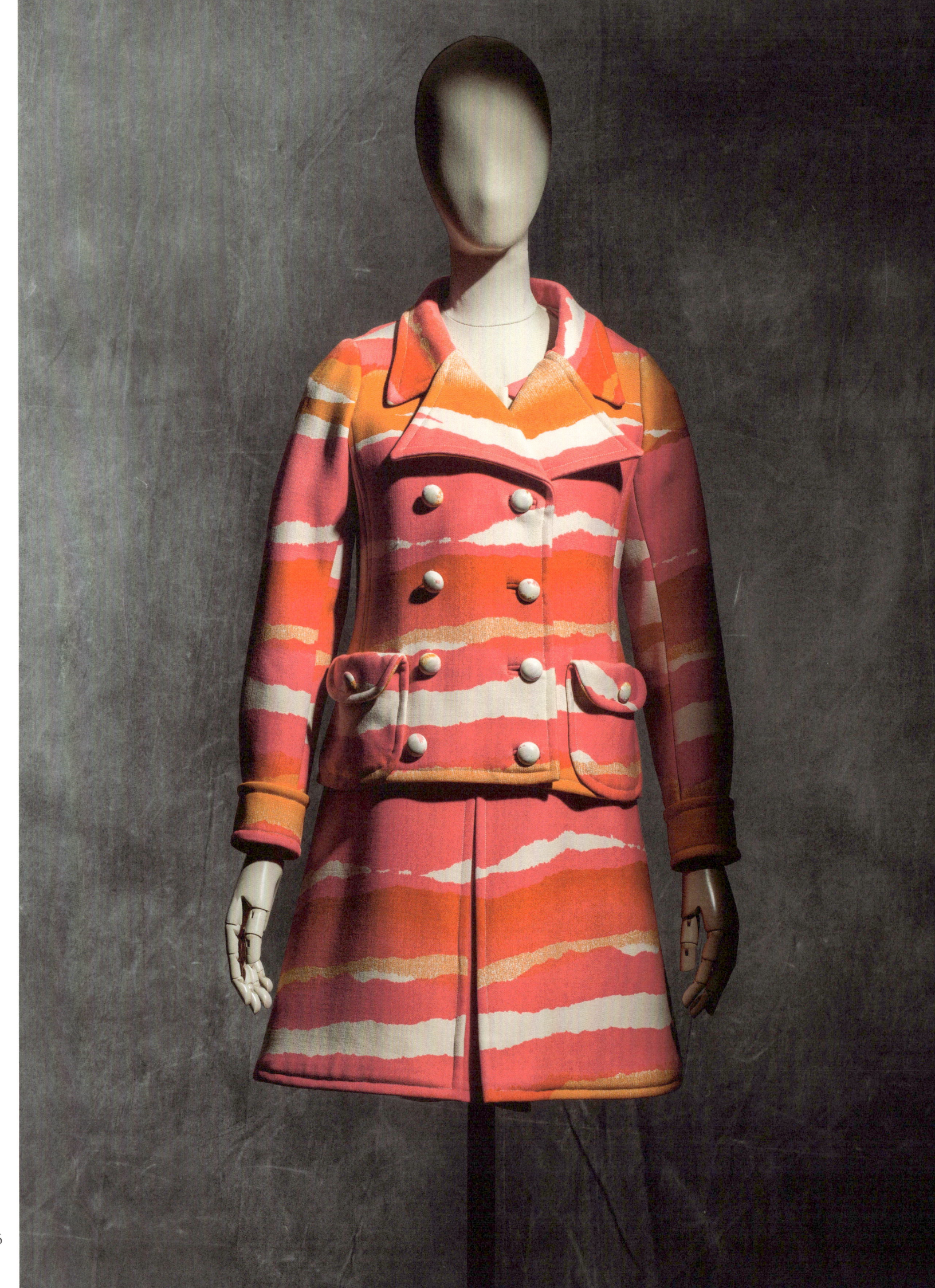

Emanuel Ungaro
Ensemble, Autumn/Winter 1969-1970

After working as head tailor at Balenciaga, then collaborating with André Courrèges, Emanuel Ungaro established his fashion house in 1965, aiming to reconcile sobriety of cut with the exuberance of ornamentation.

This trapeze-shaped ensemble follows the typical principles of composition: the garment stands slightly away from the body (as in the creations of Balenciaga) and the structure is established at the shoulders (like the dresses that made Courrèges famous). The stiff look of the outfit is typical of Nattier triple gabardine and is further accentuated with topstitching. The graphic impact of the large size and somewhat random print is emboldened by masterful tailoring. The *buvard* (blot) or *déchirure* (tear) pattern, created from a drawing by Sonia Knapp, is cleverly extended onto the sleeves, with special attention paid to the placement of the pockets and the half-belt. The overall impression is similar to a projection of color onto a screen.

E.P.-P.

PETER KNAPP, Photograph for Emanuel Ungaro published in *Elle*, September 1, 1969, page 51.
PP. 188-189 — YVES SAINT LAURENT, Collection board from the 1970 Autumn/Winter collection.
Fondation Pierre Bergé — Yves Saint Laurent, Paris.

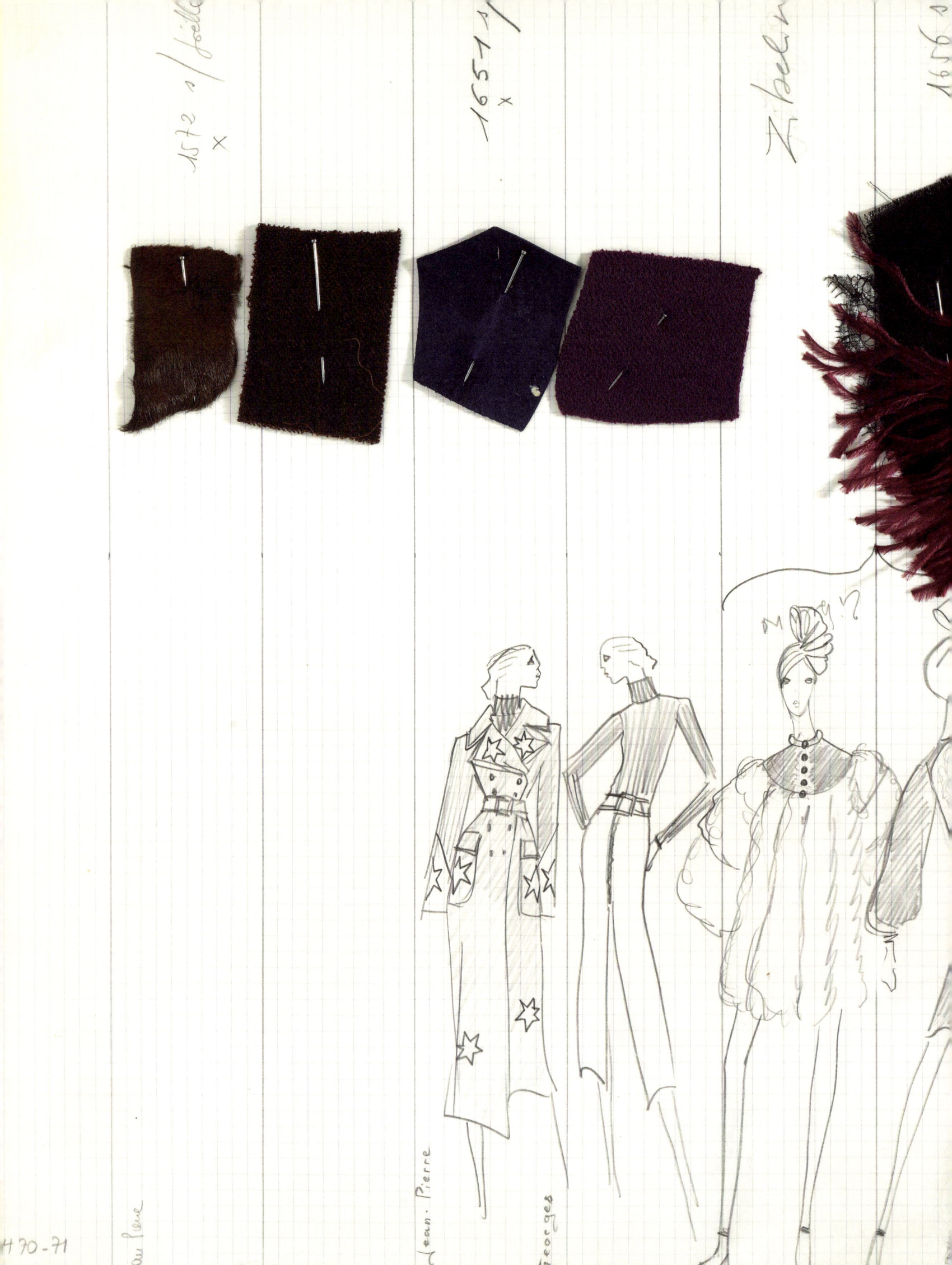

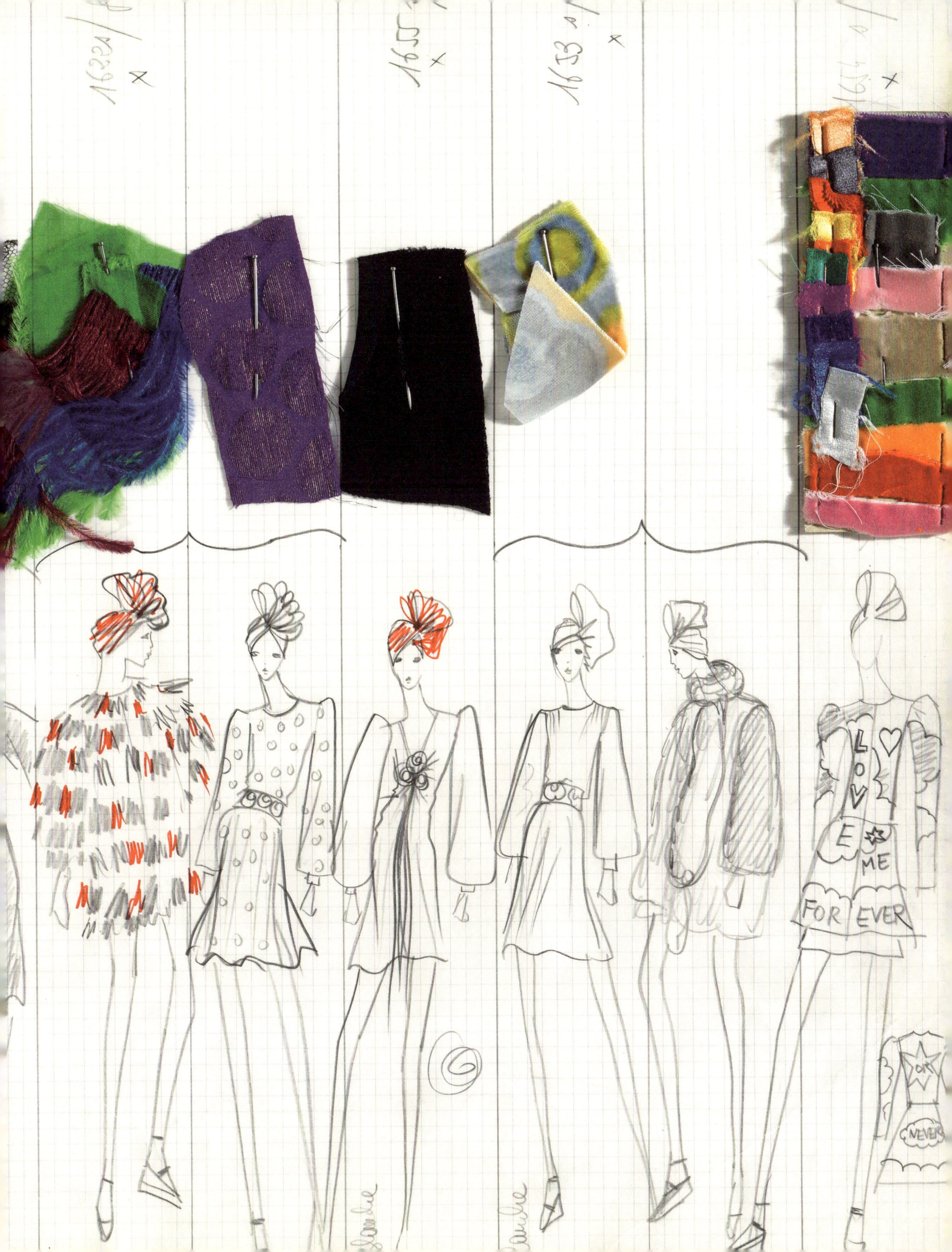

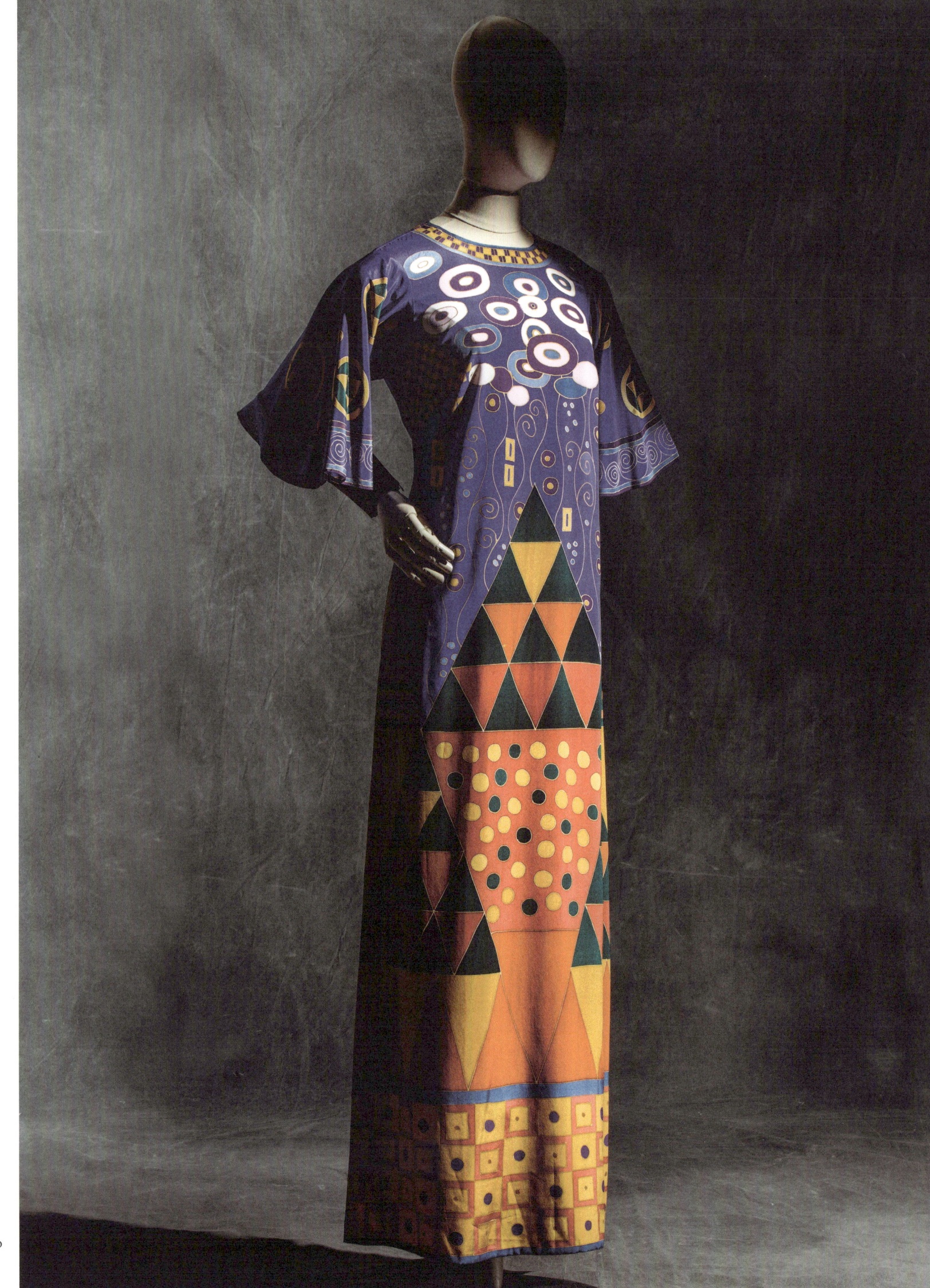

Karl Lagerfeld for Chloé
Long Dress, 1971

During the 1960s and 1970s the luxury ready-to-wear house Chloé hired several designers, including Christiane Bailly, Michèle Rosier, and Karl Lagerfeld. The singer Régine asked Lagerfeld to design this dress for the opening of her Parisian nightclub, Regineskaia. Created in the Chloé ateliers, the design represented a break with the futuristic, stiff, and monochromatic styles of the 1960s. Instead, this retro design is silky, fluid, and entirely embellished.

Inspired by the work of Gustav Klimt, Lagerfeld created a polychrome pattern that was hand painted by the textile designer Nicole Lefort. The line of this unique piece is reminiscent of the dresses worn in the early twentieth century by Émilie Flöge, the companion of the secessionist painter. This homage to the Slavic splendor of Mitteleuropa anticipated the influence of orientalism on the fashions of the 1970s.
E.P.-P.

Guy Laroche
Long Dress, 1972

Guy Laroche created this dress for French actress Mireille Darc when she starred in Yves Robert's film, *The Tall Blond Man with One Black Shoe*. The film was a blockbuster in France, due in no small part to the dress, whose plunging back exposed Darc's buttocks — leaving her tuxedo-clad lead actor speechless. The designer was probably inspired by the famous dress that Yves Saint Laurent created for his 1970 Autumn/Winter collection.

This dress was the symbol of a liberated woman who has a mischievous side. "It was neither scandalous nor shocking, simply insolent. It was a fantasy dress that many women dreamed of wearing: it definitely left its mark on my generation and the one that followed," recalled Darc in a June 1966 interview for *Elle* magazine.
E.P.-P.

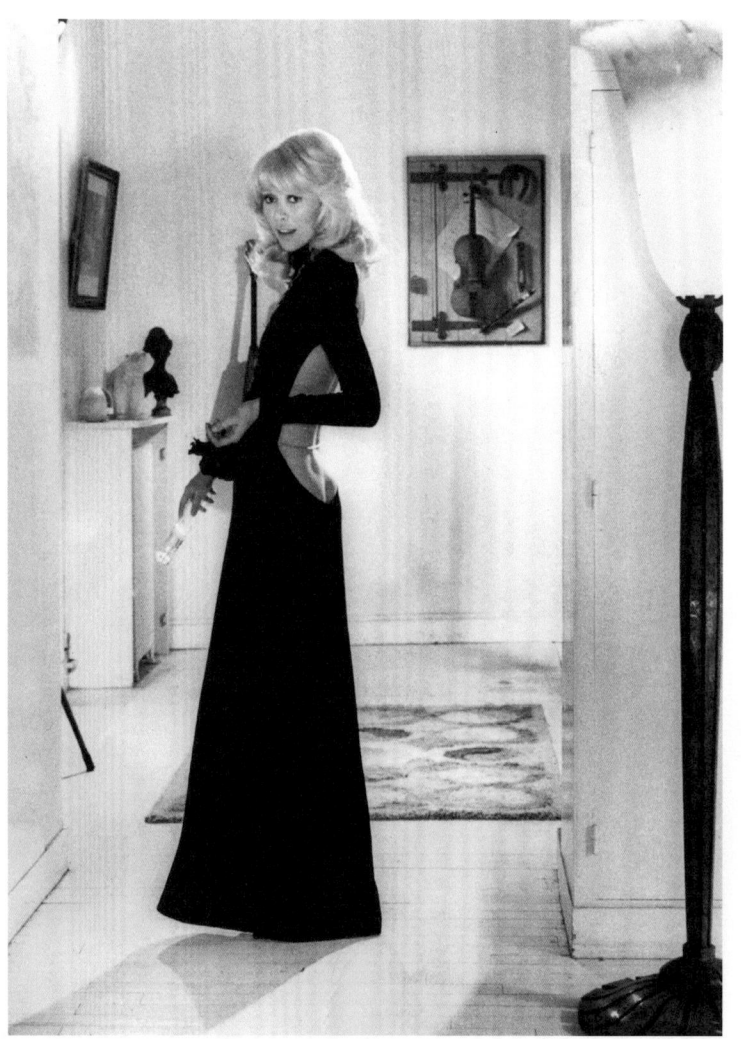

MIREILLE DARC in Yves Robert's *Tall Blond Man with One Black Shoe*, 1972.

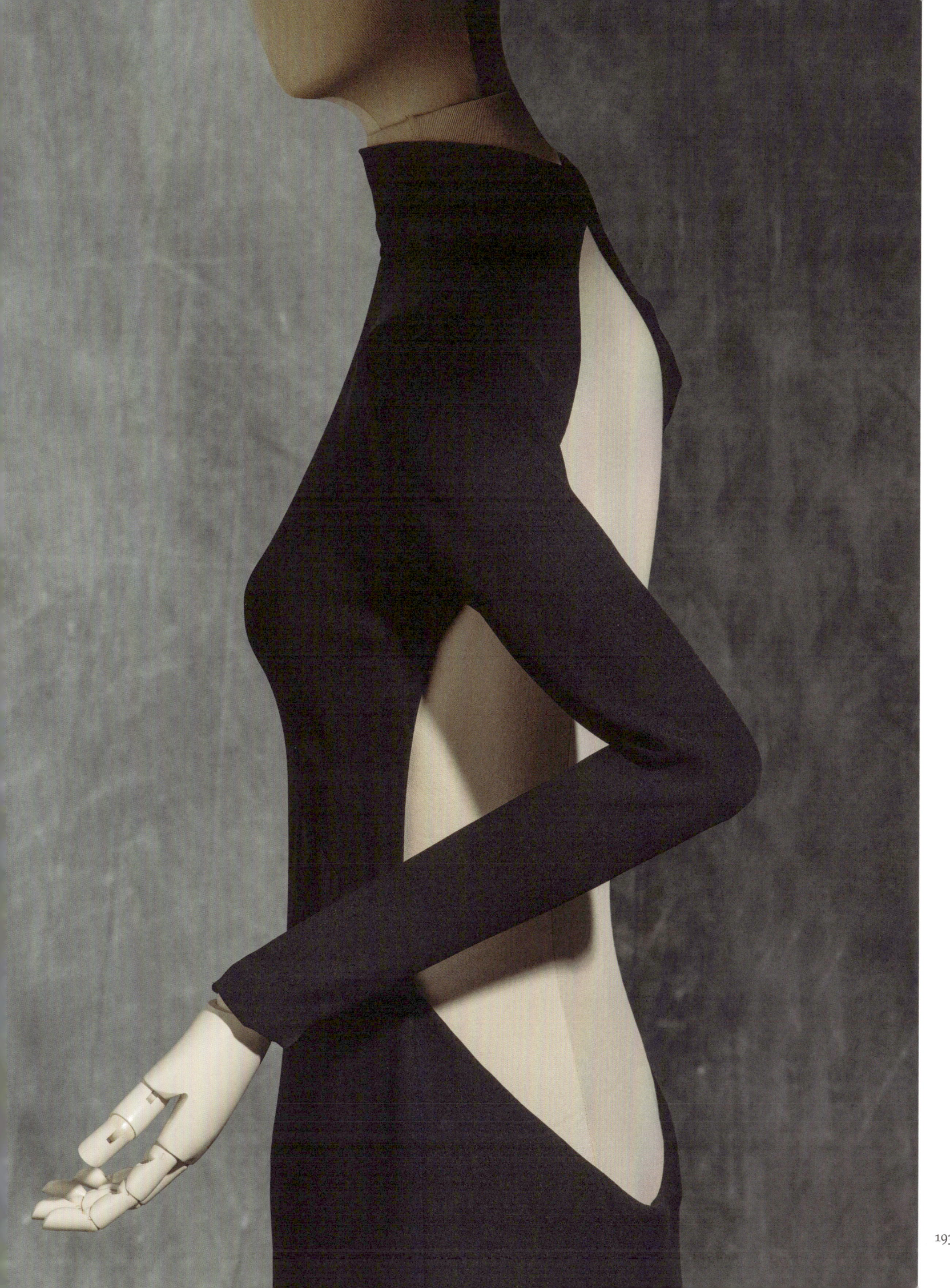

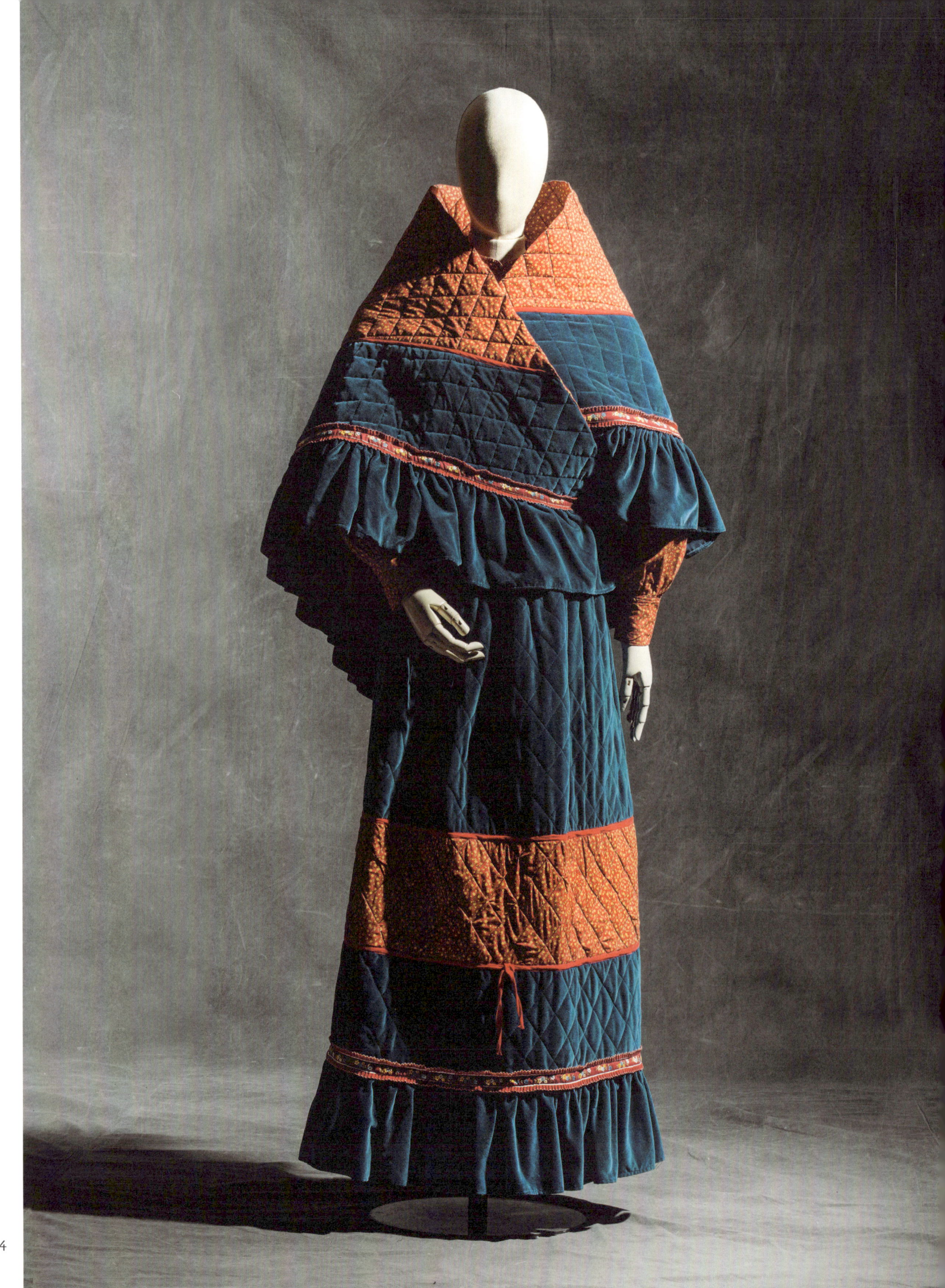

Kenzo
*Daytime Ensemble
Autumn/Winter 1970-1971*

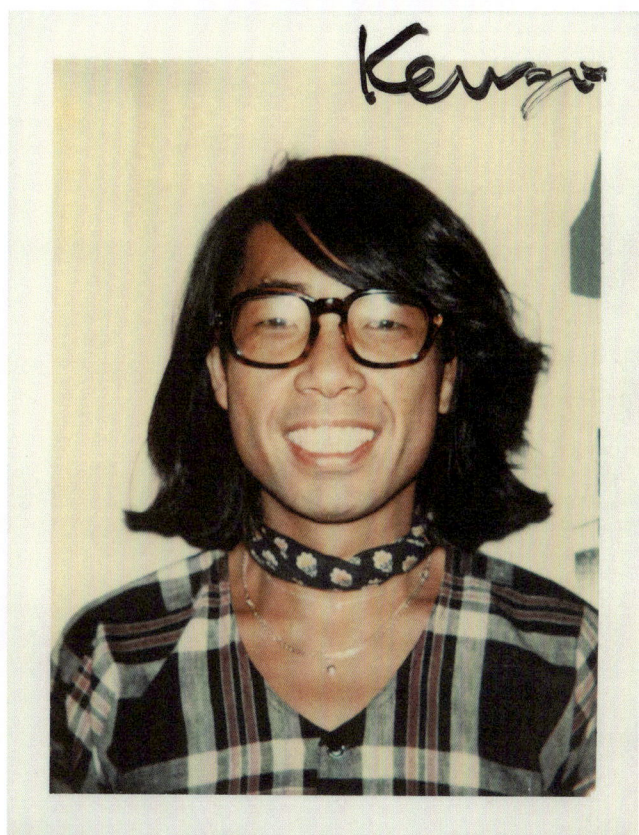

When Kenzo Takada moved to France in 1965, he began drawing sketches for newspapers and fashion publications. In 1970 he opened his first boutique, Jungle Jap, located in the Passage Vivienne, and decorated the walls with a fresco in the style of Henri Rousseau. He was the first Japanese designer to show his collection in Paris, under the aegis of Créateurs et Industriels, a company founded by Didier Grumbach that brought together young talented designers and manufacturers. Kenzo's fashion shows were exuberant, festive, and relaxed, just like Kenzo himself, who always flashed a smile behind his large glasses. His designs are characterized by the use of many different fabrics, whether traditional textiles from his native land or folk-style floral prints. The combination of patterns reflects a fusion of various popular arts and traditions.

The red floral fabric pictured here was paired with another print on a jean jacket that was featured on the cover of *Elle* in March 1971. The "patchwork" effect, as described in the magazine, was a "novel mix of materials and colors."
E.P.-P.

ANDY WARHOL, *Portrait of Kenzo*, 1975. Polaroid. The Andy Warhol Foundation.
PP. 196-197 — ANTONIO LOPEZ, *Café Society* 1 and 2, 1975. Magic Marker on paper, collages.

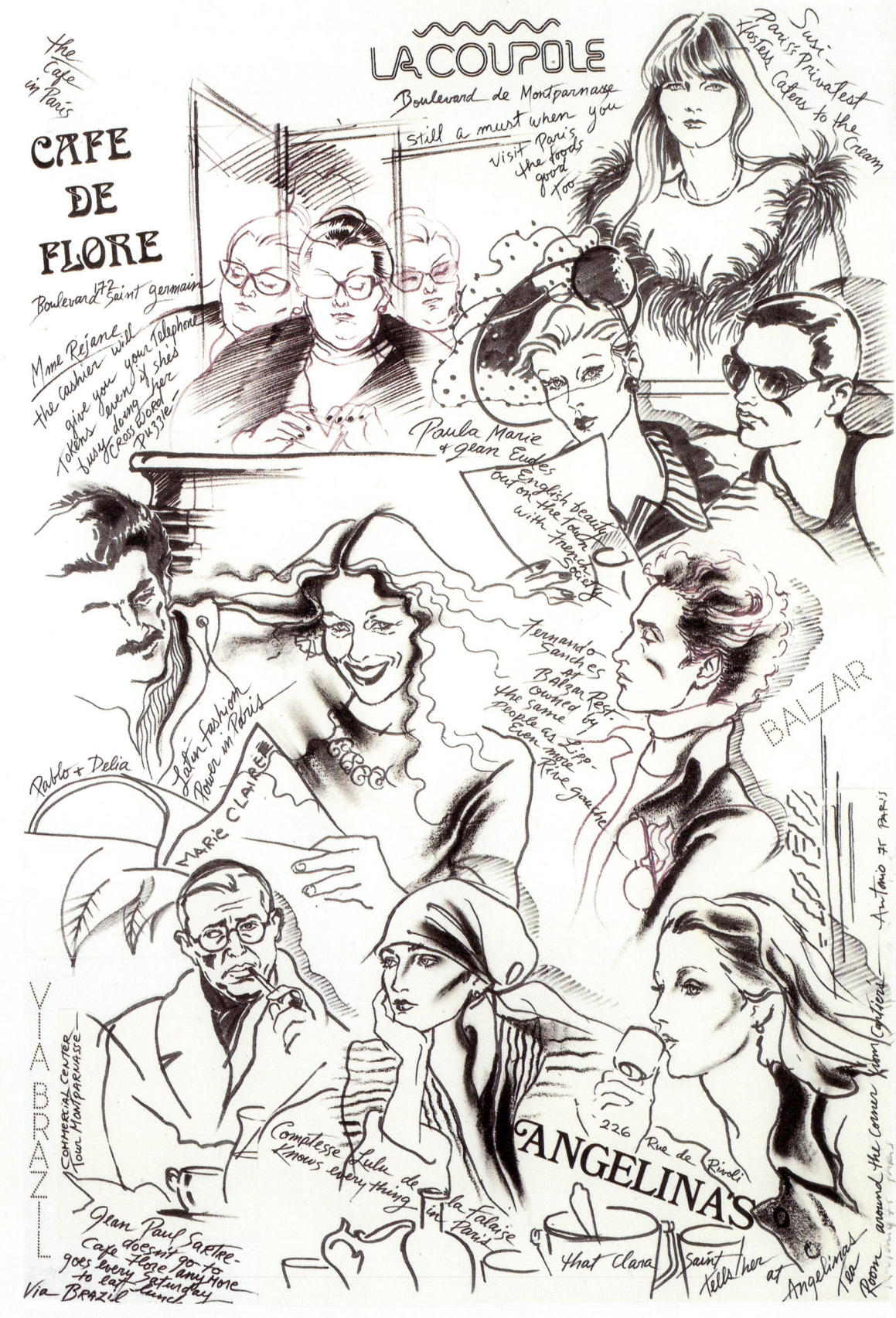

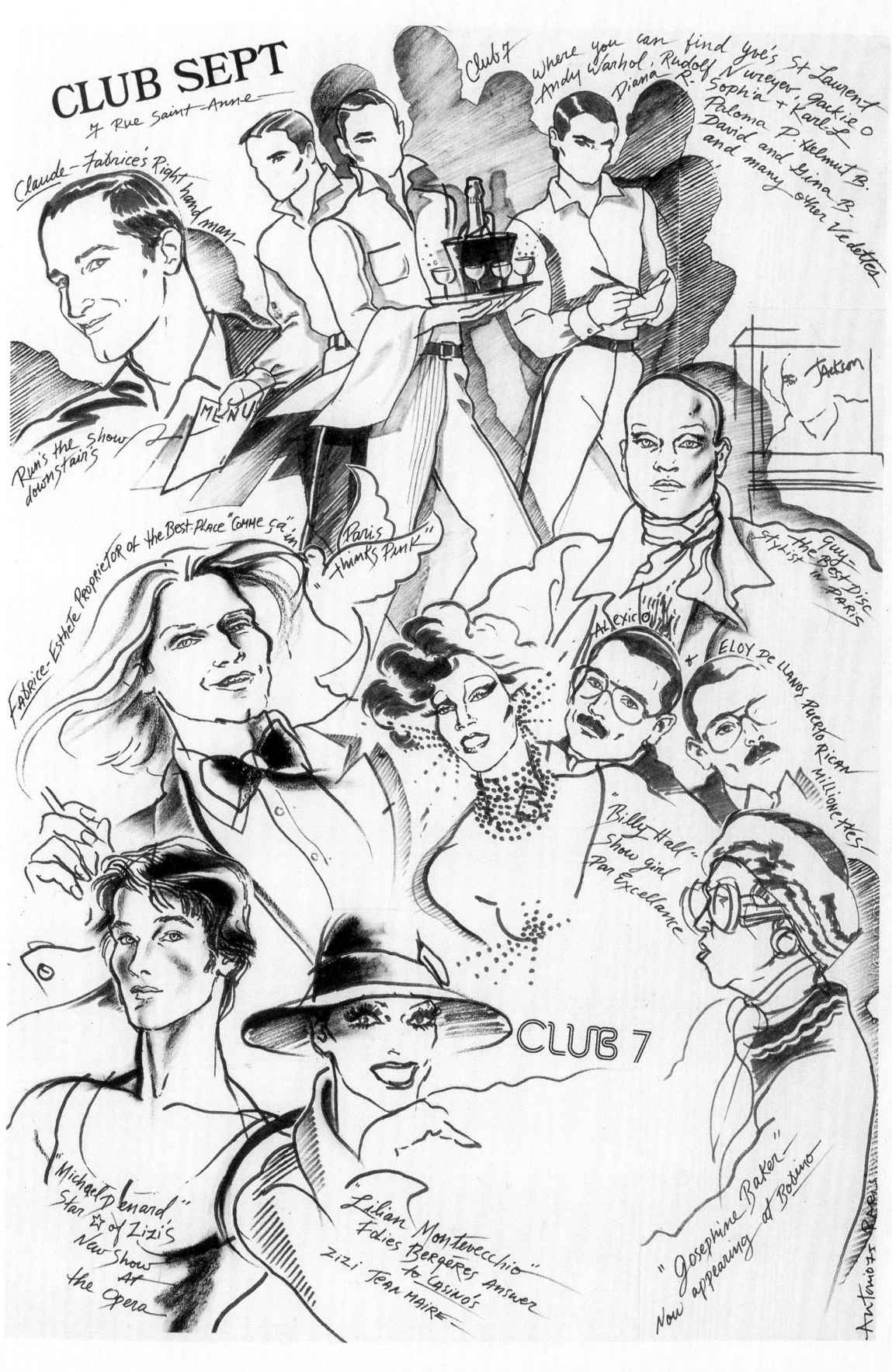

Grès
Long Dress, Spring/Summer 1976

"When I drape silk around a mannequin, it reacts in my hands and I try to understand and assess its reactions. In this way I can give the dress I am creating the line and shape that the fabric itself would choose," explained Madame Grès in a March 1984 interview for British *Vogue*. In this example, the designer selected a soft and fluid jersey that falls straight, except where it is intentionally fixed in place by tight gathers. Madame Grès typically worked with large amounts of fabric. In its static state, the dress recalls the antique wet-drapery techniques used by academic painters and sculptors. But when worn by a woman, the dress unfolds like a veil. Madame Grès's dresses emphasize the body and fill the space around it, a figurative and dynamic treatment of volume that is radically different from Balenciaga's (abstract) or Dior's (choreographic), which were based on construction and layering, respectively.

Although the drape of the dress seems to fall naturally, the designer devised many clever ways to control it (in this instance, a trompe l'oeil effect created the braided fabric on the bodice). Madame Grès's designs represent the synthesis of classic prewar couture, with its inherent sensuality (as exemplified by Madeleine Vionnet) and postwar techniques that facilitated the means of illusion.
E.P.-P.

PP. 200-201 — HELMUT NEWTON, *Dans les salons des couturiers. Chez Yves Saint Laurent* (In the salons of couturiers. Yves Saint Laurent's salon). Photograph published in French *Vogue*, March 1977.
PP. 202-203 — GUY BOURDIN, *Les robes drapées de Madame Grès* (The draped dresses of Madame Grès). Photographs published in French *Vogue*, March 1976.

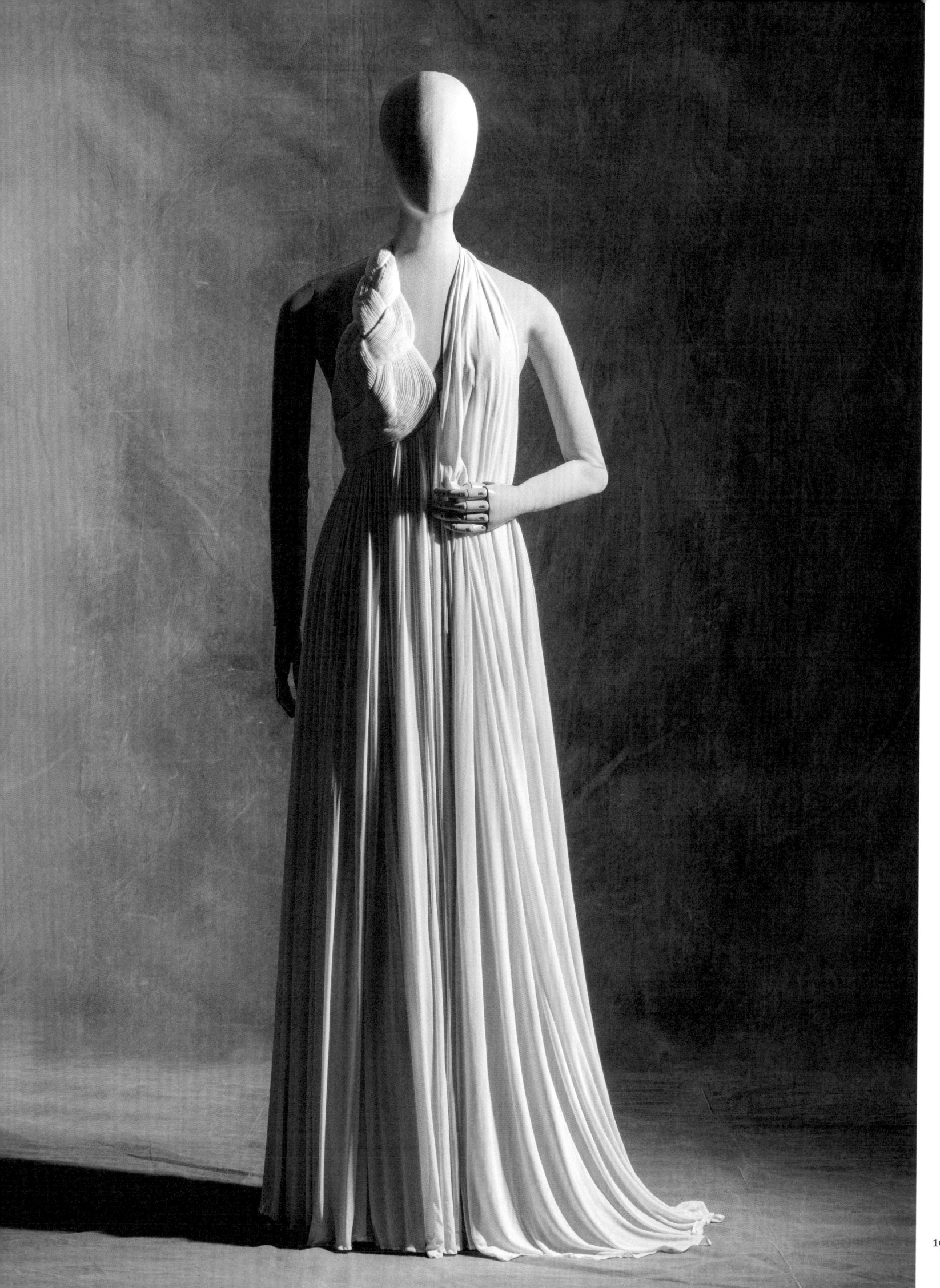

199

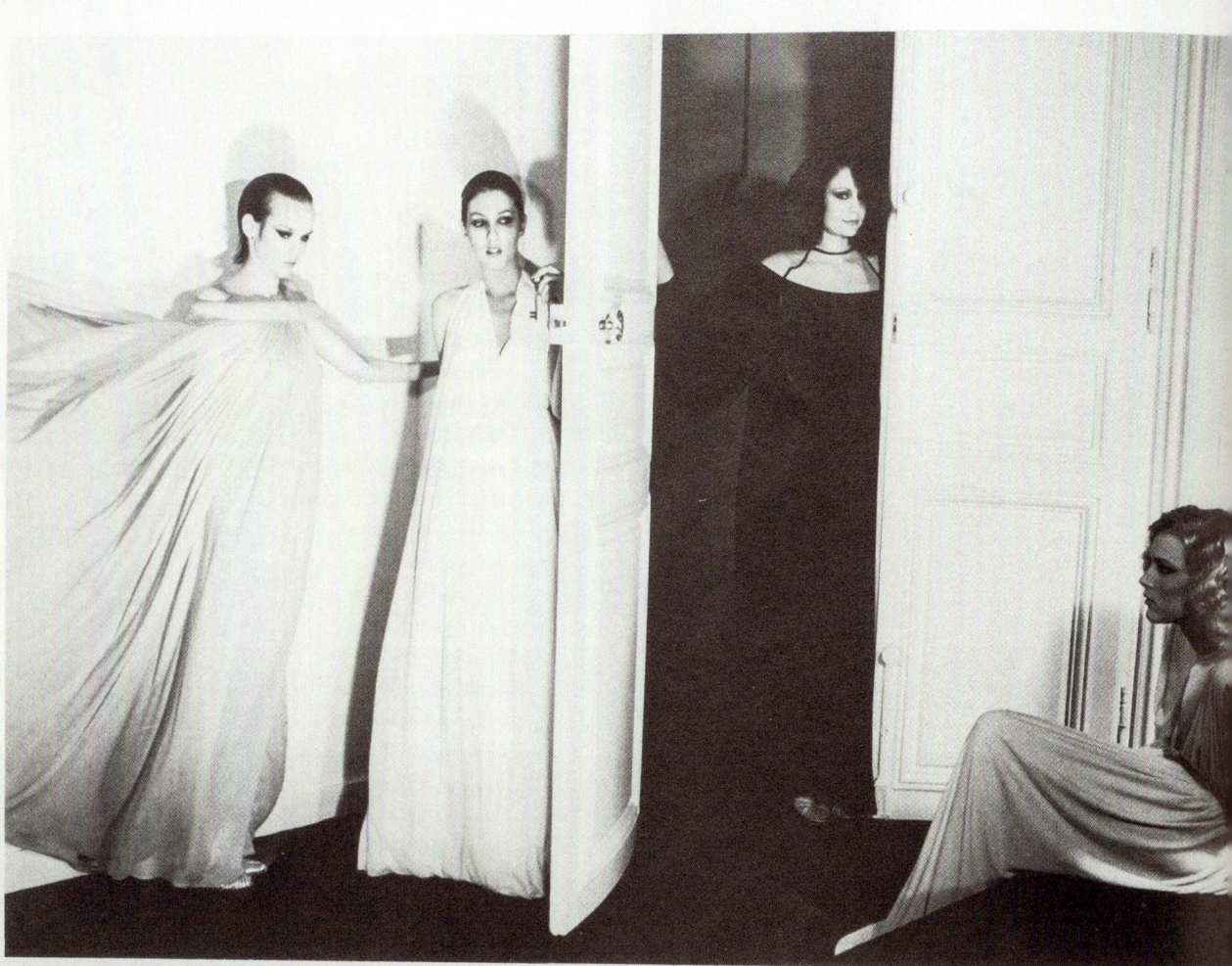

LES ROBES DRAPÉES DE MADAME GRÈS C'est le festival de l'imagination pure autour du corps de la femme avec le travail de fins drapés qui font sa gloire. "Je ne dessine jamais une robe sur le papier," dit-elle. "Elle se forme dans mon esprit; ensuite, je me laisse guider par les proportions du corps. Le rôle de la couleur est de me conduire et de m'inspirer."

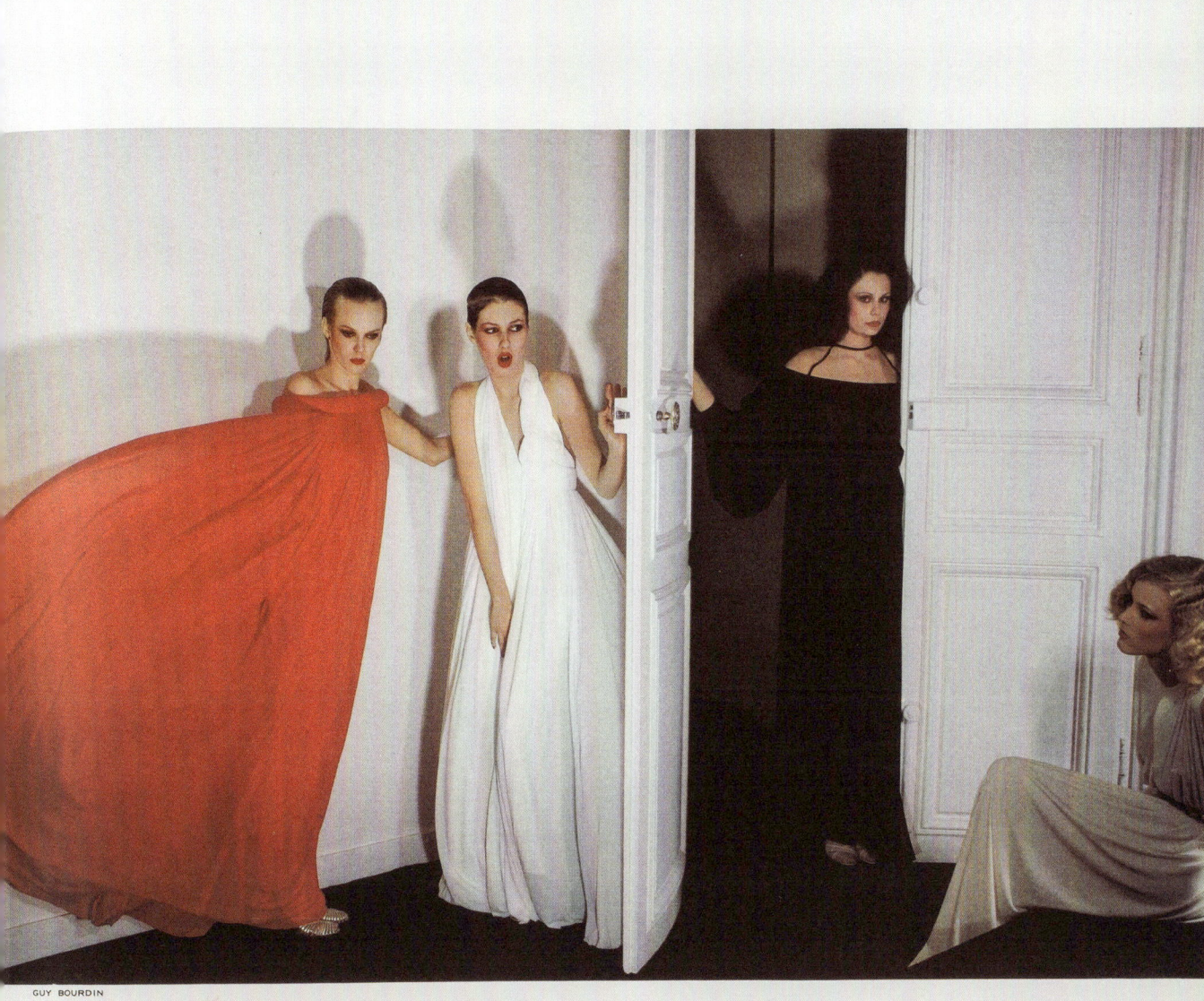

Rouge, en jersey de soie de Racine, une robe à l'encolure bateau formée d'un bourrelet finement drapé d'où partent deux pans libres devant et dans le dos, sur une jupe-fourreau et un soutien-gorge assorti. Blanche, une robe en jersey de soie de Racine, au buste formé, d'un côté, d'une torsade finement drapée, et de l'autre d'un pan libre de jersey. Coiffures Valentin pour Jean-Louis David. Maquillages Heidi Moravetz pour Lancaster.

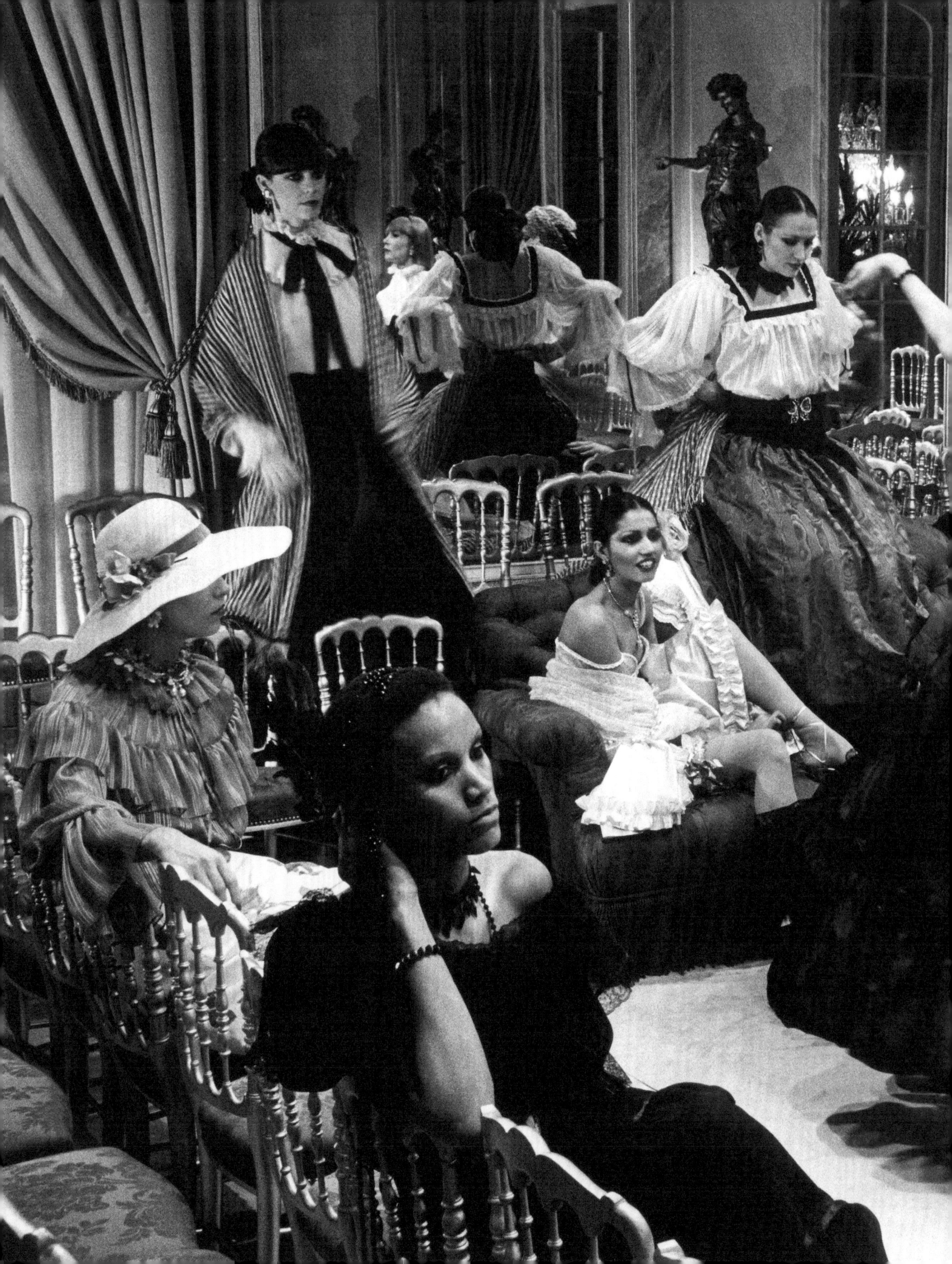

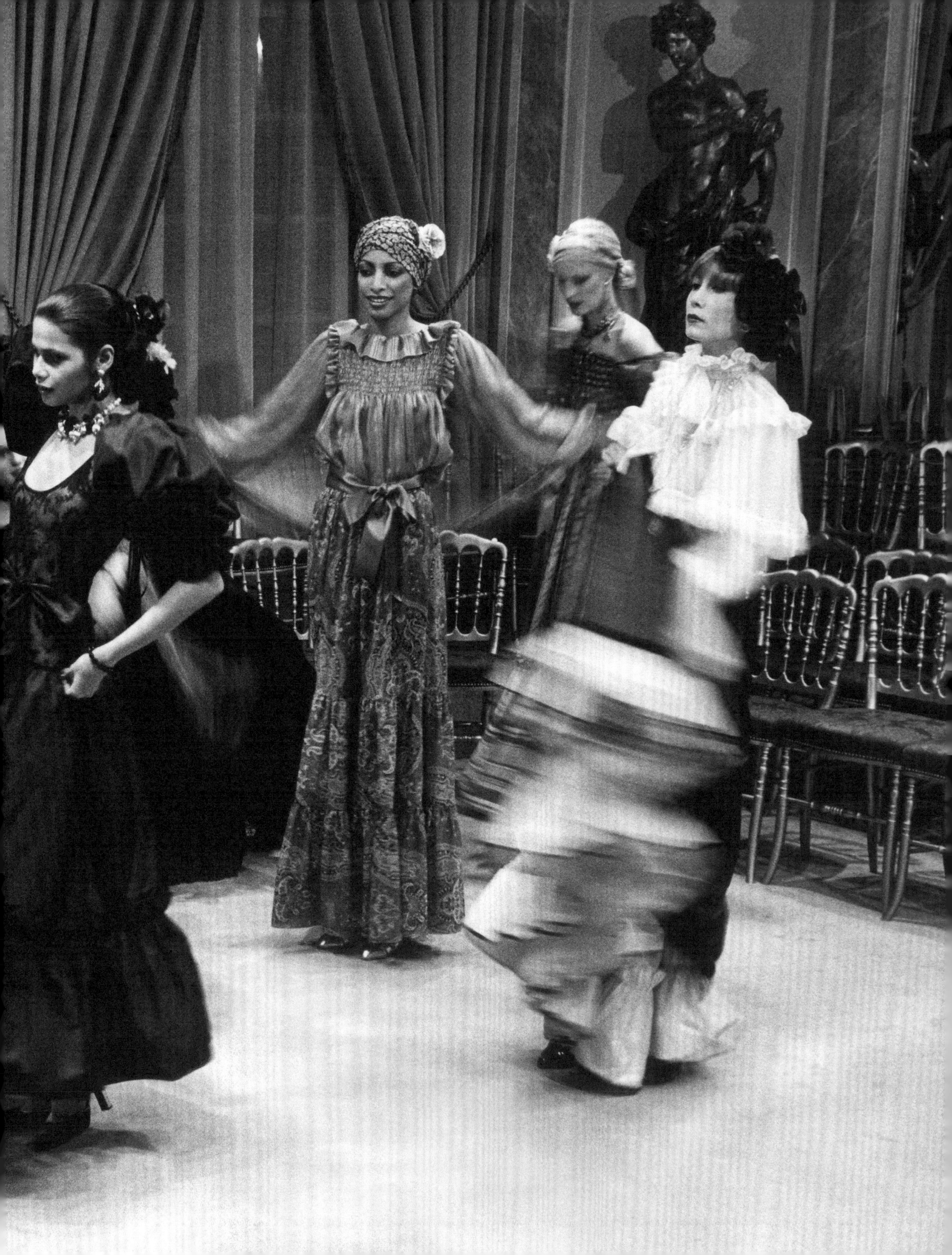

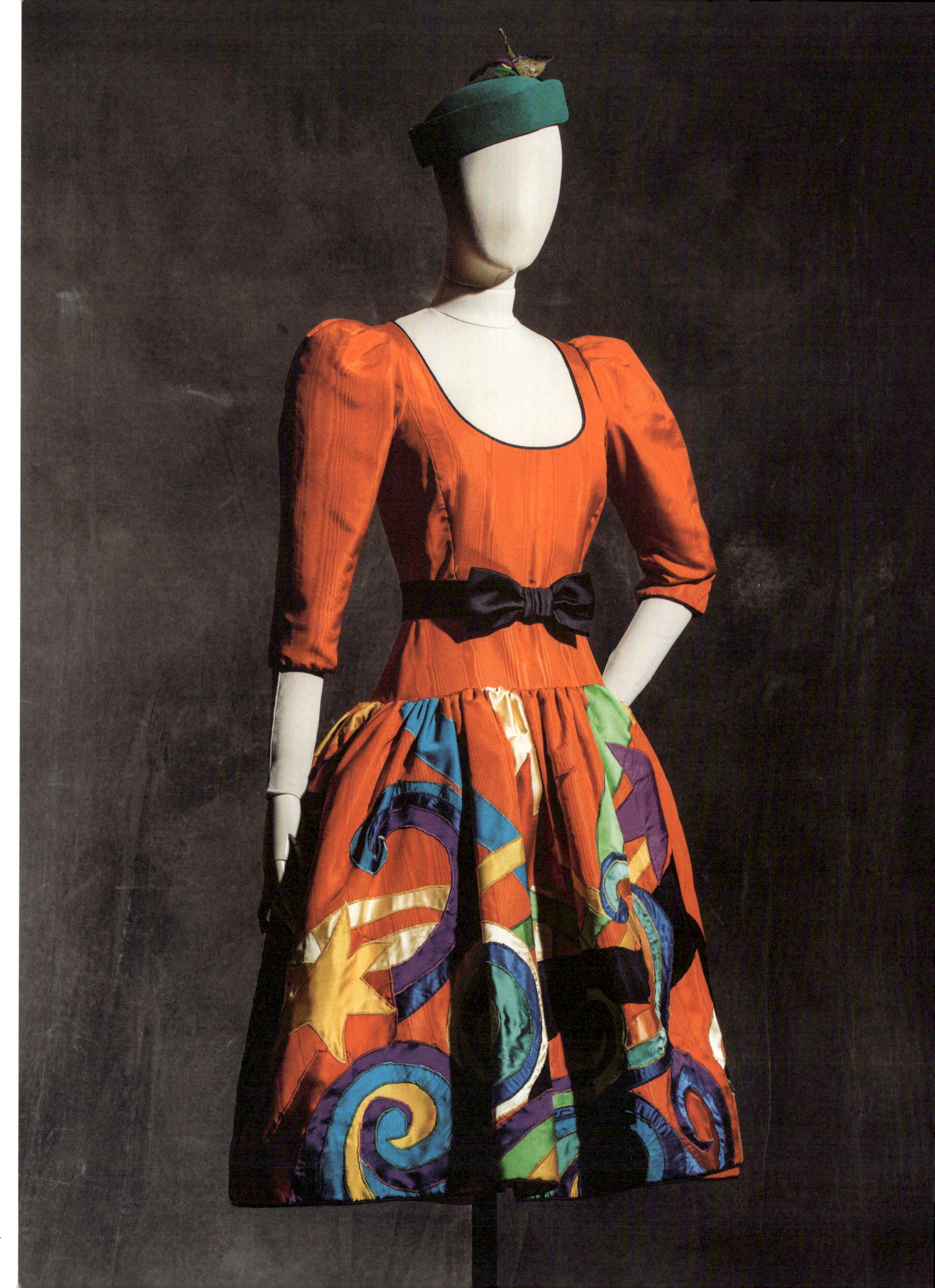

Yves Saint Laurent
Picasso Dress, Fall/Winter 1979-1980

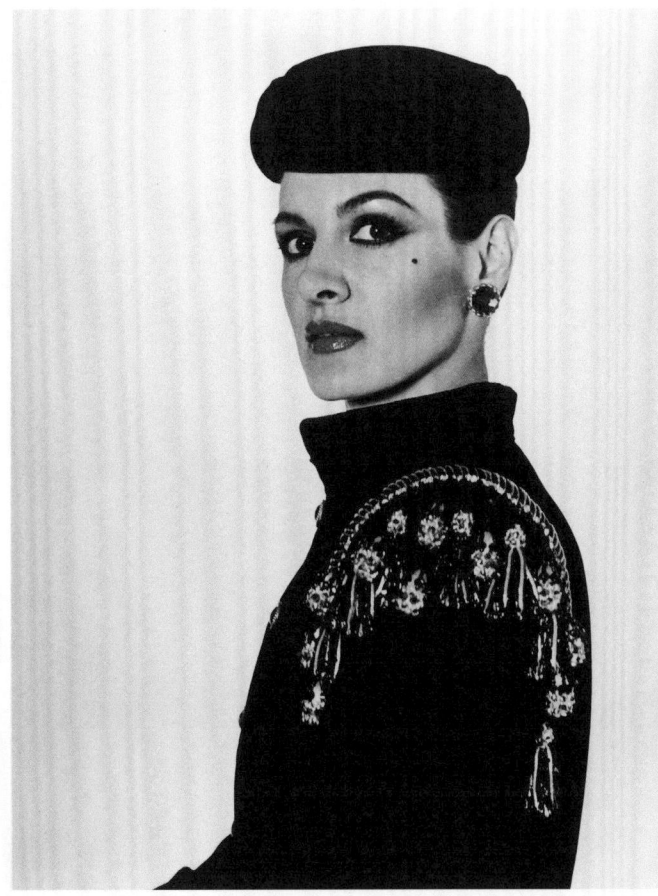

This dress was the highlight of Yves Saint Laurent's "Homage to Diaghilev and Picasso" collection. The dress was inspired by the costumes that Picasso designed for the ballet *Parade* that premiered at the Théâtre du Châtelet on May 18, 1917, and signaled, according to Guillaume Apollinaire, the "starting point of this new spirit." The tight-fitting bodice evokes the costumes worn by acrobats, whereas the skirt's appliquéd embroidery — created by the textile designer Andrée Brossin de Méré — was Yves Saint Laurent's interpretation of the scroll designs that appear on the costumes of the Chinese magician.

This tribute by Saint Laurent emphasizes the connection between couture and major art forms, both figurative and performance oriented. By 1979, when the couturier had reached his creative maturity, his brilliant oeuvre was instrumental in the recognition of fashion as art. He was the first living couturier to be given a retrospective at the Metropolitan Museum of Art in New York in 1983. The Picasso dress, photographed by Duane Michals, appeared on the cover of the exhibition catalogue.
E.P.-P.

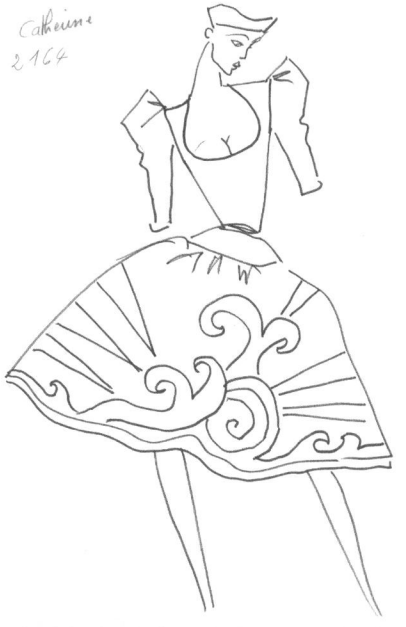

HORST P. HORST, *Paloma Picasso*, 1979. Silver-gelatin print (reprint).
Musée des Arts Décoratifs, Paris; The Photo Collection, gift from Horst P. Horst, 1993.
YVES SAINT LAURENT, Original sketch for the *Hommage à Pablo Picasso* dress, Autumn/Winter 1979.
Fondation Pierre Bergé – Yves Saint Laurent, Paris.

Claude Montana
Dress, Spring/Summer 1979

Starting in 1973, Claude Montana began designing ready-to-wear collections for Idéal-Cuir, a leather specialty company run by brothers Alain and Frédie Jochimek. Montana's creative handling of leather, especially lambskin, gave the material the cachet of couture; in return, its many variations added a unique dimension to the designer's work. In this example, the delicate leather contrasts sharply with the ornamentation—images and materials borrowed from biker jackets, such as the embroidered motif and studded belt.

This dress captures the essence of a Claude Montana woman, whose squared shoulders were inspired by the androgynous silhouettes of the 1940s. As noted in the November 1979 issue of *L'Officiel*: "Leather gains sophistication when it is embroidered by Montex. The menacing eagle across the chest adds a punk dimension to the straight leather dress that wraps around the back."
E.P.P.

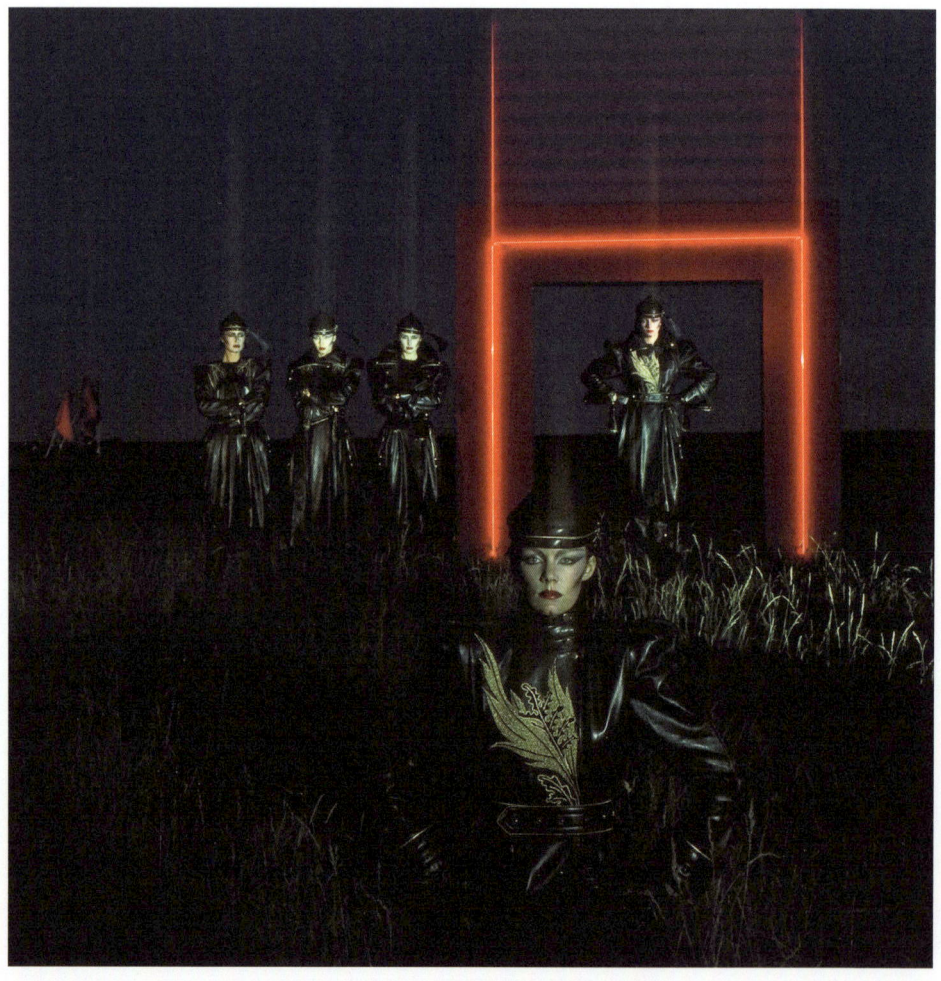

PETER KNAPP, Publicity shot for Claude Montana, 1979.
Musée des Arts Décoratifs, Paris; Advertising Department, gift from Peter Knapp.
PP. 208-209 — GUY BOURDIN, Advertisement for Charles Jourdan, 1979. Published in *Elle*, March 5, 1979.

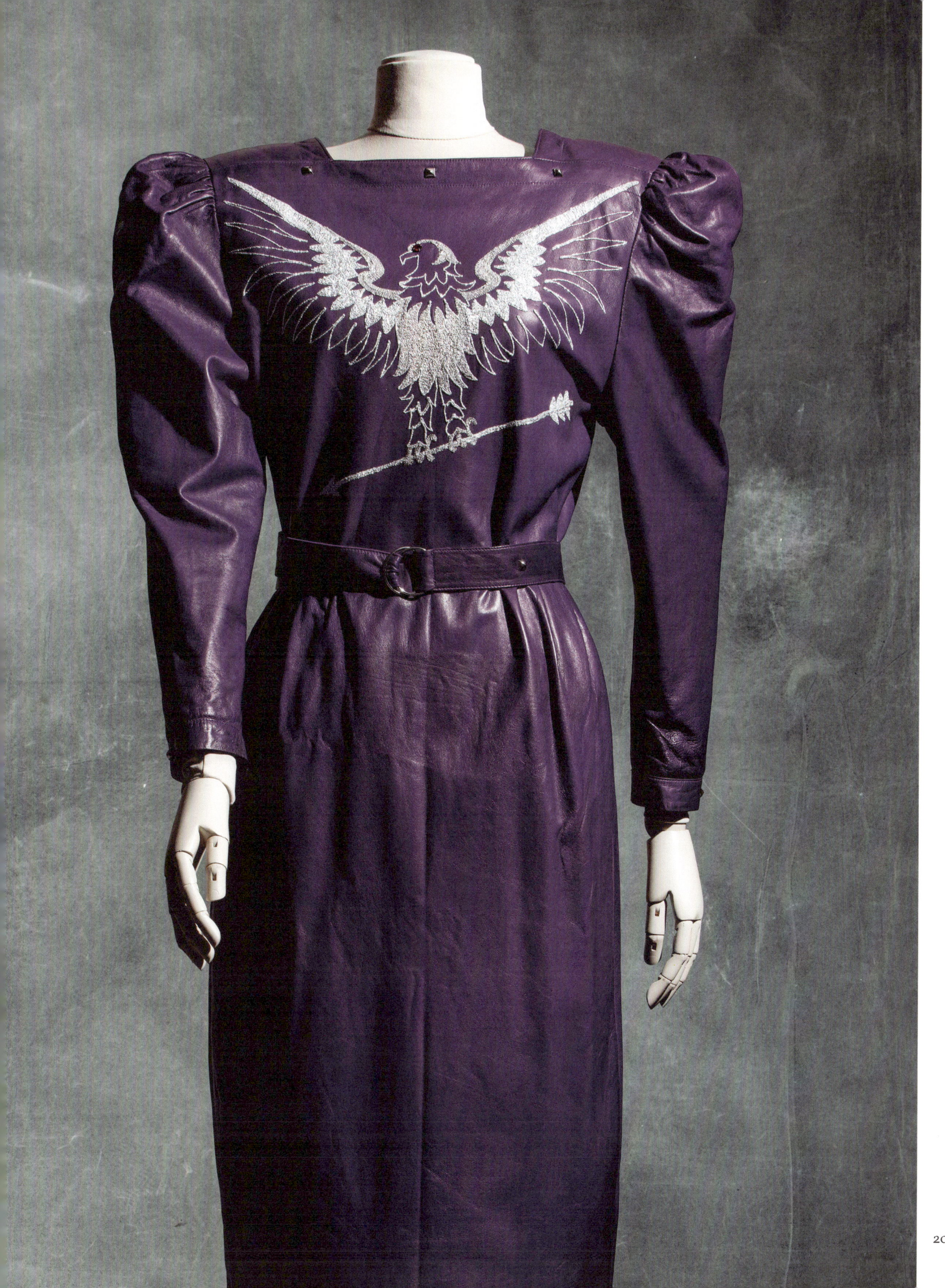

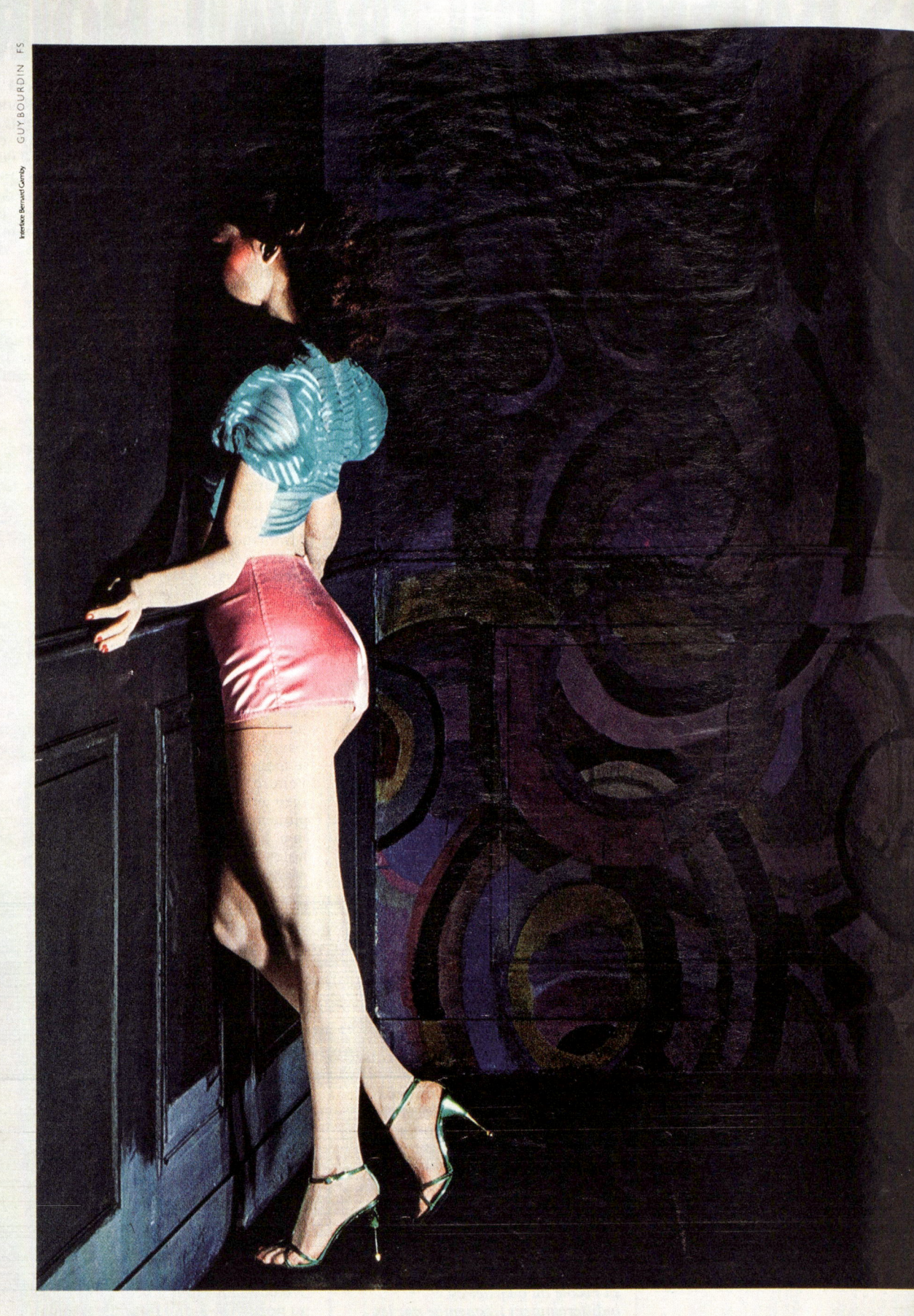

Charles Jourdan Californie 395 F

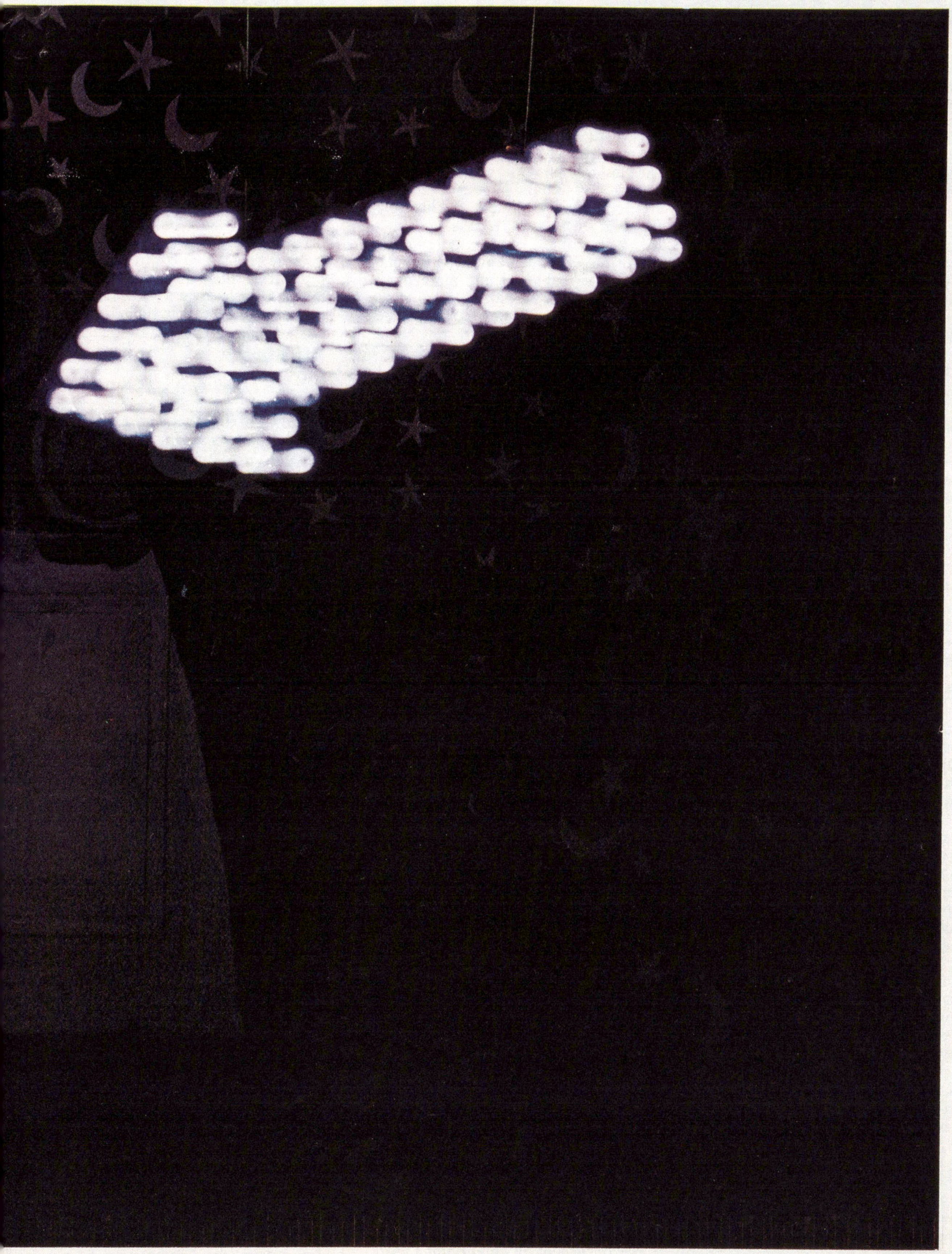

Liste des dépositaires
et catalogues sur demande
Charles Jourdan
Bureau 2
40 rue François Ier
75008 Paris

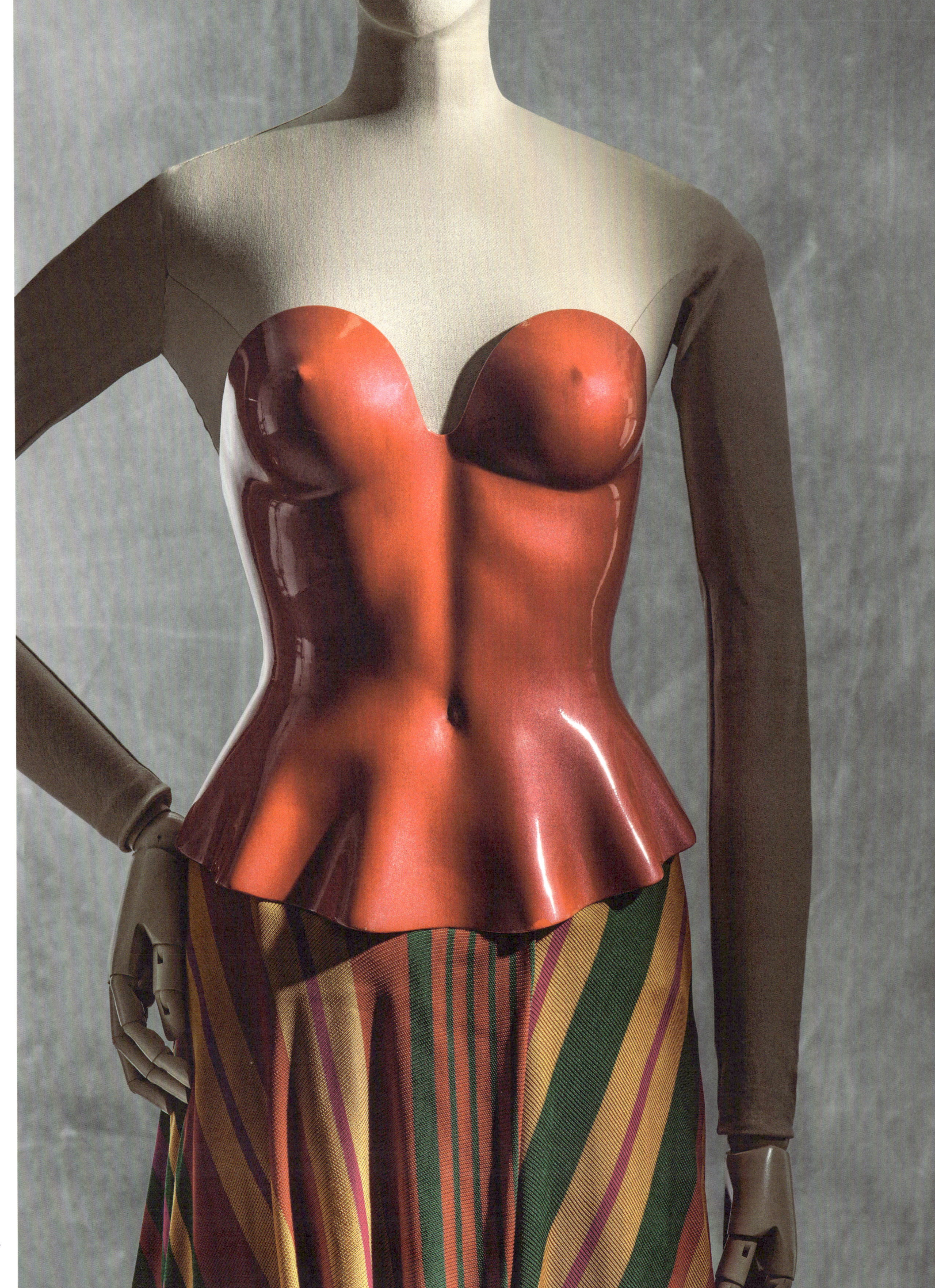

Issey Miyake
Ensemble, Autumn/Winter 1980-1981

As the French fashion magazine *L'Officiel* declared in August 1980: "When it comes to beauty, one thing is certain, the body will take on more and more importance, but only its magnetism will matter! Clothes, materials, and colors will only sublimate it further. By chance or premonition, three important couturiers (Issey Miyake, Thierry Mugler, and Kansai Yamamoto) have presented, for their winter 1981 collections, mermaids poured into 'shell-like bustiers,' a sort of second skin, a garment without a garment, a hymn to the body of a woman." This inspiration, which led many designers to revisit examples of armor, was already familiar territory for Yves Saint Laurent, who had presented gold metal bustiers, made by Claude Lalanne, in his Autumn/Winter 1969 collection.

    Issey Miyake's pairing of a bodice and harem pants offered a new sculptural vision of a woman's body, one that emphasizes the analogy between the molded body and body armor. Indeed, the shell of the bustier, made of colored resin, is a combination of anatomically correct Western armor and a samurai lacquered-leather breastplate. In the spirit of a cultural exchange between the East and the West, the Japanese designer combined the strapless bodice — a reference to the evening gowns of the 1950s — with multicolored striped harem pants. With this ensemble, Miyake celebrates the body in both its state of dress and undress.

    Lisa Lyon, a female bodybuilder and model, wore a similar outfit in a photograph taken by Robert Mapplethorpe in 1982.
E.P.-P.

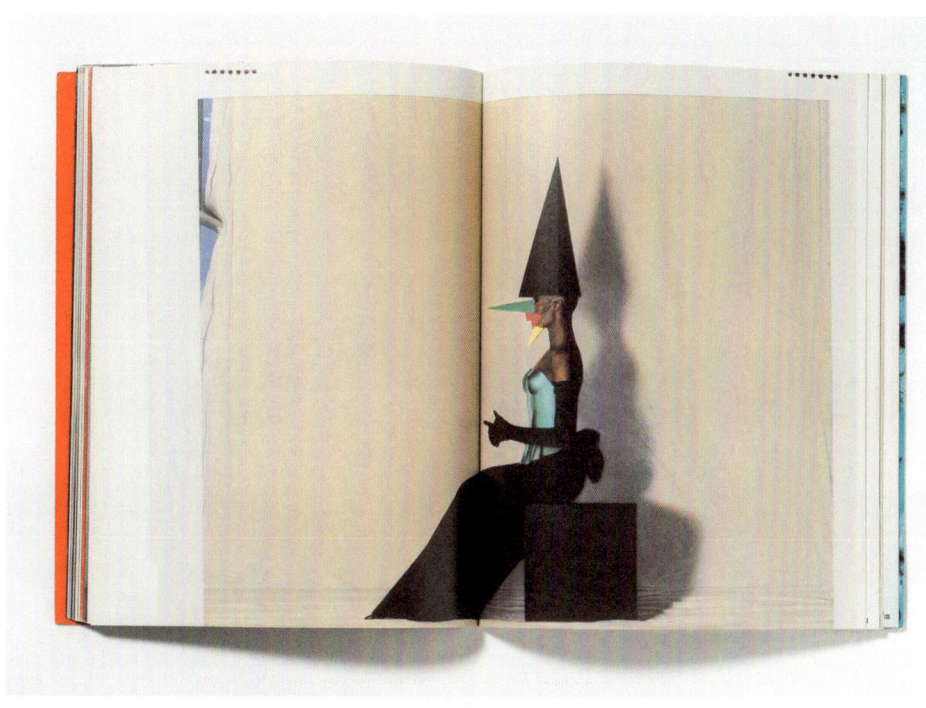

JEAN-PAUL GOUDE, *Libertango*, New York. Painted photograph.

Yves Saint Laurent
Le Smoking (Tuxedo), Spring/Summer 1982

Yves Saint Laurent presented *Le Smoking* — his first evening suit for women, inspired by the tuxedo — as part of his Fall/Winter 1966 collection. Many variations would follow: the tuxedo would be shown with pants or with a skirt, trimmed with satin, crepe, or silk moiré, in black or other colors, with a shawl or tailored collar, single or double breasted. It could be worn with or without a blouse but always retained the V neck and sharply structured shoulders.

Introduced as an alternative to cocktail dresses or evening gowns, the tuxedo's androgynous nature only increased the awareness of a woman's curves. With this design, Saint Laurent proposed a new vision of a couple — one in which a man and a woman can choose to wear similar clothes — as seen in Helmut Newton's 1981 photograph of the designer and his muse, Catherine Deneuve.
E.P.-P.

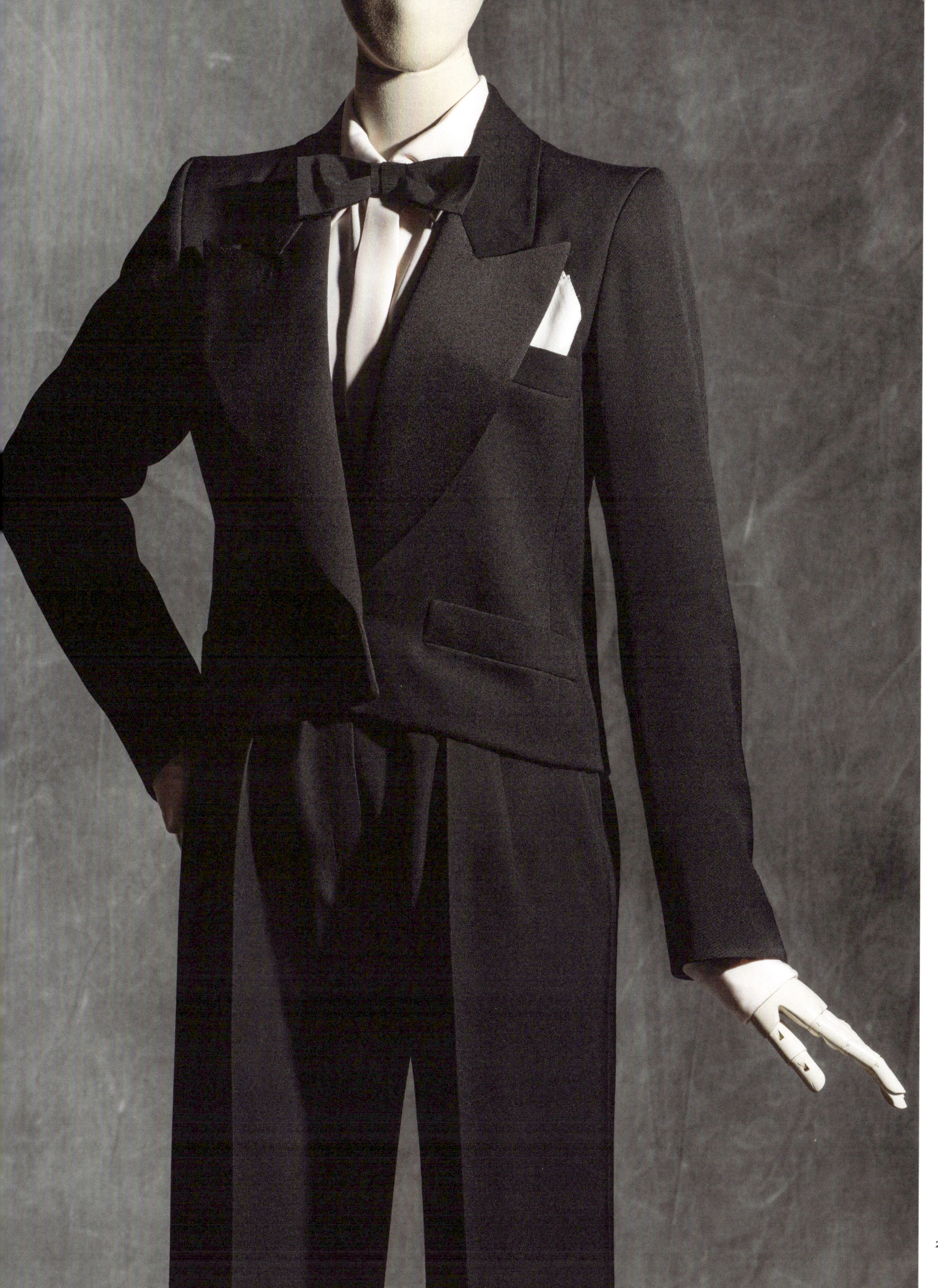

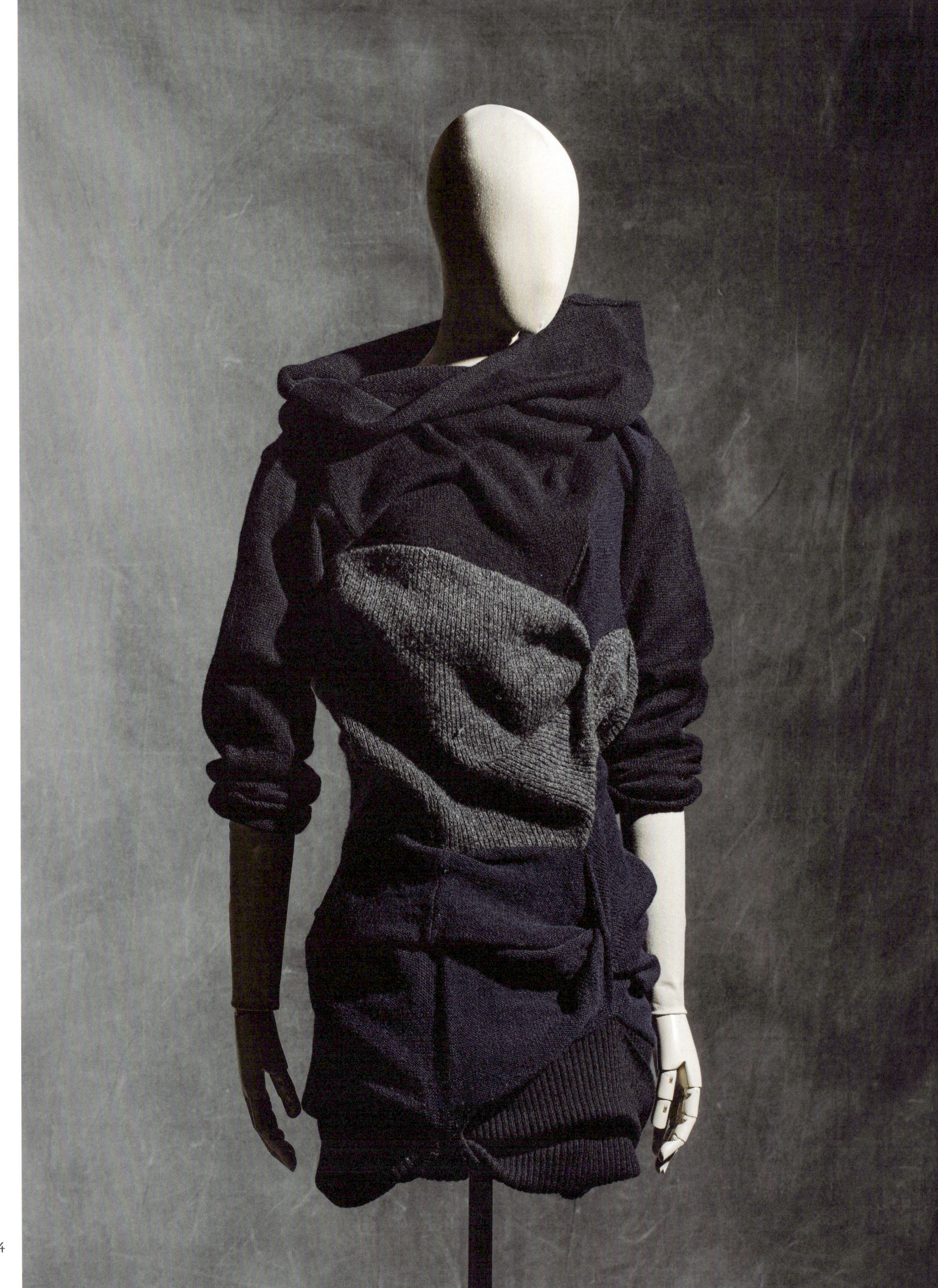

Comme des Garçons
Dress, Autumn/Winter 1984–1985

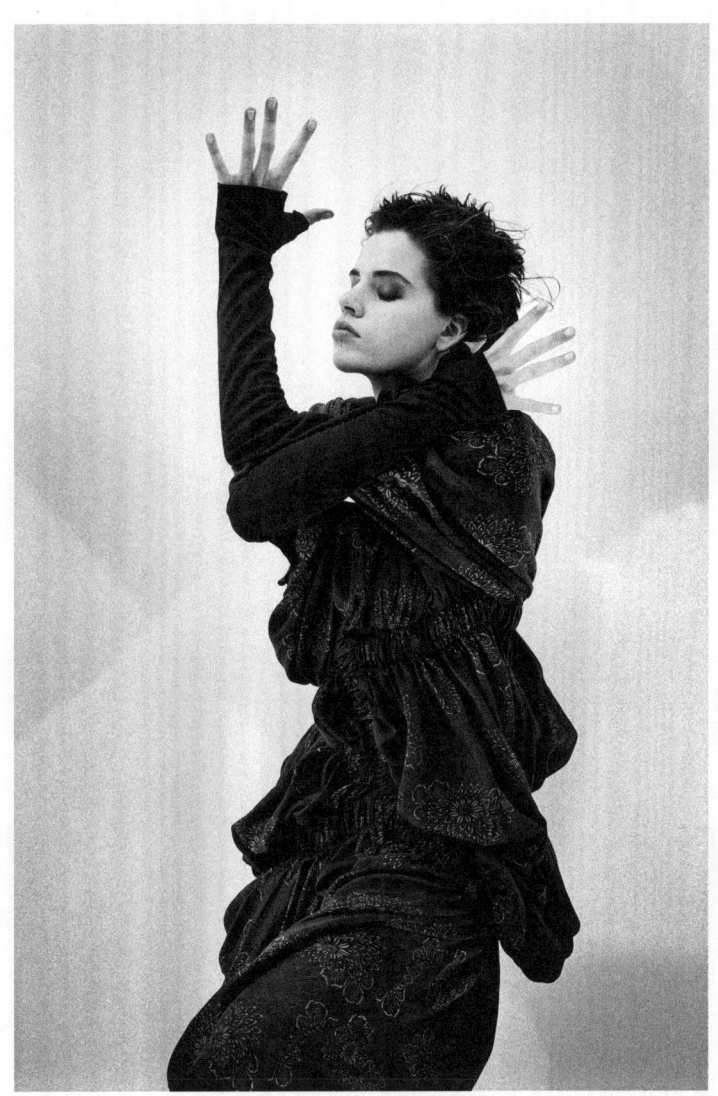

This dress illustrates the new interest in volume that would characterize the work of Rei Kawakubo, founder of the brand Comme des Garçons. Bands of black, navy, and mottled gray knitted wool are sewn together in a way that exposes the seams, overlaps, and openings. The neck, shoulders, bust, waist, and hips disappear under the distorted material, revealing only the woolly bumps of stocking and moss stitching and edge ribbing. The woven rather than sewn aspect gives the fabric the look of having been stretched and twisted. The complex design raises questions about the concept of the body: the inventive and systematic character of the dress could lead viewers to believe they are looking at a random piece of second-hand clothing. But this is, in fact, industrially produced and designed ready-to-wear.

Kawakubo's body of work has stylistically redefined femininity by upending the codes of seduction. Her reaction to the traditional aesthetics of couture and ready-to-wear is violent, perhaps because she bears its legacy. Her collections, defined by disciplined candor, have been presented in Paris since 1981.
E.P.-P.

PETER LINDBERGH, Photograph from the Comme des Garçons Fall/Winter 1984-1985 collection catalogue. Model: Claudia Huidobro.
PP. 216-217 — NICK KNIGHT, Photographs from the Yohji Yamamoto Summer 1987 collection catalogue. Model: Naomi Campbell.

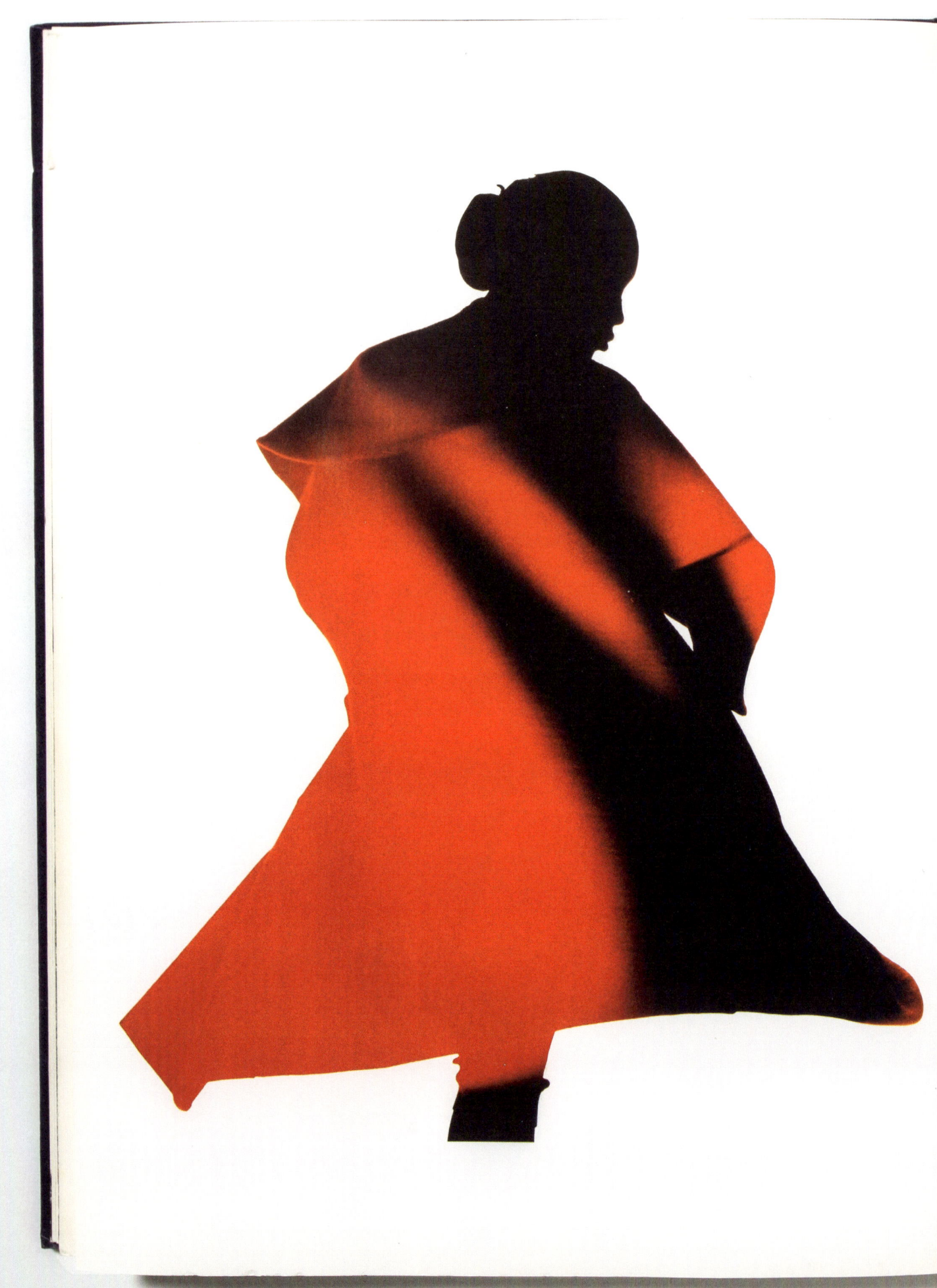

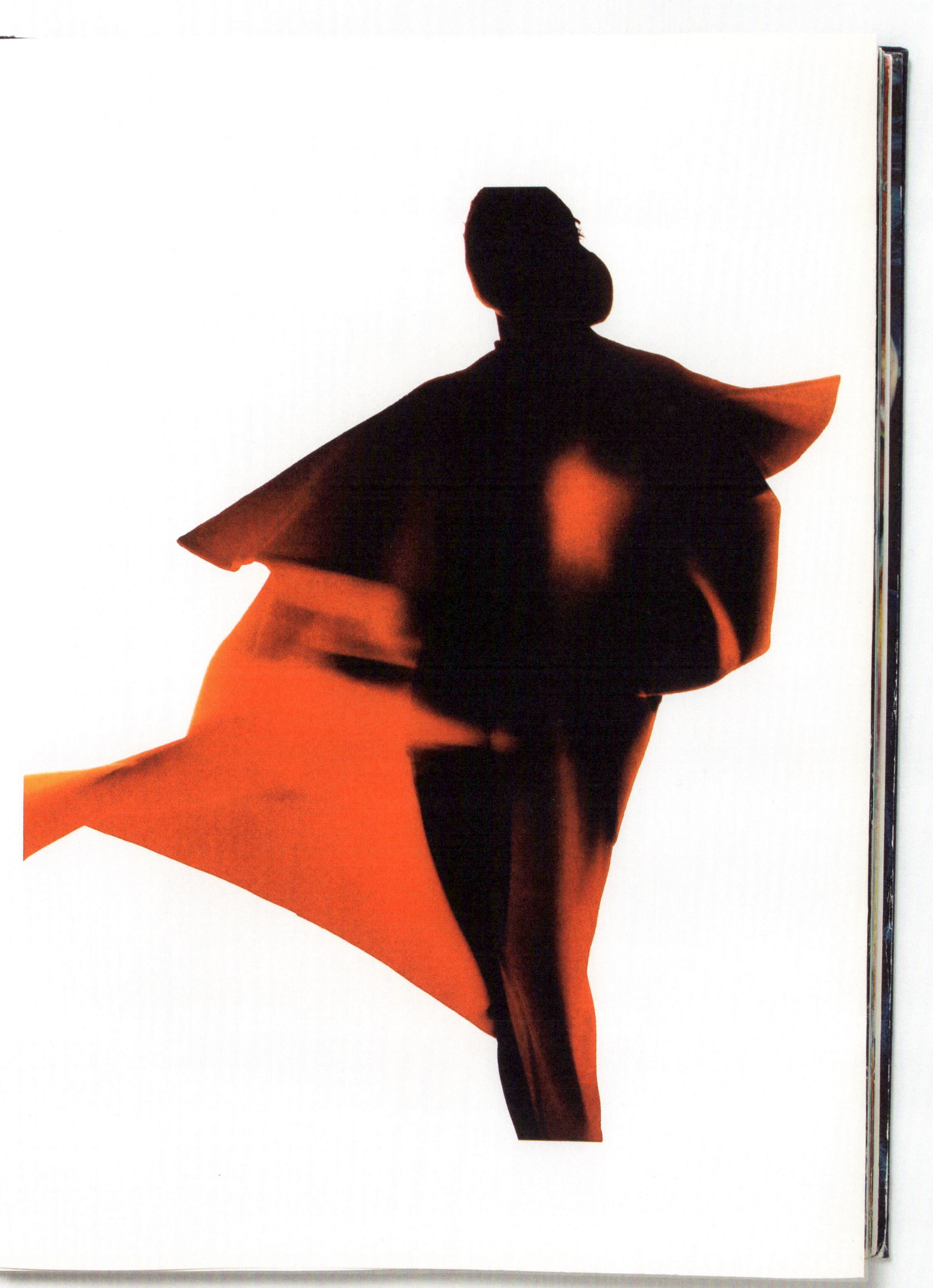

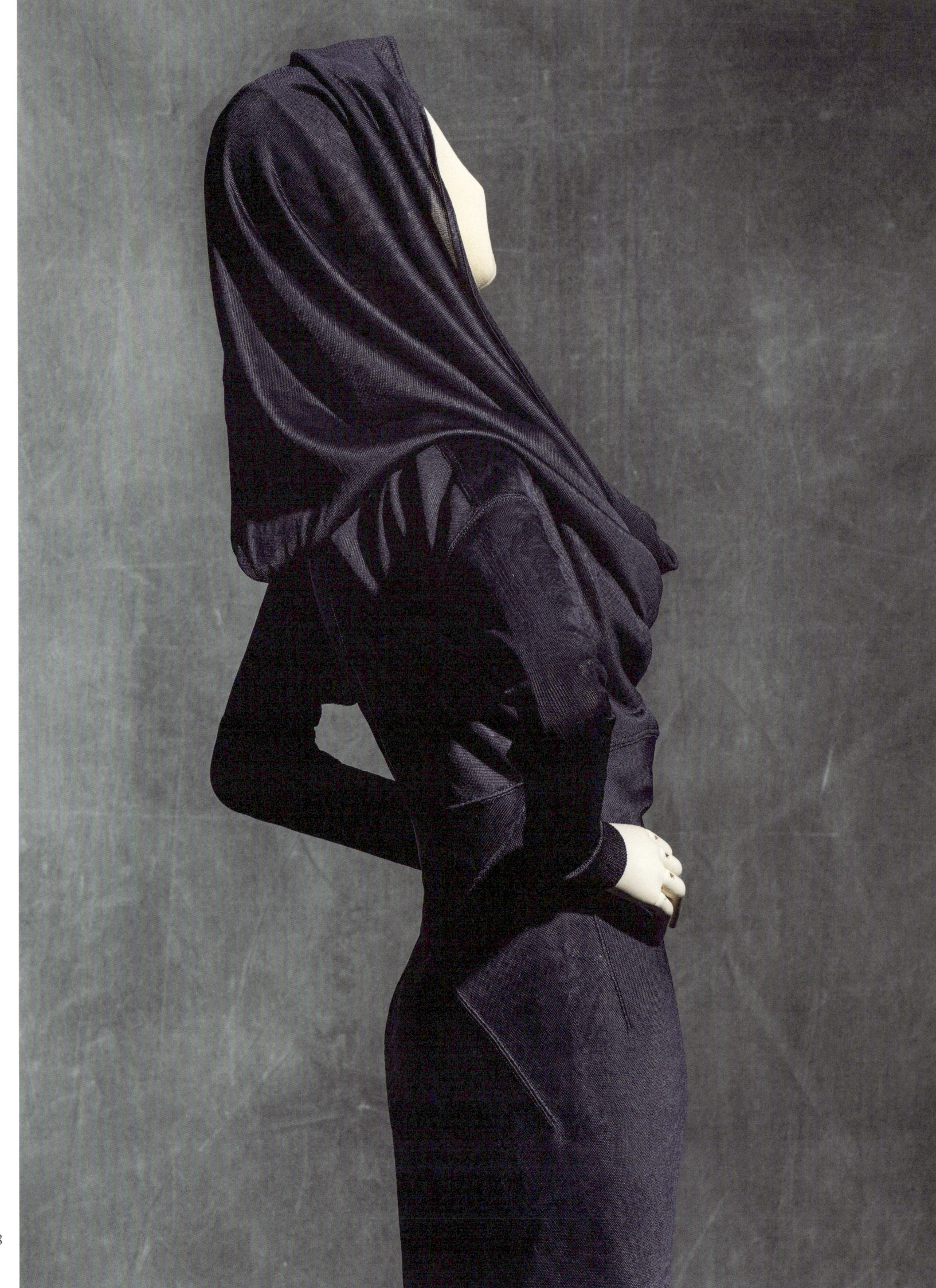

Azzedine Alaïa
Sheath Dress
Autumn/Winter 1986-1987

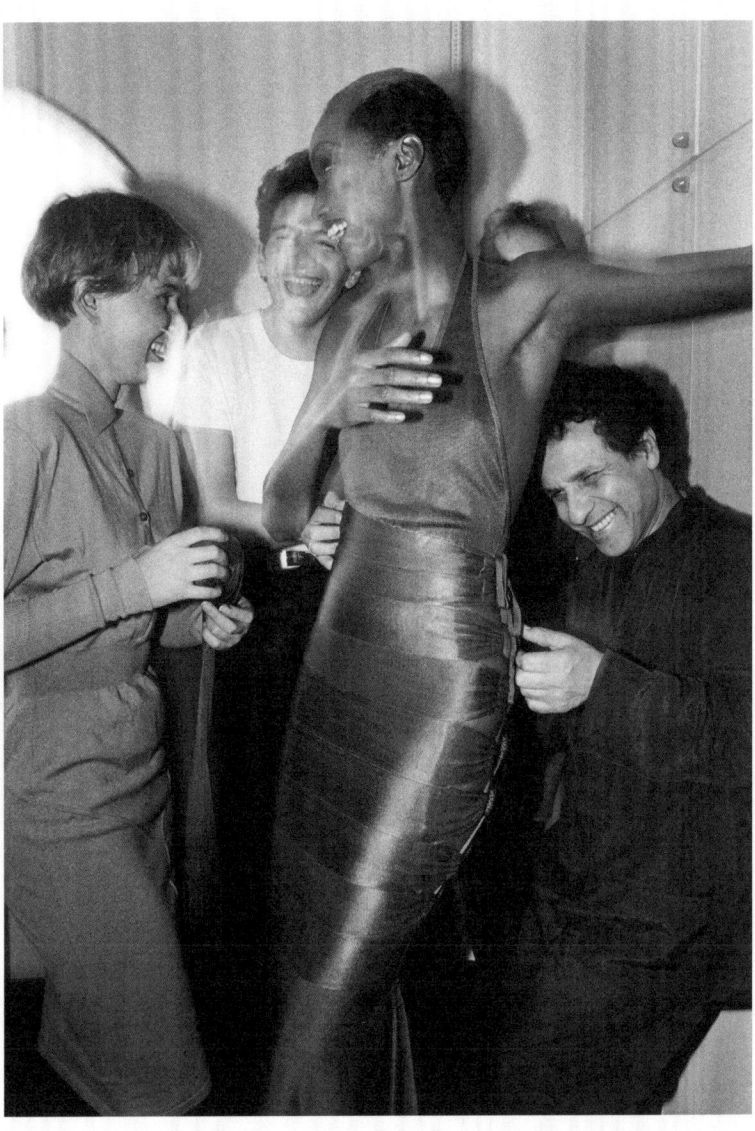

Azzedine Alaïa became famous during the 1980s for his knitwear, leather, and coated-fabric designs that clung to the body. Tina Turner, Grace Jones, and Naomi Campbell figured among his many muses, and top models were eager to wear his form-fitting designs on the runway.

This dress of acetate jersey has the gleam and moiré look of luxurious silk. The fall and slight elasticity of the fabric allow it to cling to the body or drape fluidly, as it does on the cape — the sportswear equivalent of a veil. A photograph of Princess Stephanie of Monaco wearing an identical dress appeared in *Vogue* in November 1986 with the following caption: "She swims like a fish. She sings like a siren . . ." The true essence of a woman, according to Alaïa, is both carnal and mythical — in a word, divine.
E.P.-P.

WILLIAM KLEIN, *Backstage Alaïa + Katoucha, Paris 1986*. Photograph.

Thierry Mugler
Embarquement Immédiat (Immediate Boarding) Evening Gown
Autumn/Winter 1987–1988

"Created in the spirit of baroque humor and floral mannerism, this dress lives a metaphor that reaches the pinnacle of sophistication and elegance," noted *L'Officiel* in August 1987. This ready-to-wear design is a stylistic exercise that combines many challenges and features of haute couture. The velvet, satin, and roses illustrate three different uses of silk, an emblematic fabric of couture; the drape, sheath, and train of the dress are also elements usually reserved for made-to-measure clothes.

The back of this sleek, long, and mysterious gown revealed an unexpected surprise—the return of Christian Dior's flower-woman. "Embarquement Immédiat" signaled Thierry Mugler's entry into the world of haute couture in 1992, under his own name—a first for a ready-to-wear designer.
E.P.-P.

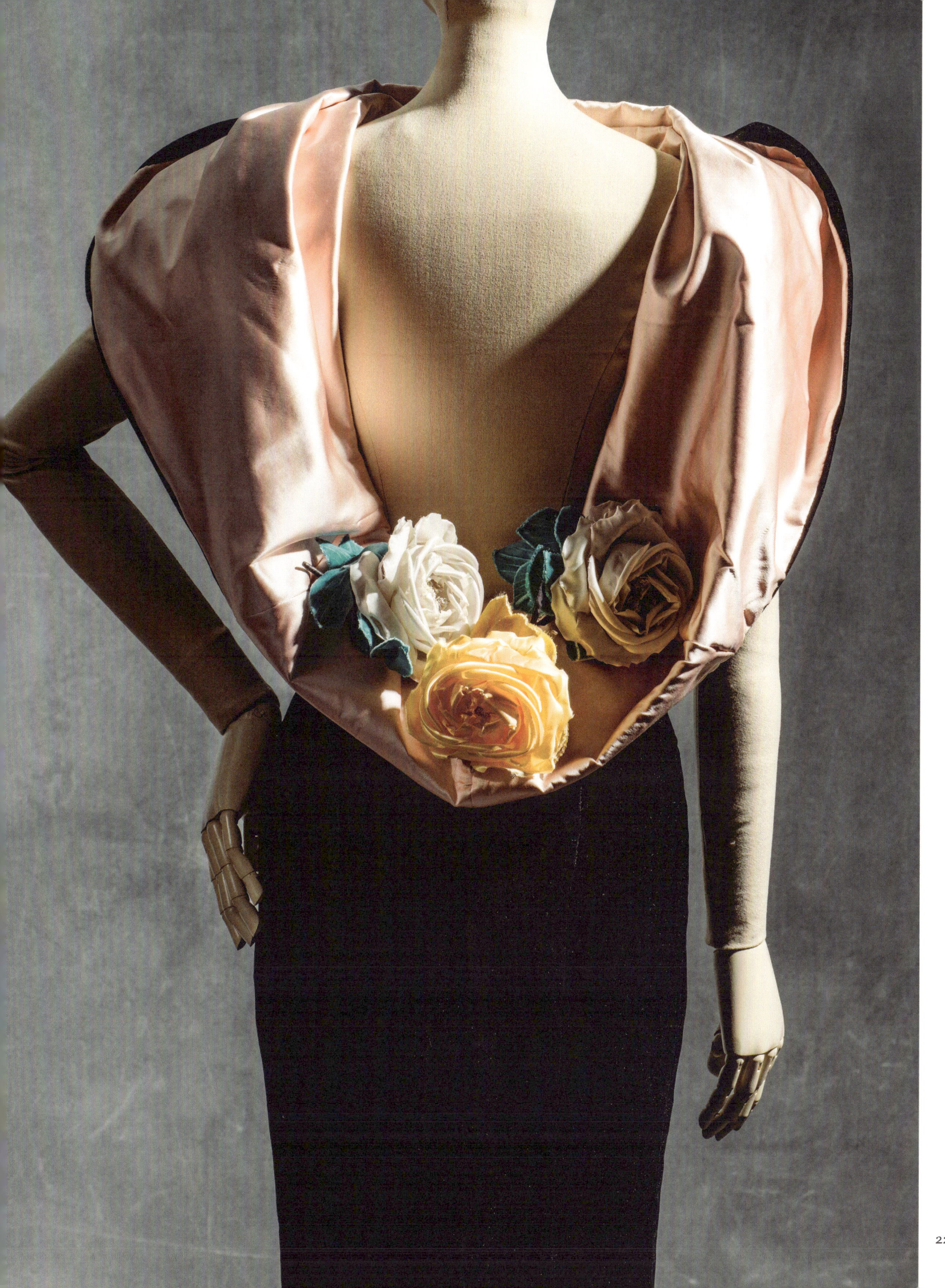

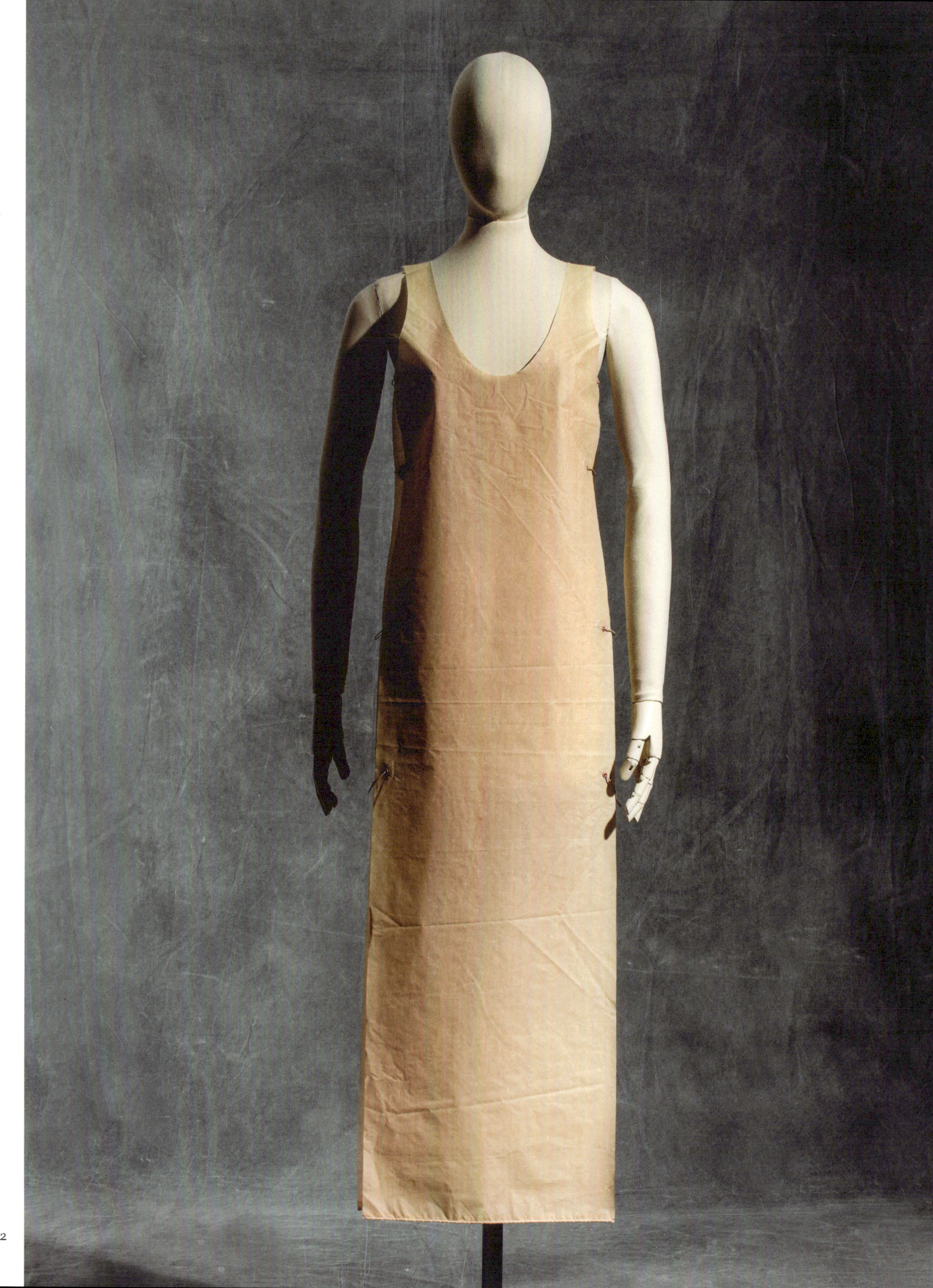

Helmut Lang
Long Dress, Spring/Summer 1991

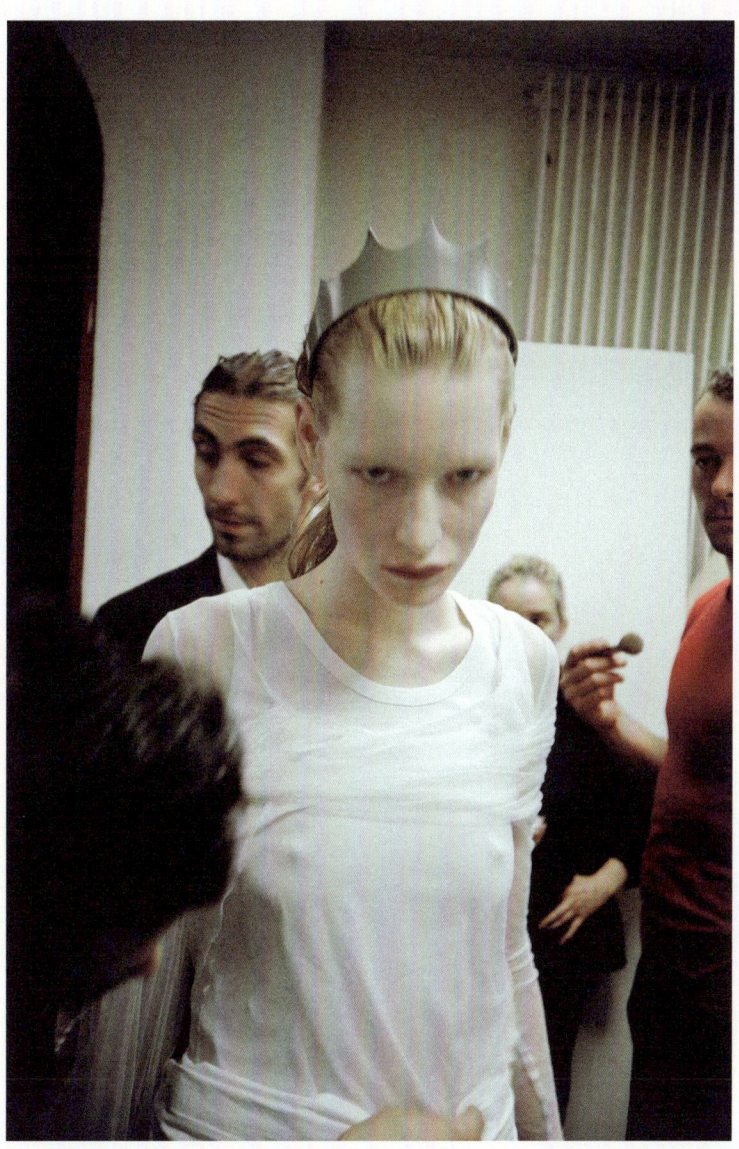

According to the *Journal du textile* of November 12, 1990, Helmut Lang had reached "an extreme point of minimalism." This dress, composed of two panels of beige polyester held together with side ties, signals a sharp reaction to the baroque trends of the 1980s. Lang's first fashion show, held in 1986 at the Centre Georges Pompidou in Paris, was part of the exhibition *Vienna: Birth of a Century, 1889-1938*. The influence of the Wiener movement and Adolf Loos — for whom ornamentation was a crime — has been evident since the designer's first "*Kollection*."

Lang's spare aesthetic would influence fashion for years to come. As he told *Elle* in an October 2003 interview: "I believe the first collection we showed in Paris in 1986 defined the silhouette of the 1990s, for men as well as for women."
E.P.-P.

JUERGEN TELLER, Helmut Lang fashion show, Spring/Summer 1997. Photograph. Model: Kirsten Owen.

Christian Lacroix
Mademoiselle Hortensia *Gown*
Autumn/Winter 1992-1993

Hoping to become a museum curator, Christian Lacroix studied at the École du Louvre. His knowledge of fashion history is evident throughout his work as he draws inspiration from the past and reconfigures it for the present. The shape of this gown recalls the *robes volantes* worn during the Regency period, while the hydrangea and tuberose brocade is reminiscent of the silk designs that were fashionable during the late nineteenth century — a time when the styles of the ancien régime were so popular. The elegance of the Age of Enlightenment and the opulence of the Third Republic would come together in a world depicted by Léon Bonnat and dresses by Charles Frederick Worth.

In this instance, Lacroix adds a lighthearted touch to his creation: the name of the dress refers to a song about a countess's humble beginnings: "*Au temps des crinolines, vivait une orpheline, toujours tendre et câline, Mlle Horsensia*" (In the days of crinolines, there lived an orphan, always kind and sweet, whose name was Mademoiselle Hortensia).

E.P.-P.

CHRISTIAN LACROIX, Notes for the "Mademoiselle Hortensia" dress, 2016.
Musée des Arts Décoratifs, Paris; The Documentation Center.

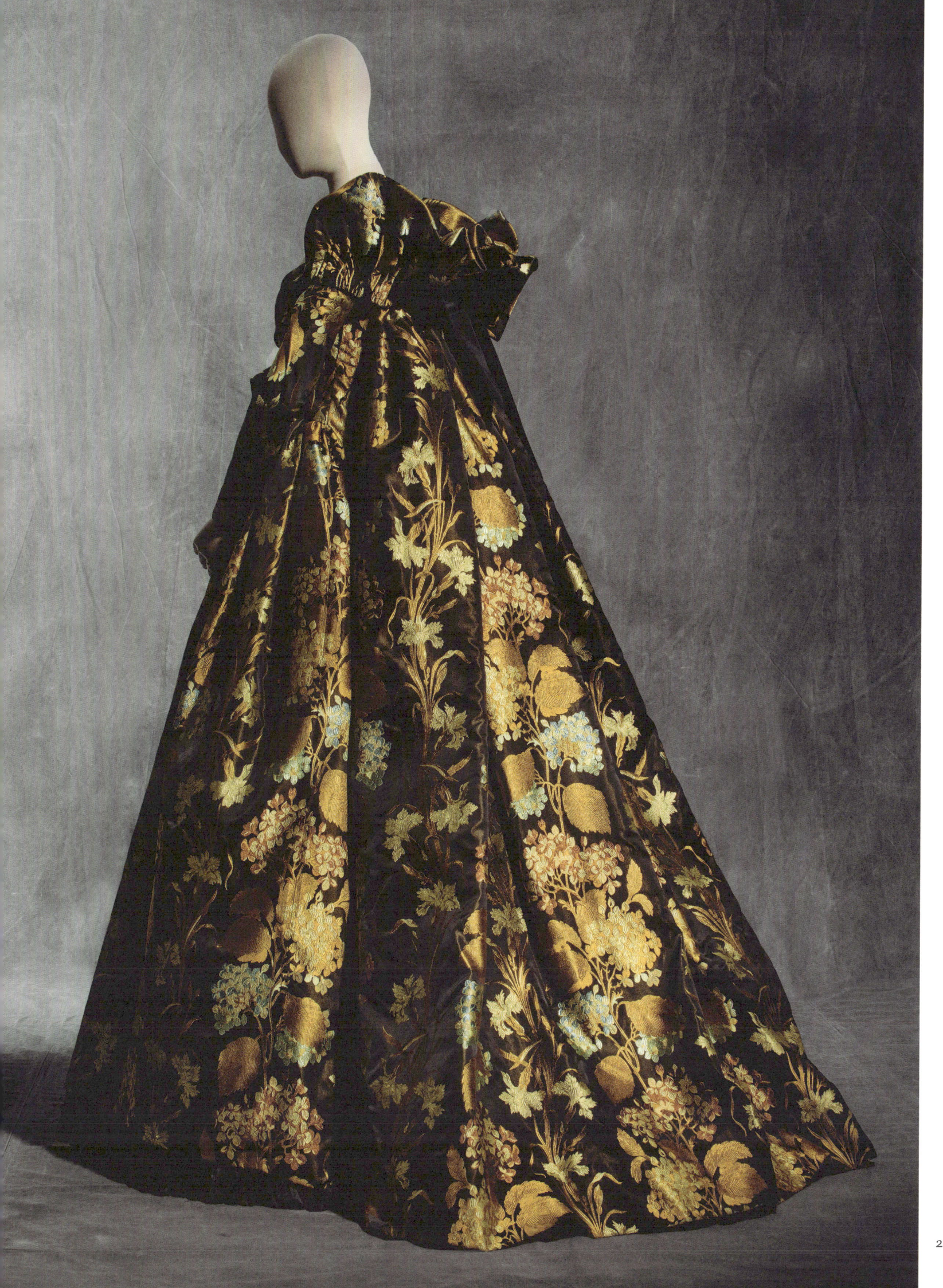

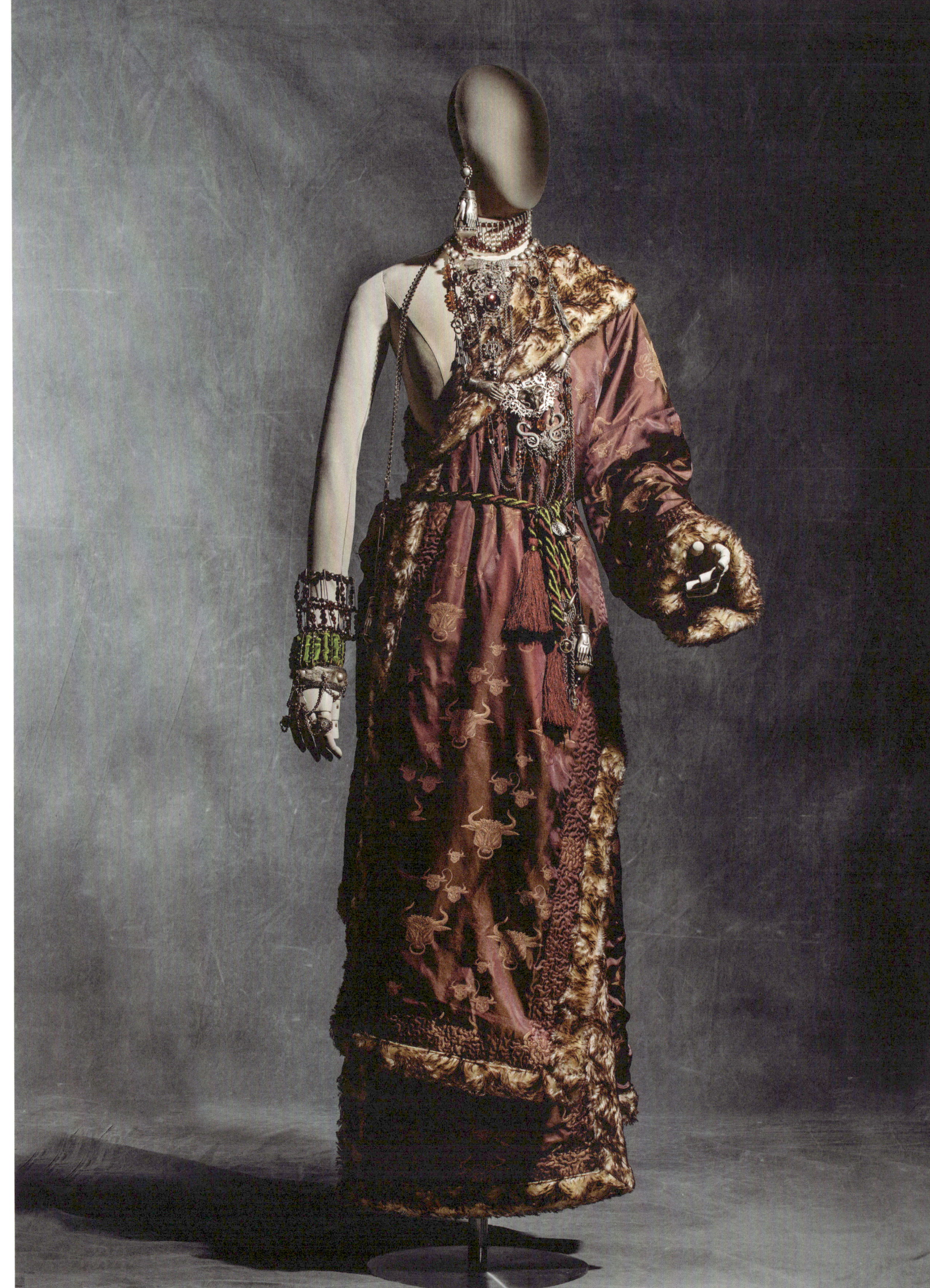

Jean Paul Gaultier
Ensemble, Autumn/Winter 1994-1995

This creation is part of a collection inspired by Eastern exoticism. Regardless of the designs' actual geographic provenance, Gaultier's genius resides in the way he combines these various elements. In his unconventional fashion shows, all types of people — men, women, large, small, with buzzed, platinum, braided, or *kokochnik*-adorned hair — walk the runway sporting dress clothes or wide caftans (such as the casual fur-lined damask coat shown here). The show is a harmony of warm colors, of velvets, satin, fur, and knits in solid tones or embellished with cultural or heraldic motifs.

This ensemble is characteristic of Gaultier's nomadic spirit — every collection is a travel adventure. Each season, the collection focuses on one or several aspects of Parisian fashion or traditional costumes (Russian Constructivism, followers of Krishna, or the Lubavitch movement, to name just a few), with the designer taking a cue from the work of Elsa Schiaparelli and upholding the principles of surrealism.

E.P.-P

Karl Lagerfeld for Chanel
Evening Gown, Spring/Summer 1996

This evening gown, from the Spring/Summer 1996 collection, was the costliest Chanel dress ever presented during a fashion show. The embroidery, created by the house of Lesage, required 1,200 hours of needlework, and assembling the dress took another ninety hours of couture work in the atelier. The design was a commercial success and was ordered by several wealthy clients, among them Mouna Ayoub. Emblematic of Lagerfeld's work for Chanel, the dress illustrates the designer's ability to reinterpret the Chanel style for current social and economic times.
E.P.-P.

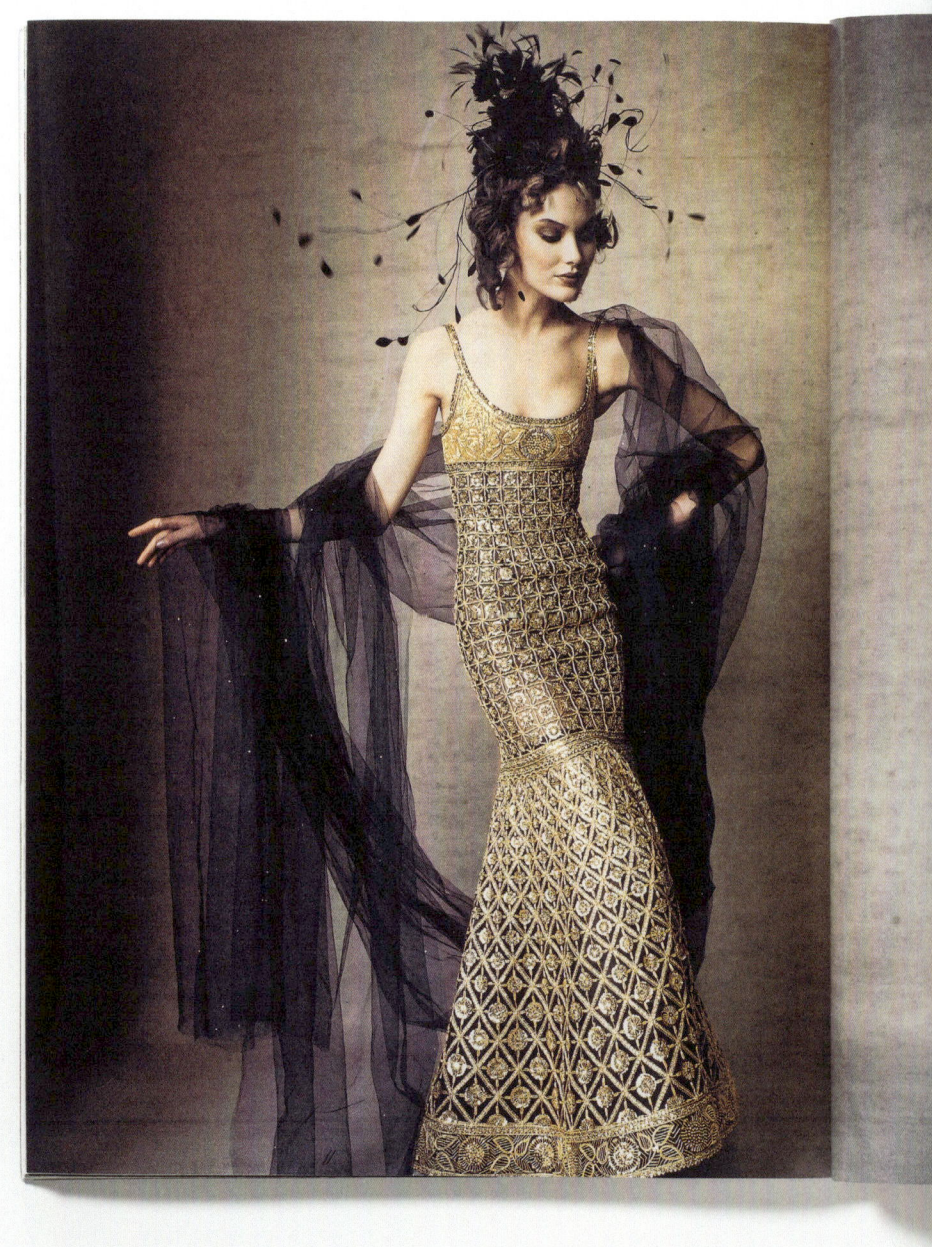

IRVING PENN, Photograph published in *Vogue*, April 1996, page 284.

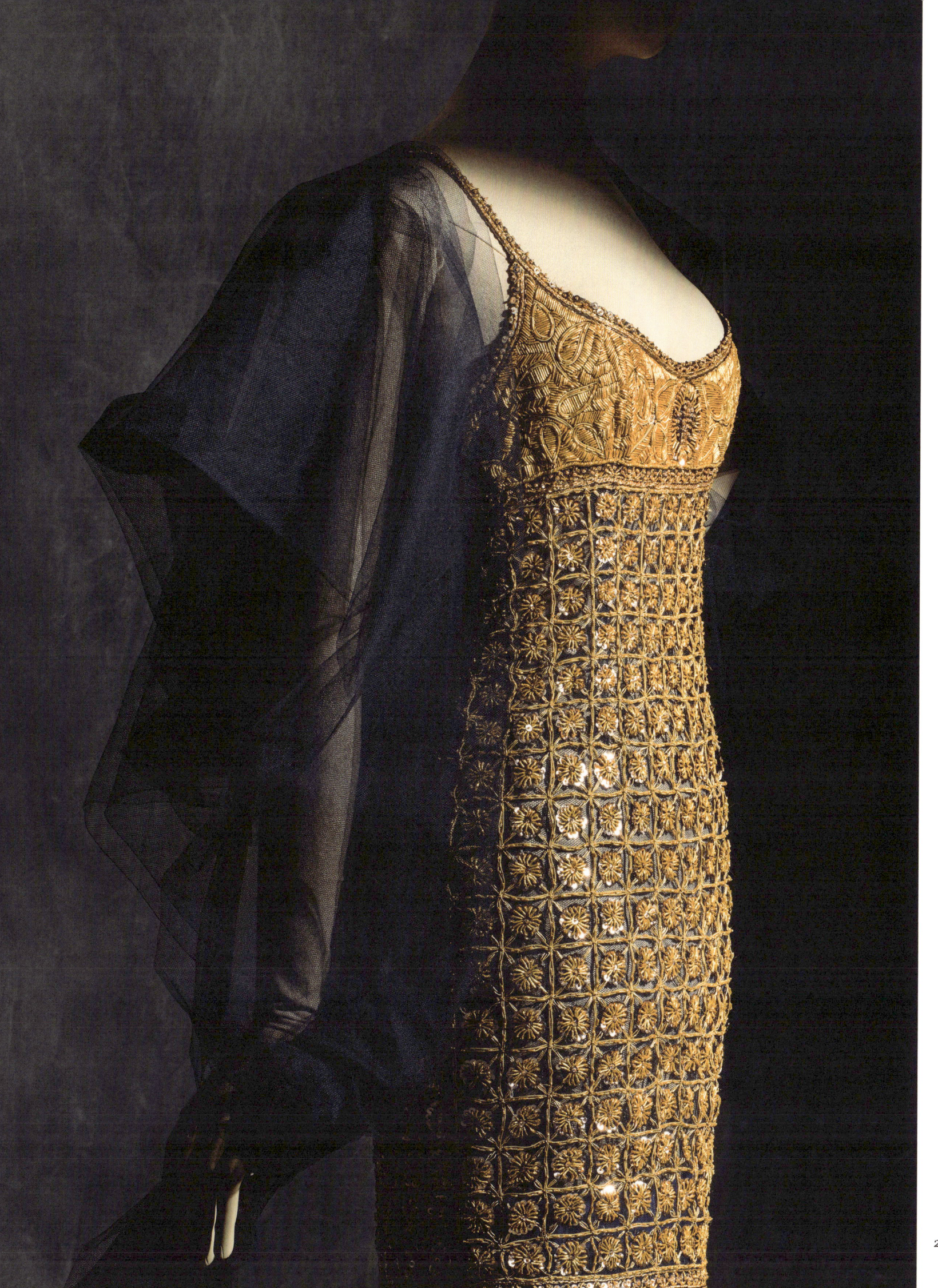

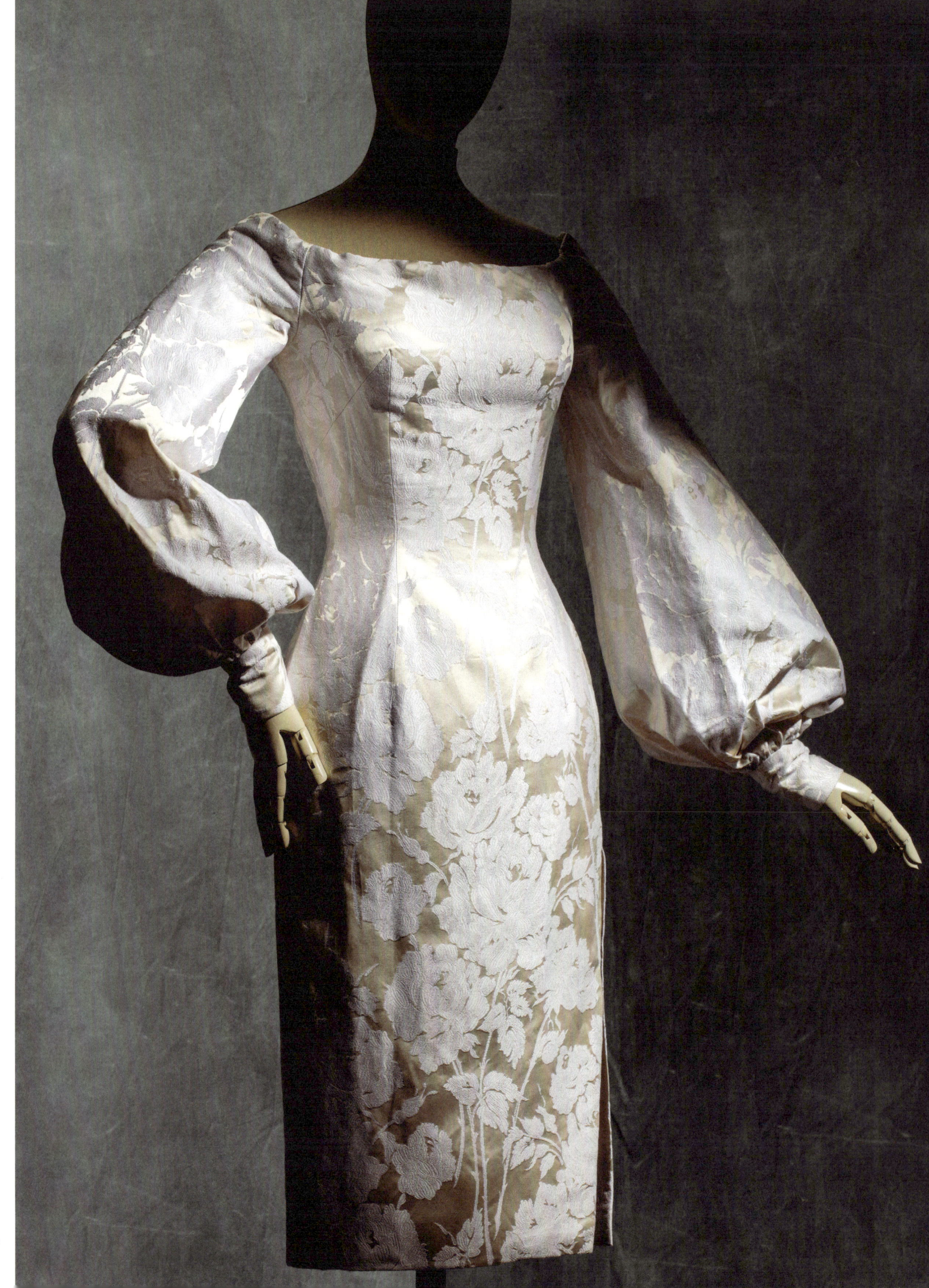

Alexander McQueen for Givenchy
Cocktail Dress, Spring/Summer 1997

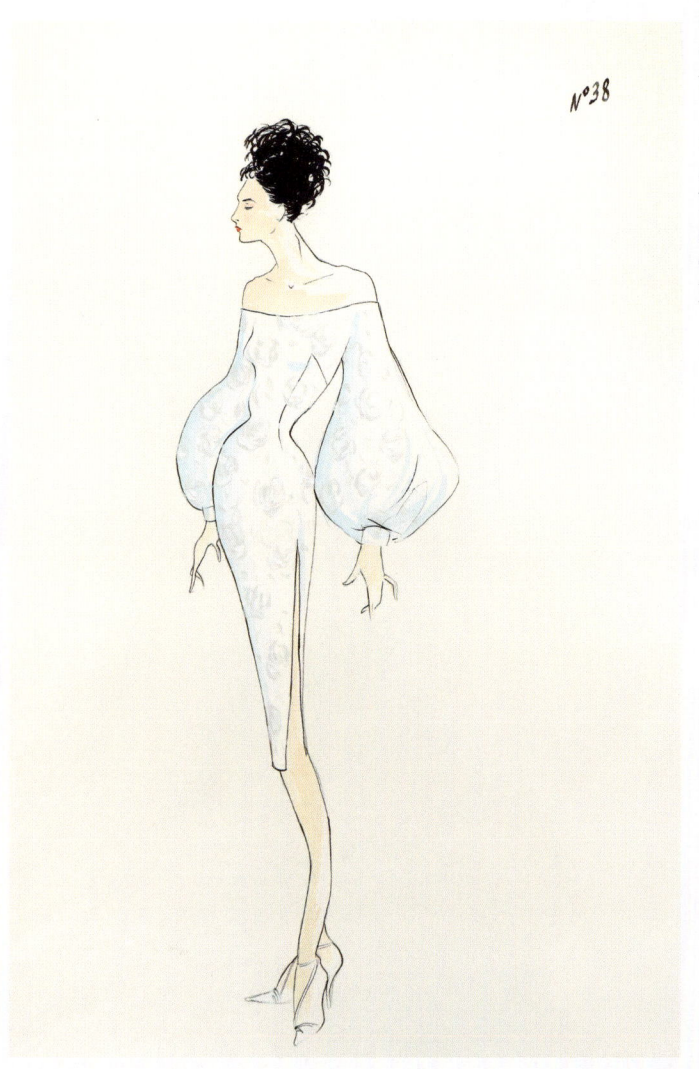

Alexander McQueen took over creative direction of the house of Givenchy when John Galliano moved to Christian Dior in 1996. For a time, both houses were under the artistic direction of British designers, who put on spectacular fashion shows that brought these brands back to the forefront of couture.
The theme of McQueen's first collection for Givenchy was Jason and the Argonauts and the Quest for the Golden Fleece. A procession of predominantly white and gold-clad silhouettes from Greek mythology or yachting walked the runway. It was an opportunity for the London designer to display his mastery of *flou* (the antique draping) and of *tailleur* (the precise tailoring of nautical uniforms).

Other designs inspired by the fashion of the 1950s and 1960s — such as this cocktail dress, with a wide décolletage, of silk damask strewn with bouquets of roses — bring to mind the many exclusive clients of the Mediterraneon region, including Maria Callas, who contributed to the fame of Givenchy.
E.P.-P.

ALEXANDER MCQUEEN, Sketch for the "In Search of the Golden Fleece" collection, Spring/Summer 1997.
PP. 236-237 — DAVID LACHAPELLE, *Burning Down the House: Alexander McQueen and Isabella Blow, Essex, England*, 1996.
Photograph published in *Vanity Fair*, 1996.

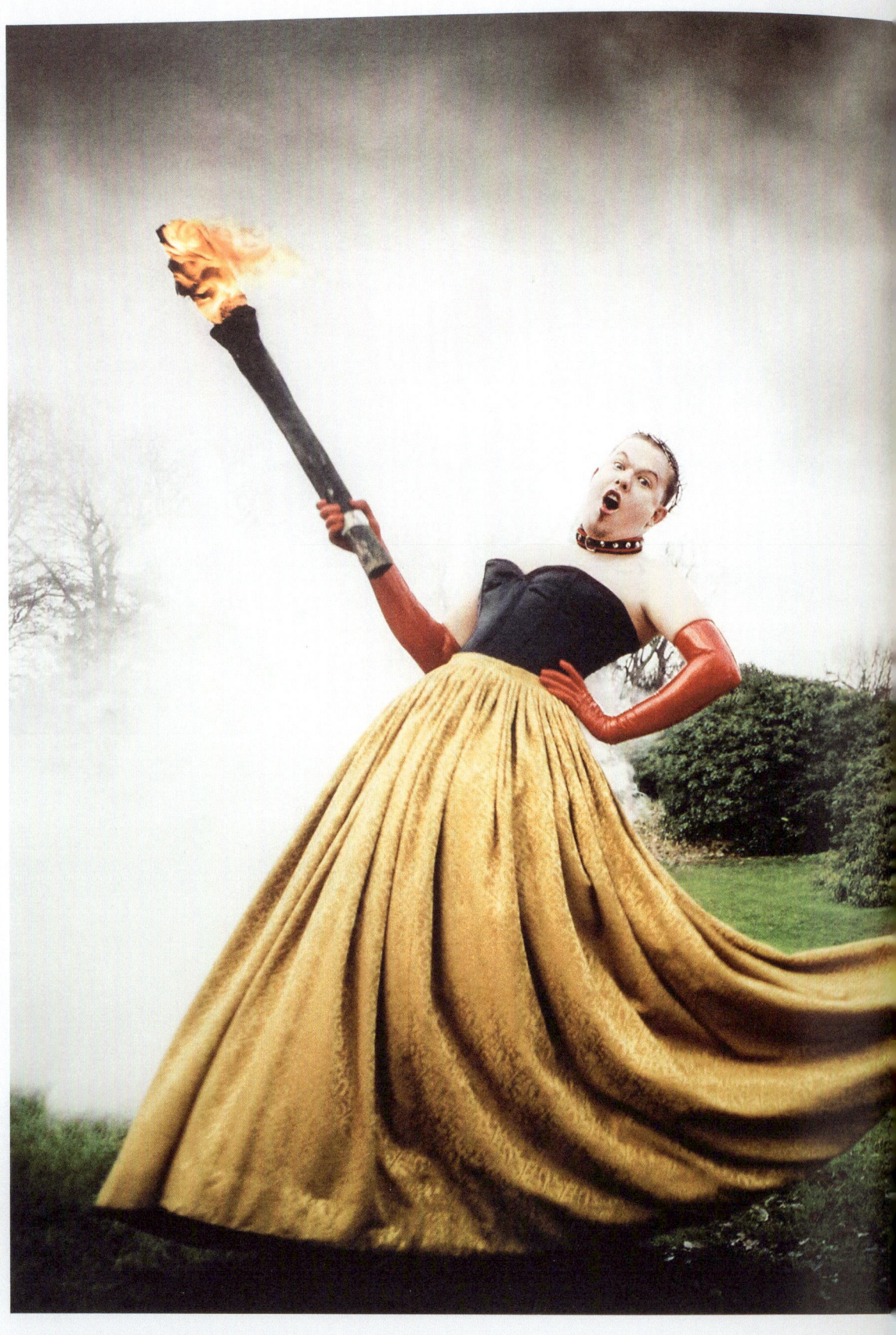

144　SENSIBILITY — A GOTHIC MIND

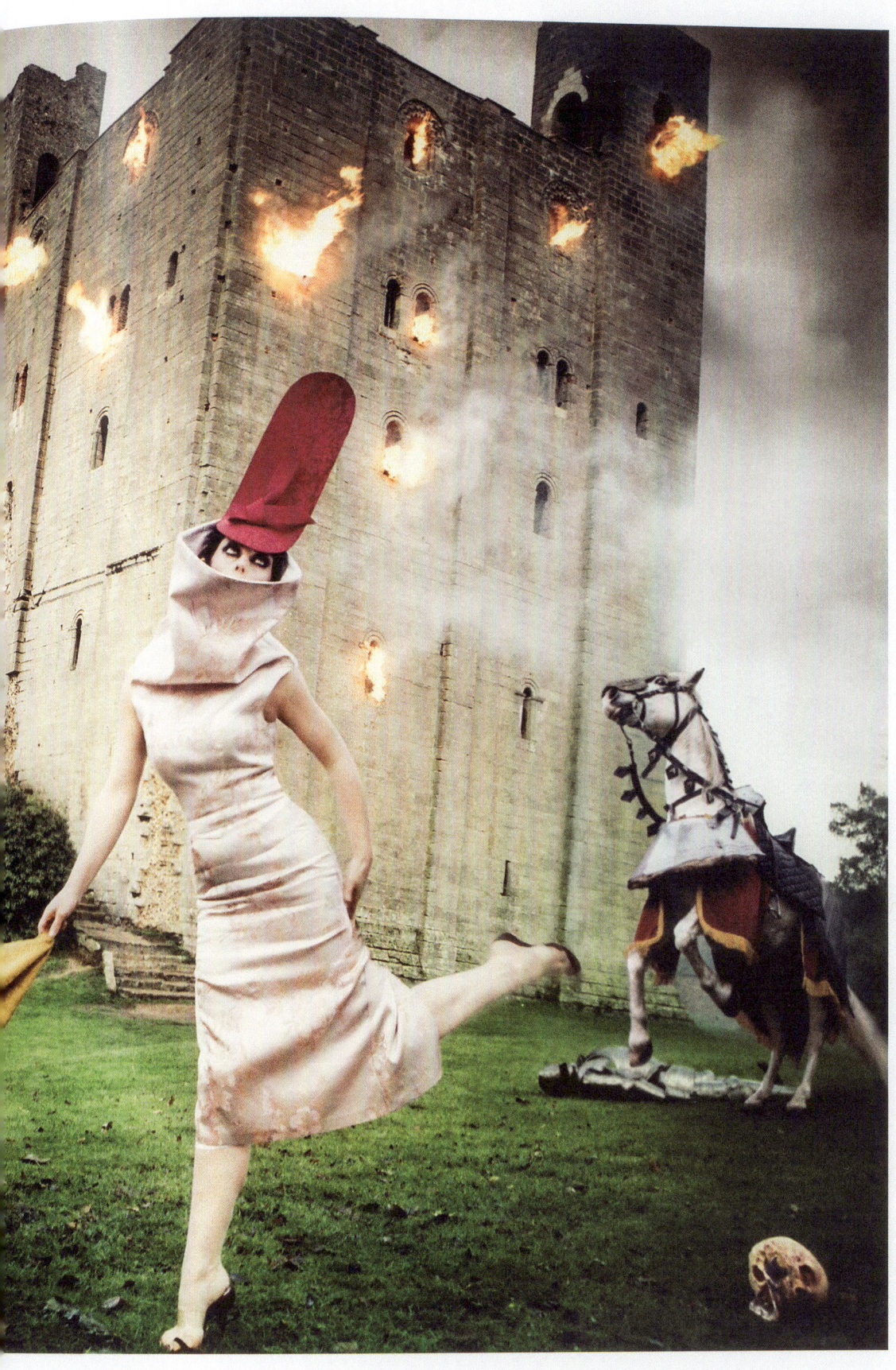

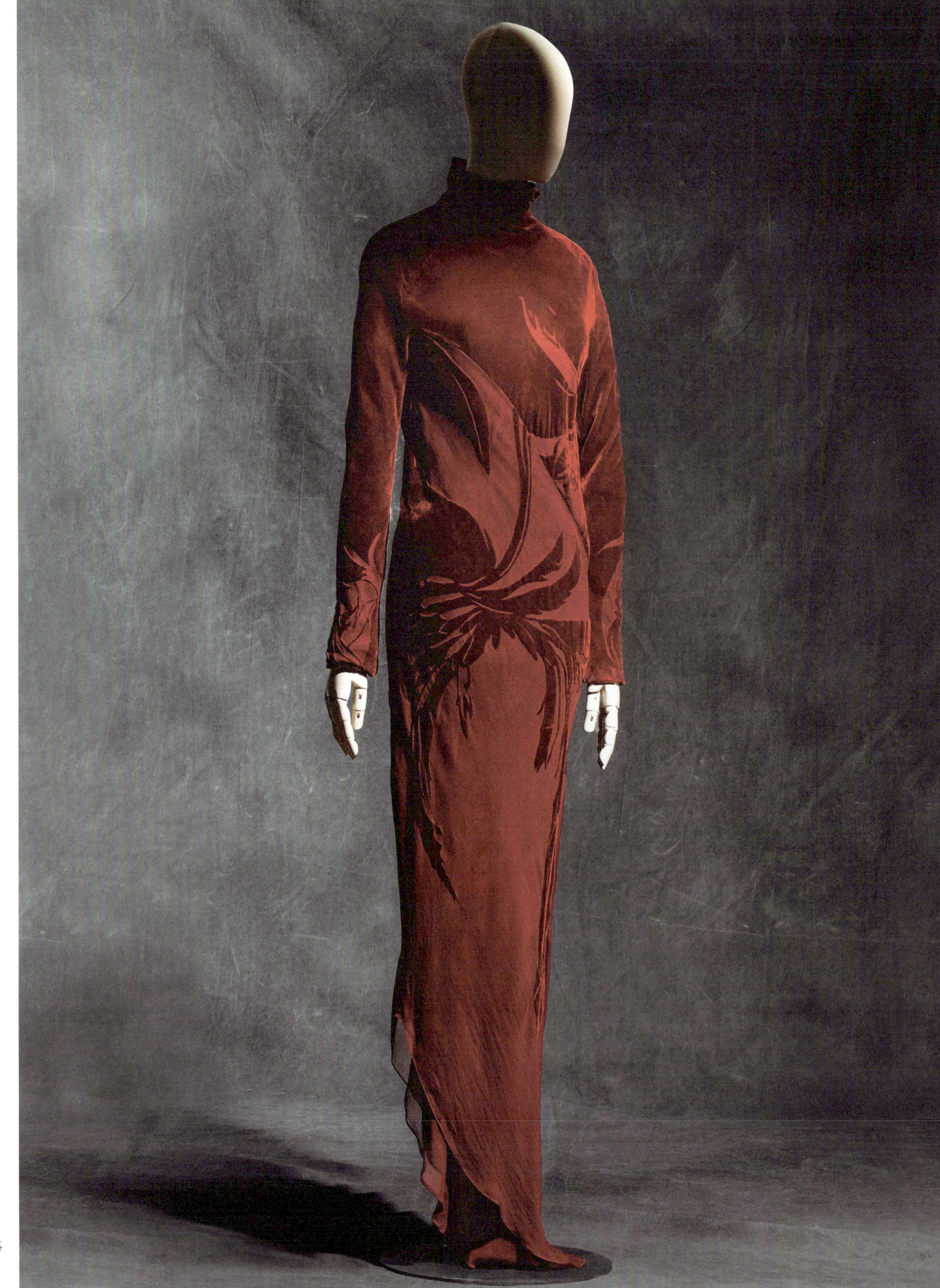

Martine Sitbon
Dress, Autumn/Winter 1997-1998

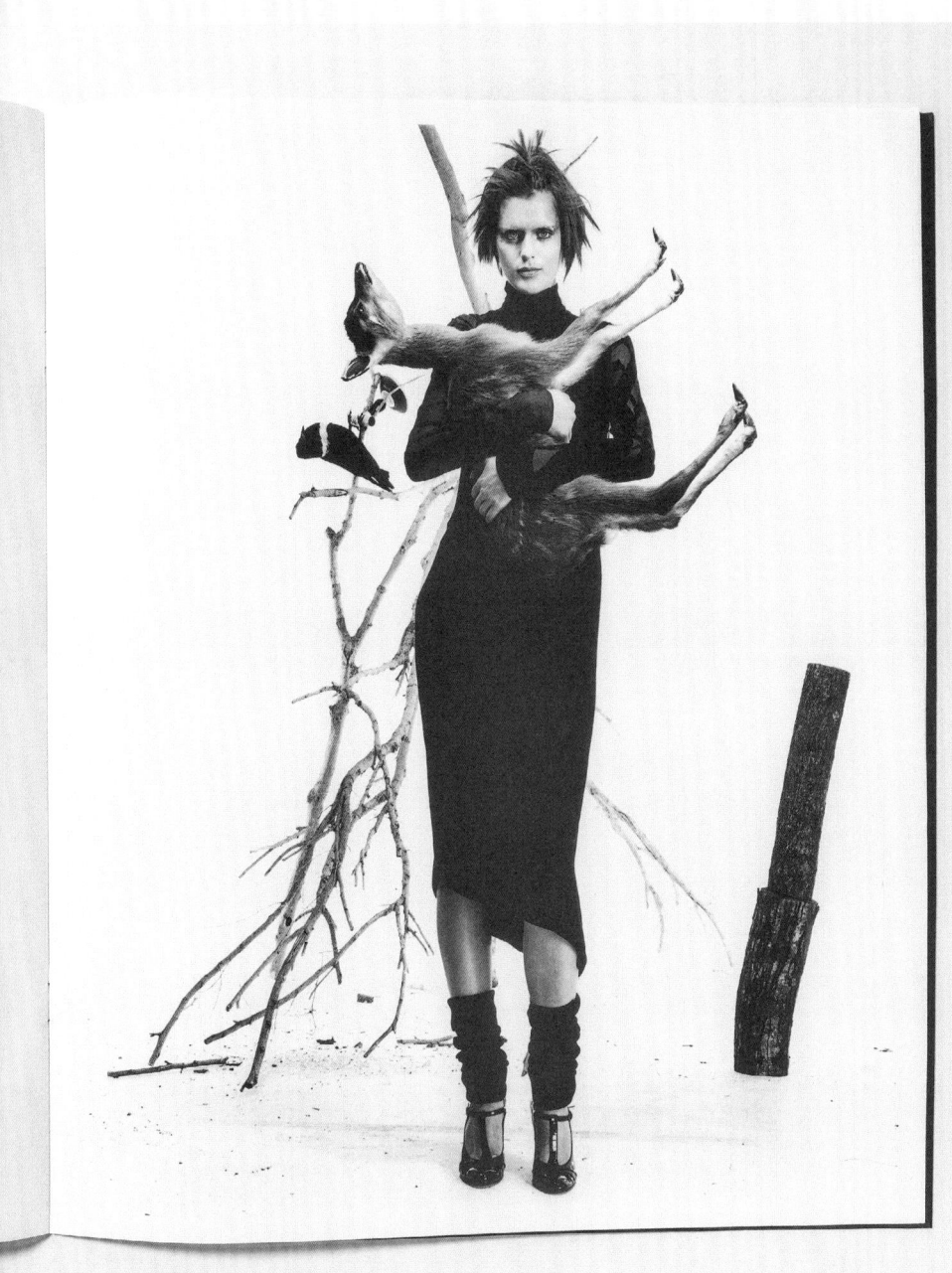

This full-length dress, with extra-long sleeves, is made of burnout velvet with sheer leaf-shaped areas of chiffon that descend the length of the asymmetric train. Martine Sitbon's tendency toward minimalism — seen in the straight shape and solid color of this design — and her interest in complex fabrics reflect the taste for shimmering materials that were appearing on the runways of Dries Van Noten, Romeo Gigli, and even Jean Paul Gaultier.

Martine Sitbon was probably referencing either historical costumes from the past — figured velvet and huge sleeves that were fashionable during the sixteenth century at the Burgundy court — or bias-cut evening dresses from the 1930s. The silhouette, both medieval and glamorous, could belong to a princess in a dark fairy tale. The mock collar, delicately zipped on a diagonal in the back, is reminiscent of the costume worn by the Wicked Queen in *Snow White*, while the velvet's shaded areas could be the terrors lurking in the forest at night.

During the 1990s, anxiety, ambiguity, and even dread had once again become references of beauty, and the end-of-century designers, with varying degrees of humor, exorcised their fascination of dark romanticism through their work.
E.P.-P.

CRAIG MCDEAN, Photograph for the Martine Sitbon Autumn/Winter 1997-1998 collection catalogue.

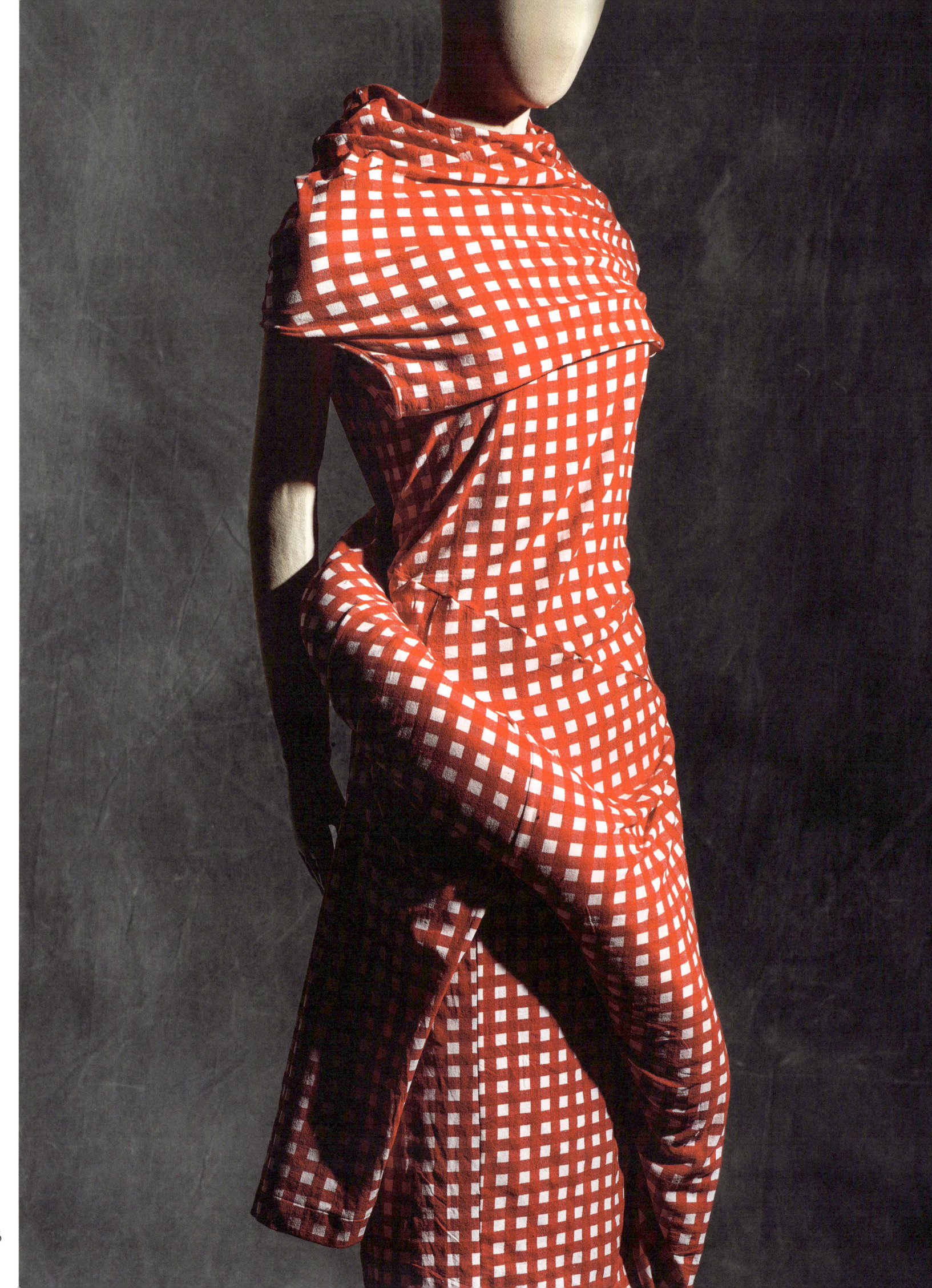

Comme des Garçons
Bump Dress, *Spring/Summer 1997*

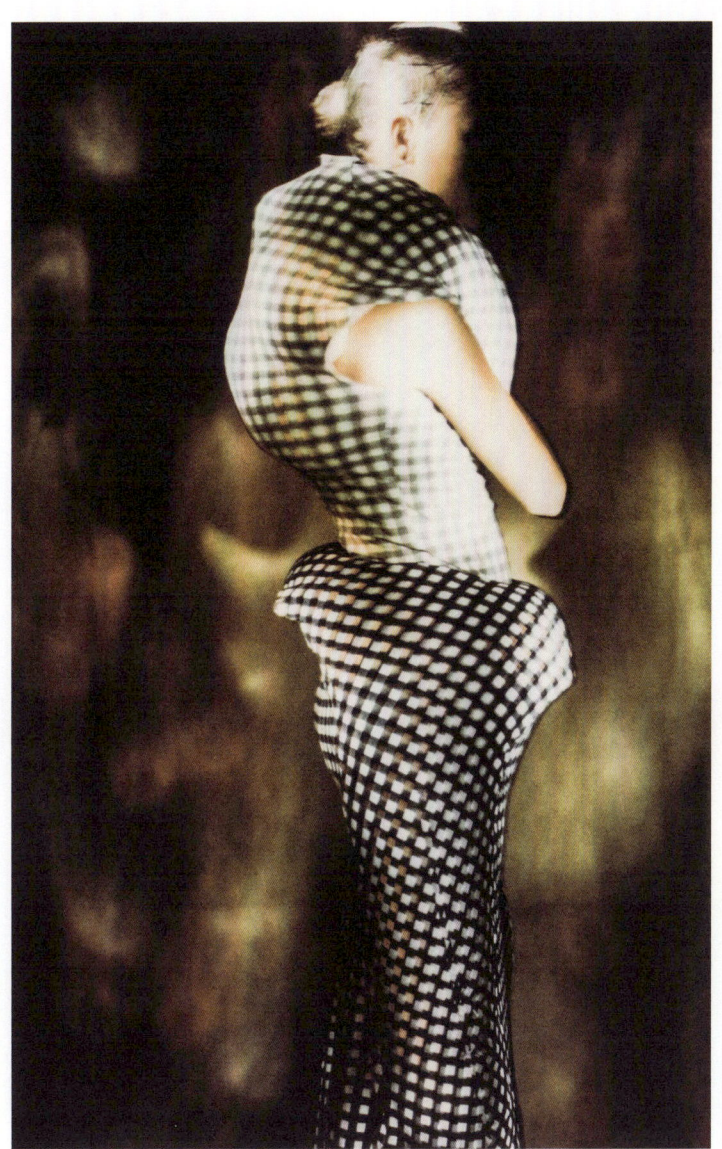

"Dress Meets Body, Body Meets Dress and They Are One" was the name of the collection that featured this dress. Also called "Lumps and Bumps," the collection presented designs with padding that randomly exaggerated the female form. The gingham Vichy jersey that covers the body's actual or artificial bumps brings to mind the pattern of Brigitte Bardot's wedding dress from 1959. Rei Kawakubo uses the padding without respect for the symmetry of anatomy or the conventions of Western tailoring that usually employ artificial volume (shoulder pads, interfacing, and padding) to enhance their designs.

In this example, the intention is not to use the polyester wadding to obtain a conventional silhouette. Instead, the silhouette develops haphazardly, following an experiment with fabric that produces voluminous shapes and unexpected images and ideas.
E. P.-P.

PAOLO ROVERSI, Photograph for Comme des Garçons published in *Visionnaire* no. 20, 1997.
Musée des Arts Décoratifs, Paris.

Martin Margiela
Ensemble, Autumn/Winter 1997-1998

Trained at the Académie royale des beaux-arts d'Anvers, Martin Margiela distinguished himself from the group of so-called Antwerp 6 designers by opening his fashion house in Paris. From his time as an assistant at Jean Paul Gaultier, he retained an interest in distorting archetypical sartorial shapes. In Margiela's non-narrative approach, recycling became a decorative concept. This jacket and its removable sleeves are made from the fabric used for the Stockman dressmaker's forms found in ateliers, giving the finished garment a real connection with the object on which it was created.

The headpiece, made from several fur collars, is of the same spirit. Indeed, Margiela often recut second-hand clothes, highlighting their beauty by flattening them, cutting, combining, and reconfiguring them, revisiting their earlier identity. By doing so, the designer offers a simultaneous perspective of a garment as it was, is, and will become.
E.P.-P.

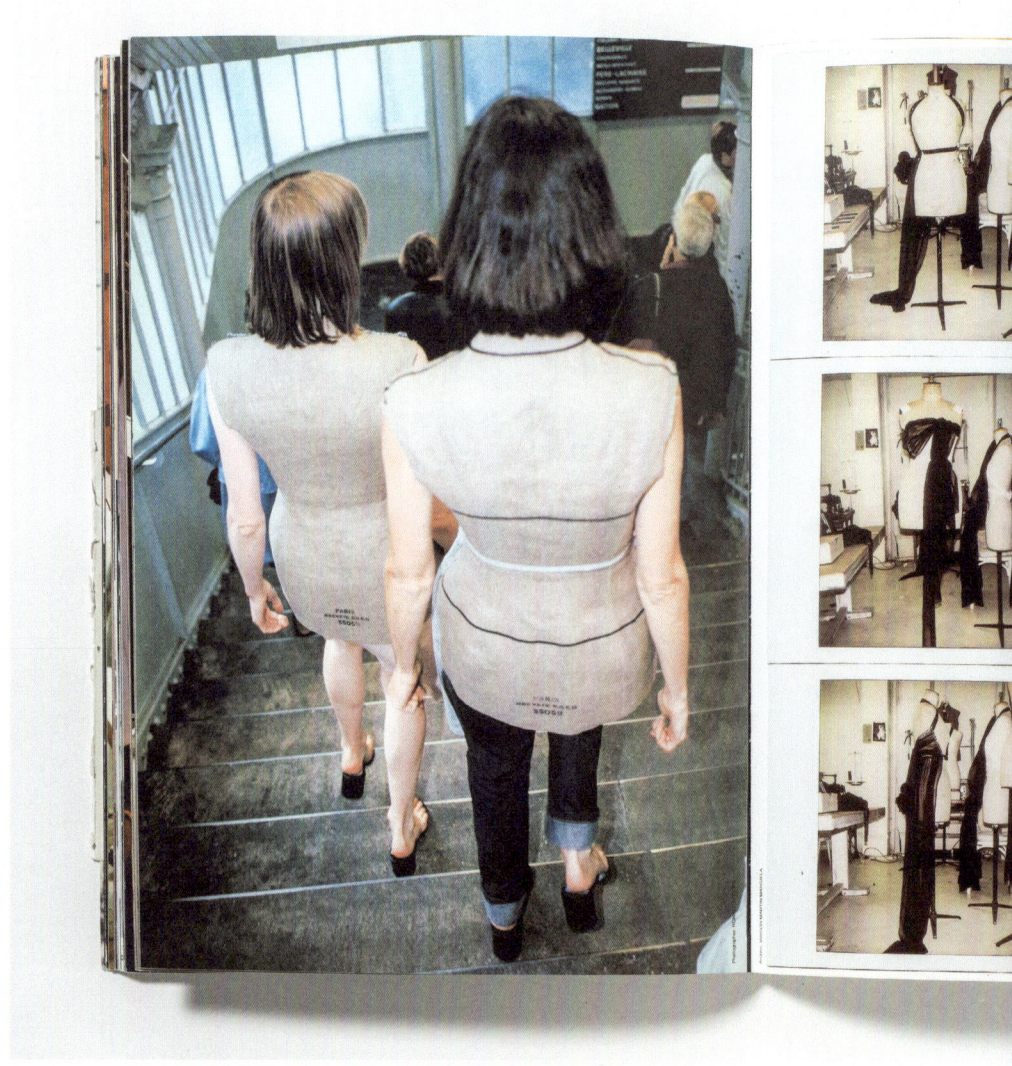

RONALD STOOPS, Photographs published in *Martin Margiela, Street Special 1 & 2*, November 1999.

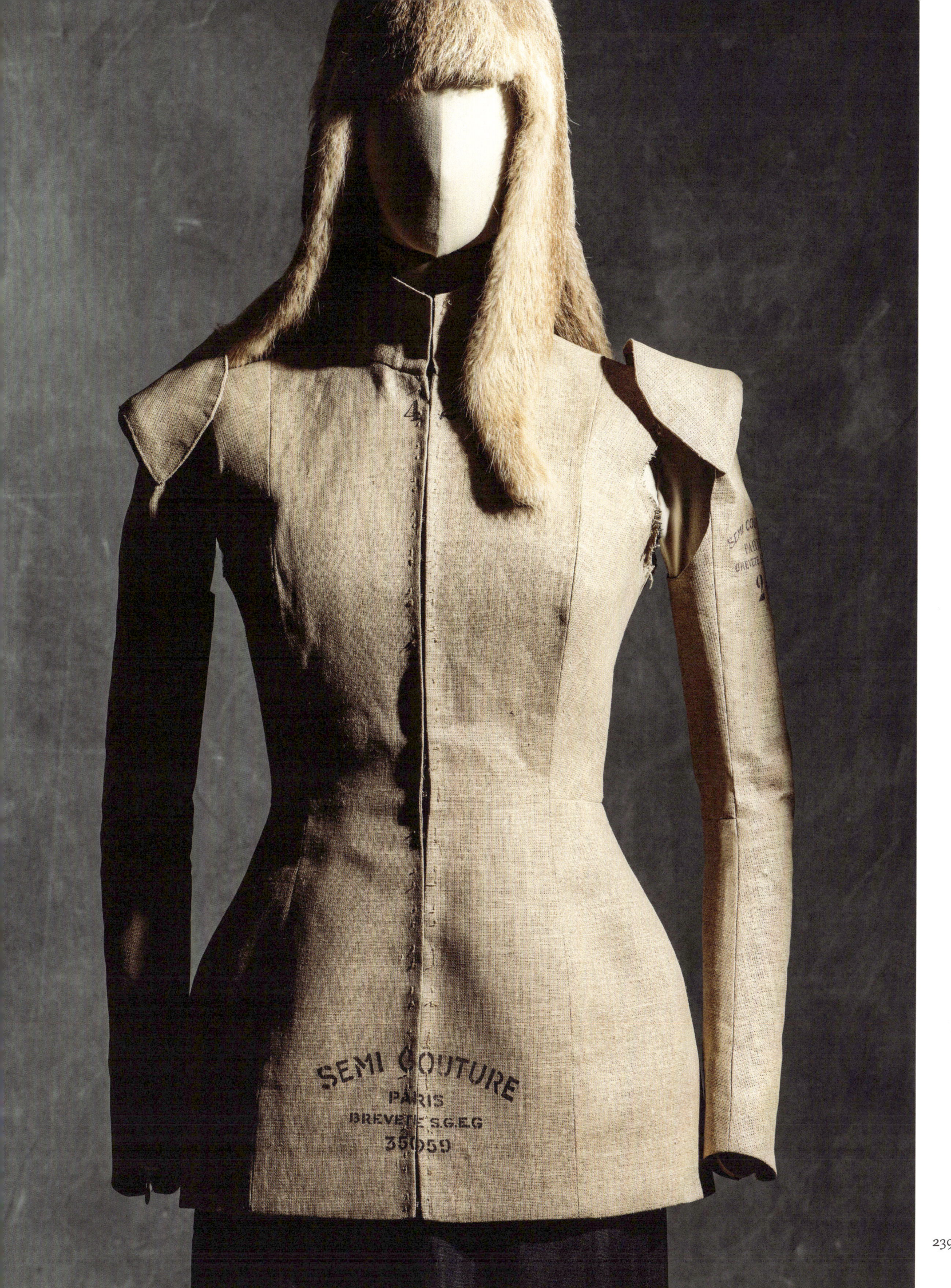

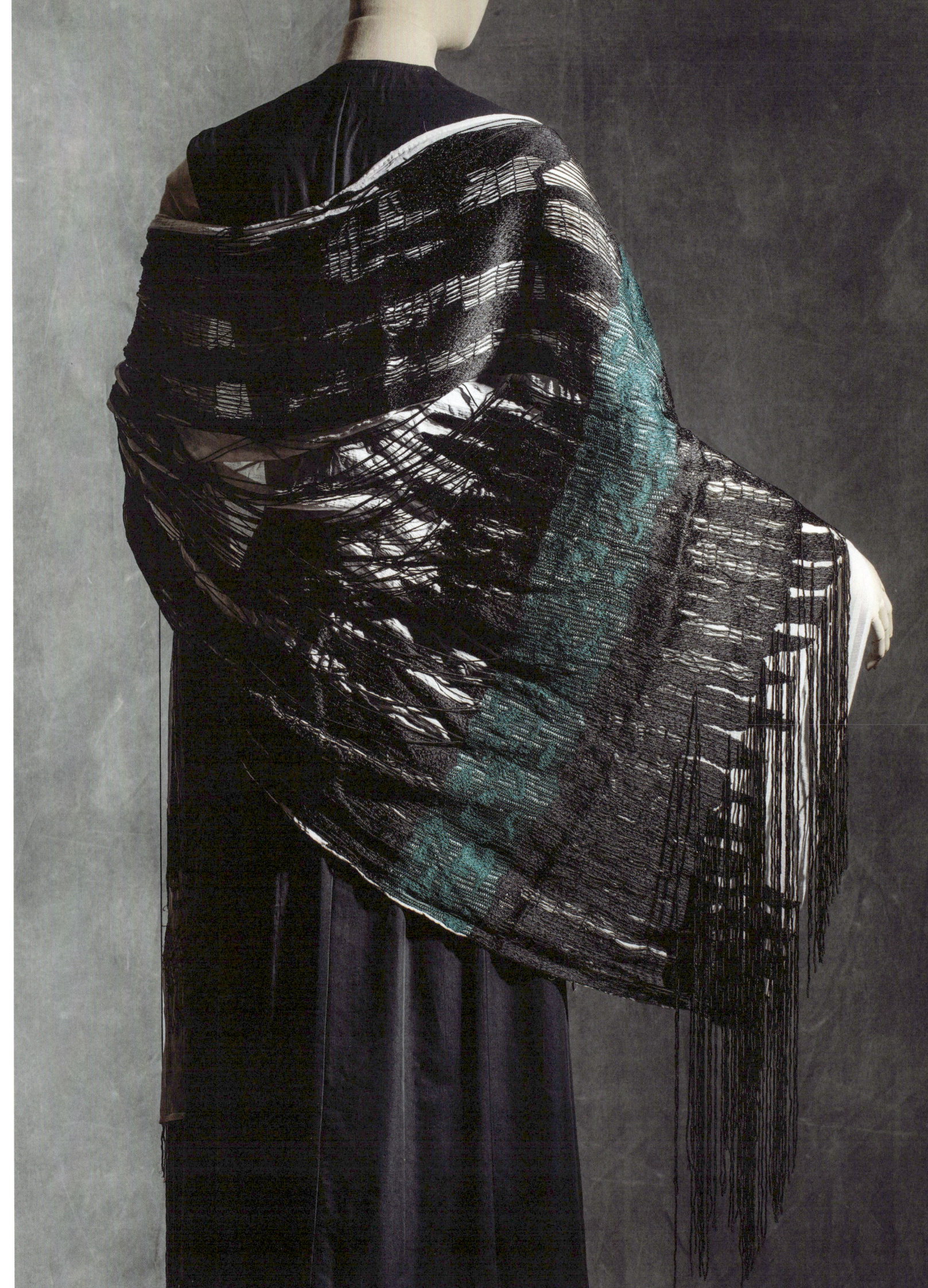

Dries Van Noten
Ensemble, Spring/Summer 1999

Dries Van Noten is a member of the Antwerp 6, a group of fashion designers (which includes Walter Van Beirendonck, Dirk Bikkembergs, Ann Demeulemeester, Dirk Van Saene, and Marina Yee) who were part of the so-called Belgian Wave. Graduates of Antwerp's Royal Academy of Fine Arts, they all presented their first collections and gained name and brand recognition at the same time.

Van Noten's work reflects his Flemish identity and its vast textile, decorative, and artistic heritage. This ensemble is part of the collection inspired by Jane Campion's film *The Piano*, whose Victorian heroine narrowly escapes death from drowning. The shawl is embroidered with long beaded fringe that flows like rushing waters. From his earliest days as a designer, Van Noten's silhouettes have reflected his penchant for exclusive and precious fabrics. Seemingly austere, the straight, sleeveless, collarless, and unlined dress with flat pleats has an understated sheen, created by the combination of two fabrics of different black shades that have a silky luster, making the dress seem almost moist.

Delicate, luxurious, and often nostalgic, Van Noten's designs reflect a timeless Ophelian femininity.
E.P.-P.

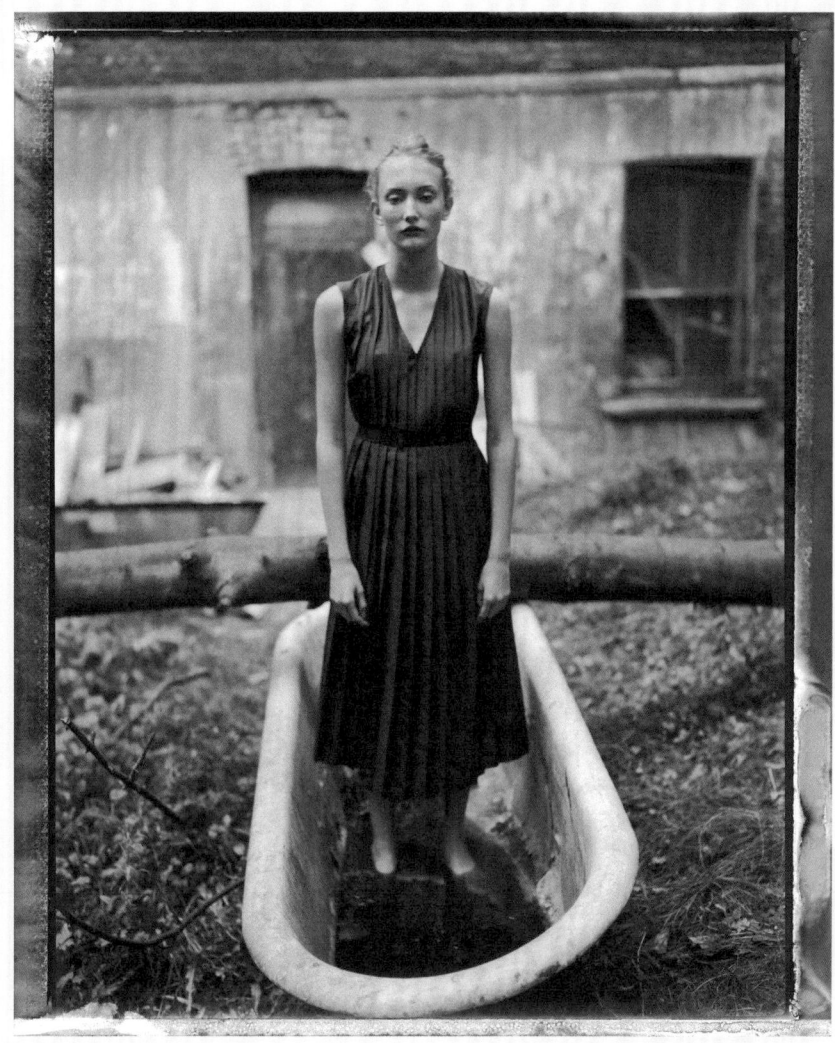

TOM MUNRO, Photograph for the Dries Van Noten Spring/Summer 1999 collection catalogue.

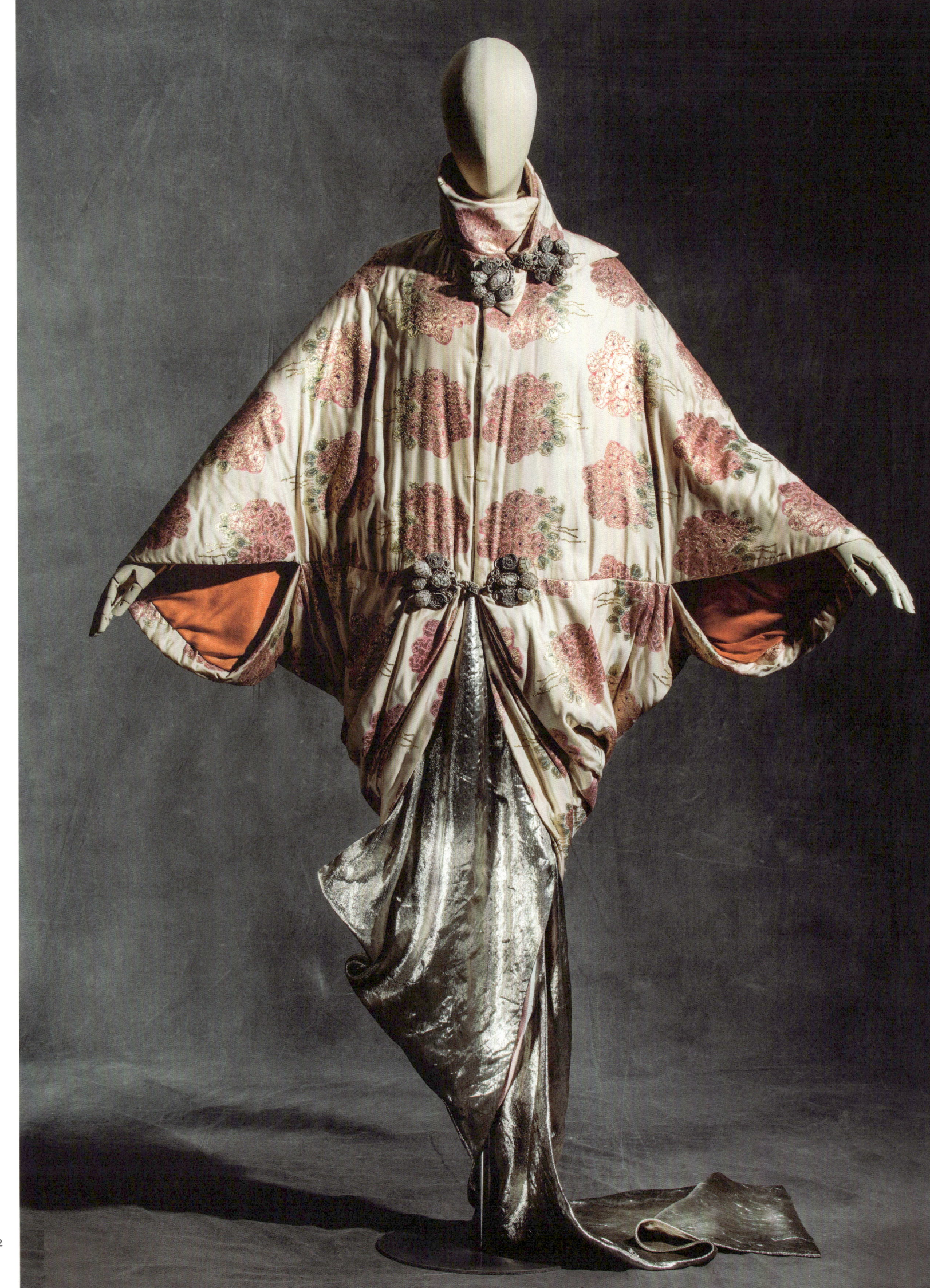

John Galliano for Christian Dior
Stourhead *Evening Ensemble*
Spring/Summer 1998

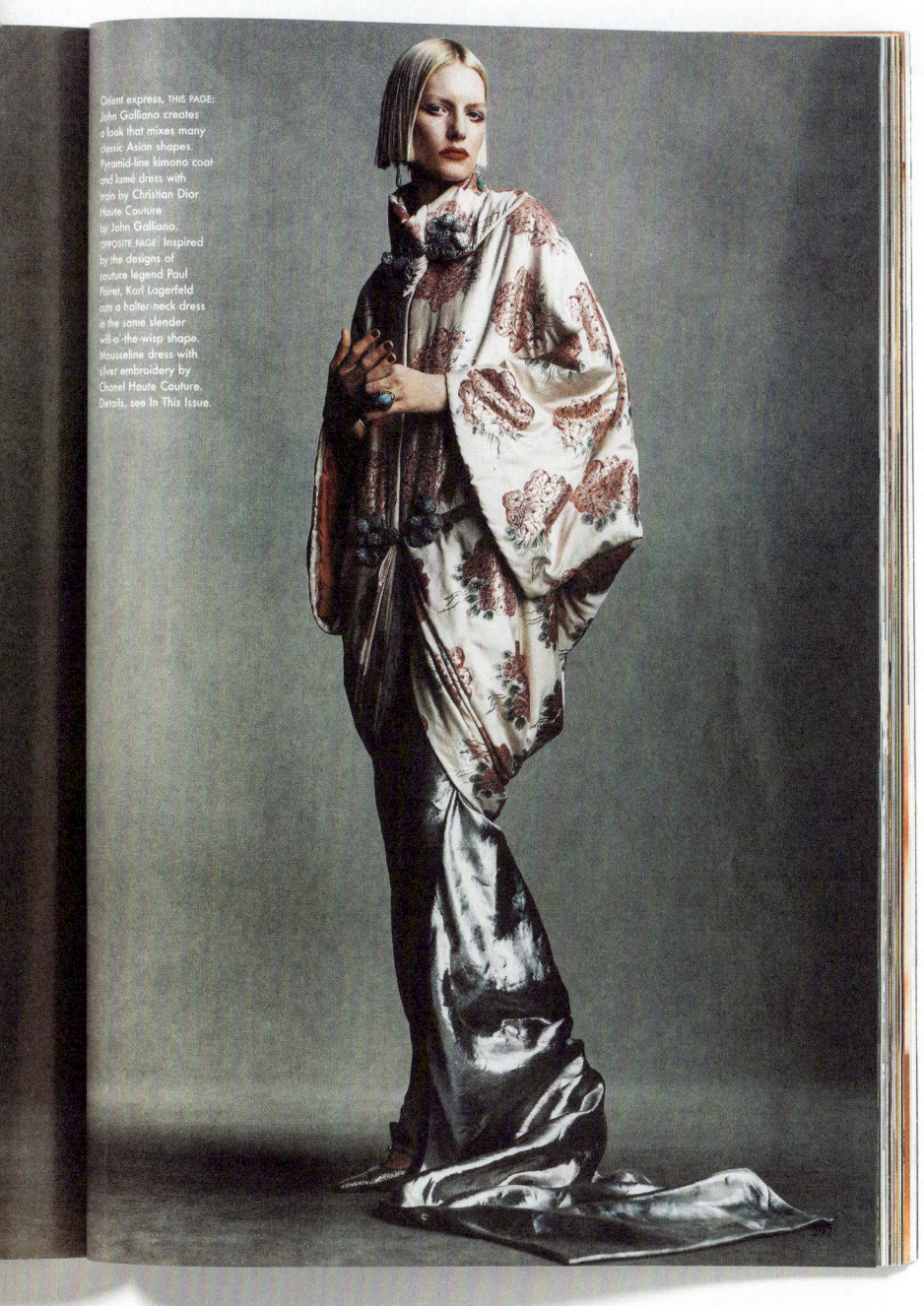

This evening ensemble is emblematic of John Galliano's work during his tenure as creative director of women's haute couture and ready-to-wear at Christian Dior, from 1996 to 2011. Pink and gray, Dior's favorite colors, are revived in a novel and gleaming fashion: bouquets of roses embroidered in gold and silver lamé embellish the *boule* coat and dress with a spiraling train — a style reminiscent of Callot Sœurs. Presented on the grand staircase of the Paris Opéra — the setting for this spectacular fashion show — this Roaring Twenties–inspired silhouette walked among others that reflected different *periods, such as the Belle Époque and New Look.

Perhaps "Stourhead" was meant to channel Christian Dior's youth through the eyes of John Galliano. The fanciful cut (unexpected volume, asymmetrical lines) and rocaille spirit represent a break with the classicism and baroque styles of Galliano's predecessors at Dior.
E.P.-P.

Hussein Chalayan
Dress, Spring/Summer 2000

Born in Nicosia, Cyprus, Hussein Chalayan trained at Central Saint Martins College of Art and Design in London. From his first postgraduate collection in 1993, Chalayan compared fashion design to the resolution of an enigma: "I believe the processes are here to serve the designer. What matters is the result and nobody needs to know the process."

This dress, from the "Before Minus Now" collection, presented at the Sadler's Wells Theatre in London, illustrates the designer's view of the invisible phenomena that sculpt nature: formation, erosion, sedimentation. Topstitched onto the rigid bustier are small wings that seem to have been carried in by the wind, and the skirt, made from a continuous panel of pleated fabric, wraps around the waist like the spiral of a shell. This silhouette is suggestive of the opposing forces of expansion and resistance that occur in nature—a phenomenon that extends to the fashion runway as a flow of warm air caused the skirt to billow during the show/performance.

This two-piece dress, composed of a corolla skirt and a structured bodice, is perhaps a tribute to the New Look or a reference to the traditional uniforms worn by Greek Evzoni guards.
E.P.-P.

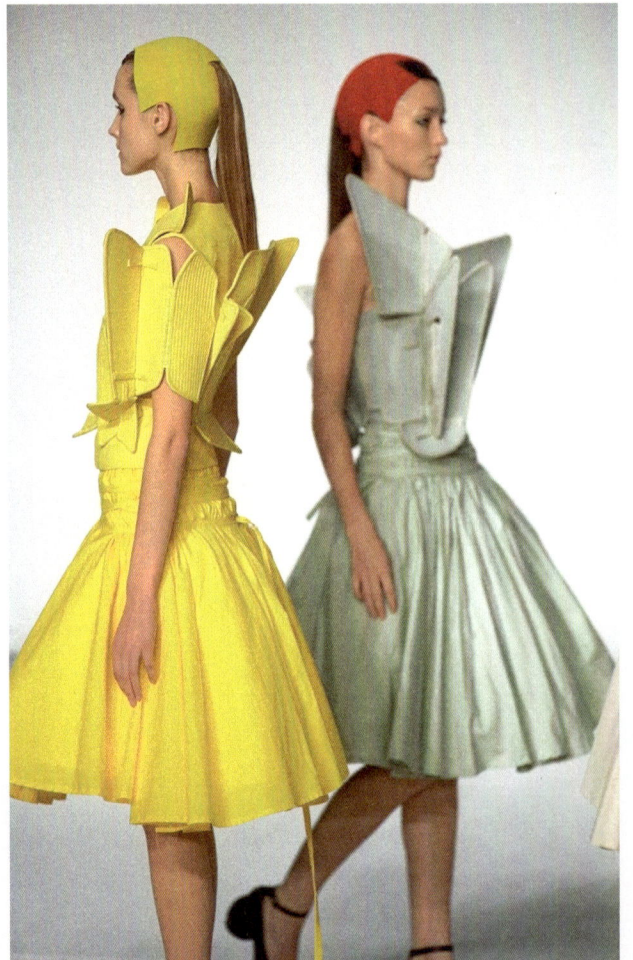

CHRIS MOORE, Photograph from Hussein Chalayan's "Before Minus Now" fashion show, Spring/Summer 2000.

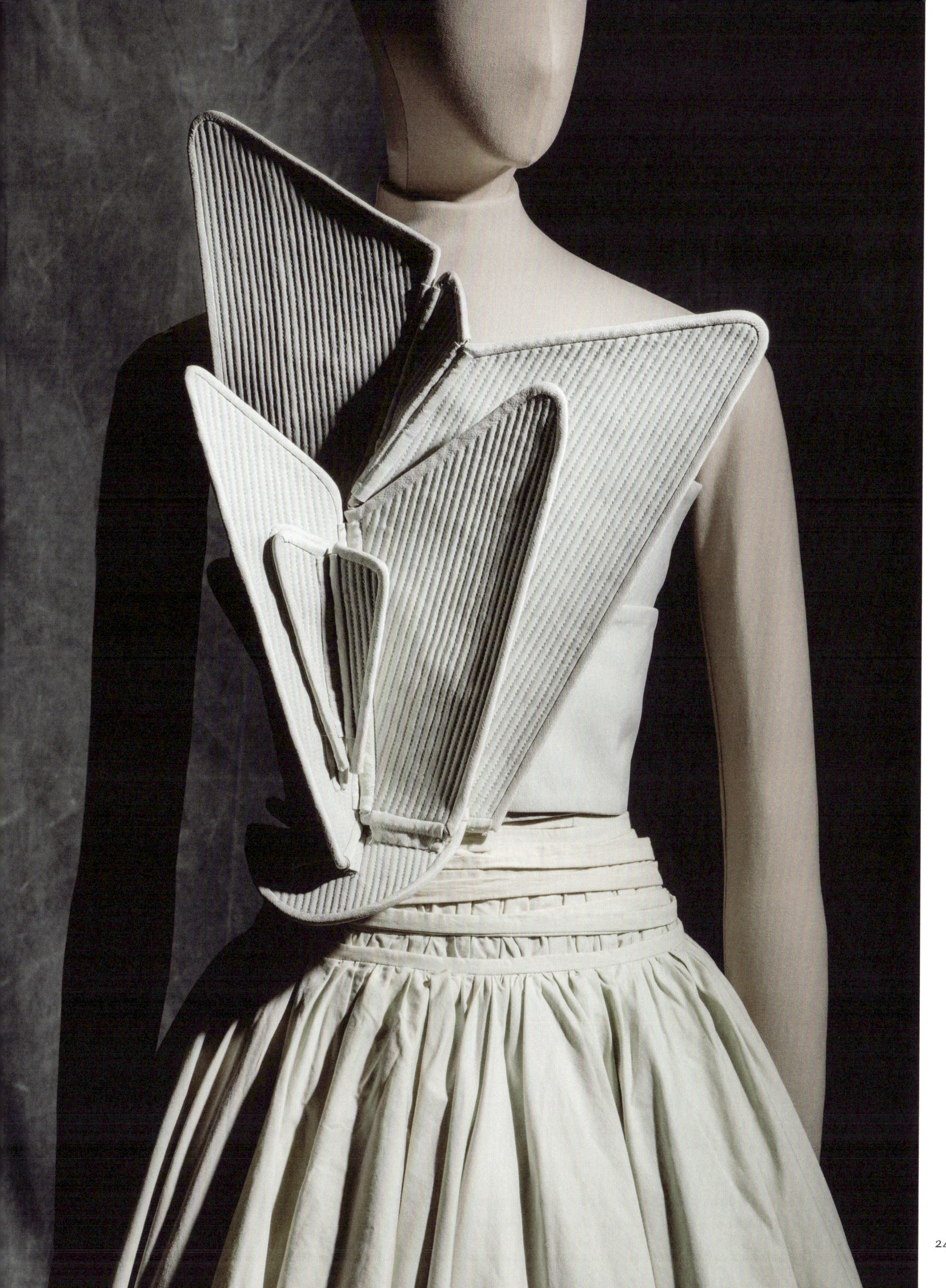

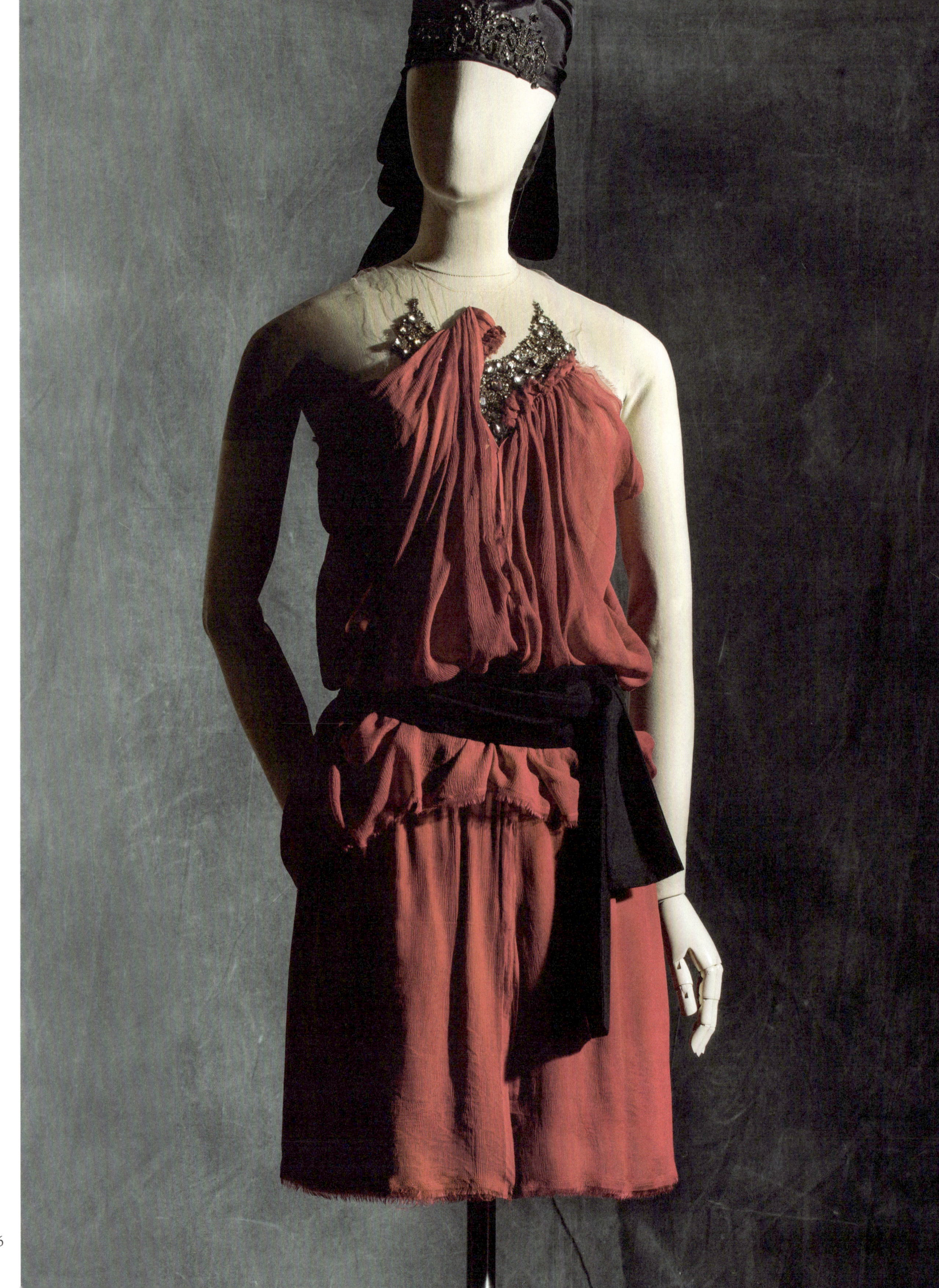

Alber Elbaz for Lanvin
Ensemble, Spring/Summer 2003

This evening ensemble speaks to the creativity of Alber Elbaz, artistic director for the House of Lanvin from 2001 to 2015. Elbaz defined himself as a stylist-designer. His creations, marketed exclusively for ready-to-wear, carry on the tradition of the fashion house founded in 1885 by Jeanne Lanvin. The House of Lanvin has been in existence longer than any other couture fashion house still in operation. Made of luxurious fabrics, Elbaz's sensual and fluid creations are emblematic of Lanvin's tradition of *flou* (dressmaking).

The dazzling effect of this jewel-dress lies in the vibrancy of the colors. Elbaz embraced luxurious fabrics and the sobriety of cut in couture, but maintained a respectful distance from bespoke traditions. A true believer in ready-to-wear, he was not proposing an alternative to hand finishing. The raw edge and machine-made pleats and seams are selected strictly for their decorative value.

E.P.-P.

Junya Watanabe Comme des Garçons
Dress, Spring/Summer 2003

A former protegé of Rei Kawabuko, Junya Watanabe first presented his own collections under the label Junya Watanabe Comme des Garçons in 1992. The print of this dress recalls the popular 1950s fabrics and wallpapers that featured eighteenth-century Toile de Jouy. The repeated motif — a rustic scene with figures wearing corolla dresses — was perhaps a tribute to Christian Dior, who admired the style of Louis XVI and rekindled the interest in old-fashioned motifs on the advice of his collaborator and friend Christian Bérard. "It was he who suggested we use Toile de Jouy fabric in the boutique," notes Dior in his 1956 autobiography.

This dress is a modern-day version of those worn in the Hameau de la Reine, Marie Antoinette's rustic retreat in Versailles. The panniers have been replaced by zippered duffels attached to the waist with straps. This pastoral outfit, composed of a shirt and a skirt-smock with detachable pockets, is held together with ties and clips commonly found on hikers' equipment. The shape and motif of the dress are reminiscent of postwar ready-to-wear designs.
E.P.-P.

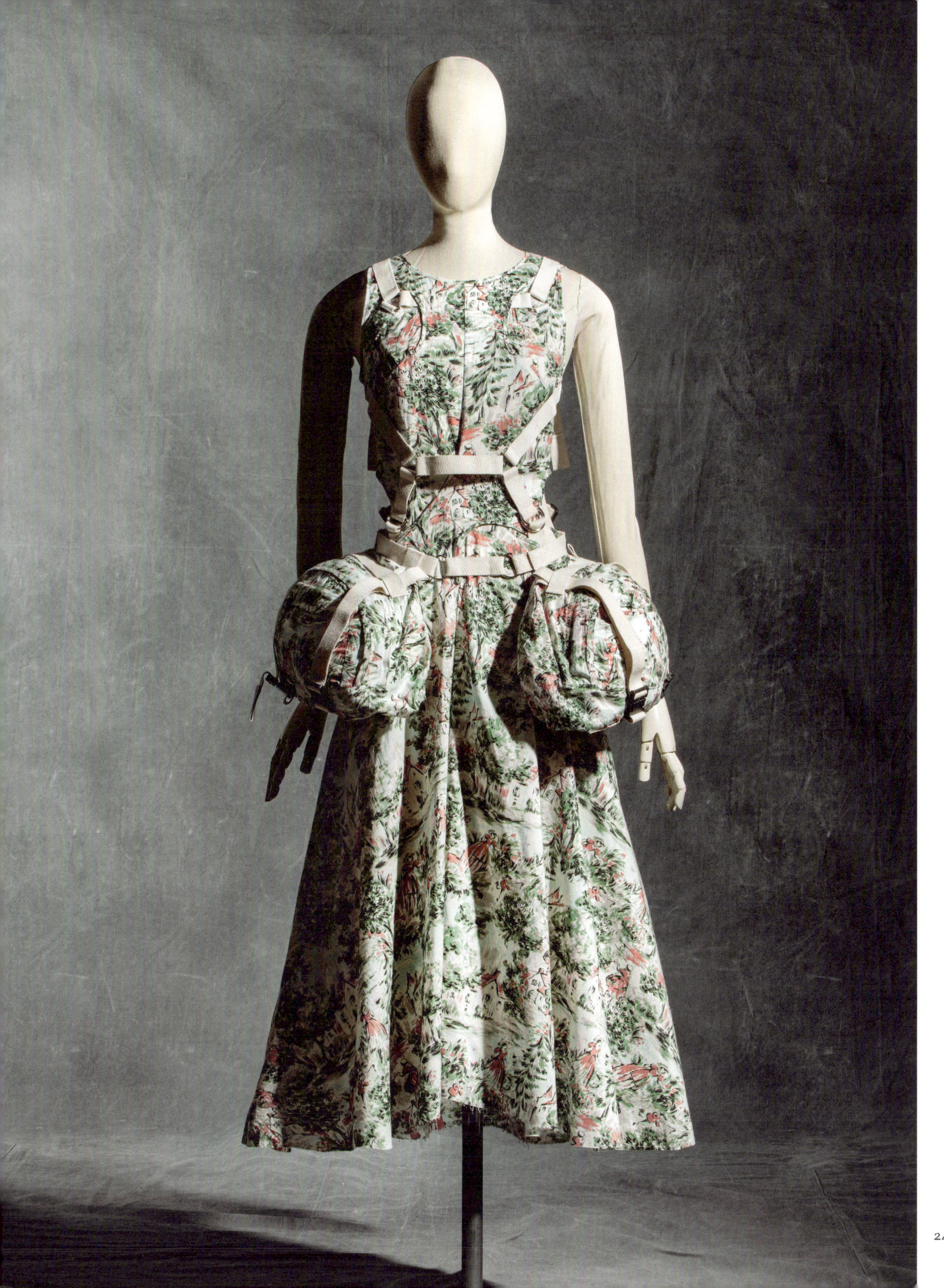

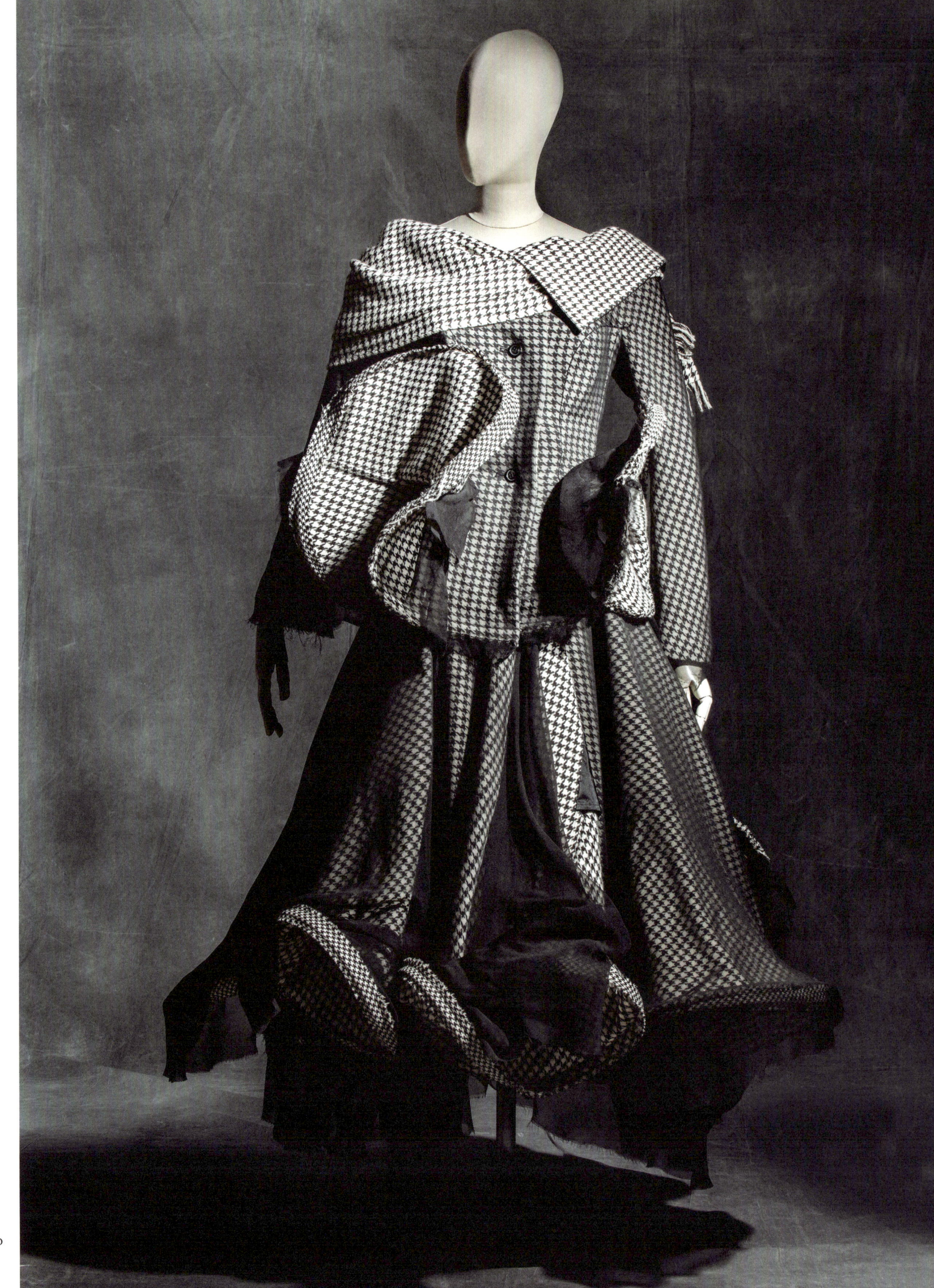

Yohji Yamamoto
Ensemble, Autumn/Winter 2003-2004

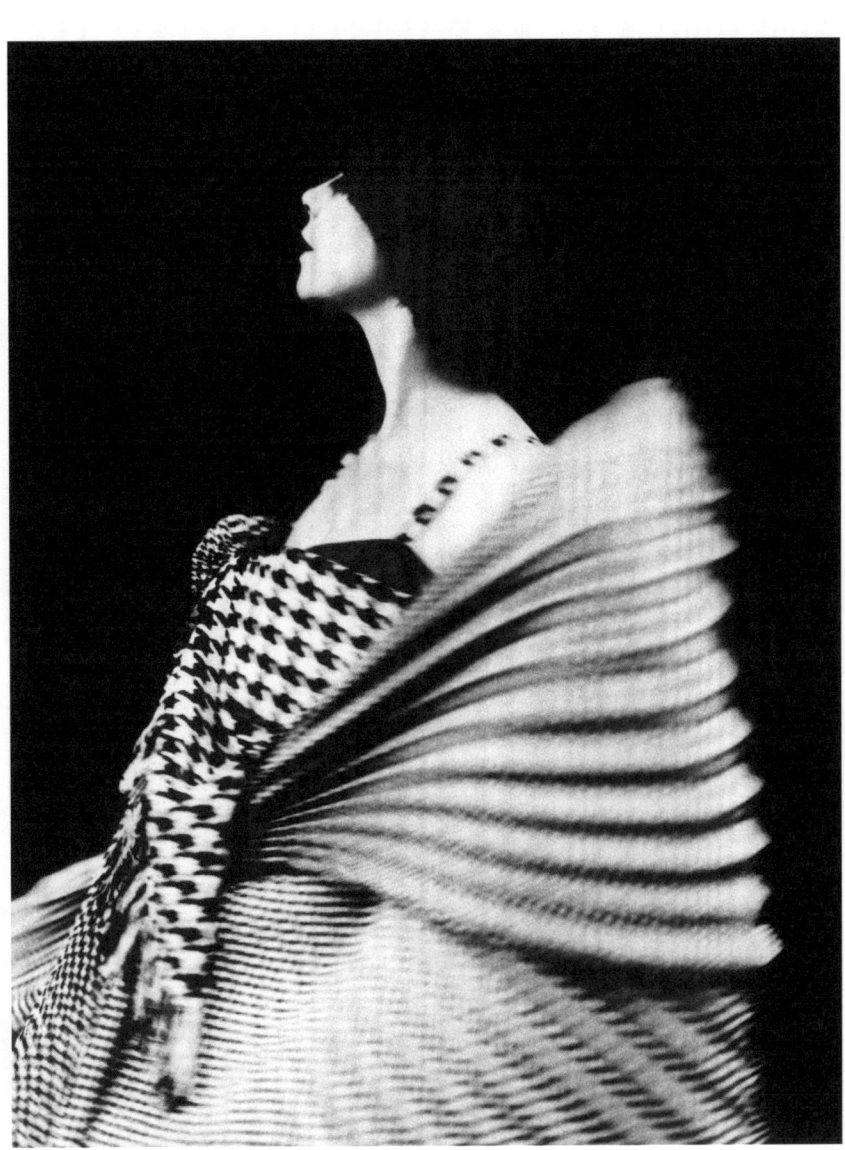

In the spirit of his earlier creations inspired by popular costumes, Yohji Yamamoto based this design on silhouettes inherited from the New Look but assimilated into a traditional culture. This collection is built around black and white houndstooth wool fabrics. By playing with the scale and variation of the pattern, Yamamoto creates a range of optical effects and shades of gray.

In this example, the complex pairing of the jacket and skirt reveals the ambivalent spirit of the entire collections — the mix of sharp contrasts with intermediary tones of gray. The composite inspiration draws from both *flou* (draped chiffon) and *tailleur* (wool); the collar is draped on the right side and flat on the left, while the hem is both raw and beautifully finished. Worn as a daytime suit or an evening dress, this creation pays homage to couture in all its variations.

E.P.-P.

CRAIG MCDEAN, Photograph published in *AnOther Magazine*, 2003.

Nicolas Ghesquière for Balenciaga
Dress, Autumn/Winter 2004-2005

Appointed creative director of Balenciaga in 1997, then-26-year-old Nicolas Ghesquière was one of the most promising designers of his generation. His ready-to-wear creations brought back to prominence the fashion house founded by Cristóbal Balenciaga. His first collections for the brand follow the minimalist trends of the late 1990s: "Austerity and rigor are my contemporary codes and I follow this radical line all the way," explained the designer in a March 1999 interview for *Elle* magazine. His later collections would include more ornamentation, a play of complex materials, and intentionally asymmetric cuts.

This approach is perhaps inspired by the couture of Balenciaga himself (famous for his use of fabric panels and volume effects created with invisible ties) and by Ghesquière's fascination with the styles of the 1980s. The designer infused his own creations with designs in vogue during his childhood. This silhouette was probably inspired by the mermaid dresses of the 1980s that were made of jersey or adorned with zippers (replaced here with colored chains). The geometric composition of black, gray, and flecked fabrics brings to mind the floors of the Balenciaga boutiques, which were designed by Dominique Gonzalez-Foerster.
E.P.-P.

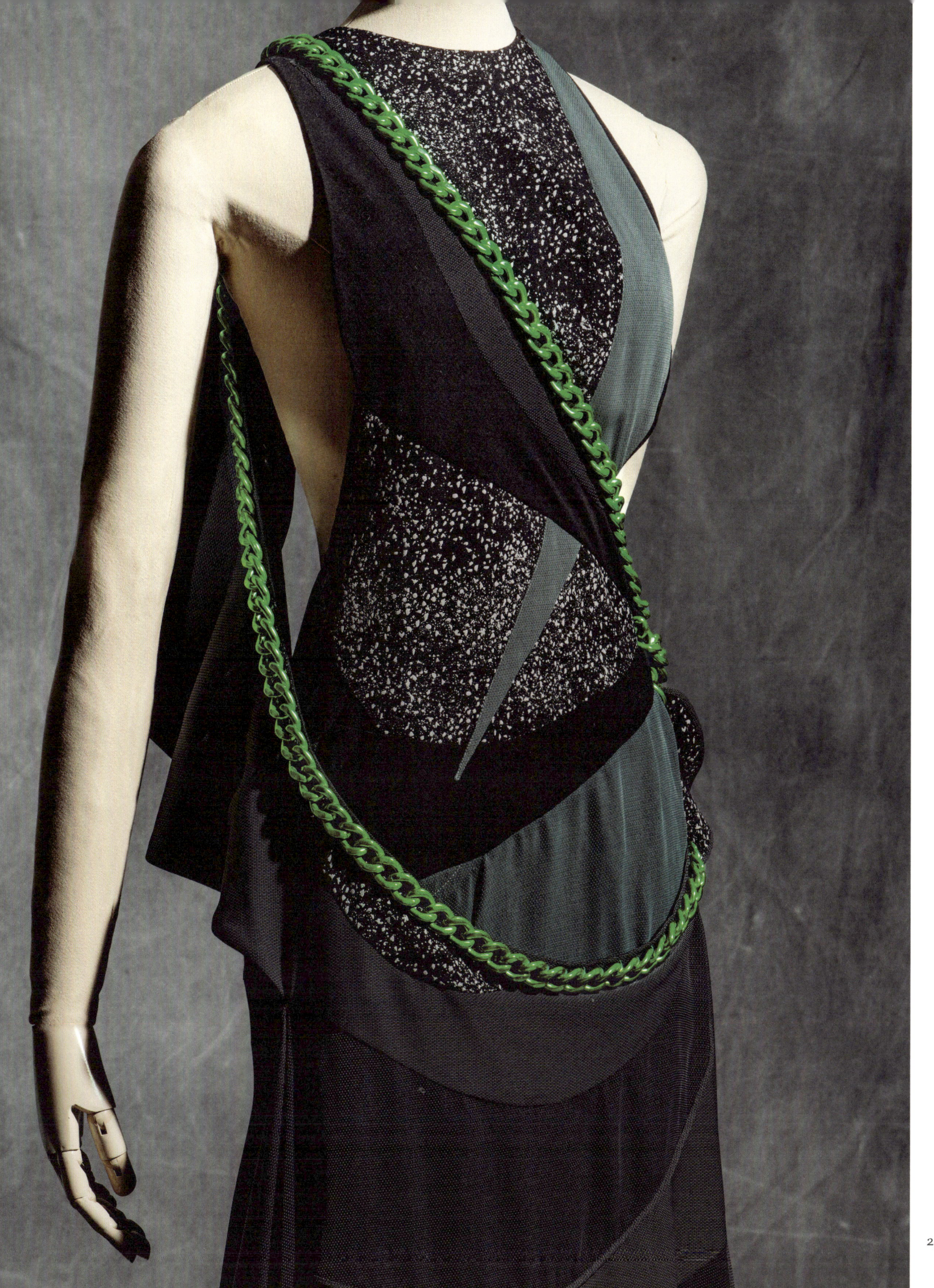

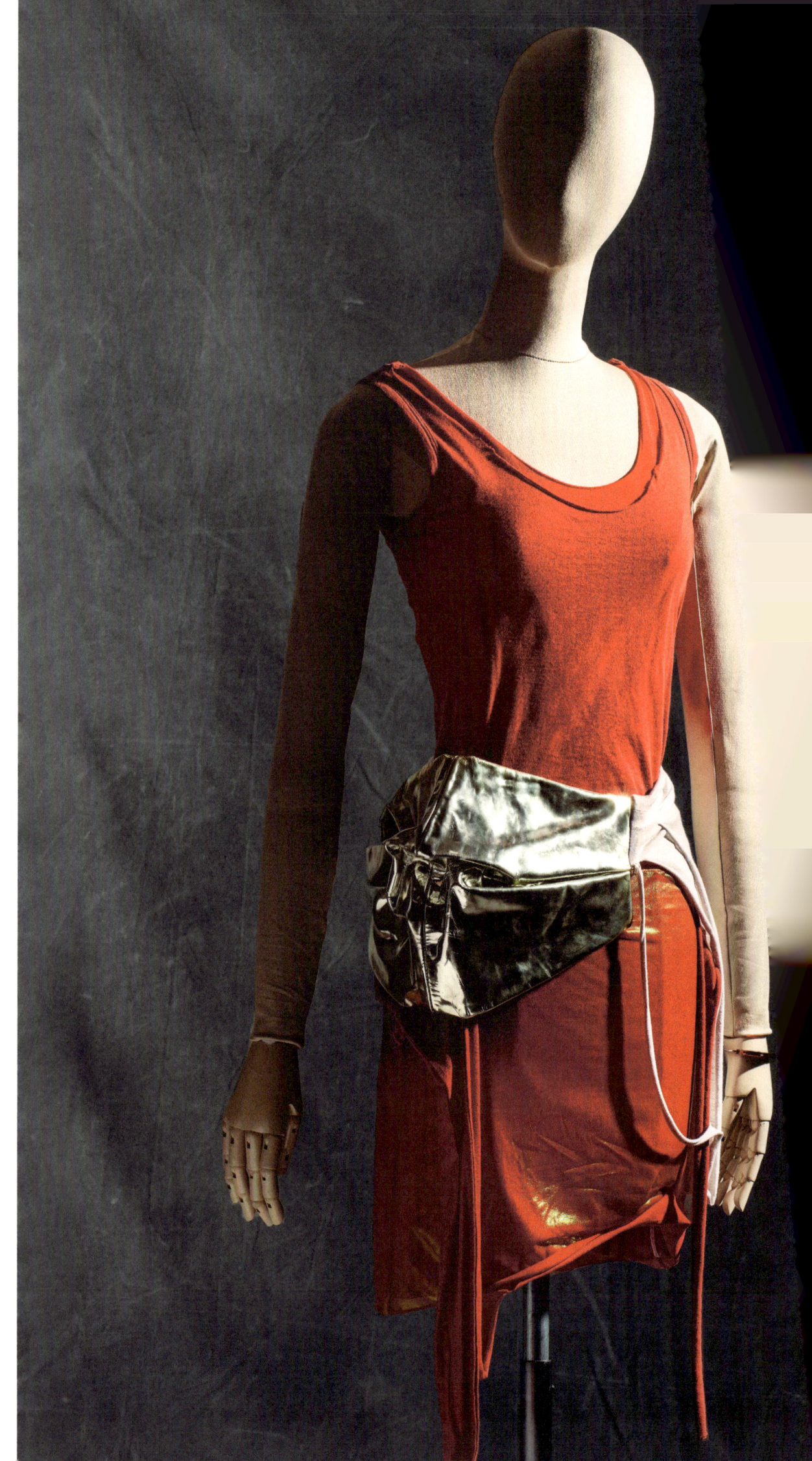

Helmut Lang
Dress, Spring/Summer 2004

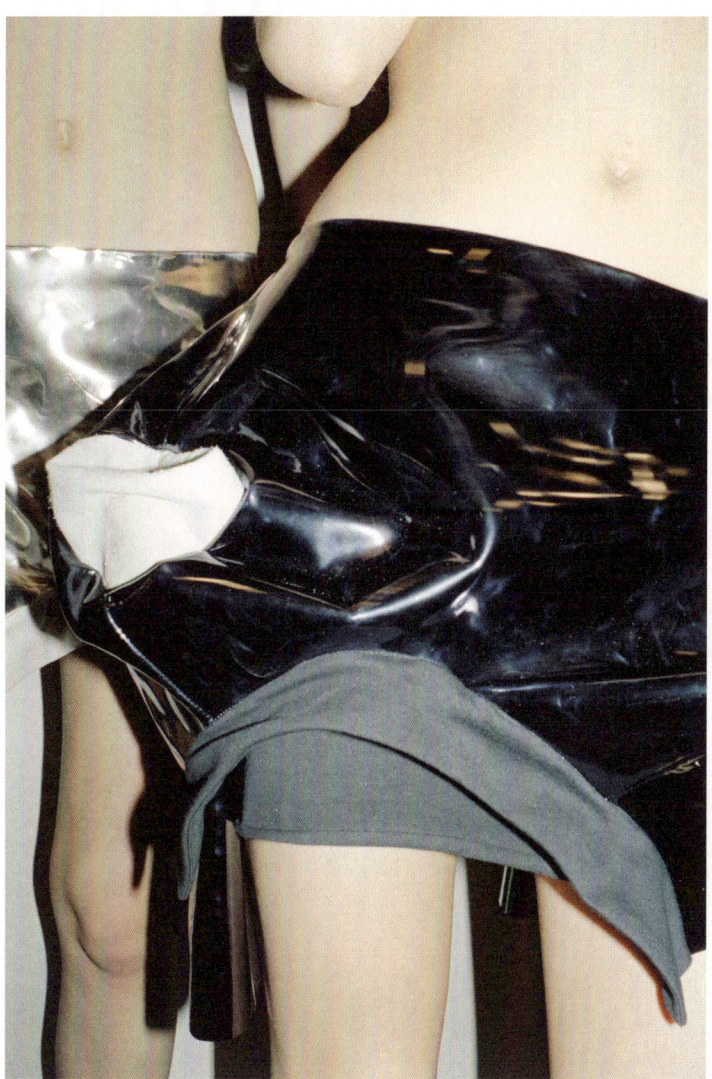

As the leader of the minimalist movement of the 1990s, Helmut Lang reintroduced the use of ornamentation in the 2000s, drawing from the decorative motifs of streetwear. For the composition of this design, Lang used different jerseys, a fabric chosen for its special decorative qualities: cut into thin strips, the jersey rolls onto itself, creating a tubular effect, while the rest of the uncut fabric can be stretched, molded against the body, or left floating freely.

The range of effects provides the designer with a decorative repertoire used to highlight the sporty image of jersey. This outfit could have been inspired by streetwear — a jogger, for instance, who might be wearing two T-shirts, one over the other, and a sweatshirt casually tied around the waist, headphone dangling from her waist pack. But the sporty look of this red dress embellished with silver leather and gold fabric is purely ornamental.
E.P.-P.

JUERGEN TELLER, Publicity shot for Helmut Lang, 2004.

Prada
Dress, Autumn/Winter 2007-2008

What is striking about this straight and sleeveless black dress is the quality of the fabric, a complex weave of different broadcloths and textures. The solid and matte wool at the top and bottom is raised, wafted, and becomes progressively silkier at the hipline, creating a frieze of irregular, puckered, and satin-like textures. Enlivened by this abstract decoration, this dress evokes the styles of the 1960s, whose simplified silhouettes took a backseat to the fabric patterns that were in turn inspired by the artistic avant-garde movement.

    The half-belt on this dress—which recalls the paintings of Pierre Soulages or the combustions of Arman—is also a reference to the styles of that period, as are the feathers that embellished the hats of Cristóbal Balenciaga. This Prada creation is filled with historical references to Parisian haute couture. The long grouse feathers embroidered onto the shoulders allude to the iconic uniforms of the Bersaglieri, the elite Italian military corps who perfected the art of a fast-paced parade.

E.P.-P.

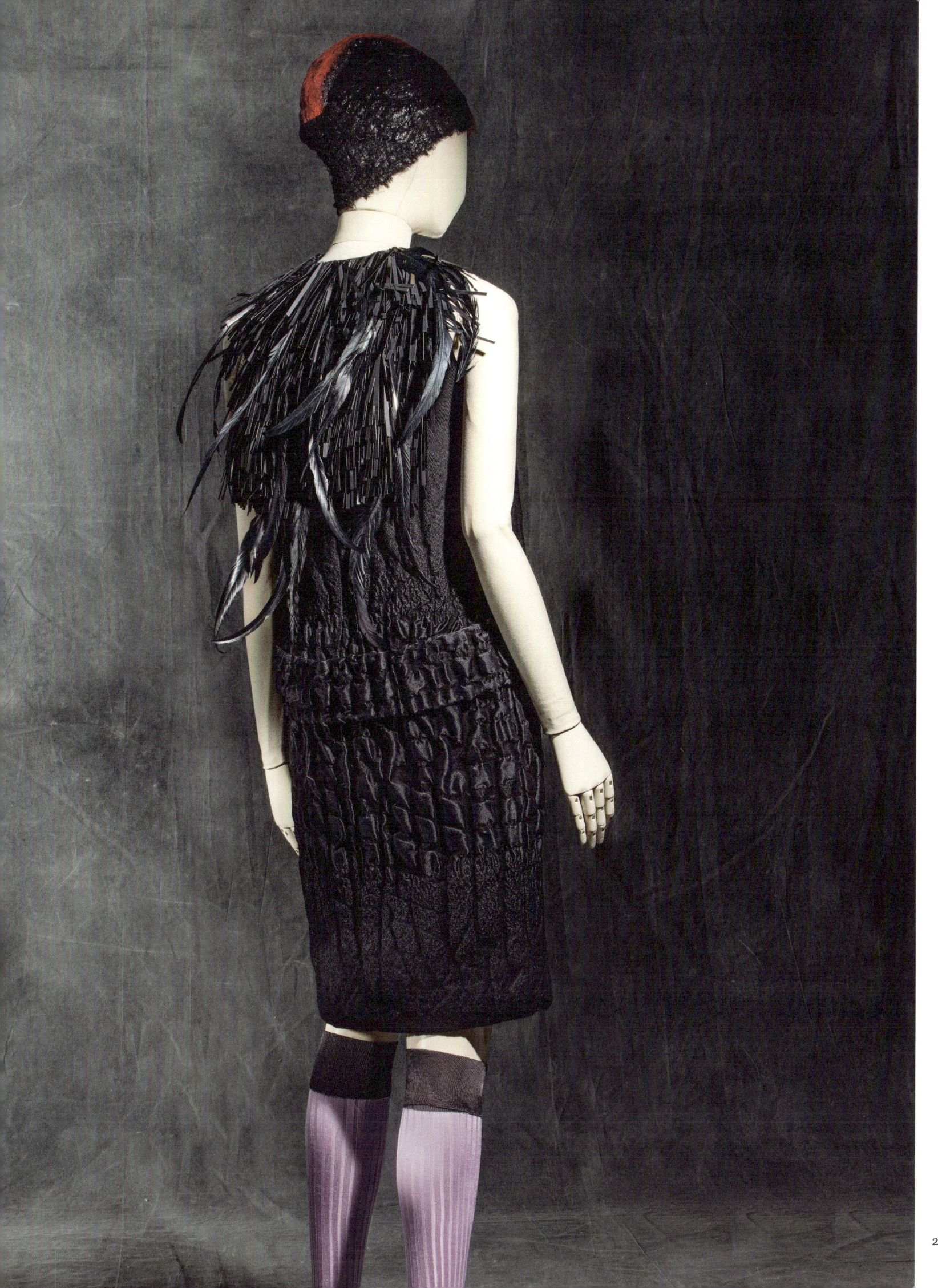

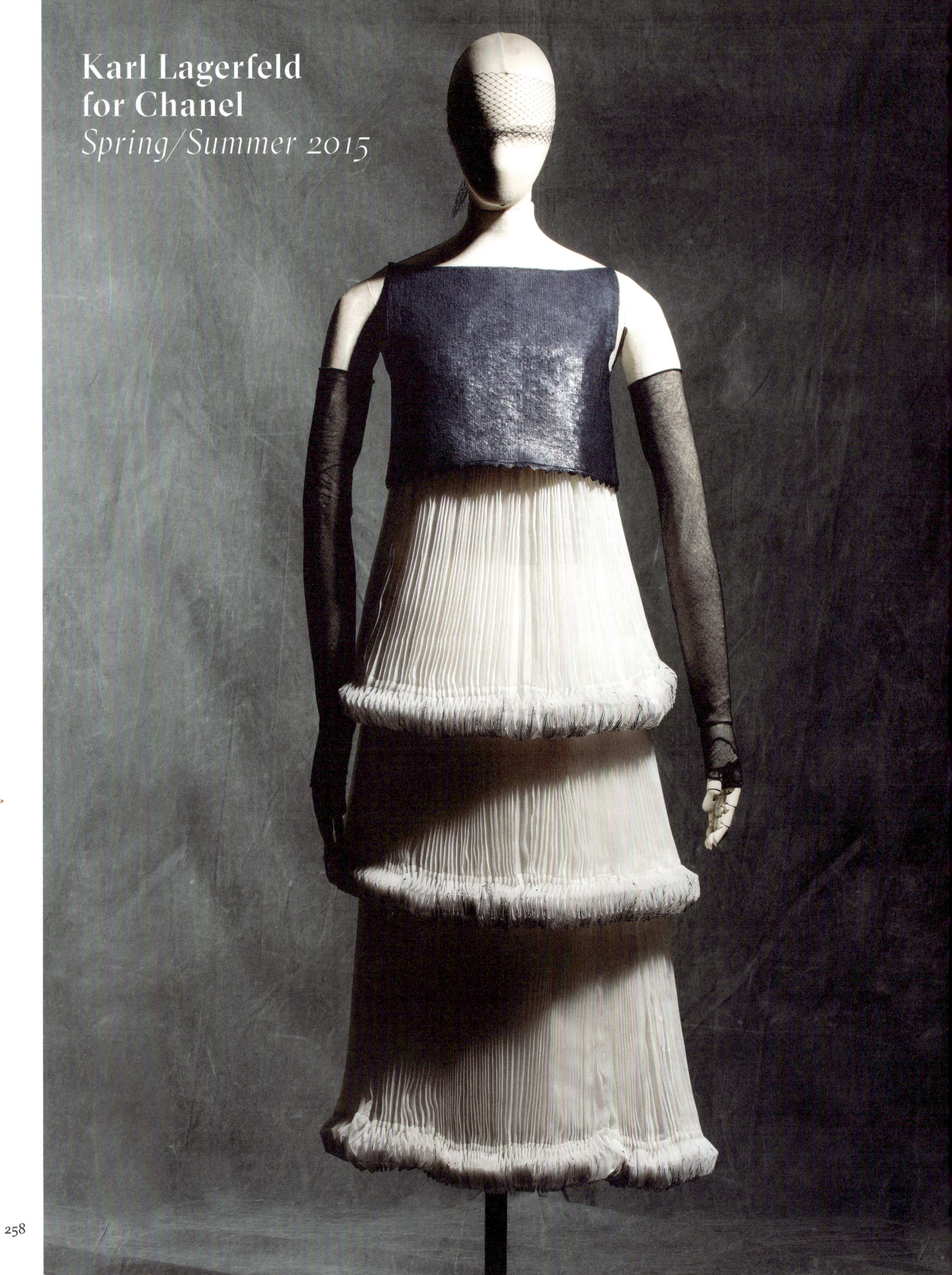

Karl Lagerfeld for Chanel
Spring/Summer 2015

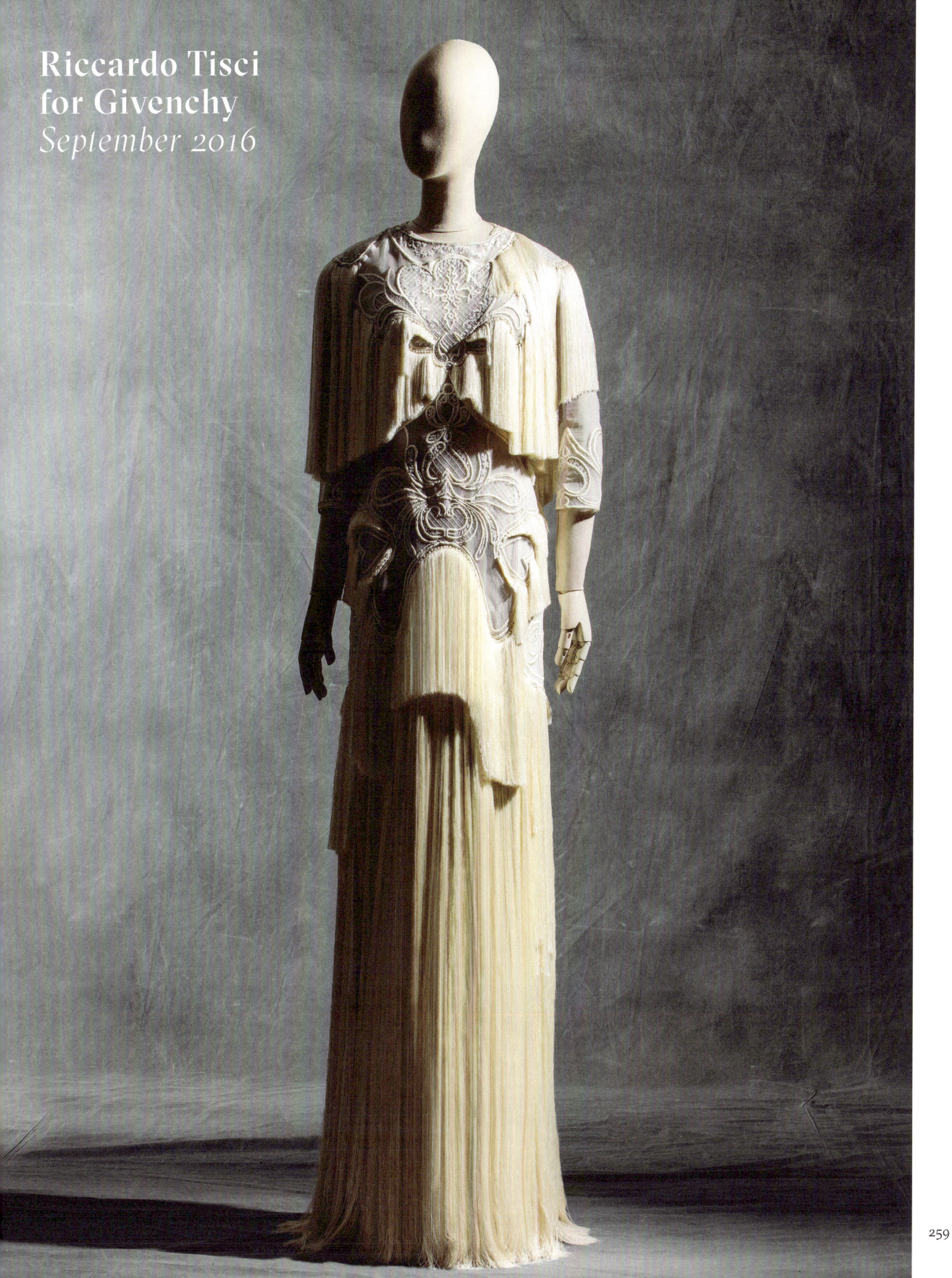

Riccardo Tisci
for Givenchy
September 2016

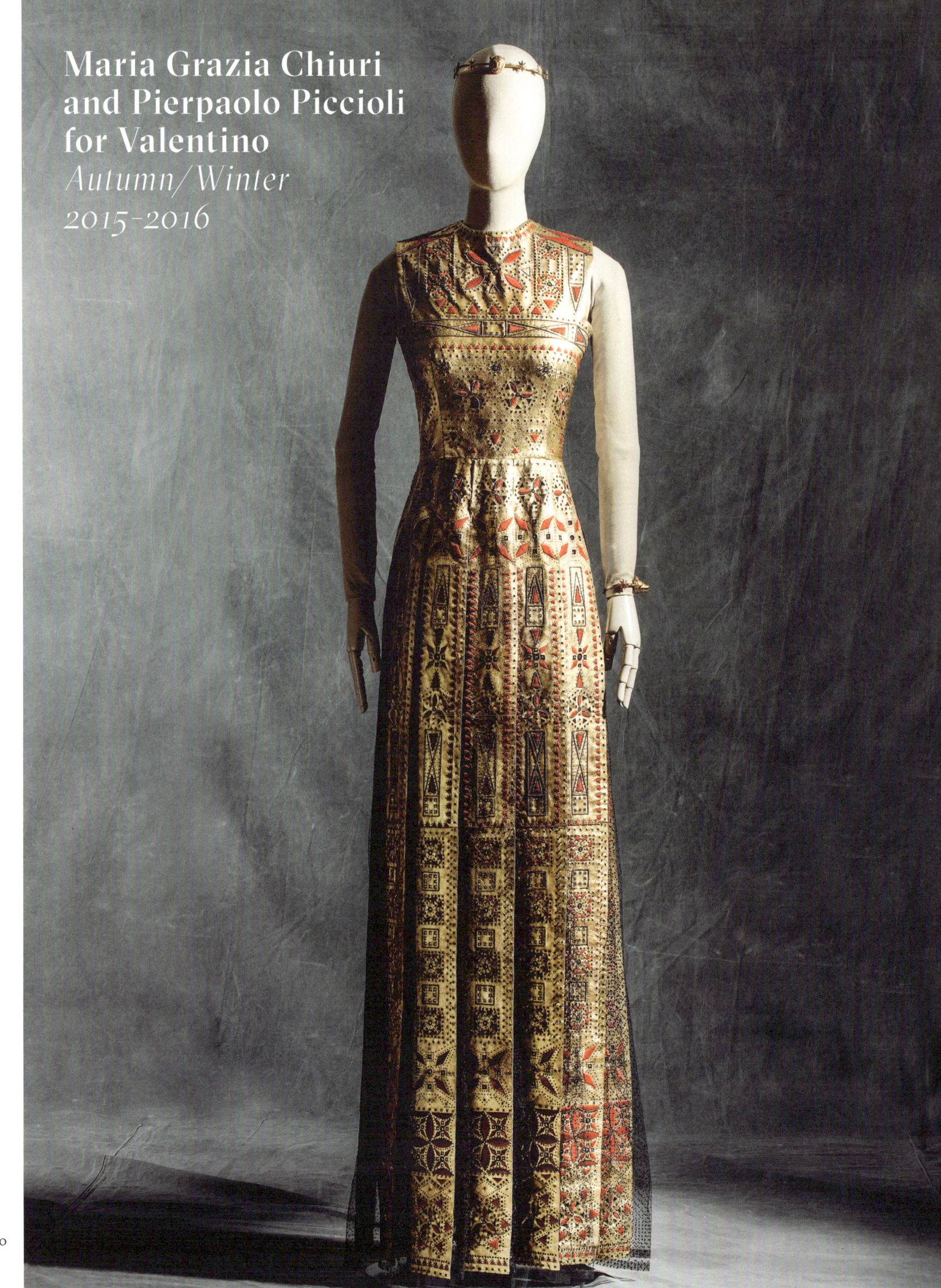

Maria Grazia Chiuri and Pierpaolo Piccioli for Valentino
Autumn/Winter 2015-2016

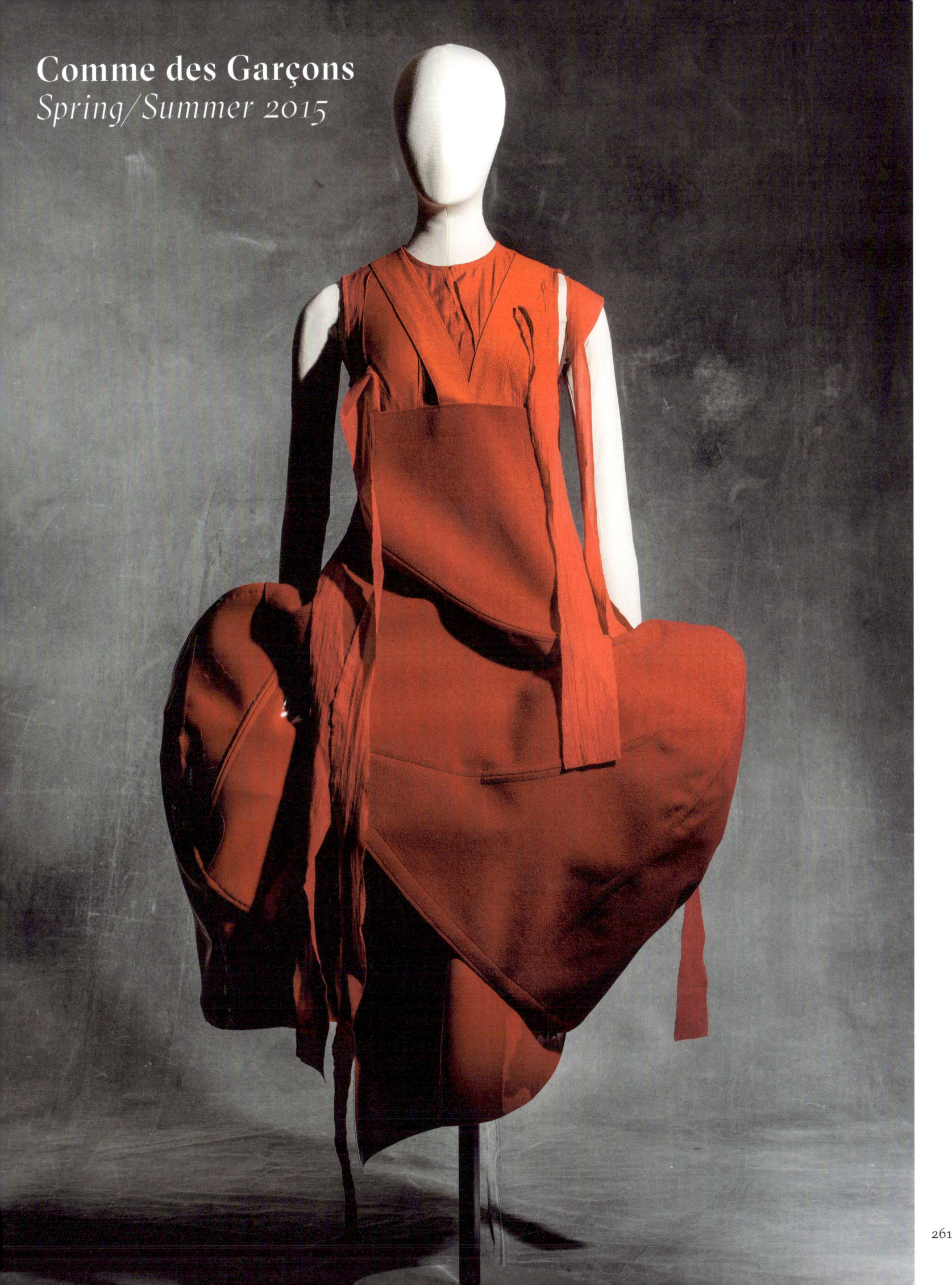

Comme des Garçons
Spring/Summer 2015

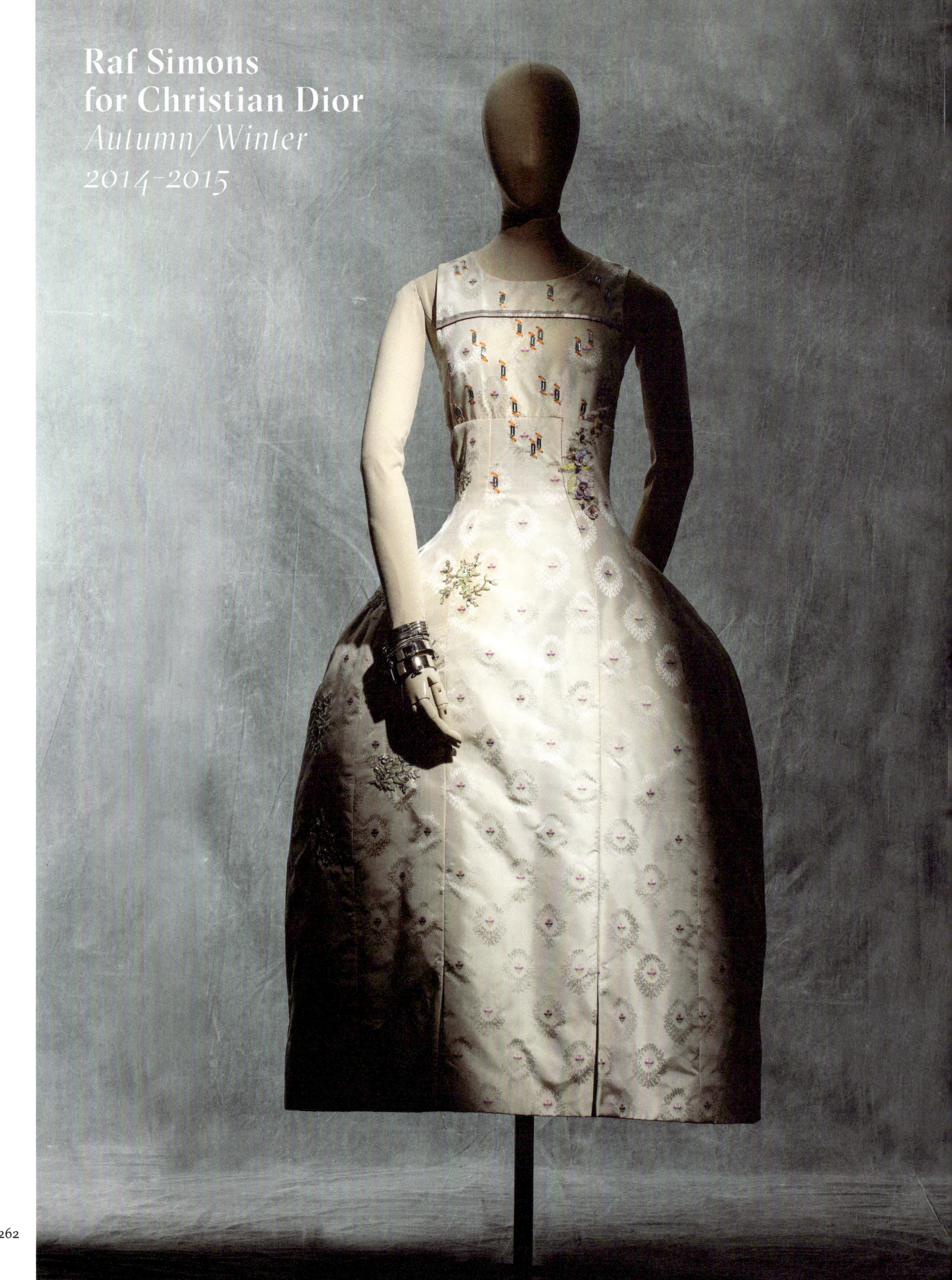

Raf Simons for Christian Dior
Autumn/Winter 2014-2015

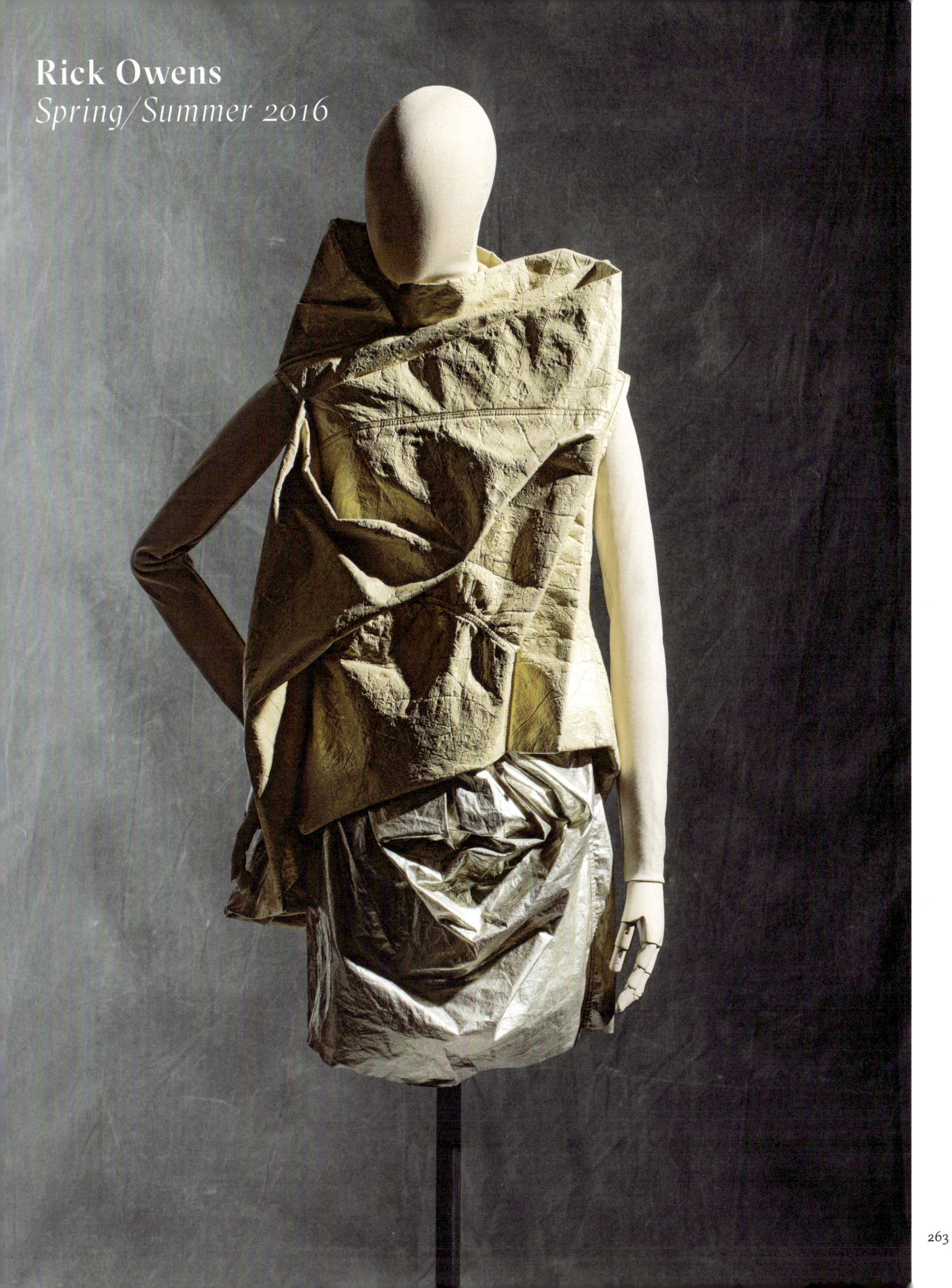

Rick Owens
Spring/Summer 2016

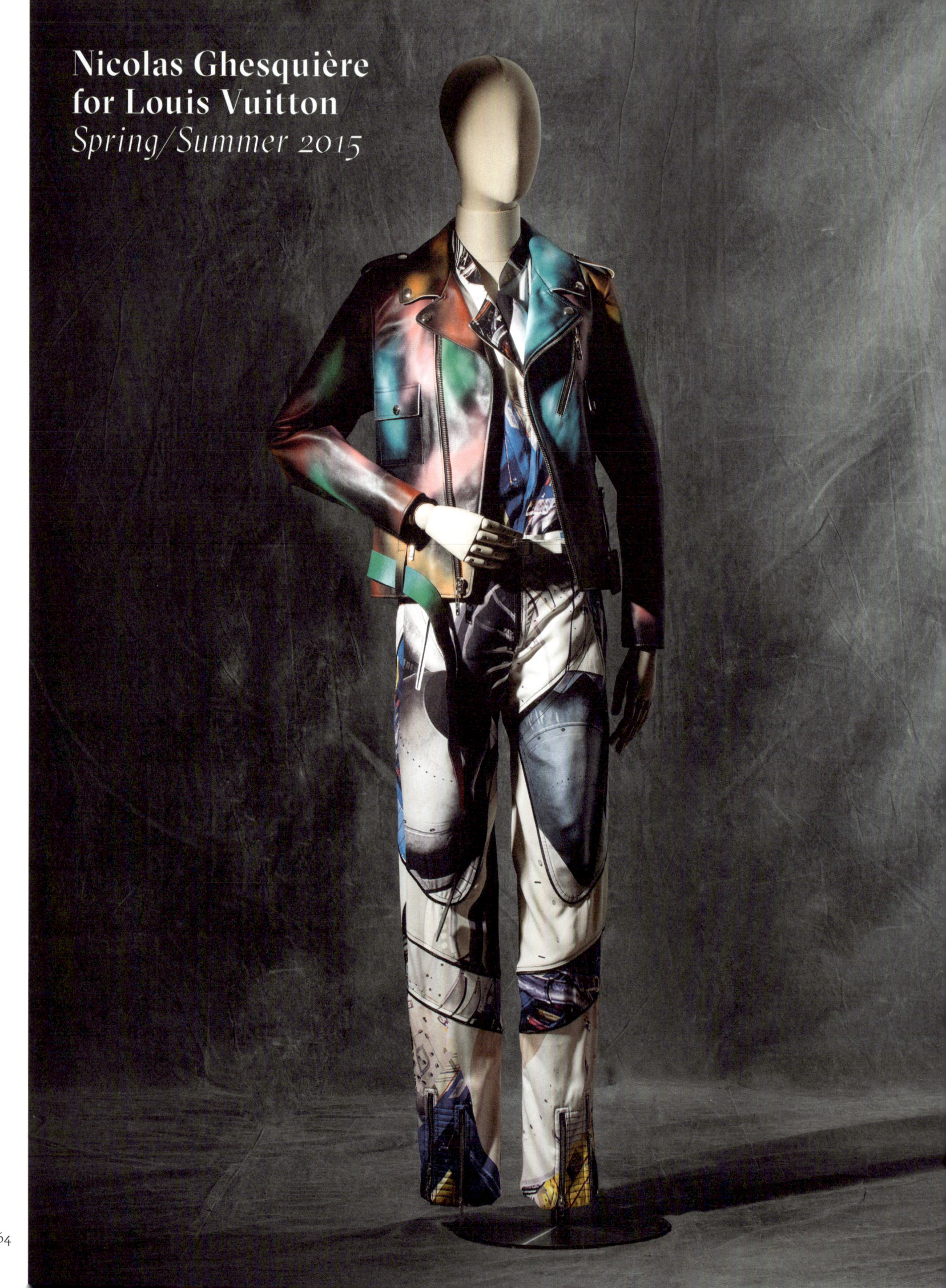

Nicolas Ghesquière for Louis Vuitton
Spring/Summer 2015

John Galliano
for Maison Margiela
Spring/Summer 2015

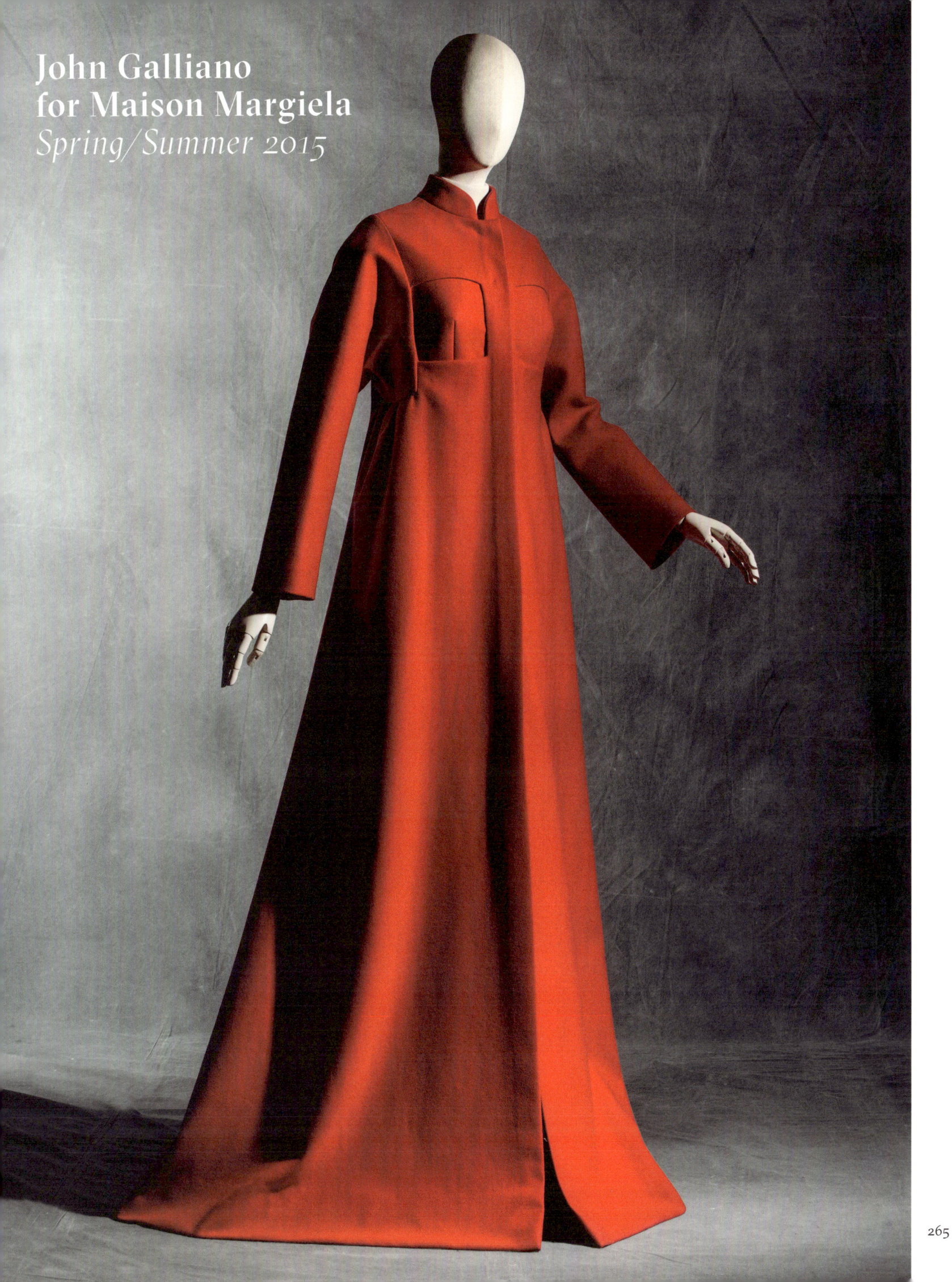

CAPTIONS

ALL WORKS ARE PART OF THE COLLECTION OF
THE MUSÉE DES ARTS DÉCORATIFS, PARIS

ABBREVIATIONS
COLL. MMT: COLLECTIONS MODE ET TEXTILES
(FASHION AND TEXTILE COLLECTIONS)
COLL. UFAC: COLLECTIONS UNION FRANÇAISE DES ARTS
DU COSTUME (FRENCH UNION
OF ARTS AND COSTUMES COLLECTIONS)

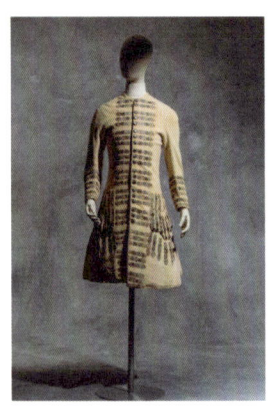

[20]

Riding Jacket
Circa 1690
Animal skin embroidered with metallic thread
Coll. MMT, deposit from the Musée du Louvre, 1991
Inv. Louvre OA P631

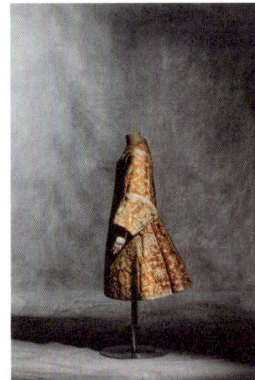

[23]

Children's Justaucorps
1715-1720
Cut silk velvet with flat, trellis, stem- and knot-stitch embroidery
Coll. MMT, bequest of Marie Augustine Goy widow Piet-Lataudrie, in memory of her husband, Charles Piet-Lataudrie, 1914
Inv. 19850

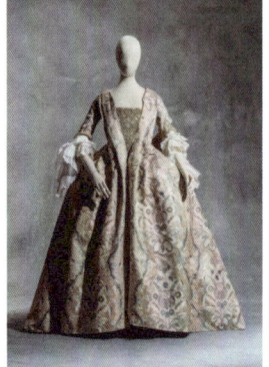

[28]

Robe Volante
Circa 1725
Silk satin with supplementary weft patterning bound in twill (lampas), with supplementary weft-float patterning and brocaded weft insertions
Coll. MMT, gift of Mme. Lionel Normant, 1902
Inv. 10103

[24]

Justaucorps and Waistcoat
1720-1725
Plain weave wool with flat- and knot-stitch silk embroidery
Coll. MMT, purchase, 1887
Inv. 3733AB

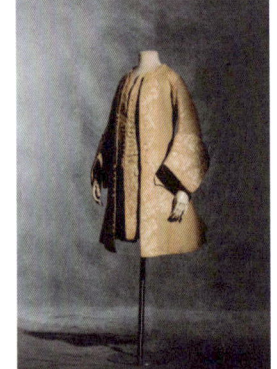

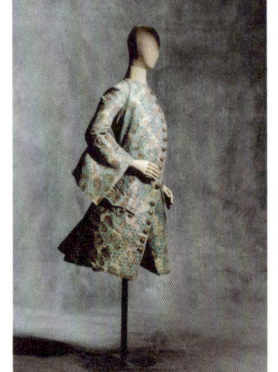

[27]

Banyan, Waistcoat, and Vest
1720-1730
Silk satin lampas with twined taffeta
Coll. UFAC, purchase, 1949
Inv. UF49-32-634A-C

[31]

Justaucorps and Breeches
1730-1740
Silk velvet with supplementary weft patterning, frisé with edging, silver brocade, silver metallic buttons, spun yarn embroidery and purls on sel-patterned silver *lamella*
Coll. MMT, deposit from the Musée du Louvre, 1991
Inv. Louvre OAP630AB

[34]

Robe à la Française
Circa 1740
Silk damask with polychrome silk brocade
Coll. UFAC, purchase, 1949
Inv. UF49-32-1AB

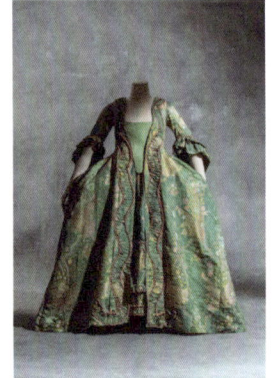

[37]

Monkey's Suit
1730-1750
Silk taffeta
Coll. MMT, gift of Hubert Taffin de Givenchy, 1986
Inv. 56580
Armchair
(*Fauteuil à la Reine*)
Stamped Cresson
Circa 1755
Inv. 24549

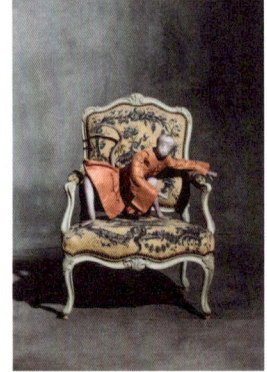

[38]

Robe à la Française
Circa 1760
Chiné à la branche silk taffeta
Coll. UFAC, gift of Mme. A. de Besombes Singla, 1972
Inv. UF72-12-1AB

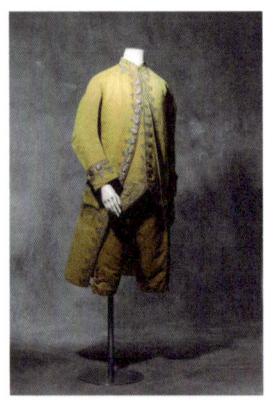

[41]

Men's Suit
(*Habit à la Française*)
1770-1780
Frisé silk velvet with supplementary warp-float patterning
Metallic thread embroidery with purls, sequins, foil, and tinsel
Coll. MMT, bequest of Augustine Bulteau, 1923
Inv. 23571A-C

[44]

Men's Suit
(*Habit à la Française*)
1775-1790
Silk satin *liseré, jaspé*
Coll. MMT, purchased with the aid of Louis Vuitton, 2014
Inv. 2014.19.1.1-3

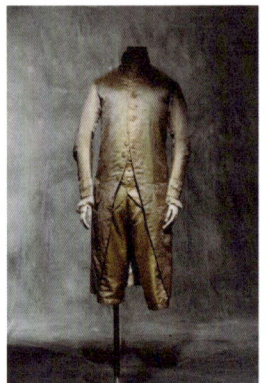

[47]

Court Dress
Circa 1778
Silk pekin, silk taffeta, silk satin, *cannelé simpleté, cannelé fantaisie*, and decorative bands with warp floats and embroidery with tinsel, sequins, and purls
Coll. MMT, purchase, 1886
Inv. 3370A-C

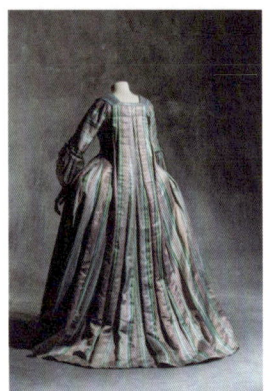

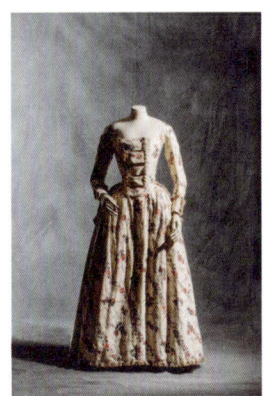

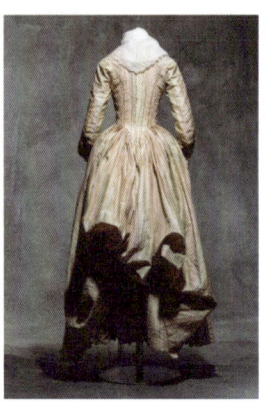

[50]

Robe à la Française
1780-1785
Striped silk satin
Coll. UFAC, purchase, 1964
Inv. UF64-51-AB

[54]

Two-Piece Ensemble
1775-1790
Hand-painted cotton percale
Coll. UFAC, gift of Mme. Osmont, 1953
Inv. UF53-49-1AB

[57]

Robe à l'Anglaise
1780-1785
Striped silk taffeta
Coll. UFAC, purchase, 1989
Inv. UF 89-6-2

[61]

Frock Coat
1789-1791
Cotton toile, carved copper buttons
Coll. UFAC, purchase, 1955
Inv. UF55-75-1

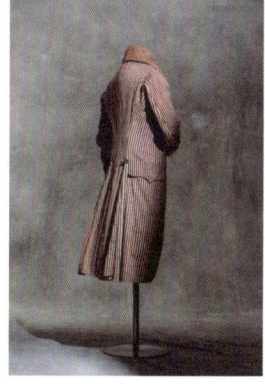

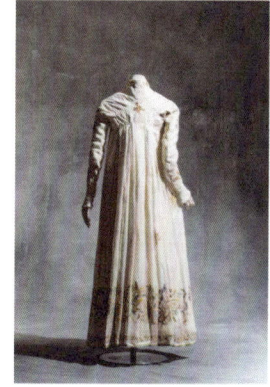

[62]

Men's Early Double-Breasted Tailcoat (Habit Dégagé)
1795-1799
Plain weave wool, painted glass, and copper buttons
Coll. UFAC, gift of Mlle. Martin and Mme. Chambolle-Tournon, 1952
Inv. UF52-17-17

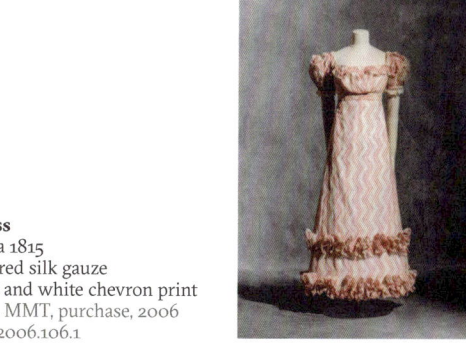

[65]

Dress
1795-1800
Embroidered cotton muslin
Coll. MMT, gift of Mme. Henri Lavedan, 1951
Inv. UF51-9-1

[69]

Men's Suit (Habit à la Française)
1804-1815
Jacket and breeches in green frisé silk velvet with miniature design on border, green liseré, polychrome silk flat-stitch embroidery. Vest in silk *cannelé simpleté* embroidered with the same materials
Coll. UFAC, purchase, 1962
Inv. UF62-25-1

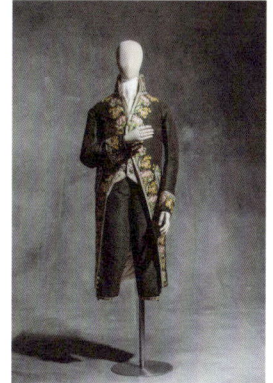

[66]

Dress and Spencer
1804-1815
White linen dress with Beauvais stitch embroidery
Black silk satin spencer with frogging
Coll. UFAC
Inv. UF87-07-1 and UF96-07-54

[73]

Dress
Circa 1815
Figured silk gauze
Pink and white chevron print
Coll. MMT, purchase, 2006
Inv. 2006.106.1

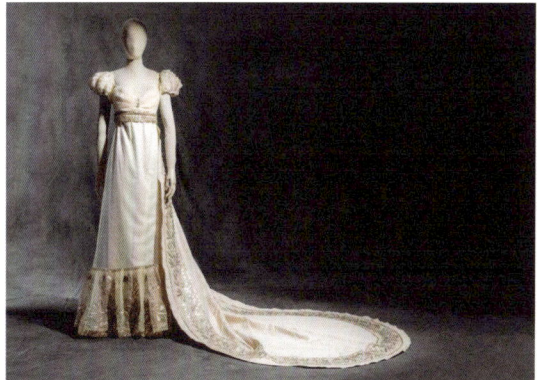

[70]

Court Dress
1815-1825
Embroidered silk tulle dress
Flat *lamella* and guilloche *lamella* with straight-stitch needlework. Overdress in silk faille, appliquéd tulle embroidered with the same materials
Coll. UFAC, gift of Comtesse de Dreux-Brézé in memory of the Compte d'Hunolstein, 1968
Inv. UF68-30-1AB

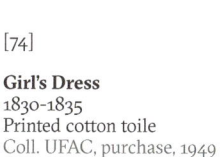

[74]

Girl's Dress
1830-1835
Printed cotton toile
Coll. UFAC, purchase, 1949
Inv. UF49-32-829

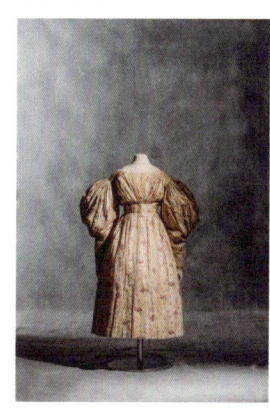

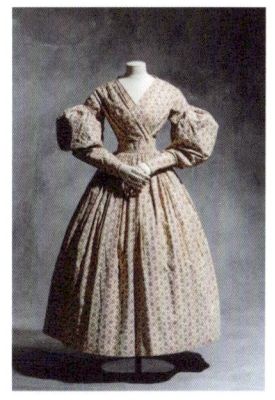

[77]

Day Dress
1830-1835
Roll-printed floral percale
Coll. UFAC, gift of Éliane Bonabel, 1970
Inv. UF70-50-1

[81]

Day Dress
1830-1835
Dotted muslin embroidered lawn
Coll. UFAC, gift of Edmonde Charles-Roux, 1975
Inv. UF75-13-1

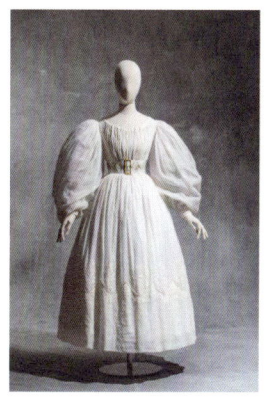

[82]

Dress
Circa 1835
Threaded white cotton muslin with polychrome flower garland print
Coll. MMT, purchase, 1989
Inv. 988.1021

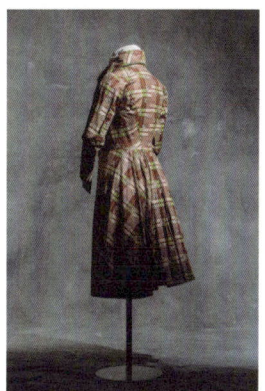

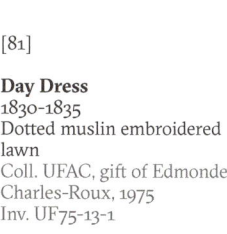

[85]

Dressing Gown
1830-1840
Block-printed glazed percale
Coll. UFAC, purchase, 1949
Inv. UF49-32-637

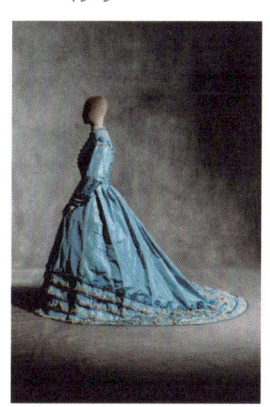

[89]

Transformation Dress (Robe à Transformation)
With Day Bodice
Circa 1862
Silk taffeta with satin appliquéd on the bias and passementerie fringe
Coll. MMT, gift of Bertrand Doncieux, 2013
Inv. 2013.11.1.1-4

[90]

Transformation Dress (Robe à Transformation)
With Day Bodice
1868-1872
Organdy, tulle, taffeta, appliquéd lace, velvet, crocheted lace
Coll. UFAC, gift of Mme. Chancrin, 1986
Inv. 86-39-2A-D

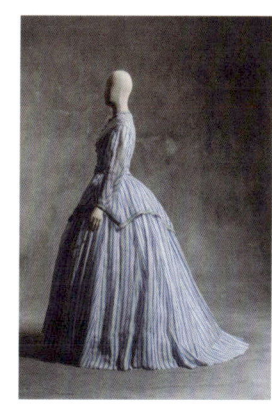

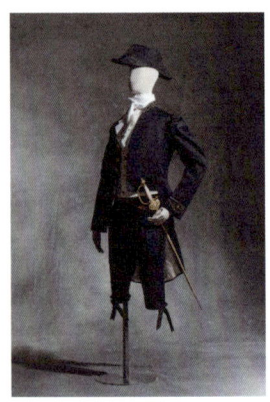

[96]
Men's Court Suit
A. Shaeffer (breeches)
1859
Early double-breasted tailcoat and breeches in plain weave wool cloth, cotton piqué vest, black felt bicorne hat
Coll. UFAC, gift of G. Baugnies, 1950
Inv. UF50-51A-G

[99]
Day Dress
Mme. Bombes
Circa 1885
Gros de Tours and block-printed paisley cotton percale
Coll. MMT, purchase, 1995
Inv. 995-85.1.1-2

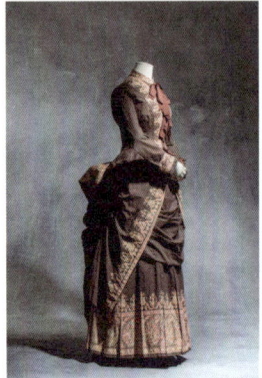

[100]
Evening Gown
Charles Frederick Worth
Circa 1885
Figured satin, metallic thread, and gold sequined embroidery
Coll. MMT, gift of Mrs. Franklin Gordon Dexter, 1920
Inv. 22014E.1-2

[103]
Dolman-Mantle
1870-1880
Paisley, appliquéd silk fringe, braiding, and tassels
Taffeta
Coll. UFAC, gift of Princess Joseph de Broglie, 1950
Inv. UF50-6-5

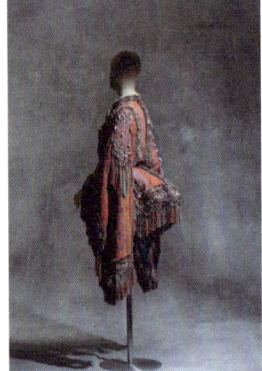

[104]
Little Boy's Outfit
Circa 1870
Tweed and tartan
Coll. UFAC, gift of Pierre de Bieville, 1982
Inv. UF82-16-1A-G

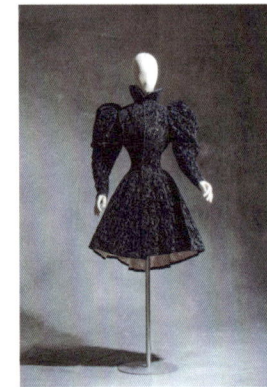

[108]
Attributed to Jacques Doucet
Jacket
1898-1900
Silk velvet, embroidery with jet beads, and sequins
Coll. UFAC, gift of Cléo de Mérode, 1949
Inv. UF41-14.1

[107]
Travel Outfit
Mme. Siebenmann
Circa 1898
Tartan, taffeta, and silk faille
Coll. UFAC, gift of Mlle. Magniol, 1955
Inv. UF55-54-1A-D

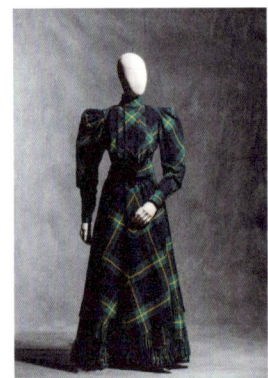

[111]
Jacques Doucet
Robe à Transformation
With day bodice
1900-1905
Silk muslin, appliquéd embroidery, embroidered designs, rhinestones, Brussels needlepoint lace
Coll. UFAC, purchase, 1955
Inv. UF54-64 bis-26AB

[114]
Babani
Kimono Robe
Circa 1905-1910
Blue pongee silk embroidered with gold thread and silk braid
Coll. MMT, purchased with the generous aid of Mrs. Jane Wrightman, 1998
Inv. 998.5.2

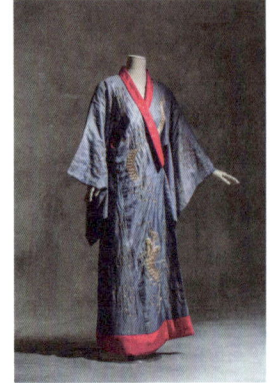

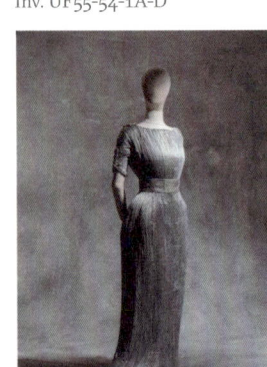

[117]
Mariano Fortuny
"Delphos" Dress
1910-1915
Pleated silk satin, Murano glass beads
Coll. UFAC, anonymous gift, 1986
Inv. UF86-62-2

[122]
Paul Poiret
"Joséphine" Dress
1907
Silk satin, silk net, metallic braid
Coll. UFAC, gift of Marcel Piccioni, 1970
Inv. UF70-38-10

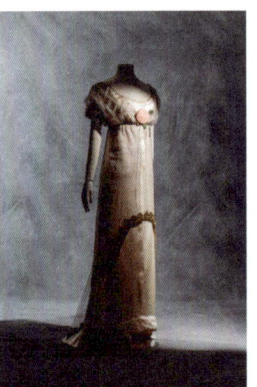

[125]
Callot Soeurs
Evening Gown
1909-1910
Silk, metallic thread, silk satin, embroidered silk tulle, metallic lace
Coll. UFAC, purchase, 1954
Inv. UF54-64bis-3

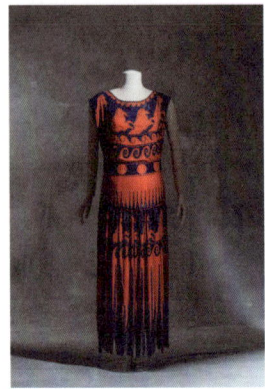

[131]
Madeleine Vionnet
"Petits chevaux" or "Greek Vase" Evening Gown
Haute couture, Winter 1921-1922
Model 1113
Silk crepe, embroidered with tubes, beads, and gold thread
Coll. UFAC, gift of Madeleine Vionnet, 1952
Inv. UH52-18-40

[132]
Gabrielle Chanel
Evening Dress
Haute couture, 1925
Silk crepe, embroidery
Coll. UFAC, gift of Madame Jean Larivière, 1972
Inv. UF72-18-1 AB

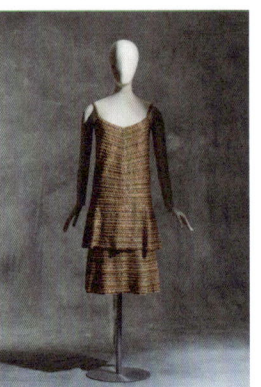

[137]
Jeanne Lanvin
Evening Cape
Haute couture, Summer 1923
Silver lamé topstitched with gold and black thread, silk satin
Coll. UFAC, purchase, 1962
Inv. UF62-8-18

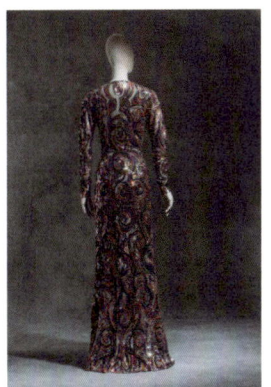

[143]
Mainbocher
Evening Dress
Haute couture, Winter
1937-1938
Rayon tulle hand embroidered with sequins, a process known as *broderie de Lunéville*
Coll. UFAC, gift of Main R. Bocher, 1961
Inv. UF61-19-17

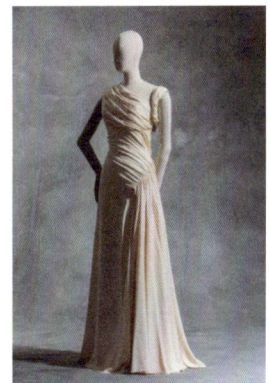

[140]
Madeleine Vionnet
Evening Gown
Haute couture,
Winter 1935-1936
Model 4062
Moroccan crepe
Coll. UFAC, gift of Madeleine Vionnet, 1952
Inv. UF52-18-94

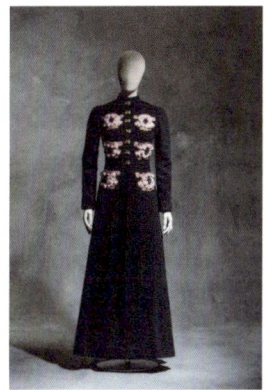

[145]
Elsa Schiaparelli
Evening Coat
Haute couture,
Winter 1938-1939
Wool, silk velvet, embroidery, metal, porcelain, resin
Coll. UFAC, gift of Patricia Lopez-Willshaw, 1966
Inv. UF66-38-6

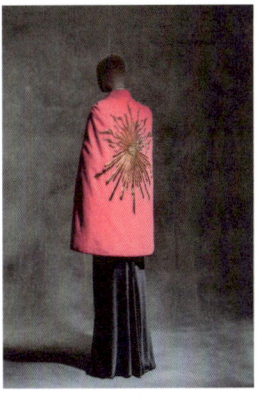

[146]
Elsa Schiaparelli
"Phoebus" Evening Cape
Haute couture,
Winter 1938-1939
Blended wool, (*drap de laine*: plain weave wool) metallic strips and thread, sequins and cuvettes, silk crepe
Coll. UFAC, gift of Elsa Schiaparelli, 1973
Inv. UF73-21-39

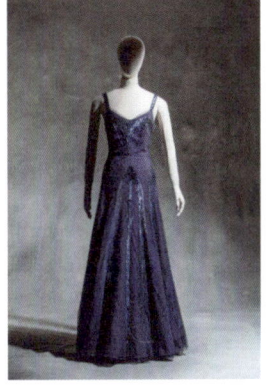

[149]
Gabrielle Chanel
Evening Gown
Haute couture,
Winter 1938-1939
Silk tulle, sequin embroidery, silk crepe
Coll. MMT, gift of Joëlle Despas, in memory of her mother, Madame Isabelle Despas, 1982
Inv. 52832

[153]
Jacques Fath
Long Evening Gown
Haute couture,
Autumn/Winter 1946-1947
Pékin silk velvet bodice
Velvet skirt
Coll. MMT, gift of Mr. Nichols, 1990
Inv. 990.877

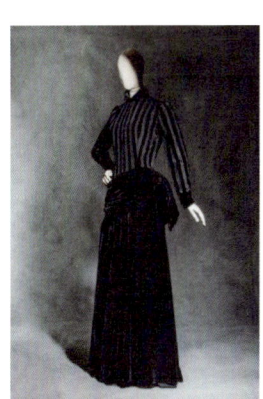

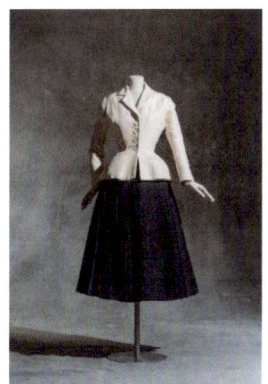

[154]
Christian Dior
"Bar" Suit
Haute couture,
Spring/Summer 1947
Shantung jacket
Skirt of wool crepe by Gérondeau et Cie.
Coll. UFAC, gift of Christian Dior, 1958
Inv. UF58-29-1

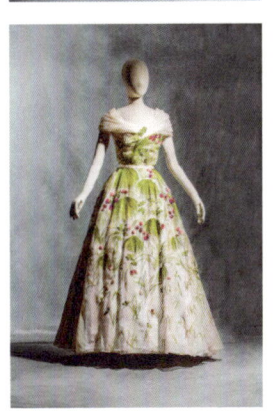

[161]
Christian Dior
"May" Evening Gown
Haute couture,
Spring/Summer 1953
Silk organza with embroidery by Rébé
Coll. UFAC, gift of Madame de Bord in memory of her mother, Madame Lazard, 1978
Inv. UF78-33-1

[157]
Christian Dior
"Adélaïde" Evening Ensemble
Haute couture,
Spring/Summer 1948
Silk satin coat with gold braid trim
Bodice and skirt of synthetic tulle embellished with satin
Coll. UFAC, gift of Elinor Brodie, 1969
Inv. UF69-28-14

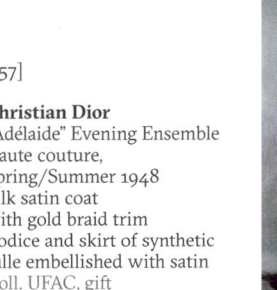

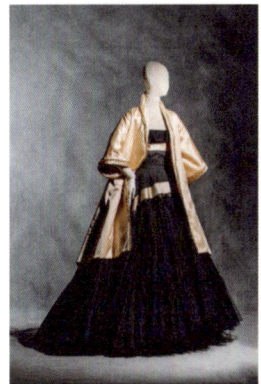

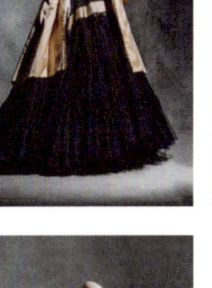

[158]
Grès
Day Dress
Haute couture,
Autumn/Winter 1948-1949
Gros de Tour silk made by Bianchini-Férier, silk flower
Coll UFAC, gift of Madame Quernel, 1967
Inv. UF67-8-1

[162]
Cristóbal Balenciaga
Long Evening Gown
Haute couture
Autumn/Winter 1954-1955
Model 176
Silk taffeta
Coll. UFAC, gift of Patricia Lopez-Willshaw, 1966
Inv. UF66-38-18

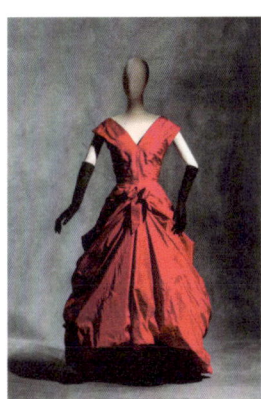

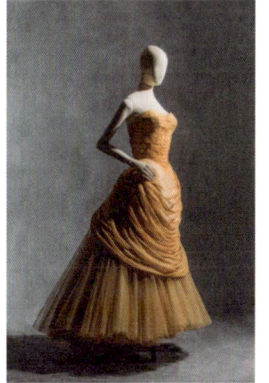

[165]
Charles James
"Swan" (Cygne) Evening Gown
Haute couture
Autumn/Winter 1955-1956
Silk crepe draped over Du Pont Nylon tulle
Coll. UFAC, gift of Patricia Lopez-Willshaw, 1966
Inv. UF66-38-23

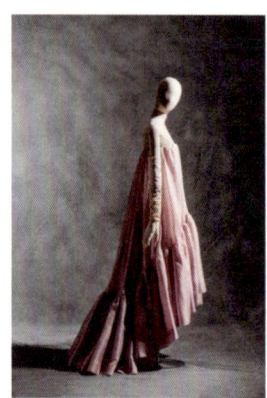

[166]
Cristóbal Balenciaga
Strapless Evening Gown
Haute couture
Spring/Summer 1958,
Model 143
Gazar Organ-laine by Perceval
Coll. MMT, purchased
with the aid of Louis Vuitton,
2015
Inv. 2015.140.5

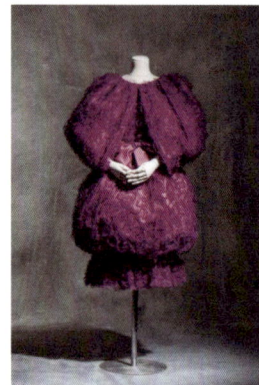

[169]
Cristóbal Balenciaga
Evening Ensemble
Cape and short strapless dress
Haute couture,
Autumn/Winter 1961-1962
Model 182
Bulle lace by Marescot,
underslip and bows
of silk satin
Coll. UFAC, gift
of Balenciaga, 1969
Inv. UF69-10-3

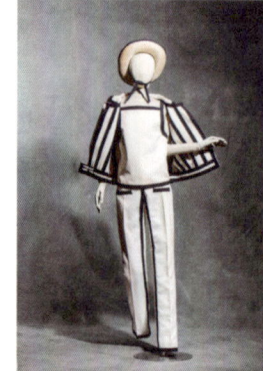

[173]
André Courrèges
Pant Suit
Haute couture,
Spring/Summer 1965
Double-face serge,
wool and cotton, cotton
grosgrain trim
Coll. UFAC,
gift of Courrèges, 1976
Inv. UF76-23-2

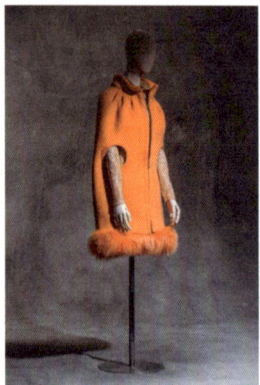

[176]
Pierre Cardin
Evening Ensemble
Haute couture,
Autumn/Winter 1966-1967
Cape of wool serge
Minidress of metallic-plastic
lamé figured silk by
Leonard trimmed with dyed
fox fur
Coll. UFAC, gift
of Michèle Rosier, 1974
Inv. UF74-33-24

[179]
Gabrielle Chanel
Evening Ensemble
Dress and jacket
Haute couture,
Spring/Summer 1967
Metallic-plastic lamé figured
Nylfrance de Bucol
Coll. UFAC,
gift of Chanel, 1976
Inv. UF76-29-20

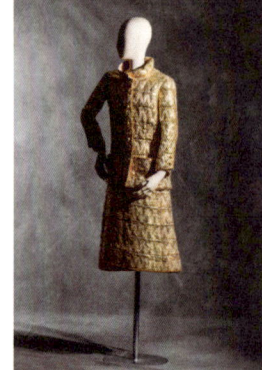

[183]
Paco Rabanne
Dress
Haute couture,
Spring/Summer 1968
Hammered or
smooth aluminum plates,
aluminum links
Coll. UFAC
Inv. UF86-07-24

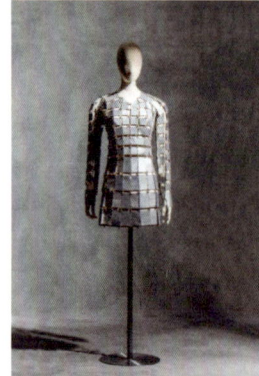

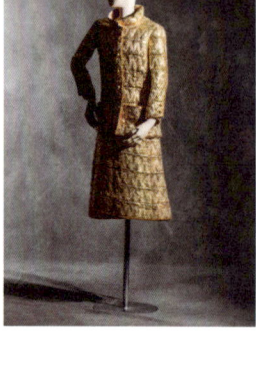

[185]
Hubert de Givenchy
Coat
Haute couture,
Spring/Summer 1969
Wool by Chatillon,
Mouly, Roussel
Coll. MMT, purchased, 2010
Inv. 2010.113.1

[180]
Emilio Pucci
Ensemble
Spring/Summer 1967
Cape of printed silk twill
in the "Vivara" print by
Stamperia Italiana
di Luisago
Coll. MMT,
gift of Régine, 1988
Inv. 988.1028

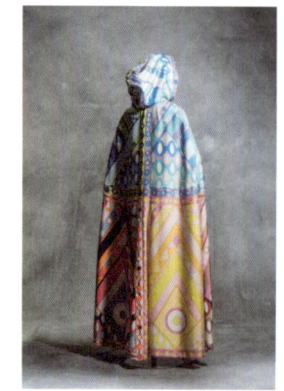

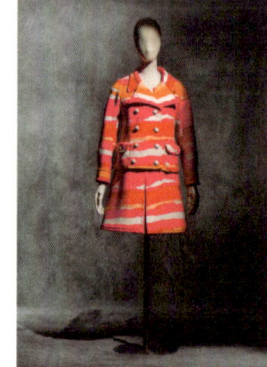

[186]
Emmanuel Ungaro
Ensemble
Minidress and jacket
Haute couture,
Autumn/Winter 1969-1970
Triple gabardine by Nattier,
printed from a design
by Sonia Knapp
Coll. MMT, gift of Hélène
David-Weill, 1997
Inv. 997.47.6

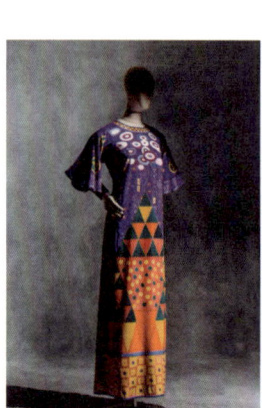

[190]
Karl Lagerfeld for Chloé
Long Dress
Special order, 1971
Bini silk crepe painted
by Nicole Lefort in the style
of Gustav Klimt
Coll. MMT,
gift of Régine, 1988
Inv. 988.1029

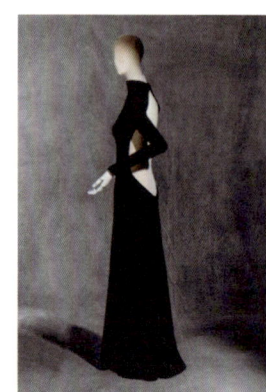

[193]
Guy Laroche
Long Dress
Dress created especially
for French actress Mireille Darc
when she starred in Yves
Robert's film *The Tall Blond Man
with One Black Shoe*, 1972
Silk crepe
Coll. MMT, gift
of Mireille Darc, 1994
Inv. 994-113.1

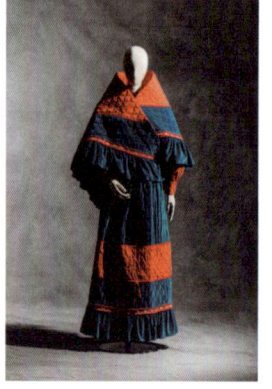

[194]
Kenzo
Day Ensemble
Shawl, shirt, and long skirt
Ready-to-wear,
Autumn/Winter 1970-1971
Cotton velvet, quilted
printed canvas, and brocade
ribbon
Coll. MMT, gift of
Maurice Bokanowski, 1988
Inv. 988.922

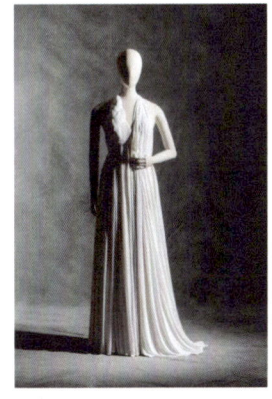
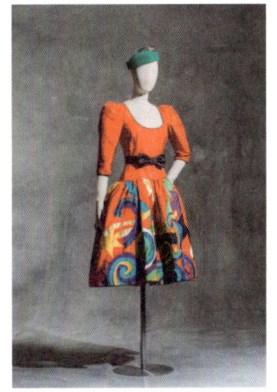
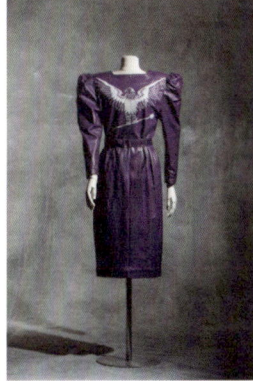

[199]
Grès
Long Dress
Haute couture,
Spring/Summer 1976
Draped silk jersey
Coll. UFAC, gift of Ira de Furstenberg, 1980
Inv. UF80-4-1

[204]
Yves Saint Laurent
"Picasso" Dress
Haute couture,
Autumn/Winter 1979-1980
Model 133
Dress of silk moiré faille by Taroni, appliquéd silk satin print by Andrée Brossin de Méré
Silk satin belt by Moreau
Wool felt hat adorned with feathers
Coll. MMT, purchased, 1993
Inv. 993.106.2

[207]
Claude Montana for Idéal-Cuir
Dress
Ready-to-wear,
Spring/Summer 1979
Lambskin, Lurex embroidery by Montex
Coll. MMT, purchased with the aid of Louis Vuitton, 2013
Inv. 2013.61.5

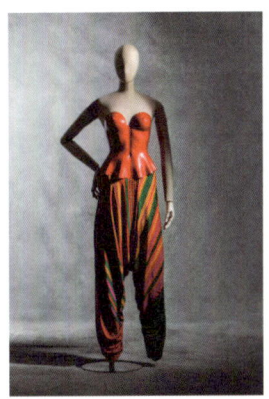
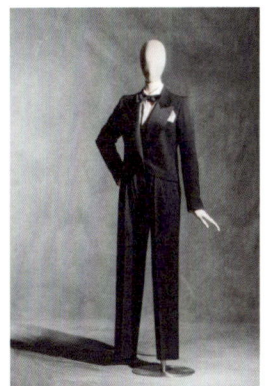

[210]
Issey Miyake
Ensemble
Ready-to-wear, Autumn/Winter 1980-1981
Bustier of molded resin
Harem pants in viscose
Coll. MMT, gift in progress
Inv. PR 2016.34.1

[213]
Yves Saint Laurent
Tuxedo
Haute couture, Spring/Summer 1982
Model 72
Spencer and trousers of barathea wool by Dormeuil
Blouse of silk crepe by Bianchini
Coll. MMT, gift of Yves Saint Laurent, 1998
Inv. 998.39.46

[214]
Comme des Garçons
Dress
Ready-to-wear,
Autumn/Winter 1984-1985
Wool knit
Coll. MMT, purchased with the aid of Louis Vuitton, 2015
Inv. 2015.181.1

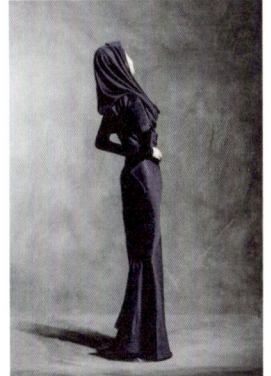

[218]
Azzedine Alaïa
Sheath Dress
Ready-to-wear,
Autumn/Winter 1986-1987
Moiré acetate jersey
Coll. MMT, gift of Azzedine Alaïa, 1990
Inv. UF90-13-6

[221]
Thierry Mugler
Evening Gown
"Embarquement immédiat"
(Immediate boarding)
Ready-to-wear,
Autumn/Winter 1987-1988
Silk velvet by Christoph Andreae, silk satin by Abraham, silk flowers
Coll. MMT, purchased with the aid of Louis Vuitton, 2013
Inv. 2013.61.15

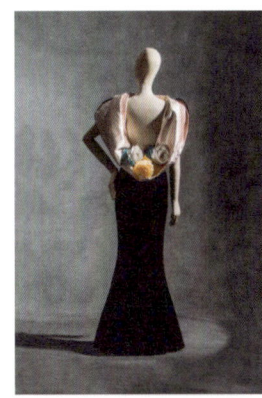

[222]
Helmut Lang
Long dress
Ready-to-wear,
Spring/Summer 1991
Coated and painted polyester fabric, elastic ties, metal eyelets
Coll. MMT, gift of Helmut Lang, 2010
Inv. 2010.115.2

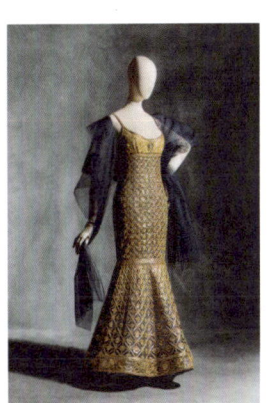

[229]
Karl Lagerfeld for Chanel
Evening Gown
Haute couture,
Spring/Summer 1996
Model 55
Tulle and silk organza by Buche, embroidered with sequins and gold metal thread by Lesage
Coll. MMT, gift of Madame Mouna Ayoub, 2014
Inv. 2014.47.1

[225]
Christian Lacroix
Evening Gown
"Mademoiselle Hortensia"
Haute couture,
Autumn/Winter 1992-1993
Model 63
Damask, faille bow, pleated taffeta flounce
Coll. MMT, gift of Christian Lacroix, 2009
Inv. 2009.66.1

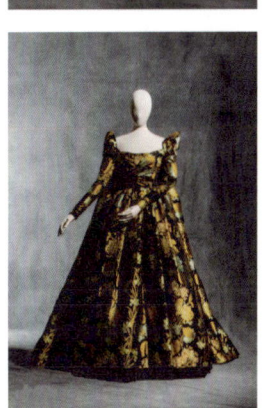

[226]
Jean Paul Gaultier
Ensemble
Ready-to-wear,
Autumn/Winter 1994-1995
Iridescent silk damask, synthetic fur
Coll. MMT, gift of Jean-Paul Gaultier, 1996
Inv. PR2011.24.2

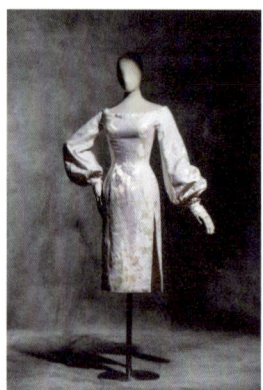

[230]

Alexander McQueen for Givenchy
Cocktail dress
Haute couture,
Spring/Summer 1997
Model 38
Ivory silk damask
Coll. MMT, purchased with the aid of Louis Vuitton, 2015
Inv. 2015.6.1

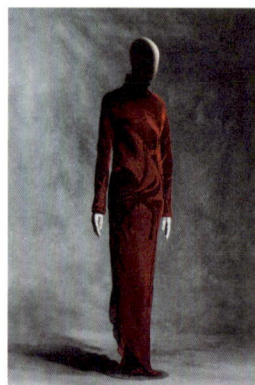

[234]

Martine Sitbon
Dress
Ready-to-wear,
Autumn/Winter 1997-1998
Silk devoré velvet
Coll. MMT, gift of Martine Sitbon, 2016
Inv. PR2016.33.1

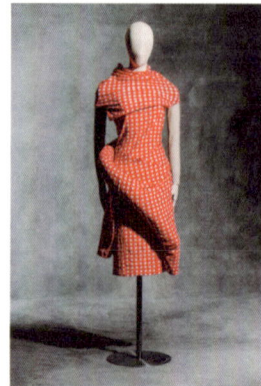

[236]

Comme des Garçons
"Bump" Dress
Ready-to-wear,
Spring/Summer 1997
Vichy print synthetic jersey, polyester wadding
Coll. MMT, purchased, 2005
Inv. 2005.7.4

[240]

Dries Van Noten
Ensemble
Ready-to-wear,
Spring/Summer 1999
Dress of cotton and pleated silk
Silk chiffon shawl embroidered with fringe strung with glass beads
Coll. MMT, gift of Dries Van Noten, 2016
Inv. PR2016.25.1

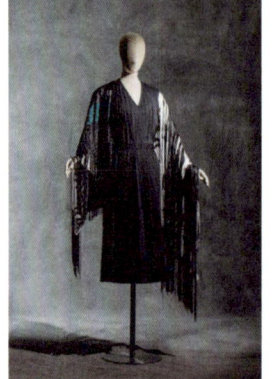

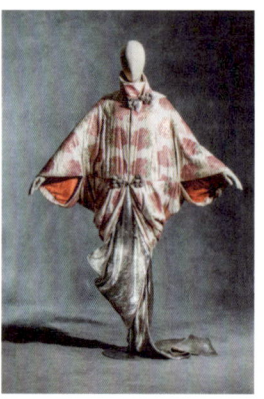

[239]

Martin Margiela
Ensemble
Vest, sleeves, skirt, and hat
Ready-to-wear,
Autumn/Winter 1997-1998
Vest, sleeves and fur hat
Dress-form cotton canvas, numbered and lettered
Coll. MMT, on loan from the Centre National des Arts Plastiques – Ministère de la Culture et de la Communication, 2015
Inv. FNAC980487-90

[242]

John Galliano for Christian Dior
"Stourhead" Evening Ensemble
Haute couture,
Spring/Summer 1998
Model 14
Quilted coat of hand-painted, gold-embroidered figured silk
Dress and train of distressed and embossed silver lamé
Straps of silk chiffon embroidered with silver metallic thread and rhinestones
Coll. MMT, gift of Christian Dior, 2005
Inv. 2005.159.1

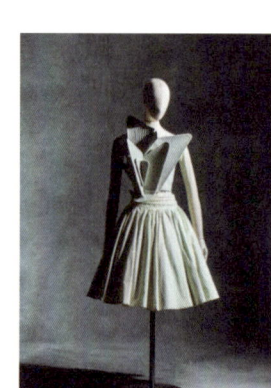

[245]

Hussein Chalayan
Dress
Ready-to-wear,
Spring/Summer 2000
Silk faille bustier
Cotton canvas skirt
Synthetic tulle slip
Coll. MMT, gift of Hussein Chalayan, 2010
Inv. 2010.127.1

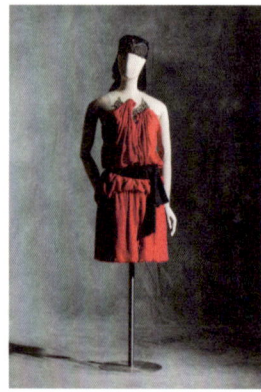

[246]

Alber Elbaz for Lanvin
Ensemble
Ready-to-wear,
Spring/Summer 2003
Tulle embroidered with rhinestones and silk chiffon
Coll. MMT, gift of Lanvin, 2006
Inv. 2006.132.24

[249]

Junya Watanabe Comme des Garçons
Dress
Ready-to-wear,
Spring/Summer 2003
Printed cotton, cotton strap
Coll. MMT, on loan from the Centre National des Arts Plastiques – Ministère de la Culture et de la Communication, 2015
Inv. FNAC03-1120

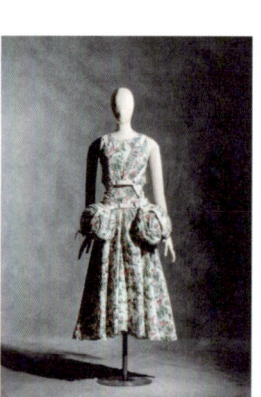

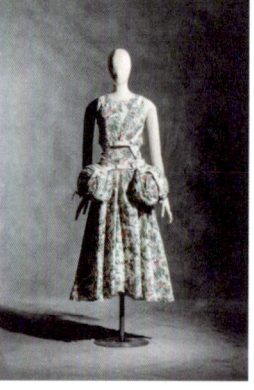

[250]

Yohji Yamamoto
Ensemble
Ready-to-wear,
Autumn/Winter 2003-2004
Houndstooth pattern wool, silk chiffon
Coll. MMT, gift of Yohji Yamamoto, 2006
Inv. 2006.11.6

[253]

Nicolas Ghesquière for Balenciaga
Dress
Ready-to-wear,
Autumn/Winter 2004-2005
Silk jersey, printed silk crepe
Lacquered colored aluminum chain
Coll. MMT, gift of Balenciaga, 2011
Inv. 2011.136.2

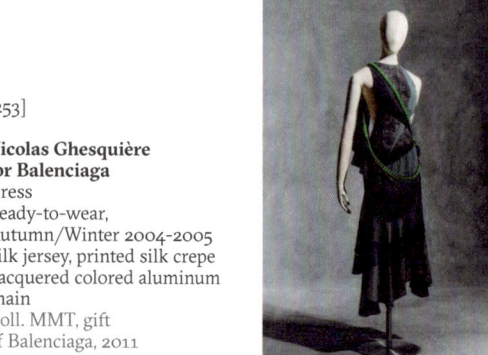

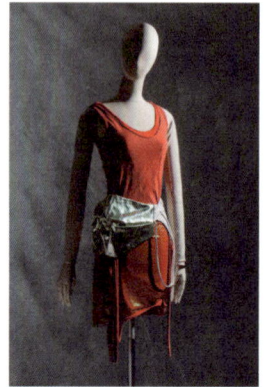

[254]

Helmut Lang
Dress
Ready-to-wear,
Spring/Summer 2004
Two T-shirts of stretch cotton jersey
Skirt of stretch cotton jersey and metallized leather
Synthetic iridescent net
Coll. MMT, gift of Helmut Lang, 2010
Inv. 2010.115.56

[257]

Prada
Dress
Ready-to-wear,
Autumn/Winter 2007-2008
Fashioned wool and cloqué silk, embroidery with rooster feathers and plastic film
Coll. MMT, gift of Prada, 2011
Inv. 2011.140.1

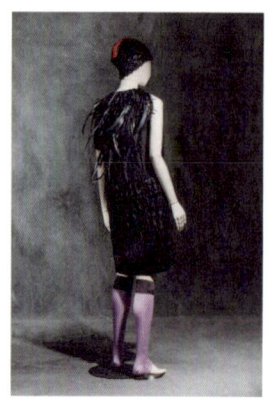

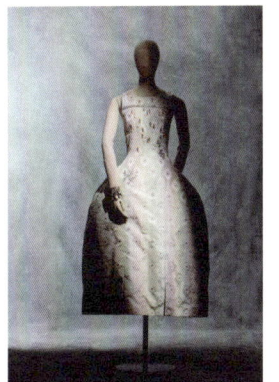

[262]

**Raf Simons
for Christian Dior**
Short Evening Dress
Haute couture,
Autumn/Winter 2014-2015
Model 3
Silk damask brocade
by Ostinelli, appliquéd by
Aurélie Lorriaux, and
embroidered by Cécile Henri
and by Montex with
thread, beads, and rhinestones
Coll. MMT, gift of
Christian Dior Couture, 2016
Inv. PR 2015.60.7

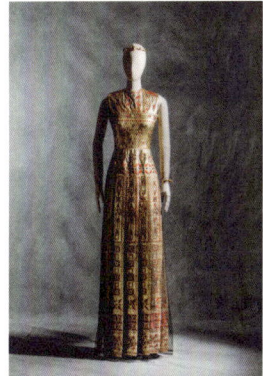

[260]

**Maria Grazia Chiuri
and Pierpaolo Piccioli
for Valentino**
Long Evening Gown
Haute couture,
Autumn/Winter 2015-2016
Model 46
Gold kidskin with embroidery
and beads appliquéd on tulle
Coll. MMT, gift
of Valentino S.p.A. 2016
Inv. PR 2016.21.1

[258]

Karl Lagerfeld for Chanel
Evening Ensemble
Bodice and skirt
Model 54
Haute couture,
Spring/Summer 2015
Organza embroidered with
sequins by Montex,
printed silk chiffon pleated by
Lemarié
Coll. MMT, gift of Chanel, 2016
Inv. PR 2016.32.1

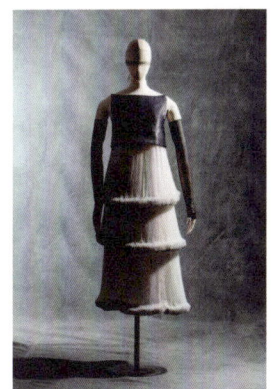

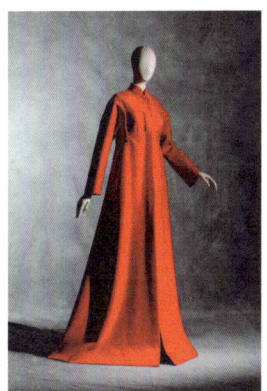

[259]

Riccardo Tisci for Givenchy
Long Evening Dress
Haute couture,
"Essentials" collection,
September 2016
Model 46
Presented at New York
fashion show
Organza with tulle, embroidery,
and silk fringes
Coll. MMT, gift of Givenchy,
2016
Inv. PR 2016.27.1

[261]

Comme des Garçons
Ensemble
Ready-to-wear,
Spring/Summer 2015
Short dress in silk crepe
and cotton voile
Vinyl and wool panniers,
cotton strap
Coll. MMT, purchased with the
aid of Louis Vuitton, 2015
Inv. 2015.98.1

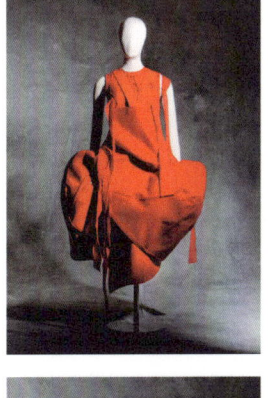

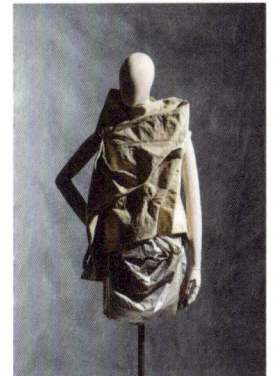

[265]

**John Galliano
for Maison Margiela**
Coat-Dress with a Train
Haute couture, Spring/Summer
2015
Model 21
Wool
Coll. MMT, gift of Maison
Margiela, 2016
Inv. PR 2016.26.1

[264]

**Nicolas Ghesquière
for Louis Vuitton**
Ensemble
Ready-to-wear,
Spring/Summer 2015
Painted leather jacket
Blouse and pants
of printed twill
Ready-to-wear
Coll. MMT, gift of
Louis Vuitton, 2016
Inv. PR 2016.28.3

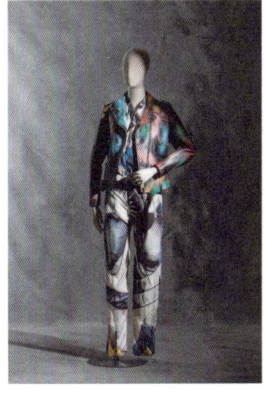

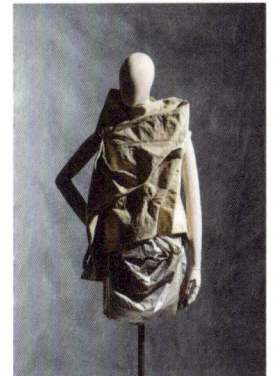

[263]

Rick Owens
Ensemble
Vest and Dress
Ready-to-wear,
Spring/Summer 2016
Metallic silver nylon
and cotton fabric coated
with polyurethane
Coll. MMT, gift
of Rick Owens, 2016
INV. PR 2016.24.1

EXHIBITIONS

A selection of exhibitions held at the Musée des Arts Décoratifs since the opening of the Musée des Arts de la Mode in 1986

Moments de Mode (Fashion moments)
January 28–May 4, 1986
CURATOR — Edmonde Charles-Roux
SCENOGRAPHY — Alfredo Arias

Yves Saint Laurent : 28 années de création
(Yves Saint Laurent: Twenty-eight years of fashion)
May 30–October 26, 1986
CURATOR — Yvonnes Deslandres
DÉCOR — Jacques Grange
STAGING — Stephen de Pietri

Yves Saint Laurent et le théâtre
(Yves Saint Laurent and the theater)
June 27–September 8, 1986

Hommage à Christian Dior (Homage to Christian Dior)
March 22–October 4, 1987
CURATOR — Pierre Provoyeur
SCENOGRAPHY — Roberto Plate

Les souliers de Roger Vivier (Shoes by Roger Vivier)
December 10, 1987–March 13, 1988
CURATOR — Pierre Provoyeur
SCENOGRAPHY — Guillaume de Fontenay

Issey Miyake: A UN
October 4–December 31, 1988
CURATORS — Yvonne Brunhammer
and Véronique de Bruignac
ARTISTIC DIRECTOR — Tomio Mohri
GRAPHIC DESIGNER — Ikko Tanaka

L'Étoffe des héros : 1789-1815
(The fabric of heroes: 1789-1815)
April 27–July 30, 1989
CURATORS — Pierre Provoyeur and Claudette Joannis

Nos années 80 (The '80s)
November 29, 1989–April 1, 1990
CURATORS — Pierre Provoyeur and Florence Müeller
SCENOGRAPHY AND GRAPHIC DESIGN —
Hilton McConico, in collaboration with Gilles LeGall

Le théâtre de la mode (The theater of fashion)
May 10–September 9, 1990
CURATORS — Nadine Gasc and Pierre Provoyeur
SCENOGRAPHY AND GRAPHIC DESIGN — Anne Sugers

Hymne au parfum : Deux siècles d'histoire dans les arts décoratifs et la mode (Ode to perfume: Two centuries of history in decorative arts and fashion)
October 7, 1990–February 3, 1991
CURATORS — Yvonne Brunhammer and Pierre Provoyeur

Horst, 60 ans de photographie
(Horst, Sixty Years of Photography)
March 6–September 9, 1991
CURATOR — Pierre Provoyeur
SCENOGRAPHY — Ezechiel

Élégances et modes en France au XVIIe siècle
(Elegance and fashion in France during the 17th century)
November 22, 1991–March 29, 1992
CURATOR — Nadine Gasc
SCENOGRAPHY — Masao Nihei

Mode et libertés, 1492-1992
(Fashion and Freedom, 1492-1992)
June 25–October 26, 1992
CURATORS — Nadine Gasc and Florence Müller
SCENOGRAPHY — Batispace
GRAPHIC DESIGNERS — Lucio Fanti, Stephen Gan,
Jacques Davis

Man Ray, les années Bazaar
(Man Ray, the *Bazaar* Years)
October 14, 1992–January 31, 1993
CURATOR — Katell Le Bourhis

*La Renaissance de la mode italienne :
Florence, la Sala Bianca, 1952-1973*
(The Renaissance of Italian fashion:
Florence, the Sala Bianca, 1952-1973)
March 20–August 1, 1993
CURATOR — Pamela Golbin
SCENOGRAPHY — Gae Aulenti and Luca Ronconi
GRAPHICS — Ipa Patoux

Antonio, images de mode (Antonio, Fashion Images)
October 15, 1994–February 26, 1995
CURATORS — Pamela Golbin and Olivier Saillard

Inauguration du Musée de la Mode et du Textile
(Inauguration of the Musée de la Mode
et du Textile)
January 28, 1997–January 1, 1998
SCENOGRAPHY — Bob Verhelst

Touches d'exotisme : XIVe-XXe siècle
(Exotic accents: 14th–20th Centuries)
January 4, 1998–March 1, 1999
CURATOR — Sylvie Legrand
SCENOGRAPHY — Ezio Frigerio

Garde-robes (Wardrobes)
May 18, 1999–October 22, 2000
CURATOR — Pamela Golbin
SCENOGRAPHY — Radi Designers et Éric Benqué

Beaux-restes (Beautiful remains)
May 4–October 22, 2000
CURATORS — Pamela Golbin and Macha Makeïeff
SCENOGRAPHY — Macha Makeïeff

Jouer la lumière (Play with light)
January 25, 2001–February 3, 2002
CURATOR — Jean-Paul Leclercq
SCENOGRAPHY — Bob Verhelst
GRAPHIC DESIGNER — Pascal Guedin

Couturier superstar
June 5–September 29, 2002
CURATOR AND SCENOGRAPHY — Olivier Saillard
GRAPHIC DESIGN — Antoine Jean, TDM

Jacqueline Kennedy : Les années Maison-Blanche
(Jacqueline Kennedy: The White House Years)
November 20, 2002–March 16, 2003
CURATOR — Pamela Golbin
SCENOGRAPHY — Pierre Charpin
GRAPHIC DESIGN — Denis Coueignoux
and Frédéric de Brugada

*Sixties mode d'emploi : Collections du musée
de la Mode et du Textile*
(A manual for the sixties: Collections
from the Musée de la Mode et du Textile)
November 19, 2002–March 16, 2003
CURATOR — Pamela Golbin
SCENOGRAPHY — Pierre Charpin
GRAPHIC DESIGN — Denis Coueignoux
and Frédéric de Brugada

Trop (Over-the-top)
April 30–August 31, 2003
CURATOR — Olivier Saillard
SCENOGRAPHY — Patrick Jouin
GRAPHIC DESIGNER — Philippe David

Bijoux fantaisie : Collection Barbara Berger
(Costume jewelry: Barbara Berger Collection)
April 30–August 31, 2003
CURATOR — Pamela Golbin
SCENOGRAPHY — Patrick Jouin
GRAPHIC DESIGNER — Philippe David

Viktor & Rolf par Viktor & Rolf
(Viktor & Rolf by Viktor & Rolf)
October 8, 2003–January 25, 2004
CURATOR — Olivier Saillard
SCENOGRAPHY — Viktor & Rolf
GRAPHIC DESIGNER — Linda Van Deursen

Elsa Schiaparelli
March 17–August 29, 2004
CURATOR — Pamela Golbin
SCENOGRAPHY — Jacques Grange
GRAPHIC DESIGNER — Nicolas Hubert

Le cas du sac (All about handbags)
October 7–February 20, 2005
CURATOR — Olivier Saillard
SCENOGRAPHY — Christian Rizzo
GRAPHIC DESIGNER — Ludivine Billaud

Yohji Yamamoto. « Juste des vêtements »
(Yohji Yamamoto: "Just clothes")
April 13–August 28, 2005
CURATOR — Olivier Saillard
SCENOGRAPHY — Masao Nihei
GRAPHIC DESIGNER — Éric Pillault

L'homme paré (Men's dresswear)
October 20, 2005–April 30, 2006
CURATORS — Jean-Paul Leclerq, Olivier Saillard, Pamela Golbin
SCENOGRAPHY — Jean-François Dingjian
GRAPHIC DESIGNER — Sandra Chamaret

Balenciaga Paris
July 6, 2006–January 28, 2007
CURATOR — Pamela Golbin
ARTISTIC DIRECTION — Nicolas Ghesquière
SCENOGRAPHY — Dominique Gonzalez-Foerster and Benoît Lalloz
GRAPHIC DESIGNER — Fabien Baron

Jean Paul Gaultier/Régine Chopinot : Le Défilé
(The Fashion Show)
March 22–September 23, 2007
CURATOR — Olivier Saillard
SCENOGRAPHY — Raphael Navarro and Clément Debailleul
GRAPHIC DESIGNER — Laurent Fétis

Christian Lacroix — Histoires de mode
(Christian Lacroix — Fashion stories)
November 8, 2007–April 20, 2008
CURATOR — Olivier Saillard
SCENOGRAPHY — Jean-Michel Bertin
GRAPHIC DESIGNER — Philippe Lebihan

Valentino — Thèmes et variations
(Valentino — Themes and variations)
June 17–September 21, 2008
CURATOR — Pamela Golbin
SCENOGRAPHY — Patrick Kinmonth and Alberto Monfreda
GRAPHIC DESIGNER — Sam Shahid

Sonia Rykiel, « Exhibition » (Sonia Rykiel, "Exhibition")
November 20, 2008–April 19, 2009
CURATOR — Olivier Saillard
SCENOGRAPHY — Jean-Christophe Poggioli and Pierre Beucler
GRAPHIC DESIGNER — Bianca Gumbrecht

Madeleine Vionnet, puriste de la mode
(Madeleine Vionnet, fashion purist)
June 24, 2009–January 31, 2010
CURATOR — Pamela Golbin
SCENOGRAPHY — Andrée Putman
GRAPHIC DESIGNER — Rodolphe Parente

*Histoire idéale de la mode contemporaine :
Vol. I : Les années 1970-1980*
(An ideal history of contemporary fashion:
Vol. 1: 1970-1980)
April 1–October 10, 2010
CURATOR AND SCENOGRAPHY — Olivier Saillard
GRAPHIC DESIGN — Funny Bones, Antoine Jean, and Sylvestre Hovart

*Histoire idéale de la mode contemporaine :
Vol. II : Les années 1990-2000*
(An ideal history of contemporary fashion:
Vol 2: 1990-2000)
November 25, 2010–May 8, 2011
CURATOR AND SCENOGRAPHY — Olivier Saillard
GRAPHIC DESIGN — Antoine Sreuemol and Antoine Stevenot, in collaboration with the Funnybones Agency

Hussein Chalayan : Récits de mode
(Hussein Chalayan: Fashion tales)
July 5–December 11, 2011
CURATOR — Pamela Golbin
SCENOGRAPHY — Block Architecture
GRAPHIC DESIGN — Frith Kerr, Studio Frith

Louis Vuitton – Marc Jacobs
March 8–September 16, 2012
CURATOR — Pamela Golbin
SCENOGRAPHY — Samantha Gainsbury and Joseph Bennett
GRAPHIC DESIGNER — Jonathan Lu

Fashioning Fashion
December 13, 2012–April 14, 2013
CURATORS — Véronique Belloir and Denis Bruna
SCENOGRAPHY — Frédéric Beauclair
GRAPHIC DESIGNERS — Bernard Lagacé and Agnès Rousseau

La mécanique des dessous. Une histoire indiscrete de la silhouette (Fashioning the body: An intimate history of the silhouette)
July 5–November 24, 2013
CURATOR — Denis Bruna
SCENOGRAPHY — Constance Guisset
GRAPHIC DESIGNER — Agnès Dahan

Dries Van Noten : Inspirations
March 1–November 2, 2014
CURATOR — Pamela Golbin
ARTISTIC DIRECTION — Dries Van Noten
SCENOGRAPHY — Jean-Dominique Segondi
GRAPHICS — GR20 Paris

*Fashion Icons : Chefs-d'œuvre de la collection
Mode et Textile des Arts Décoratifs*
(Fashion icons: Masterpieces from the collection of the Musée des Arts Décoratifs)
October 25, 2014–February 15, 2015
CURATOR — Pamela Golbin
SCENOGRAPHY — Christian Biecher
GRAPHICS — Les Graphiquants

Déboutonner la mode
(Unbuttoning fashion)
February 10, 2014–July 19, 2015
CURATOR — Véronique Belloir
SCENOGRAPHY — Éric Benqué
GRAPHIC DESIGNER — Agnès Dahan

This book was produced for the exhibition *Fashion Forward: Three Centuries of Fashion* presented at the Musée des Arts Décoratifs, Paris, from April 7, 2016 until August 14, 2016.

The exposition was curated by Les Arts Décoratifs, Paris, with the exclusive support of H&M.

The fashion pieces presented at the exhibition have been restored with the support of Friends of the Musées des Arts Décoratifs.
Ms. Susan Bloomberg
Mr. and Mrs. Glenn Fuhrman
Mr. and Mrs. John Phelan

The Fashion and Textiles collections of the Musée des Arts Décoratifs benefit from the constant support of the DEFI.

LES ARTS DÉCORATIFS

PRESIDENT
Pierre-Alexis Dumas

VICE PRESIDENT OF FASHION
Pierre Bergé

GENERAL MANAGER
David Caméo

DIRECTOR OF THE MUSÉE DES ARTS DÉCORATIFS
Olivier Gabet

DIRECTOR OF COMMUNICATION
Pascale de Seze

CATALOGUE

HEAD OF PUBLICATIONS
Chloé Demey

Assisted by
Lola Carsault

CREATIVE DIRECTION
Marc Ascoli

GRAPHIC DESIGN
Atelier 32 – Diego Fellay
& Chloé Berthaudin

Assisted by
Marin Muteaud

PHOTOGRAPHY
Photographer Jean Tholance
Lighting Federico Berardi
& Tom de Peyret

EXPOSITION

GENERAL CURATOR
Pamela Golbin
Chief Curator of Fashion and Textiles collections, 1940 to the present

Assisted by
Lola Barillot
Éric Pujalet-Plaà

ASSOCIATE CURATORS
Denis Bruna
Curator, before 19th Century Fashion and Textiles collections

Assisted by
Hélène Renaudin

Marie-Sophie Carron de la Carrière
Curator in Chief, Fashion and Textiles collections, 1800-1939

Assisted by
Marie-Pierre Ribère

With the contribution of the curators of the Musée des Arts Décoratifs: Réjane Bargiel, Monique Blanc, Agnès Callu, Dominique Forest, Anne-Forray-Carlier, Amélie Gastaut, Audrey Gay-Mazuel, Véronique de La Hougue, Anne Monier, Jean-Luc Olivié, Évelyne Possémé

HEAD OF EXHIBITIONS DEPARTMENT
Jérôme Recours

ARTISTIC DIRECTION
Christopher Wheeldon

SCENOGRAPHY
Jérôme Kaplan

Assisted by
Isabelle Vartan

GRAPHIC DESIGN
Atelier 32